# HISTORY OF TWIGGS COUNTY, GEORGIA

Compiled By

J. Lanette O'Neal Faulk
(Mrs. Hugh Lawson)

and

Billy Walker Jones

PUBLISHED BY
MAJOR GENERAL JOHN TWIGGS CHAPTER,
DAUGHTERS OF THE AMERICAN REVOLUTION,
JEFFERSONVILLE, GEORGIA

This volume was reproduced from
An 1960 edition located in the
Publisher's private library,
Greenville, South Carolina

All rights reserved.  No part of this publication
may be reproduced, stored in a retrieval system,
transmitted in any form, posted on to the web
in any form or by any means without the
prior written permission of the publisher.

Please direct all correspondence and orders to:

www.southernhistoricalpress.com
or
SOUTHERN HISTORICAL PRESS, Inc.
PO BOX 1267
375 West Broad Street
Greenville, SC   29601
southernhistoricalpress@gmail.com

Originally published: GA. 1960
Reprinted with New material by:
Southern Historical Press, Inc.
Greenville, SC
New Material Copyright 1971 by:
Southern Historical Press, Inc.
ISBN #0-89308-009-8
All rights Reserved.
*Printed in the United States of America*

DEDICATION

This volume is dedicated to the men and women of the past and present who have done much to leave an impress of their individuality upon the history of their county and to future generations.

LANETTE O'NEAL FAULK
(Mrs. Hugh Lawson)
For sketch see page 381

BILLY WALKER JONES

## ABOUT THE CO-COMPILER

BILLY WALKER JONES was born in Twiggs County, Georgia, the eldest of three sons born to Stephen Shedrick Jones and Opal Tharpe Jones, and was reared in the Dry Branch, Georgia Community, in Twiggs. He was graduated from Smith High School, Georgia Teachers College and the University of Georgia. From Teachers College he received his Bachelor of Science Degree in Education, and from the University of Georgia he obtained his Master of Education Degree. He taught in Houston and Twiggs Counties; served as the first County Instructional Supervisor in Twiggs and Bleckley Counties. The past six years he has been the Georgia Representative of American Book Company, publishers of school and college textbooks, library books and audio-visual teaching aids.

Mr. Jones has had several articles published in newspapers, magazines, and books. During World War II he served in the U. S. Navy and saw action in the Asiatic-Pacific War Theater. He is a member of the Georgia Society of the National Society, Sons of the American Revolution, accepted on his maternal Tharpe line and paternal Jones line.

Like his grandfather, B. D. Tharpe, Sr., and his great-great-grandfather, J. A. Tharpe, he is a member and deacon of historic Stone Creek Baptist Church in Twiggs County. His paternal grandfather, J. Walker Jones, was a church leader; he being a steward in the Methodist Church, and a promoter and organizer of the Rosebud Methodist Church at Fitzpatrick. The author is married to the former Bernice Jeanette Lindsey of Sumter and Ben Hill Counties. Children born of this union: Janet Elise and Elizabeth Rachel.

## HISTORY PLANNING BOARD

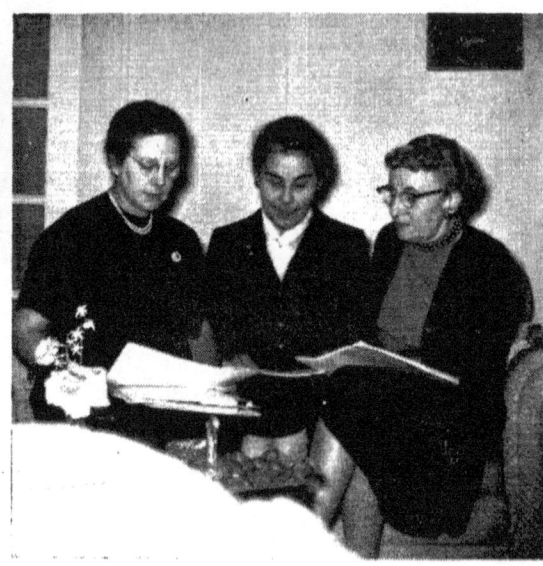

Mrs. Helen Domingos Wimberly, Chapter Regent
Mrs. Lanette O'Neal Faulk, General Chairman
Mrs. Cornelia Johnston McCormick, Treasurer
Mrs. Irene Wimberly Gleeson, Genealogical Chairman

History is the essence of human experience. Its knowledge is indispensable in man's struggle for self-government. "Not to know what happened before one was born is always to be a child," said Cicero.

—Selected

## ACKNOWLEDGMENTS

The members of the chapter and the compilers are grateful to everyone who gave cash donations and other material aid. They are also indebted to those who aided in the preparation of the manuscript and who assisted in the proof reading and offered constructive criticism.

Especially noteworthy, mentioning a few, who made valuable materials and records available and for their assistance: Mrs. Mary G. Bryan, Director of Georgia Department of Archives and History; Mrs. Philip W. Bryant, Officer in Charge, Georgia Surveyor General Department; Miss Ruth Corry, Law Librarian, formerly at Georgia Law Library; Miss Margaret Solomon, for permitting the use of her father's, Dr. J. C. Solomon, history material as resource material; Herbert Martin, Clerk of Twiggs Superior Court; T. H. Mercer, Twiggs County Ordinary; Ivey F. Collins; Mrs. James E. Powers, Librarian at Washington Memorial Library; John Bonner, Research Department, University of Georgia Library; Dr. Johnnye V. Cox, College of Education, University of Georgia; Mrs. Sara Robertson Dixon, Mrs. Virginia Speer Harris and Mrs. Ruby Dobson Bollinger for reading the manuscript; Miss Jewel B. Adams for her diligent typing parts of the manuscript; and to the local newspapers.

The compilers wish to recognize and are indebted to Hugh Lawson Faulk and Bernice Lindsey Jones, husband and wife respectively of Lanette and Billy, for their patience, inspiration, understanding and aid in the vast amount of research and the many miles of traveling required to complete the manuscript, and to Mrs. Kathleen J. Carswell and Mrs. Cornelia J. McCormick for their assistance.

## PREFACE

A trek through Volume I of Twiggs County's history may be likened to that of Janus, a Roman god, looking two ways—backward and forward. To gain some knowledge from the living past which can lead to an understanding that the past is conversant with the present and the present with the future.

The compilers are cognizant that in Volume I much of the rich history of Twiggs County will remain unrecorded due to many elder citizens who have answered God's summons and with them passed a storehouse of information, the fire on February 6, 1901 which destroyed the Court House with many valuable records, and the chapter with a limited budget with which to finance publication. The omissions from this volume and any corrections must be woven into a Volume II.

Although information was scant, the compilers have endeavored to collect data from every available source. Since the task was first begun the months have rolled into years, these years seem to mount into decades. It has been necessary to burn the midnight oil in order to assimilate and portray some insight into the stories, big and little, wrought by the men and women of yesteryear and today. Stories which in the light of full history are not important, but to the individuals concerned are of major import. Lives of those who have lived and died for the most part unknown outside of their own circle or county.

In tracing the development of County history it would be impossible to name all of those who have participated. No effort has been made to embellish the picture with rhetorical phrases, only facts stated.

Some of the dates and details may conflict with other versions of the same story. This may be attributed to faults of the human mind and time rather than a direct error. A combination of the two factors have a way of recounting the pleasant, discounting the unpleasant, and expounding the sensational.

Pessimistic by nature and cynical by experience, the compilers anticipate many varied criticisms for we realize and deplore more than anyone the imperfections necessarily prevalent in a book of this nature.

On the eve of the County's Sesquicentennial year this volume comes as an outgrowth of the pertinent need for lost records and to bring some of the legend-laden past into more permanent and more cohesive form. Perhaps the era for Twiggs County will arrive when this publication will achieve its worth.

To the student as well as to the casual reader, the compilers hope that each reader who browses through these pages will find some satisfaction and some enjoyment.

A hearty clasp of the hand and a sincere "thank you" to each friend who made any contribution or participated in any way to make possible the publication of Volume I. It has been our proudest privilege to have had an opportunity to present a portion of the story of Twiggs County People.

This volume is a labor of love, love for the courage and devotion of those who pioneered into Twiggs County, the love for the clean land in which they lived and developed, because "where there is no vision, the people perish".—Proverbs 29:18.

May the citizens of the County ever be thankful for God's blessings. "Blessed is the nation whose God is the Lord".—Psalm 33:12.

Lanette O. Faulk
B. W. Jones
Dry Branch, Georgia
August 1, 1959

# ERRATA

"To err is human . . ." Making due allowance for the weakness of human flesh, unavoidably typographical errors have appeared in this book. A book passes through many hands before the final release—the researcher, the contributor, the compiler, the copyist, the typist, the proof reader, and the printer.

Will you please mark the following corrections noted herein which have appeared after the galley was proof read?

Page 17—For sums she, read *he*.

Page 21—For Dudley H. Hughes, read Dudley M. Hughes

Page 26—For Balckom, read *Balkcom*.

Page 42—For Buzzarrd, read *Buzzard*.

Page 43—For mail to Jeffersonville, January 15, 1930, read to *Adams Park, January 31, 1925*.
For mail to Adams Park, read *mail to Jeffersonville, January 15, 1930*.

Page 44—For site, read *cite*.

Page 45—For Ftzpatrick, read *Fitzpatrick*.

Page 46—For Huber of, read J. M. Huber *on*.

Page 50—For Gargrove, read *Hargrove*.

Page 68—For Chairman, read *Chairmen*.

Page 72—For ditto marks at top of page, read *Lashley's*   323

Page 81—For B. F. Carden #325, read #326.
For W. T. Chappell #326, read #325.

Page 85—Delete (,) *comma* after court of the county.

Page 86—After for heated, delete *because*.

Page 87—For Herald issue, read Herald (,) *comma* issue.

Page 105—Omitted: after Sandiford, Geo. W., read *Sandiford, Henry T.; Sandiford, James A.*
Omitted: after Thompson, Heywood, read *Thompson, Thomas*.

Page 109—Omitted: *Majors, Solomon*.
Omitted: *Vinson, John P.*

Page 111—For Robt. H. Annington, read *Arrington*.

Page 123—Delete *Arnold* from first paragraph.
For Mrs. C. L. Fullilore, read *Mrs. C. L. Fullilove*.
For Mrs. Mackie Lou James, read *Mrs. Mackie Lou Jones*.

Page 128—For leave her, read to leave *for*.

Page 133—For Jane L. Duross, read *Jane L. and Duross.*

Page 137—For John Walker Joness read John Walker *Jones.*
Omitted: *Comma* (,) after therefore.
For Sepp, read *Sapp.*

Page 155—For News Era, read *New Era.*

Page 159—For at ths, read at *this* office.

Page 160—For otained, read data *obtained* from

Page 172—For coton, read *cotton.*

Page 190—Omitted: *Fort, Arthur*
For Rort, read *Fort.*

Page 195—For Wm. Buts', read *Wm. Butts'.*

Page 196—Place in alphabetical order, *G's, H's* and *I's.*

Page 205—Omitted: *Granberry, John M.* and *Granberry, Henry.*

Page 206—Omitted: *Truluck, Bryan.*

Page 207—For Moases, read *Moses.*

Page 208—For Waler, Arnold J., read *Walker,* Arnold J.

Page 209—For Christtopher, read *Christopher.*

Page 219—Delete 112, opposite Finch. Wm. C. acres of land; read 1112

Page 225—Omitted: 202 under Smith District, opposite Ashley, John—Acres of land. Delete 202 on line below.

Page 226—For Bery F., opposite Goldin, read BENJ.
For Bery, opposite Jessop, read BENJ. F.

Page 228—Opposite Wall, James B., under Poll *insert* 1, *delete* 404
Opposite William, Abraham—under acres of land, delete 308, use 404
Opposite Woodall, James W., under Polls use 1, Acres of land 303
Opposite Agt. for Needham Parker, delete the No. 1 and 2000
TARVERSVILLE DISTRICT—opposite Carter, Henry, delete 202—use 282 for acres of land

Page 245—For Rupell F. Read, read *Russell F. Read.*

Page 276—For t confirm, read *to.*

Page 278—For Sec. IV Be ot, read *Be it further.*

Page 285—Omitted: #3,583,330 for Anderson, James Allen, Pvt.
For Carson, #3,417,920, read #3,417,929.

Page 286—For Dal, read *Day.*

Page 289—Read, Jones (,) Henry Grady.
Read, Monroe (,) Price.

Page 293—For Sept. 10, 1911, read Sept. 10, 1910. (Infant son of H. G. & Anna Atkins.)

Page 295—For husbands, read Kennedy, *husband of*.

Page 300—For RiRchland, read *Richland Church*.

Page 301—For ChCurch, read New Haven *Church*.
   For copies, read *copied* by.

Page 305—For Mrs. Estelte, read Mrs. *Estelle* J. Balcom.

Page 307—Omitted: Dates for Lillie B. Goins, *Nov.* 1, 1895—*June* 30, 1896.

Page 309—Omitted: Dates for Walker, W. H., *May* 27, 1848—*March* 10, 1910.

Page 324—Omitted: Dates for Mary Adelaide, *Sept.* 7, 1874—*May* 28, 1913.
   Delete line, *Cox. USNRF—World War 1.*

Page 362—Omitted (,) *comma*—after Food Administrator.

Page 370—For droping, read *dropping.*
   Omitted: in Cook Family Skektch, read, *at Baldwin County, Georgia, May* 5, 1847; *Belle (Arabelle); Sallie; Lula; Wm. Arnold;*

Page 385—For Henry Gordon, born August 14, 1935, read 1936.

Page 394—For Dennie, read *Dennis.*

Page 395—Omitted: after second paragraph, read *Dudley M.*, 1908-1910.

Page 405—For Vose, read *Voss.*

Page 410—For educated a, read educated *at.*

Page 420—Omitted: *Period* (.) after county.

Page 422—Delete line, *Aug.* 3, 1942.

Page 427—For knowns, read *known.*

Page 429—Delete removed to Alabama, read *moved to Texas.*
   Delete all in the first *No.* 10, read this which was omitted: 8. *John E. Hudson born* 1-27-1823 *moved to Hancock County, Ga.* (on first line).
   For Sarrah, read *Sarah* Ann Lewis.

Page 432—For when this, read when *his* third child.

See page 480 for additional errata
Compiled for this reprint edition

# TABLE OF CONTENTS

| | Page |
|---|---|
| **CHAPTER I** Early History of Twiggs County | 15 |
| **CHAPTER II** Indian History | 23 |
| **CHAPTER III** Settlements of the County | 39 |
| **CHAPTER IV** Officers, Representatives, Senators Serving Twiggs County | 58 |
| **CHAPTER V** Court House and Government | 85 |
| **CHAPTER VI** Natural Resources of Twiggs County | 91 |
| **CHAPTER VII** War Between the States—1861-1865 | 99 |
| **CHAPTER VIII** The Schools of Twiggs County | 115 |
| **CHAPTER IX** Churches | 127 |
| **CHAPTER X** Old Homes | 143 |
| **CHAPTER XI** Communication | 157 |
| **CHAPTER XII** Organizations of Twiggs County | 164 |
| **CHAPTER XIII** Doctors and Nurses | 185 |
| **GENERAL APPENDIX** | 187 |
| Census and Population Chart | 188 |
| Abstract of Twiggs County Tax Digest for 1818-1826-1853 | 194 |
| Abstract of Deed Records, 1809-1900 | 231 |
| Abstract of Deeds from other Index Books to 1901 | 251 |
| Letters Testamentary | 259 |
| Pickin's from the Press | 262 |
| Legislative Acts Relating to Twiggs County | 272 |
| Revolutionary War Records | 280 |
| The LaFayette Volunteers | 282 |
| World War I | 285 |

| | |
|---|---|
| World War II | 290 |
| Cemeteries in Twiggs County | 292 |
| Land Lottery—Wilkinson County 1805 (now Twiggs) 23rd District through 28th District | 325-358 |
| GENEALOGIAL APPENDIX (Biographies) | 359 |
| Andrews Family | 361 |
| Asbell, F. B. | 361 |
| Beddingfield, Gideon | 363 |
| Bullard, Wiley | 363 |
| Bull Family | 364 |
| Califf, W. H. | 365 |
| Carswell, Kathleen J. | 372 |
| Chapman | 367 |
| Chapman, Dr. G. E. | 365 |
| Chapman, John | 366 |
| Chance, W. H. | 374 |
| Chappell | 376 |
| Childers | 373 |
| Clark-Wilkinson | 371 |
| Collins-Gilder | 368 |
| Cook Family | 370 |
| Cook, J. R. | 369 |
| Everett, T. L. | 378 |
| Faulk, The Co-Compiler | 381 |
| Faulk, Mark | 381 |
| Faulk, Judge W. C. | 387 |
| Fitzpatrick Family | 387 |
| Gallemore Family | 389 |
| Gates | 391 |
| Gettys | 392 |
| Griffin, L. L. | 393 |
| Hendricks Family | 395 |
| Holliday | 397 |
| Horne, Rev. W. D. | 397 |
| Hughes, D. M. and Mary D. | 399 |
| Hughes, H. L. D. | 404 |
| Johnston Family | 405 |
| Jones, C. E. | 411 |
| Jones, J. W. | 412 |

| | |
|---|---:|
| Jones, S. E. | 416 |
| Lamb Family | 417 |
| Latson | 420 |
| Long and Crocker Families | 423 |
| Lowe-Mims | 430 |
| McCallum, J. A. | 432 |
| McCoy, J. T. | 437 |
| McCrea-Hendricks | 433 |
| McNair Family | 436 |
| Maxwell, I. N. | 438 |
| Nelson, Alexander | 438 |
| O'Daniel, William | 440 |
| Paul Family | 441 |
| Pope Family | 442 |
| Read, R. F. | 443 |
| Read, Genealogy | 444 |
| Sauls | 445 |
| Shannon, D. H. | 445 |
| Shannon, J. D. | 446 |
| Shannon, John C. | 447 |
| Slappey, Dr. J. G. | 447 |
| Solomon, Dr. and Mrs. J. C. | 447 |
| Tharpe, B. D., Sr. | 452 |
| Vaughn, H. J. | 452 |
| Watson, W. V. | 454 |
| Whitehurst, W. M. | 454 |
| Wimberly, Ezekiel, Maj. Gen. | 455 |
| Wimberly, E. J. | 457 |
| Wimberly | 459 |
| Wimberly, J. L. | 460 |
| Wimberly, Dr. J. R. | 460 |
| Wood, I. W. | 461 |
| INDEX | 465 |

## ILLUSTRATIONS

| | |
|---|---:|
| Lanette O'Neal Faulk | Frontispiece IV |
| Billy Walker Jones | Frontispiece IV |
| History Planning Board | Frontispiece VI |
| Maps, Twiggs County | 11-12 |
| Marker, Twiggs County | 13 |

| | |
|---|---|
| Marker, Marion | 13 |
| Centennial and School Fair, 1909 | 22 |
| Marker, DeSoto Trail | 23 |
| Sketch, Bluff Trail | 25 |
| Myricks Mill | 40 |
| Jeffersonville Business District | 46 |
| Mayor D. Y. Califf | 48 |
| Plat, Town of Marion | 49 |
| The Court House | 85 |
| Kaolin Mining | 94 |
| Pictorial Picture, Kaolin | 96 |
| Oath by Confederate Citizen | 101 |
| Conscript of Service, Georgia | 102 |
| Copy of Amnesty | 113 |
| Auburn Institute | 118 |
| Twiggs County Board of Education, 1907 | 120 |
| School Map, 1907 | 121 |
| Twiggs County High School | 125 |
| Superintendents of Education | 126 |
| Jeffersonville Baptist Church | 129 |
| Richland Baptist Church | 131 |
| Marker, Richland Baptist Church | 133 |
| Stone Creek Baptist Church | 134 |
| Beech Springs M.E. Church | 136 |
| Carswell-Beck Home | 144 |
| John Chapman Home | 144 |
| Epps-Finney Home | 146 |
| Benjamin S. Fitzpatrick Home | 146 |
| Gleesom Hall | 147 |
| Thomas Glover Home | 148 |
| Higgs-Horne Home | 149 |
| Magnolia Plantation | 150 |
| Reynolds-Fitzpatrick Home | 151 |
| Daniel Whitaker Shine Home | 152 |
| Mark Faulk, Sr. Home | 153 |
| J. A. Tharpe Home | 154 |
| Rev. V. A. Tharpe Home, erected 1809 | 154 |
| Wimberly-Jones Home | 155 |

| | |
|---|---|
| Ezekiel Wimberly Home | 156 |
| First Trip, Macon and Dublin Train | 159 |
| U. S. Mail Cart | 163 |
| Maj. Gen. John Twiggs Chapter Officers | 165 |
| First Chapter Project | 166 |
| Float of D. A. R. | 166 |
| County Library | 167 |
| Changes in Militia Districts | 230 |
| Flag, LaFayette Volunteers | 284 |
| George E. Chapman | 365 |
| Mrs. Minnie L. Pettey Chapman | 365 |
| Mr. and Mrs. O. T. Chapman | 367 |
| Mrs. Kathleen J. Carswell | 372 |
| Taylor Lamar Everett, Sr. | 378 |
| Mrs. Mark Faulk, Sr. | 382 |
| Faulk Brothers | 382 |
| Mark W. Fitzpatrick Home | 387 |
| Luther L. Griffin | 393 |
| Mrs. Claudia F. Hendricks | 395 |
| Dudley Mays Hughes | 397 |
| Mrs. Dudley M. Hughes | 397 |
| William Warren Johnston | 406 |
| Mary Jones Lowe | 406 |
| Chart, John Jones | 415 |
| Shedrick E. Jones | 416 |
| Mary E. Solomon | 416 |
| Anna T. "Mitt" Carswell | 417 |
| Mrs. Mary Shine Johnston Lamb | 418 |
| William Crocker Cemetery | 425 |
| J. T. McCoy | 437 |
| William O'Daniel, M.D. | 440 |
| Russell Floyd Read | 443 |
| James C. Solomon, M.D. & D.D. | 449 |
| Mrs. Maggie Tharpe Solomon | 449 |
| W. M. Whitehurst | 454 |
| W. M. Whitehurst Car | 455 |
| E. J. Wimberly | 458 |
| Dr. Arthur E. Wood | 462 |

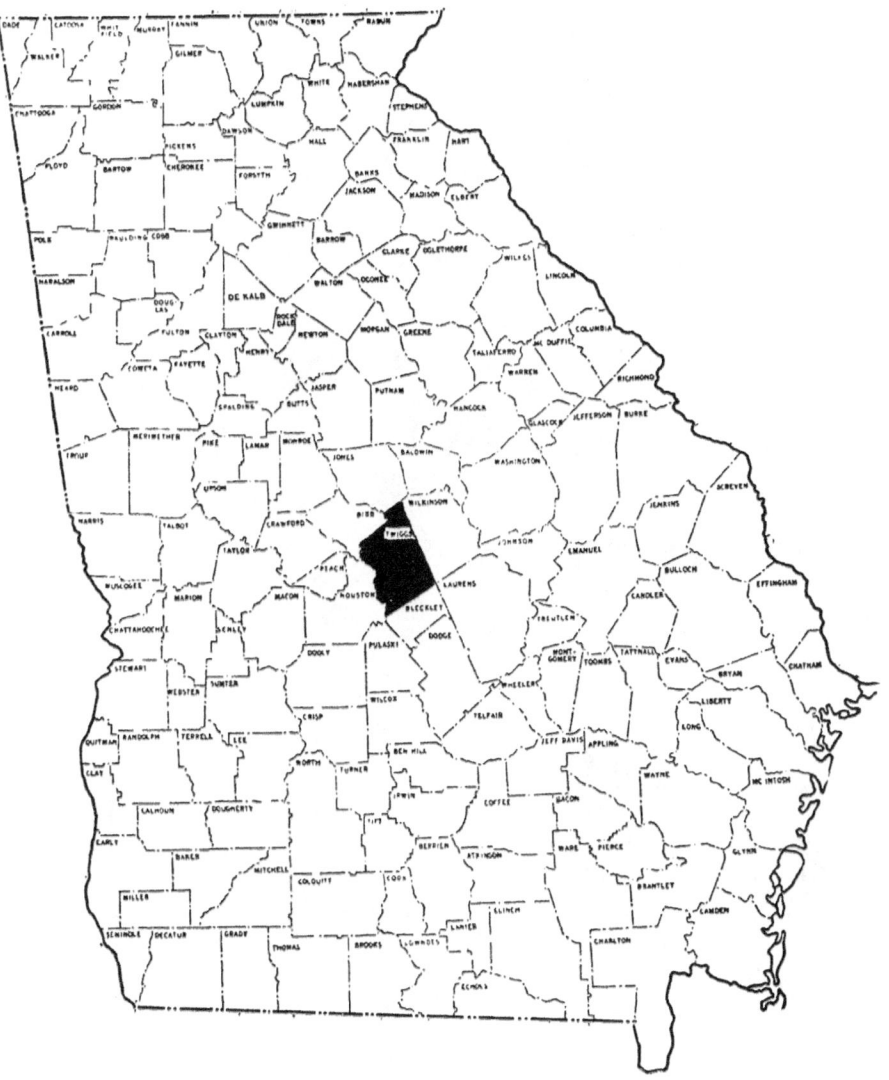

TWIGGS COUNTY, THE HEART OF GEORGIA.
37th in Order of Creation—Carved from Wilkinson County, 1809.

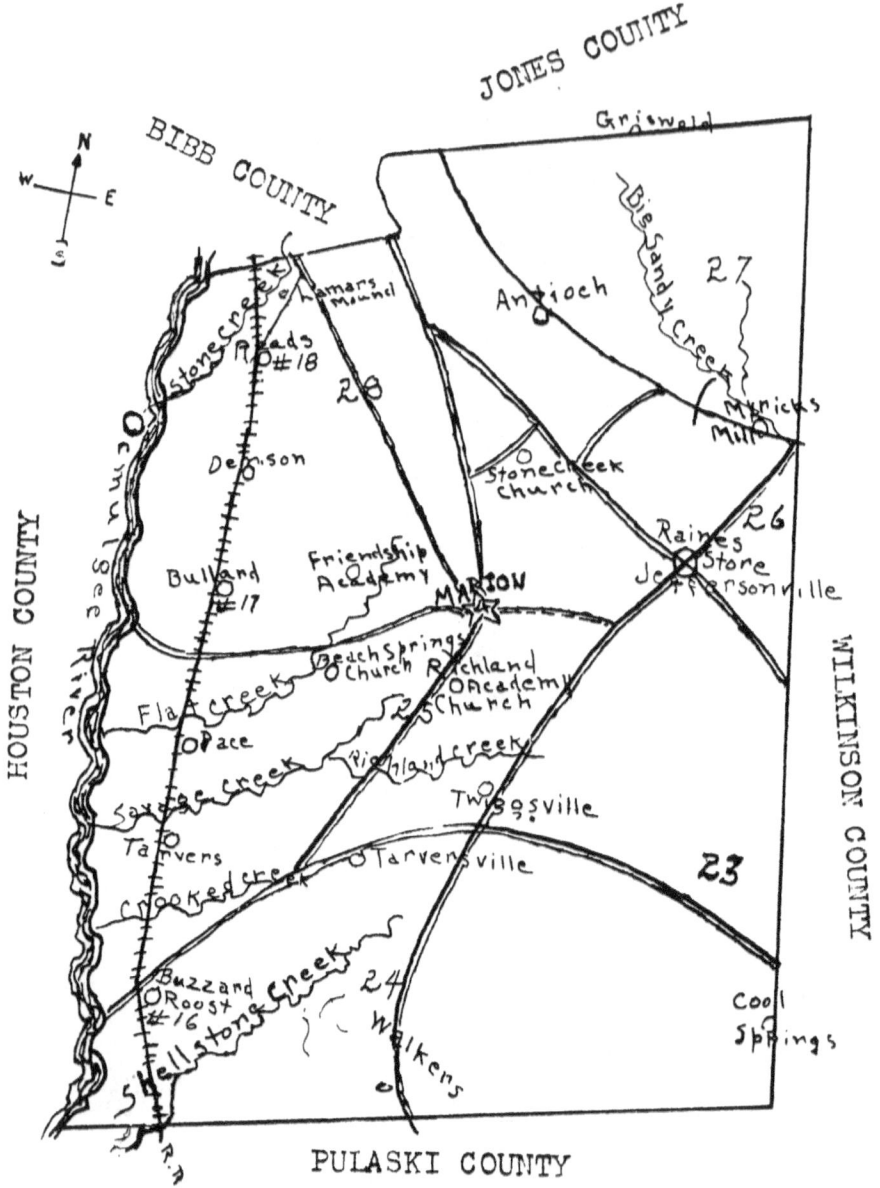

TWIGGS COUNTY

Copied from a map of GEORGIA, 1859, by J. R. Butts.
Revised by A. G. Butts in 1870.
This rare map was presented to Bibb County by Charles J. Haden. It hangs in the office of the Clerk of Superior Court, Bibb County, Georgia.

(*Map not drawn to scale.*)

*"No man is fit to be entrusted with the control of the PRESENT who is ignorant of the PAST, and no PEOPLE who are indifferent to their PAST, need hope to make their FUTURE great."*

—Selected

# CHAPTER I
# EARLY HISTORY OF TWIGGS COUNTY

Twiggs County has prospered and grown as families have pioneered into the county, settled and established themselves. Her background in legend, religion, morals and many unsung accounts is designed with variegated colors. An interesting tapestry, with 150 years of struggle, has been woven for admiration, not only of her growth, but for her contribution to the progress of the State and Nation.

County court house records must be antedated, and the true beginning of Twiggs County must be sought in the early history of Georgia. The current of which affects the whole commonwealth.

Recall the framework laid by some of the forebears who came with General James Edward Oglethorpe to the eastern shores of Georgia. They came to a land in the wilderness, inhabited by Indians, in which to build log homes and find means of earning a livelihood for the families. Within a short time other settlers migrated into Georgia whose contributions have led to the development of many counties. In due course, Twiggs County was created from one of these counties.

Twiggs County, Georgia, developed from a dissatisfaction over the proper location of the county seat of Wilkinson County and from the hardships that a virgin wilderness imposed upon its citizens.

The proposed site for the capital city of Wilkinson was to be as near the geographical center of that county as possible. This was near Ball's Church, or about five miles distant from the present town of Jeffersonville. In conformity with the prescribed law, in a resolution passed by the Georgia Legislature in 1807, land was acquired and public buildings put under construction on lands purchased from Samuel Dick. The construction of the court house and jail had hardly begun before a storm of opposition to its location arose, which helped to lead to the division of Wilkinson County and the formation of Twiggs.

On November 14, 1809, Mr. Arthur Fort, of Wilkinson County, introduced in the Georgia Legislature a bill to set Twiggs County apart from Wilkinson, and on December 14, 1809, the bill became law. Due to the large number of citizens who were disappointed over the selected location of the Wilkinson County seat, news of the formation of a new county was generally greeted with approval.

Except as a memorial to a proposed county-seat town that never came into existence, the creation of Twiggs in 1809 made useless the Wilkinson County court house, then under construction in the extreme eastern part of Twiggs. The legislative bill establishing Twiggs County stipulated that both Twiggs and Wilkinson Counties share equally in the payment of the public buildings already constructed in the proposed county-seat town of Wilkinson.

The immense size of original Wilkinson was another reason for its division. The terrain of the county, mode of travel, and the distance the frontiersmen lived from the seat of government all played their part in helping to create Twiggs. It was not uncommon for citizens living in large counties to protest and petition the Legislature to carve small counties. (Ref: House and Senate Journal 1808).

The establishment of Twiggs was aided by the wisdom and foresight of the citizens of Wilkinson who realized that the seat of government needed to be more accessible to greater number of citizens. It was with this and other things in mind that the notable Arthur Fort, Wilkinson County Representative, introduced the bill on November 14, 1809 in the Georgia Legislature, meeting at Milledgeville, to lay out a new county from Wilkinson. The following is a copy: An Act—

"To divide the County of Wilkinson, and to form one other new county.

1. Be it enacted by the Senate and House of Representatives of the State of

Georgia, in General Assembly met, and by the authority of the same, That the county of Wilkinson shall be divided and formed into two new counties, in the following manner, that is to say; beginning on the Ocmulgee river, where the upper line of said county of Wilkinson strikes the river, thence on the upper line of said county to where the same crosses the main south fork of Commissioners creek, thence a straight line to the first branch, which the present line crosses, dividing Pulaski and Wilkinson, on a south west direction from the corner that divides Laurens and Pulaski counties and lower line of Wilkinson, thence with said line as it now runs, until it strikes the Ocmulgee river, thence up the meanders thereof to the place of beginning on said river; and all that part of Wilkinson County, comprehended within the lines aforesaid shall form a new county to be known by the name of Twiggs, and that all the remaining part of said county shall form one new county to be known by the name of Wilkinson.

2. And be it further enacted, That the Justices of the Inferior Court already commissioned, and hereafter to be appointed for said counties, shall be vested with full power and authority to fix on, and purchase for the county of Twiggs for county uses, a tract of land not less than one hundred, or more than two hundred two and a half acres, at the most convenient place within said county, for the site of public buildings, which shall be at the centre or within two miles thereof; at which place, the courts and elections shall be held, as soon as suitable buildings are erected thereat, and the said commissioners or a majority of them, are hereby authorized and empowered to contract with a fit and proper person or persons, for the purpose of building a courthouse and jail in said county, at such place as is made choice of as the site of public buildings, after giving at least thirty days notice in some one of the public gazettes of this state, and at three or more public places in the county; provided nevertheless, that until the court house shall be completed, the elections and courts for said county shall be held at such place as the Inferior Courts respectively shall point out, until the public buildings shall be complete.

3. And be it further enacted by the authority aforesaid, That the Justices of the Inferior Court or a majority of them, for the county of Twiggs, be, and they are hereby authorized to lay off out of such land as may be purchased for the county use, such number of lots and they, or a majority of them, may think proper, and sell on twelve months credit, taking bond and good personal security, to said courts and their successors in office, for the amount of such sales, which net proceeds is hereby appropriated to the defraying the expenses of erecting the public buildings in said county, and to other county demands as are common.

4. And be it further enacted, That Stephen Johnson, John Eady, Senior, Elkanah Lofton, Philip Pitman and William Cauley, be, and they are hereby appointed commissioners to fix on a site of public buildings for the county of Wilkinson, and to purchase for the county use, not less than one hundred acres of land,

5. And be it further enacted, that all officers, civil and military, shall hold and enjoy their respective appointments, in whichever county they may fall, as fully as though such division had not taken place, and that the county of Twiggs shall at her own expense run and plainly mark the dividing lines as heretofore pointed out; and whereas, the county of Wilkinson have employed men to build a court house in said county, which shall be rendered useless by this division;

6. Be it enacted by the authority aforesaid, That the Inferior Court in each county is hereby authorized and required to levy an extra tax in proportion to their respective taxes, to compensate the undertaker of said court house, and to pay other debts which may now exist, and that the house shall be sold for the mutual interest of each county by the courts thereof.

7. And be it further enacted by the authority aforesaid, That that lot of land

in the twenty-sixth district of Wilkinson County, number one hundred and eleven, conveyed by Samuel Dick to the county aforesaid is hereby declared to be vested in said Dick, his heirs and assigns, his refunding to said county, whatever sum or sums she may have advanced to him in consideration thereof.

8. Be it enacted by the authority aforesaid, That all the public records of Wilkinson County shall remain and belong to the County of Wilkinson. Benjamin Whitaker, Speaker of the House of Representatives. Henry Mitchell, President of the Senate. Executive Department, Georgia, assented to, 14th December, 1809, David B. Mitchell, Governor." Ref: Laws of Georgia 1809, pages 75 - 78.

This bill to create a new county from Wilkinson County was read in the House of Representatives on November 14, 1809. The Act entitled "An Act to divide the County of Wilkinson and to form one other new county" was passed and concurred in by both houses of the General Assembly on December 12, 1809 and was assented to by the Governor on December 14, 1809.

Excerpts of the following Acts show the changes which have been made in the boundaries of Twiggs over a period of years:
Act of December 9, 1822—
                    Dawson Compilation, page 121
Houston, Jones, Monroe, and Twiggs Counties shall be divided as hereinafter pointed out, viz, and all that tract of country hereinafter pointed out:
beginning at Waller's or Torrentine's Ferry on the Ocmulgee River, running a direct line to the corner of the 12th and 13th Districts of Monroe County, on the line dividing Monroe and Houston Counties, thence due South to Ichuconna Creek, thence down said Creek to where it enters into the Ocmulgee River, thence beginning at Waller's or Torrentine's Ferry, running down the Ocmulgee River to the mouth of a small branch below Wm. W. Brown's shoals, thence a direct line to the corner of the Reserve near Mrs. Lavania Hawkins' old mill, thence down the Reserve line to the corner, thence to the corner of Land Lots Numbers 96 and 86 in the 7th District of originally Baldwin, now Twiggs County, thence a direct line to Stone Creek, thence down said Creek until it strikes the dividing line of Land Lots Numbers 108 and 107, thence a direct line to the Ocmulgee River, thence down said River to the mouth of Ichuconna Creek, forming a County to be called "Bibb".

Act of December 23, 1833, page 51—Land Lots Number 90 and 91 in the 7th District of originally Baldwin, now Twiggs, are added to and become a part of the County of Bibb.

Act of December 26, 1842, page 61—The residence of Isaac Watts who now lives in the County of Twiggs, distinguished as Land Lot Number 61 of the 7th District of originally Baldwin, now Twiggs, is hereby added to the County of Bibb.

Other Acts have been passed to include certain land lots in the County of Bibb which were in the 7th District of orignally Baldwin, now Twiggs County, which changed the line were: Act of Dec. 21, 1849, Lot Numbers 70 and 89; Act of Jan. 20, 1852, Land Lot Number 62, the same being part of the plantation of Elisha Davis; Acts of Mar. 2, 1875, Land Lot Numbers 134, 135, 143, 144, 145, 146, 149, 150, 151, 152 and 161; Act of Feb. 25, 1876, Land Lot Numbers 132, 133, 122, 123, 120, 121, 110, 111, and parts of numbers 108, 109 and 92 west of Stone Creek; Act of Feb. 19, 1877, Land Lot Numbers 63 and 64.

## ORIGIN OF THE NAME OF TWIGGS COUNTY

The county was named for the illustrious Revolutionary hero, Major General John Twiggs, who was a soldier of Georgia during the Revolution. Not long before the War started he came to Georgia from Maryland as a young mechanic. He entered the army as captain and rose rapidly to the rank of Brigadier-General. Brave, active, talented, and influential, he was a tower of strength to the patriots. No partisan

leader in Georgia was engaged in more fights and battles with the enemy and never once did he suffer defeat. He lived for twenty-five years after the war closed, and filled many positions of honor and trust in Georgia. He was a member of the State Legislature for a number of years and was a trustee both of Richmond Academy, Augusta, and of the University of Georgia. He died in Richmond County, Georgia.
Ref: Chappell, J. H., GEORGIA HISTORY SERIES.

Ten miles below Augusta, near the line of the Central of Georgia Railroad, at a point reached by driving a mile into the country from Allen's Station is a private burial ground of the noted Twiggs Family. On the tombstone of the Revolutionary patriot reads this inscription:

Major-General John Twiggs
Born 5th of June 1750
Died 29th March 1816
Aged 65 years, 10 months and 24 days

## ARTHUR FORT

Arthur Fort, Senior, of English stock, born January 15, 1750 in North Carolina, was married to Susuannah Tomlinson and reared several children: Tomlinson, Moses, Arthur, Jr., Sarah, Elizabeth, Zachariah, and Owen Charlton.

He came to Georgia before the Revolutionary War in which he served as a defender for the cause of freedom.

His integrity and concern for his fellowman led him, with opinions of his neighbors, to realize the hardships imposed on the citizens in such a large county as Wilkinson. It was on November 14, 1809, that he, as representative of Wilkinson County, introduced the bill in the Georgia Legislature to carve a new county out of this vast territory which became an act one month later, thus Twiggs County was created. After the division, he resided in Twiggs County until his death November 5, 1833, and his immortal remains were interred in the family burying ground in the vicinity of Bullard, but a sad fate befell this cemetery a few years ago when the owner of the property obliberated it.

He served as a member of the Committee of Safety, to whom the State Government was entrusted during the darkest hours of struggle.

For many years, he was retained in honorable stations by the people. He was appointed the first Justice of the Inferior Court of Twiggs County on December 15, 1809, a Justice of Peace for Twiggs in 1818 and 1821.

A fervid, patriotic Christian zeal, characterized his life to its latest hour.
Ref: White, George, HISTORY OF GEORGIA, page 687—The National Cyclopaedia of American Biography—Vol. II.

## PIONEERS

Twiggs County was settled largely by immigrants from eastern counties, some of whom had migrated from Virginia, North Carolina, and South Carolina.

The sturdy, pious pioneer settlers, who came into Twiggs settled on the rich wilderness lands. They built their crude hand-hewn log houses in scattered communities. The small log house had dirt floors with a stick and dirt chimney at one end on which most of the meals were cooked in iron pots hanging from hooks. This crude house served the family until a larger and more commodious house could be constructed. Usually this new house was built in front of or to the side of the log house which then served as a kitchen connected by a gang-plank without any cover.

There were in Twiggs, as in other sections, three major groupings or divisions of material wealth among the Twiggs County people during the ante-bellum or pre-

Civil War Era. The three categories were: plantation owner, independent planter, and slave labor.

PLANTATION SYSTEM. The plantation system refers to the family ownership of vast tracts of land, supervised by the master of the household. The master placed the initial responsibility of operation on the plantation overseer, who carried out the master's request, and acted as foreman over the slave laborers. This type of system was not uncommon to certain Twiggs families prior to the War-Between-the-States.

Plantation owners usually lived in spacious houses, often called the "Big House", and were possessed with aristocratic inclinations, which meant they were a privileged group due to their wealth and rank. Their families were given those privileges denied the less money class, such as schooling by private tutors who taught the three 'R's" and the social graces becoming the status of a plantation owner's family. And too, the members of the master's household were generally exempt from all manual duties of labor. The human relationship between the families of wealth and the families of lesser stations were usually cordial.

INDEPENDENT PLANTER. The independent planters and artisans settled in numbers in all parts of the county. Perhaps they are best described by George Gillman Smith in his book entitled, THE STORY OF GEORGIA AND THE GEORGIA PEOPLE.

As yet society in new Georgia had most of the features which belong to all newly settled countries. The houses were still in the main of logs, and most of the people very plain in their style of living. Nearly all of the people with families owned their homestead, and while many of them were in humble circumstances, they were very independent.

The Middle Georgia society differed from that of lower Georgia in that the latter was an American of long descent.—The good women of middle Georgia society were the best and busiest of their kind. They had married in the early years of the century, and had known but little of the school teacher and had never seen a dancing master. Reaching womanhood before they ever saw a town or city, they had the simple, genial manners learned from their old Virginia mothers. They had culture, but it had not come from books. They knew all kinds of domestic work; they could weave and spin and knit, and, if need be, cook and wash; but they had too much to do to attend to these homely duties themselves. They saw to the welfare of the Negroes, especially the ailing women and little children. They knew the virtues of bone-set and sage and catnip; they could dress a blister or make a poultice or bind a bandage with the skill of a physician. These matrons led busy lives in attending such duties as to see to the making up of Negro clothing; too see after the kitchen garden and flower garden; to go to week-day meetings and to get ready for camp meeting; to spread a generous table every day. They were proud of their Virginia lineage, and spoke of the old commonwealth as if no spot on earth could ever be like that. They had read no book but the Bible and "Pilgrim's Progress," and possibly "Charlotte Temple" or "Alonzo and Melissa"; took no magazine and had no flashing plates. Many of them had no Negroes at all, a great many had only a few. They owned land and livestock, and by hard work made an abundant living. The middle class family lived in simplicity.

SLAVE. The third major division in society was that of the slave, a status of those persons possessed as property of another person. The slave had a monetary value of from about $150.00 upward to about $1,500.00, and was on occasions used as a medium of exchange. Wealthy planters often owned several hundred slaves while the most modest farmer possessed only a few. Most of the able-bodied male slaves were used for field work and other such duties requiring strength and endurance. The very young and extremely old male slaves performed chores less strenuous, such as caring for the animals and chopping of firewood. On several large plantations select slaves were taught to be blacksmiths, masons and other similar trades and practiced these learned skills exclusively.

Slave women and girls generally performed tasks pertaining to household duties, as weaving, cooking, sewing and yard jobs, but on occasions the women were used as field laborers.

The slave was looked upon as a piece of property or a tool used to produce an end product at a profit to the master. So long as the owner received remunerations in return for the cost, board, clothing, and lodging of the slave, he was usually retained, but when the end product was less than the cost of production over a period of time, then slavery ceased to be an asset to the owner and the slave was sold, or given in payment for a debt.

The mode of travel from one community to another was by horse back, ox cart, wagon, road cart, the fringed top surry and stage coach. The settlers used the old trails blazed by the Indians for the most part until they could survey and improve roads.

The pioneer settlers were men of enterprise and intelligence, who despite the hardships and privations that existed, learned how to find their way around, developed business and farming interests and a county where their progeny and later settlers have had a chance to live a rewarding and useful life, contributing in part to the building of a great State and Nation.

The newcomers were welcomed by those who had previously settled here. As the settlements grew in size, a log church was built to care for the spiritual needs of all. The minister was a circuit rider, who besides providing for the spiritual needs of his flock, was often an adviser on many daily problems. Often churches had to be used for schools. The school master was an important person in the community.

The following surnames of the first settlers according to George White in HISTORICAL COLLECTIONS OF GEORGIA are: Fort, Wimberly, Perry, Crocker, Peck, Wall, Tarver, Everett, Williams, Denson, Jones, Hodgins, Wilder, Murphy, Lowery, Johnson, Thorp, Davis, Ray, Harrell, Harrington, Sullivan, Melton. In other sources the following family names were listed among the early settlers: Fannin, Griffin, Lawson, Ware, Hughes, Chappell, Powell, Wood, Smith, Jamison, Wilkinson, Joiner, Pearce, Andrews, Bull, Young, Hawthorn, Dick, Evans, Shine, Solomon, Hinson, Bullard, Beckom, and Ricks. Soon other families settled in the county, purchasing land as noted on the 1818 Tax Digest, which was the earliest available digest.

An interesting article appeared in THE TWIGGS HERALD in February, 1903, J. J. Wimberly, editor. Captioned—OBSERVATIONS. "Twiggs is one of the grandest counties of this, or any other state. The blood of Glovers, Burns, Wimberlys, Hughes, Jones, Faulks, O'Daniels, Williams, Asbells, Johnstons, Slappeys, Burketts, Whitehursts, Fitzpatricks, Walters, Griffins, Stevens, Shannons, Solomons, and many other distinguished men who have made Georgia History, flow through the veins of the younger generation of Twiggs County citizens, many of whom are worthy of their distinguished sires."

From the early sires passed a heritage undaunted to progeny—thus the cycle of history moves.

THE HERITAGE

Diana Kearney Powell

By permission from N.S.D.A.R.

Hold me not boastful that I take a pride
    In what my forefathers have achieved;
I honor, not myself, but them, who gave
    A priceless heritage on which to build.
Not selfishness—for they knew sacrifice;
    Not cowardice—but courage for the right:
Not boldness—but a quiet dignity;
    Not false pride—but a love of high ideals
And reverence for things to be revered.
    Heir to these qualities, so may I prove
More worthy of the blood that flows in me.
    The great foundation of my life today,
Which by the toil of patriots has been formed.

## NOTABLE CITIZENS OF TWIGGS

The list of notable citizens of Twiggs County is lengthy. Herein mention is made of a few persons who have attained prominent stations in life. (In mentioning these outstanding citizens no person has been inadvertently omitted.)

Several outstanding personalities during the last century and a half were: Stephen F. Miller, outstanding lawyer and authority on law, and author of THE BENCH AND BAR OF GEORGIA; Robert Perryman, lawyer by profession and writer by vocation, his best known writing being THE LIFE AND PUBLIC SERVICE OF MAJOR-GENERAL ANDREW JACKSON. Also living in the early period of the county was Thaddeus Oliver, lawyer and poet. Mr. Oliver is given credit in several sources of information for having written the famous poem, "All Quiet Along the Potomac Tonight."

Other outstanding citizens of Twiggs were: General Hartwell Tarver, a wealthy planter; Colonel Ezekiel Wimberly, a planter, head of the State Militia, and State Legislator; Governor James M. Smith, Governor of Georgia from 1872-1877; James W. Fannin, a West Point appointee from Twiggs and martyr to the cause of Texas Independence and after whom Fannin County, Georgia was named; Doctor James E. Dickey, president of Emory College; General Philip Cook, Secretary of State, Congressman and veteran of the War Between the States; General L. L. Griffin for whom the town of Griffin was named, later a resident of Monroe County, and first president of the old Monroe Road; Robert A. Everett, lawyer and debater.

Some of the more recent notable citizens were Dudley M. Hughes, United States Congressman; Benjamin S. Fitzpatrick, commissioner and superintendent of Twiggs Schools; Dr. J. C. Solomon, scholar, physician, minister, and author; Dr. Albert M. Gates, Sr., professor and president of Brewton-Parker Junior College, president of Georgia Teachers College, and Superintendent of Twiggs Schools; and James D. Shannon, lawyer, County School Superintendent, Representative, Senator, and collector of historical data.

## CENTENNIAL 1909

### CELEBRATION OF 100 YEARS GROWTH

The centennial celebration of the county was a colorful day in the history of the county. It was held on October 22, 1909, the day of the annual School Fair. At that time as the county's main interest was agricultural it seemed practical to celebrate the School Fair and the Centennial on the same date, although this date was not the actual date of the constitution of the county. The following reference to this gala event was found in the Annual School Statement of 1909 by B. S. Fitzpatrick, County School Commissioner: "The court house was appropriately decorated, the Dublin band played, and a suitable program was arranged. The day was bright and pleasant, everyone seemed happy. A mammouth dinner was spread on the court house square. Among those who made addresses on this occasion were Supt. B. S. Fitzpatrick, H. F. Griffin, Jr., Honorable Dudley M. Hughes, Rev. J. C. Solomon, Honorable James M. Dupree and Rev. G. W. Thorpe. The history of the county, prepared by Dan G. Hughes, was read by Honorable J. C. Shannon. A paper on the County's resources was read by Colonel M. J. Carswell. The evening program, which was enjoyed by a large crowd in the spacious courtroom, consisted of music by the Dublin band and readings by Misses Clara Wimberly, Marianna Slappy and Fleta Fitzpatrick."

Centennial and School Fair, 1909

# CHAPTER II
# INDIAN HISTORY

The first inhabitants in this section were Indians. The white man made much use of the framework laid by them and many towns and villages now occupy sites of former Indian settlements. The Indians planned to halt the influx of the white man, but failed.

The compilers feel it needless to repeat the Indian history which ante-dates the formation of Twiggs County, formerly a part of Wilkinson County, because of the complete data in the HISTORY OF WILKINSON COUNTY by the late Honorable Victor Davidson and in the HISTORY OF PULASKI AND BLECKLEY COUNTIES by Mrs. Virginia Speer Harris.

A few old Twiggs County records substantiate Indian habitation here, even though the information is scarce and practically all evidence is obscure.

## DE SOTO TRAIL

About 1538-40, Hernando De Soto, a Spanish nobleman, led an expedition of well-armed men through Florida passing through Georgia in search of riches. The course of his zig-zag route led these fortune seekers through a section of what is presently Twiggs County. How different might have been the story today, if De Soto had remained longer here and found wealth in these parts. A probability, had it not been that an Indian chief informed him that further north more wealth abounded. DeSoto's eager desire for treasure caused he and his men to move onward seeking fortune. A DeSoto Quadri Centennial marker stands near Tarversville giving facts about his visit.

Marker Erected—on U. S. Highway 23-129, Ga. 87

## BLUFF TRAIL

In 1807 when William Dowsing, Sr. surveyed the Twenty-fourth Land District of Wilkinson County, presently Twiggs, he traced a trail on his plat which he labeled "Bluff Trail". The trail begins in the northern part of lot number 43 moving westward across the district, crossing waters of Crooked Creek on the south side, on through lot numbers 269 and 292 leading into the Ocmulgee Swamp. South of this trail ran another trail known as Jameson's trail which passed through the town of Danville, on by Mount Zion Baptist Church westward to the River. Many surveyors did not indicate Indian trails on their original survey of a district.

Dr. John H. Goff, Emory University, an authority on old trails in Georgia, gave the following information on "Bluff Trail" also known as the "Upper Uchee Path": "It ran from Uchee Town on the west side of the Chattahoochee River, at the mouth of Uchee Creek, below Columbus to present Montezuma. Thence it passed eastward to the crossing on the Ocmulgee at the mouth of Crooked Creek, near the West Lake Station. It went on past the area of Tarversville then turned more northward for a stretch. Apparently it went by or through old Marion District passing somewhat to the west of today's Jeffersonville. From there to a juncture with the main Lower Creek Trading path, at or near where the latter crossed the Oconee River at the Rock Landing, about four miles below Milledgeville. Later no doubt at the Oconee, it was changed to lead to Fort Wilkinson, when that stockade was built. There was a fork in the trail between Tarversville and Marion to the southward of Jeffersonville. This trail is bound to have existed, because records of old eastern Wilkinson show a trail leading westward from Oconee toward such a junction.

As far as is known, this Uchee trail must have received its name about 1729. It was called the "Upper Uchee Path" in contrast to the "Lower Uchee Path", a fork which ran from Montezuma via today's Hawkinsville, Cochran and near Dublin to "Old Town," on the east side of the Ogeechee below Louisville.

It should be stated that two trails reached the west side of the Ocmulgee and joined at the crossing below the mouth of Crooked Creek. One of these came from the direction of Montezuma where the Timothy Barnard sons' settlement was located. The other route is not so clear as to its entire course, but I believe it led from Patsiliga, an Uchee town located on the Flint River, to the west of today's Reynolds, Georgia.

I have never seen the name, "Bluff Trail", applied to the "Upper Uchee Path" before receiving your letter (Mrs. Faulk). Since the general area along the Ocmulgee opposite the ford at the mouth of Crooked Creek is called "The Bluff", there is a suggestion that the route received its name because it led past this bluff."

Part of the Twenty-fourth District of Wilkinson County, now Twiggs, Georgia, showing Bluff Trail. Traced from original map surveyed by William Dowsing, Sr., Feb. 10, 1807. Trail—dotted line.

Courtesy: Mrs. Philip W. Bryant, Georgia Surveyor General Department

## OTHER TRAILS

Mrs. Sallie Balckom Kitchens, an elderly Twiggs Countian, related information about the signs of an Indian trail she remembered from childhood days which led to an out-post for trading from Fort Hawkins, located near the present site of Antioch Baptist Church. The trail ran through lot number 41, the property once owned by the late Daniel Travis Epps.

According to legend, Savage Creek bears the name because white families living near were massacred by savage Indians. Today signs of small mounds of earth in the vicinity can be seen.

Indian paths, packed hard by the runners, became the trails which the white men followed and eventually widened to accommodate their ox carts and crude wagons on which they moved their supplies and other cargo as they moved inland. At a bluff on the Ocmulgee River, known as Durham's Bluff, cargo was loaded and unloaded to freight boats that plied the river between Darien and Macon. A road led from Marion to this bluff. Reference to this old road is made in an old deed made by Allen Bullard dated November 14, 1844. An old stage road that led from Savannah northward through Marion has visible signs of the old bed near historic Richland Church. Over this road, known as the Northern State Road, the beautiful marble monument that marks the grave of Amanda Beckom Richardson in the Church Cemetery was hauled by ox-cart from Savannah.

## HARTFORD ROAD

The old military road constructed from Milledgeville to Hartford passed through Twiggs County, running through the present town of Jeffersonville, followed in part, the road bed that is commonly referred to as the Longstreet Road. The Hartford Road has been referred to since it served its military purpose as the Milledgeville-Hartford Public Road as shown in a deed made by the late Mrs. Julia Burns and in a deed made by the late H. B. Burns as the Milledgeville-Hawkinsville dirt road, both of whom owned land in the Twenty-fourth Land District. In later years it also served as a stage road for mail service and passengers between these points.

The Hartford to Milledgeville Road was an important line of communication during the War of 1812 for Brigadier General David Blackshear's couriers carrying dispatches to and from Hartford, in Pulaski County, to Milledgeville, the Capitol of the State. Hartford was then a Georgia frontier town situated at the head of navigation on the Ocmulgee River and an important point for political and military operations. The crisis which was threatening the destiny of Georgia citizens was responsible for the building of the Hartford Road. British agents stationed just beyond the Ocmulgee River were constantly stirring up trouble among the Creek Indians. Georgians realized the dangerous position of the State in that the British could attack from several strategic points. Thus it was necessary for Georgia officials to make hurried preparations to be able to rush troops, artillery, and ammunition to Hartford as well as to other points. An act of the Georgia Legislature in 1810 ordered the construction of the road, naming as commissioners, Aaron Feagan and B. McCrary of Baldwin County, John King, Thomas McGinity and Thomas Durham of Wilkinson, Robert Sherrod, John Hays and Thomas Dennard of Twiggs. Very soon along this road the tramp of General Blackshear's troops, the rumble of artillery wagons and the roll of drums were heard. The Hartford Road had to serve as a military road again when trouble broke out with the Indians in 1818 and again in 1836.

## THE WAR OF 1812

The citizens of Georgia realized the peril that now faced them as news reached the inhabitants that the British were planning to land troops on American shores. They were aware that if the British landed troops in Indian territory hostile Indians would rally to their standard and would probably march through the State. The uneasy inhabitants in the section between the Ocmulgee and the Oconee rivers feared this area would be in the threatened line of march if the British were to use Florida as a base or if they were to attack along the coast below Savannah. This section as well as the frontier was totally unprepared for any invading forces such as might burst forth upon it.

The British grasped every opportunity to arouse the Indians in religious beliefs against the Americans. Tecumesh, the powerful agent, was selected to devise every conceivable means to convert the Indian chieftains of the various tribes until they joined in a war party against the Americans.

Here and there, an Indian chieftain would remain loyal to the Americans and hold his followers in line. Chiefest of these was Big Warrior of the Tuckabatches, Chief Speaker of the nation. He treated the teachings of Tecumesh and his converts with derision. Regardless of the prophecies made by Tecumesh and the outcome of these fantastic threats that peril would befall those who did not believe in them, the old chieftain refused to take sides against his American friends.. With him remained the greater part of the Tuckabatchee tribe, the Coweta, the Cusseta and a few other tribes.

The British had planned for the Indian outbreak to coincide with the arrival of their fleet and land forces. But the outbreak throughout the Indian Nation came earlier than they expected. In 1813 a civil war among the Creeks was evident. Hoboheilthle, the Tallassee King, now took the war club. He vowed to capture and destroy all the Indian towns lying between him and the Georgia frontiers and would not stop until he had reached the Ogeechee, with his bows and arrows and magic powers, aided by the British and Shawnees, he would crush the Americans.

Civil war burst forth. The weight of Indian vengeance could be felt. The Cussetah and Coweta warriors succeeded in saving Big Warrior and his tribesmen and brought them back to the Indian towns along the Chattahoochee. The towns along the Chattahoochee now constituted the first line of defense for the inhabitants. Yet, the Governor of Georgia and federal officials seemed unaware of the crisis facing the people. The sudden massacree at Fort Mims filled the nation with horror and awakened the leaders to the crisis. The date set to storm Coweta town was about October 1st, 1813. News reached the friendly Indians that the Seminoles were on the march. Appeals were sent to the Governor of Georgia. He, now being alarmed, hastened General Floyd with the Georgia Militia to Coweta and arrived in time to prevent its fall.    (Ref.: Indian Affairs.)

The inhabitants in the section living along the Ocmulgee frontier were in a panic of fear and were fleeing inland because they were aware of the ability of Hoboheilthle to make good his threat, with his thousands of warriors, and that the small forces of Militia in the area would be no match for these redskin tribesmen.

Brigadier General David Blackshear, of Laurens County, was in command of the Second Brigade of the Fifth Division, composed of the regiments of Wilkinson, Twiggs, Laurens, Pulaski, and Telfair counties.

In the early part of August, 1813, the situation along the frontier guarded by this brigade became so serious that Governor David Mitchell ordered him to repair at once to the Ocmulgee and take such necessary steps as would make the inhabitants safe. He hastened to Twiggs County and laid out three forts along the river frontier at strategic points. Colonel Ezekiel Wimberly, commanding the militia of Twiggs, was ordered to assemble sufficient men to garrison the forts along the

Twiggs border and to provide mounted spies to patrol the territory lying between. Similar orders were given to Colonel Tooke of Pulaski and Major Cawthorn of Telfair to garrison forts in their respective counties. The forts in Twiggs County were to be in line with these forts along the river and with Fort Hawkins (now at Macon).

## LOCAL COMMANDER'S REQUEST FOR ARMAMENT—WAR 1812
Georgia Military Affairs, Hays, Vol. 3, 1801-1813—Page 163

Marion, 9 Apl. 1813

Sir.

I have engaged the bearer hereof Mr. Harrol to bring the arms which I requested of you some days ago agreeable to the message you sent me by Major Hardin; If there is any ammunition in the public arsenal I would be glad you would send the amount before requested, for that article is as much wanted as the guns. I have agreed to waggoner three dollars per day provided he is not gone more than four days, or detained in Milledgeville, you may therefore know how to settle with him. Any directions which you may give respecting the disposal of the arms here shall be punctually attended to.

I am sir, with the highest
respect your most ob sevt.
Ezek. Wimberly

His Excellency
Govr. Mitchell

On reverse
His Excellency Governor Mitchell
Milledgeville

Letter from Col. Ezekiel Wimberly of Twiggs County on subj of Public Arms. Ordered to be filled 12th April 1813.

Received the 12th April 1813 of His Excellency David B. Mitchell, Governor of Georgia, 100 public muskets, bayonets, cartouch boxes, bets ec. and 50 pounds Gun powder, also 50 horsemens swords and scabbords all which I promise to deliver safe (the dangers of the road excepted) to Colo. Ezekiel Wimberly of Twiggs County.

his
David  x  Harrel
mark

## ORDERS TO OFFICERS IN COMMAND RELATING TO THE WAR OF 1812
Ref.: Bench and Bar of Georgia.

XII—Gen. Blackshear to Lt. Col. E. Wimberly, August 7, 1813. (General Orders). Sir:—Agreeably to orders from his Excellency the Governor, of the 4th instant, you will proceed without delay to call out of your regiment one subaltern, one sergeant, one corporal, and fifteen privates to each of the three forts to be built on the frontier of your county, whose duty it will be to erect the said forts agreeable to the plan enclosed. You will relieve the said detachments once every week by the same number, until you receive further orders. Those at Forts Telfair and Twiggs will be furnished with rations by Mr. Drury Williams, and Fort Jackson by Mr. William Jemison. Should any thing transpire to further alarms, you will communicate it to me without further delay.

You will call on some expert captain, in whom you have confidence, to take command of the whole detachment, whose duty it will be to superintend the aforesaid works and the discipline of the troops.

I am, &c.,
D. Blackshear,
Brigadier-General 2d Brigade 5th Division.

XIII—Gen. Blackshear to Gov. Mitchell. Oconee, August 13, 1813.
Sir:—I have just returned from my tour on the frontier of my brigade, where I found the inhabitants in a high state of alarm,—an immense number of whom had left and fled to the interior.

I proceeded to lay off three forts on the frontier of Twiggs County, at about ten miles distant from each other, about one hundred feet square, to have two block-houses, and enclosed with a stockade eight feet above ground,—and ordered one subaltern, a sergeant, a corporal, and fifteen privates to each, and a captain to command and superintend the buildings, and discipline of the men.

In Pulaski, having a greater extent of frontier, I laid out four, to be built in the same manner as those in Twiggs, and the same number of men to each, commanded by a captain.

I then proceeded to Telfair, and laid out three, ninety feet square and ordered one sergeant, a corporal, and twelve privates to each, and a subaltern to command the whole, to be relieved every ten days until further orders. I employed persons to furnish those men called out with meat, meal, and salt until some arrangement can be made.

This plan of defense, with the addition of two horsemen to each fort to reconnoitre on the other side of the river as far as the next fort, I should deem sufficient even in time of actual danger, which protection will be a great inducement to those who have left their homes to return. Those in Telfair should have the same force as the other counties; but that county is thinly inhabited, and the men called out are from the frontier counties.

Should this plan meet your Excellency's approbation, I shall immediately order men from Wilkinson and Laurens to relieve them; and, if it should be deemed proper to reduce or augment the force thus ordered out, any other order your Excellency may think proper to give shall be attended to with utmost promptness. My exertions, together with your letter to Col. Tooke reiterating that the frontier should be protected, had great effect in removing the apprehension of danger. Should there be any arms and ammunition to spare, those forts in Telfair County will stand in need of some.

I am, &c., D. Blackshear,
Brigadier-General

XVI—Gen. Blackshear to Col. Wimberly. Fort Twiggs, September 14, 1813.
Sir:—The danger of an immediate invasion on the frontier appears to have subsided for the present. A detachment of troops having marched out to the Flint River will, in my opinion, give security to the frontier. You will therefore discharge the men ordered out on the frontier of your county.

I am, sir, &c., D. Blackshear, Brigadier-General
Ref: Miller, S. F., BENCH AND BAR OF GEORGIA.

## SPIES IN SERVICE

Names of spies employed by Maj. Patton at the several forts on the Indian frontier.

| County | Forts | Spies' Names | When Commenced | Price Pr. Day |
|---|---|---|---|---|
| Twiggs | Telfair | William Griffin and Robert Johnson | Dec. 30th, 1813 | $1.00 |
| Twiggs | Twiggs | William Hemphill and Isaac Dennard | Dec. 22nd, 1813 | $1.00 |

| Twiggs | Jackson | William Davison (Davidson) and William Barker and/or William Burke | Dec. 22nd, 1813 | $1.00 |

I do certify the above to be a correct list of the spies as employed by me this 22nd of February 1814.

Jas. Patton, Major

Ref: CREEK INDIAN LETTERS—Hays—Part Three    1813-1829, Page 827.

Department of Archives and History, Atlanta, Ga.

Drury Williams had a Government contract to furnish rations to Fort Telfair and Fort Twiggs; William Jemison (Jameson) a contract to furnish rations to Fort Jackson. The contracts were signed by Lovett B. Smith, Brevet. Lieut.

The following is a copy of a contract:
"Fort Jackson 9th August 1813. The contractor will issue to Sergt. Simpson eight days rations for this detachment of Georgia Militia commencing the 9th and ending the 16th Inst. Number men 17; Number days 8; Number rations 17; complete rations Aug. 9th, 1813.    L. B. Smith, Brevt. Lieut."

The names of the spies for the forts and those who furnished rations are listed on an early Tax Digest in the 25th, 26th and 28th districts—Drury Williams, William Griffin, Isaac Dennard, William Hemphill and Robert Johnson (Johnston). The men, who had other military duties—James Patton, Caleb McKinney, Samuel Alexander and Ezekiel Wimberly—are listed on the early Tax Digest as property owners in the above named districts. Richard Smith, William Jameson (Jemison) and William Davidson are listed on the Tax Digest in the 24th district.

Below is a verbatim copy of a spy's letter to his commanding officer making a report: CREEK INDIAN LETTERS, by Hays, page 783.

"Georgia, Twiggs County, 7 June 1813

Sir:

In pursuance of orders to me delivered by Col. Samuel Alexander I set out in company with Calip McKinna over the Ocmulgee River on the 26 of May last continued fore days we found an Indian camp oppersit the Bluff called Dennimus Bluff (near the swamp) we saw none of them we did see wheair they had drove a number of cattle from the upper parts of his state down the river—we saw corn in the camp in the year—we saw an ax that we did suppose was taken from R. Johnstons field from the description of it. No savage partys (or the sine) discovered but hear of a great deal of sine bin seene since that date.

I remain with dew Rspect yours,<br>Richard Smith

On reserve side appeared; Richard Smith, Twiggs County, 7th June, 1813, Enclosing an account for services as a Spie & C    $12 orders taken 12 June, 1813."

## ROSTER OF MEN WHO SERVED AT TWIGGS COUNTY FORTS, WAR OF 1812
### Lieutenant Lovett B. Smith's Company

Pay-roll of the first detachment of militia ordered out on the frontier of Twiggs County, in pursuance of orders from Brigadier General Blackshear, dated August 7, 1813, for the protection of the inhabitants residing in the Ocmulgee area, and to build Fort Jackson.

## OFFICERS

Brevet-Lieutenant, Lovett B. Smith
1st Sergeant, Solomon Simpson
2d Sergeant, Daniel Jordan
3d Sergeant, Edward Land
1st Corporal, Elijah Bryan
2st Corporal, Benjamin Mobley
3d Corporal, John Conner

## PRIVATES

| | | |
|---|---|---|
| Thomas Smith | George Jemison | Young Vickars |
| John Bateman | Holman Stephens | Harman Mock |
| James Dunwoody | James Stephens | Amos Haughton |
| Simon Simpson | John Morgan | Robert Underwood |
| Lewis Daniel | John Wolf | Rowland Tate |
| Thomas Matthews | Joel Carter | James Garrett |
| Thornton Perry | Simon Bateman | John Upton |
| James Graham | George Opry | Thomas Underwood |
| Thomas Hunt | Uriah Simpson | John Hughlen |
| David Neeland | David Bozeman | Eleazar Galloway |
| John Williams | John Smith | James Daniel |
| Samuel Wells | James Vickars | James L. Craig |
| Robert W. McKinney | Benjamin Johnson | Willis Ward |
| William Coach | Charles Sutton | Charles Wolf |
| Benjamin Grantham | Ephriam Hightower | Lemuel Lanier |

The end of service, September 14, 1813, I do certify upon honor that the service for the above pay-roll was performed under my command.

Ezekiel Wimberly
Lieutenant-Colonel

## CAPTAIN JOHN THOMAS' COMPANY

Fort Mitchell, February 22, 1814. A muster-roll of Captain John Thomas' Company, under the command of Major James Patton, ordered into service on the 22d December, 1813, and terminated on the 19th of February, 1814, both days inclusive, to guard the frontiers in the different counties and forts: Twiggs County: Fort Twiggs, Fort Jackson; Pulaski County: Fort Mitchell, Fort Laurens; Telfair County: Fort Adams and Fort McIntosh.

## OFFICERS

Captain, John Thomas
Lieutenant, James G. Haines
Ensign, Eli Collins
1st Sergeant, John Fenn
2d Sergeant, Sampson Culpepper
3d Sergeant, Daniel Lewis
4th Sergeant, Nathan Maddox
1st Corporal, John Dean
2d Corporal, Uriah Kinchen
3d Corporal, Allaway Roach
4th Corporal, Simon Woodson

## PRIVATES

| | | |
|---|---|---|
| William H. Paramore | John Garrard | James Simmons |
| B. McLendon | Abram Bush | Isaac Wade |
| Moses E. Bush | Levin Gilstrap | James Mayo |
| Thomas Swearingen | Dawson Webb | Jacob Kanahest |
| Alexander Varner | E. Webb | Arahibald H. Odom |
| Thomas Gilbert | Lemuel Pruett | James Caldwell |
| James Yarborough | Joseph Culpepper | Samuel Miller |
| John Lawson | John Sims | M. Lewis |

| | | |
|---|---|---|
| John Martin | William Smith | Isaac Kirksey |
| Seth Ward | Harris Hicks | Needham Bedingham |
| Jesse Harris | Alexander Mars | Jesse Murphrey |
| Thomas W. Benson | George Morgan | William Barker |
| Mills Ezell | Levi Elsley | Josiah Stewart |
| Jonathan Jones | Jeremiach Allman | Isaac Dennard |
| John Harrel | John Truluck | William Hemphill |
| J. Kingsley | John Harris | William Griffin |
| Abram Nipper | Alexander Shepherd | James Ward |
| James Cain | Sampson Dickson | Dennis Posey |
| Edwin Moye | James W. McCullers | William Studfield |
| Herod Mills | Lemon Johnson | Moses Kirkland |
| Gidon Bush | Edward Johnson | Reuben Wheeler |
| Britton Sanford | John Nelson | Prior Prewett |
| James Collins | John Tharp | James Clark |
| Thomas Newberry | Martin Livingston | A. Lassiter |
| Thomas N. Singletery | Benjamin Watkins | J. A. William |
| Benjamin Salter | Abram Adams | William Lester |
| Joshua Cobb | James Bailey | Lemuel Evans |
| James Johnson | Henry Bailey | |

## FRONTIER OF TWIGGS COUNTY

Pay-roll of a detachment of militia ordered on the frontier of Twiggs County, for the protection of the inhabitants and for the erection of a fort called Telfair, by Brig. Gen. Blackshear, from the 9th of August to 13th September, 1813.

### OFFICERS

Lieutenant, John Keener  
1st Sergeant, Lewis Moore  
2d Sergeant, William White  
3rd Sergeant, Nimrod Busby  
4th Sergeant, John Hair  

5th Sergeant, Henry Summerall  
1st Corporal, Powell Smith  
2d Corporal, James Howard  
3d Corporal, Jeremiah Dunn  
4th Corporal, James Jones  

### PRIVATES

| | | |
|---|---|---|
| Kinney Powell | Michael Carlisle | William Solomon |
| John Jones | Frederick G. Herring | John Dean |
| Samuel Streetman | James Randall | Thomas Hair |
| William Streetman | Ezekiel Wall | William Burke |
| James Hollingsworth | Thomas Bird | Joshua Hawthorn |
| James Smith | John Hinson | John Burke |
| Henry Conrad | Mark Pettis | Minton Dean |
| Henry Troutman | A. Pate | Hardy Bedingfield |
| William Johnston | John Hollingsworth | Jethro Holland |
| J. Matthews | John Fullwood | Isaac Brown |
| William Stanford | William Fullingame | Frederick Watson |
| William Griffin | William Crawford | John Frederick |
| William Summerall | Johnathan West | Charles Stewart |
| William Dunn | C. Leonard | Josiah Davis |
| Reuben Anderson | John Wilson | Samuel Stanford |
| Lewis Coppage | Stephen Bostick | Clement Milton |
| John Adkins | James Bailey | Caleb McKinney |
| John Lamb | Henry Fortner | Robert Atkinson |
| Elisha Tarver | William Todd | Moses Hill |
| Joshua Sloan | | |

I do certify upon honor that the service for the above pay-roll was performed under my command.

Ezekiel Wimberly
Lieutenant-Colonel

## GEORGIA MILITARY RECORD BOOK 1779-1839

Page 162-163

Pay roll of a detachment of Militia ordered on the frontier of Twiggs County for the protection of the inhabitants and for the erection of a Fort called Telfair by Brig. Gen. D. Blackshear from the ninth of August 1813, to the thirteenth of September inclusive.

| RANK | NAMES | COMMENCEMENT OF SERVICE | EXPIRATION OF SERVICE |
|---|---|---|---|
| Brig. Lieut. | John Kener | Aug. 9, 1813 | Sept. 13, 1813 |
| Sergt. | Lewis Moore | " | Aug. 16, 1813 |
| Corpl. | Powel Smith | " | " |
| Pvt. | Quincy Powell | | |
| | John Jones | | |
| | Samuel Streetman | | |
| | William Streetman | | |
| | James Hollingsworth | | |
| | James Smith | | |
| | Henry Coward | | |
| | Henry Trentman | | |
| | William Johnston | | |
| | J. Mathews | | |
| | William Stanford | | |
| | William Griffin | | |
| | William Summeral | | |
| | William Dunn | | |
| | Reuben Anderson | | |
| Sergt. | Nimrod Busby | Aug. 17 | Aug. 24 |
| | Powel Smith | | |
| | Thomas Bird | | |
| | John Hinson | | |
| | Mark Petis | | |
| | A. Pate | | |
| | John Holingsworth | | |
| | John Fulwood | | |
| | William Griffin | | |
| | William Fullingame | | |
| | William Crawford | | |
| | Caleb Hinson | | |
| | James Smith | | |
| | Johnathan West | | |
| | C. Leonard | | |
| | John Wilson | | |
| | Stephen Bostwick | | |
| Sergt. | William White | Aug. 24 | Aug. 31 |
| Corpl. | James Howard | " | " |
| Pvt. | Lewis Coppage | | |
| | John Adkins | | |
| | John Lamb | | |
| | Elisha Tare | | |

|  |  |  |  |
|---|---|---|---|
|  | Joshua Sloan |  |  |
|  | M. Carlisle |  |  |
|  | Fredrick G. Herring |  |  |
|  | James Randle |  |  |
|  | E. Wall |  |  |
|  | James Bailey |  |  |
|  | Henry Fortner |  |  |
|  | William Todd |  |  |
|  | William Solomon |  |  |
|  | John Jones |  |  |
| Sergt. | John Hair | Sept. 1 | Sept. 7 |
| Pvt. | Jeremiah Dunn | " | " |
|  | John Dean |  |  |
|  | Thomas Hair |  |  |
|  | William Burke |  |  |
|  | Joshua Hathern |  |  |
|  | John Burke |  |  |
|  | Minton Dean |  |  |
|  | Hardy Bedingfield |  |  |
|  | Jethro Holland |  |  |
|  | Robert Bedingfield |  |  |
|  | Isaac Brown |  |  |
|  | Frederick Watson |  |  |
|  | James Hollingsworth |  |  |
|  | John Fedrick |  |  |
| Sergt. | Henry Somersall | Sept. 7 | Sept. 14 |
| Corpl. | James Jones | " | " |
| Pvt. | William Stanford |  |  |
|  | Charles Stuart |  |  |
|  | Josiah Davis |  |  |
|  | Samuel Stanford |  |  |
|  | Clement Milton |  |  |
|  | Caleb McKinney |  |  |
|  | Robert Adkinson |  |  |
|  | Moses Hill |  |  |
|  | James Holingsworth |  |  |

I do certify upon Honor that the service for the above pay roll was performed under my command Brevet Captain.
      E. Wimberly

 I do certify that the services performed in the above pay roll was by my order.
      B. Gen. 2nd B.B.D.
      D. Blackshear

             Marion 30th May 1816
Sir.
 I have the honor of again informing your excellency that my spies continue to report that no appearance of any enemy upon diligent examination has been made on the other side of Ockmulgee and no other discovery of a nature necessary to be communciated to your excellency. I hope I shall be excused for suggesting the propriety of discharging them as soon as the safety of the country will admit, in the meanwhile be assured the utmost diligence will be observed, to avoid a surprise, or other misfortunes should we be (?) by the enemy.

 I am your excellency' most obedient svt.,
      Ezekiel Wimberly, Lt. Col.

## THE SEMINOLE INDIAN WAR

The white man's desire for westward expansion was marked by a series of Indian cessions. The last Indian menace came in 1836 after which this race was forcefully moved to reservations. The following information shows the participation of Twiggs County in the Seminole Indian War.

Headquarters, Georgia
Milledgeville, January 13, 1836

"To the Commanders of Volunteer Corps:

The hostile conduct of the Indians on our western frontier, and the actual state of war now enlisting in Florida between our fellow-citizens of that territory and the Seminole Indians, render it proper that Georgia should place herself in a state of defence to meet any emergency that may grow out of this state of things. You will, therefore, immediately proceed to cause the volunteers Company under your command to be prepared to serve their country if they should be required, and to hold themselves in readiness at a moments warning.

You will also, without delay, make report to Headquarters, of the effective force under your command. With the names of the officers and privates, and of the number, nature and condition of their arms and accouterments.
By order of the Commander-in-Chief,
Boling H. Robinson
Aide-de-Camp

J. C. Butler,*History of Macon and Central Georgia*, page 124.

The following information was copied from a loose file on Twiggs County's Military Records at the State Department of Archives and History.

Georgia, Twiggs County. In pursuance of orders from headquarters, the men subject to Militia duty paraded at Marion said county on Thursday the fourth, Inst, for the purpose of standing a (Doaft?) to be in readiness at a minutes notice to march against the hostile Seminoles in Florida—when on the day sixty seven persons turned out as volunteers, who this day met at the Court House in said county to organize the Company, where an election was held for officers and after counting the votes the result was as follows, to-wit:
James Pearson was duly elected as Captain
Josiah Atteway, 1st Lieut.
Nathan Land, 2d Lieut.
Richard Myrick, Ensign
All of which will more fully appear by the enclosed check and list of voters—this Feby 6, 1836.
Given under our hands who superintended the election.
Ben. B. Smith
Elam Hinson
Richard Desazo J. P. Freeholders
List of Marion Volunteers not available.

## TWIGGS COUNTY CALVARY

Twiggs County Cavalry attached to the 37th Regiment. List of names as reported by Captain Harrison composing the Twiggs County Cavalry who enlisted on February 4, 1836.

| | | |
|---|---|---|
| James Harrison, Captain | William C. Harrison, 2nd Lieut. | |
| Ethelred Griffin, 1st Lieut. | Hayden Hughes, Cormt. | |
| Josiah Daniel | H. Hughes | Arthur Lucas |
| Wm. Bryan | C. Hodges | R. Minshaw |
| Joseph T. Saxon | Thomas I. Perryman | R. J. Hodges |

John Raly
Wm. Sawyers
C. Butler
Daniel Coombs
Greenwood Bateman
A. Stephens
John E. Bateman
Henry Carter
L. F. Bateman
Jno. Dennard
Hugh Opry
Wm. C. Harrison
E. Pearce
W. C. Anderson
Joseph Martin
Alfred Thompson
Reecy Street
Simeon Frasier
Lawrence Jenkins
Wm. Nelson
George W. Welch, Jr.

Wm. G. Wilkinson
David Young
Jno. B. Moon
Jas. Radford
Wm. Methvin
T. L. Guerry
L. W. Ward
James Harrison
Lewis Barnett
George W. Wardlaw
L. Ezell
Ethelred Griffin
Wm. H. Ezell
R. A. Nash
Levi Bryan
Alex Pearce
John C. Sheehan
George Taylor
Joseph Sawyer
Sidney Bryan
James M. Watkins

F. L. Bowman
Obidah Adams
Wm. Wimberly
Jno. L. Hodges
Hardy Durham
Jno. J. Wimberly
Richard Adams
Marshall Dennard
Joseph L. Lenton
Wm. Street
R. Mincy
Abishia Horn
James P. Blount
Edward D. Crosland
M. M. Granny
Jonas Lucas
Harmon Bedingfield
Howard Peacock
Robert H. Raines
Nathan Anglin
Jno. F. Simmons

The above officers for the Twiggs Cavalry were commisioned 8th Feby. 1836 by his Excellency Wm. Schley, Milledgeville, Geo.

At an election this day held in the town of Marion, Twiggs County, Georgia for the officers of the Twiggs County Cavalry. We do certify that on counting out the votes that James Harrison was duly and unanimously elected captain of the Twiggs County Cavalry, and that Ethelred Griffin was duly elected first Lieutenant. William C. Harrison was elected as second Lieutenant and Hayden Hughes, Cormt.

Georgia : We certify the above and foregoing to be true given un-
Twiggs County : der our hand and seal this 4th day of February, 1836.
               Henry Bunn (Seal)

                                       Free
             W. C. Harrison (Seal) : Holders
             Levi Ezell, J. P. :

## ELECTION RETURN FOR A MAJOR TO COMMAND THE SQUADRON OF CAVALRY FOR THE FLORIDA SERVICE

The Twiggs County Cavalry together with companies from Hall, Putnam, Walton, Twiggs, Butts and Dooly counties joined a Battalion of horse for Florida service during the Seminole uprising. In an election held at Hawkinsville, Pulaski County, to select a Major and Surgeon, the results were as follows:

James Harrison, 142 votes; David Ross, 239 votes; Slappey, 132 votes; Baily, 228 votes. Camp Hall, Hawkinsville, David Ross, Major, Commissioned, 17th March, 1836.

We do certify that the election for Major and Surgeon held at this place by order of your Excellency the above is a just and true return and that Capt. David Ross is duly elected Major and Stephen Baily, Surgeon.

Given under our hand and Seal, March 17th, 1836.

Jon. Jos. Taylor, J. I. C.; John J. Anderson, J. P.; James B. Stevens, freeholder. To His Excellency William Schley, Milledgeville, Georgia

Refer to the complete list of CAVALRY UNITS (Hall, Putnam, Walton, Twiggs, Butts and Dooley Counties) given in HISTORY OF PULASKI AND BLECKLEY COUNTIES, GEORGIA, pages 50-53.

## PASSPORTS 1785-1820

The following information concerning passports was copied from the Volume on Passports at the State Department of Archives and History.

Passports issued by Governors of Georgia 1785 to 1820 was compiled with authority of John B. Wilson, Secretary of State, under direction of Mrs. J. E. Hays, State Historian, 1940.

"In going through the million loose papers in the Georgia Department of Archives and History, many papers of all sizes and with all manner of handwriting, they proved to be recommendations to the Governors of Georgia for passports for certain persons to go through the Indian nation. These recommendations were from neighbors, friends and Justices of the Peace, who vouched for the industry, sobriety and good character of the person desiring to go through the Indian Nation. The earliest ones found (1785) were recommendations for men to go into the Indian Nation to recover stolen horses, or slaves, or collect debts. Later the object was to "view the country" with an eye to moving; then they began to ask for passports to go as settlers, sometimes to the "strange western countries" to "Tombigbee" or the "Dunbigbee", or "Bigby Country"; to the "Louisiana Country", "The Mississippi Territory" "Orleans", Natchees Territory" or Natchey Country"; to east Florida or the Spanish Province of West Florida. One request was to go into "the foreign country of West Georgia".

In 1809 and 1810 many passports were issued to citizens of North Carolina and South Carolina, who were passing through Georgia in large groups with their families, their household goods on pack horses, their slaves, also their mother-in-law and sisters-in-law, whose names they always failed to mention. In these original papers are two passports prepared for delivery and perhaps never called for, but these are a valuable find to show just the form in which they were issued. The passports seem to stop in 1813, only two issued in 1816, two in 1817, one in 1819, and four in 1820. This was probably due to the fact that many of the Indians had become Allies of England in the War of 1812 and it was dangerous to go through the Indian Nation. By the time it was safe to go through the Indian Nation the last lands in Georgia were secured from the Indians, and there was no need for passports."

From Minutes of the Executive Department on passports. (Excerpts)
PAGE 246, MONDAY 10TH SEPT. 1810. On Application—Ordered—That a passport be prepared for Mr. Mathew Wood from the County of Twiggs in this State to travel through the Creek Nation of Indians.
PAGE 248, SATURDAY, 29TH SEPT. 1810. On application and recommendation, Ordered.—That passports be prepared for the following persons to travel through the Creek Nation of Indians, to-wit, one for John West with his wife and 4 children from the County of Twiggs; one for William Thomas Le Grand from the city of Philadelphia.
PAGE 248, TUESDAY, 2D OCT. 1810. Mr. Joseph Bell with wife and 5 children from Beaufort District, S. C.; Messers Leonard Scott and Aaron Clark and also Budcaid Matthews from Edgefield Dist., S. C., and for Messers John Roberts and Christopher Dyess from the County of Twiggs.
PAGE 252, THURSDAY, 18TH OCT. 1810. Mathew Rushing with his wife and seven children from Beaufort Dist., S. C., one for Loftin Fairchild with his wife and one child and two negroes from Twiggs County in this State.
PAGE 265, FRIDAY, 4TH JAN. 1811. For Mr. Joseph Harly, Twiggs County.
PAGE 265, 15TH FEB. 1811. for Mr. William Davidson with his wife, from Beaufort Dist., S. C., for Mr. Abraham Wood from Twiggs County.

PAGE 279, MONDAY, 18TH MARCH 1811. for Mr. Charles Smith with his wife and 9 children from County of Twiggs, for Mr. Samuel Vernado with his wife and 7 children and 2 negroes; for Mr. John O. Macker with his wife and 3 children; Mr. James Hughes with his wife and 9 children and 2 negroes; Mrs. Sarah Macker and 9 negroes, all from Orangeburgh Dist., S. C.

PAGE 290, MONDAY 12TH AUG. 1811. for Messers Craven P. Moffett and Henry Moffett, the former with wife and 2 children and 2 negroes, all from County of Twiggs.

PAGE 295, FRIDAY, 18TH OCT. 1811. for Mr. Elias Woodruff with his wife, from County of Twiggs . . . to travel through Indian Nation to the Western County.
PAGE 296, WED. 23RD OCT. 1811 . . . to travel through Indian Nations to the Western County, viz: Mr. Francis H. Wellman from County of Chatham, Ga.; for Messers Moses Collins with his wife and 3 children and 13 negroes and Arcy McMannus with his wife, all from County of Twiggs.

PAGE 307, SATURDAY, 4TH JAN. 1812. to travel to the Western Country, for Mathew Bryan and his wife from County of Jefferson, Ga.; one for Mr. Straham with his wife and 4 children and 6 negroes from the County of Effingham; for Mr. David Hines and his wife and 6 children from County of Jefferson in State of Georgia; for Messers Alexander Smith with his wife and 6 children; Samuel Rulk with his wife and 7 negroes, his sister-in-law and her 2 children and the Widow Hall and her 2 sons, and also Peter Rulk with his wife and 2 children and one negro, all from County of Twiggs in this State.

PAGE 307, WED. 8TH JAN. 1812 . . . travel to Western Country, for Robert Jamison and Joseph Burnes, for Martin Wood, Esquire, all from County of Twiggs, Ga. Copy of how recommendations were made to obtain a passport . . .
Original Document in File Two, under West, John
"Recommendation for passport—
Sir—

John West and Family is about to move to the Western Country of corse he will have need os a passport I have been acquainted with him these ten or fifteen years past he has always supported the character of an honest Industris Good Citizen

                      I am your most obdt Humble Servt
                      George Evans
28th Sept. 1810
Reverse—
Recommendation in favor of John West of Twiggs County for the purpose of obtaining a passport to travel through the Creek Nation. Order taken 29—Sept.—1810. His Excellency, David B. Mitchell, Esqr."
Passport Book, page 86, form of another recommendation used . . .
"State of Georgia, Washington County—Know all men by thes presence that this is to certify that the barer hearof Nathan Jiner. Jiner has resided in the State afoarsaid fer twenty Ears and upward During which time we have been acquainted with him, and do consider him to be honest Peaceable good meaning man and recommend Him to all persons to Whome these preasents Shall come,—Given under our handes this 11th February 1807.
Daniel Frazer; Krenchec Newsom: Wm. Hogins; Jno Collins, Capt., J. P.; David Smith; Samuel Salter; John Falk: Eli Comme; Joshua Collins; Jas. Salter; John Roughton; Abeom Frebrel; Wm. Smith; Zacharias Roughton; John Cash; Thomas McDowell; Edmond Price; Dread May; Isaiah Coleman; Jno Curru, J. P.
Reverse: Nathan Jiner, recommendation from State of Georgia; in favor of Nathan Jiner for a passport through the Creek Nation; order taken 18th Feby, 1807."

## CHAPTER III
## SETTLEMENTS OF THE COUNTY

Twiggs County settlements are widely distributed. The information on several of the communities is fragmentary. In relating data about the villages the establishment date of a post office is given, as it helps determine the age of many of the communities. All information given about the post offices and the list of post masters at each was obtained from records at the National Archives in Washington, D. C.

ADAMS PARK (PACE'S STATION). The Adams Park settlement was located in the western part of the county along the Southern Railroad. It was a small settlement, but the local citizens had strong expectations for its future development. A city was planned, streets laid off and named. The town encouraged native Georgians, as well as persons living out of the State, to purchase lots in the anticipated city. The community had a beautiful flowing spring with a pavilion located in its vicinity which attracted numerous visitors. On occasions, trains would make special runs to Adams Park to transport persons desiring to attend certain festivities at which there would be music by visiting bands. During the summer months Adams Park was used as a summer resort. There were visitors from other states, as well as from Georgia.

The first post office for the settlement was established as Pace's Station; later called Adams Park.

Post Masters:
April 6, 1870—Nathanel W. Pulsifer (Pace's Station)
    Discontinued—July 25, 1870
June 14, 1892    Anthony Hoegen (Adams Park)
Sept. 25, 1893    William Rolland
Feb. 24, 1897    Roy C. Adams
May 4, 1897    Irvin Fitzpatrick
May 17, 1899    W. H. Maclese
    Discontinued—Mail to Bullards—Nov. 30, 1899
Re-established
June 16, 1900    Clare B. Fitzpatrick
May 18, 1901    David Barkwell *
        (* A probable postmaster here. U. S. Post Office records show his name incorrectly listed on line with another office)
    Discontinued—Mail to Bullards—March 26, 1902
Re-established
May 2, 1903    Edwin H. Fitzpatrick
Nov. 24, 1906    John F. Allen
July 2, 1914    John D. Scott
April 5, 1915    Clare B. Fitzpatrick
    Discontinued—Mail to Bullards—Jan. 31, 1916
Re-established
Sept. 28, 1916    Benjamin P. O'Neal
Dec. 8, 1916    Walter M. Laine
Sept. 10, 1919    William A. Hoss
Nov. 12, 1920    David Hillman
April 5, 1921    Oscar Paul
July 27, 1922    Xillo Y. McCann
Feb. 15, 1927    Mrs. Bell B. Anderson
    Discontinued—Mail to Drybranch—Jan. 15, 1930

Note: On Sept. 28, 1916, the name of the Philip Post Office, established in 1912, was changed to Adams Park, following the closing of the first Adams Park Office, Jan. 31, 1916.

ASA. Asa was a settlement in the northeast section of the County. The community had a general store with a post office located in one part of the building. The post office was established March 25, 1896, and continued to operate until its merger with the Griswoldville Office on January 14, 1904. All mail to Asa came by the Central of Georgia Railroad and was taken to the local office by horseback rider. The families living in the area derived their livelihood from agricultural enterprises.

Post Masters were:

| | |
|---|---|
| March 25, 1896 | Tullie G. Crosby |
| Nov. 1, 1897 | Richard E. Thompson |
| May 8, 1901 | Zachariah Harrison |

Discontinued—Mail to Griswoldville—Jan. 14, 1904.

BIGOAK (BIG OAK). The Bigoak settlement and post office was in the northern part of the county. A United States Post Office was established for the settlement on December 28, 1895, but it was discontinued after about nine years when a new rural free delivery route from Griswoldville, in neighboring Jones County, began operation.

Post Masters were:

| | |
|---|---|
| Dec. 28, 1895 | Edward F. Cranford |
| May 8, 1896 | John H. Jessup |
| Feb. 8, 1900 | Henry J. Cranford |
| Oct. 23, 1903 | Edward F. Cranford |

Discontinued—Mail to Griswoldville—Jan. 14, 1904.

Historic Myricks Mill as it appears today
(Courtesy: W. C. Humphries)

BIG SANDY. The Big Sandy Post Office was applicably named as it was located near the banks of the Big Sandy Creek in the northeast section of the county. The post office was established June 2, 1879, and was in continuous operation until

May 15, 1903. One of the historic old landmarks of Twiggs stands here, Myrick's Mill. When General Lafayette, hero of Colonial American Forces, made his official State visit to Georgia in 1825 he learned of Myrick's Mill and the coarse or unbolted flour the mill produced. Upon his return to his native France, he sent the miller at Myrick's Mill a bolt of silk to improve the quality of the local flour.

Post Masters:

| | | |
|---|---|---|
| June 2, | 1879 | Lewis Cranford |
| Dec. 6, | 1881 | Yancy Griffin |
| March 26, | 1883 | John S. Crosby |
| June 1, | 1885 | John D. Noles |
| Nov. 9, | 1886 | Levenia B. Epps |
| Nov. 23, | 1889 | Mary J. Crawford |
| Dec. 27, | 1895 | Ichabod Balkcom |
| April 1, | 1896 | Louis F. Crawford |

Discontinued—Mail to Gordon—May 15, 1903.

BULLARD(S). The Bullard settlement was named for the Daniel Bullard Family who acquired land along the eastern bank of the Ocmulgee River. Mr. Bullard operated a large mercantile business at the "Station" and a small boat up and down the Ocmulgee River buying and selling wares. He was a shrewd trader and knew the worth of a dollar. He, too, was agent for the steamboat line at the ferry where boats were used to carry passengers from Twiggs to Houston and vice versa. Mr. Bullard, a successful planter and businessman, was also a financier. He accumulated much wealth through investments and personal loans.

When the Macon and Brunswick Railway, now Southern, made its appearance in this part of the County, the River Boat freight traffic soon ceased. Eventually the Bullard Depot, located near the River, was removed to the railway line where it became the Bullard Railroad Depot with Mr. Bullard, the agent.

In May, 1870 the United States Government established for the Bullard Settlement a post office that operated continuously for more than fifty years.

The present site of the Bullard community is to the east of the original settlement. The shift of the site was due to the location of Georgia Highway 87. The school and several stores have now been built along this highway.

As in generations of the past, landowners continue to possess large tracts of property, several family estates exceeding 1,000 acres. The lands of the area have good stands of both soft and hardwood trees. In many instances the tree's roots penetrate beneath the surface of the earth into known mineral deposit pockets of clay and rock. Today families of this section engage in tree farming, and general farming enterprises, although some of the citizens work in local kaolin mines and plants.

Post Masters were:

| | | |
|---|---|---|
| May 10, | 1870 | Daniel Bullard |
| Dec. 14, | 1881 | W. H. Harrell |
| Jan. 16, | 1882 | Daniel Bullard |
| Feb. 1, | 1882 | W. H. Harrell |
| July 27, | 1882 | T. S. Marcy |
| Jan. 11, | 1887 | William Z. Marcy |
| Jan. 15, | 1889 | John L. Harrell |
| Jan. 14, | 1890 | John A. Barclay |
| Sept. 20, | 1890 | James T. Harrell |

Discontinued mail to Macon—January 4, 1892
Order Rescinded January 9, 1892
Jan. 9, 1892 Reese Ramey

Discontinued mail to Adams Park—August 31, 1899
Order Rescinded September 9, 1899

| | | |
|---|---|---|
| Jan. 28, | 1901 | Stephen C. Jones |
| Dec. 22, | 1902 | Reese Ramey |
| Jan. 17, | 1911 | Frank Harrell |
| Feb. 4, | 1918 | Sparks H. Ramey |

Discontinued mail to Drybranch—January 31, 1923

BUZZARD ROOST AND/OR WESTLAKE. Early citizens, who located in this southwest corner of Twiggs County, knew their settlement as Buzzard Roost, Georgia. It was under this name that the first post office was established on May 20, 1872.

What's in the name? Mrs. G. Walker Jordan, granddaughter of General Hartwell H. Tarver, relates this story. In pioneer days Indians were plentiful on the west side of the Ocmulgee River, and would cross over to regale themselves at the "grog-shop" on the east side. It is an old tradition that so many Indians were always lying around on the ground sleeping off intoxication, that gradually the place acquired the name of Buzzard Roost.

A second story relating to the naming of the local settlement centers around the railroad. The survey for the Macon and Brunswick Railway (Southern) followed the course of the Ocmulgee as far as Buzzarrd Roost, and when right-of-way at that point was solicited from the landowner, Robert R. Slappey, the request was granted provided he be given the privilege of naming the station. Mr. Slappey, being a practical joker and teaser, named the station Buzzard Roost to infuriate his friends and kinsmen. Time marched on without change in the town name, until two ladies went off to school and had to list Buzzard Roost as their home address; then came the blitz to get the town name changed. The outlook for change appeared unfavorable, because Mr. Slappey wouldn't consider such a thought. However, sometime fate is kind to youth! Indeed it was in this instant, for it so happened that Mr. Slappey's granddaughter was visiting in a neighboring town and in the newspaper it was announced that "The belle of Buzzard Roost was in Town". The newspaper caption so aroused old Mr. Slappey's indignation that he was ready for a change in the village name.

Another story involving the name of the community has to do with a remark made by two passengers on the train while stopped at Buzzard Roost. Two men were standing on the rear platform of the passenger train when one man was heard to say, "So this is Buzzard Roost," to which his companion replied, "And there sit two Buzzard Roosters." The remark referred to Mr. Slappey and his son who were sitting in pleasantly tilted chairs enjoying the sun on the depot platform. Following this the last barrier to changing the name of Buzzard Roost went down. The new name agreed upon was Westlake as a lake was located just to the west of the settlement.

In early days an important ferry was operated near Westlake on the River to assist persons in crossing. Here, too, was located a shipping point for cotton.

Post Masters:

| | | |
|---|---|---|
| May 20, | 1872 | Mrs. Mary E. Coley |
| Jan. 16, | 1873 | Mark F. Slappey |
| Feb. 12, | 1874 | Robert F. Brown |
| Jan. 20, | 1876 | J. W. Trunnell |
| March 10, | 1876 | R. R. Slappey |
| Jan. 18, | 1877 | J. W. Trunnell |
| March 7, | 1878 | Andrew Y. Allen |
| Jan. 24, | 1879 | Frank P. McClendon |
| Feb. 11, | 1884 | John F. Carter |

Name changed from Buzzard Roost to Westlake—March 3, 1885.

| | | |
|---|---|---|
| March 3, | 1885 | John F. Carter |

Discontinued mail to Longstreet—January 6, 1891

Re-established  February 19, 1891
Feb. 19, 1891  Robert R. Slappey
Sept. 14, 1908  Aaron T. Woodward
Dec. 13, 1912  Mary H. Sistrunk
May 2, 1913  Robert J. Fullerton
Aug. 28, 1913  Nell M. Bartee
June 26, 1920  John M. Rush
Oct. 7, 1920  Clarence Howell
Nov. 27, 1922  Alton V. White (acting)
June 11, 1924  Howard P. Hamrick (acting)
   Discontinued mail to Jeffersonville—January 15, 1930
Re-established  August 27, 1925
Aug. 27, 1925  Alfred Mabry
   Discontinued mail to Adams Park—January 31, 1925

DANVILLE. The Danville Community was named for Daniel Greenwood Hughes, father of Congressman Dudley M. Hughes. A post office was established for the settlement in April, 1892 and has functioned continually since its creation. The Macon, Dublin, and Savannah Railroad helped in changing Danville from open country into a thriving community of more than 400 persons. Located here was the Crossland Academy, an outstanding rural school in its day. The Academy building continues to stand though aged with years.

During the last phases of the great War-Between-the-States, the Honorable Robert Toombs, spent several days in hiding at the "White House" (old Hughes Homestead) near Danville.

Today most families living in the Danville area derive their livelihood from the soil. Land in the area ranges from level to rolling and is well suited to agricultural pursuits.

Post Masters:
April 1, 1892  Isaac N. Maxwell
Oct. 29, 1914  Harvey H. Maxwell
Nov. 21, 1921  Lelia W. Maxwell
March 31, 1952  H. J. Chance (acting)
July 6, 1953  M. H. Stevens, Jr.
Sept. 6, 1958  Mrs. Laura Dominy (Acting)
Aug. 31, 1959  Mrs. Laura M. Dominy

(United States Post Office records show a David Barkwell's name on line of Danville postmasters as having received an appointment on May 18, 1901. Post Office line above his name was for Adams Park. He could have served at Adams Park. Local citizens of the town state no Barkwell has served at Danville.)

DRY BRANCH. The Dry Branch Community is widely spread. It is located about nine miles from Macon in Bibb and Twiggs Counties and covers an area several miles square. The community is not new; instead, it dates back several generations. The oldest house in Twiggs is found in this settlement. The house was built in 1808 for the Rev. V. A. Tharp. The first post office was established in 1879, but the community itself antedates this office by more than a half century. Today the community is an important kaolin and fullers earth mining center.

What's In The Name? There are several theories regarding the naming of the United States Post Office Dry Branch, Georgia. One might suggest that it was named for a stream of water called Dry Branch! There is today a local "wet weather" branch by that name. This stream antedates both Bibb and Twiggs Counties as it was used to describe or identify a Government land grant drawn by Edmund Shackleford in May, 1807. The Shackleford property was described as being "202½ acres on the Waters of Dry Branch". It is quite uncomprehensible to suggest a post office located in Bibb County being named for a stream of water located in Twiggs County some five miles removed from the site of the post office. Instead, if a body or stream of water was to embrace the post office name its most logical name would have been Stone Creek, Georgia. The Dry Branch post office has been virtually located on or near the banks of Stone Creek, a tributary of the Ocmulgee, for its entire history. Therefore, it must be resolved, that the evidence seems to warrant little or no connection between the post office, Dry Branch and stream called Dry Branch.

Another belief about the naming of the post office concerns the weather. Perhaps one of the most often quoted unauthenticated stories insists the post office was given the name "Dry Branch" due to the lack of rainfall preceding its establishment date in 1879. This mythical story implies that the lack of rain caused the creeks and branches to weaken and often times become dry.—And so the name Dry Branch, Georgia was thought to have been coined.

The United States Weather Bureau records do not substantiate the folk-tale regarding the post office having been named Dry Branch due to unusual dry weather conditions. The precipitation for the year preceding and the year during the establishment of the office was only slightly below an established average for rainfall. For comparative purposes the following precipitation data for the Middle Division of Georgia are given: Average precipitation for the year 1878 was 41.61 inches; for the year 1879 it was 45.48 inches. The average normal precipitation as established by the Macon Weather Bureau is 46.31 inches. One can compare these figures with the year 1954, when the average precipitation for the Macon Area was only 26.05 inches, and see that the general conditions did not wararnt the name Dry Branch.

The best and most authoritative sources indicate a prohibition influence in the naming of Dry Branch, Georgia. It is said that many of the local streams, prior to the establishment date of the post office, contained many moonshine stills. These distilleries must have done a thriving business as the church records of the period site numerous cases of members being called before the church to answer to the charge of intoxication. In the Stone Creek Baptist Church record book, for instance, under the date of January 23, 1875 this entry appears: "A committee was appointed to investigate reports for dancing and selling ardent spirits." Under the date of November 25, 1876 appears this notation: "A resolution was read declaring any member getting drunk expelled." (This resolution was never voted upon, but instead, a substitute was offered and approved).

The churches alone were apparently unable to cope with the liquor traffic, for in the year 1876 an Act was passed by the Georgia Legislature to govern the sale of liquor in Twiggs County: "Be it enacted, that—an Act—granting license to sell intoxicating liquors—be so amended as to embrace in said Act the County of Twiggs. 'Be it enacted by the General Assembly of the State of Georgia, that it shall not be lawful for the Ordinaries of—Twiggs County to grant a license to any person to sell intoxicating liquors—, in any quantity, unless requisites of the law as it now stand, present to said Ordinaries to be filed in their office the written consent to granting of said license, signed by two-thirds of the citizens free holders living within three miles of the place at which the applicant proposes to sell. . . '"

The law enforcement agencies must have done their duty enforcing the Twiggs Liquor Law in 1876, because many of the distilleries in what is now Dry Branch began to dry up and the "drying up" is thus said by some to have given rise to the community which now bears the designation Dry Branch, Georgia.

The Dry Branch economy is based largely on the kaolin mines and plants located in the vicinity. The community has several general stores, a tourist court, a candy manufacturing plant, and is listed by Rand McNally as having a citizenry of five hundred.

Post Masters:
| | | |
|---|---|---|
| June 17, | 1879 | Jasper Bullock |
| Nov. 8, | 1880 | J. H. Nelson |
| Sept. 27, | 1881 | Elizabeth S. Burkett |
| Dec. 17, | 1883 | Mary E. Lingo |
| March 10, | 1886 | Joseph U. Burkett |
| Jan. 18, | 1890 | J. O. Marcy |
| Jan. 29, | 1890 | John A. Herring |
| April 24, | 1890 | George W. Tharp |
| April 13, | 1892 | Thomas J. Butler |
| Nov. 15, | 1892 | Washington J. Burkett |

Name changed to Drybranch—Jan. 17, 1895
| | | |
|---|---|---|
| Jan. 17, | 1895 | William S. Burkett |
| Sept. 13, | 1895 | Joseph B. Burkett |

Post Office moved into Twiggs County—Dec. 3, 1895
Dec. 3, 1895 Joseph B. Burkett
Name of Post Office changed to Bernita—April 14, 1900
Post Office re-established in Bibb County under the name of Drybranch—April 6, 1902**

| | | |
|---|---|---|
| Sept. 17, | 1910 | James M. Rogers |
| Jan. 13, | 1915 | George W. Burkett |
| 1942 and 1942 | | Mrs. Edna Tharpe Powell (acting) |
| 1942 and 1943 | | F. H. Treadwell (acting) |
| April 16, 1943 | | Mack B. Smith |

**Spelling changed, two words on July 1, 1950, Dry Branch.
| | | |
|---|---|---|
| Nov. 1, | 1957 | Mrs. Olline N. Wood (acting) |
| July 11, | 1959 | William Thomas Wood (acting) |
| Oct. 3, | 1959 | William Thomas Wood |

FITZPATRICK. The Fitzpatrick settlement is situated along U. S. Highway 80, paralleling the Macon, Dublin and Savannah Railroad in the interior of the county. The original post office at Fitzpatrick was created in March, 1891 and was called Elmwood. The name was changed to Fitzpatrick in April, 1891 and was so called until its discontinuance date, August 31, 1934.

Today the community looks very much as it did in earlier times with several of its old landmarks still intact; among the landmarks are the Fitzpatrick Home dating back to the Jeffersonian Era, and the Old Epps House, dating back to about the same period of time. The older homes and the newer residences located in their vicinity, make up the Fitzpatrick community of today. Citizens of this area farm, work in neighboring industrial plants, and in defense jobs.

Post Masters: (Elmwood & Fitzpatrick)
| | | |
|---|---|---|
| May 19, | 1879 | Benjamin S. Fitzpatrick |
| March 23, | 1880 | Miss Henrietta V. Epps |
| Discontinued | | June 17, 1881 |

Name changed to Ftzpatrick April 25, 1891
| | | |
|---|---|---|
| April 25, | 1891 | Benjamin S. Fitzpatrick April 25, 1891 |
| Feb. 1, | 1918 | Miss Fleta Fitzpatrick |

Discontinued August 31, 1934

HUBER (Philip). Huber is the newest industrial settlement of the County, an outgrowth of old Philip Station. It is located in the northwest section of Twiggs, just off Georgia Highway 87, and along the Southern Railway, near the Ocmulgee River. The community was created with the establishment of the J. M. Huber Company. The post office also was named after J. M. Huber of June 8, 1939. Huber is one of the two industrial areas of the county, with almost all of the local citizens being associated with the local kaolin mines, plants and/or ink factory.

Post Masters: (Philip & Huber)
Oct. 7, 1912 Walter M. Lain
Aug. 26, 1913 Benjamin P. O'Neal
    Name changed to Adams Park—Sept. 28, 1916
    Huber established June 8, 1939
June 8, 1939 Mrs. Mamie R. Denson

JEFFERSONVILLE. The county-seat town of Jeffersonville was originally established as Rain's Store on September 3, 1828, and was not officially changed to Jeffersonville until 1849. The village got its name from the Jefferson Family, who were leaders here during the early development of the settlement. The first known community school was Jefferson's Academy, incorporated in 1828, and it was likewise named for the same Jefferson Family as the village.

Lots were sold in 1836 at a time when there were few stores in the settlement. The Jeffersonville Community took on real vigor on February 11, 1850 when an Act was approved authorizing the removal of the county seat from Marion to such a place as the Inferior Court might decide on lands owned by Mr. Henry Solomon. The Act also stipulated that the new county site was to be known as Marion. Due to the lack of rapidity in selecting a county site, an election for that purpose was held in 1868 at which time Jeffersonville was agreed upon by the majority of those expressing an opinion.

The selection of a new county capitol was just one obstacle out of the way, for next came the responsibility of erecting public buildings. This obligation was met by removing the usable public buildings from old Marion to Jeffersonville, some six miles distant, by teams of oxen. Not only were the public buildings moved from Marion, but business men also moved a hotel and several stores, to the county-seat town. These buildings were first dismantled at Marion by laborers, and hauled by teams of oxen to the new county site, Jeffersonville.

One of the most noted and interesting cases tried in the Courts of Twiggs occured in the frame court house at Jeffersonville in 1896. In a book by W. F. Combs he called it THE STONE CREEK WRECK. The story centered around the trial of two men who planned to kill their wives in a train accident by wrecking a train and collecting insurance.

In February, 1901 the old wooden courthouse, once removed from Marion, burned, and in April, 1903 the present brick building was constructed.

A Portion of the Jeffersonville Business District, 1959

Jeffersonville has been a cultural and educational center down through the years. Its high moral, spiritual, and educational values have set a fine cultural record. The community has held in high esteem its schools—outstanding was the old Jefferson Academy, famous was old Auburn, creditable was the original Twiggs High, praiseworthy was the Twiggs High brick school of 1922, later destroyed by fire, and certainly the Consolidated Twiggs County High School of this generation is indeed laudable.

In 1852 Rev. W. D. Horne, in a personal letter, had this to say about the local school, "We have an excellent school, I suppose there are very few better in the State." In another latter dated 1852 from Anna Higgs of Jeffersonville to relatives in North Carolina she writes, "We have an excellent school here at Jeffersonville. . . . Society here is very fine, children can't get from home without being in the very best of society. Good churches, school and society all exist here."

The incorporated town of Jeffersonville has a population of 787 (1950 census). The town is located in the upper Coastal Plains Region of Georgia and has an altitude of approximately 526 feet. The fine water system that the city today enjoys dates back to 1918 when the town authorized a $15,000.00 bonded indebtedness for establishing a system of water works and a lighting system for the city. Most of the available employable citizens work in the local lumber industry, neighboring kaolin mines and plants, and in government jobs in nearby towns. The prosperity of the town is based upon an agricultural economy, including field crops, dairying, and forestry enterprises.

Post Masters: First post office established Sept. 3, 1828. (Postmaster's name not available).

|  |  |
|---|---|
| Jan. 28, 1832 | Josiah Murphy |
| April 29, 1837 | E. Wimberly and R. H. Raines |
| June 7, 1841 | Ellis Long |

Name changed to Jeffersonville, Sept. 24, 1849

|  |  |
|---|---|
| Sept. 24, 1849 | Ellis Long |
| Aug. 8, 1860 | John T. Smith |
| March 9, 1866 | Mrs. Ullysses A. Rice |
| May 29, 1866 | Mrs. Isabella A. L. McCoy |
| May 24, 1872 | John F. Shine |
| Aug. 1, 1872 | C. A. Solomon |
| Nov. 7, 1872 | Thomas J. Tharp |
| May 20, 1874 | William H. Crocker |
| Jan. 20, 1876 | H. C. Ward |
| Feb. 1, 1876 | William H. Crocker |
| Feb. 5, 1877 | Sidney H. Boynton |
| Sept. 17, 1877 | Joshua R. Wimberly |
| Aug. 4, 1879 | William B. Carver |
| Feb. 16, 1880 | William H. Holzandorf |
| Jan. 4, 1882 | Marcus E. Solomon |
| Dec. 27, 1886 | Augustus F. Martin |
| Dec. 29, 1887 | Henry F. Griffin |
| Aug. 13, 1889 | Jane Bell |
| Oct. 8, 1890 | Mrs. Sallie D. Pettis |
| Sept. 27, 1901 | DeWitt Carswell |
| May 28, 1906 | Mary L. Carswell |
| June 16, 1916 | Joseph G. Rockmore |
| April 16, 1917 | Joshua R. Wimberly |
| July 20, 1924 | Addie W. Griffin (acting) |
| July 31, 1924 | William F. Shannon (acting) |
| March 2, 1925 | Miss Fannie M. Vaughn |
| | Miss Jennie Wimberly (acting) |
| | Ralph Smith |

Dec. 1,    1956        Mrs. Sue W. Sanders (acting)
Sept. 6,   1957        Mrs. Sue W. Sanders

## MAYORS OF CITY OF JEFFERSONVILLE, GEORGIA 1903-1959

(Ref.: The minute books in the office of the City of Jeffersonville by Mrs. Johnnie Sanders, Clerk).

| | | | | |
|---|---|---|---|---|
| 1903-1908 | Dr. T. S. Jones | | 1922-1923 | W. E. Hoyle (Resigned) |
| 1908-1912 | J. C. Shannon | | 1923-1944 | W. M. Whitehurst |
| 1912-1916 | Dr. T. S. Jones | | 1944-1946 | D. C. Adams |
| 1916-1920 | J. G. Rockmore | | 1946-1959 | D. Y. Califf |
| 1920-1922 | S. E. Jones | | | |

Mayor D. Y. Califf with great-niece, Sara E. Beck, looking on as he signs a proclamation.

MARION. Historic old Marion was the first county-seat town of Twiggs County. It was established by the Georgia Legislature December, 1810. "Be it enacted—that the Courthouse and other public buildings for the County of Twiggs shall be erected at or near Joiner's Spring above Savage Creek, on Lot No. 73, in the 25th district, late Wilkinson, now Twiggs County. And be it further enacted— to purchase as a site for public buildings not less than 75 nor more than 200 acres of said lot 73 above described.—Authorized to lay off on such land as may be purchased as aforesaid, such number of lots as may be proper, and the same to expose to public sale. The proceeds of said sales to be applied to the erection of the public buildings in said County, and for other county purposes." Thus was Marion created.

The town was situated 36 miles south west of Milledgeville, 20 miles south east of Macon, 30 miles north of old Hartford, 28 miles south of Clinton, 20 miles west of Irwinton, and 6 miles west of Jeffersonville. The township was named for General Francis Marion, the "Swamp Fox" of Revolutionary fame.

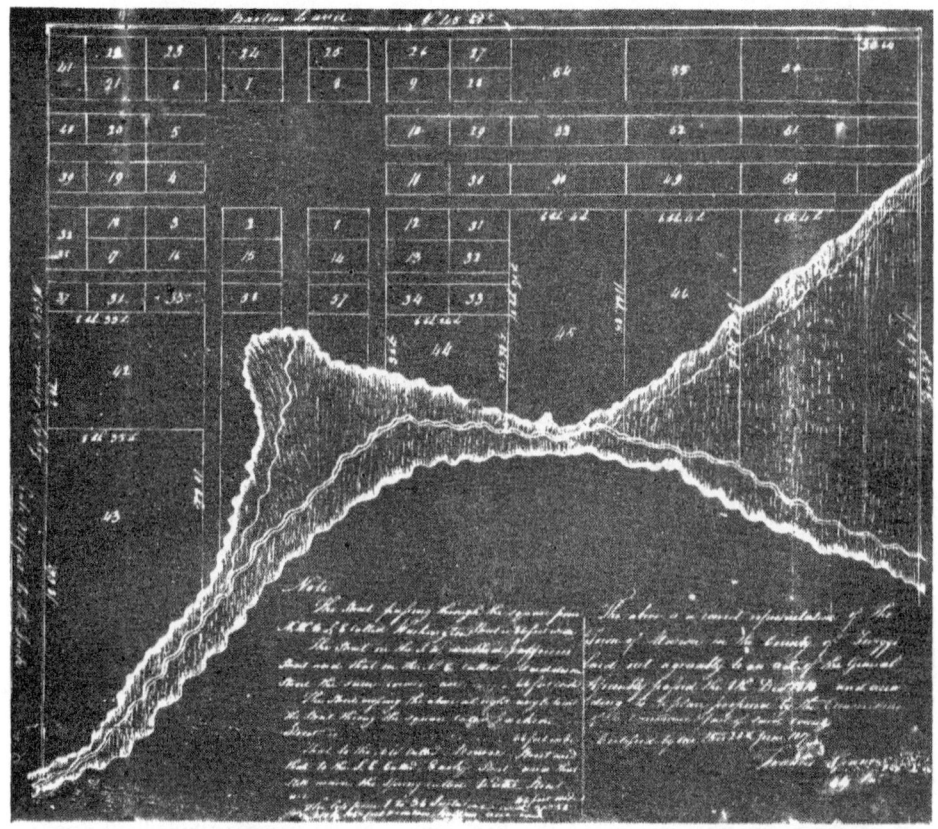

Plat. Town of Marion (Certified by Francis Spann. Cty. Sur., 27th June, 1817.)

Marion was hardly established before the War of 1812 caused the town and entire countryside alarm because of its location near the frontier. Marion was only eight miles distant from the Ocmulgee River, the western frontier of Georgia. Not far removed from the eastern bank of the River were Indian villages. Within the Indian ranks were whites called "squawmen"—whites who had married Indian women and who affiliated themselves with the Redman's race. The Indians, the squaw-men—who practically to a man served as spies for the British—and the British soldiers composed the threat to Marion. To help defend the area three forts, Jackson, Telfair, and Twiggs, were laid out in Twiggs County near the Ocmulgee River at about ten miles distance from each other. These forts composed a general line of defense stretching from Fort Hawkins to the Twiggs forts from thence southward into old Pulaski and Telfair Counties. Although the Twiggs forts were never under seize by the enemy, they served to reassure the citizenry that the area was in readiness should eventualities demand defense.

With War threats over, Marion and the surrounding country returned to a state of normalcy. Old Marion began to grow into a town endowed with a promising future. It was the capital of Twiggs County located in the geographical centers of both the county and the State. In addition to the court house and the jail, it had several stores, a post office, academy, boarding house, a fine hotel, bank, church house, stage stop, law offices, doctors' shops, several saloons and a citizenry of several hundred souls. One of the more interesting places of business was the bakery or cake-beer shop. It was operated by an old Negro who specialized in molasses, cakes and beer.

All legends indicate the town enjoyed a gay society. In the 1820's and 1830's, when money was plentiful and the laws not so strict, the gentlemen of Marion and surrounding neighborhood were frequent guests at the saloons with their alcoholic drinks, gambling dens and wild conversations. Here indeed social merriment was the order of business. On more than one occasion the gay-hearted Lotharios ended their merry-making in street brawls.

The most noted merchant of Marion was the sprightly Ira Peck, a New Yorker. He came to Marion, like several of his neighbors, from the North. Over the years at Marion he grew immensely wealthy and enjoyed a lucrative business. In addition to carrying on his mercantile business he was a money lender and banking institution to many of the local citizens. But as the abolition movement gained momentum, and old Marion began to fade away, Mr. Peck sold all his property and returned to the north from which he came.

The courts of justice were organized with capable judges, and the character and ability of some of the lawyers who practiced in the courts remain of renown in Middle Georgia today. The early Bar at Marion was composed of Lawyers Robert Perryman, Robert Evans, Thaddeus G. Holt, Robert A. Beall, Samuel Griner, Thomas Harris, Zachariah B. Gargrove, William Crocker, Moses Fort, S. Delk, Stephen F. Miller and others. Miller was an outstanding lawyer and authority on law, and author of, THE BENCH AND BAR OF GEORGIA. Another of the Marion lawyers, Perryman, was also a writer by vocation, his best known writing being, THE LIFE AND PUBLIC SERVICE OF MAJOR-GENERAL ANDREW JACKSON.

The Court House at Marion was a large, two-story, square frame building with blinds and three entrances. The first floor was one great room, and from which ascended steps to the various county offices above. In front of the main entrance was the judge's elevated desk; to the right and left were jury benches. The front half of the room was devoted to the Bar, which by courtesy included all leading citizens, and the remainder of the space in the rear of the courtroom was for spectators.

Marion was for many years the most important town in the Southern Judicial Circuit. Here lived the first Judges of the circuit, Harris, Holt, and Fort, and here, too, was born Judge A. T. McIntyre, Sr. During court sessions some of the best legal minds Georgia could muster assembled at Marion. At times an incidental remark made during the course of a trial would lead to a thunderous outburst of voices that would rattle the very windows, and make chills run down the lofty rafters. Marion was a mecca to the legal profession in early middle Georgia History.

Three middle Georgia towns bade for dominance of the early mid-Georgia trade area. The pretenders were Clinton in Jones County, Macon in Bibb County, and Marion in Twiggs County; but Clinton and Marion soon fumbled in the race. Both Clinton and Marion banked on the prosperity of the past, and the good days of the present while Macon worked, planned and gambled on the future. Macon was accessible to river boat transportation and the only town to show an interest in railroad construction.

The citizens of Marion fought the railroad and the progress it might have brought the community. The town wanted no part of the new "puffing" machine and the so-called advantages it offered as a modern media of transportation. The majority of the town people and country folks were ladies and gentlemen schooled to leisure who disliked the idea of change. The people were satisfied with their customary oxen, buggy, surrey and stage type transportation and saw no advantage of building a railroad to and through the county capitol. Many citizens feared the advent of the horseless carriage, believed it to be a curse upon their welfare, and stated publicly and emphatically that they wanted no part of any untried gadget running loose in their midst! Lucian Lamar Knight states in, GEORGIA LANDMARKS, MEMORIALS AND LEGENDS, "The original survey of the Central Railroad was made to Marion; but the iron horse was an untried experiment— and the people objected to the intruder on the ground that it might endanger livestock and demoralize the poultry yard." The good people of Marion and Twiggs County wanted no part in constructing any railroads or railroad. And so, in obedience to their request the Central Railroad bypassed Marion. But it was not long before Marion and Twiggs citizens realized their error. The merchants and planters soon became aware of the fact that merchandise and cotton could be hauled more efficiently and less expensively by rail than wagon team and river barge. Years later when a second railroad was proposed through western Twiggs County, the Macon and Brunswick, now Southern Railway, the anti-railroad sentiment was gone and the people wished it well.

Marion made its exit as a leading Middle Georgia town during the 1840's as Macon, 20 miles north, provided the magnetic pull for the business and professional men. It was during this period that several business men and their families, and several "colonels" and their plantation families began to leave Marion and vicinity looking for a golden opportunity to succeed. Thus, Marion was soon reduced to a "Deserted Village".

During the 1850's Marion was so devastated that the people of the County decided to move the public buildings to another site. The new proposed countyseat was to be named Marion but the delay in carrying out the plans fixed the new county capital at Jeffersonville. The old residents who remained at Marion and their friends in the County fought to keep the public buildings from being relocated at Jeffersonville. On August 10, 1867 a special order from Headquarters, Third Military District, Atlanta was issued halting the dismantling of the public buildings at Marion. "The taking down of the Court House, at Marion, Twiggs County, State of Georgia, and its removal from Marion to Jeffersonville, in the same County, are hereby ordered to be suspended until after the completion of Registration, when an election will be ordered to decide upon the question of the removal of the County site from Marion." This order only delayed matters for a short period of time as the removal of public buildings to Jeffersonville was soon completed. The old frame court house once removed from old Marion to Jeffersonville continued to serve the County well until it burned February 6, 1901. Not only were public buildings moved from Marion to Jeffersonville, but several families moved their private buildings, including the fine old two story hotel. The hotel building stood in Jeffersonville until 1953 when it was purchased by an individual of Danville, Georgia who had it wrecked in order to salvage the choice heart timbers for another building.

Marion no longer exists as a town, the name does not appear on a modern map of Georgia. The contributions made by the two generations of Georgians who lived in this Middle Georgia village will live through the annals of history as a part of the growth and expansion of the Piedmont area of the State.

Post Masters:   Post office was established Oct. 26, 1812
(Information not available on former postmasters.)

Aug. 31, 1831   Allen Fleming
Oct. 12, 1835   Edward B. Young
Jan. 28, 1837   Allen Edwards
June 1, 1838    Peyton Reynolds
April 23, 1841  Charles Eason

| | | |
|---|---|---|
| June 23, | 1844 | Elijah E. Crocker |
| Feb. 4, | 1845 | William J. Stephens |
| July 2, | 1845 | Andrew Anderson |
| Nov. 30, | 1848 | Benjamin T. Smith |
| Feb. 15, | 1849 | Ira Peck |
| Jan. 13, | 1855 | Henry K. Peck |
| March 28, | 1856 | Wright Neel |
| Dec. 19, | 1859 | Marcus E. Solomon |
| May 18, | 1860 | Henry C. Keys |
| March 9, | 1866 | W. H. Bichum |
| May 8, | 1866 | Mrs. Abigail Jordan |
| Jan. 8, | 1867 | E. E. Crocker |
| Feb. 19, | 1867 | Lou Land |

Discontinued—May 15, 1868

RIPLEY. Ripley was first established as Ripling June 11, 1892, but was changed to Ripley August 6, 1892. The community was named by John Walker Jones, a leading citizen of the settlement. The establishment of the local post office and the development of the settlement came as a result of the successful completion of the Macon, Dublin and Savannah Railroad. The Ripley Community is located on United States Highway 80 about six miles north of Jeffersonville. Near here stood one of the early churches of the County, Wood's Meetinghouse (Baptist). Ripley, from the time of its creation until its abandonment as a railroad stop, was used primarily as a shipping point for farm and forest products.

Post Masters:

| | | |
|---|---|---|
| June 11, | 1891 | John Walker Jones |

Name changed from Ripling to Ripley August 6, 1892

| | | |
|---|---|---|
| Aug. 6, | 1892 | John Walker Jones |

Discontinued—Mail to Solomon—November 23, 1893

| | | |
|---|---|---|
| Re-established | | March 17, 1894 |
| March 17, 1894 | | R. A. Lyles |
| July 2, | 1895 | John Walker Jones |
| Feb. 9, | 1909 | James F. Hinson |
| June 5, | 1912 | John Walker Jones |

Discontinued—Mail to Jeffersonville—July 16, 1921

SABINE. The Sabine settlement was located in the northeast section of the County. A post office was established in 1896. The Office became antiquated with the introduction of the Macon, Dublin and Savannah Railroad in the immediate vicinity, and the improved public road conditions. In January, 1904 Sabine, together with Asa and Bigoak, were absorbed by the Griswoldville rural free delivery route.

Post Masters:

| | | |
|---|---|---|
| Aug. 1, | 1896 | Thomas S. Tharpe |

Discontinued—Mail to Griswoldville—January 14, 1904

TARVERSVILLE. Tarversville was the name given two post offices of Twiggs. The original Tarversville post office was opened September 26, 1826 as Tarver's Store. The second Tarversville post office was established February 29, 1876.

The Tarversville settlement is old and has many hallowed memories. In this community lived several wealthy planters with large holdings in land and slaves. The largest planter and most noted citizen of the settlement was General Hartwell H. Tarver. Mr. Tarver was given the title of General by the Georgia Legislature in 1842 when that body named him General of the Georgia Militia. The General is reputed to have been one of the largest slave owners in the South. For many years he maintained a race track for horse enthusiasts of Georgia and nearby states.

In addition to the post office and race track, the settlement had several stores and an Academy for both local and boarding students. The local school was the Ocmulgee Academy incorporated by the State in 1819. In 1838 the Academy Trustees were: Henry Bunn, D. W. Shine, Ira E. Dupree, Hartwell H. Tarver, and John G. Slappey.

Post Masters:
Sept. 27, 1826       H. H. Tarver
    Name changed from Tarver's Store to Tarversville March 24, 1831
Nov. 24, 1831        William M. Tarver
March 24, 1838       Hartwell H. Tarver
Oct. 22, 1841        John G. Slappey
April 13, 1842       William H. Exam
July 24, 1843        William S. Townsend
March 20, 1844       John W. Myrick
Sept. 19, 1845       Hartwell H. Tarver
Dec. 11, 1851        Frederick R. Tarver
Nov. 10, 1852        Robert R. Slappey
May 31, 1855         Thomas E. McCrea
    Discontinued—July 7, 1866
Re-established
Feb. 29, 1876        Benjamin M. Tarver
    Discontinued—February 24, 1880

TWIGGSVILLE. The Twiggsville settlement was located in the southern part of the county along the old federal road connecting Jeffersonville and Hartford (Pulaski County). A post office was established for the settlement in June, 1853 and, except for short periods of time on four occasions, lasted for about forty years. The families of the community, like their neighbors, derived their living from the soil. The settlement had several large planters who accumulated considerable wealth.

Post Masters:
June 1, 1853         James T. Evans
March 31, 1856       Green B. Bridger
Jan. 16, 1858        John S. Evans
March 26, 1859       John A. Clements
Dec. 27, 1860        Mrs. Eliza Jane Evans
March 9, 1866        James T. Evans
May 29, 1866         Robert C. Carroll
July 7, 1871         J. R. Asbell
Sept. 12, 1871       John S. Evans
    Discontinued—October 4, 1872
Re-established       Nov. 19, 1872
Nov. 19, 1872        John S. Evans
Oct. 1, 1877         J. T. Land
Dec. 21, 1881        John S. Evans
    Discontinued—Mail to New Providence (Wilkinson Co.) Jan. 20, 1882
Re-established       June 7, 1882
June 7, 1882         John S. Evans
June 10, 1884        Henry J. Newby
Jan. 15, 1885        Mrs. Willie J. Newby
Aug. 3, 1887         John S. Vaughn
Nov. 15, 1887        Francis B. Asbell

Discontinued—Mail to Burns—Dec. 2, 1887
Re-established           Jan. 18, 1888
Jan. 18,   1888          Alexander E. King
Discontinued—Feb. 16, 1888
Re-established           March 27, 1888
March 27, 1888           Hilliard S. Newby
March 31, 1891           Robert R. Newby
Dec. 2,    1891          John Vaughn
Discontinued—Mail to Longstreet—Oct. 31, 1903

WILLIS. The Willis settlement was located about five miles south of Jeffersonville in the vicinity of the Gallemore and Palmetto settlements near Turkey Creek. The first post office was established March 25, 1893 in the old Stephen Jones Home. Families living in the community were planters and depended upon the soil for a living. A grist mill, called Gallemore's Mill, was maintained at nearby Turkey Creek.

Post Masters:
March 25, 1893           Will Ernest Jones
Nov. 9,    1901          John S. Gallemore
Discontinued—Mail to Jeffersonville—Feb. 14, 1906

## OTHER POST OFFICES OF TWIGGS COUNTY

BESSINA
Post Masters:
May 29,   1891           John W. Jones
Discontinued—June 10, 1895

BONDS MILL
Post Masters:
June 19,  1877           John T. Bond
Discontinued—Mail to Big Sandy

BURNS
Post Masters:
                         Joseph K. Burns
                         Christopher D. Findlay
Discontinued—Mail to Twiggsville—Oct. 28, 1897

CHAPEL HILL
Post Masters:
April 14, 1837           Thomas Chapel

DELPHAS
No post office established here, however, a village was planned and lots sold in 1845.

DELZEL
Post Masters:
May 1,    1890           Thomas J. Robertson
May 25,   1895           Isham G. Asbell
Nov. 29,  1897           Nancy S. Sims
Discontinued—Mail to Delight (Bibb Co.) Dec. 17, 1897
Re-established           March 17, 1898
March 17, 1898           James T. Robertson
Dec. 6,   1905           Andrew J. Land
Discontinued—Mail to Drybranch—May 15, 1907

DENSON'S MILL
Post Masters:
June 15,  1869           Elias J. Denson
Discontinued—August 4, 1869

**DIANA**
  Post Masters:
  June 29, 1899        Dudley H. Bozeman
     Rescinded—Oct. 13, 1899
**DURHAM**
  Post Masters:
  April 14, 1896       Joseph A. Stokes
     Changed to McKinley—March 28, 1902
**FAULK**
  Post Masters:
  June 16, 1885        John C. Shannon
  Feb. 5, 1887         William C. Faulk
     Discontinued—Mail to Bullards—Feb. 10, 1888
**GRANBERY**
  Post Masters:
  May 7, 1830          James M. Granbery
     Name changed to Sonicera
**HIGGSVILLE**
  Post Masters:
  July 19, 1833        A. Higgs
  June 26, 1835        Alfred Blacke
  Sept. 30, 1835       Hayden Hughes and Hardy Durham
         1837          B. R. (not known)
  Dec. 5, 1839         Nathan Berry
     Discontinued—July 24, 1843
**IRMA**
  Post Masters:
  March 12, 1902       James W. Jones
     Discontinued—Mail to Bullards—May 15, 1903
**McKINLEY**
  Post Masters:
  March 28, 1902       Joseph A. Stokes
     Discontinued—Mail to Jefferson City (Jeffersonville)—Feb. 28, 1903
**PINE RIDGE**
  Post Masters:
  May 15, 1879         Mrs. Louisa Burkett
     Discontinued—Mail to Big Sandy
**READS**
  Post Masters:
  June 7, 1902         Russell F. Read
     Rescinded—Jan. 29, 1903
**SOLOMON**
  Post Masters:
  April 2, 1888        Shedrick E. Jones
  Jan. 26, 1892        John E. McDonald
  Jan. 17, 1900        Mary A. Stokes
     Discontinued—Mail to Fitzpatrick—July 15, 1901
  Re-established       April 25, 1905
  April 25, 1905       Luther S. Griffin
     Discontinued—Mail to Drybranch—Oct. 15, 1906
**SONICERA**
  Post Masters:
  April 9, 1836        John Eanes
     Discontinued—June 20, 1837

The following names were copied from the newspaper "GEORGIA MESSENGER" of Macon, Georgia, issues of April 14, 1832 and July 12, 1832 listing uncalled for letters at the Marion Post Office, Twiggs County, Georgia.

Such lists can be found in other issues of newspapers on file at the Washington Memorial Library, Macon, Georgia.

## GEORGIA MESSENGER, MACON, GEORGIA
### Saturday, April 14, 1832

List of Letters remaining at the Marion Post Office which will be sent to the General Post Office Department as dead letters.

Angelly, Mills
Butts, Gartrell and Co. 10
Alfred Blackle
Geo. W. Bostick
Wm. Brown
H. Brown
Dempsey Brown 2
Leonard Bowman
Robt. Bedingfield
Wiley Bullard
Benjamin Bryan, Sr.
Thos. Chappell, Sr. 2
Allen Courtney
Cata Cooper
Clerk Superior Court
John Calcord
Hardy Durham 2
Wm. H. Dupree
Robt. A. Evans
Wm. H. Exum
Rhesa J. Ellis 3
Raiford Fulghum
Joseph Francis
John Fulton
John Ford
Moses Fort
Elisha Howell or Jas. Parks

Bud Ham
Joseph Hardyman
Wm. Hamilton
James Hayden 2
M. B. Headen
Thads G. Holt 2
Wm. Hatcher
John Hardin
Amos Harris
Patrick Hays
James Hughes
James Harrell
Ezekiel Johnston
James R. Lowey
Matthew M. Lockhart
Anthony McCarty
John Morris
Benjamin Matthews
Wm. Martin
Alexander McFadden
McCormick Neal
Little B. Nix
James Oliver
Wm. Oliver
James Pearson 2
Samuel Passmore 2
Harmon Perryman

Moses Petis
Ira Peck 2
Enos Powell
Hardy Pace
Jesse Pope
John W. Raines or Levi Ezell
John Rutherford
Matthew Robertson
James Solomon
Henry Solomon
J. A. and D. W. Shine 2
Abraham Sapp
Dennis Sanders
Thos. R. Sandiford
James M. Smith
George D. Tharpe
James Vincent
E. Wimberly 3
F. D. Wimberly 2
George W. Welch
Wm. Wortus
Nancy Williams
David Walker
Isaac Wood
Michael Young
Allen Fleming, Post Master
April 1, 1832    6-32

## GEORGIA MESSENGER, MACON, GEORGIA
### Thursday, July 12, 1832

List of Letters, remaining in the Post Office, Marion, Georgia which if not taken out by First of October will be sent to the General Post Office as dead letters.

Butts Gartsell and Co.
Robt. Belcher 2
Geo. Barker
Benj. Bryan
Joseph Blackshear
J. D. Bostick
John F. Ball
David Bontecore
Wm. Cook
Phillip Cook

Mark Faulk
James P. Guerry
John Gallimore
James Hayden
James Harrison
Charity Harrison
Josiah Hodges
Isaac Holley
Andrew Howard
John R. Hunt

Jesse Pope
Samuel Passmore
Richard S. Rogers
James R. Rouse
Wm. Robinson
James Radford
Thos. Sandiford
D. D. Sanders
B. B. Smith
Thos. Terrell

Allen Courtney
Joseph Collins
Wm. Choice
Ira F. Dupree 2
John S. Darby
John Davis
John E. Dennard
Wm. Dennard
Lewis Dupree
Isaac Daniel
John Denson
Ephriam Ellis
Isham Edwards
James D. Edwards
Robt. A. Evans
John Fort
Thomas M. Fort
Raiford Fulghum

Lieut. Wiley Jordan
John James
T. Johnston
Nathan King
John Kent
James Lipsey
Richard Myrick
Joseph Minshew
Edward Montgomery
Richard Morris
Mrs. I. I. Munro
John Nelson
Wm. Oliver
Samuel Pate 2
Miss P. M. Phillips 2
Mr. Pittman
Wm. Prescott

John Williams
John Wilson
James Wall
James Wimberly
Isaac Wood
Mrs. Mary Wimberly
James H. Webb
James Wright
Wm. Wells
David Young
Allen Fleming, Post Master
7 - 1 - 1832
St. - 18
Letters
Jan. 1, 1833
John Pearce
Allen Fleming, P. M.

## CHAPTER IV
## OFFICERS, REPRESENTATIVES, SENATORS SERVING
## TWIGGS COUNTY

DURING HER 150 YEAR HISTORY—DEC. 14, 1809-DEC. 14, 1959
Reference: GEORGIA'S OFFICIAL AND STATISTICAL REGISTER
Department of Archives and History, Atlanta, Georgia

### SHERIFFS

| | When Commissioned | When Succeeded |
|---|---|---|
| Edmund Nunn | *Oct. 9, 1809 | |
| Mathew Hodges | Oct. 22, 1811 | |
| Roger Lawson | Jan. 24, 1814 | |
| Andrew Lawson | Jan. 3, 1816 | April 24, 1816** |
| Samuel Dick | April 24, 1816 | |
| Moses Wheat | Jan. 13, 1818 | |
| Wiley Belcher | Jan. 11, 1820 | |
| James Harrison | Jan. 14, 1822 | |
| Robert Hodges | Jan. 12, 1824 | |
| James Harrison | Jan. 13, 1826 | |
| Robert Hodges | Jan. 11, 1828 | |
| James Harrison | Feb. 12, 1830 | Jan. 5, 1832 |
| Peyton Reynolds | Jan. 5, 1832 | Jan. 18, 1834 |
| John Fitzpatrick | Jan. 18, 1834 | Jan. 13, 1836 |
| Josiah Daniel | Jan. 13, 1836 | Jan. 9, 1838 |
| Joseph Martin | Jan. 9, 1838 | |
| Tillman Denson | Jan. 10, 1840 | |
| Cornelius Hollingsworth | Jan. 20, 1842 | |
| Harden T. Smith | Jan. 5, 1844 | |
| James Hamock | Jan. 15, 1846 | Jan. 22, 1848 |
| Harden T. Smith | Jan. 22, 1848 | |
| James Hammock | Jan. 12, 1850 | Jan. 14, 1852 |
| Eli S. Griffin | Jan. 14, 1852 | Jan. 11, 1854 |

*Commissioned Sheriff of Wilkinson County on this date. Declared legal Sheriff of Twiggs County, Dec. 14, 1809, when Twiggs was cut off from Wilkinson.

| | | |
|---|---|---|
| Charles P. Reynolds | Jan. 11, 1854 | Jan. 11, 1856 |
| John Raley | Jan. 11, 1856 | Jan. 11, 1858 |
| William W. Bozeman | Jan. 11, 1858 | Jan. 10, 1860 |
| Jeremiah Sanders | Jan. 10, 1860 | |
| William H. Stokes | Jan. 23, 1862 | Feb. 16, 1864 |
| L. A. Nash | Feb. 16, 1864 | Jan. 22, 1866 |
| William H. Stokes | Jan. 22, 1866 | |
| Jeremiah Sanders | Aug. 26, 1868 | |
| James T. Evans | Jan. 25, 1871 | |
| " | Jan. 18, 1873 | |
| " | Jan. 20, 1875 | |

| | | |
|---|---|---|
| W. H. Stokes | Jan. 18, | 1877 |
| " | Jan. 4, | 1879 |
| William H. Stokes | Jan. 14, | 1881 |
| T. J. Robertson | Jan. 16, | 1883 |
| Frank Pettis | Jan. 13, | 1885 |
| Elijah F. Pettis | Jan. 8, | 1887 |
| E. F. Pettis | Jan. 11, | 1889 |
| W. H. Fitzpatrick | Jan. 12, | 1891 |
| ** " | Jan. 9, | 1893 |
| Henry S. Griffin | Nov. 11, | 1893 |
| S. E. Jones | Jan. 9, | 1895 |
| " | Oct. 16, | 1896 |
| S. W. Yopp | Oct. 20, | 1898 |
| D. S. Faulk | Oct. 17, | 1900 |
| | Term of Service | |
| F. E. Wimberly | 1902 - 1916 | |
| E. J. Griffin | 1916 - 1929 | |
| S. G. Kitchens | 1902 - 1941 | |
| W. E. Hamrick | 1941 - Incumbent | |

**Deceased.

## JUSTICES—INFERIOR COURT

| Name | When Commissioned | When Succeeded |
|---|---|---|
| Francis Powell | Dec. 27, 1809 | Dec. 14, 1811* |
| John Lawson | " " " | |
| Robert Glenn | " " " | |
| Arthur Fort | " " " | Dec. 13, 1811* |
| Jacob Ricks | Dec. 11, 1810 | April 21, 1812* |
| ***John Faulk | Dec. 13, 1811 | |
| ****John Hardin | Dec. 14, 1811 | |
| **Jeremiah Dupree | April 21, 1812 | |
| Samuel Alexander | Nov. 30, 1812 | |
| Jeremiah Dupree | " " " | |
| Harmon Perrymon | Nov. 9, 1813 | |
| Willoughby Hill | " " " | Aug. 22, 1815* |
| Robert Glenn | " " " | |
| William Melton | " " " | |
| John Faulk | " " " | June 20, 1814* |
| *****Gabriel Moffet | June 20, 1814 | |
| ******Samuel Dick | Aug. 22, 1815 | July 16, 1816* |
| *******James Hutchinson | July 16, 1816 | |
| Abram Miles | Nov. 1, 1817 | |
| Robert Glenn | " " " | |
| John Davis | " " " | March 8, 1819* |
| Jesse Brown | " " " | Jan. 6, 1819 |
| Moses Moore | " " " | Jan. 6, 1819* |

*Resigned.  ****Vice Francis Powell resigned.
**Vice Jacob Ricks resigned.  *****Vice John Faulk resigned.
***Vice Arthur Fort resigned.  ******Vice Willoughby Hill resigned.
*******Vice Samuel Dick resigned.

| | | |
|---|---|---|
| *Wm. W. Williamson | Jan. 6, | 1819 |
| **Archibald McIntyre | " " | " |
| ***James Brown | March 8, | 1819 |
| James B. Wimberly | Oct. 26, | 1821 |

| | | |
|---|---|---|
| Henry Bunn | Oct. 26, 1821 | |
| John Harden | ,, ,, ,, | |
| William Melton | ,, ,, ,, | |
| Robert Glenn | ,, ,, ,, | |
| Henry Bunn | Jan. 8, 1825 | |
| William Melton | ,, ,, ,, | |
| James Wimberly | ,, ,, ,, | |
| Henry Solomon | ,, ,, ,, | |
| Robert Glenn | ,, ,, ,, | |
| Kelly Glover | Jan. 22, 1829 | April 19, 1831 |
| Nimrod W. Long | ,, ,, ,, | Jan. 15, 1833 |
| James Ware | ,, ,, ,, | ,, ,, ,, |
| Dennis D. Sanders | ,, ,, ,, | ,, ,, ,, |
| Ira E. Dupree | ,, ,, ,, | July 20, 1831 |
| James Oliver | April 19, 1831 | Jan. 15, 1833 |
| Joshua R. Wimberly | July 20, 1831 | ,, ,, ,, |
| Henry Solomon | Jan. 15, 1833 | Jan. 9, 1837 |
| Hartwell H. Tarver | ,, ,, ,, | ,, ,, ,, |
| Peter G. Thompson | ,, ,, ,, | ,, ,, ,, |
| Thomas G. Perryman | ,, ,, ,, | Oct. 8, 1835 |
| John E. Daniel | ,, ,, ,, | Feb. 5, 1835 |

\*Vice Moses Moore resigned
\*\*Vice Jesse Brown resigned
\*\*\*Vice John Davis resigned

| | | |
|---|---|---|
| Joseph J. Chappell | Feb. 5, 1835 | Jan. 9, 1837 |
| Jordan W. Lee | Oct. 8, 1835 | ,, ,, ,, |
| Hartwell H. Tarver | Jan. 9, 1837 | Jan. 14, 1841 |
| Henry Solomon | ,, ,, ,, | ,, ,, ,, |
| Jordan W. Lee | ,, ,, ,, | ,, ,, ,, |
| George W. Welch | ,, ,, ,, | ,, ,, ,, |
| Gideon Bedingfield | ,, ,, ,, | ,, ,, ,, |
| Jesse Bateman | Jan. 21, 1839 | ,, ,, ,, |
| Henry Solomon | Jan. 14, 1841 | |
| Peyton Reynolds | ,, ,, ,, | |
| Benjamin B. Smith | ,, ,, ,, | June 18, 1842 |
| William A. Thorpe | ,, ,, ,, | June 20, 1842 |
| John L. Hodges | ,, ,, ,, | June 18, 1842 |
| James Ware | Jan. 20, 1842 | |
| John Fitzpatrick | June 18, 1842 | |
| John M. Nelson | ,, ,, ,, | |
| Thomas Glover | Jan. 15, 1845 | |
| Peyton Reynolds | ,, ,, ,, | |
| John Fitzpatrick | ,, ,, ,, | |
| Elisha Davis | ,, ,, ,, | Jan. 26, 1847 |
| Henry Solomon | ,, ,, ,, | April 20, 1847 |
| William Crittenden | April 20, 1847 | |
| Benjamin B. Smith | Jan. 26, 1847 | |
| ,, | Jan. 6, 1849 | |
| John Fitzpatrick | ,, ,, ,, | |
| James S. Miller | ,, ,, ,, | Feb. 7, 1852 |
| Thomas Glover | ,, ,, ,, | |
| Peyton Reynolds | Jan. 6, 1849 | |
| Henry Faulk | Feb. 7, 1852 | |
| Benjamin B. Smith | Jan. 8, 1853 | |

| | | |
|---|---|---|
| John Fitzpatrick | Jan. 8, 1853 | |
| Thomas Glover | " " " | |
| Henry Faulk | " " " | |
| Peyton Reynolds | " " " | |
| John D. Sharp | Jan. 24, 1854 | |
| Peyton Reynolds | Jan. 12, 1857 | Jan. 11, 1859 |
| Henry Faulk | " " " | April 9, 1860 |
| Levi Gallimore | " " " | Jan. 11, 1861 |
| Hardy Solomon | " " " | " " " |
| Wright Neel | " " " | " " " |
| John C. Epps | Jan. 11, 1859 | " " " |
| William S. Kelly | April 9, 1860 | " " " |
| Wright Neel | Jan. 10, 1861 | March 26, 1864 |
| *Hardy Solomon | " " " | Jan. 23, 1865 |
| Levi Gallimore | " " " | " " " |
| James T. Glover | " " " | " " " |
| William S. Kelly | " " " | " " " |
| Simeon Tharpe | March 26, 1864 | |
| J. T. Glover | Jan. 23, 1865 | |
| Levi Gallimore | " " " | |
| Simeon Tharpe | " " " | |
| W. L. Solomon | " " " | |
| T. S. Jones | " " " | |

*Incorrectly recorded as Hardy Johnson in the Justices of Inferior Court Book, 1861-1869.

## CLERKS, COURT OF ORDINARY, ORDINARIES

| Name | When Commissioned | When Succeeded |
|---|---|---|
| Micajah Fulgham | Jan. 5, 1815 | |
| " " | May 28, 1817 | |
| " " | Feb. 25, 1819 | |
| Edwin Hart | Jan. 4, 1821 | |
| " " | Jan. 22, 1823 | |
| Larkin Griffin | Feb. 10, 1825 | |
| Peter Solomon | Jan. 17, 1827 | |
| Richard Ricks | Jan. 6, 1829 | Feb. 17, 1831 |
| " " | Feb. 17, 1831 | Jan. 17, 1833 |
| " " | Jan. 17, 1833 | Jan. 14, 1835 |
| Nathan Land | Jan. 14, 1835 | Jan. 17, 1837 |
| William Crittenden | Jan. 17, 1837 | |
| Lewis Solomon | Jan. 11, 1841 | Jan. 20, 1843 |
| " " | Jan. 20, 1843 | |
| " " | Feb. 4, 1845 | |
| " " | Jan. 25, 1847 | Jan. 17, 1849 |
| Benjamin T. Smtih | Jan. 17, 1849 | |
| Lewis Solomon | Jan. 20, 1851 | Jan. 27, 1852 |
| " " | Jan. 27, 1852 | Jan. 11, 1856 |
| " " | Jan. 11, 1856 | Jan. 10, 1860 |
| " " | *Jan. 10, 1860 | |
| J. E. McDonald | Feb. 16, 1864 | Feb. 23, 1866 |
| John T. Glover | Feb. 23, 1866 | |
| William S. Kelly | Aug. 26, 1868 | Jan. 22, 1869** |
| John T. Shine | Jan. 22, 1869 | Jan. 25, 1871*** |

| | | |
|---|---|---|
| Joseph M. Burkett | Jan. 26, | 1871 |
| C. A. Solomon | Jan. 18, | 1873 |
| " " | Jan. 18, | 1877 |
| " " | **Jan. 14, | 1881 |
| William Griffin | Dec. 26, | 1883 |
| Joshua R. Wimberly | Jan. 13, | 1885 |
| J. R. Wimberly | Jan. 11, | 1889 |
| " " | Jan. 9, | 1893 |
| " " | Oct. 16, | 1896 |
| W. C. Faulk | Oct. 17, | 1900 |
| " " | Oct. 17, | 1904 |
| " " | Nov. 10, | 1908 |
| " " | Oct. 19, | 1912 |
| " " | Dec. 4, | 1916 |
| " " | Dec. 9, | 1920 |

| | Term of Service |
|---|---|
| H. F. Griffin, Sr. | 1922 - 1925 |
| S. J. Faulk | 1925 - 1938 (died in office) |
| W. W. Wood | 1938 - 1946 (died in office) |
| Mrs. W. W. Wood | 1946 - 1949 |
| J. R. Wimberly | 1949 - 1953 |
| T. H. Mercer | 1953 - Incumbent |

*Incorrectly marked 1861 on page 85 of the County Officers' Book, 1850-1851.
**Deceased.
***Resigned.

## CLERKS—INFERIOR COURT

| Name | When Commissioned | When Succeeded |
|---|---|---|
| Edwin Hart | May 29, 1810 | |
| Martin Kolb | Oct. 22, 1811 | |
| Edwin Hart | Jan. 24, 1814 | |
| " " | Jan. 3, 1816 | |
| " " | Jan. 13, 1818 | |
| " " | Jan. 11, 1820 | |
| " " | Jan. 14, 1822 | |
| Larkin Griffin | Jan. 12, 1824 | |
| " " | Jan. 13, 1826 | |
| John H. Blount | Jan. 11, 1828 | |
| Peter Solomon | Feb. 12, 1830 | Jan. 5, 1832 |
| Joshua M. Thigpen | Jan. 5, 1832 | Jan. 18, 1834 |
| John Fleming | Jan. 18, 1834 | Jan. 13, 1836 |
| Abel Stephens | Jan. 13, 1836 | Jan. 9, 1838 |
| James G. Oliver | Jan. 9, 1838 | |
| Thomas B. Pace | Jan. 10, 1840 | |
| Lewis Solomon | Jan. 20, 1842 | |
| " " | Jan. 5, 1844 | |
| Luallen Griffin | Jan. 15, 1846 | Jan. 22, 1843 |
| Richard Dashazo | Jan. 22, 1848 | |
| Lewis Solomon | Jan. 12, 1850 | Jan. 14, 1852 |
| William E. A. Wall | Jan. 14, 1852 | Jan. 11, 1854 |
| " " | Jan. 11, 1854 | Jan. 11, 1856 |
| Robert Belsher | Jan. 11, 1856 | Jan. 11, 1858 |
| " " | Jan. 11, 1858 | Jan. 10, 1860 |

| | | |
|---|---|---|
| John P. Vinson | *Jan. 10, 1860 | |
| John A. Clements | Jan. 23, 1862 | Feb. 16, 1864 |
| J. H. Ray | Feb. 16, 1864 | Jan. 22, 1866 |
| Joseph H. Ray | Jan. 22, 1866 | |

*Incorrectly marked 1861 on page 85 of the County Officers' Book 1850-1861.

## CLERKS, SUPERIOR COURT

| Name | When Commissioned | When Succeeded |
|---|---|---|
| Archibald McIntyre | *April 29, 1811 | |
| " " | Oct. 22, 1811 | |
| " " | Jan. 24, 1814 | |
| " " | Jan. 3, 1816 | |
| " " | Jan. 13, 1818 | |
| " " | Jan. 11, 1820 | |
| Wiley Belsher | Jan. 14, 1822 | |
| James Spullock | Jan. 12, 1824 | |
| Thomas Arrington | Jan. 13, 1826 | |
| " " | Jan. 11, 1828 | |
| Peyton Reynolds | Nov. 8, 1828 | |
| Allen Fleming | Feb. 12, 1830 | Jan. 5, 1832 |
| Peter Solomon | Jan. 5, 1832 | Jan. 18, 1834 |
| " " | Jan. 18, 1834 | Jan. 14, 1835 |
| Henry Loyless | Jan. 14, 1835 | Jan. 13, 1836 |
| " " | Jan. 13, 1836 | Jan. 9, 1838 |
| Josiah Martin | Jan. 9, 1838 | |
| Lemuel P. Hoskins | Jan. 10, 1840 | |
| Josiah Daniel | Jan. 20, 1840 | |
| Peyton Reynolds | Jan. 5, 1844 | |
| " " | Jan. 15, 1846 | Jan. 22, 1848 |
| " " | Jan. 22, 1848 | |
| " " | Jan. 12, 1850 | Jan. 14, 1852 |
| " " | Jan. 14, 1852 | Jan. 11, 1854 |

*Elected Apr. 20, 1811 in consequence of an Act passed Dec. 15, 1810, directing the Jusices of the Inferior Court to hold an election of a Clerk of the Superior Court for Twiggs County.

| | | |
|---|---|---|
| Wright Neel | Jan. 11, 1854 | Jan. 11, 1856 |
| " " | Jan. 11, 1856 | Jan. 11, 1858 |
| " " | Jan. 11, 1858 | Jan. 10, 1860 |
| " " | *Jan. 10, 1860 | |
| " " | Jan. 23, 1862 | Feb. 16, 1864 |
| W. Neal | Feb. 16, 1864 | Jan. 22, 1866 |
| William A. Daniel | Jan. 22, 1866 | |
| J. M. Burkett | Aug. 26, 1868 | |
| ***John H. Fitzpatrick | Jan. 25, 1871 | |
| William B. Steeley | Jan. 3, 1872 | |
| " " | Jan. 18, 1873 | |
| Elbert W. Hughes | Jan. 20, 1875 | |
| E. W. Hughes | Jan. 18, 1877 | |
| James B. Peacock | Jan. 4, 1879 | |
| " " | ****Jan. 14, 1881 | |
| John R. Nelson | March 2, 1881 | |
| " " | Jan. 16, 1883 | |
| Frank Johnson | Jan. 13, 1885 | |

| Name | Date | |
|---|---|---|
| F. M. Johnston | Jan. 8, | 1887 |
| F. M. Johnston | Jan. 11, | 1889 |
| F. M. Johnston | Jan. 12, | 1891 |
| D. S. Faulk | Jan. 9, | 1893 |
| " " | Jan. 9, | 1895 |
| " " | Oct. 16, | 1896 |
| A. F. Martin | Oct. 20, | 1898 |
| " " | Oct. 17, | 1900 |
| " " | Oct. 13, | 1902 |
| A. F. Martin | Oct. 17, | 1904 |
| " " | Nov. 1, | 1906 |
| " " | Nov. 3, | 1908 |
| " " | Nov. 5, | 1910 |
| A. F. Martin, Sr. | Oct. 19, | 1912 |
| A. F. Martin | Nov. 30, | 1914 |

| Name | Term of Service |
|---|---|
| W. C. Stokes | 1916 - 1928 |
| J. H. Whitehurst | 1929 - 1952, Deceased |
| Elmina B. Hamrick (Mrs.) | 1952 unexpired term. |
| W. H. Martin | 1953 - Incumbent |

*Incorrectly marked 1861 on page 85 of the County Officers' Book, 1850-1861.
***Resigned No. 17, 1871
****Died Jan. 14, 1881; William Griffin appointed to fill vacancy till election.

## TAX RECEIVERS

| Name | When Commissioned | When Succeeded |
|---|---|---|
| James Patton | May 5, 1810 | |
| " " | April 29, 1811 | |
| Jonathan Bell | Jan. 16. 1812 | |
| William Hawkins | Jan. 19, 1813 | |
| Nathaniel Tatum | Jan. 24, 1814 | |
| " " | Jan. 10, 1815 | |
| Robert Hodges | Jan. 3, 1816 | |
| " " | Jan. 20. 1817 | |
| " " | Jan. 13. 1818 | |
| Allen Summers | Jan. 13, 1819 | |
| Robert Hodges | Jan. 11. 1820 | |
| " " | March 7, 1821 | |
| " " | March 14, 1822 | |
| Larkin Griffin | Jan. 15, 1823 | |
| James Pearson | Jan. 12. 1824 | |
| " " | Jan. 8. 1825 | |
| " " | Jan. 13. 1826 | |
| Charles Cardin | Jan. 23, 1827 | |
| " " | Jan. 11, 1828 | |
| " " | Jan. 22, 1829 | |
| " " | Feb. 12, 1830 | |
| Holiday H. Harrell | Nov. 15, 1830 | |
| " " | Jan. 12, 1831 | |
| " " | Jan. 5, 1832 | |
| Joseph Martin | Jan. 18, 1834 | |
| " " | Jan. 14, 1835 | |
| Sovereign Ellis | Jan. 13, 1836 | |

| | | |
|---|---|---|
| Daniel Duncan | Jan. 9, | 1837 |
| William Kelly | Jan. 9, | 1838 |
| Silas Brown | Jan. 21, | 1839 |
| Daniel Wall | Jan. 25, | 1841 |
| Richard Deshazo | Jan. 20, | 1842 |
| Amos Harris | Jan. 20, | 1843 |
| Joseph Blackshear | Jan. 5, | 1844 |
| ″ ″ | Feb. 1, | 1845 |
| William C. Finch | Jan. 12, | 1847 |
| William Fitzpatrick | Jan. 22, | 1848 |
| Jacob Pearce | Jan. 8, | 1849 |
| Reuben A. Waters | Jan. 12, | 1850 |
| Joseph Blackshear | Jan. 16, | 1851 |
| Edward C. Epps | Jan. 14, | 1852 |
| Wright Neel | Jan. 17, | 1853 |
| John F. Paul | Jan. 11, | 1854 |
| Thomas H. Jones | Jan. 9, | 1855 |
| Abraham S. Alexander | Jan. 11, | 1856 |
| Jeremiah Sanders | Jan. 12, | 1857 |
| John P. Vinson | Jan. 11, | 1858 |
| James T. Evans | Jan. 10, | 1859 |
| Henry Crawford | *Jan. 10, | 1860 |
| E. C. Epps | Jan. 10, | 1861 |
| William Griffin | March 1, | 1862 |
| ″ ″ | Feb. 16, | 1864 |
| John Cribb | March 8, | 1866 |
| M. W. Kitchens | Sept. 18, | 1868 |
| Lewis Solomon | *Jan. 25, | 1871 |
| William C. Solomon | **April 24, | 1871 |
| E. A. Nash | Jan. 27, | 1873 |
| Thomas J. Robertson | Feb. 1, | 1875 |
| R. F. Reed | Jan. 18, | 1877 |
| Thomas H. Jones | Jan. 4, | 1879 |
| ″ ″ | Jan. 14, | 1881 |
| T. H. Jones | Jan. 16, | 1883 |
| George R. Asbell | Jan. 13, | 1885 |
| ″ ″ | Jan. 8, | 1887 |
| R. H. Arrington | Feb. 14, | 1889 |
| ″ ″ | Jan. 12, | 1891 |
| H. M. Jones | Jan. 9, | 1893 |
| ″ ″ | Jan. 9, | 1895 |
| ″ ″ | Oct. 16, | 1896 |
| S. T. Burkett | Oct. 20, | 1898 |
| ″ ″ | Oct. 17, | 1900 |
| H. J. Williams | Oct. 13, | 1902 |
| R. R. Slappey | Oct. 17, | 1904 |
| ″ ″ | Nov. 1, | 1906 |

| | | |
|---|---|---|
| | Jan. 16, | 1851 |
| | Jan. 14, | 1852 |
| | Jan. 17, | 1853 |
| | Jan. 11, | 1854 |
| | Jan. 9, | 1855 |
| | Jan. 11, | 1856 |
| | Jan. 12, | 1857 |
| | Jan. 11, | 1858 |
| | Jan. 10, | 1859 |
| | Jan. 10, | 1860 |
| | Jan. 10, | 1861 |
| | Feb. 16, | 1864 |
| | March 8, | 1866 |

*Failed to qualify.
**Appointed by Ordinary.

| | | |
|---|---|---|
| R. R. Slappy Sr. | Nov. 3, | 1908 |
| ″ ″ | *Nov. 5, | 1910 |
| J. A. Wimberly | April 16, | 1912 |
| L. L. Griffin | Oct. 17, | 1912 |

L. L. Griffin                Nov. 30, 1914
E. L. Hill                   Dec. 4,   1916
                             Term of Service
L. L. Griffin                1920 - 1925
H. V. Jackson                1925 - 1936
Tax Receiver office discontinued merged with Tax Commissioner.
*Resigned April 13, 1912.

## TAX COLLECTORS

| Name | When Commissioned | When Succeeded |
|---|---|---|
| James Spann | May 5, 1810 | |
| Theophilus Pearce | April 29, 1811 | |
| " " | Jan. 16, 1812 | |
| Jonathan Bell | Jan. 19, 1813 | |
| William Joiner | Jan. 24, 1814 | |
| Lewis L. Griffin | Jan. 10, 1815 | |
| Henry Solomon | Jan. 3, 1816 | |
| " " | Jan. 20, 1817 | |
| " " | Jan. 13, 1818 | |
| Moses Moore | Jan. 13, 1819 | |
| Allen Summers | Jan. 11, 1820 | |
| Moses Moore | March 7, 1821 | |
| " " | March 14, 1822 | |
| Theophilus Pearce | Jan. 15, 1823 | |
| " " | Jan. 12, 1824 | |
| " " | Jan. 8, 1825 | |
| Jourdan W. Lee | Jan. 13, 1826 | |
| John Fort | Jan. 23, 1827 | |
| " " | Feb. 26, 1828 | |
| " " | Jan. 22, 1829 | |
| William Wimberly | Feb. 12, 1830 | |
| John Fitzpatrick | Jan. 5, 1832 | |
| Isham G. Andrews | Jan. 18, 1834 | |
| " " | Jan. 14, 1835 | |
| " " | Jan. 13, 1836 | |
| " " | Jan. 9, 1837 | |
| Richard Deshazo | Jan. 9, 1838 | |
| " " | Jan. 21, 1839 | |
| S. Streetman | Jan. 25, 1841 | |
| Jacob Pearce Jr. | June 18, 1842 | |
| John Holly | Jan. 20, 1843 | |
| Richard Deshazo | Jan. 5, 1844 | |
| " " | May 16, 1845 | |
| " " | April 23, 1846 | |
| Uriah Maxwell | Jan. 12, 1847 | |
| John S. Pearce | Jan. 22, 1848 | |
| Isham Edwards | Jan. 8, 1849 | |
| Benjamin Tharp | Jan. 12, 1850 | Jan. 16, 1851 |
| John Martin | Jan. 16, 1851 | Jan. 14, 1852 |
| Henry Oneal | Jan. 14, 1852 | Jan. 17, 1853 |
| William J. Martin | Jan. 17, 1853 | Jan. 11, 1854 |
| Benjamin Tharp | Jan. 11, 1854 | Jan. 9, 1855 |
| Isham Edwards | Jan. 9, 1855 | Jan. 11, 1856 |

| | | |
|---|---|---|
| John Henderson | Jan. 11, 1856 | Jan. 12, 1857 |
| John Martin | Jan. 12, 1857 | Jan. 11, 1858 |
| William H. Stokes | Jan. 11, 1858 | Jan. 10, 1859 |
| James Bobitt | Jan. 10, 1859 | Jan. 10, 1860 |
| Thomas H. Jones | *Jan. 10, 1860 | Jan. 10, 1861 |
| W. J. Hammock | Jan. 10, 1861 | |
| William Griffin | March 1, 1862 | Feb. 16, 1864 |

*Incorrectly marked 1861 on page 85 of the County Officers' Book, 1850-1861.

| | | |
|---|---|---|
| J. Hammock | Feb. 16, 1864 | Mar. 8, 1866 |
| Henry Martin | March 8, 1866 | |
| R. A. Waters | Sept. 8, 1868 | |
| Thomas Jones | Jan. 25, 1871 | |
| Henry Martin | Jan. 18, 1873 | |
| Thomas H. Jones | March 20, 1875 | |
| W. J. Pitts | Jan. 18, 1877 | |
| John S. Johnson | Jan. 4, 1879 | |
| Charles G. Johnson | Jan. 14, 1881 | |
| R. R. Slappy Sr. | Jan. 16, 1883 | |
| George R. Gallemore | Jan. 13, 1885 | |
| " " | Jan. 8, 1887 | |
| G. R. Gallemore | Jan. 11, 1889 | |
| " " | Jan. 12, 1891 | |
| W. F. Slappey | Jan. 9, 1893 | |
| " " | Jan. 9, 1895 | |
| " " | *Oct. 16, 1896 | |
| W. C. Faulk | Aug. 5, 1897 | |
| J. C. Everett | Oct. 20, 1898 | |
| " " | **Oct. 17, 1900 | |
| S. E. Jones | ***Nov. 7, 1901 | |
| " " | Oct. 13, 1902 | |
| T. F. Everett | Oct. 17, 1904 | |
| T. F. Everett | Nov. 1, 1906 | |
| " " | Nov. 3, 1908 | |
| C. A. Vaughn | Nov. 5, 1910 | |
| " " | Oct. 18, 1912 | |
| S. M. Gallemore | Nov. 16, 1914 | |
| " " | Dec. 4, 1916 | |

| | Term of Service |
|---|---|
| H. F. Kennington | 1920 - 1925 |
| J. H. Vaughn | 1925 - 1935 |

Change of title for Office to Tax Commissioner

| | |
|---|---|
| J. H. Vaughn | 1936 - 1950 |
| M. W. Fitzpatrick | 1950 - Incumbent |

*Resigned Apr. 26, 1897, to take effect on qualification of successor.
**Resigned Oct. 18, 1901.
***Listed in the column under 1900 for Twiggs County in the County Officers' Book, 1896-1904, but stands to reason that the year is 1901.

## TWIGGS COUNTY TREASURERS

| | |
|---|---|
| C. A. Solomon | 1866 - 1868 |
| S. K. Long | 1868 - 1871 |
| Robert H. Arrington | 1871 - 1875 |
| Floyd A. Finch | 1875 - 1879 |

| | |
|---|---|
| Hayward Hughes | 1879 - |

(Office of County Treasurer abolished during this period by Law. Ordinary served as Treasurer.)

| | |
|---|---|
| Stephen Jones | 1895 - 1904 |
| J. Walker Jones | 1904 - 1912 |
| J. H. Solomon | 1912 - 1914 |

(Law enacted for County Commissioners to act as County Treasurer)

## CHAIRMAN, TWIGGS CO. COMMISSIONERS OF ROADS AND REVENUE

(According to Georgia Laws this Board was organized and abolished several times between 1875 - 1915.)

| | |
|---|---|
| I. N. Maxwell | Holding office in 1901 |
| H. F. Griffin, Sr. | 1914 - 1915 |
| F. J. Ray | 1915 - 1921 |
| Linton Hatcher | 1921 - 1924 |
| S. C. Jones | 1924 - 1927 |
| Linton Hatcher | 1927 - 1929 |
| D. S. McGee | 1929 - 1930 |
| W. W. Howell | 1931 - 1936 |
| W. H. Mercer | 1936 - 1939 |
| C. A. Duggan | 1939 - 1951 |
| Olin C. Cannon | 1951 - 1956 |
| W. V. Watson | 1957 - Incumbent |

Some of the Laws creating and abolishing the Board of Commissioners: (Excerpts)
Georgia Laws 1876   Page 296   No. CCCXVI   (0 No. 228)
An Act to amend an Act entitled an Act to organize a Board of Commissioners for the County of Twiggs, approved March 2, 1875.
Georgia Laws   1884-5   Page 430   No. 190
An Act to abolish the Board of County Commissioners for the County of Twiggs, and duties imposed upon the Ordinary of said County, approved 23rd day of Sept. 1885.
Georgia Laws   1898   Page 381
An Act to create a Board of Commissioners of Roads and Revenues for County of Twiggs, to define their powers and etc. . . . Consist of 5 persons as follows: Jas. W. Jones, W. A. Joyner, I. N. Maxwell, George W. Waters, E. F. Pettis, citizens of Twiggs County.
Georgia Laws   1915   Part II   Title II   County Matters, Page 389
Act Number 70: Twiggs Board of Commissioners created—Part of Sec. 1 and Sec. 2: An Act to create a Board of Commissioners of Roads and Revenues for Twiggs County consisting of three members—F. J. Ray, T. S. Tharpe, Linton Hatcher, citizens of said County. Shall hold office to January 1, 1917 and until their successors are elected and qualified—.
Georgia Laws   1923   Page 324, On County Matters
Act Number 163 relative to Twiggs Boards of Commissioners of Roads and Revenues—five members—Sec. 2 enacted, that S. C. Jones, B. D. Melton, W. W. Harrell, G. F. Cannon and M. S. Faulk—term, begin immediately upon taking oath and giving bond—continue until Jan. 1, 1925.

## CLERKS OF TWIGGS COUNTY COMMISSIONERS OF ROADS AND REVENUES 1915 - 1959

F. J. Ray, 1915-1920; J. H. Vaughn, 1921-1923; J. P. Califf, 1924-1926; J. D. Shannon, 1927-1934; W. F. Maxwell, 1935-1942; Mrs. Johnnie Sanders, 1943-1944; Florrie H. McKinnon, 1945-1950; Mrs. Johnnie Sanders, 1951—to the present time.

Furnished by Mrs. Johnnie Sanders, Clerk.

## CORONER

| Name | When Commissioned | When Succeeded |
|---|---|---|
| James Wheeler | May 29, 1810 | |
| Robert Cummins | Oct. 22, 1811 | |
| " " | Jan. 24, 1814 | |
| " " | Jan. 3, 1816 | |
| " " | Jan. 13, 1818 | |
| George T. Jameson | Jan. 11, 1820 | |
| Robert Cummins | Jan. 14, 1822 | |
| " " | Jan. 12, 1824 | |
| " " | Jan. 13, 1826 | |
| John G. Lefoy | Jan 11, 1828 | |
| " " | Feb. 12, 1830 | Jan. 5, 1832 |
| Samuel Jourdan | Jan. 5, 1832 | Jan. 18, 1834 |
| " " | Jan. 18, 1834 | Feb. 5, 1835 |
| Abram Davis | Feb. 5, 1835 | Jan. 13, 1836 |
| Abraham Davis | Jan. 13, 1836 | Jan. 9, 1838 |
| John Linton | Jan. 9, 1838 | |
| John Rains | Jan. 10, 1840 | |
| John Raines | Jan. 20, 1842 | |
| Rhesa J. Ellis | Jan. 5, 1844 | |
| Abraham S. Alexander | Jan. 25, 1845 | |
| Abraham B. Alexander | Jan. 15, 1846 | Jan. 25, 1847 |
| John Raines | Jan. 25, 1847 | Jan. 22, 1848 |
| " " | Jan. 22, 1848 | Jan. 8, 1849 |
| Thomas P. Lavar | Jan. 8, 1849 | |
| Alexander Pierce | Jan. 12, 1850 | Jan. 14, 1852 |
| James J. Arnold | Jan. 14, 1852 | Jan. 11, 1854 |
| James Arnold | Jan. 11, 1854 | Jan. 11, 1856 |
| James J. Arnold | Jan. 11, 1856 | Jan. 11, 1858 |
| John Henderson | Jan. 11, 1858 | Jan. 10, 1860 |
| *Henry Newberry | Jan. 10, 1860 | |
| James Liles | Jan. 23, 1862 | Feb. 16, 1864 |
| S. L. Alexander | Feb. 16, 1864 | Jan. 22, 1866 |
| Elbert Kent | Jan. 22, 1866 | |
| J. C. McGaugh | Aug. 26, 1868 | |
| Hardy Bennett | Jan. 25, 1871 | |
| Alexander Thompson | Jan. 18, 1873 | |
| " " | Jan. 20, 1875 | |
| " " | Jan. 18, 1877 | |
| " " | Jan. 4, 1879 | |
| " " | Jan. 14, 1881 | |
| Zachariah Floyd | Jan. 16, 1883 | |
| " " | Jan. 13, 1885 | |
| " " | Jan. 8, 1887 | |
| " " | Jan. 11, 1889 | |
| " " | Jan. 12, 1891 | |
| " " | Jan. 9, 1893 | |
| " " | Jan. 9, 1895 | |
| J. C. Bozeman | Oct. 16, 1896 | |
| William Dye | Oct. 20, 1898 | |

*Incorrectly marked 1861 on page 85 of the County Officers' Book, 1850-1861.

| | | |
|---|---|---|
| W. M. Dye | Oct. 17, | 1900 |
| J. W. Crossey | Oct. 13, | 1902 |
| J. W. Crosby | Oct. 17, | 1904 |
| " " | Nov. 1, | 1906 |
| " " | Nov. 3, | 1908 |
| J. W. Crosby | Nov. 5, | 1910 |
| R. M. Johnson | Oct. 14, | 1912 |
| " " | Nov. 30, | 1914 |
| E. B. Sauls | Dec. 4, | 1916 |

| | Term of Service |
|---|---|
| C. W. Libbey | 1920 - 1925 |
| E. B. Sauls | 1925 - 1943 |
| W. M. Little | 1945 - Incumbent |

## COUNTY SURVEYORS

| Name | When Commissioned | When Succeeded |
|---|---|---|
| Peter L. Livingston | May 29, 1810 | |
| Hartwell L. Harris | Oct. 22, 1811 | |
| Osborn Childers | Jan. 24, 1814 | |
| Robert Johnson | Jan. 3, 1816 | July 16, 1816 |
| Francis Spann | July 16, 1816 | |
| Matthew R. Grace | Jan. 18, 1818 | |
| " " | Jan. 11, 1820 | |
| " " | Jan. 14, 1822 | |
| Abraham Adams | Jan. 12, 1824 | |
| William Hunt | Jan. 13, 1826 | |
| " " | Jan. 11, 1828 | |
| " " | Feb. 12, 1830 | Jan. 5, 1832 |
| George W. Welch | Jan. 5, 1832 | Jan. 18, 1834 |
| Richard Whitehead | Jan. 18, 1834 | Jan. 13, 1836 |
| Robins Andrews | Jan. 13, 1836 | Jan. 9, 1838 |
| Robin Andrews | Jan. 9, 1838 | |
| Robins Andrews | Jan. 10, 1840 | |
| Ira E. Dupree | June 18, 1842 | |
| " " | Jan. 5, 1844 | |
| Elisha Davis | Jan. 15, 1846 | Jan. 25, 1847 |
| Charles R. Wright | Jan. 25, 1847 | |
| " " | Jan. 22, 1848 | |
| Levi Gallamore | Jan. 12, 1850 | |
| Acton E. Nash | Jan. 16, 1851 | Jan. 14, 1852 |
| " " | Jan. 14, 1852 | Jan. 11, 1854 |
| " " | Jan. 11, 1854 | Jan. 11, 1856 |
| A. E. Nash | Jan. 11, 1856 | Jan. 11, 1858 |
| Acton E. Nash | Jan. 11, 1858 | Jan. 10, 1860 |
| " " | Jan. 10, 1860 | |
| A. E. Nash | Jan. 23, 1862 | Feb. 16, 1864 |
| " " | Feb. 16, 1864 | Jan. 22, 1866 |

| | | |
|---|---|---|
| E. A. Nash | Jan. 22, | 1866 |
| " " | Aug. 26, | 1868 |
| Edwin A. Nash | Jan. 25, | 1871 |
| A. W. Astell | Jan. 18, | 1873 |
| Edwin A. Nash | Jan. 20, | 1875 |
| E. A. Nash | Jan. 18, | 1877 |
| " " | Jan. 4, | 1879 |
| George R. Gallemore | Jan. 14, | 1881 |
| G. R. Galimore | Jan. 14, | 1883 |
| Benjamin S. Fitzpatrick | Jan. 13, | 1885 |
| Tilman I. Joyner | Jan. 8, | 1887 |
| Frank Sanders | Jan. 11, | 1889 |
| B. F. Finch | Jan. 12, | 1891 |
| S. A. Bryant | Jan. 9, | 1893 |
| G. R. Gallemore | Jan. 9, | 1895 |
| " " | Oct. 16, | 1896 |
| " " | Oct. 20, | 1898 |
| G. R. Gallemore | Oct. 17, | 1900 |
| " " | Oct. 13, | 1902 |
| Charles B. Lamb | Oct. 17, | 1904 |
| A. T. Pope | Nov. 1, | 1906 |
| H. T. Pope | Nov. 3, | 1908 |
| *H. T. Polk | Nov. 5, | 1910 |
| Joe Nobles | **Oct. 14, | 1912 |

| | Term of Service |
|---|---|
| H. T. Pope | 1914 - 1937 |
| C. B. Lamb | 1939 - 1952 |
| W. D. Dean, Acting | 1953 - 1954 |
| W. D. Dean, Acting, Res. | 1955 - 1956 |
| Mark B. Faulk | 1956 - |

*probably Pope.
**Resigned April 25, 1913.

## JUSTICES OF THE PEACE

| Name | Captain's District | No. of District | When Commissioned | When Succeeded |
|---|---|---|---|---|
| Theophilus Pierce[1,2] | | | June 14, 1808 | June 17, 1811 |
| James Brown[1,2] | | | " " " | Aug. 6, 1811 |
| William Hawthorn[1,2] | | | " " " | July 21, 1812 |
| John Faulk[1,2] | | | " " " | " " " |
| William Hemphill | Slaughter's | 356 | Nov. 17, 1810 | |
| William Melton | " | " | " " " | |
| James McCormick | Parker's | 355 | " " " | |
| Jonathan Bell | " | " | " " " | |
| Arthur Fort | | | " " " | |
| James Vickers | Wood's | 354 | " " " | |
| Lovett B. Smith[3] | L. Smith's | 326 | " " " | Feb. 6, 1812 |
| Seaborn Mimms[2] | " | " | " " " | " " " |
| James Ware[6] | R. Lawson's | 324 | " " " | " " " |
| Joseph Braddy | Lashley's | 323 | Nov. 23, 1810 | |

| Name | District | No. | Commissioned | Terminated |
|---|---|---|---|---|
| Robins Andrews[4] | " | " | June 17, 1811 | |
| Isaac Dennard[5] | Ford's | 325 | Aug. 16, 1811 | |
| John Harden[9] | Lawson's | 324 | Feb. 6, 1812 | |
| William H. Dupree[7] | Jo. Jamieson's | 326 | " " " | |
| Robert Curry[8] | " | " | " " " | |

1. Commissioned Justices of the Peace for Wilkinson County and became Justices of the Peace for Twiggs County, Dec. 14, 1809, when Twiggs was cut off from Wilkinson.
2. Resigned.      3. Removed.      6. Cut off into another district.
4. Vice Theophilus Pierce resigned.      7. Vice Lovett B. Smith removed.
5. Vice James Brown resigned.      8. Vice Seaborn Mimms resigned.
9. Vice James Ware cut off into another district.

| Name | District | No. | Commissioned | Terminated |
|---|---|---|---|---|
| *Benjamin Mitchell | Wood's | 354 | July 21, 1812 | |
| **Bryant Edmundson | Lawson's | 324 | " " " | |
| Timothy Mathews | Keener's | 323 | Jan. 19, 1813 | |
| Jacob Ricks | Lawson's | 324 | " " " | Apr. 12, 1816 |
| Abner Bishop | " | " | " " " | Aug. 22, 1815 |
| Moses Wheat | And. Smith's | 326 | " " " | Apr. 6, 1815 |
| Jonathan Bell | Simmons' | 355 | " " " | Aug. 14, 1815 |
| John H. Powell | " | " | " " " | |
| Nathaniel Tatum | Tatum's | 356 | " " " | Apr. 22, 1816 |
| James Buckelew | " | " | " " " | |
| Lovett B. Smith | L. B. Smith's | 376 | " " " | |
| John Cooper | " | " | " " " | |
| Isaac Dennard | Ford's | 325 | Jan. 30, 1813 | |
| George McKigney | " | " | " " " | May 31, 1815 |
| Arthur Fort Jr. | Harden's | 372 | " " " | Sept. 15, 1815 |
| James Durham | " | " | " " " | June 20, 1814 |
| Silas Wood | Wood's | 354 | Mar. 11, 1813 | Jan. 17, 1816 |
| Benjamin Mitchell | " | " | " " " | June 28, 1815 |
| Drury Williams | Keener's | 323 | Mar. 15, 1813 | |
| Robert Sharrard | And. Smith's | 326 | June 14, 1813 | July 10, 1816 |
| John Moffett | Fort's | 372 | June 20, 1814 | |
| William Davis | And. Smith's | 326 | Apr. 6, 1815 | |
| Richard C. Spann | Childer's | 325 | May 31, 1815 | |
| James N. Sutton | Gates' | 354 | June 28, 1815 | |
| Micajah Harrington | Filligen's | 355 | Aug. 14, 1815 | |
| Joseph Hutchinson | Lawson's | 324 | Aug. 22, 1815 | Apr. 12, 1816 |
| John Harrinton | Stevens' | 372 | Sept. 13, 1815 | |

*Vice William Hawthorn resigned.      **Vice John Faulk resigned.

| Name | District | No. | Commissioned | Terminated |
|---|---|---|---|---|
| William Clopton | Gates' | 354 | Jan. 17, 1816 | |
| James Ware | Hodge's | 324 | Apr. 12, 1816 | |
| Hardy Durham | " | " | " " " | |
| William Jones | Joiner's | 356 | Apr. 22, 1816 | |
| Andrew Smith | Bozeman's | 326 | July 10, 1816 | |
| Drury Williams | Belcher's | 323 | Jan. 9, 1817 | Mar. 4, 1818 |
| Timothy Matthews | " | " | " " " | " " " |
| Little B. Bostick | " | 372 | " " " | |
| Samuel P. Hargrave | " | " | " " " | Apr. 6, 1818 |
| Isaac Dennard | Wimberly's | 325 | Jan. 31, 1817 | |
| Richard C. Spann | " | " | " " " | Sept. 15, 1819 |
| James Ware | " | " | " " " | Mar. 4, 1818 |
| Moses Wheat | Hodge's | 324 | " " " | |

| | | | | | |
|---|---|---|---|---|---|
| John Davis | Bulloch's | 355 | Jan. 31, 1817 | Mar. 16, 1818 | |
| William T. Jenkins | ,, | ,, | ,, ,, ,, | ,, ,, ,, | |
| John N. Thompson | Ellis' | 354 | ,, ,, ,, | Mar 8, 1819 | |
| Thomas Beaty | ,, | ,, | ,, ,, ,, | ,, ,, ,, | |
| James Buckelew | Joiner's | 356 | ,, ,, ,, | | |
| William Hemphill | ,, | ,, | ,, ,, ,, | Sept. 9, 1818 | |
| Wm. W. Williamson | Smith's | 376 | Feb. 26, 1817 | Oct. 9, 1818 | |
| Andrew Smith | Bozeman's | 326 | ,, ,, ,, | Apr. 6, 1818 | |
| Martin Wood | ,, | ,, | ,, ,, ,, | ,, ,, ,, | |
| Lovet B. Smith | Smith's | 376 | May 28, 1817 | | |
| John Keener | Belcher's | 323 | Mar. 4, 1818 | | |
| James Patton | ,, | ,, | ,, ,, ,, | Mar. 8, 1819 | |
| John H. Gilmore | Hodge's | 324 | ,, ,, ,, | Apr. 8, 1819 | |
| John Liles | Bulloch's | 355 | Mar. 16, 1818 | June 21, 1819 | |
| Moses Fillingame | ,, | ,, | Mar. 16, 1818 | Jan. 29, 1819 | |
| Arthur Fort Jr. | Belcher's | 373 | Apr. 6, 1818 | | |
| Benjamin Harvey | Bozeman's | 326 | ,, ,, ,, | Feb. 18, 1819 | |
| Wm. W. Williamson | ,, | ,, | ,, ,, ,, | | |
| Isaac Lindsey | Jefferson's | 356 | Sept. 9, 1818 | | |
| Henry Bunn | Smith's | 376 | Oct. 9, 1818 | | |
| Robert Fleming | Evans' | 355 | Jan. 29, 1819 | | |
| Dennis D. Sanders | Bozeman's | 356 | Feb. 18, 1819 | July 25, 1820** | |
| Wiley Belcher | Belcher's | 323 | Mar. 8, 1819 | Mar. 6, 1820 | |
| William Grimsley | ,, | 354 | ,, ,, ,, | | |
| Joab Tison | ,, | ,, | ,, ,, ,, | | |
| John Womack | Johnson's | 326 | June 15, 1819 | | |
| John Davis | Barrow's | 355 | June 21, 1819 | | |
| David Graham | Wimberly's | 325 | Sept. 15, 1819 | | |
| Matthew R. Grace | Belcher's | 372 | Sept. 29, 1819 | | |
| Samuel Williams | Griffin's | 423 | Jan. 19, 1820 | | |
| Nicholas Lloyd | Irwin's | 323 | Mar. 6, 1820 | | |
| James C. Dozier | Wimberly's | 324 | Apr. 8, 1820 | | |
| Jabez Curry | Oliver's | 326 | May 25, 1820 | | |
| *David Jamison | Evans' | 355 | July 25, 1820 | | |
| ,, ,, | Barrow's | 355 | Jan. 10, 1821 | Feb. 28, 1826 | |
| Harmon Pearson | ,, | ,, | ,, ,, ,, | | |
| James Buckelew | Blackshear's | 356 | Jan. 11, 1821 | | |
| Elkanah Powell | ,, | ,, | ,, ,, ,, | Jan. 9, 1822 | |
| Samuel Williams | Griffin's | 423 | ,, ,, ,, | | |
| Abraham Zuber | ,, | ,, | ,, ,, ,, | Nov. 12, 1821 | |
| *Vice Robert Fleming resigned. | | | **Resigned. | | |
| James Pearson | Thames' | 323 | Jan. 11, 1821 | | |
| James B. Smith | ,, | ,, | ,, ,, ,, | Jan. 19, 1824 | |
| Hardy Durham | Wimberly's | 324 | ,, ,, ,, | | |
| James Ware | ,, | ,, | ,, ,, ,, | | |
| Lovett B. Smith | Smith's | 376 | ,, ,, ,, | Jan. 15, 1823 | |
| John M. Smith | ,, | ,, | ,, ,, ,, | | |
| David Graham | Brown's | 325 | Jan. 26, 1821 | | |
| Isaac Dennard | ,, | ,, | ,, ,, ,, | | |
| Matthew R. Grace | Chain's | 372 | ,, ,, ,, | Mar. 5, 1824 | |
| Arthur Fort Jr. | ,, | ,, | ,, ,, ,, | | |
| Littleton Tison | Tison's | 354 | ,, ,, ,, | May 30, 1822 | |
| Alexander Carswell | ,, | ,, | ,, ,, ,, | | |
| Dennis D. Sanders | Oliver's | 326 | ,, ,, ,, | Nov. 20, 1823 | |

| | | | | | |
|---|---|---|---|---|---|
| James N. Sutton | Olivers | 326 | Jan. 26, 1821 | | |
| Laird McMurrey | Griffin's | 423 | Nov. 12, 1821 | May 7, 1823 | |
| Davis Hayes | Blackshear's | 356 | Jan. 9, 1822 | Nov. 1, 1822 | |
| Joab Tison | Tyson's | 354 | May 30, 1822 | | |
| John Fort | Blackshear's | 356 | Nov. 1, 1822 | | |
| Chesley Bradshaw | Tyson's | 354 | Dec. 3, 1822 | Feb. 26, 1823 | |
| T. M. Chamberlain | Smith's | 376 | Jan. 15, 1823 | | |
| John E. Dennard | Wimberly's | 354 | Feb. 26, 1823 | | |
| Lovett B. Smith | Griffin's | 423 | May 7, 1823 | | |
| James M. Kelly | Kelly's | 326 | Nov. 20, 1823 | | |
| John Campbell | Pearson's | 323 | Jan. 19, 1824 | | |
| William Davis | Bostick's | 355 | Feb. 28, 1824 | | |
| Holiday H. Harrell | Harrell's | 372 | Mar. 5, 1824 | | |
| James Ware | Holiday's | 324 | Jan. 22, 1825 | | |
| James Pearson | Pearson's | 323 | Jan. 22, 1825 | | |
| John Evans | " | " | " " " | Jan. 26, 1826 | |
| David Graham | Lee's | 325 | " " " | Jan. 24, 1828 | |
| George W. Welch | " | " | " " " | | |
| Jacob W. Pearce | Streetman's | 372 | " " " | Mar. 5, 1827 | |
| Nathan Grimes | " | " | " " " | | |
| Elijah Pearce | Bostick's | 355 | " " " | Aug. 14, 1827 | |
| David B. Perryman | " | " | " " " | Apr. 29, 1826 | |
| Dennis D. Sanders | Kelley's | 326 | " " " | | |
| James M. Kelly | " | " | " " " | Mar. 14, 1826 | |
| Samuel Williams | Farnum's | 423 | " " " | | |
| Thomas Arington | " | " | " " " | Mar. 7, 1826 | |
| Rhisa J. Ellis | Wimberly's | 354 | " " " | Mar. 14, 1828 | |
| Linkfield Perkins | " | " | " " " | Feb. 13, 1826 | |
| Kelly Glover | Fulton's | 356 | " " " | | |
| John Fort | " | " | " " " | Feb. 6, 1828 | |
| T. M. Chamberlain | Chamberlain's | 376 | " " " | Jan. 17, 1827 | |
| Ira E. Dupree | " | " | " " " | Mar. 14, 1826 | |
| Joel Denson | Holliday's | 324 | Feb. 25, 1825 | | |
| Robins Andrews | Person's | 323 | Jan. 26, 1826 | | |
| Joshua D. Bostick | Solomon's | 423 | Feb. 1, 1826 | | |
| Daniel Joyce | Wimberly's | 354 | Feb. 13, 1826 | | |
| William Solomon | Solomon's | 423 | Mar. 7, 1826 | | |
| Henry Saxon | Anderson's | 376 | Mar. 14, 1826 | | |
| John W. Barkwell | Kelly's | 326 | " " " | Mar. 13, 1827 | |
| William Crawford | Bostick's | 355 | Apr. 29, 1826 | Dec. 29, 1827 | |
| James A. Bryan | | 376 | Jan. 17, 1827 | | |
| Thomas Dozier | Streetman's | 372 | Mar. 5, 1827 | | |
| Hardy Brown | Kelley's | 326 | Mar. 12, 1827 | | |
| George Jameson | Bostick's | 355 | Aug. 14, 1827 | | |
| William Davis | Rall's | 355 | Dec. 29, 1827 | | |
| John Crocker | Johnston's | 325 | Jan. 24, 1828 | | |
| John Fitzpatrick | | 356 | Feb. 6, 1828 | | |
| Benjamin J. Lane | Grimsley's | 354 | Mar. 14, 1828 | | |
| Joel Denson | | 324 | Jan. 7, 1829 | Jan. 8, 1833 | |
| Thomas Glover | | " | " " " | " " " | |
| James McCroan | | 325 | " " " | Feb. 29, 1832 | |
| Isaac Dennard | | " | " " " | Jan. 25, 1832 | |
| Alfred Blacke | | 354 | " " " | Jan. 10, 1833 | |
| Benjamin J. Lane | | " | " " " | Nov. 5, 1829 | |

| Name | | | | |
|---|---|---|---|---|
| Daniel Massey | 376 | Jan. 7, 1829 | Jan. 8, 1833 |
| James Oliver | ” | ” ” ” | Sept. 16, 1830 |
| James Solomon | 423 | ” ” ” | |
| Henry Moffett | ” | ” ” ” | Apr. 5, 1830 |
| James M. Granbery | 323 | Jan. 10, 1829 | Jan. 8, 1833 |
| William H. Perkins | ” | ” ” ” | ” ” ” |
| R. W. W. Wynne | 326 | Jan. 13, 1829 | Feb. 3, 1830 |
| Rix Arrington | ” | ” ” ” | Nov. 15, 1830 |
| William Davis | 355 | ” ” ” | Jan. 10, 1833 |
| Sampson Bell | ” | ” ” ” | Jan. 29, 1830 |
| John Fitzpatrick | 356 | ” ” ” | Jan. 31, 1832 |
| Joseph Blackshear | ” | ” ” ” | Aug. 14, 1829 |
| Holliday H. Harrell | 372 | ” ” ” | Feb. 25, 1831 |
| Nathan Grimes | ” | ” ” ” | Dec. 21, 1831 |
| William Fitzpatrick | 356 | Aug. 14, 1829 | Feb. 29, 1832 |
| Isaiah Attaway | 354 | Nov. 5, 1829 | Oct. 20, 1830 |
| James Hammock | 355 | Jan. 29, 1830 | Jan. 10, 1833 |
| William Herring | 326 | Feb. 3, 1830 | Sept. 17, 1831 |
| Edward B. Young | 423 | Apr. 5, 1830 | |
| Hartwell H. Tarver | 376 | Sept. 16, 1930 | Jan. 8, 1833 |
| Jacob Smith | 354 | Oct. 20, 1830 | Jan. 10, 1833 |
| Hardy Brown | 326 | Nov. 15, 1830 | Sept. 17, 1831 |
| Jordan W. Lee | 372 | Nov. 25, 1831 | |
| William P. Gilbert | 326 | Sept. 17, 1831 | Jan. 8, 1833 |
| John A. Shine | ” | ” ” ” | Feb. 29, 1832 |
| Richard Deshazo | 372 | Dec. 21, 1831 | |
| Josiah Murphy | 325 | Jan. 25, 1832 | Jan. 8, 1833 |
| Joseph Martin | 356 | Jan. 31, 1832 | |
| William Epps | ” | Feb. 29, 1832 | |
| James P. Guerry | 325 | ” ” ” | Jan. 8, 1833 |
| Green B. Johnston | 326 | ” ” ” | ” ” ” |
| Edmund Pierce | 372 | Jan. 7, 1832 | Feb. 22, 1834 |
| Jordan W. Lee | ” | ” ” ” | May 21, 1835 |
| Josiah Murphy | 325 | Jan. 8, 1833 | June 25, 1834 |
| James P. Guerry | ” | ” ” ” | Aug. 12, 1835 |
| Joel Denson | 324 | ” ” ” | |
| Thomas Glover | ” | ” ” ” | |
| William Herring | 326 | ” ” ” | July 23, 1835 |
| Green B. Johnston | ” | ” ” ” | Apr. 10, 1834 |
| James M. Granbery | 323 | ” ” ” | Mar. 3, 1836 |
| James Evans | ” | ” ” ” | |
| Daniel Massey | 376 | ” ” ” | |
| Josiah Daniel | ” | ” ” ” | Nov. 11, 1834 |
| Alfred Blacke | 354 | Jan. 10, 1833 | |
| Rhesa J. Ellis | ” | ” ” ” | |
| James Hammock | 355 | ” ” ” | Apr. 30, 1834 |
| Thomas C. Chappell | ” | ” ” ” | Aug. 14, 1833 |
| James Solomon | 323 | Jan. 10, 1833 | |
| Joseph Martin | 356 | Feb. 27, 1833 | Oct. 15, 1835 |
| Joseph J. Chappell | ” | ” ” ” | Feb. 20, 1835 |
| Henry W. Terry | 323 | Mar. 5, 1833 | Feb. 12, 1834 |
| Jacob Pearce | 355 | Aug. 14, 1833 | Aug. 20, 1835 |
| Richard Deshazo | 323 | Feb. 12, 1834 | Jan. 14, 1835 |
| Jesse J. Wall | 372 | Feb. 22, 1834 | |

| | | | |
|---|---|---|---|
| John A. Learry | 326 | Apr. 10, 1834 | July 23, 1835 |
| Daniel Duncan | 355 | Apr. 30, 1834 | |
| Levi Ezell | 325 | June 25, 1834 | |
| Thomas Kinsey | 376 | Nov. 11, 1834 | |
| John B. Hodges | 323 | Jan. 14, 1835 | Jan. 22, 1836 |
| Kinchen Martin | 356 | Feb. 20, 1835 | |
| Nathan Grimes | 372 | May 21, 1835 | Mar. 3, 1836 |
| James C. Burns | 326 | July 23, 1835 | |
| Arthur B. Horne | ,, | ,, ,, ,, | Feb. 6, 1836 |
| Joshua R. Wimberly | 325 | Aug. 12, 1835 | |
| Samuel Taylor | 355 | Aug. 20, 1835 | |
| Thomas Moore | 356 | Oct. 15, 1835 | |
| Benjamin Peck | 323 | Jan. 22, 1836 | |
| William Herring | 326 | Feb. 6, 1836 | |
| Abisha Andrews | 323 | Mar. 3, 1836 | |
| Pleasant Moon | 372 | ,, ,, ,, | |
| Abisha Andrews | 323 | Jan. 20, 1837 | June 11, 1838 |
| Cornelius | ,, | | Feb. 3, 1840 |
| Hollingsworth | | ,, ,, ,, | |
| Benjamin Blount | 324 | ,, ,, ,, | May 24, 1837 |
| Jacob Harris | ,, | ,, ,, ,, | |
| Israel Gragg | 325 | ,, ,, ,, | |
| Levi Ezell | ,, | ,, ,, ,, | Feb. 24, 1840 |
| James C. Burns | 326 | ,, ,, ,, | |
| James S. Miller | ,, | ,, ,, ,, | |
| Aley Hughes | 354 | ,, ,, ,, | Aug. 6, 1838 |
| Nathan Berry | ,, | ,, ,, ,, | Jan. 13, 1841 |
| Daniel Duncan | 355 | ,, ,, ,, | |
| Wiley Clance | ,, | ,, ,, ,, | Jan. 20, 1840 |
| Joseph Blackshear | 356 | ,, ,, ,, | |
| Thomas Moore | ,, | ,, ,, ,, | |
| Josiah Hodges | 372 | ,, ,, ,, | Feb. 25, 1839 |
| Richard Deshazo | ,, | ,, ,, ,, | Mar. 12, 1838 |
| Daniel Massey | 376 | ,, ,, ,, | |
| William K. Hall | ,, | ,, ,, ,, | Feb. 12, 1838 |
| James Solomon | 423 | ,, ,, ,, | |
| Jesse J. Wall | ,, | ,, ,, ,, | |
| Thomas Glover | 324 | May 24, 1837 | |
| William J. Horne | 423 | Jan. 25, 1838 | Jan. 20, 1840 |
| Signal Raney | 376 | Feb. 12, 1838 | |
| Thomas Dozier | 372 | Mar. 12, 1838 | Jan. 20, 1840 |
| Samuel Steelman | 323 | June 11, 1838 | |
| Hayden Hughes | 354 | Aug. 6, 1838 | |
| Alfred Blacke | 354 | Jan. 21, 1839 | Jan. 13, 1841 |
| Will Brown | 372 | Feb. 25, 1839 | |
| Isaiah Attaway | 354 | Jan. 13, 1840 | |
| William Watters | ,, | ,, ,, ,, | |
| Henry Holmes | 423 | Jan. 20, 1840 | |
| Uriah Maxwell | 355 | ,, ,, ,, | |
| John W. Pearson | 323 | Feb. 3, 1840 | |
| Arthur Lucas | 325 | Feb. 24, 1840 | |
| Richard Deshazo | 372 | July 1, 1840 | |
| John W. Russell | 376 | Jan. 14, 1841 | Mar. 12, 1842 |
| Signal Rainey | ,, | ,, ,, ,, | |

| Name | Col1 | Col2 | Col3 |
|---|---|---|---|
| William S. Kelly | 423 | Jan. 14, 1841 | |
| James Solomon | " | " " " | May 18, 1842 |
| B. J. Ellis | 354 | " " " | |
| H. Hughs | " | " " " | |
| William Brown | 372 | " " " | |
| Henry Perry | " | " " " | |
| Amos Harris | 325 | " " " | Oct. 29, 1842 |
| Josiah Murphy | " | " " " | |
| Samuel Streetman | 323 | " " " | June 18, 1842 |
| John Holly | " | " " " | |
| Joseph Blackshear | 356 | " " " | |
| Lewis Martin | " | " " " | Mar. 7, 1844 |
| Jacob Harris | 324 | " " " | |
| John H. Denson | " | " " " | Apr. 15, 1843 |
| James Hammock | 355 | " " " | Dec. 27, 1843 |
| Wiley Clance | " | " " " | Mar. 25, 1842 |
| Daniel H. Coombs | 326 | Feb. 27, 1841 | Mar. 25, 1842 |
| Daniel M. Vaughn | " | " " " | Jan. 28, 1843 |
| John G. Slappy | 376 | Mar. 12, 1842 | |
| William Herring | 326 | Mar. 25, 1842 | |
| Beverly D. Parker | 355 | " " " | Aug. 12, 1843 |
| Allen Edwards | 423 | May 18, 1842 | |
| Abisha Andrews | 323 | June 18, 1842 | |
| Bryant Asbill | 325 | Oct. 29, 1842 | |
| Arthur B. Horn | 326 | Jan. 28, 1843 | |
| John H. Denson | 324 | Apr. 15, 1843 | |
| Samuel Taylor | 355 | Aug. 12, 1843 | |
| Hinton Duncan | " | Dec. 27, 1843 | |
| William Fitzpatrick | 356 | Mar. 7, 1844 | |
| Signal Raney | 376 | Jan. 24, 1845 | |
| Gustavus McCrew | " | " " " | Mar. 24, 1846 |
| Rhesa J. Ellis | 354 | " " " | July 5, 1847 |
| Nathan Berry | " | " " " | Feb. 6, 1847 |
| Henry J. Perry | 372 | " " " | |
| Albert Surls | " | " " " | May 25, 1846 |
| William Fitzpatrick | 356 | " " " | |
| Benjamin D. White | " | " " " | Oct. 2, 1845 |
| William Stephens | 423 | " " " | Jan. 20, 1846 |
| Daniel Wall | " | " " " | " " " |
| Abisha Andrews | 323 | " " " | |
| Benjamin Tharp | " | " " " | Mar. 30, 1847 |
| Thomas C. McGonugh | 355 | " " " | |
| Hinton Duncan | " | " " " | Mar. 24, 1846 |
| Josiah Murphy | 325 | Jan. 24, 1845 | June 27, 1848 |
| Henry Radford | " | " " " | May 8, 1847 |
| John H. Denson | " | " " " | |
| Daniel H. Coombs | 326 | " " " | |
| William Herring | " | Sept. 15, 1845 | Jan. 27, 1848 |
| James C. Burns | 356 | " " " | " " " |
| Reuben A. Waters | 324 | Oct. 2, 1845 | |
| Ira E. Dupree | 423 | Jan. 20, 1846 | |
| James Land | " | " " " | |
| A. S. Alexander | 355 | Mar. 24, 1846 | |
| Daniel Massey | 376 | " " " | |

# History of Twiggs County

| Name | Page | Date | Date | Successor |
|---|---|---|---|---|
| Richard Deshazo | 372 | May 25, 1846 | Mar. 10, 1848 | By whom Succeeded |
| William P. Collins | 354 | Feb. 6, 1847 | | |
| John Davis | 323 | Mar. 30, 1847 | | |
| Nathan Berry | 325 | May 8, 1847 | | |
| Haywood Hughes | 354 | July 5, 1847 | | |
| Daniel G. Hughes | 325 | Jan. 27, 1848 | | |
| Daniel H. Coombs | 326 | Jan. 27, 1848 | | |
| Thomas Grimsly | " | " " " | | |
| Pleasant Gentry | 372 | Mar. 10, 1848 | | |
| Tilman R. Denson | 324 | Jan. 27, 1849 | | |
| Joseph J. Boynton | " | " " " | Apr. 1, 1850 | Tucker Mauldin |
| Amos Lasseter | 325 | " " " | Feb. 26, 1850 | Josiah Murphey |
| Charles E. Mallory | " | " " " | | |
| John F. Pearce | 355 | " " " | Dec. 31, 1850 | O. H. P. Barclay |
| Hinton Duncan | " | " " " | Sept. 28, 1849 | Abraham S. Alexander |
| William Fitzpatrick | 356 | " " " | | |
| Reuben A. Waters | 372 | " " " | | |
| Henry H. Perry | " | " " " | | |
| Signal Rainey | 376 | " " " | | |
| Alexander H. Pearce | 372 | " " " | | |
| Joseph W. Rowland | 423 | " " " | Aug. 16, 1851 | Samuel D. Scovill |
| Henry Faulk | " | " " " | | |
| John Davis | 323 | " " " | | |
| William H. Bull | " | " " " | | |
| Daniel H. Coombs | 326 | Feb. 21, 1849 | May 26, 1852 | Isaac H. Meadows |
| John A. Clements | " | " " " | " " " | Daniel Johnson |
| Abraham S. Alexander | 355 | Sept. 28, 1849 | | |
| Simeon Harris | 325 | Jan. 15, 1950 | | |
| Josiah Murphey | " | Feb. 25, 1850 | | |
| Tucker Mauldin | 324 | Apr. 1, 1850 | July 23, 1852 | A. W. Asbell |
| O. H. P. Barclay | 355 | Dec. 31, 1950 | | |
| Samuel D. Scovill | 423 | Aug. 16, 1851 | | |
| Signal Rainey | 376 | Mar. 1, 1852 | | |
| Gustavua McRae | " | " " " | | |
| Isaac H. Meadows | 326 | May 26, 1852 | | |
| Daniel Johnson | " | " " " | | |
| Andrew W. Asbell | 324 | July 23, 1852 | | |
| J. Edwards | 326 | Jan. 10, 1853 | Apr. 8, 1857 | John A. Clements |
| J. H. Meadows | " | " " " | Jan. 15, 1857 | J. H. Meadows |
| Samuel D. Scovill | 423 | " " " | Feb. 8, 1864 | C. R. Faulk |
| John S. Goodwin | " | " " " | " " " | H. M. Loyless |
| Joseph Blackshear | 372 | " " " | Jan. 15, 1857 | Joseph B. Blackshear |
| Henry H. Perry | " | " " " | " " " | Henry H. Perry |
| John H. Denson | 323 | " " " | " " " | John H. Denson |
| John D. Tharp | " | " " " | " " " | Edward B. Latson |
| Matthew R. Murphey | 325 | " " " | " " " | Robert B. Wimberly |
| John L. Sinclair | " | " " " | " " " | John Methvin |
| A. S. Alexander | 355 | " " " | " " " | Abraham S. Alexander |
| John Martin | " | " " " | Jan. 17, 1854 | James Hammock |
| Warren S. McCoy | 323 | Aug. 22, 1853 | | |
| Seaborn V. Sauls | " | " " " | | |
| William Fitzpatrick | 356 | Mar. 20, 1853 | Jan. 15, 1857 | Charles G. Johnson |
| Reuben A. Nash | 355 | " " " | Mar. 14, 1856 | Archibald H. Moore |
| James Hammock | " | Jan. 17, 1854 | Jan. 15, 1857 | James Hammock |

| | | | | | | | |
|---|---|---|---|---|---|---|---|
| Andrew W. Asbell | 324 | Apr. 17, | 1854 | Feb. 8, | 1864 | A. W. Asbell | |
| Tilmon R. Denson | " | " " | " | " " | " | John F. Shine | |
| Warren S. McCoy | 354 | Nov. 8, | 1854 | | | | |
| Seaborn V. Sauls | " | " " | " | | | | |
| William Barnes | 323 | " " | " | Nov. 4, | 1862 | James H. Wilkes | |
| Archibald H. Moore | 355 | Mar. 14, | 1856 | Jan. 15, | 1857 | Thomas H. Jones | |
| John H. Denson | 323 | Jan. 15, | 1857 | Jan. 16, | 1863 | John H. Benson | |
| Edward B. Latson | " | " " | " | " " | " | James H. Wilkes | |
| Robert R. Wimberly | 325 | " " | " | | | | |
| John Methvin | " | " " | " | | | | |
| Isaac Meadows | 326 | " " | " | | | | |
| Charles G. Johnson | 356 | " " | " | Feb. 20, | 1869 | William Griffin | |
| Thomas H. Jones | " | " " | " | | | | |
| James Hammock | 355 | " " | " | | | | |
| Abram S. Alexander | " | " " | " | | | | |
| Henry H. Perry | 372 | " " | " | | | | |
| Joseph B. Blackshear | " | " " | " | Oct. 11, | 1862 | W. O. Daniel | |
| John A. Clements | 326 | Apr. 8, | 1857 | | | | |
| William Griffin | 356 | Feb. 20, | 1860 | | | | |
| " " | " | Jan. 28, | 1861 | Mar. 24, | 1864 | R. A. Waters | |
| Thomas H. Jones | " | " " | " | | | | |
| A. S. Alexander | 355 | " " | " | | | | |
| James Hammock | " | " " | " | Apr. 10, | 1864 | James Lockhart | |
| Isaac H. Meadows | 326 | Apr. 10, | 1861 | | | | |
| George R. Asbell | " | " " | " | | | | |
| William O. Daniel | 372 | Oct. 11, | 1862 | | | | |
| Enoch J. Collins | 326 | Nov. 3, | 1862 | | | | |
| James H. Wilkes | 323 | Nov. 4, | 1862 | | | | |
| John H. Benson | " | Jan. 16, | 1863 | | | | |
| James H. Wilkes | " | " " | " | | | | |
| A. W. Asbell | 324 | Feb. 8, | 1864 | | | | |
| John F. Shine | " | " " | " | | | | |
| Charles R. Faulk | 423 | " " | " | | | | |
| H. M. Loveless | " | " " | " | | | | |
| R. A. Waters | 356 | Mar. 24, | 1864 | | | | |
| James Lockhart | 355 | Apr. 10, | 1864 | | | | |
| E. L. Croker | 325 | May 19, | 1864 | Apr. 6, | 1865 | Jasper Bulloch | |
| W. O. Daniel | 372 | Jan. 28, | 1865 | | | | |
| W. M. Pearce | " | " " | " | | | | |
| C. R. Faulk | 425 | " " | " | | | | |
| F. A. Finch | " | " " | " | | | | |
| A. W. Asbell | 324 | " " | " | | | | |
| J. F. Shine | " | " " | " | | | | |
| W. A. Anderson | 323 | " " | " | | | | |
| W. H. Bull | " | " " | " | | | | |
| E. J. Collins | 326 | " " | " | | | | |
| J. C. Burns | 226 | " " | " | | | | |
| James Lockhart | 355 | " " | " | Mar. 20, | 1866 | A. E. Nash | |
| K. F. Burkett | " | " " | " | | | | |
| R. A. Waters | 356 | " " | " | Apr. 10, | 1865 | John H. Fitzpatrick | |
| William H. Stokes | " | " " | " | Sept. 10, | 1866 | William Griffin | |
| M. E. Slappey | 376 | Mar. 20, | 1865 | | | | |
| Jasper Bulloch | 325 | Apr. 6, | 1865 | | | | |

| | | | | |
|---|---|---|---|---|
| John H. Fitzpatrick | 356 | Apr. 10, 1865 | Sept. 10, 1866 | R. A. Waters |
| William J. Gallamore | 354 | Apr. 19, 1865 | | |
| John A. Clements | ,, | ,, ,, ,, | | |
| A. E. Nash | 355 | Mar. 20, 1866 | | |
| William Griffin | 356 | Sept. 10, 1866 | | |
| R. A. Waters | ,, | ,, ,, ,, | | |
| John H. Jones | 325 | May 1, 1869 | | |
| H. S. Newby | 324 | ,, ,, ,, | | |
| Simeon Tharp | 355 | ,, ,, ,, | | |
| Robert H. Averett | 425 | ,, ,, ,, | | |
| William W. Bozeman | 326 | ,, ,, ,, | | |
| James F. Land | 323 | ,, ,, ,, | Apr. 28, 1870 | William Melton |
| E. M. Floyd | 356 | Aug. 26, 1869 | | |
| William Melton | 323 | Apr. 28, 1870 | | |
| John H. Strong | 372 | July 15, 1870 | | |
| Alexander Pearce[1] | 325 | Jan. 20, 1873 | | |
| W. E. Hill[2] | 354 | Jan. 21, 1873 | | |
| J. A. Bush | 355 | Jan. 28, 1873 | | |

1. Deceased.    2. Resigned Jan. 20, 1875.

| | | |
|---|---|---|
| T. M. Hughes[1] | 356 | Feb. 10, 1873 |
| Pleasant Gentry | 373 | Feb. 20, 1873 |
| J. K. Burns | 326 | Feb. 18, 1873 |
| H. S. Newby | 324 | ,, ,, ,, |
| B. H. Melton | 323 | Mar. 11, 1873 |
| L. C. Furse | 356 | Jan. 26, 1874 |
| T. J. Robertson[2] | 323 | Mar. 16, 1874 |
| J. C. Andrews | ,, | Jan. 26, 1874 |
| F. M. Jones | 256 | Mar. 3, 1876 |
| Pleasant Gentry | 372 | Feb. 8, 1877 |
| J. K. Burns[3] | 326 | ,, ,, ,, |
| Alexander Pearce | 325 | ,, ,, ,, |
| M. E. Slappy | 396 | ,, ,, ,, |
| J. E. Andrews | 323 | ,, ,, ,, |
| William Griffin[4] | 356 | ,, ,, ,, |
| James E. Stokes | 354 | Aug. 17, 1878 |
| John S. Crosby | 1322 | Feb. 13, 1880 |
| John S. Vaughn | 326 | Jan. 18, 1881 |
| William Griffin | 356 | ,, ,, ,, |
| James A. Bush | 355 | Jan. 28, 1881 |
| Alexander Pearce | 325 | Jan. 30, 1881 |
| B. F. Read | 323 | Feb. 4, 1881 |
| G. W. Lee | 372 | June 14, 1883 |
| Iverson L. Hunter[5] | 325 | Sept. 20, 1883 |
| George T. Barrentine[6] | 1322 | Feb. 15, 1884 |
| Freeman L. Stokes[7] | 356 | Feb. 23, 1884 |

1. Resigned Dec. 12, 1875.
2. Resigned Mar. 8, 1875.
3. Resigned Dec. 6, 1880.
4. Resigned Jan. 3, 1884.
5. Vice Alexander Pearce deceased.
6. Vice John S. Crosby resigned.
7. Appointed by Ordinary.

| | | |
|---|---|---|
| F. A. Cochran[1] | 325 | Nov. 3, 1884 |
| M. E. Slappey | 396 | Jan. 23, 1885 |
| John H. Jessup | 355 | ,, ,, ,, |
| F. A. Cochran[2] | 325 | ,, ,, ,, |

| | | |
|---|---|---|
| B. F. Read | 323 | Jan. 23, 1885 |
| Robert R. Wimberly | 325 | May 19, 1885 |
| Thomas H. Holliday | 354 | Mar. 3, 1886 |
| H. F. Griffin[3] | 325 | Jan. 23, 1889 |
| James H. Sanders | 354 | ,, ,, ,, |
| J. S. Williams | 1322 | ,, ,, ,, |
| W. T. Latson | 323 | ,, ,, ,, |
| C. M. Asbell | 324 | June 27, 1890 |
| W. T. Chappell | 325 | Apr. 29, 1891 |
| J. T. Harrell | 372 | Feb. 5, 1891 |
| B. F. Read | 323 | Jan. 27, 1893 |
| C. M. Asbell | 324 | ,, ,, ,, |
| W. T. Chappell | 325 | ,, ,, ,, |
| F. M. Brown[4] | 354 | ,, ,, ,, |
| J. H. Jesup | 355 | ,, ,, ,, |
| M. E. Slappey | 376 | ,, ,, ,, |
| J. S. Williams | 1322 | ,, ,, ,, |
| C. M. Bull | 323 | Oct. 18, 1893 |
| J. T. Balkcom | 325 | Jan. 8, 1897 |
| J. H. Jessup | 355 | ,, ,, ,, |
| J. C. Johnson | 354 | ,, ,, ,, |
| M. E. Slappey | 376 | ,, ,, ,, |

1. Appointed by Ordinary.
2. Resigned Apr. 8, 1885.
3. Resigned Mar. 30, 1891.
4. Resigned Mar. 6, 1894.

| | | |
|---|---|---|
| C. M. Asbell | 324 | Dec. 21, 1900 |
| J. H. Jessup | 355 | ,, ,, ,, |
| G. F. Leslie | 1322 | ,, ,, ,, |
| M. E. Slappey | 376 | ,, ,, ,, |
| J. C. Johnston | 354 | ,, ,, ,, |
| James P. Califf[1] | 325 | ,, ,, ,, |
| J. W. Bradshaw | ,, | Aug. 27, 1904 |
| J. T. Newby | 354 | May 25, 1906 |
| J. J. Arnold | 326 | Oct. 20, 1906 |
| W. T. Chappell | 325 | Dec. 19, 1908 |
| E. A. Word | 1322 | ,, ,, ,, |
| E. J. Jones | 425 | ,, ,, ,, |
| J. I. Newby[2] | 354 | ,, ,, ,, |
| B. F. Carden | 326 | ,, ,, ,, |
| G. M. Bull[3] | 323 | ,, ,, ,, |
| James H. Bull | ,, | Feb. 6, 1909 |
| W. F. Epps | 355 | Dec. 20, 1910 |
| Emory Harrell | 372 | July 5, 1911 |
| W. J. Sheppard[4] | 354 | July 13, 1911 |
| R. C. Hatcher | 354 | Sept. 26, 1912 |
| W. O. Birdsong | 1322 | Dec. 20, 1912 |
| J. H. Bull | 323 | ,, ,, ,, |
| C. T. Epps | 425 | ,, ,, ,, |
| R. C. Hatcher | 354 | Jan. 1, 1913 |
| W. T. Chappell | 125 | ,, ,, ,, |
| J. H. Bull | 323 | Dec. 21, 1916 |

1. Resigned Sept. 1, 1903.
2. Resigned Jan. 1, 1910.
3. Died.
4. To fill unexpired term.

| | | |
|---|---|---|
| B. F. Carden | 325 | Dec. 21, 1916 |
| W. T. Chappell | 326 | ,, ,, ,, |

| | | |
|---|---|---|
| R. E. Kitchens | 355 | Dec. 21, 1916 |
| J. D. Johnson | 372 | ″ ″ ″ |
| M. P. Sapp | 425 | ″ ″ ″ |
| W. O. Birdsong | 1322 | ″ ″ ″ |
| T. L. Hill | 354 | Oct. 23, 1919 |
| J. T. Holloway | ″ | Jan. 1, 1921 |
| F. E. Killebrew | 323 | ″ ″ ″ |
| W. O. Birdsong | 1322 | ″ ″ ″ |
| R. L. Kitchens | 355 | ″ ″ ″ |
| W. T. Chapell | 325 | ″ ″ ″ |
| E. L. Hill | 354 | May 30, 1921 |
| J. S. Cowart | 325 | ″ ″ ″ |
| H. M. King | 354 | Feb. 27, 1924 |

The spelling of names which vary have been used as recorded on original records.

## TWIGGS COUNTY SCHOOL COMMISSIONERS

| | |
|---|---|
| George W. Tharpe | 1871 |
| A. E. Nash | 1872-1877 |
| J. A. Barclay, Jr. | 1877-___ |
| W. Y. Griffin | ___ -1886 |
| A. J. Glover | 1886-1892  (died in office) |
| B. S. Fitzpatrick | 1892-1917 |
| A. M. Gates | 1917-1921 |
| B. S. Fitzpatrick | 1921-1944  (died in office) |
| James D. Shannon | 1944-1949 |
| Dr. A. M. Gates | 1949-1953 |
| A. T. Wimberly | 1953-Incumbent |

## TWIGGS

Senators in the General Assembly of Georgia since the County's Organization Dec. 14, 1809.

Twiggs had representation first in the 35th Session of The General Assembly.

| | |
|---|---|
| Session | 1829—Benj. B. Smith |
| 1810—James Johnson | 1830—Lott Warren |
| 1811—John Lawson | 1831-1832—Benjamin B. Smith |
| 1812—John Tharpe | 1833—James Pearson |
| 1813—Arthur Fort | 1834-1836—Benjamin B. Smith |
| 1814—Wm. Hawthorn | 1837-1838—James Pearson |
| 1815-1824—Ezekiel Wimberly | 1839-1840—Benjamin B. Smith |
| 1825—Lewis L. Griffin | 1841—James Pearson |
| 1826-1828—Ezekiel Wimberly | 1842-1843—Wm. M. Tarver |

From 1845 until 1853, Twiggs and Bibb constituted the old 20th District, at which time, the State was divided into 47 Senatorial Districts, and during this interval of 8 years, the Senators from the 20th District were as follows:

| | |
|---|---|
| 1845—Absalom H. Chappell | 1849-1850—Leroy Napier |
| 1847—Wm. M. Wiggins | 1851-1852—Joseph Day |

From 1853 until 1861, there was a return to the old basis of representation, namely: one senator from each county chosen biennially by the electors thereof, and during this interval, the senators from Twiggs were as follows:

1853-1854—Peyton Reynolds         1855-1860—Eli S. Griffin

In 1861, Georgia was organized into 44 Senatorial Districts, of which Twiggs, Wilkinson, and Jones constituted the 21st; Senators have been as follows: Beginning the 77th Session—

1861-62-63 Ex.—D. N. Smith
1863-64 Ex.—64-65—Ex.—E. S. Griffin
1865-66-66—Eli S. Griffin
1868 Ex. 69-70 Ex.—Wm. Griffin (Rev.)
1871-72
   72 Adj.—James B. Deveaux (Col.)
1873-74—James B. Deveaux (Col.)
1875-76-77
   (83rd & 84th)—W. O. Daniel
1878-79 Adj.—A. S. Hamilton
1880-81 Adj.—Richard Lawson Story
1882-83 Ex. 83 Ann.-Adj.—D. M. Hughes
1884-85 Adj.—H. B. Ridley
1886-87—D. N. Smith (died 6-28-1887)
1887 Adj—Joel A. Smith
1888-89 Adj.—L. D. Shannon
1890-91 Adj.—Richard Johnson
1892-93—Frank Chambers
1894-95—W. J. Harrison
1896-97-97 Adj.—James R. VanBuren
1898-99—J. S. Wood
1900-01—S. W. Yopp

1902-03-04—James R. VanBuren
1905-06—G. H. Carswell
1907-08-08 Ex.—H. F. Griffin
1909-10—J. B. Jackson
1911-12-12 Ex.—J. D. Davis
1913-14—S. E. Jones
1915-15 Ex. 16-17.—T. R. Jones
1917-18—G. H. Carswell
1919-20—Andrew J. Wood (M.D.)
1921-22—Joseph Benj. Jackson
1923-23 Ex. 24—George H. Carswell
1925-26 Ex. 26 Ex.—Hugh L. D. Hughes
1927—Joseph Benj. Jackson
1929-31 Ex.—John S. Davis
1931—Wilkinson Maberry Whitehurst
1933—Joseph Benj. Jackson
1937-38 Ex.—James D. Shannon
1939—Carlton C. Williams
1941—Allen W. Daughtry
1943—J. D. Shannon
1945-45 Ex. 46—Alvah M. Greene

Beginning the 119th Session Twiggs, Bibb and Houston constituted the 51st Senatorial District, the Senators have been as follows:

1947-48 Ex. 48—Alexander H. S. Weaver
1949-49 Ex. 50—Grover C. Land
1951-52—Mayo Davis
1953-54—J. Douglas Carlisle

1955-56—Homer L. Chance
1957-58—Charlie L. Williams
1959-60—J. Douglas Carlisle
   (The 125th Sesssion)

## TWIGGS

Representatives in the General Assembly of Georgia since the County's organization, Dec. 14th, 1809.
Beginning with the 35th Session.

Sessions
Representatives
1810—Robert Glenn
1811—Willis Anderson,
   Ezekiel Wimberly
1812—Ezekiel Wimberly,
   Harman Perryman
1813—Willis Anderson
   Ezekiel Wimberly
1814—Willis Anderson, Jonathan Bell
1815—Timothy Mathews,
   Willis Anderson
1816—Roger Lawson, Matthew Hodges
1817—Roger Lawson, Wm. Crocker
1818—Roger Lawson,
   Robert Glenn, Moses Fort
1819—Roger Lawson,
   Robert Glenn, Wm. W. Williamson
1820-21—Robert Glenn,
   Ex. Wm. W. Williamson,
   Roger Lawson

1821—Roger Lawson,
   Robert Glenn, Timothy Matthews
1822—Roger Lawson,
   Robert Glenn, Timothy Matthews
1823—Roger Lawson,
   Wm. Crocker, Moses Wheat
1824-25 Ex.—Roger Lawson
   Wm. Crocker, Moses Fort
1825—James Willis,
   Robert A. Beall, Roger Lawson
1826—Henry Bunn,
   Robert A. Beall, Jared Dennard
1827—Henry Bunn,
   Hardy Durham, Jarred Dennard
1828—Henry Bunn,
   Hardy Durham, James Pearson
1829—James Pearson,
   Larkin Griffin, Wm. Davis
1830—Robert A. Beall,
   Robert Hodges, Larkin Griffin

1831—Henry Solomon,
   James Pearson, Hartwell H. Tarver
1832—Henry Solomon,
   Daniel W. Shine
1833—Henry Solomon,
   Daniel W. Shine
1834—Henry Solomon,
   Hartwell H. Tarver
1835—Henry Solomon,
   Hartwell H. Tarver
1836—Henry Solomon,
   John Fitzpatrick
1837—Henry Solomon,
   John Fitzpatrick
1838—John Fitzpatrick,
   Josiah Daniel
1839—Hartwell H. Tarver,
   Josiah Daniel
1840—John Fitzpatrick, W. H. Tarver
1841—Peyton Reynolds,
   John Fitzpatrick
1842—John Gallemore, John A. Nelson
1843—John Gallemore, John A. Nelson
1845—Theodore L. Guerry
1847—John Fitzpatrick
1849-50—William W. Wiggins
1851-52—Josiah Wall
1853-54—Eli S. Griffin
1855-56—Henry Faulk
1857-58—Henry Faulk
1859-60—H. T. Smith
1861-62-63 Ex.—R. R. Slappey
1863-64 Ex. 64--65 Ex.—W. Faulk
1865-66-66—Daniel G. Hughes
1868 Ex. 69-70 Ex.—Hayden Hughes
1871-72-72 Adj.—Eli S. Griffin
1873-74—William Griffin
1875-76—J. Nelson
1877—James T. Glover
1878-79 Adj.—James T. Glover
1880-81 Adj.—James T. Glover
   (died 9-4-81)
1882-83 Ex. 83 Ann. Adj.—S. E. Jones

1884-85 Adj.—Hubbard Reynolds
1886-87 Adj.—Hubbard Reynolds
1888-89 Adj.—Eli S. Griffin
1890—Eli S. Griffin (died)
1891 Adj.—W. J. Harrison
1892-93—W. J. Harrison
1894-95 Adj.—J. T. Vaughn
1896-97 Adj. 97—J. T. Vaughn
1898-99—Henry Faulk Griffin
1900-01—Henry Faulk Griffin
1902-03-04—Henry Faulk Griffin
1905-06—I. N. Maxwell
1907-08-08 Ex.—I. N. Maxwell
1909-10—Henry Faulk Griffin
1911-12 Ex. 12—Andrew J. Wood, M.D.
1913-14—Andrew Jackson Wood, M.D.
1915-15 Ex. 16-17 Ex.—James Douglas
                           Shannon
1917-18—James Douglas Shannon
1919-20—James D. Shannon
1921-22—A. J. Wood
1923-23 Ex. 24—F. E. Wimberly
1925-26 Ex. 26-2nd Ex.—L. L. Griffin
1927—L. L. Griffin
1929-31 Ex.—Will C. Stokes
1931—Jones Ira Mercer
1933—Wm. Carswell Stokes
1935—Edgar Y. Mallory, Jr.
1937-38 Ex.—Jesse Ivey Newby
1939—Hugh Virgil Jackson
1941—J. D. Shannon
1943—Homer L. Chance
1945-45 Ex.—Homer L. Chance
1947-48 Ex. 48-2nd Ex.—Homer L. Chance
1949-49 Ex. 50—Claude S. Kitchens
1951-52—Claude S. Kitchens
1953-54—Jesse B. Johnson
1955-56—Claude S. Kitchens
1957-58—Jerre Chappell Miller, Jr.
1959—Jerre C. Miller, Jr.
   (died Jan. 26, 1959)
1959—Homer L. Chance

# CHAPTER V
# COURT HOUSE AND GOVERNMENT
## COURT HOUSES AND FIRE OF 1901

The act assented to on the 8th of December 1810, by David B. Mitchell, Governor of Georgia, provided that a site be established for a Court House and other public buildings for Twiggs County. The site to be located at or near Joiner's Spring above Savage Creek on lot Number 73 in the Twenty-fifth District, originally Wilkinson County, now Twiggs.

The site selected not to be less than 75 acres nor more than 200 acres was laid off in lots. Marion was chosen as the name for the new site which became the first county site and seat of government.

The following persons, John Harden, Jacob Ricks, William Davis, Lovet B. Smith, and James McCormick were appointed as Commissioners to contract for and to superintend the building of a Court House and jail. Also in order to help raise funds for building the public buildings, lots which were not needed could be exposed to public sale after properly advertising in the public Gazettes.

In due time work began on the public buildings, but the Court House was not completed in time for the first Superior Court of the County, to be held in the Court House. The first term of Court was held at John Harden's house.

The Court House which was removed from Marion to Jeffersonville
(Refer to page ■ for description)
50

The court house was a large frame building two stories high painted with green blinds. Doubtless, there were a number of court scenes that were aired in this building which was used for almost a century. The court house was made the scene of a murder trial graphically described by Harry Stilwell Edwards in one of his stories,

"De Valley and De Shaddow." Also here was held the prolonged trail of the wreckers of the ill-fated Southern Train which occured on Saturday night, February 29, 1896, in the western part of the County at the Stone Creek trestle.

For over a half century Marion had remained the county site. Then for varied reasons the center of population shifted to other areas. In 1867 the question arose among the citizens—Should the court house be moved from Marion to Jeffersonville and establish this small place as the county site? The argument for the proposed move to the small town, just six miles east, was: Jeffersonville would be more accessible and a healthier place in which to live. After much debate, evidently heated, because an injunction was filed to prevent removal of the court house as shown by a copy of the order:

"HEADQUARTERS, THIRD MILITARY DISTRICT, ATLANTA, GEORGIA, AUGUST 10, 1867. Special orders no. 103. 'The taking down of the court house, at Marion, Twiggs County, State of Georgia, and its removal from Marion to Jeffersonville, in the same county, are hereby ordered to be suspended until after the completion of Registration, when an election will be ordered to decide upon the question of the removal of the County site from Marion.' By Command of Brevt Major General Pope. G. K. Sanderson, Capt. 33d U. S. Inf. & A. A. A. G. Countersigned and recorded August 12, 1867. Chief of Bureau, Civil Affairs." Reference: Department of Archives and History, Atlanta, Georgia.

In 1868 Jeffersonville became the County-site, thence the removal of the court house and jail by ox cart from Marion, now destined to become a ghost-town. The court house and jail were rebuilt and continued to be used as public buildings until February 6, 1901 when the ill-fated fire completely destroyed the old court house and many valuable records.

The Board of Commissioners were in a dilemma without a court house and records in ashes. Several matters relating to the welfare of the County were now mandatory. At once they secured permission from the Trustees of Auburn Institute for the March term of Court to convene in the school building. A revised jury was drawn for this term of Court. The jurors' names are listed in an old ledger in the Clerk of Twiggs Superior Court's Office.

Realizing the necessity for a court house, the Grand Jury in session at the March term of Court immediately drew a resolution requesting the County Commissioners to promptly make plans for building another court house. The following excerpt from THE TWIGGS HERALD shows some of the presentments:
THE TWIGGS HERALD, JEFFERSONVILLE, GEORGIA, MARCH 15, 1901, Vol V.

"General Presentments of the Grand Jury, March Term 1901.

We, chosen and sworn as Grand Jurors for the March Term of Superior Court, of the County of Twiggs, submit — — —. We recommend that a new court house and jail be built as may be practicable; that funds to offset the expense of the same be obtained through an issue of 35 bonds, value of each $1000. We request the Board of Commissioners of Roads and Revenue to use all haste in carrying into effect this recommendation. . . . Think best to rebuild on the same lot used by the one recently burned. County School Commissioners books examined and found in perfect condition. Treasurer's report made of receipts and disbursements, owing to destruction of the County Clerk's books we are utterly unable to make any investigation of their books. . . . For the kindness of the Trustees of Auburn Institute in allowing us to use their building we cordially thank them — — — . In taking leave of his Honor Judge D. M. Roberts and Solicitor, J. F. Delacy, we express appreciation.

Respectfully submitted, J. S. Vaughn, Foreman." Court was held in Auburn Institute's building until the present court house was completed, April, 1903.

In order to comply with the request of the Grand Jury the Board of Commissioners of Roads and Revenues began to formulate plans on the paramount question of the hour—how to raise funds to finance building a court house and jail. The question was most difficult to settle as can be ascertained from the following excerpts which were copied from several issues of THE TWIGGS HERALD. "March 22, 1901, an election notice to the qualified voters of Twiggs County—By virtue of an order of the Board of Commissioners of Roads and Revenue of Twiggs County an election will be held in every precinct within limits of said county . . . on Thursday, April 18, 1901, to determine the question of whether Bonds shall be issued by the County for the purpose of a court house and jail. I. N. Maxwell, Chairman." This order was revoked due to a decision of the Supreme Court of Georgia. The next election notice that was placed in the paper set May 28, 1901 as the date for an election to be held at the precincts, amount of Bond would be $30,000. After tabulation of all precinct returns the bond question was defeated. In August some of the citizens petitioned the County Board of Commissioners to set another date and call for an election. The date set for the second vote to be taken on the issue was the 25th day of Sept., 1901. The consolidated returns from the precincts revealed the issue was again defeated by thirty-two votes. Some of the citizens were disheartened. Many made open comments, one such comment on the question which was printed in the local paper September 27, 1901, "This is the second trial on the question, both being a failure to carry bonds, which now leaves the prospects for a court house gloomy, as a direct tax is a myth."

In spite of the gloomy outlook, the optimistic Board of Commissioners set March 6, 1902 as the date on which qualified voters of the county were to return to their respective precincts and cast ballots for or against a bond issue. When these precinct returns were tabulated the bond question had won a victory—670 votes for, 25 votes against, out of 710 qualified voters. It was on Monday, March 31, 1902, that Judge D. M. Roberts validated the Bond issue for the County court house and jail as the election returns were favorable. J. W. Golucke and Company of Atlanta were the architects and Fred Wagner, contractor.

Upon completion of the court house the keys were turned over to the Board of Commissioners of Roads and Revenue who arranged for a dedicatory service, naming B. S. Fitzpatrick, Chairman.

The following program was copied from THE TWIGGS HERALD issue, April 10, 1903, Editor: Samuel Lowrie.

Court House Dedicated

Wednesday afternoon at 1:30, 500 representative citizens in attendance. Prayer—Rev. R. M. Booth.

Chairman—Mr. B. S. Fitzpatrick, C. S. S.

Speaker—Colonel L. D. Shannon of the local bar, who presented the building to the County on behalf of the Board of County Commissioners of Roads and Revenue.

Col. John F. DeLacy of Eastman, Solicitor-General of the Oconee Circuit, a short address on the judicial system in relation to Church and State.

Judge D. M. Roberts of Eastman, spoke in feeling terms of the old Court House upon the ashes of which the present structure has been erected. The old building made famous by the legal battles of such men as Ben Hill, Alex H. Stephens and Judge Twiggs. He paid glowing tribute to the County's citizenry past and present, congratulated the County Commissioners upon their wise and judicious expenditure of funds for the erection of the new building, not a dollar of which was malevolently disposed of. The Chairman then presented Honorable D. M. Hughes, President, Georgia State Agricultural Society.

## GOVERNMENT

The two basic reasons for government are the protection of the citizens from foreign invasion and the maintenance of internal order. For the first objective we depend on our military establishment. For the second we rely on courts, law enforcement officers, and lawyers.

Twiggs County has been blessed by a series of good judges and able attorneys. The lives and property of her citizens have been well protected by those who have been responsible for the administration of justice.

The Twiggs County Superior Court has been the scene of many dramatic trials. The normal proportion of murders, thefts, and other crimes have been aired at the bar.

The General Assembly in session on December 13, 1809, elected the following Justices of the Inferior Court of Twiggs, namely, Francis Powell, John Lawson, Arthur Fort, and Robert Glenn, who were commissioned by Governor Mitchell on December 27, 1809.

The General Assembly in session December 1810, set the first Monday in February and October of each year as the time that the Inferior Court should be holden. By passage of a Legislative Act the Superior and Inferior Courts and County elections were to be held at the house of John Harden until a court house could be erected. The records that had been kept by Archibald McIntier, acting clerk of the court, which pertained to the County were made legal by passage of an act on December 15, 1810. (From Georgia Laws.)

An act passed on December 13, 1810 provided that the Justices of the Inferior Court along with the sheriff of the County draw Grand and Petit Jurors.

The first Superior Court was held on November 11, 1811 with General Peter Early as Judge. Those who composed the Jury were, namely, Francis Powell, N. Bugby, A. Wood, William Ford, Thomas C. Heidleburge, J. Wilkinson, B. Joiner, B. Barnabee, William Herrishall, T. Pearce, William Carr, William Grimes, Robin Andrews, William Cloud, John Matthews, John Young, Arthur Fort, Jr., John Hawthorne, Ashlet Wood, S. Belk, and John Evans. Reference: Smith, G. C., THE STORY OF GEORGIA AND GEORGIA PEOPLE.

Twiggs County was embraced in the Ocmulgee Judicial Circuit from December 15, 1809 to December 19, 1818. Some of the Judges other than General Early, who served the county were: Stephen W. Harris and Christopher B. Strong.

The Southern Judicial Circuit was created by an act of the Georgia Legislature on December 19, 1818 which included a large territory in southern and southwest Georgia, also it embraced five older counties to the north, Laurens and Montgomery on the Oconee River, Telfair, Pulaski, and Twiggs on the Ocmulgee River.

The enterprising town of Marion on Savage Creek, twenty miles southeast of Fort Hawkins, was for many years the most important town in the Southern Circuit.

Marion was the first county site and the first incorporated town in the county to be regulated by an act of Georgia Legislature on December 13, 1811, which remained the county seat of government for 58 years. Robert Cumins, James Spann, Thomas W. Harris, Martin Kolb, and Henry Loyless, Esquires, were the first commissioners with full power and authority to make and ordain such by-laws and regulations as deemed necessary for good government. Reference: Georgia Laws 1811 and 1816, Volume III.

Court week at Marion was a rendezvous for many eminent lawyers. There lived the first Judge of the Southern Circuit, Thomas W. Harris. He served as judge until December 20, 1824. Also, the town was the residence of Thaddeus Goode Holt, the first Solicitor-General. Near this inland town, a thrifty center of trade in the antebellum day, was the home of Archibald MacIntyre, the first Clerk of Twiggs Superior Court.

Stephen F. Miller in BENCH AND BAR OF GEORGIA, Volume I, names many lawyers, who were regular practioners in Twiggs Superior Court. From 1810 to 1825 the old dockets show that the local bar at Marion was made up in part of the following lawyers: Major William Crocker of Marion, who at the 1820 spring term of Court, was retained in 300 cases. Moses Fort, the brothers, Stephen W. Harris, Thomas W. Harris, Eli Shorter, Robert Rutherford, Bedney Franklin, Seaborn Jones, Thomas Fitch, Christopher B. Strong, Adam G. Safford, James S. Frierson, James Smith, Samuel Rockwell, Lucius Q. C. Lamar, Joel Crawford, John H. Howard, Albert G. Clopton, Charles J. McDonald, William H. Torrence, Alfred Iverson, Charles F. M. Betton, Samuel Lowther, Zachariah B. Hargrove, Thaddeus G. Holt, Robert A. Beall, Samuel Gainer, Robert L. Perryman and Robert A. Evans. The last six being resident attorneys. In an address delivered before the 46th Session of the Georgia Bar Association, at Atlanta, on May 31, 1929, by J. N. Talley of Macon, entitled "The Southern Circuit," he referred to the following lawyers who had practiced in Twiggs Courts: Major Stephen F. Miller, Oliver H. Prince, Edward T. Tracy, Washington Poe and at one term was Walter T. Colquitt and Hiram Warner.

Other judges who have served the Southern Circuit succeeding Thomas W. Harris are: Thaddeus G. Holt, Moses Fort, Lott Warren, James Polhill, Carleton B. Cole, Arthur A. Morgan, James J. Scarborough, and Augustin H. Hansell.

Twiggs transferred to the Macon Judicial Circuit on November 24, 1851. Judges of the Macon Circuit serving the county from November 28, 1851 to 1876 were: Abner P. Powers, Richard H. Clark, Henry G. Lamar, Osborne A. Lochrane, Carlton B. Cole, and Barnard Hill.

On February 23, 1876 Twiggs County was transferred by an act of the General Assembly to the Oconee Circuit and finally on January 1, 1912 to the Dublin Circuit where it remains today.

During the thirty-six years that the Oconee Circuit embraced Twiggs County, the county was served by the following Superior Court Judges: Anthony C. Pate, Charles C. Kibbee, David M. Roberts, Christopher C. Smith, John H. Martin, and Elisha D. Graham. Those who have served as judges since Twiggs has been a part of the Dublin Circuit, beginning January 1, 1912 are: K. J. Hawkins, W. W. Larsen, J. L. Kent, R. Earl Camp, Rufus I. Stephens, incumbent.

The compilers are grateful for information furnished on some of the Judicial Circuits of the county by two distinguished Twiggs Countians: the late James D. (Jim) Shannon, who had his law office at Jeffersonville, and R. Archie Chappell, presently a partner with the law firm, Chappell-Barfield-Hasty, at Macon, Georgia.

The following comments with reference to members of the local bar were contributed by Mr. Chappell:

"One of the ablest judges sitting in the county during the early 1900's was John H. Martin[1]. It is noteworthy that he always had court opened by prayer, usually by a local minister. An interesting story has it that on one occasion Judge Martin, not knowing the relationship, called on a minister in another county and circuit to open prayer. At the time there was on trial a man for murder, and the minister called upon was a near relative of the defendant. The minister in his prayer prayed for the widow and the orphaned children of the deceased. He asked that the jury be led by Divine Guidance to do the duty toward the accused and not be swayed by the eloquence of lawyers to let him escape his just punishment. Because of the tenure of the prayer the judge found it necessary to declare a mistrial.

Among the lawyers who practiced in the Twiggs County Bar are the following: During the lifetime of the writer of this section of the history, he recalls most vividly H. F. Griffin, Jr., a colorful character who was noted for his humor, oratory, and ability to sway a jury. Affectionately known as Bud to all of his friends, he practiced in Twiggs County for many years and spent the last years of his life in Macon in poor health. He was a descendant of the Griffins and Faulks, both prominent Twiggs County families.

Richard A. Harrison, who passed away in 1956, was a quiet-spoken gentleman, who was an authority on title and real estate law. He was married to Mary Faulk and was the father of Henry Faulk Harrison, a hero of World War II who was

[1]THE GEORGIA BENCH AND BAR. Volume 1. Page 231.—By Grice.

awarded the Purple Heart for wounds received in the Battle of the Bulge. Henry is an important official in the personnel office of the Warner Robins Air Material Command and is at present District Commander of the American Legion.

The third member, whom I knew best of all, was James D. Shannon who practiced in Jeffersonville. A more charming and interesting friend and conversationalist would be difficult to imagine. Judge Shannon, as he was known, began the practice of law in partnership with Richard Harrison with offices in the Twiggs County jail. The partnership was dissolved after a few years, and he continued practicing alone. His office was equipped with an excellent library and located on the second floor of the Shannon Building in Jeffersonville. Judge Shannon served in the Georgia legislature under Governors Harris, Dorsey, Walker, Eugene Talmadge, Rivers, Thompson, and Arnall. He served on a number of committees of the House and the Senate and at one time was Chairman of the Judicial Committee of the Senate.

The writer also remembers faintly an uncle of James D. Shannon, L. D. (Nonie) Shannon, who was Judge of the City Court of Jeffersonville during the entire life of that court. He died many years ago when the writer was still a boy.

In recent years a promising young man in the Twiggs County Bar was Jerre Chappell Miller whose grandparents and parents lived near Fitzpatrick in Twiggs County. A promising career in the Bar was ended abruptly when Jerre Miller suffered a heart attack in Atlanta, Georgia in January, 1959. At the time he was the representative from Twiggs County in the State General Assembly and County Attorney.

James G. Maddox recently located in Jeffersonville for the practice of law, and he will be a fine addition to the Bar of the county. He graduated from Mercer University Law School near the top of his class, and he occupies the office in the court house, which was formerly used by Jerre C. Miller.

The writer is indebted to Judge James D. Shannon for additional information on attorneys who practiced in the Twiggs County Bar and resided in the county before the time that this writer can remember. In a letter written to me, Judge Shannon mentions Peter W. Edge, who he says was a contemporary of his father and mine; and he points out that he did a most unusual thing. "He was a Baptist pastor of considerable ability and influence and left the ministry for the law. We often hear of it the other way. It was said of him that he had considerable oratorical powers and was convincing from the pulpit or before trial juries. His residence, the old Edge Place, lay adjacent to lands of Old Stone Creek Church. He was pastor for many years of Old Stone Creek Church."

Mr. Shannon also refers to Honorable Thomas Glover, resident of Jeffersonville who owned the property now in possession of Mr. Hugh A. McCallum on the Jeffersonville-Warner Robins Highway. Mr. Glover was said to be an excellent farmer as well as a splendid lawyer. After a few years he removed to Alabama where he was an outstanding member of the Bar."

Among some of the other distinguished lawyers who have practiced in Twiggs County Courts were Matthew James Carswell and Minter Wimberly of whom Hugh L. Faulk contributes the following comments. From his boyhood days he recalls their wise counsel and the pleasant hours spent with them.

"Mathew James Carswell, more familiarly known as "Jim", was endowed with rare ability and talent. He was married to Mary Wimberly, daughter of Dr. J. R. Wimberly and Adelaide Steely. To this union were born three children. Judge Carswell was a personality of little or no refute.

Minter Wimberly, legislator, humorest, orator, a successful attorney, and a friend of man, was born on Capt'n. Fred Wimberly's (his father) homeplace often referred to as "Bunn's Folly" but in more recent years as "Inglehurst," the name chosen by his mother, Isolene Minter. Although he had a home and law office in Macon he spent much time in retreat at his Twiggs County farm. All that was mortal of Minter now reposes in historic Richland Baptist Church cemetery."

# CHAPTER VI
# NATURAL RESOURCES OF TWIGGS COUNTY

Twiggs County has a land area of about 365 square miles or 233,600 acres. The County is located in the geographical center of the State of Georgia as established and published by T. J. Jones in his *Handbook Of Georgia* in 1876. Again in 1947 this fact was verified by Captain Charles M. Thomas in his U. S. Coast and Geodetic Survey. In a letter to Angus Hart, Jr., Jeffersonville, dated September 25, 1950 from Captain Thomas this information was given: "The United States Coast and Geodetic Survey of 1947 based on a survey by Charles E. Lamb, Twiggs County engineer, and Captain Charles N. Thomas of the U. S. Coast and Geodetic Survey, give the geographic center of Georgia as follows: Latitude 32° 38.5' N., Longitude 83° 25.4' W., which is believed to be within a quarter of a mile of the true position, the point about seventeen and a half miles southeast of Macon." The point described above is near where Turvin Creek flows into Savage Creek at the site of old Marion.

Twiggs is bounded North by Jones and Bibb Counties, East by Wilkinson, South by Bleckley and West by the Ocmulgee River.

Natural resources are defined by Dr. Reba Burnham, University of Georgia, in her *Teacher's Guide And Aid To Conserving Soil Resources* as, "Those gifts of nature—air, water, soil, sunshine, minerals, plant life, animal life—upon which man depends for sustenance." To exemplify several of the natural resources of Twiggs County, Georgia, a brief account of several of the nature-produced resources is related in this section.

## I. FOREST

Seventy-five per cent of the total acreage of the County is in forest, as compared to about 61 per cent forest land in Georgia, and 33 per cent forest land in the United States. The principal trees growing in Twiggs are pine, oak, gum, hickory, bay and poplar, although there are possibly more than one hundred different kinds of trees in the County.

When the County was first settled by the white race, it contained some of the most valuable timber to be found in America. Longleaf and loblolly pine covered most of the highland, while oak, gum, bay and poplar were found in abundance along the lowlands. Today only a few acres of the original forest remain. Most of the land suitable to agriculture has been cleared and cultivated.

Either directly or indirectly the forest furnishes jobs and financial benefits to many Twiggs citizens. The 1952 market value of the local products include: lumber, veneer, pulpwood, paper products, and fuel. Then there is the added value of beauty, recreation, and protection. The local and distant wood-processing plants, sawmills, and other consumers of forest resources have greatly depleted the once vast stands of giant trees. The production, however, remains generally good despite the removing of the sizable sawtimber for market. The greatest enemy to the forest and natural reforestation is man, he is responsible for the annual loss of many acres of young trees through human carelessness. In 1953 more than 400 acres were burned over in the County, considerably less than a decade ago. To help combat this forest fire menace the County has established a forestry conservation unit. This public-supported forestry protection service is supplemented by the good work in forestry management practiced by several large landowners who have constructed fire-breaks, purchased personal fire fighting equipment, exercised practices of cutting only marked timber, and the removal of undesirable trees.

Twiggs County citizens are becoming increasingly aware that if forest go, soil may go too, along with birds and animals, the water supply, and finally the people.

To help nature mend its wounds inflicted upon her by the encroachment and carelessness of man, landowners are planting seedlings (small trees) on sections of their property where the forest are depleted. During the 1958-59 planting season the state shipped to Twiggs County 3,371,500 seedlings for distribution to landowners to help replenish their forest.

## II. SOILS

Twiggs County lies in the Upper Coastal Plain region of Georgia. The northern portion of the county is for the most part rolling and hilly. The southern portion consists of rather smooth, gently rolling plains which slope gradually southward. The soils of the county are derived from beds of impure limestone, sands, and clays with a considerable amount of the Greenville soil series. The Greenville soil is predominantly sandy, containing a moderately low content of mineral plant nutrients and organic matter, which ranges from mild to strong acid in reaction.

The land surface of Twiggs County is drained principally by two rivers, the Ocmulgee and the Oconee. The Ocmulgee River forms the western boundary of Twiggs County. The Oconee River does not touch Twiggs, but flows through neighboring Wilkinson and Laurens Counties. Some of the Oconee tributaries flow into Twiggs; Big Sandy Creek is such a tributary.

Erosion is a constant menace to the land of Twiggs. Erosion ranging from moderate to severe sheet, as well as to gully erosion, is evident throughout the county. The amount of erosion is generally related to the slope, soil type, and vegetation. Usually the lower the per cent of slope, the smaller the loss by erosion; and the greater the per cent of slope, the greater the loss by erosion. But soil types also affect erosion condition.

For the past several years the federal, state and local governments have cooperated in providing trained personnel to assist landowners and tenants in practicing conservation and good land utilization. Through the cooperation of all levels of government and the trained field personnel, an improved agricultural doctrine in Twiggs County is being realized.

## III. FARMING

Twiggs County is endowed with many natural wonders conducive to good farming. Mild weather, adequate rainfall, productive soil, long-growing season, and a ready market for produce are encouraging to the farmer. The County is so geographically located that it can grow almost any plant not requiring tropical or frigid conditions.

For generations Twiggs Countians have depended upon agriculture as a means of livelihood. During the past two decades many changes have occurred in the agricultural economy of local farmers. The more forward-looking people have continually sought to better their farm practices and to improve their conservation program. Many farmers who formerly planted only one cash crop, cotton, have increased their annual earnings through a diversified program. In 1953, as a result of past experiences either practiced or observed, several prominent farmers raised fine herds of beef and dairy cattle; other farmers increased their annual income by planting several cash crops instead of only one. Some of the extra crops planted to increase production and family income were: pepper, peanuts, corn, pecans, grains, and vegetables. It can truly be said that Twiggs County farmers are deviating from the one-crop system of farming, the dependence upon the mule as a farm animal, and are substituting a multiform type farming through mechanized equipment.

## IV. WILDLIFE

Abundance is the word with which to describe the original animal life that stocked this area only a short century ago. Animal life has suffered as man has made progress. The clearing of forest, the draining of swamps, the damming of rivers, and other steps taken for the development of agriculture, mining, and industry have been of great benefit to civilization when these activities were wisely planned. But one of the bad results has been the disappearance of much wild animal life because of the destruction of their natural homes.

Twiggs County, like many other local governmental divisions, does not have an abundance of wildlife as it did a few generations ago. The County has many types of native animals, and animal kingdom groupings, as fish, birds, insects, and worms. But through inadequate legislation, weak laws, laws without proper enforcement, and civilized man with an uncivilized greed, many desirable wildlife animals have become rare, or are showing a considerable decrease in number. Several persons in positions of leadership are seeking ways of preserving our wildlife friends. The federal, state, and local governments are cooperating to assist nature restock the depleted wildlife kingdom and thus avoid extension of certain species. Several Twiggs County landowners are helping to conserve wildlife by planting sericeas lespedeza and bi-color lespediza as border strips around field and woodland areas for wildlife food and cover. Local citizens offer further protection to animal life by posting their property against trespassers, building ponds and lakes, releasing pen-raised wildlife, and punishing law violators.

## V. MINERALS

Minerals, unlike the animal or plant kingdoms, have no life, and therefore cannot die. Minerals can increase in size only by additions from the outside. Any special kind of mineral occurs naturally and very seldom, if ever, as the result of living processes.

Nature was generous in locating her mineral deposits throughout the earth and exceedingly liberal to Twiggs County. Despite the known mineral wealth of Twiggs it has not yet been developed to its fullest extent; and too, the area has not been sufficiently explored to determine the availability of all mineral deposits.

The story of the mineral resources in Twiggs County dates back to the time when the red men lived and roamed the area, using rocks for tools of labor and weapons, and local clays for making pottery. It is recorded that the first known use of a local mineral by the white race was in the late 1700s when some kaolin was shipped to England for use in that nation's ceramic industry. The 1957 edition of the *Bureau of Mines and Minerals Yearbook* list Twiggs above all Georgia counties in the value of mineral production.

The topics that follow are concerned with an explanation of some of the mineral resources of Twiggs County, Georgia.

KAOLIN. The story of kaolin dates back centuries ago to ancient China where this white clay was first discovered. The word kaolin comes from the Chinese word "Kaoling" meaning high place. It was from the high places or hills that the Chinese got a white clay for making porcelain and pottery. Today there are large kaolin mines and plants in the British Isles, France and Germany, as well as in the United States. The leading kaolin-producing states in the United States are Georgia, South Carolina, North Carolina, Pennsylvania, and California. Georgia is the chief producer of kaolin clays for the American market. Georgia furnishes about 70 per cent of the value of all kaolin mined and sold in the United States.

One of the chief kaolin-producing sections of Georgia is Twiggs County. From her clay pits and plants go the "White Gold" that serves American industry so well. It has been only within recent times that local citizens have realized the value of kaolin. Several generations ago local residents considered the impure kaolin surface clays a hindrance. The story is told of how early residents detested the "clay-gall" road area during wet seasons. This clay would adhere to the wagon wheels and make traveling almost impossible unless the occupants were continually cleaning the wheels along the journey.

KAOLIN MINING. Heavy mining machinery removes overburden and cleans the kaolin surface for subsequent mining operation.

KAOLIN MINING. Mobile blunger and pumping station (to make kaolin suspension).

Kaolin in Twiggs County is mined from the earth by first removing by modern machinery the topsoil and subsoils overlying the kaolin deposits. After the partial or complete uncovering of the kaolin bed, the crude kaolin is then removed from the bed by diesel shovels to large trucks, or small trains for transportation to the nearby processing plant. Several kaolin companies have eliminated the necessity of hauling the crude clay to the mines; instead, the clay undergoes a processing treatment at the pit and is piped to the nearby plant for final purification.

After the crude clay completes its orbit of refinement it is shipped in railroad carload lots, either bulk or bags, to customers throughout the United States and foreign countries. The local companies have a few regional customers who receive their kaolin supply directly from the plant, and transport same to their place of business.

Numerous products in which kaolin is an ingredient, as established in part by the 1943 Macon Chamber of Commerce Post-War Study, include:

CERAMIC USES

Tableware (hotel china, semi-porcelain and porcelain)
Pottery and art ware
Vitreous china sanitary ware
Electrical porcelain
Electronic porcelain
 Spark plugs
Floor and wall tile
Chemical porcelain
Dentures
Refractories:
 Firebrick and block
 Special shapes
 Pots
 Crucibles
 Ladle brick
 Saggers
 Kiln furniture
 Refractory mortar

COSMETICS

Face powder
Dusting powder
Rouge
Clay packs

FILLERS AND COATING

Paper
Linoleum
Oilcloth
Textiles
Tires
Rubber goods
Phonograph records
Lead pencils
Polishing compounds
Plaster
Soap
Dentrifices
Calcimines
Casein paints
Other paints
Insecticides
Plastics

METALS

Aluminum (There is a possibility that Kaolin may become a practical source of aluminum.)

MEDICAL

Clay "drawing" Compounds (Antiphlogistine)
Stomach and diarrhea compounds.

A single issue of many slick-paged pictorial magazines contains as much kaolin as shown in the pile. (Picture, courtesy Georgia Kaolin Handbook, Bulletin 1, 1956, Georgia Kaolin Co., Elizabeth, N. J.—Dry Branch, Ga.)

BRICK AND TILE CLAY. Local brick and tile-type clays are generally reddish in color. The brick-type clays of Twiggs are unmolested, due to the lack of processing plants in the area. The county has no manufacturing plants utilizing the brick-type clay; however, in neighboring Bibb County, at Macon, are located several manufacturing plants. Clays of the brick and tile consistency are used in making brick, roofing tile, drain tile, flue pipe, and sewer pipe.

BAUXITE. Bauxite is a mineral found in clay-like deposits, and ranges in color from its gray-white pure state to a rust-like appearance when affected by impurities as iron. Deposits of bauxite are known to exist in Twiggs County; however, its mineral content ratio is low compared to some other areas of the world. The greatest consumer of bauxite ore is the aluminum industry.

FULLERS EARTH. The term fullers earth gets it name from the word "fulling" which came to America from the Eurasia continent. "Fulling" in its original locale meant the cleaning of woolen goods, but later it also came to mean the rubbing and squeezing of woolen and cloth goods by a mill process to make the product tougher and the weave more coherent. The fulling process would usually last about two days. This process consisted of placing the cloth product in a fuller's earth solution, which was a part of the entire procedure that caused the product to shrink and lessen its proclivity to unravel. Due to the closeness of threads brought about by shrinkage and the resistance to unraveling, the cloth was usually made more valuable by undergoing the "fulling" treatment.

Fullers earth is the general name applied to a type of impure clay containing properties making it porous and absorbent. The clay mineral component in fullers earth is different from kaolin. The color of the fullers earth clays range from ivory to a brownish-gray. The mining operation used in obtaining fullers earth is very similar to the methods used in kaolin mining.

Fullers earth deposits are found in many parts of the world, the United States being the leading producer and consumer, followed by such foreign producers as Japan and Great Britain. An important source of the American supply comes from Twiggs County which has vast deposits of this non-metallic mineral.

The main uses found for this clay product are in the refining of petroleum and vegetable oils, although some other uses include floorsweeping compound, insecticide blending, and dry cleaning.

LIMESTONE. Limestone is a rock formation of organic remnants, as shells, which produces lime when burned. It is widely spread throughout Twiggs County. The mineral is used in fertilizer, building materials, road work, cement, and other products.

Twiggs County has no commercial concern utilizing the limestone in the county. The nearest consuming plant for limestone is Clinchfield, Georgia, in Houston County. The Clinchfield plant uses limestone as a principal ingredient in the manufacturing of cement.

SAND. Sand is generally well spread throughout sections of the County, and is especially evident in the eastern portion of Twiggs in the vicinity of Big Sandy Creek. Little native sand has been used for commercial purposes outside the bounds of the county.

Locally, sand has been dug, washed, and sold near Myrick's Mill during the construction of several miles of concrete highway in Twiggs and vicinity. In the proximity of Dry Branch Community is located an abandoned sand pit that once supplied local demand.

## VI. WATER

Water is the giver of life, and without it an area will soon become barren. The Twiggs County area has an annual rainfall of about 46 inches. In years past there was little water run-off and the earth received maximum benefit. The encroachment of settlers caused vast tracts of land to be cleared without regard to loss of water or soil. The county gained in population and thus caused a continual clearing of lands. Oftentimes least productive fields were abandoned and erosion was soon evident with water run-off high. Civil man has too frequently laid waste to the land through poor judgment and carelessness. This weakness on the part of local citizens has caused the loss of much desirable topsoil, the pollution of streams, a high per cent of surface water run-off, and erosion.

Within recent times steps have been taken to teach landowners the value of surface water run-off control and other good conservation practices. Several people taking the lead in these efforts have been the soil conservation technician, extension agent, public school leaders, and leading landowners. Farm fish ponds are one evidence of the conservation-reeducation program. The ponds furnish fish for the family table, water for the livestock, irrigation possibilities, wildlife retreat, and recreation for the family and friends.

Twiggs County is well drained by several creeks, the Ocmulgee and the Oconee

Rivers—though the latter river does not touch the county. The county has numerous ponds and streams. Several of the major streams of the county include:

| | |
|---|---|
| Alligator Creek | Little Shellstone Creek |
| Big Sandy Creek | Richland Creek |
| Buck Creek | Rocky Creek |
| Crooked Creek | Royston Creek |
| Dry Branch Creek | Savage Creek |
| Flat Creek | Shellstone Creek |
| Game Creek | Stone Creek |
| Gum Swamp Creek | Turvin Creek |
| Little Rocky Creek | Turkey Creek |
| Little Sandy Creek | Ugly Creek |

Water for homes and businesses comes from deep wells. Several artesian wells are known to flow in the vicinity of the Ocmulgee River. Indeed Twiggs is fortunate in having such a plentiful water resource.

## VI. CLIMATE

Twiggs County normally has a rather pleasant climate. The winters are usually short and the summers long, although the county sometimes has sudden cold waves that last for a few days. The United States Weather Station at Macon list the area as having an average growing season of 246 days with the last killing freeze in spring falling on the average about March 15, and the first killing freeze in autumn occurring about November 16. The most recent available information lists the area as having a normal annual temperature of about 66 degrees Fahrenheit, and having a normal rainfall of about 46 inches annually.

For the purpose of comparing Twiggs, a middle Georgia county, with the state at large, the following data was furnished:

Georgia has an average of 235 growing days a year, free from frost, ranging from 200 growing days in the mountains of north Georgia to 270 such days in south Georgia. The average annual rainfall in the state is about 50 inches; the average temperature is 63.8 degrees Fahrenheit.

## CHAPTER VII
## WAR BETWEEN THE STATES 1861 - 1865

"Blow, bugles of battle, the marches of peace;
East, west, north and south let the long quarrel cease;
Sing the song of great joy that the angels began,
Sing the glory of God and of good-will to man!
—Whittier

The question of States Rights and Slavery which were causing discontent in the United States in 1860 were also of great local interest. Georgians and fellow Southerners felt that since the various states had made the Constitution and the Union and had given the Union only certain powers, then what they had not given the Union they still had for themselves. This interpretation meant that the states had a great many rights left to them, and that in many ways the states were more important than the Union. This was defined as "States Rights," and Southerners felt that these rights were her most valuable asset.

The slavery issue was a close ally to States Rights. The position taken by the Southern States on the slavery question was very simple. They maintained that the holding of slaves was a question that each State had a right to decide for itself, and that this right was one of the things reserved by the Constitution of the United States to the States themselves.

The slave owners were anxious to increase the area of slaveholding not necessarily because of any anticipated benefits to the territory secured, but in order to gain more representative strength for the slave interest, so as to prevent the possibility of the overthrow of the institution by the powerful North against the opposition of the Southern minority. The free States had long controlled the lower House of Congress, but with great effort the South was able to keep the balance in the Senate. Anti-slavery sentiment had become very powerful in the North, showing itself in abolition petitions, in the obstructions to the capture of fugitive slaves, and in efforts to restrict the area of slavery. Compromises reached between Northern and Southern political leaders held the Union together until 1860.

The defeat of the Democratic candidates for the presidency in 1860 and the election of Abraham Lincoln as President caused much excitement in Twiggs County and all the Southland. Lincoln was feared, for the Republicans were made up chiefly of Northern people; and Southerners believed that Lincoln would take away their rights and free their slaves when he took office. Excitement mounted, the question, "To Secede or Not To Secede," was the topic of conversation in every Georgia Community.

The Georgia Legislature voted to have a meeting in January, 1861, which should decide what Georgia would do. The people then would have a voice in settling the question. If they did not want to secede they could elect members to the meeting to vote against secession. Twiggs Countians heard speeches favoring both sides, but elected representatives who favored secession. When the State meeting convened there were many speeches both for and against secession, but when the final roll call was taken on January 19, 1861, most of the members voted to secede. Other states also seceded, until the number finally reached eleven.

Before President Lincoln was inaugurated as president of the United States, representatives from five of the seceding Southern States met at Montgomery, Alabama, in February, 1861, and organized a provisional government which they called the "Confederate States of America", with Jefferson Davis as president and Alexander H. Stephens as vice president. In March, 1861, a permanent constitution was drafted which granted full sovereignty to the states. Later they were joined by delegates from six other Southern States. The capital was then moved from Montgomery to Richmond, Virginia. A Confederate flag was adopted. (The historic Confederate Constitution is housed at the University of Georgia Library at Athens.)

The United States Government would not allow the several Southern States to leave the Union in peace. War clouds had begun to gather. Preparations for war had to be made in all the seceding states. The governor of Georgia, Joseph E. Brown, had organized two regiments of soldiers to be ready for any call that might be made upon the State.

In nearly every county in the State volunteer companies were formed. Available men, young and old, volunteered for service. With limited weapons they were often drilled with old shotguns and rifles. A gun which was used by a Confederate soldier, manufactured at Athens, Georgia, is owned by B. W. Jones. The more elderly and disabled men, women and children were loyal on the home front and did much to aid in the cause. They produced as much food as possible, knitted socks and clothes, prepared first-aid kits, gave as much of their means as they could, also gave some of their pewter and silverware to help make weapons.

Sherman's army made sure that all of Georgia would feel the effects of war. Wherever his troops marched from the mountains to the sea they devasted and left a cinder path.

Twiggs County was no exception for the Federal troops. Skirmishes took place in sections of the county. Fragments of Yankee soldiers would raid and pillage homesteads in all sections of the county. Some of the available old church records mention that no services were held at the church due to raids by Yankee soldiers. An old clipping in the possession of Mrs. J. T. McCormick gives an account of the raid at the home of Robert Paul about one mile from Marion.

Limitations of funds for printing a larger volume as well as insufficient material on the era of the War and the reconstruction days in the county make it difficult to recount lengthy episodes of war's privations and hardships endured by men, women and children.

The loyalty and patriotism of Twiggs Countians bade them do no less than rally to the call of the Confederate States of America which were defending a principle they believed right. These four companies from Twiggs were formed: The Twiggs Guards, Co. I, 6th Georgia Regiment; The Slappey Guards, Co. G, 48th Georgia Regiment; The Faulk Invincibles, Co. I, 26th Georgia Regiment; The Twiggs Volunteers, Co. C, 4th Georgia Regiment.

The departing soldiers were sometimes paid a farewell tribute at a ceremony by loved ones and friends before they left to join other troops. A record of this appears in *Historical Collections of Richland Baptist Church.* In June, 1861, Mrs. Isolene Minter (F. D.) Wimberly made a farewell address from the steps of Richland Church and presented a flag to the departing soldiers of Company I, 6th Georgia Regiment, Confederate States of America. The color-bearer, Sergeant Warren of Company I, received the Confederate Flag in behalf of the Twiggs Guards. According to tradition a similar service was held at Antioch Baptist Church located in the northeastern part of the county and perhaps at other central points in the county.

The War-Between-the-States raged with great blood-letting on both sides, the Southern populous suffered, the South was subdued, the Union of United States of America was preserved.

## BACK TO THE UNION

The battlefields were quiet, the war was over, and Georgians faced new problems. Her one greatest need now was to get back into the Union. Many of the once proud soldiers of the late Confederate States were now returning home weary, footsore and ragged from distant camps to face a devasted and distraught land. In order for many Southern leaders, both civil and military, to enjoy full American citizenship they were required to take an oath of allegiance to the United States Government pledging to support the constitution. The following is a copy of such an oath by a Twiggs Countian:

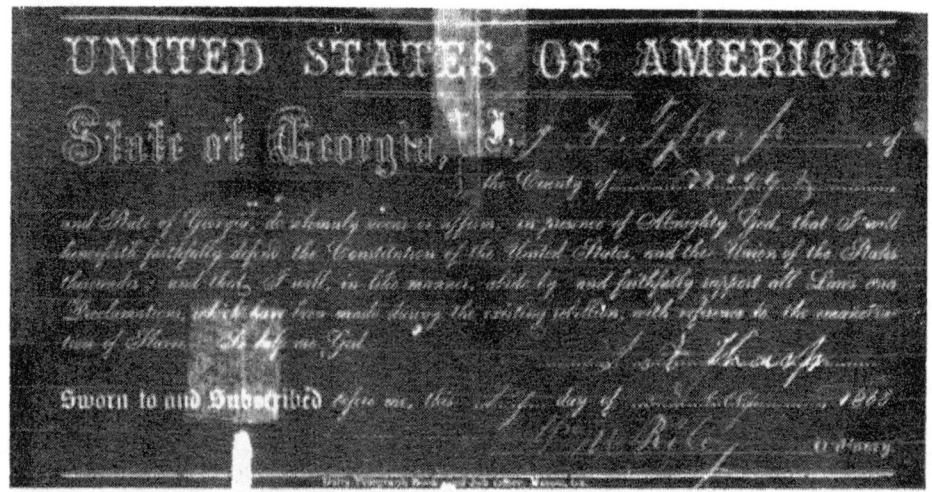

Oath taken by late Confederate citizens to regain their U. S. Citizenship Rights.

## SLAVERY QUESTION

The slavery issue as seen and recorded by a major religious denomination is listed below. The data was selected from the published minute books of the Ebenezer Baptist Association on file at Mercer University.

1835: Recent events have taught us that there is a number of fanatics in the North, who wish to disturb the peace and union of this country, by publishing and circulating incendiary papers and pamphlets, therefore, Resolved unanimously, That this body look upon the conduct of the Abolistionists as an unjust and impolitic interference with the private interests of the whole Southern people.

1840: That we recommend to our brethern of the South, to speak out their sentiments fully on the subject (of slaves), and let Northern Baptists, so called, know distinctly, that we cannot co-operate with those who stigmatize, and excommunicate us. If those Northern Baptist are as sympathetic and philanthropic as they profess to be, let them relieve the indigent circumstances of the poorer class of their own communities, and they will have enough to do. Resolved, That this Association (Ebenezer) disapprobate the conduct of the Northern Abolistionists, and we will have no correspondence or co-operation with them, or those elsewhere, and that the above resolution be published in the SOUTHERN RECORDER, FEDERAL UNION, and CHRISTIAN INDEX; and that they be inserted in our minutes as the sense of this body.

1845: Resolved, That in view of the unwarrantable ground assumed by the action of the Board at Boston, in relation to the subject of slavery, and the importance of greater harmony and energy amongst our Southern Churches, in the support of the Missionary cause. We most heartily approve of the organization of the Southern Baptist Convention and commend that body to the favorable notice of the Churches composing our Association.

1845: The Committee appointed to take into consideration the religious instruction of our colored population, report through their Chairman C. A. Tharp, as follows, viz: Your Committee regards this subject as involving solemn obligations.

In the relation which we sustain to our servants, and to this portion of our population in general, positive claims are presented and urged, which may not be disregarded with impunity. In a certain sense, they constitute a part of our respective families, and where proper effort on our part, will secure for them that instruction which will promote their happiness, make them more faithful, and therefore more valuable, and which under the divine blessing will lead to their spiritual and eternal good, and that effort should be made, and our Master in Heaven, will hold us accountable for the discharge of the trust thus committed to us. It is apprehended there has been heretofore a remissness upon this subject which the world of God does not justify, and in order that the claims which are presented may be more consistently answered, it is recommended respectfully, and earnestly, (1) That the Ministers connected with this Association, at their regular appointment, devote a part of the afternoon of the Lord's day to the special religious instruction of the Negroes belonging to their respective congregations. (2) That such individual Planters that feel interested in the matter and have it in their power, proceed as early as practicable, to provide proper instruction for their servants on their own plantations, by obtaining the services of some Minister who will visit them, and teach them at stated periods according to the word of God.

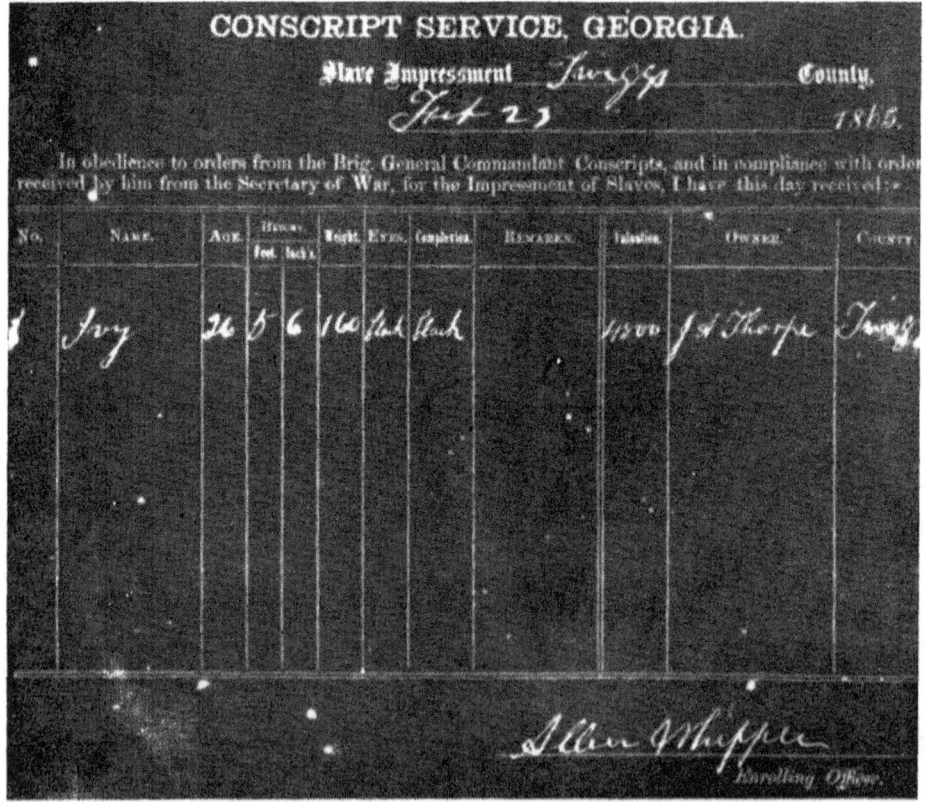

REPORT: STATE OF THE COUNTRY 1861-65

The data for this report on the conditions of the Confederate States of America was selected from the published minute books of the Ebenezer Baptist Association on file at Mercer University.

1863: Whereas, Our common country is still involved in a mighty revolution, and whereas our past successes against such vast numbers, so well equipped and thoroughly disciplined an army, almost unlimited in their resources, convinces us that we are on the side of truth and justice, be it therefore,

Resolved, That we acknowledge the hand of Almighty God in our afflictions and calamities, and humbly submit to his chastening rod, believing that he will ultimately deliver.

Resolved, That we, believing that the God of our fathers is with us, and that we are right in maintaining the cause we have espoused, we are still determined with the help of God, and in reliance upon his aid, to press onward with unyielding energy, until the nations of earth, and our sanguinary enemies, shall have acknowledged our rights, and the justice of our cause.

Resolved, That we commend to all Baptist the cause of the South, and trust that we may never falter, but be found ever ready to yield personal property, or to make whatever sacrifices that will be auxiliary to our cause.

Resolved, That this Association observe Friday before the 4th Sabbath in January next (1864), as a day of fasting, humiliation and prayer to God in behalf of our Country.

1864: Whereas, We as a denomination, have ever planted ourselves upon the broad principles of truth, and justice in the prosecution of any unholy war waged against us by a merciless foe; and whereas, we believe that in successes as well as in reverses, in adversity as well as in prosperity, the footprints of a just God are ever visible to a Christian people. Be it therefore,

Resolved, That in the series of reverses with which we have met in the last year, we acknowledge the justice of an Allwise Ruler who doeth all things well.

Resolved, That while the chastising rod of God has been visited upon us, a wicked people, we still believe we are on the side of truth and justice; and while we humbly bow to an Allwise Providence, we humbly trust in God, hoping and believing that success will yet attend our cause.

Resolved, That while we would make no effort to blend Church and State, we believe that our final success depends upon the will of God, and to this end believing we are right, we commend our cause to all Baptists and Christians everywhere, exhorting our brethren to be ever vigilant in the discharge of duty, both in the field and at home.

REPUBLIC OF GEORGIA
ORDINANCE OF SECESSION
PASSED JANUARY 19, 1861

(The names of the signers on this document from other counties were omitted.)

AN ORDINANCE to dissolve the Union between the State of Georgia and other States united with her under a compact of government, entitled THE CONSTITUTION OF THE UNITED STATES OF AMERICA:

WE, THE PEOPLE OF THE STATE OF GEORGIA, in Convention assembled, do declare and ordain, and it is hereby declared and ordained, that the Ordinance adopted by the people of the State of Georgia, in Convention on the Second Day of January, in the Year of Our Lord Seventeen Hundred and Eighty-eight, whereby the Constitution of the United States of America was assented to, ratified, and adopted; and also, all acts, and parts of acts of the General Assembly of this State, ratifying and adopting amendments of the said Constitution, are hereby REPEALED, RESCINDED, and ABROGATED.

We do further Declare and Ordain, that the Union now subsisting between the State of Georgia and other States, under the name of the United States of America, IS HEREBY DISSOLVED, and that the State of Georgia is in full possession and exercise of all those rights of Sovereignty which belong and appertain to a Free and Independent State.

George W. Crawford, of Richmond, President.

Signers' names from Twiggs County:
John Fitzpatrick, Stephen L. Richardson.
Attest: this January 21, 1861

A. R. Lamar, Secretary

## BATTLE OF GRISWOLDVILLE, GEORGIA

During the spring of 1865 a bloody battle was fought near Griswoldville located on the Jones and Twiggs County line. Mrs. Sallie Balkcom Kitchens of the Antioch community related a grim account of the battle as recounted to her by her mother, Martha Ann E. Reynolds, Mrs. Ichabod Balkcom, who was born in Twiggs County in 1850. Ichabod Balkcom was born in 1844.

Mrs. Kitchens remembered that the battle was fought on a hundred acre field on the northern edge of Twiggs County near a hill located between Little Sandy Creek and Big Sandy Creek and known as Duncan's old battlefield.

Wheeler's Calvary had warned the inhabitants that Sherman's army was approaching but they were not prepared for the destruction of the property perpetrated by his men. On Sunday following the battle it was necessary for the old men, women and boys of the community to bury the many who were killed. The cattle, swine, and other stock massacred by the northerners were piled in huge piles and burned.

The following is a partial list of Confederate soldiers who served in the War Between the States, compiled from combined sources of Confederate Records of Georgia by Miss Lillian Henderson and Confederate records at the Georgia Department Archives and History, Atlanta. (For a more complete record check the above mentioned sources.)

## TWIGGS COUNTY GUARDS
## MUSTER ROLL OF COMPANY I, 6TH REGIMENT
## GEORGIA VOLUNTEER INFANTRY
## ARMY OF TENNESSEE
## C. S. A.
## GEORGIA VOLUNTEER INFANTRY ARMY OF TENNESSEE
## TWIGGS COUNTY, GEORGIA

Ref: Henderson, Lillian, ROSTER OF THE CONFEDERATE SOLDIERS OF GEORGIA, 1861-1865, Vol. I, pp. 817-824.

### OFFICERS

Barclay, John, Captain
Crocker, William H., 1st Lieut.
Wimberly, Frederick D., 2d Lieut.
Slappey, Mathew E., 2d Lieut.
Nelson, Jared M., 1st Sergeant
Whitehead, Ronald R., 2d Sergeant

Brown, James N., 3d Sergeant
Bush, Moses H., 4th Sergeant
Tharpe, Simon, 1st Corporal
Whitehead, Henry J., 2d Corporal
Ellis, John B., 3d Corporal
Jarvis, Daniel W., 4th Corporal

### PRIVATES

Anderson, Christopher C.
Andrews, John C.
Andrews, Joseph B.
Arnold, George F.
Arnold, William H.
Arrintgon, Thomas
Banks, John R.
Barclay, Francis S.
Beall, William
Bennett, Felix

Boynton, Sidney H.
Bozeman, J. William
Bryan, Clem
Bullard, Charles
Bullard, Henry H.
Bullard, Ira
Bullard, Wiley
Bunn, Henry
Bunn, Judson S.
Chance, William B.

Chance, William C.
Chapman, John C.
Chapman, John Iverson
Chapman, William M.
Chitty, Nathan G.
Chitty, William J.
Coley, John B.
Coley, Richard H.
Coley, W. H. H.
Collins, Jacob
Coombs, James T.
Coombs, William H.
Crocker, Evans L.
Davis, Andrew J.
Davis, Daniel D.
Davis, Jonathan
Davis, Wiley W.
Dye, William M.
Edmonds, William A.
Edwards, Washington
Evans, John S.
Evans, William C.
Everett, John B.
Floyd, Everett
Gilmore, George W.
Glover, George R.
Glover, John T.
Glover, William Walker
Harrell, William H.
Hasty, Henry C.
Hasty, Josiah W.
Herrington, Obediah A.
Holland, James B.
Holliday, Thomas H.
Horton, Isaac J.
Horton, John
Hughes, Elbert W.
Johnston, Francis M.
Johnston, John S.
Jones, Archibald Baldwin
King, Thomas M.
Kitchens, David H.
Kitchens, John F.
Kitchens, William L.
Lamb, Arthur
Lamb, Samuel D.
Lamb, Thomas R.
Lamb, William F.
Latson, Francis M.
Lee, Needham S.
Lowe, Franklin
Lowe, Thomas A.
Maddox, William
McCoy, James M.
McCoy, Warren S.

McCrea, John A.
McMillian, Milton
Melton, Daniel B.
Melton, Jasper (or James) H.
Methvin, William F.
Nelson, Franklin C.
Nelson, John
Newby, Josiah
Nobles, Bryant E.
Norris, Isaac
Norris, Isaiah B.
O'Brien, Francis T.
Pace, William H.
Paul, James R.
Pearce, Theophilus A.
Phillips, William T.
Price, Franklin
Puckett, James W.
Puckett, John E.
Radford, James L.
Raspberry, Sanders
Roberts, William H.
Rogers, John
Rogers, Peter
Rogers, Stephen
Rooks, William J.
Sandiford, George W.
Sandiford, Joseph J.
Sauls, Theophilus
Sessions, Abner D.
Slappey, Robert R.
Smallwood, Wilkinson
Solomon, John W.
Solomon, Ruffin A.
Tharpe, Alexander C.
Tharpe, Charnick
Tharpe, Judson
Thompson, Heywood
Thompson, Tucker
Wade, Dock
Warren, Thomas Abner
White, Nelson C.
Williams, John
Wimberly, Edward
Wimberly, Fred D.
Wimberly, Fred E.
Wimberly, George E.
Wimberly, John L.
Wynne, Aleanon R.
Wynne, Needham W.

Additional names appearing on loose sheets in a Confederate Folder at Georgia Department of Archives, Atlanta:

Grantham, Henry G.
Walters, J. A. J.

## TWIGGS COUNTY VOLUNTEERS
## MUSTER ROLL OF COMPANY C, 4TH REGIMENT
## GEORGIA VOLUNTEER INFANTRY
## ARMY NORTHERN VIRGINIA
## C. S. A.

(This company left Twiggs County, Georgia April 25, 1861 and arrived at Augusta, Ga. same day. Left Augusta, Ga. May 2, 1861 for Portsmouth, Va. and arrived there May 3, 1861).

Ref: Henderson, Lillian, ROSTER OF THE CONFEDERATE SOLDIERS OF GEORGIA 1861-1865, Vol. I, pp 571-579. (a brief notation is made about each soldier).

### OFFICERS

Folsom, James M., Captain
Champion, E. F., 1st Lieut.
Nash, Edwin A., 2d Lieut.
Morton, Charles G., Jr., 2d Lieut.
Solomon, Marcus E., 1st Sergeant
Nash, Linton A., 2d Sergeant
Epps, Edward C., 3d Sergeant
Sanders, Jeremiah, 4th Sergeant

Williams, Allen, 5th Sergeant
Tharpe, Simeon, 1st Corporal
Epps, John J., 1st Corporal
Jessup, Benjamin, 2d Corporal
Jessup, Samuel, 3d Corporal
Donnally, Patrick. 4th Corporal
Balkcom, Bryant W., Musician
Lockhart, James, Musician

### PRIVATES

Adkins, Calvin
Adkins, John H.
Alexander, Franklin
Alexander, Samuel
Anderson, Lawrence W.
Andrews, J. B.
Andrews, Thomas H.
Arrington, Robert H.
Balkcom, LaFayette
Balkcom, W. T.
Barrentine, William
Beckcom
Birdsong, Benjamin F.
Blalock, Sanders
Bobbitt, Joseph
Bobbitt, William J.
Boone, Robert H.
Burkett, Asa
Burkett, Solomon
Calhoun, Branson D.
Cannon, James
Chisholm, Albert F.
Clance, John
Clance, Reuben M.
Clance, Wiley
Clance, William H.
Collins, Acrael J.
Collins, Ethridge
Collins, Jacob
Collins, James Durham

Collins, John O.
Collins, Levin M.
Cook, George W.
Cranford, Benjamin (or Crawford)
Cranford, James
Cranford, John
Cranford. Stephen
Cranford, Washington
Cranford, William F.
Davis, John
Day, William F.
Dennington, Charles
Denson, Elias J.
Denson, Joel J.
Denson, John Berrien
Denson, Tillman S.
Dyer, John D.
Dyer, Thomas
Dykes, J. D.
English, J. M.
Epps, Daniel T.
Epps, Elbert D.
Evans, Daniel
Evans, Robert
Evans, William N.
Flowers, Martin
Fowler, Samuel Robert
Gorman, J. B.
Green, Robert
Green, Wesley

Hammerick, William J.
Hammock, Albert
Hammock, John
Hammock, J.
Hammock, William J.
Hardy, William B.
Harrison, J. H.
Harrison, William J.
Henderson, Brady
Henderson, Ephraim
Henderson, John
Hinson, Tillman
Howell, Wright S.
Jessup, John H.
Kennington, Hiram
Kennington, James
Kennington, John
Kennington, William G.
LaGrange, Eugene
Lamb, Andrew J.
Lanier, Alexander
Lanier, Avery
Lewis, Whitfield
Lord, Jesse M.
Martin, E. Branton
Martin, Green B.
Martin, Henry M.
Martin, Hiram J.
Martin, James W.
Martin, John M.
Martin, William F.
Mathis, William D. (or Mathews)
Maxwell, John T.
Maxwell, Joseph
McGee, William K.
Mims, David
Moore, George

Moore, John T.
Moore, P. T.
Murphy, M. N.
Nichols, Raney
Nichols, Yancy
Pettis, William J.
Pettis, William M.
Proctor, Thomas
Proctor, Witt
Reynolds, John
Rhodes, William H.
Richardson, Edmond A.
Robertson, Thomas J.
Rogers, Stephen
Ryle, Coates
Ryle, David J.
Sketoe, William S.
Smith, George
Smith, Thomas
Southall, Benjamin F.
Stafford, Joshua
Taylor, Charnick
Tharp, M. A.
Tidwell, Jonathan
Vann Appling
Vann, Reuben
West, John W.
Wester, Hezekiah
Whitfield, Lewis
Williams, Benjamin
Williams, Franklin
Williams, John W.
Williams, Joseph
Willingham, D. S.
Witt, James F.
Wyse, Joseph W.
Young, John B.

## THE FAULK INVINCIBLES
## COMPANY I, 26TH REGIMENT GEORGIA VOLUNTEERS, INF.

This company was named in honor of William Faulk, a large landowner and prominent citizen of Twiggs County, who outfitted this company at his own expense. During the entire period of the war he gave material aid to the families of the men in service. As shown in the following extract from his obituary.

"While in common with the rest of his countrymen, loyally accepting the situation, he often referred with tenderness to the days before the fratricidal and cruel war; and to those of that gigantic struggle, when his country lost all save honor. During those dark days and years of revolution, the products of his fields were turned into the lap of the Confederacy and to feed the soldiers' wives and children at home while the husbands were at the front battling for their country."

There were seventy-one men who signed a tender of service as FAULK INVINCIBLES, commissioned July 22, 1861. No arms, accoutrements, no tents. Jeffersonville. Stated last on the tender of service, a copy of which follows: "Georgia,

Twiggs County. We hereby tender our services to the Governor of Georgia, for the defense of this State, or the Confederate States, and agree in case we have arms and accoutrements from the State, that we will hold ourselves in readiness to enter the service for the term of the war, unless sooner discharged; and, that we will march on short notice, at any time, until our difficulties with the Government of the United States are settled. This tender of service is made by the persons whose names are included on the Muster Roll of the Company.   E. S. Griffin, Capt.

MUSTER ROLL OF THE COMPANY (The 71 original volunteers)

E. L. Griffin, Captain
Haywood Hughes
Henry M. Loyless
Ezekiel W. Crocker
J. U. Burkett
Jack Lowe
William Blackshear
Danl. Bullard
John S. Wood
Henry West
H. T. Smith
I. F. Crosby
A. G. Crosby
T. D. Crosby
W. F. Martin
R. J. Lavan
Joshua Myers
John Birdsong
Franklin Adkins
F. M. Williams
Henry Martin
Thomas H. Jones
Thomas Bobbit
John Linton
C. H. Carter
A. J. Stockley
J. T. Hughes
Simeon McWilliams
Hull Bridger
Simon Cuttingham
Robert Evans
Hezekiah Evans
David Blackshear
Isaac Blackshear
John P. Vincent
William Churchwell

P. H. Read
James Pruitt
Lewis Adkins
William Crawford
Newman Nelson
J. W. Hodges
Sherrod Lyles
Wilson Pettis
Jesse Williams
William Lyles
William Clance
William E. Lamb
Robert Brown
James Meadows
Thomas Vincent
D. H. Kitchens
Everett Floyd
Lewis Bennett
Elijah McDonald
John Kitchens
Gabriel Farmer
Franklin F. Pierson
Joseph Bond
James Barnes
Benjamin Vincent
James Newberry
A. D. Myers
W. W. Bozeman
H. H. Manning
H. C. Hasty
J. H. Marchman
J. W. Wilkinson
Levi Newberry
J. H. Harrison
George Crosby

Ref: Confederate File at the Georgia Dept. of Archives, Atlanta.

Muster Roll of COMPANY I, THE FAULK INVINCIBLES, 26th Regiment, Georgia Volunteers, Inf., commanded by Captain Eli S. Griffin, later by E. W. Crocker, last mustered from the 25th day of September, 1861, to the 31st day of October, 1861.

E. S. Griffin, Capt.
E. W. Crocker, 1st Lt.
J. U. Burkett, 2nd Lt.
J. E. McDonald, 2nd Lt.
J. T. Hughes, 1st Sergt.
C. H. Carter, 2nd Sergt.

D. N. Melton, 3rd Sergt.
A. J. Shockley, 4th Sergt.
J. W. Hodges, 1st Corporal
G. W. Lee, 2nd Corporal
J. W. Wilkinson, 3rd Corporal
Irby H. Marchman, 4th Corporal

## PRIVATES

| | | |
|---|---|---|
| Adkins, Henry | Day, James | Myers, Joshua |
| Adkins, Lewis | Dyer, Wm. | Myers, A. D. |
| Blackshear, Isaac | Evans, Robert | Manning, H. H. |
| Blackshear, Wm. | Tanner, Gabriel | McWilliams, Simeon |
| Blackshear, David | Floyd, E. M. | Newberry, Levi |
| Birdsong, John | Haywood, Wm. H. | Newberry, James |
| Bobbit, Thomas | Hanison, J. H. A. | Newberry, Columbus |
| Bridges, B. H. | Hitson, Henry | Pate, Isaac |
| Bennett, Lewis | Harden, James | Pruitt, James |
| Balkcom, Wm. | Howell, John M. | Smith, John T. |
| Blalock, Wm. | Ives, Daniel I. | Smith, H. J. |
| Batchler, John | Jarvis, Wm. | Thompson, Carden |
| Bateman, Robert W. | Johnson, Kinchan | Vinson, Benjamin |
| Barclay, Wm. | Kent, Elbert | Vinson, Joseph |
| Crosby, A. G. | Lamb, Benj. | Wall, Trusset |
| Crosby, George | Lamb, Wm. E. | West, Henry |
| Churchwell, Wm. | Lamb, Wm. D. | Williams, Jesse |
| Cranford, Wm. | Levane, Robert J. | Williams, John |
| Cranford, Martin | Linton, John | |
| Crocker, D. E. | Loyless, Wm. | |
| Cuttingham, Simon | Lee, B. F. | |
| Clarke, Henry, Jr. | Morris, Solomon | |

Station: Camp Styles, St. Simons Island
Date: Oct. 31st, 1861
Capt. Eli S. Griffin

This Company rendezvoused in Twiggs County under orders from Colonel Wm. B. Golden on the 25th day of September and took up line of march same day for Camp Stoddard and reported to General Lawton the 5th of October, arrived same day, was ordered by General Lawton on the 13th of October to report to Camp Styles 13th Regiment, Georgia Volunteers on St. Simons Island. Reported to Colonel Styles 16th of October, 1861. This Company was mustered into the service of the Confederate States of America for twelve months at Savannah by Colonel Wm. S. Rockwell on the 12th day of October.

E. S. Griffin
Captain, commanding

Ref: Microfilm Reel No. 15.

### THE SLAPPEY GUARDS
### MUSTER ROLL OF COMPANY G, 48 REGIMENT, GEORGIA VOLUNTEERS ARMY OF THE CONFEDERATE STATES OF AMERICA

Colonel Wm. Gibson, from 30th day of June, 1862, when last mustered to the 31st October, 1862.

Station: Near Winchester, Va.
Date: October 31, 1862.
T. L. Polhill, Inspecting and Mustering Officer.
U. A. Rice, Capt.
Wm. A. Kendricks, 1st Lt.
Daniel W. Jarvis, 2nd Lt.
Robert F. Averet, 1st Sgt.

John F. Bond, 2nd Sgt.
Wm. Goodman, 3rd Sgt.
Joseph H. Read, 4th Sgt.
Geo. L. Vaughn, 5th Sgt.
Russell F. Read, 1st Cpl.
Thomas J. Robertson, 2nd Cpl.
John Tidwell, 3rd Cpl.
Lewis M. Crawford, 4th Cpl.

## PRIVATES

| | | |
|---|---|---|
| Isham G. Andrews | John W. Ard | Jas. Barnes |
| Robins Andrews | Jas. W. Ard | Green W. Bateman |
| Andrew A. Ard | Thos. Ard | Robert Birdsong |
| Geo. W. Ard | Geo. R. Asbell | Warren R. Bond |
| Henry Ard | John L. Asbell | Wm. W. Bowden |

Geo. F. Bryant
Lewis F. Cranford
Aaron Davidson
James Davidson
Elias J. Denson
John B. Denson
Matthew A. Ellis
Willis E. Epps
J. B. M. Ellison
Jno. H. Fountain
Jno. F. Fowler
Michael A. Fowler
Martin L. Harden
Josiah W. Hasty
Jno. Hearn
J. Willis Hearn
Wm. Hearn
Jas. C. Herrin
Joseph B. Hinson
J. C. Howinton
J. C. Land
Newton Land
Wm. R. Lee
Jno. H. Liles
Jno Linton
K. G. Manning
Henry Martin
Jno Martin
J. Henry McCrady
James Meadows

Jasper Melton
Geo. J. Moon
Henry Moon
Lewis M. Mobton
Moses Neal
Obadiah O'Neal
Thomas O'Neal
Benj. Parker
Henry Parker
Isaac Pate
Robert W. Paul
Franklin H. Pearson
Wm. H. Read
Jas M. Reynolds
Jas. N. Rodgers
Joseph Rodgers
John F. Shine
Jno. Smith
Wm. B. Steely
Hartwell Stephens
Josiah Stephens
Sanborn Taylor
Roland Tidwell
Jas. Ward
Patrick H. Ward
Henry Watts
Henry J. Whitehead
Jno. L. Wood
Philip J. Wood
Haywood H. Wynne

Jno. Young
Discharged:
Joel D. Jones
Thos. E. McCrea
Wm. H. Pace
Elijah Pate
Transferred:
E. W. Hughes
Resigned:
Henry M. Loyless
Died:
Tilman S. Denson, June 7,
  Richmond, Va.
Jas. D. Ellis, March 4,
  Marion, Ga.
Haywood Hammock, May 14
  Charleston, S. C.
A. A. Herring, Mar. 4,
  Marion, Ga.
Martin Millandy, Mar. 4,
  Marion, Ga.
B. G. McCrea, Mar. 4,
  Marion, Ga.
Wm. B. Lane, May 8,
  Grahamville, S. C.
Hartwell L. Soloman, Mar. 4,
  Marion, Ga.
Deserted:
J. D. Gardner
Benj. F. Southall

Bounty pay and receipt roll of the Slappey Guards of the Army of the Confederate States of America, Company G, 48th Regiment, Georgia Volunteers, commanded by Captain Ulysses A. Rice.

Ulysses A. Rice, Capt., Twiggs Co., Mar. 11
Henry M. Loyless, 1st Lt.
Hartwell S. Solomon, 2nd Lt.
James B. Wall, 2nd Lt.
Robt. F. Everet, 1st Sgt., Marion, Ga.
Thos. J. Bond, 1st Sgt.

Wm. Goodman, 1st Sgt.
Joseph Read, 1st Sgt.
Geo. L. Vaughn, 1st Sgt.
Lewis M. Cranford, Cpl.
Arthur A. Herring, Cpl.
John Tidwell, Cpl.
R. Floyd Reed, Cpl.

## PRIVATES

Isham G. Andrews
John Ard
Thos. Ard
Andrew W. Asbell
Geo. R. Asbell
John Asbell
Stephen F. Asbell
James Barnes
Green W. Bateman
Thos. A. Berry
Wm. W. Bowden
Geo. T. Bryant
Robt. Birdsong

James S. Crawford
Lewis F. Cranford
Wm. I. Cranford
Aaron Davidson
Willis E. Epps
Jackson Evans
John M. Fountain
John S. Fowler
John C. Howington
Willis Hearn
Wm. Hearn
John Hearn
Martin L. Hardin

Josiah W. Hasty
Wm. Hinson
Elam Hinson, Jr.
John A. Hammock
James C. Herring
Joel D. Jones
Stephen Jones
Wm. N. Kendrick
John Kennington
James Kennington
Wm. Lee
Newton Land
Whitefield Lewis

Thos. P. Moore
Benj. G. McGrady
Jasper Melton
James Meadows
Martin Mellanny
Wm. H. Mims (not on muster sheet)
Joseph Martin
Robt. W. Paul
Elijah Pate

Henry Parker
Franklin F. Pearson
James M. Rogers
Wm. J. Rooks
Wm. B. Stiles
John F. Shine
John Smith
Roland Tidwell
Seoborn Taylor
Judson Tharpe

P. H. Ward
James Ward
Philip Wood
John L. Wood
Haywood H. Wynn
Franklin Williams
John Young
Wm. L. Zachary
D. H. Yearty
Wm. A. Pace

Muster Roll of Capt. James M. Folsom's Co. C. of the 4th Regiment of Ga. Vols., Army of the Confederate States. Colonel George Doles, from the 30th June, 1861, when last mustered to the 30th day of Aug., 1861.

James M. Folsom, Capt.
Edwin A. Nash, 1st Lt.
Marion E. Solomon, 2nd Lt.
Linton A. Nash, 3rd Lt.
Jeremiah Saunders, 1st Sgt.
Edward C. Eprs, 2nd Sgt.

Samuel Jessup, 3rd Sgt.
Marcellas A. Tharp, 4th Sgt.
Patrick Donnally, 1st Cpl.
Wm. J. Hammock, 2nd Cpl.
Robt. H. Annington, 3rd Cpl.
Branson D. Calhoun, 4th Cpl.

### PRIVATES

Samuel Alexander
Franklin Alexander
John Adkins
Calvin Adkins
Thos. H. Andrews
Joseph B. Andrews
Asa Burkett
Solomon Burkett
Wm. Bobbett
Wm. Barrentine
Benj. Birdsong
Wyley Clance
Wm. F. Cranford
John Cranford
Geo. Cook
Thos. Dyer
Wm. Day
Joel Denson
Tilman S. Denson
J. B. Denson
Elias J. Denson
John Epps
Wm. A. Evans
Daniel Evans
Samuel Fowler
Robt. Green
Wm. B. Hardy

Ephriam Henderson
Tilman Hinson
Wm. J. Harrison
Andrew J. Lamb, Dr.
Alexander Lanier
Henry M. Martin
J. Madison Martin
H. Jefferson Martin
Joseph Maxwell
David Mims
John T. Moore
Geo. Moore
M. N. Murphy
Thomas Protor
Wm. Pettis
Wm. H. Rhodes
Stephen Rogers
Thomas Robertson
Geo. Smith
Thos. Smith
Joshua Stafford
Benj. Southall
Charnie Taylor
Hezakiah Wister
James Witt
James Lockhart
Bryant W. Balkcom

Recruits:
Wm. F. Balkcom
Durham Collins
Martin Fowler
Appling Vann
John West
Frank Williams
Resigned:
E. F. Chapman
C. G. Morton
Deaths:
James H. Harrison
Saunders Blalock
Washington Cranford
Discharged:
James W. Martin
Joseph Williams
Albert Epps
John F. Maxwell
Wm. G. Kennington
Jonathan Tidwell
Wesley Green
A. F. Beckcom
Station: Camp Jackson, Nansemond Co., Va.
Date: Aug. 31, 1861

STATE OF GEORGIA
TWIGGS COUNTY

TO HIS EXCELLENCY
JOSEPH E. BROWN, GOVERNOR OF GEORGIA

We, the undersigned Petitioners and former patrons of Wm. O'Daniel, Teacher of said State and County (now a member of Captain Jones' Company E., 8th Regiment, G. M.) Respectfully sheweth that we believe said teacher's services, as such will be of more benefit to the young and rising generation, than his individual services as a soldier in the Militia of Georgia. Said teacher has an experience of six successive years in his profession and is well qualified to impart useful knowledge and is physically disabled to perform the duties of a soldier and as his services, or the services of some efficient teacher is almost indispensable in the County aforesaid. We pray therefore that if in your power under the law you grant to us on his behalf a detail for the purpose herein contemplated and in duty your petitioners will ever pray and etc.

Marion, March 2nd, 1865

Wm. Faulk, M. L.
Henry Durden
Elisha Melton
Milenda C. Durden
C. R. Faulk, J. P.
C. A. Solomon
M. A. Howell
Lewis Solomon

John M. Pearce
Wm. H. Beckam
Wiley M. Pearce
H. M. Loyless
Thos. S. Jones, J. I. C.
W. L. Solomon, J. I. C.
J. T. Glover, J. I. C.

Febry. 26, 1861

To His Excellency, Joseph E. Brown
Dear Sir.

The condition of the Twiggs Volunteers are rather in a deplorable condition at the present time to be ordered out by your Honorable Self; the majority of the Company are men of large families and no one to labor but themselves for a support, yet I believe that the major part of them are at your command at any moment you may need their services; and I pray you in their behalf to let them remain at home to support said families until your excellency may need said Company for actual service if you can supply the needs of the State without them, if not let us know and we will come forward at 2 or 5 days notice.

I would state to your excellency that the Company is made up nearly entirely of the poorest men in the County.

Your most obedient servant,
Simeon Tharp.

Ref: Original letter in Confederate Records, State Department of Archives, Atlanta.

## CONFEDERATE MUSTER ROLLS ON MICROFILM
## AT THE GEORGIA ARCHIVES, ATLANTA

FAULK INVINCIBLES, Company I, INFANTRY REEL #15
Captain E. S. Griffin, 26th Georgia Regiment
SLAPPEY GUARDS, Company G, INFANTRY REEL #21
Captain U. A. Rice, 48th Georgia Regiment
TWIGGS VOLUNTEERS, Company C, INFANTRY REEL #5
Captain James Folsom, 4th Georgia Regiment
TWIGGS GUARDS, Company I, INFANTRY REEL #6
Captain John Barclay, 6th Georgia Regiment

As early as December 8, 1863, President Lincoln had issued his Proclamation of Amnesty and Reconstruction, in which he offered pardon to all except those who had resigned civil or military positions to accept positions in the Confederacy.

Pardon was not extended to Confederate officers above the rank of colonel in the army and of lieutenant in the navy. The President was willing to offer amnesty and aid to others who would take the oath of allegiance and accept the abolition of slavery. After President Lincoln's death Andrew Johnson was inaugurated as President of the United States of America. In the main, he accepted Lincoln's plan of reconstruction. Reference: United States History Revised Edition, by F. P. Wirth.

The following is a copy* of an amnesty granted by President Johnson to William Faulk of Twiggs County:
*Courtesy, D. H. Shannon.

# ANDREW JOHNSON,
## PRESIDENT OF THE UNITED STATES OF AMERICA,
### TO ALL TO WHOM THESE PRESENTS SHALL COME, GREETING:

**Whereas,** *William Faulk* of *Twiggs County, Georgia*, by taking part in the late rebellion against the Government of the United States, has made himself liable to heavy pains and penalties;

**And whereas,** the circumstances of his case render him a proper object of Executive clemency;

**Now, therefore, be it known,** that I, ANDREW JOHNSON, **President of the United States of America,** in consideration of the premises, divers other good and sufficient reasons me thereunto moving, do hereby grant to the said *William Faulk* a full pardon and amnesty for all offences by him committed, arising from participation, direct or implied, in the said rebellion, conditioned as follows, viz.: this pardon to begin and take effect from the day on which the said *William Faulk* shall take the oath prescribed in the Proclamation of the President, dated May 29th, 1865, and to be void and of no effect if the said *William Faulk* shall hereafter, at any time, acquire any property whatever in slaves, or make use of slave labor;

and that he first pay all costs which may have accrued in any proceedings hitherto instituted against his person or property:—

**And upon the further condition** that the said William Faulk shall notify the Secretary of State, in writing, that he has received and accepted the foregoing pardon.—

**In testimony whereof,** I have hereunto signed my name and caused the Seal of the United States to be affixed.—

Done at the City of Washington, this Fourth day of August A. D. 1865, and of the Independence of the United States the Ninetieth

Andrew Johnson

By the President:
W. Hunter.
Acting Secretary of State.

# CHAPTER VIII

# THE SCHOOLS OF TWIGGS COUNTY

Free public schools were non-existent in the early history of Twiggs County. The first schools in the County were either private or academies. Families with means provided private schools and tutors for their children; the less fortunate families provided few learning experiences for their children beyond those mastered from the parents. Education, with its three "R's" and social graces, was looked upon more as a luxury than as a necessity by many of the laboring class. It was not until 1852 that the State authorized local taxation for education, and then labeled it the Poor School Fund as an earlier State Fund had been known in 1823. The name, Poor School Fund, as it was unfortunately called, antagonized the pride of many parents who considered they were objects of charity whenever they accepted schooling for their children paid by this fund.

The only known existing records on the establishment of early schools in the County of Twiggs are contained in the Acts passed by the Georgia Legislature incorporating certain academies. The academy was usually incorporated by the state and a board of trustees or commissioners named with vested power for operation. Students who attended the academy were charged tuition and boarding places were available for those who came from distant areas.

## SOME EARLY ACADEMIES OF TWIGGS

The first known school in the County was the Twiggs Academy, established in 1810 by the Georgia Legislature. The original Board of Commissioners for the school was James Ricks, James McCormick, James Johnston, Thomas Daniel and Abraham Wood.

The Twiggs County Academy or Marion Academy was incorporated by the State in 1816 with Archibald McIntye, Moses Fort, Samuel Dick, Dr. Robert Cummins, and William Crocker, Trustees. According to Stephen F. Miller in *Bench And Bar of Georgia* the trustees of Marion Academy employed Patrick Henry, a grandson of the patriot, Patrick Henry, to take charge of the institution about the year 1830. At this time young Patrick was visiting his aunt, Mrs. Christopher B. Strong in Macon, Georgia, for several months.

The Ocmulgee Academy at Tarvers was incorporated in 1819 with Benjamin Dupree, Edmund Dupree, William W. Williamson, Henry Bunn and Robert Glenn, Trustees. In December, 1838 a school advertisement appeared in a local paper to attract students. The school was operated for ten months each year with tuition as follows: spelling, reading or writing, $16; definition and derivation, history, geography, arithmetic, geometry, elements of nature and of moral philosophy, Grammar; rhetoric, logic or composition, $25; music on the piano, $60, and the use of the piano (practice), $10. The school had an enrollment of 78 students in 1835.

The Jefferson Academy was incorporated in 1828 with Thomas W. Terrell, John R. Lowry, James Guerry, Sr., James Willis, and John F. Dennard, Trustees. This school was located near Raine's Store, now Jeffersonville. The academy reported an enrollment of 75 students in 1836.

The Stone Creek Academy was incorporated by the State in 1831 with William A. Tharp, Elisha Davis, Jeremiah A. Tharp, William Davis, and Thomas Chappel, Trustees. The school house stood near the site of the present Stone Creek Baptist

Church on land owned by the Rev. Charnick A. Tharp. Fifty students were enrolled here in 1837, 31 male, 19 female.

The Planters Academy was incorporated by the State in 1833 with William A. Cowan, Joseph J. Chappel, Reuben A. Nash, James G. Wall and Champion Butler, Trustees.

The Richland Academy was established in 1837 with Joseph R. Hand, John Asbell, Hardy Durham, John H. Denson, Thomas Glover, Thomas W. Anderson and Joel Denson, Trustees. The school had an enrollment of 56 students in 1838.

The Pleasant Grove Academy was established in 1837 with Richard S. Rogers, James Pearson, Abishia Andrews, William Read and Cornelius Hollingsworth, Trustees. The school reported an enrollment of 46 in 1838.

The Union Hill Academy was incorporated by the State in 1837 with Thomas S. Chappel; John A. Nelson; William Nelson; John C. Epps, and James W. Collins. Trustees. The academy had an enrollment of 40 students in 1838.

The Friendship Academy was incorporated in 1854 with Joseph Davidson, Joseph Blackshear, John H. Denson, Abner Hammond, and Peyton Reynolds, Trustees.

The Crosland Academy was built by Dan Hughes at Danville in 1863. It was named for its first teacher, James Evander Crosland, who taught here until 1869. The men instrumental in locating the school and engaging Professor Crosland were: Col. Hughes and Col. Ashley Vickers. Prof. Crosland was not a native son, however, his wife was the daughter of Judge Peyton Reynolds of Twiggs. From about 1858 to 1861 Mr. Crosland was principal at the Jeffersonville School, then removing with his family to Alabama for two years before locating at Danville.

The Davidson Academy was located near Friendship Baptist Church. The Academy was standing in 1868 because Friendship Church was constituted at this school building. No other known information available.

The first move toward a uniform school system in each county was in 1823 when the General Assembly provided for the distribution of the poor school fund in each county by three trustees chosen by the inferior court. In 1838 a legislative enactment became effective providing for five school commissioners in each county to be known as "Commissioners of the Common School."

With the creation in 1852 of the office of ordinary in each county, this officer, in addition to his other duties, was made ex officio school commissioner, bringing the school administrative officers in each school division to a total of six. County boards of education were created by the legislature in 1859 and the board membership was set at seven by provision of the act that the five justices of the inferior court and the ordinary were members of the board and vested with authority to appoint an additional member. Henry Faulk, Representative of Twiggs County, introduced a bill on November 26, 1858 in the General Assembly, entitled an Act to establish a board of education in Twiggs County. (Ga. House Journal, 1858.) Uniformity in the number of board members in the various counties, was, in effect, eliminated by the General Assembly in 1866 when it provided that grand juries elect a commissioner of schools in each division (county) and that he lay out school districts from each of which were elected three commissioners who, with the county commissioner, directed the county educational program. The structural organization was changed again by the legislature in 1870 to provide for county boards of education consisting of one person from each militia district. This law, too, provided for the board to elect a president and a secretary, the latter officer serving as county school commissioner. Uniformity of number on the board was restored in 1871 by an act which empowered each county grand jury to elect five free holders to serve as the county board of education. This is the law governing appointment of members to the Twiggs County Board of Education. The title of county school commissioner was changed to that of superintendent in 1911.

In accordance with an Act passed by the General Assembly the public school system of Twiggs County began functioning in 1872. The Twiggs Grand Jury at the April term of court 1872, elected the following men as the first Board of Education: William Griffin, F. D. Wimberly, William Bull, James T. Glover, and D. M. Hughes, with A. E. Nash as County School Commissioner. However, information obtained from the First Annual Report of the State School Commissioners 1871, Table I, List of County School Commissioners, G. W. Tharp was named as Twiggs County School Commissioner for that term. In 1872 he was succeeded by A. E. Nash.

Extracts from State School Reports show public school funds for Twiggs as follows:

First Apportionment For 1872

| Counties | School Population | Entire Debt as reported | County's Pro Rata |
|---|---|---|---|
| Twiggs | 2388 | $2249.00 | $651.78 |
| " | 2388 | Second Apportionment $2249.00 | $651.78 on 12-21—1872 $479.54 on 9 -13—1873 |
| " | 2334 | Third Apportionment—1873 | $1587.26 |

School Population this year included Confederate Soldiers under 30 years of age.

Fourth Apportionment—1874

| | | | |
|---|---|---|---|
| " | 2276 | | $1498 on 9 - 2—1874 |

The most noted school in Twiggs during the late 1800's was Auburn Institute. Its fame as a school was not limited to Twiggs. Instead, it was one of the most outstanding private schools of Middle Georgia and it enjoyed great influence. Students were charged tuition. Auburn was located at Jeffersonville and it came into existance shortly after the relocation of the County Site at Jeffersonville in 1868. For the year 1874 the school reported 41 students enrolled with J. A. Barclay, Jr., principal. It was the only high school in the County and was noted for its thorough preparation of boys and girls who planned to enter college. It was one of the few high schools that had a course in Greek which was at that time a required subject for scholars who wanted the AB degree at graduation. The school also offered a four-year course in Latin and higher mathmatics including algebra, geometry, trigonometry and surveying, together with the usual other subjects necessary for college entrance.

A high percentage of Auburn graduates went to college, and so well were they prepared that no entrance examination was required by University of Georgia, Emory, Wesleyan or Mercer. Its students made good college grades because they had already studied many of the subjects taught in the Freshman College class.

There were very few extra-class activities, however, the boys played baseball, and the girls attended music lessons and painting classes under the supervision of expert teachers. The local school dramatic club put on some very elaborate plays and musicals.

AUBURN INSTITUTE—CLASS OF 1897

Reading left to right, front row: Henry Bunn Burns, Tom Faulk, Crosby Williams, Denson Martin, Charlie Faulk, Tom Methvin, William S. Jones, Willie E. Jones, Cecil Jones, Lula Joiner, Mattie Sinquefield, Kathleen Jones, Everett Harrell, Lelia Cranford (holding the slate), Annie Nutting, Iris Jones, Theo Sinquefield, Belle Harrell, Johnny Griffin, Effie Burke, Avie Wimberly.
2nd row: Carter Slappey, Gus Martin, Wilbur Reynolds, Fred Slappey, Ellington Burke, Clayborn King, Willie Joe Burns, Spurgeon Rutland, John Vaughn, Robert Methvin, Albert Gates, Rufus Carswell, Mary Faulk, Mary Lou Harrell, Lucy McCrary, Eunice Harrell, Miss Lillian Bonner (music teacher), Miss Annie Sims (elementary teacher), M. J. Carswell (high school teacher), Iverson Carswell ( a visitor).
Top row: Mary Burns, Mable McCoy, Maggie Wimberly, Bessie Harrell.

AUBURN INSTITUTE—1904

The pupils attending Auburn were both local and boarding. The student body came from miles around in wagons, on horseback and by surrey to attend the Institute. This famous old school ceased to operate as Auburn at the close of the 1903-1904 term when the Twiggs High School was established. J. C. McEachin was the last principal at old Auburn and the first at Twiggs High School.

The following is a list of students enrolled at Auburn the Spring term 1890, J. E. McRee, Principal:

*High School Dept.*
Lizzie Balcom
Bessie Burke
Norman Burke
Anna Carswell
Iverson Carswell
Annie Dyer
Mamie Gates
Oscar Chapman
Willie Harrell
Dan Hughes
Dennard Hughes
Clarence Jones
Steve Jones
Erastus King
William King
Andrew McCoy
Willey McNair
John Maxwell
James Pettis
Minnie Pettis
Moses Pettis
Mamie Solomon
Minnie Stevens
Claude Todd
George Wimberly
Hal Wimberly
Plane Wimberly
*Intermediate Dept.*
Ida Balcom
Mamie Balcom
Sallie Balcom
Pauline Burke
Evie Burns
Gussie Califf
Luther Califf
Lizzie Carswell
Jones Griffin
Mary Lizzie Hall
Eugene Johnson
Bessie Jones
Gertruge McCoy
Emmie McNair
Louis Edge Solomon
Cicero Walker
Freeman Walker
Earnest Williams
Maude Williams
Mazzie Williams
Minnie Williams
Carrie Wimberly
Courtney Wimberly
*Primary Dept.*
Frank Balcom
Will Balcom
Charlie Brown
Lemuel Burkette
Glover Burns
Mary Burns
Willie Joe Burns
Rufus Carswell
Iverson Chapman
Will Chapman
George Gallemore, Jr.
Ruppert Gallemore
Albert M. Gates
Henry Griffin
Mary Yancey Griffin
Ben Jones
Robert Methvin
Maybelle McCoy
Lucy McCrary
Mattie McCrary
Walter McCrary
Hattie Pettis
Mark Pettis
Ross Pettis
Carey Shannon, Jr.
Edgar Stevens
Luther Stevens
Maggie Wimberly

After the turn of the century the Twiggs School System was in a period of transition. The school leadership and patrons realized more than ever the need of good school buildings, better furniture, more textbooks and library books, an improved curriculum, better qualified teachers and a greater holding power on its students. Also the idea of providing transportation to pupils and of consolidating certain schools were voiced. In the year 1909 the first public school transportation for Twiggs children was provided, although mention of offering transportation to pupils attending Richland School was reported in 1907. It was in 1909 that the Board of Education, upon the recommendation of Superintendent B. S. Fitzpatrick, a pioneer in school transportation and consolidation, employed a mule team for transporting students who lived beyond a safe walking distance. This team was the beginning of public school transportation in the County. The number of schools has steadily decreased as a result of improved roads and public school transportation to the present day.

### NAMES OF COUNTY TEACHERS EMPLOYED FOR THE 1902 TERM

Antioch—Miss Kate Burkett
Arnold—Miss Hattie James
Auburn—(Not available)
Bond—Miss Fidell Miller
Bullard—Miss Ruth Toole
Cool Springs—Miss Mary L. Hall
Crosby—Miss Hattie Pettis
Danville—Prin. A. J. Clark
       Ass't. Miss Abi Clarke
Fitzpatrick—R. H. Kimball
Friendship—Miss Nannie Burkett
Jessup—Miss Lizzie Burkett
Mt. Zion—Miss Minnie Pettis
O'Neal—Miss Maggie Wimberly
Oakdale—J. H. Vaughn
Prospect—C. R. Gallemore
Stokes—Miss Clif Miller
Williams—Miss Lizzie King
Tarversville—(To be supplied)

TWIGGS COUNTY BOARD OF EDUCATION.

1907 — Picture, courtesy J. T. McCoy

(From published annual statement of B. S. Fitzpatrick, Superintendent.)

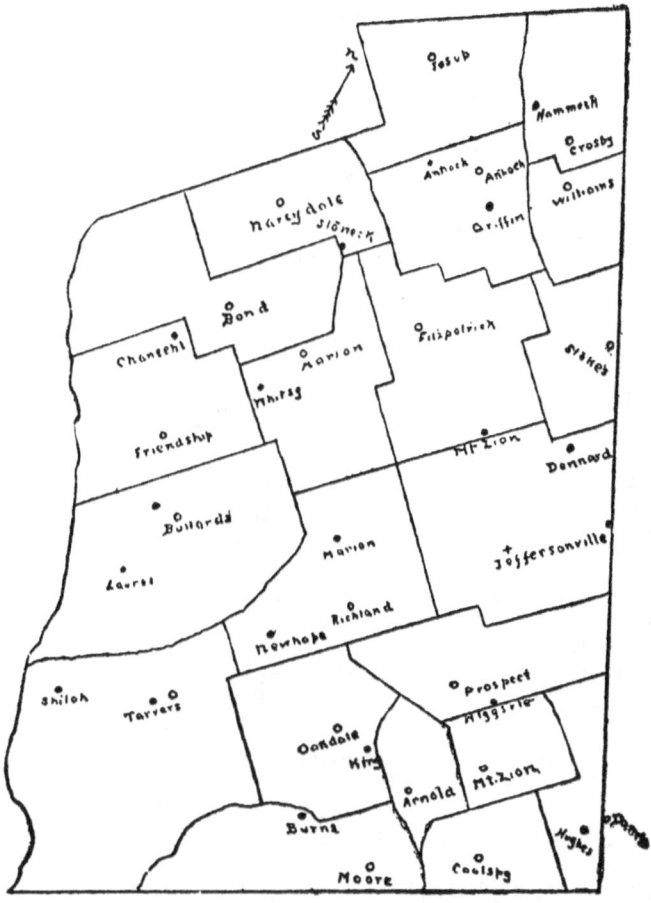

TWIGGS COUNTY SCHOOL MAP—1907
White School o — Colored School ●
Courtesy, Mrs. Bruce Richardson
(From published annual statement of B. S. Fitzpatrick, Supt.)

SCHOOL DIRECTORY FOR 1908

| School | Teacher | Enrollment |
|---|---|---|
| Antioch | Miss Annie Briley | 38 |
| Arnold | Miss Lollis Combess | 38 |
| Bond | Miss Myrtle Haygood | 9 |
| Bullards | Mrs. C. L. Fullilove | No Report |
| Coolspring | Miss Maude Mosley and Miss Mabel Haigler | 66 |
| Crosby | F. M. Butler | 41 |
| Fitzpatrick | Miss Hortense Briggs | 30 |
| Friendship | Miss Mary McKibben | 13 |
| Jesup | (Not open) | |
| Marion | Miss Clay | 24 |
| Mt. Zion | Miss Helen Brundage | 33 |

| | | |
|---|---|---|
| Narcydale | R. A. Nash | 17 |
| Oakdale | Miss Issie Rankin | 20 |
| Prospect | Miss Essie Stokes | 39 |
| Richland | Miss Avie Wimberly | |
| Stokes | Miss Effie Lovell | 18 |
| Tarvers | Miss Madge Fitzpatrick | 16 |
| Williams | Miss Fannie Vaughn | 37 |
| Danville | Miss Eula Barrett and Miss Gurley | 25* |
| Twiggs High | Prof. H. L. Worsham | |
| | Miss Kathleen Jones | |
| | Mrs. Lucy Coombs | 122 |

* Line School, enrollment from Twiggs

## LOCAL SCHOOL TRUSTEES IN 1909

Antioch—B. C. Tharpe, S. T. Burkett, T. S. Tharpe
Arnold—John Lucas, W. M. Little, J. J. Arnold
Cool Spring—J. G. Sanders, W. J. Pettis, B. F. Carden
Crosby—A. F. Crosby, Ed Ward, E. F. Hammock
Everett—W. E. Everett, H. M. Kitchens, C. F. Johnson
Fitpatrick—W. V. Epps, J. T. Day, H. A. Jones
Friendship—J. W. Jones, J. W. Paul, W. B. Johnson
Jesup—W. G. Kitchens, M. C. Kitchens, E. F. Cranford
Glenland—A. J. Land, L. L. Griffin, Alonzo Simmons
Moore—J. S. Hardie, J. E. Ward, S. M. Moore
Mt. Zion—E. L. Hill, A. U. Ham, E. N. Stephens
Narcydale—H. F. DeFore, F. M. Smith, B. M. Latson
Oakdale—(Election to be held)
Richland—J. H. Arnold, J. T. Davis, G. W. Faulk
Prospect—J. F. DeFore, J. T. Holiday, J. R. Sanders
Tarversville—S. H. Griffin, C. H. Bozeman, John Rice
Williams—J. W. Crosby, W. C. Hamm, C. B. Barrentine

For the several decades following the above report on schools, consolidation continued, when practicable, and school transportion expanded. Four permanent school centers finally emerged: Bullards, Danville, Jeffersonville and Smith at Dry Branch. In 1956 the frame schools at Smith and Jeffersonville were replaced with a permanent type structure, as were all the Negro schools, under the State School Building Authority. All high school pupils of the County, white and Negro, were transported to the two separate but equal centralized high schools at Jeffersonville.

The SMITH CONSOLIDATED JR. HIGH SCHOOL opened in 1921 with three teachers: Miss Kate Ingram, Mrs. Walter Burkett, and Miss Ruth Emerson. A school bus was provided by the Board and driven this first term by Mrs. Opal Tharpe (S. S.) Jones, a student at the school. The first Board of Trustees were J. D. Grace, B. D. Tharpe, Sr. and D. S. McGee. The first graduating class was in 1925, the graduates: Corrine Lewis (Mrs. E. G. Dallmus), Grady Kitchens and Elizabeth Cranford. A fire destroyed the original building in 1929 and a new school plant, located at the present site, was occupied in 1931. The new school had four large classrooms, coat rooms, large hall and a kitchen in the rear of the hall. The teachers were Mrs. Mary (Poole) Cranford, Principal, Mrs. Edna Tharpe Powell, Mrs. Ottie W. Wells and Mrs. Jennye W. Brown. In 1935 Crosby School was consolidated with Smith School and Smith Junior High was made a Senior High Institution. From an original three teacher consolidated school, Smith grew into an eleven teacher Georgia accredited elementary and high school.

In 1956 the frame school house of 1931 was replaced by a modern brick seven grade-seven teacher elementary school plant constructed by the State School Building Authority. The high school pupils were transported to the county consolidated high school at Jeffersonville. Smith is the culmination of many earlier schools in the Northern section of the County—Stone Creek Academy, Splintersville, Shackelford, O'Neal, Narcydale, Herring, Fairview, Glenland, Antioch, Arnold, Crosby, Williams, Jesup and others.

The principals at Smith from 1921 to the present:

| | | | |
|---|---|---|---|
| Miss Kate Ingram | 1921-1923 | J. N. Vinson | -1943 |
| Mrs. Mary Dunlap | 1923-1924 | A. L. Clark | 1944-1945 |
| Mrs. Mary Poole Cranford | 1924-1928 | Mrs. Manta A. Lester | 1945-** |
| H. Lunceford | 1928-1929 | H. O. Cravey | -1946 |
| Miss Frances Luke | 1929-1930 | J. L. Claxton | 1946-1947 |
| Mrs. Mary Poole Cranford | 1930-1936 | T. E. Allen | 1947-1948 |
| Joe A. Andrews | 1936-1937 | Joe A. Andrews | 1948-1950 |
| Dr. C. C. Goss | 1937-1941 | B. W. Jones | 1950-1951 |
| H. O. Cravey | 1941-1942* | Charles Tornabene | 1951-1956 |
| Mrs. Lenora T. Dudley | 1943-1944 | Mrs. Jennye Wood Brown | 1956- |

*Cravey called into Armed Forces during 1942-43 term—Vinson made principal
**Mrs. Lester acting Principal until Mr. Cravey's discharge from Armed Forces

The present BULLARD SCHOOL is an outgrowth of Pine Grove, Ocmulgee, (name later changed to Everett), Adams Park, Bond-Ray, and Bullard. Pine Grove, a one-room building with a chimney at one end for heating and home-made tables and benches for the children's desks, began operation about 1890. Insufficient school material on the past history of these non-existant schools makes it difficult to recount events, but mention is made of a few former teachers who taught at some of these schools, namely: Misses B. Cook, G. McCoy, F. Miller, W. W. Johnston, Kate Snipes, R. Toole, H. Doughtrey, Mrs. C. L. Fullilore, Mrs. Mackie Lou James, J. E. Everett, and G. L. Perryman. It was due to the former location of the schools which were being operated about 1920 and other factors which brought about the consolidation of the schools and a new site. The old buildings of Everett, Bullard and Bond-Ray were dismantled and the salvaged material from these buildings was used in the construction of the present school buliding which was located on Georgia Highway No. 27. The new school first operated as an elementary-high for a number of years. Local school taxation in Bluff District which came about through the efforts of a teacher at Everett school, Miss Kate Snipes, and the patrons of Bullard Community, helped support the new school for a number of years in addition to county and state funds. The last school to be consolidated with Bullard was the Tarversville School in September, 1930.

It was about 1938 when community population began to shift to other areas that the high school enrollment began to decrease. At this turn of events, for the 1939-40 school term, the County Board of Education transported the high school students to Twiggs High School at Jeffersonville. The school then operated with two teachers and seven grades until the 1954-1955 term. It was on August 26, 1954 that pupils from the fifth through the seventh grades registered at Twiggs Elementary School. Currently the school is in session with one teacher and four grades.

Bullard School was the first school in the county to serve hot lunches to school children.

The following persons have served as principals at Bullard including the high school era and elementary grades, though not given in the order of service:

Miss Lucy Fleming
Miss Daisy Reese
Miss Florine Sappington
Lamar Woodward
Miss Marion Laine
B. S. Smith
Miss Pearl Phillips
Mrs. Mildred J. Richerson
Mrs. J. H. Aldredge
Mrs. Elizabeth H. Pierce

R. L. Johnson
Miss Mary M. Johnson
Mrs. E. A. Haskins
Mrs. Alice W. Durden
Miss Frances Cochran
W. O. Brown
Mrs. Marie M. Johnson
Mrs. Lanette O. Faulk
Mrs. Clara W. Sanders

## HIGH SCHOOLS AT JEFFERSONVILLE

The origin of the first public Twiggs High School dates back to 1904 according to records available; a small entrance fee was charged each child at this time to help defray expenses for some supplies. This sketch begins with the year 1922 when the second school plant, of brick construction, was occupied. The school building was located on the same campus as the present consolidated county high school. It was during the school term of 1945 that the building was destroyed by fire. It was not possible to construct another building before the ensuing term. School work went on in spite of the catastrophe. During the interium, teachers and pupils labored under strenuous conditions in make-shift class rooms set up in the gymnasium, the Shannon Building and in one or two other available centers. In 1949 another building was erected for temporary use which was used until the 1956 term. The enrollment and certain other factors at the three high schools in the county did not meet the required standard for high school accreditation. In 1955 the three high schools in the county were consolidated for the first time on a county-wide basis as the Twiggs County High School. In 1955 ground was broken on the same campus where the old building burned to begin construction of a modern high school plant under the supervision of the State School Building Authority. In October 1956 the students moved into this streamlined plant.

The following principals who served at Twiggs High from 1922 were:

J. H. Howard, 1922-24
C. E. Bryson, 1924-25
W. O. Johnson, 1925-26
W. A. Dean, 1926-27
C. W. Walker, 1927-29
W. A. Womack, Jr., 1929-31
V. E. Wessinger, 1931-32
H. H. Kellogg, 1932-33
L. H. Fargason, 1933-34

H. R. Bowles, 1934-36
W. D. Oxford, 1936-41
C. C. Crooms, 1941-42
J. M. Cochran, 1942-45
George Clay, 1945-48
J. L. Claxton, 1948-49
J. F. Lindsey, 1949-53
H. M. Fulbright, 1953-56

Principal who has served since consolidation of Twiggs County High School: H. M. Fulbright, 1956 and presently serving the 1959-60 school term.

TWIGGS COUNTY HIGH SCHOOL
H. M. Fulbright. Principal

## SCHOOLS OF DANVILLE

The first known school at *Danville* was the Crosland Academy of 1863. After the doors of Crosland Academy were closed (about 1892), a one-room school came into operation at Danville. The one-room school was built principally through the efforts of Dudley M. Hughes and Dr. Ira E. Dupree. Rabun C. Sanders, an educator, a gentleman of culture, and a minister, was the first teacher employed at the one-room school. A few of the early families who patronized the school were Chapman, Dupree, Hughes, Johnston, and Williams.

There were several one-teacher schools in the Danville area which over a period of years have had to close their doors for various reasons to be consolidated with the school at Danville. The following known schools are a few which have been consolidated: Moore, Ida Hill, Allentown, Cool Spring, Mount Zion.

The *Danville or Twiggs-Wilkinson School* opened at its present location during the term of 1933-34 following the destruction of a prior school by fire in 1931. Land for the school site was given by the Hughes Family. The principals at the Danville School from 1933-1934 to the present:

| | | | |
|---|---|---|---|
| S. E. Goss | 1933-1936 | Wade Watson | 1948-1949 |
| E. A. Edwards | 1936-1937 | H K. Adams | 1949-1951 |
| W. C. Cox | 1937-1940 | David Griffin | 1951-1952 |
| Holland Strother | 1940-1942* | T. W. Jones | 1952-1954* |
| M. B. Branscomb | Nov. 1942-1945 | Spencer Teal | 1954-1957 |
| S. G. Cornish | 1945 (3 mos.) | J. E. Lee | 1957-Jan. 1959 |
| W. D. Compton | Nov. 1945-1946 | Mrs. Faye R. Holliday | Jan.-June 1959 |
| H. F. Luckett | 1946-1948 | | |

*Served only part of this year

## SUPERINTENDENTS OF EDUCATION IN TWIGGS COUNTY

George W. Tharp
(?) -1871

Acton E. Nash
1872-1877

J. A. Barclay
1878- (?)

W. Yancey Griffin
(?) -1886

A. J. Glover
1886-1892
(died in office)

Benj. S. Fitzpatrick
1892-1917, 1921-1944
(died in office)

Albert M. Gates, LLD
1917-1921, 1949-1953

James D. Shannon
1944-1949

A. Turner Wimberly
1953- Incumbent

# CHAPTER IX
# CHURCHES

The pious settlers, men of broad vision and being concerned with the religious care of the people, established meeting houses as places of worship. These buildings were usually one room, log houses, with hand hewn logs for seats. The principal denominations were the Baptists and Methodists. The early minister was a circuit rider, going from church to church, as services were not held too often at the meeting houses, due to the terrain of the country and mode of travel, the members could not attend too often.

As these pious settlers were blessed and prospered better houses of worship were constructed, still using hand hewn timber and pegs. Among the earliest Baptist churches in the county were Stone Creek, constituted 1808, then in Wilkinson County, Woods Meeting House, non-existant today, Richland, constituted 1811. Formerly these churches were in other Associations before coming into the Ebenezer Baptist Association which was organized in 1814 at Cool Springs Church. Others of early constitution dates are Antioch in 1817 and Jeffersonville in 1850. Several of the early churches that ceased to function in later years were: New Hope, Bersheba (later the name was changed to Beach Springs), Mount Moriah, and Mount Pleasant, these last two were active churches in 1816.

However, during the county's years of progress many churches have been erected. Services have been held more regularly. Their style of architecture changed from the small log meeting houses to more comfortable buildings and were more elaborate in design.

Some of the early notable divines who served the early Baptist churches at various years were: Henry Hooten, Micajah Fulghum, David Wood, Vincent A. Tharp, Charnic A. Tharp, J. H. Campbell, Theo. Pearce, Lewis Solomon, Charles D. Mallory, William D. Horne, George R. McCall and probably others whose names are not available.

## ANTIOCH BAPTIST CHURCH
### Dry Branch, Georgia

Antioch numbers among the oldest churches of Twiggs. The church was received into the Ebenezer Association in 1817 with the notation "recently constituted" being entered in the published minutes of that body. The church claims 1811 as the year of its birth, however, the date can't be verified since all church records were lost in a fire. Like many of the frontier churches, Antioch's first meeting house was of log construction with a stick and mud chimney. Numbered among the early membership were the following family names: Clance, Taylor, Bobbitt, Jessup, Hammock, Griffin, Davis, Pearce, Myrick, Wood, Champion and Epps. The land for the church site was given by Travis Epps.

In 1857 the congregation was of such size that a larger and better meetinghouse was decided upon. The new church was built under the supervision of Levi Mathis and was financed to a large degree by Lunce Riggins of Riggin's Mill, who sawed the timber at his mill and hauled it to the church site in ox carts. Leading members during the building of the 1857 church were Bill Lingo, Dr. Nash, Hen Solomon, Issac Jessup. Jeremiah Sanders, Reuben Clance, Issac Maxwell, Isaac Carroll, Jimmie Hammock, Travis Epps and a Mr. Ham.

During the early months of the great War-Between-the States a sizeable group of local men assembled at this church prior to leaving for the Confederate Army. As the War progressed and the men continued to leave her military service, the church revenue decreased until soon there was no money in the treasury to pay Mr. Riggins on the indebtedness. He therefore is said to have threatened to close the church doors unless the debt was paid.

Following the end of the great civil strife several of the local church leaders met to decide on a course of action for repaying Mr. Riggins—among them were: H. Solomon, Dr. Nash, J. Sanders, Short Griffin and J. Hammock. These men couldn't arrive at a satisfactory way of raising the necessary funds to repay the debt; however, it is said that Mr. Hammock personally paid Mr. Riggins the $500.00 due him and cleared the church of all indebtedness.

In 1913 the church agreed to let the Liberty Hill Masonic Lodge add a second story to the old church for a meeting place. The once proud frame church of 1857 was sold and dismantled in 1956, but not before the present new brick sanctuary was occupied in the same year.

The Board of Deacons (1959): Cliff Epps, Herbert Epps, Hubert Epps, Winfred Epps, W. C. Humphries, J. B. Joiner, Cecil Jones, Roy Jones, Hardy Lee Kitchens, James Lyles, Walter Rawlins, Grady Spillers, and Hansel Williams.

## FRIENDSHIP BAPTIST CHURCH

The Church was constituted at Davidson's Academy November 14, 1868. The presbytery consisted of Brethern G. R. McCall, Lewis Solomon and W. D. Horne. After preaching by Rev. G. R. McCall the Presbytery organized the church by appointing Rev. W. D. Horne, Chairman and Rev. Lewis Solomon, Secretary. The letters of the Brethern and Sisters were called for, when those of the undersigned were handed in and read: Elias J. Denson, A. M. Denson, John H. Denson, Elizabeth Denson, James M. Dye, Mary Dye, Eliza J. Denson, John M. Pearce, and G. M. Melton. Brethern E. J. Denson and J. M. Pearce were unanimously chosen and ordained the first deacons of the Church; the Rev. Lewis Solomon unanimously chosen the first pastor.

On September 18, 1870 James Pearce and E. J. Denson were elected to take up subscriptions to build a church. In September 1872 a committee was appointed to select a location for the Church; members were: J. H. Denson, B. H. Melton, Bennet Jones, D. B. Melton, H. Durden, J. W. Paul, Reese Ramey, J. M. Dye and William Davidson.

The Church stands on a two-acre lot of land in the extreme northeastern corner of the old original Pearce Place, Lot 158, District 28 of original Wilkinson, now Twiggs.

The church lot was purchased March 2, 1872, by the deacons and members of the Church from Mrs. Addie Robertson Pearce, who granted the deed to Elias J. Denson and deacons of Friendship Church and their successors in office for the consideration of the sum of Ten Dollars and the further consideration of assisting in the matter of expounding God's Holy Law. A. Baldwin Jones was the executive and financial chairman of the building committee in erecting the present church building.

Prepared from an article by Mrs. Sarah Hendry (James Wilson) Jones, January 20, 1940, and the Original Church Minute Book in custody of Mark D. Durden, Jr.

## JEFFERSONVILLE BAPTIST CHURCH

The Church was constituted December 15, 1849 with Brethren Charles D. Mallary, Jones E. Sharpe and J. H. Campbell as the Presbytery. The charter members were: Dr. Ira E. Dupree, Mrs. Frances Dupree, Archibald McCallum, John Barksdale, Mrs. Mary Brazeal, Mrs. Caroline Wimberly and Haywood Hughes. The pastors to 1900 were: Jones E. Sharpe, Bro. McCall, Franklin Tharp, J. L. Warren, Bro. Cooper, Wm. Steeley, Edward Coats, W. D. Horne, G. B. Hughes, J. L. Harrell, P. W. Edge, J. E. Powell, F. C. McConnell, J. M. Hall, J. H. Oliver, J. C. Solomon, G. W. Tharpe, W. S. Ramsey, and R.A. Lansdell. Several of the above pastors were called to serve the church at different times. Church clerks to 1900 were: John Barksdale, J. H. Denean, Haywood Hughes, S. R. Long, John L. Wimberly, J. L. Harrell, J. B. Burgess, S. H. Boynton, J. T. Horne, M. E. Solomon, J. Wimberly, J. R. Wimberly, Jr., J. H. Wimberly and J. P. Califf.

In 1917 a new church was built on the same site as the former building. J. T. B. Anderson, pastor; the Board of Deacons at this time were: W. C. Faulk, W. H. Harrell, D. S. Faulk, J. G. Rockmore, J. C. Shannon Jr., A. M. Gates Sr., and Linton Hatcher. Members of the Building Committee for the new church were: D. S. Faulk, J. G. Rockmore and A. M. Gates, Sr. The Architect, J. J. Baldwin; the Building, R. E. Mayfield.

An Education Building was dedicated February 23, 1958. Members of the Educational Building Committee were: A. T. Wimberly, D. H. Shannon, J. D. Shannon, H. A. McCallum, J. E. Beck, D. Y. Califf, O. C. Cannon, and C. A. Duggan.

Officiating at the dedicatory serice were the Reverends M. R. Gaddis and E. N. Swinney, Jr.

The Missionary Society for the church was instituted October 9, 1886 with Sisters W. D. Walker, Lucy G. Wimberly, Lucy Solomon, and Sallie Joyner.

Compiled from: Church Records and sketch by Miss Clyde Martin.

## MT. ZION MISSIONARY BAPTIST CHURCH
### Route 1
### Danville, Georgia

The Mt. Zion Baptist Church, located in the southern section of Twiggs County, on the old West Lake Public Road, was founded on December 9, 1860, according to the minutes of the church that have been preserved through all these years. Rev. William R. Steely preached the organizational sermon with the Rev. Green B. Hughes serving as Moderator and J. R. Coombs as Secretary. Charter members of the church were B. W. Godwin, who acted as pastor until the Rev. Steely was called, Julian Godwin, Briton S. Ware, Mary T. Ware, Martha Hargrove and Sarah Chance.

In November, 1880, four progressive minded members of the church organized the first Sunday School. Mr. and Mrs. Dudley M. Hughes, William Chance and John Lee were responsible for this step in the progress of the church.

For a number of years, preaching services, as well as classes for children attending the Mt. Zion public school, were held in the same building; but in 1890 the church members realized another of their dreams when they constructed a church building in which Sunday School and preaching services were to be held.

In 1948, Mt. Zion members added eight Sunday School rooms to the church auditorium; and, in 1956, the Educational Building Annex was completed and dedicated.

Some 23 ministers have been called to serve the church from its organization through 1958, many of them returning to the church year after year as they would be recalled for service. Members of the church have gone forth to serve in national, state, and county government positions, establishing homes throughout the nation, and carrying forth the teachings of the church that stands as a beacon light in its community.

Approved for Publication in the Twiggs County History by: S. M. Gallemore (Deacon), Clerk and Treasurer; R. L. Stevens (Deacon), Chairman of Board; M. H. Stevens Sr. (Deacon), Sunday School Superintendent.

## NEW HAVEN BAPTIST CHURCH

The New Haven Church grew out of a bush arbor located across the road from the present sanctuary. New Haven was received into the Ebenezer Association in 1887. The Association met here in 1898. Numbered among the early membership were James I. Dykes, J. D. Collins, George Leslie, Frank Cannon and Marcus Read.

To purchase their first piano for the new church, the membership sponsored a "Womanless Wedding" and other stunts, to the enjoyment of audiences at several of the local schools.

The first Extension or Short Course Camp for Twiggs was held at this Church by Mrs. Kathleen Jones Carswell. She and certain other members of the Troop slept overnight on the church floor.

## NEW RICHLAND BAPTIST CHURCH

On the 30th day of May in the year of our Lord one thousand nine hundred fifteen (1915), the Reverend Brethrens G. W. Tharpe and J. E. Townsend met as a Presbytery for the purpose of organizing the Church. Rev. George W. Tharpe preached the introductory sermon and acted as moderator, J. E. Townsend served as Secretary.

Bro. J. E. Townsend was elected first pastor. Deacons were R. E. Carrol, A. V. Washburn, and C. E. Vaughn. Officers were: C. E. Vaughn, treasurer; A. V. Washburn, Clerk; Miss Inez Asbell (now Mrs. Thomas Lee), Organist; and C. O. Asbel, Sexton. Members were: Mr. and Mrs. M. S. Faulk Sr., Mr. and Mrs. J. E. Burns, C. R. Faulk, C. E. Vaughn, R. E. Carroll, C. O. Asbel, B. L. Hawkins, A. C. Washburn, Miss Georgia Asbel, Mrs. Clora Asbel, and Dessie Hawkins.

The church requested admittance into the Ebenezer Association in 1915 with the following delegates appointed to represent the Church: M. S. Faulk Sr., L. Z. Asbel and R. E. Carroll.

Under the pastorate of Rev. E. N. Swinney, Jr., the Church went to full time. Deacons are Mercer Burns, George W. Faulk, Coley Walters, Alton White, Jr., Joe W. Faulk, Jr., and C. R. Faulk, Jr. Some of the present church officers are: Shine Faulk, Secretary-Treasurer; Miss Dorothy Faulk, Organist; Coley Walters, Sunday School Superintendent; Mrs. Joe Faulk, Sr., W.M.S. President; and Mrs. Dan Vaughn, Young People's Director.

By Mrs. Joseph W. Faulk, Sr.

## RICHLAND BAPTIST CHURCH

Richland Baptist Church is located six miles west of Jeffersonville on a country road commonly known as "Old Richland Road." A few hundred yards from the church is the "Old Stage Road" trail that led from Savannah, north through Georgia. The northern soldiers traveled this road on their return home after the War-Between-the-States, and camped within the vicinity.

In regard to the constitution of Richland Baptist Church, following is a quotation from an Ocmulgee Association Minute Book: "The Ocmulgee Association met at Sugar Creek Church in Morgan County the 31st day of August, 1811. John Denson and Jacob Ricks were messengers, coming from Richland Creek, asking to be constituted as a church into their Association with twelve members." "Monday, Sept. 2d, 1811—The Association was informed that the Church at Richland Creek, Twiggs County was not regularly constituted, because the Presbytery called to do the same were not sufficiently authorized, for this reason, to-wit, that brother Elijah Hammock, one of the Presbytery was ordained by brother William Lord, whose ordination was invalid, and there being but one other, to-wit. Brother Is'ah Shire, the Association unanimously decided that the constitution of said Church and the ordination of Brother Hammock were invalid and the letter was again returned to the messengers." "Immediately the proper Presbytery was secured by the members and then the Ocmulgee Association accepted the 12 charter members of Richland Creek as a constituted Baptist Church." According to information obtained from records and minute books at Mercer University Library, the most dependable data fixes the date of constitution as October 5, 1811, with twelve charter members. An old church record book that has been preserved dates back to October 5, 1811, on the roster of members with twelve white names listed as charter members, namely: four males, John Denson, Jacob Ricks, the first clerk of the church; Edward Nix, William Coates; eight females, Sarah Denson, Susannah Ricks, Elizabeth Lipham, Elizabeth Truluck, Sally Parrott, Anna Hammock, Sara Glenn, Nancy Powell, and a colored woman, Cloe Hodges.

The first pastor of the church was Rev. Micajah Fulghum, serving from 1811 until October, 1820. Of the many pastors in the annuals of the church, two seem to be most outstanding. Rev. Jesse H. Campbell, of Clinton, Georgia, serving the church fourteen years. He was called as pastor January 12, 1836. The church expressed their esteem for Brother Campbell at a church conference November 6, 1841. A preamble and resolution of tribute for his untiring devotion and influence was recorded in the church minutes. Today one often hears the name of the beloved Rev. George Robert McCall, an outstanding minister in the Baptist work. He graduated from Mercer University and was ordained to the ministry September, 1854. Soon after this, he was called to serve Richland Church. He accepted the call and here he began his first pastorate. The spiritual growth of the church continued during his twenty-eight consecutive years as pastor.

The limitation of space and lack of material make it impossible to trace the labors of all the pastors who served the church.

The beacon light of the church shone brightly until 1911. On August 9, 1911, a deacon and an active member, George W. Faulk, Jr., passed away, then in October, 1911, the pastor, Rev. F. Bartow Asbell, resigned. No other pastor was called. The center of population for church membership shifted to other Baptist churches including Jeffersonville and Evergreen. Therefore, no regular services, then the church doors were closed.

Note: All of the above information was taken from the publication, *Historical Collections of Richland Baptist Church* compiled by Lanette O'Neal Faulk (Mrs. Hugh L.). Attention is invited to that publication for further detailed information.

### RICHLAND RESTORATION LEAGUE, INC.

On July 2, 1948 the Richland Restoration League, Inc., was chartered under the State of Georgia, Twiggs County. Names of the petitioners follow: Miss Sara Faulk, Mary Faulk Harrison, Irene Wimberly Gleeson, A. V. White, Mrs. A. V. White, Sr., John Ball Chapter Daughters of the American Revolution by (Mrs. C. G.) Julia P. Kitchens, Regent, F. B. Asbell, Hallie Wimberly Faulk, E. J. Wimberly, Jas. D. Shannon, Ellen Huff Carswell, Norwood Waterhouse, Mark W. Fitzpatrick, Elizabeth Pierce, Ken Pierce, Claude Fitzpatrick Hendricks, B. K. Richardson, Clara Wimberly Pope, Isoline Wimberly Robbins, Lucile A. Fitzpatrick, Irvin Fitzpatrick,

R. A. Harrison, Mercer Burns, C. R. Faulk, Jr., Laura W. Faulk, Jane L. Duross Fitzpatrick, Rebecca Slappey Whitehurst, Mrs. H. Durham Faulk, Ellen Faulk Califf, Alice Lowery Wimberly, Marcia Griffin Faulk, Louise Ivey Whitehurst, Margaret V. Larsen and Fannie M. Vaughn. Attorneys for the petitioners were R. A. Harrison and Jas. D. Shannon.

The first League officers were:

President
Mrs. Mary Faulk Harrison
1st Vice President
Mrs. Irene Wimberly Gleeson
2nd Vice President
Mrs. Clara W. Pope
Treasurer
Miss Sara Faulk
Secretary
Mrs. H. Durham Faulk

Regular services at Richland Baptist Church were discontinued in 1911 and the old building lay in a state of disrepair for 37 years, until restoration was begun by the League in 1948.

The publication, *Historical Collections of Richland Baptist Church*, was published by the Richland Restoration League, Inc., in 1949. The proceeds from the sale of this book along with individual contributions were used for the restoration of the church. The names of League members and others who made donations are listed in that publication.

The John Ball Chapter, Daughters of the American Revolution, erected a Marker at Richland Baptist Church.

Open house and ceremonies for unveiling this marker were held on September 12, 1954.

Homecoming Day services are held each year when interested members and friends from far and near gather and enjoy the interesting programs, with dinner served under the beautiful trees on the church grounds.

William Thomas Faulk,
Secretary-Treasurer of the League

Church — 1850

Church — 1953

## STONE CREEK BAPTIST CHURCH
### Dry Branch, Georgia

Stone Creek Church is the oldest active church in Twiggs County, having been constituted September 3, 1808. The Church was first located two miles from the present site on a rocky hill overlooking Stone Creek, a tributary of the Ocmulgee. In 1842 the meetings were moved to an Academy which was located on the present church site, and in 1850 the members and community "Deeming it expedient and advisable" built a stately and beautiful church with galleries, to accommodate both white and colored. The colored withdrew August, 1872, and built a church for Negroes; naming it, too, Stone Creek. The old church was destroyed by a tornado April 30, 1953, and the present brick sanctuary was occupied in November of the same year. In 1827 a committee from this Church helped to organize the First Baptist of Macon. In the records for November, 1865, appears the entry, "No conference owing to the enemy's raid near the Church."

Thirty-eight pastors have served the church. Deacons from 1808 to 1959: Theopilus Pearce, Stansel Barbree, Alexander Nelson, John Shawes, John A. Tharp, Hiram McMullars, Samuel Jessop, Jeremiah A. Tharp, James Pearson, T. S. Chappell, Abisha Andrews, Isham G. Andrews, Isaac Horn, Joseph Tharp, William Davis, William Solomon, William H. Andrews, Henry Pearce, John R. Herring, Sr., John O'Neal, H. Alex Jones, H. A. Ezell, H. F. Solomon, A. J. Land, Sr., H. A. Burkett, T. S. Tharpe, G. B. Wood, B. C. Tharpe, G. A. O'Neal, Sr., B. D. Tharpe, Sr., G. W. Burkett, Sr., J. T. O'Neal, Mack B. Smith, Mose P. Sapp, R. L. Powell, H. L. Symonds, Jr., J. C. Miller, Sr., V. Elton Wood, Arthur J. Land, Will Cannon, C. T. Rooks, J. Hollis Cannon, J. G. Lyles, Jones Wood, Adam H. Greene, Madison T. DeFore, B. Grady Kitchens, G. W. Burkett, Jr., Edward N. Nivens, Calvin Renfroe, F. J. Thomason, George E. Willey, James E. Beck, Billy Walker Jones, Bernice A. Leslie, Curtis S. Welch, William H. Wester.

The Church is full time and provides a pastorium for the pastor. In 1954 Stone Creek placed third in Georgia in the annual Town and Country Church Development Program which was under the supervision of Emory University. The current 1959 budget is about $10,000 and the membership numbers over 400. All church records (Minute Books) from 1808 to the present are available.

## THE STORY OF METHODISM IN TWIGGS COUNTY

The influence of Methodism in Twiggs County has been felt since its beginning. They came on horseback to lay deep the foundations upon which has been built the Wesleyan faith. We have seen the seeds planted by our forebears grow to a towering spiritual tree, sheltering hundreds of communicants. Francis Asbury, the itenerant preacher, later Bishop, in the early days of our country, set the example of Christian evangelism. His type of ministry was early adopted and never abandoned. Bishop Pierce's efforts were most influential in establishing edifices over the County of Twiggs. He had a Camp Ground near Jeffersonville and labored diligently among his flock. Other ardent divines among the Methodists were Reverends Bill Griffin and Charlie Johnson, local preachers who were fired with religious fervor and zeal.

The Jeffersonville Charge now comprises five churches, namely, Beech Spring, Jeffersonville, Lucy Chapel, Prospect and Rosebud. Three other churches were once on the circuit. Concord, now abandoned, was once the church of the Gallemore family and others. Ball's Church, in Wilkinson County, and sketched in Wilkinson County History by Victor Davidson, was until later years a part of the Jeffersonville Circuit. Loyal members of Ball's were the Kings, the W. T. Walls, the Hatfields, Stinsons, Sapps and others. The membership and attendance gradually diminished, due to families moving away. The remaining members placed their church letters in Jeffersonville and services were discontinued. Recently a neat iron fence has been built, enclosing Ball's Church Cemetery.

Another of the Methodist churches once on the Circuit was Mary Chapel, near West Lake. This was in horse and buggy days and distance had to be considered so it was changed to the Cochran Circuit, which was nearer. After Cochran Church was made a station, Mary Chapel became a part of the Empire Circuit. Many of Twiggs County's oldest and best families worshipped at its altars, the Slappeys, Fitzpatricks, Carters, to mention a few. Mary Chapel was built by Mary Faulk Slappey, who solicited donations and when completed, was named for her. The historic shrine burned to the ground in later years but its influence is felt by many who hold fond memories of earlier years. A coincidence was, that three days before it burned, Dr. John G. Slappey, son of the one for whom the church was named, was making a professional call and passing, saw the door open. This was after the church was abandoned. He removed the large pulpit Bible and one of the hymn books, taking them to his home. His daughter Rebecca (Mrs. Morgan Whitehurst), of Jeffersonville, now has them in her possession. Dr. Slappey felt that he was prompted by a premonition of disaster to the beloved church of his family, to remove the Sacred Word to safety. (This information about Mary Chapel furnished by Rebecca Slappey Whitehurst.)

## HISTORY OF BEECH SPRING METHODIST EPISCOPAL CHURCH

Founded in 1878, Beech Spring Methodist Episcopal Church, the name by which it was known in earlier days, is located three miles east of Bullard Station in Twiggs County. It derived its name from a cold, bubbling spring, surrounded by large beech trees, at the foot of the hill below the church.

The acre of land on which it stands had formerly been the site of two and possibly three Baptist churches, according to Twiggs County Court House Records.

On Nov. 14, 1844 a transaction is recorded between the deacons of Christ Baptist Church and the deacons of Bersheba Baptist Church, conveying the tract of land, one to the other. Deed Book "B", page 61.

Deed Book "D", p. 62, states that on Nov. 11, 1872, E. J. Denson, deacon of Friendship Baptist Church sold to Dr. William O'Daniel the one acre of land on which the Beach Spring Baptist Church stood (note the difference in spelling). This was signed by H. Durden and J. H. Denson. The name was changed from Bersheba to Beach Spring Baptist, as shown in Ebenezer Association Minutes.

Prior to this time there was no Methodist Church in this section, the nearest one being at Jeffersonville, a full half days' journey. Old Marion was then the county seat. The Methodist people living in this area felt the need of a place of worship nearer home and a group of families, headed by Dr. William O'Daniel, went to work to supply this need. Dr. O'Daniel first giving the acre of land he had previously purchased. These families who were to become its charter members included those of Dr. Allen F. Beckcom, Julian R. Cook, Thomas Lowe, Elbert Millirons and Dr. O'Daniel.

Mr. Millirons, with the help of two Negro carpenters, Joe Sears and Uzell Sherman, was responsible for the construction of the building and upon completion, it was dedicated and placed on the Jeffersonville Circuit. The dedication was made by Julian Toole, who in turn became its first pastor.

BEECH SPRINGS M.E. CHURCH

The same building has served the congregation since its founding except for the addition of class rooms, the first of which were built in 1916 during the ministry of the Rev. L. E. Brady. Having great concern for adequate Sunday School facilities he, with the strong support of G. W. Christian, long time faithful superintendent of the Sunday School, enlisted the help of all those who could use a hammer and saw and soon the dream became a reality. As a result, Beech Spring Church proudly boasted four classrooms, the very first to be had on the circuit. This addition continued in use until 1931, when under the leadership of the Rev. C. D. Harrington, the congregation, with assistance from the Board of Church Extension, remodeled the church, removing the annex from the front and rebuilding six new classrooms on the sides and across the back of the original structure. This was a great improvement over the old plan. In its beautiful setting of native trees and shrubs it is often called "The Church in the Wildwood" by passers-by and visitors who see it for the first time.

In the early history of the church, and some years before, Beech Spring Academy stood nearby and was an institution of learning for many boys and girls of that day. Some of the instructors who had a hand in the academic training of the young were, namely: Dr. Boderick Jones, who later became head physician at the State Hospital at Milledgeville, Dr. J. C. Solomon, Dr. John G. Slappey, all of Twiggs County; Miss Helen Sassnett, of Jackson, who later became the wife of John Land of Twiggs County; Miss Susie Land of Cassville, Ga., sister of Mrs. Henry Land, a charter member of Beech Spring, Miss Imogene Lovejoy, of Ellijay, Ga., Miss Anna Belle Methvin and Mrs. Jane Beall, both of Jeffersonville. There was an old Indian burial ground joining the school yard to add interest to the usual pursuit of the three R's. To this day signs of the early tribes are frequently found around the premises.

The first Register of Beech Spring Methodist Church records these names: Dr. Allen F. Beckom, Mrs. Ella J. Beckom, Delia R. Billhimer, Mrs. Nancy E. Barclay, Mr. and Mrs. James W. Brown. Nettie A. Collins, Julian R. Cook, Mrs. Laura J. Cook, Thomas Jones Cook, Laura Alberta Cook, Cornelius E. Cook, Temperance E. Gammel, Thomas Gammel, Pleas Gentry, W. F. Fitzpatrick, Mrs. T. E. Fitzpatrick, John W. Holder, Nancy Ann Jones, Henry Freeman Land, Mrs. Mouring L. Land, James Thomas Land, William R. Lawrence, Mrs. Lila R. Lawrence, Mrs. Cornelia Ann Lowe, Mary Jones Lowe, John Mims Lowe, Cornelia Elizabeth Lowe, E. Martin Lowe, Elbert Millirons, Mrs. Arkansas Jane Millirons, Della V. Millirons, Mrs. Samantha Ann Methvin, Mary Lee Methvin, Frances C. Methvin, Sarah J. Methvin, Dr. William A. O'Daniel, Mrs. Elizabeth Land O'Daniel, Mary C. O'Daniel, Marcus Henry O'Daniel, William A. O'Daniel, Jr., John W. Paul, Sr., Mrs. Laura Tankersley Paul, Sarah Paul, George Paul, John W. Paul, Jr., Mrs. Sallie Lou Paul, James E. Paul, Mary S. Paul, David M. Perry, Mrs. Cordelia Perry, Ida Belle Perry, Mrs. Cora Solomon Perry, Dr. Stephen L. Richardson. Mrs. Susan A. Richardson, Reese Ramey, Mrs. Hennie Land Ramey, Mrs. M. W. Wood, Laura Wood.

Later members were: Dora Bullard, Victoria Bullard, Cora Bullard, Mrs. Minnie N. Cook, Mrs. Lula Shearouse Cook, Lulie Cook, Julian Roswell Cook, Jr., John L. Harrell, James S. Hutchins, John Walker Joness, William W. Johnston. Robert E. Johnson, Mrs. Nancy S. Johnson, Ann E. Johnson, Andrew Johnson, Madison Johnson, Carrie D. Johnson, C. F. Johnson, Mrs. Martha F. Johnson, John D. Johnson, Otelia Johnson, Laura Johnson, Benjamin F. Johnson, Evie Johnson, Jackson Johnson, Virginia Solomon, Willard H. Spence, Mrs. Sarah M. Spence, Leon Spence.

Pastors who served the church from its beginning to the turn of the century were: Dr. Julian Toole, J. W. Domingos, Thomas E. Leonard, Joseph Carr, John G. Harrison, Wesley Lane, J. S. Lewis, W. E. Vaughan, James D. Maulden, C. E. Crawley, I. C. G. Rabun, C. T. Bickley, T. D. Strong, J. M. Outler, Whitley Langston, and R. M. Dixon.

The years 1900-1910 found the roll containing the family names. Cook, O'Daniel, Smith, Harrell, Johnston, Lowe, Johnson, Phillips, Gilbert, Stevens, Shore, Schaeffer, Kitchens, Ramey, King, Hodge, Akin, Sepp, Bloodworth, Millirons, Lewis, Ward, Cordle, Durden, Christian.

Pastors were: Simon A. Hearn, R. M. Booth, Guy D. Moses, Paul W. Ellis, George F. Austin, J. R. Jordan.

In more recent years the following family names composed the church membership: Cook, Denson, Laine, Rogers, Christian, Cranford, Durden, Johnson, Phillips, Ramey, Haskins, Hendry, Boland, Davis, Warner, Johnston, Burch, Ray, McCormick, Hartley, Fitzpatrick, Tinsley, Dykes, Gresham, Edwards, Edmonson, Griffin, Myrick, Stringfield, Simpson, Sanders, Suddeth, Yaughn, Woodruff, Woodward, White, Johnston, Rogers, Finney, Dixon, Russell, Ransom, Renfroe, Salter, Williams.

Pastors ministering to the flock during this period came in this order: A. S. Adams, W. H. Ketchum, J. W. Reese, J. G. Harrison, L. E. Brady, Corley L. Nease, J. M. Hancock, T. E. Murray, J. E. Channel, C. D. Herrington, H. P. Langlois, J. E. Buchannon, James D. Reese, J. Frederick Wilson, I. L. Bishop, Vernon Edwards, McCoy Johnson, Howard G. McCrary and the pastor in charge, H. W. Scoates, Jr. Under his leadership the church was redecorated last year, and is endeavoring to carry on a full program.

Currently, the membership numbers approximately seventy-two. The Board of Stewards consists of Johnnie M. Johnston, Frank Simpson, Brady Johnson, A. N. Simpson and J. T. McCormick. The parsonage Steward is Mrs. A. N. Simpson and the Communion Steward, Mrs. J. T. McCormick.

This sketch has dealt primarily with facts and figures, and the physical aspect of Beech Spring Church.

Only eternity can reveal and evaluate the spiritual victories that have been won at its altars nor the devotion of its consecrated ministers and laymen.

Since the writing of this history in 1954, the Rev. Gordon King served the church as pastor for two years and was succeeded by the Rev. C. S. Easom, who is now completing his second year. The official board remains the same with the addition of G. F. Rogers as steward. Trustees are John M. Johnston, G. F. Rogers and Brady Johnson. Chairman of the Official Board is Mrs. Ora Belle Fitzpatrick. The only surviving charter member is Mrs. W. W. Johnston (Mary Jones Lowe), who is now in her eighty-seventh year.

Cornelia Johnston McCormick

## LIBERTY HILL METHODIST CHURCH

Liberty Hill Church was organized in 1871, preparations for building began in 1871, finished in 1872. Charter members, families of Pink Mercer, Tilman Joiner Dan Ryles, Bill Edmonson, William Griffin and W. H. Stokes. First Pastor, Rev. Dennis O. Driscal in 1873.

The completion of the Church was celebrated with a Masonic rally and barbecue, with well over a hundred in attendance.

The original Church was destroyed by a tornado April 30th, 1953, but was rebuilt by December 25th, 1953. Reverend J. R. Thomas, present pastor.

By Mrs. W. H. Mercer, in 1956.

## JEFFERSONVILLE METHODIST CHURCH

Although the Jeffersonville Methodist charge is now in the Macon district, records show that it has also been in the Sandersville, Dublin and North Georgia districts. The charge consists of five churches: Jeffersonville, Prospect, Beech Spring, Lucy Chapel and Rosebud. Balls church which was in this charge was dropped some several years ago.

The late Mrs. Jane Beall told Mrs. O. T. Chapman that the first Methodist Church here was built by Mr. "Coot" McCoy and was located back of the houses on the west end of Magnolia Street on the side of the T. S. Jones' home. Years later a frame church building was erected on the present site.

The church was a very plain, frame building with a large front porch supported by a column at each corner. Two doors opened into the sanctuary from the porch— men entering by the right and the ladies by the left and sitting in their respective portion of the auditorium which was divided down the middle by a four foot high partition.

About 1918 this building was torn down and the present structure was begun by the late Miss Ella Gena Beckom as a memorial to her parents, and was completed by the congregation. The church building of cream brick, consists of a beautiful sanctuary, a balcony, a basement and four Sunday School rooms. The bell from the original church hangs in the belfry. The sanctuary is lighted by neon lighting.

The land for the church and parsonage, in the present location, was said to be given by the late Bob Wimberly, who is listed among the early officials along with John Chapman, Dr. Henry Wimberly and Mr. McCoy. The records of the South Georgia Conference give the preachers from the year 1841 to date.

The first parsonage of the Jeffersonville charge, perhaps in the 1870's, was the house which is now occupied by Mr. and Mrs. W. H. Harrell. The parsonage, built adjacent to the church grounds, was burned in 1895 and the present frame building was erected in 1896.

In 1945, during the pastorate of the Reverend Vernon Edwards, a Wesley House was constructed at the rear of the church lawn. This building consists of an assembly room, a dining room, a kitchen and two restrooms. For further expansion of the church program, the Asbury Building was erected during the time the Reverend H. W. Scoates, Jr. was pastor. This building, located on the church grounds, has the pastor's study, the charge secretary's office and assembly room.

In 1864 Bishop James E. Dickey of Southern Methodism first saw the light in the Jeffersonville Methodist parsonage when he was born to his parents, the Reverend J. M. Dickey, who was serving as pastor of the Jeffersonville circuit, and Mrs. Dickey. Four years later the Reverend J. T. Ainsworth was located here. He is the father of the late Bishop W. N. Ainsworth.

Compiled by Lois W. McCrory

## PROSPECT METHODIST CHURCH
### 1790-1958

After the American Revolution, between 1790 and 1810, the following original settlers—Floyds, Sauls, Johnsons, Vinsons, DeFores, and others—met and, with their combined efforts built a small log structure to fill the spiritual needs of the settlers of this new and promising section of Middle Georgia—a Methodist Episcopal Church.

The materials used were of virgin pine. The sills, sleepers, walls, and flooring were hewn into desired shape with a foot adz and a broad axe. The boards used for the roof were riven with a frow and the use of a small wooden mallet or maul, and finished with a drawing knife.

Roads and trails were bad; transportation was by foot, horseback, ox cart, and wagons.

The people were loyal and attendance was good for those days. They named this little sanctuary "Hopewell." It was situated about two miles west of the present church building.

After a period of time, this building was abandoned and a new site and another log structure church was built just across the road from the present church building, this being a larger and more conveniently located structure than the old Hopewell Methodist Church; and it was more suitable to meet the demands of that day. The surrounding territory gave promise of a bright future, so the people named the new church "Prospect."

A portion of this land for the church and cemetery was donated by Theophalaus Sauls, Sr. The other contributors are unknown. The first burial in the Prospect Cemetery was John Stokes.

After many years, this log structure was supplanted by a frame building.

After more than thirty years had passed, during which time interest in the church and church membership grew, this structure proved inadequate.

This structure was torn down and replaced by the present building about the year 1892.

Some of the earliest preachers were: Charlie Johnson and William Griffin. Many of the community men were named for the pastors of Prospect Church; for instance; Rabun, Lewis, Outler, Reece, Glynn, Ellis, Brady, and others.

In 1950, four Sunday School rooms were added; in 1952, the inside of the sanctuary was remodeled, hardwood floors, new ceiling, walls, etc., were also added. In 1954, new clear pine pews were placed in the church which added much to the beauty of the sanctuary.

Early in 1956, the church began a movement to enclose the church with a new brick wall, add porch, and make other repairs to the outside of Prospect Church.

In 1958, the main sanctuary was renovated by completely brick veneering the outside; one Sunday School room was added and a vestibule, all windows and doors were replaced and refaced inside and outside.

A building was purchased from the Board of Education of Twiggs County and moved to the Church grounds, and was repainted on the outside and completely refinished on the inside with plywood walls, celotex overhead, and hardwood floors; gas heat was also added. (This building to be used as Educational Building.)

From 1950 until July 20, 1958 a total of $41,842.77 was spent on the improvement of the Church and Church property of Prespect Methodist Church.

Compiled by John H. Holliday, with the cooperation of the members of Prospect Church, Official Board, and other members.

## LUCY CHAPEL METHODIST CHURCH
### (near Danville, Georgia)

Under the able direction of a layman, Felix J. Johnson, this congregation was organized and the church built. This was about 1876. The church was built with the money and materials given by the congregation, Colonel Daniel G. Hughes and the Cool Springs Masonic Lodge. Thomas G. Hill gave four acres of land on which the church now stands. The structure was two stories with the Cool Springs Masonic Lodge using the second story. Later the upper story was torn off. The church was named in honor of Colonel D. G. Hughes' daughter, Lucy. Rev. J. G. Harrison was the first pastor.

Ref.: TWIGGS COUNTY NEW ERA—April 16, 1953

## ROSEBUD METHODIST CHURCH
### (Fitzpatrick, Georgia)

This church was organized in 1895. The church building was constructed under the direction of the church organizers: J. P. Mercer, B. S. Fitzpatrick and J. Walker Jones. The work was done by Joe Cowart. The church was dedicated in 1896 by Dr. Monk and was named in honor of Mr. B. S. Fatzpatrick's daughter, Rose. The land on which the church building is located was later given to the Methodist Church by Mrs. J. W. (Rose) Harwell. In 1950, two Sunday School rooms were constructed in the rear of the building. This was made possible by the efforts and gifts of the members and of two Christian laymen from the Centenary Methodist Church in Macon, L. E. Floyd and Mr. Shell. Another Sunday School room was made available by the use of a former, small plyboard house from Camp Wheeler which was located on the church property next to the church. The church is located in the community of Fitzpatrick, on U. S. Highway 80.

Ref.: TWIGGS COUNTY NEW ERA—April 16, 1953

## COOL SPRINGS CHURCH

Cool Springs Primitive Baptist Church was constituted June 11, 1809 in Wilkinson County at Allentown, and later moved to its present site. The following names appeared in the constitution: Moses Tyson, David Holmes, Samuel Pouncey, Sion Davis, John Davis, Sion Davis Fern, Stephen Bryan, Silvey Tyson, Abigail Holmes, Melenchia Hathhorn, Sarah Armstrong, Sarah Pouncey, Sister Davis.

Elder David Smith (father of Elders Jim Henry and Doss Smith) preached that day. He resigned the pastoral care of the church Dec. 1, 1838. Two of his grandchildren, two of his great-grandchildren, one of his great-great-grandchildren are members there now.

Elder Jackson Nobles was ordained May 5, 1879. The following ministers were ordained here: William Howell, Josh Chance, Jim Henry Smith, Jim Nobles, Rupert Nobles, John Felton (Dock) Little, Corliss Watkins, Robert Sanders.

Elder Elzie D. Bryant now serving this church, has served since Dec. 1, 1934. Mary Johnston Lamb was a member of this church over seventy years.

Submitted by Mrs. Bruce Richardson

## NON-EXISTENT CHURCHES

Reference: Published Ebenezer Baptist Association Minutes filed at Mercer University Library, Macon, Georgia.

### BAPTIST CHURCHES

Bersheba

This church was constituted in 1820 before September 9th. Messengers to the Association in 1820 were John Young, James Hollingsworth, Cullen Dorman and N. Wheeler. The Ebenezer Baptist Association split occurred while in session at Bersheba Church September 24, 1836 over the question of, "Are the institutions of the day such as missions, temperance, etc. consistant with the articles of faith of this association?" After a debate, answered in the affirmative on this decision, delegates from seven churches left the house demanding the records and declaring themselves to be the true Ebenezer Association. The records were denied. Here the split occurred between Missionary Baptist and Anti-Missionary Baptist (Primitive Baptist). At the 1845 Association meeting in session at Richland Church the messengers from Bersheba, Lewis Solomon, D. Bullard. J. Pope and Jas. James, reported the name of the church had been changed to Beach Spring.

Hopewell

This church was constituted in 1837. Messengers were John Davis, J. Evans. and Wiley Page. The church is listed in 1856 but not in 1869. (Published Associational Minute Books missing from Mercer Library from 1856-1869). Church dissolved.

Mount Moriah

This was one of the original churches constituting the Ebenezer Association Saturday the 6th of March, 1814. (Churches of Twiggs in other Baptist Associations sent messengers to the convention held at Cool Springs in Wilkinson County, Wednesday before the first Sabbath in August, 1813.—Reference: Richland Baptist Church Record Book, Vol. I, 1812-1835). Messengers to the Association in 1814 were: Rev. Micajah Fulghum and Rev. Jesse Bullock. Dissolved in 1833.

Mount Pleasant

This church was received into the Association in 1816. Messengers were Edwin Hart, Abil Etheridge; in 1819 William Rhodes and Jesse Hollingsworth. Dissolved in 1820.

New Hope

Constituted during 1830, but prior to September 11, 1830. The messengers to the Association in 1830 were: Wiley Oliver, Dennis S. Sanders. Dissolved September 18, 1844.

Wood's Meetinghouse

Constituted prior to 1810. This church was originally in the Hephziah Association until September 22, 1810, when it joined Ocmulgee Association. It was received into the Ebenezer Association in 1815; messengers were David Wood, Blake Bryan. The last time the church name appears in the Association minutes was 1853. Dissolved. Church stood near Ripley.

## METHODIST
Concord Church

This church was established prior to 1850 on Gallemore Road about four miles from Jeffersonville on land given by the Gallemore family. Services were held there for a number of years, finally being discontinued with the membership dying out and the younger people moving to other communities.

The building stood for several years deteriorating and finally dismantled. Only the cemetery remains to mark the location of the once proud little meetinghouse. Early families associated with the church were: McNair, William, Gainey, Smith, White, Rutherford, Gallemore, and Collins. In 1903 in the Methodist Church Directory, appearing in the Twiggs Herald, the church was listed as active with Rev. Guy Moses, pastor.

Submitted by Samuel Methvin Gallemore

Mary Chapel

Located near the West Lake Road. This church was destroyed by fire early in the Twentieth Century. In 1903 it was on the Jeffersonville Circuit, Rev. R. M. Booth, pastor. Family names associated with this church were Fitzpatricks, Slappeys, Carters and others.

# CHAPTER X

# OLD HOMES

"Through wisdom is an house builded; and by understanding it is established; And by knowledge shall the chambers be filled with all precious and pleasant riches." Proverbs 24: 3-4.

The few remaining ante-bellum homes in the county built prior to 1860, standing to date, are not forgotten landmarks. Nostalgia takes one back to the scenes of the elegant, spacious, or humble home which reverbrated with an atmosphere of Southern hospitality.

In the glorious days, days of the past, when cotton was king and king was every planter, the ante-bellum homes of Twiggs were beehives of activity. The early homes were a factory in which regular workers made or produced nearly everything that was used. Seldom was plantation life so demanding that one could not enjoy some form of recreation at certain times. For the women, the social charms included the quilting bee, square dances, the Virginia Reel, and candy pulling; for the young children, games of some kind; for the men it was political meetings, wrestling, corn shucking, horse racing, barbecues, fox hunting, the exchanging of lively jokes, Muster Day, on these days people came out in large numbers to see the marching, and the occasional church gatherings in which young and old joined in fellowship.

The home setting was not complete without the hoop-skirted belles and the sideburns, ruffled shirts and tight fitting suits.

Many of the old houses, show places in the hey-day, stand in a state of decay, have been destroyed by fire or they have been dismantled. Materials from some of the dismantled homes, such as the heart timbers, the beautiful wainscoting, the ornamental mantels (some hand carved), the balusters and the newel post of the staircases, have been used in the building of a few modern homes. (Some of the material from these old homes has been shipped to other counties.)

"Mid pleasures and palaces tho' we may roam,
Be it ever so humble there's no place like home."
From "Home, Sweet Home" by John H. Payne.

### CARROLL HOME
(Near Dry Branch, Ga.)

On the 12th day of December, 1849, Joseph G. Stiles of Jones County, Georgia, sold 490 acres of land to Ruben Clance, Hugh Maxwell, James Maxwell, James M. Cranford and Isaac Carroll of the County of Twiggs. Isaac Carroll obtained possession of the whole tract and lived on this land with his wife in their sturdy log house. The land and the house remained in possession of Carroll descendants until 1927 when it was purchased by Mrs. Georgia S. Mann. This house is in a good state of preservation; the interior provides an excellent view of an ante-bellum home of the mid-eighteen hundred era.

CARSWELL-BECK HOME

This house was built by Dr. Beniah Carswell at Jeffersonville, Georgia about 1850. The original structure had five rooms and a hall downstairs with two rooms and a hall upstairs. The house was later owned by Nelson Carswell, a grandson of Dr. Carswell. In 1948, Mr. and Mrs. James Edward Beck bought the house from Nelson Carswell which they later remodeled. the timbers used in the renovation having come from "Todd Hall," later known as the Wall Place in Wilkinson County.

JOHN CHAPMAN HOME

The Georgia Colonial House (now known as Hollywood) built in 1858 by John Chapman is located one mile northeast of Jeffersonville on the Irwinton Highway. The massive two-story, ten room house with six square Grecian columns in front, has been preserved in the original state of its intended beauty and magnificent style. This house was in the process of being built for eight years. The best building materials were used and the most skillful architects and carpenters were employed. In the double parlors with sixteen-foot ceilings elaborate friezes and medallions used for chandeliers placed in the center of the plastered ceilings were hand-carved in a grape design by an Italian sculptor; they are still intact. Back of the ten spacious rooms there was a large kitchen connected to the main house by a ramp. Cabins of the house servants were also built back of the house.

This picturesque ante-bellum home is currently owned and occupied by the Charles A. Duggan, Sr. Family.
(See sketch on John Chapman)

Courtesy, Ruth Chapman

## WILLIAM CROCKER HOME

Major William Crocker, born in Virginia, pioneered to Twiggs County about 1810. He purchased land about a mile north of Marion, the County site, and built a typical southern colonial home. The house was spacious enough to accommodate his many friends and members of his family with a warm welcome. Being from Virginia no doubt the early Virginia style home was his pattern for his house and manner of life.

He and his wife, Mary Evans Long, reared a large family of children.

He was a teacher, merchant and lawyer. He concentrated on his law practice and attained fame in the profession. He practiced in the courts held in Marion court house. His slab bears the following inscription: "He was honest, benevolent and charitable, for 25 years an honorable member of the bar, having no enemies and many friends." He died at this home on June 6, 1835 and was laid to rest in the family cemetery.

Heirs of Thomas Jones Faulk presently own the place.

## HARDY DURHAM HOME

Hardy Durham came to Georgia from North Carolina about 1805. He purchased wild lands in Twiggs County about 1813 and built a home on land that he cleared. He married Sabrina Lawson, daughter of Davenport, about 1814-1815.

The two-story structure was built with a colonnade extending around the lower portion of the house. The roof was covered with large pieces of block tin. Typical of the early colonial homes, the kitchen stood off from the main house, here beside it was a dry, covered well used for storing fruits, food and to keep milk cool. The house is located at the junction of a crossroad on State Highway No. 96, about four miles west from Jeffersonville. The upper story was removed by the present owner, John W. Faulk, who lived there until he built a modern home on the same plot just to the right of the house in the cedar grove.

Hardy Durham acquired a large estate, owned a mercantile business, and operated a freight line on the Ocmulgee River from Durhams Bluff. He was the son of Samuel and Mary Durham, born Sept. 8, 1786, died July 26, 1860. He sleeps beneath the sod in the Durham-Wimberly Cemetery, enclosed in a heavy iron grilled fence, east across the road from the old home place.

### EPPS-FINNEY HOME
(Fitzpatrick, Georgia)

This two-story house with its early nineteenth century architectural lines, numbers among the oldest houses of Twiggs. The first known occupant was the Chappell Epps Family, later it became the property of his son, Will Epps, and in 1916, Charles Finney purchased the house which he and his sister, Bessie, now occupy.

### BENJAMIN S. FITZPATRICK HOME
(Fitzpatrick, Georgia)

This house was built during the Jeffersonian Era and numbers among the oldest in the County. It was remodeled in the late eighteen eighties. John B. Fitzpatrick moved into the house which was already built long before the War-Between-the-States. He was a rabid sessionist and a member of the Committee which met in Milledgeville to decide whether Georgia should secede from the Union. Benjamin S., son of John B. Fitzpatrick, was born here in 1855. He was the beloved County School Superintendent of Twiggs County for almost a half century.

### GAINEY-ARD HOME
(Near Danville, Georgia)

The Dr. Andrew W. Ard Home is one of the few remaining houses dating back to the early eighteen hundreds still standing in Twiggs. The old-fashioned, two-story house is built in the prevailing style of architecture of its day, two bedrooms upstairs, four rooms downstairs with a long hall connecting the main body of the house with two rooms in the rear used as a dining room and kitchen.

An unusual feature of this house was the early cooling or refrigerating system. Water was piped into the house from a spring to a receptacle in the pantry which had coiled pipes to help create a cooler place for food.

The Ard Place was formerly owned by William Henry Gainey whose daughter, Amanda, was born in this house on January 31, 1844. The Cannons owned it later; the present owner is Mrs. E. D. Maxwell, Sr.

         Courtesy: Mrs. Agnes G. (H. L. D.) Hughes
               Mrs. Clara B. Porter

## GLEESOM HALL

Hardy Durham had "Gleesom Hall" built between 1845-1850 for his only daughter, Caroline, who married Henry Slappey Wimberly, M.D. They reared a large family here.

This typical two-story ante-bellum home is located within a few hundred yards of Hardy's home east across Highway No. 96, about four miles west from Jeffersonville. The picturesque house stands a few yards from the road in a park of majestic trees. The grounds were landscaped by a Scotch landscape gardner. A school room was built on the north side of the house leading off the porch which was used as a private school for the Wimberly children taught by private tutors. The nursery was on the southeast side of the house and the milk or storage house was also on the southeast side, off from the kitchen.

Tradition runs that the Architect, Mr. Sessions, had the house and historic Richland Church under construction at the same time, working alternately, using the material at hand for one while waiting for a new supply of material to be delivered to the other place, then vice versa. Freight by wagon was slow in those days.

The home, once a show place, presently is the home of Miss Jane Faulk.

GLEESOM HALL, l. to r., Mrs. Laura Wimberly Faulk and niece, Miss Jane Faulk

## THOMAS GLOVER HOME

Thomas Glover, born August 27, 1799, Nash County, North Carolina, pioneered to Georgia when a young man and settled in Twiggs County about 1830 in the vicinity of Richland Baptist Church. In 1832 he joined this Church and served as a deacon and as treasurer many years. His first home was about one-half of a mile from the Church. After 1843 the old Meeting House was pulled down and a new building was erected, the present historic Richland Church, then he resolved to build him another home. He purchased a site nearer the Church and within one-eighth of a mile he erected a most commodious two-story country home. He was a man with genuine southern hospitality and of deep religious convictions. In his elegant home he delighted to entertain his pastor and other friends at Richland Meetings. Tradition has it that friends spoke of his home as "The Baptist Hotel." The architecture is peculiar to the style of colonial homes of that era. An unusual feature—the front and back of the house was almost identical. In bygone years the old Northern Stage road ran in front of the old house.

Thomas Glover died September, 1878, and was interred in the Church cemetery where other members of his family reposed.

When Jeffreys-McElrath Mfg. Company purchased the property they restored the old delapidated house.

## JAMES HAMMOCK HOME
### (Hammock G.M.D.—near New Haven Church)

This home was built by James Hammock of North Carolina for he and his family about 1840. Mr. Hammock was twice married and the father of 22 children. Following the death of his first wife, he married Mary Cranford. During his life Mr. Hammock accumulated considerable wealth, among it being 2200 acres of land

and 63 slaves. The house, now in a poor state of repair, is a two-story structure with six rooms and an open hall downstairs and four rooms upstairs. The timber and lumber for the house is said to have been sawed at Water's sawmill near Durham's Mill. The brick for the chimney was homemade by Mr. Hammock and fired at his kiln on the creek near his home. To the rear of the old home once stood a gin and spinning-weaving house.

## ANNA HORNE HIGGS HOME

The home built by Mrs. Anna Horne Higgs was most interestingly described in a letter written to her stepmother, Mrs. Joseph Horne, Britton's Store, Bertie County, North Carolina, dated 16th Feb., 1852, Jeffersonville, Ga. The following description was copied from this letter which is presently in the possession of J. Malcolm Browne, Kelford, N. C., a descendant of Joseph Horne.

## HIGGS-HORNE HOME

"First, I built me a kitchen 36 feet long and 18 feet wide, making two rooms, chimney running up in the center with a fireplace in each room. I have a shed on one side the length of the house 12 feet wide, one-half of which is open piaza, the other half is a pantry room. Have a framed painted carriage house. My dwelling house is 47 feet by 36 feet, making four, plastered, 18-foot rooms with a 10-foot passage extending through the center, in front, one of the prettiest porticos I ever saw. The fluted columns and caps cost me $60. My furniture is all new, purchased in New Haven, Connecticut at a cost much lower than it could be bought here."

Mrs. Higgs was born in Bertie County, N. C. and moved to Georgia in the early 1800's with her husband to Wilknson County which later became a part of Twiggs, where they settled.

She willed this home and property to her favorite nephew, Reverend William D. Horne, which later became known as the "Horne Place." It is located about four miles northeast of Jeffersonville, off State Highway No. 18.

## MAGNOLIA PLANTATION

When Mr. Dudley Mays Hughes purchased twelve and a quarter acres of land in 1883 from Stephen E. Moore, there was on the property a four-room house that had been built and occupied by Robert J. Smith and family. Mr. Moore lived in the house six years, having bought it from the Smiths in 1877. According to best available information, the Smiths had made this their home for more than twenty years.

Upon occupancy, Mrs. Hughes secured plans from Mississippi and copied a plantation house she admired. The original rooms were remodeled and additions built in the rear. From time to time, improvements in the house have been made, but the original rooms ceiled with twelve inch heart pine boards hand-planed have remained as built in the long ago.

Magnolia trees were planted by Mr. and Mrs. Hughes, and extensive land was acquired—so the name Magnolia Plantation was given to this home known far and near for its gracious hospitality and deep rooted Christianity.

This home is located on coast to coast Highway 80 at Danville and is occupied by descendants of Mr. and Mrs. Dudley Mays Hughes.

Courtesy: Henrietta Louise Hughes

## OLD O'DANIEL HOME

Daniel O'Daniel, born in 1806, spent his entire life in Twiggs, his old home still standing on the spot where the family lived. This is located in the large field midway between Bullard Station and Old Marion, just off the Jeffersonville Road. Although in a state of decay, it has until recently been occupied. The house was built after the fashion of most farm homes of that day; four large rooms, each having a wide fireplace, and front porch reaching across the length. All of the material was of the very best heart timber—the sills hewn out by hand, mortised and pinned together with large wooden pegs. It was built of logs, also hand-hewn and weather-boarded. The tall brick chimneys, long exposed to wind and weather, have deteriorated to the point of collapse. Having been occupied since early days by colored tenant farmers, no effort was made to preserve it. This property is now owned by John T. McCormick.

History has it that Daniel's father was born in Ireland and settled in Georgia where his son was born, and that Daniel lived all his life in Twiggs County, dying here at the age of sixty-five. Markers on the graves of him and his wife, Louisa, found in the O'Daniel Cemetery, certify this fact.

Dr. William O'Daniel, one of Twiggs County and Georgia's most illustrious sons, was the only child of this couple. He was well known to the medical profession, having filled offices in both state and national medical associations and was a frequent contributor to medical journals. His sketch is found elsewhere in this volume.

Courtesy: Cornelia J. McCormick

### REYNOLDS-FITZPATRICK HOME

Among the old homes in western Twiggs County which were built when this fertile land was being settled is the former Peyton Reynolds house. It was built of original long leaf pine, in the early part of the 19th century. It is now owned and occupied by Ora Belle Travis Fitzpatrick. This property was purchased from Mrs. Loulie Cook Woodruff in 1932, being at that time a part of the J. R. Cook estate, and was appreciated as home by Mrs. Fitzpatrick and her husband, Clare Brown Fitzpatrick until his death in 1939.

The house, originally of eight rooms, is two stories, built in traditionally Southern style, with wide hall, porches, and the kitchen located on the side. The front porch was built across the entire front of the house with six columns and wide steps. All of the porch area at back and a part of the front porch is now enclosed with glass windows, making two comfortable rooms.

The large pine trees that formerly surrounded the premises have been replaced with a grove of bearing pecan trees. Presently, the house contains modern conveniences, and is kept in good state of repair.

The house is located a few hundred yards off U.S. Highway No. 129-23, about twenty miles south from Macon.

Courtesy: Mrs. Ora Belle T. Fitzpatrick

### ROBERTSON-LAND HOME

The original part of the house is of log construction, but its erection date is unknown. However, here lived Thomas J. Robertson, soldier of the Confederacy from Twiggs County, and his family and J. T. Robertson and his family. During the early nineteen hundreds, Andrew J. Land purchased the house, remodeled it and here reared his family.

The house is located on the old Marion Road in what once was known as the Delzel Community.

Courtesy: Mr. and Mrs. Arthur J. Land

### JAMES D. SHANNON HOME
Jeffersonville, Ga.

The oldest known residence erected in Jeffersonville is the J. D. Shannon home. Originally owned a century ago by the late Robert Wimberly, grandfather of Jim and Forrest Wimberly, whose late father, B. B. Wimberly, was born there. Heyward Hughes, grandfather of J. H. Balcom and Mrs. Joel Whitehurst, later owned the house. Mr. Shannon bought the house in 1920 and remodeled it about 1931.

The sills and girders were hewn from yellow pine with broadax and morticed and pined together with wooden pegs. Slave labor was used in the work.
Reference: The Twiggs County New Era—Sept 29, 1939

D. W. Shine

### DANIEL WHITAKER SHINE HOME

Lieutenant Daniel W. Shine moved to Twiggs County about 1814-1815 from Pulaski County, Georgia. He came to Georgia from North Carolina about 1810 and settled in Pulaski County where he served in the War of 1812.

The old home was a two-story structure built on the architectural style of most homes of that day, several large rooms on the first floor with high ceilings and a wide hall through the center, chimney at each end, rooms on the upper story, the kitchen was built off from the main part of the house connected by a "cat-walk." The unoccupied building—once a show place—stands at present in an old oak grove a short distance off State Highway No. 96 not far from New Richland Baptist Church.

Daniel was born July 30, 1786, North Carolina, died Oct. 13, 1868, Twiggs County. He was the son of John Shine, a Revolutionary soldier and a LaFayette Volunteer in 1825 when General LaFayette was entertained at Milledgeville, Georgia, and Clarissa Williams. Both soldiers' graves are in the old family burying ground near the old home.

The old home remains the property of a grandson of Mary Ann Shine who married George Watkins Faulk.

MARK FAULK, SR. HOME

## SUNNYSIDE

Mark Faulk, Sr., was an early settler in Twiggs County. He came here from Washington County, Georgia, when a young man and acquired a tract of land on which he built a small house. He became a successful planter and about 1819 he built a two-story frame house typical of early Virginia homes. There are two large rooms on the second floor with the five main rooms on the first floor divided by a wide hall which is closed at both ends with wide double doors. The front entrance to the hall from the long porch around the house has wide paneled doors with a graceful fan light and reeded pilasters.

Mark and his second wife, Nancy, reared a large family in the hospitable home. He died here February 3, 1836. Their son, George Watkins, bought the home place from other heirs and remodeled the house. Sally Virginia, the oldest daughter of George Watkins Faulk, Sr. and wife, Mary Ann Shine, named their home "Sunnyside."

The property is presently owned by heirs of Henry Glenn Faulk, a grandson of Mark Sr. The house was recently restored.

Courtesy: Mrs. Hallie W. Faulk

## JEREMIAH A. THARPE HOME
Riggins Mill Road
Dry Branch, Ga.

This historic house was first built about one mile from where it now stands. An old family cemetery marks the general vicinity of where the original house once stood. Some years prior to 1850 Jeremiah had his old house dismantled and removed to its present location. The house has undergone certain structural changes through the years. The house as it was originally built at its present location had eight rooms and a kitchen, no hall. The main structure had six rooms, four downstairs and two upstairs, with two additional rooms (a two-story affair) attached—giving the house an "L" shape appearance. The kitchen, as was customary for the day, stood separate from the house. In 1907 B. D. Tharpe, Sr., grandson of Jeremiah, remodeled the house by dismantling certain portions and adding four new rooms and a hall.

The last major structural change occurred in 1923 when a large front porch was added. Other occupants and direct descendants of J. A. Tharpe were: The Alexander C. Tharpe Family and the Bill Dunn Tharpe, Sr. Family.

J. A. THARPE HOME
REV. VINCENT A. THARP HOME (1809)
Dry Branch, Georgia

"This historic house, built for Rev. V. A. Tharp, soldier of the Revolution, by his sons, John and Charnick, with slave labor in 1809, is the oldest known house in Twiggs County, then Wilkinson. The Tharp Family, who occupied this house-in-the-wilderness in 1811, helped to supply Baptist leadership in the surrounding area and the Ebenezer Baptist Association. Baptist notables were guest in this hospitable home—Rev. Polhill, Franklin, Ross, Rhodes, Baker, McGinity, Mercer and others. In 1832, the property was sold to John Parker for $600. Later owners have been Joe Burkett, P. W. Martin, American Clay Company, and Stone Creek Baptist Church. The hand hewn timbers and logs remain in this pioneer landmark."

—From the Marker erected in front of the house.

The house was recently remodeled inside and outside and presently being used as a pastorium for Stone Creek Baptist Church.

REV. V. A. THARPE HOME. ERECTED 1809

## THE WHITE HOUSE

August 30, 1847 in Athens, Georgia, Col. Daniel Greenwood Hughes and Miss Henrietta Cary Moore were married. Immediately, they left the Classic City, driving two horses to a carriage on a four-day trip over nigh impassable roads to a new house in Twiggs County, forty miles southeast of Macon near the present town of Danville.

The house of a most unusual architecture—six rooms with each two rooms a separate unit opening onto wide verandas (wonderful in summer but very uncomfortable in winter), an outside kitchen, not a closet in the house, and painted white with green blinds—welcomed the bride. Because the house was white, which was unusual at the time, it was soon known far and near as "The White House."

Among distinguished visitors to this home before and during the War-Between-the State was General Robert Toombs. Because of the warm friendship between General Toombs and Colonel Hughes, he escaped capture by the Yankees who came to this house on a searching expedition for this loyal patriot of the South, but failed in their secret mission.

"The White House," now a faded green, is still standing on Highway 80, near Danville, recalling days of long ago and pioneer builders of the County of Twiggs and the State of Georggia.

Courtesy: Henrietta Louise (Hennilu) Hughes

## WIMBERLY-JONES HOME
### Jeffersonville, Georgia

It is estimated that the original of this house, a log cabin, was built more than one hundred years ago. The two lower front rooms are the original structure. It has been remodeled and added to three times. The house now consists of 11 rooms and an attic. Many of the sills are of cedar.

The original structure was the home of Dr. Joshua Rhodes Wimberly and wife, Caroline H. Starr. Presently owned by W. E. Jones.

Ref.: The Twiggs County News Era, Sept. 29, 1939, and other sources.

### EZEKIEL WIMBERLY HOME

The second home built by Major General Ezekiel Wimberly in 1819 was a two-story log structure covered with wide boards. Typical of most southern homes, a large chimney was built at each end of the house. A wide, open hallway on the first floor divided the four main rooms on this level. The house was built on a ridge which divide the waters of the Oconee River and the Ocmulgee River. The ridge runs through the central part of the county. A spring was back of the house and one in front of the house from which the family brought their water until an open well was dug. The present location is two miles north from Jeffersonville on the east side of the Macon-Dublin-Savannah Railroad which parallels U.S. Highway No. 80.

When General LaFayette visited Macon in 1825, by request, General Wimberly's fine mahogany furniture was used at the Wayside Inn in entertaining the distinguished guests.

An unusual traditional story recounted by a granddaughter relating to the visits of Indians to this home runs: "Indians would come at times to General Wimberly's home seeking counsel. They trusted him as a friend. If they happened to be there at mealtime Mrs. Wimberly would feed them. At first she put the food in crockery dishes but they never would return the dish. They would break it when they finished eating because they sat in the open. Not wanting to have all of her dishes broken she put the food in a tin plate, this they washed and returned. She learned to serve their food in tin ware, always having the plates returned."

Two prized possessions of a granddaughter, Mrs. J. T. O'Neal, that her grandfather Ezekiel used during the War of 1812 are: a billy barlow knife and a brass button from his uniform.

The homeplace is currently owned by heirs of a great grandson, Ezekiel Jenkins Wimberly, Sr. No member of the family occupies the house.

Courtesy: Robert H. Bollinger, a great-great-grandson.

These old homes yet stand, some are occupied and some are not. It is almost impracticable to do other than name the following old homes since sufficient information was not available for a short sketch—(There may be other old houses in the county, but they were not submitted to the writers)—Barclay, Beckom, Bond, Balkcom, Cook, Maxwell, McCoy, Nelson, Epps, Ward, Gibson, LeGrande, Guerry, and according to tradition, the old house known as Jefferson's Inn, used as an inn during stagecoach days, presently stands in Jeffersonville.

## CHAPTER XI
## COMMUNICATION

Modern communication is a boost to progress. A town, community, or city cannot move forward and keep pace with neighboring competitive areas without adequate access to communications. Twiggs County affords a moderate system of communications.

TRANSPORTATION. The Southern Railway, Central of Georgia, and the Macon, Dublin and Savannah Railroad provide adequate rail service to most parts of the county. To supplement the rail service are the highway, bus and truck lines, which provide both through and local service to all parts of Twiggs, with ample connections to distant points.

### RAILROADS

CENTRAL OF GEORGIA RAILROAD. This railroad from Macon to Savannah winds its route through the northern section of Twiggs. The first rail of this line was laid in Savannah in 1835. In 1843, the roadbed and rails laid were completed to Macon. On October 13, 1843, an elaborate celebration was held in Macon given by the Company in honor of the surviving projectors of the enterprise. Many of the participants of the occasion who arrived on the first train passed over the entire length of the road.

During the War-Between-the-States General Sherman's troops destroyed the road as well as other properties from Gordon to Savannah during their march through this section of the country. Hardly had the enemy forces departed before the officials of the Central began to make preparation to rebuild the railroad.

SOUTHERN RAILROAD. The Southern tranverses the western part of Twiggs. It was chartered as the Macon and Brunswick Railroad on March 1, 1856. From 1882 until in 1894 it was known as the East Tennessee, Virginia and Georgia Railroad; in 1894 it became known as the Southern Railroad.

E. E. Crocker, of Twiggs County, was on the original Board of Directors. Grading of the road began in 1859 and was completed in 1869. J. C. Butler states in Historical Record of Macon and Central Georgia: "Mr. W. R. Phillips of Twiggs shipped the first cotton to Macon over this railroad to Coats and Wolfork."

As early as February, 1861, there was a regular train schedule from Macon to Bluff Road, the present Bullard Station, and by May of that year a regular schedule had been extended to Buzzard Roast, now West Lake. At certain times during the summer months, the Southern would run excursions to Adams Park, a planned town, then a vacationers' playground.

Over this railroad Confederate Soldiers leaving for service were transported to other points. The first company to leave from Pulaski County, Co. G. 8th Reg., Georgia Volunteers under Captain Ryan, camped at Buzzard Roost and was transported from this point to Macon over the railroad.

This road continued to progress during the great War period as shown by its station schedules within the borders of Twiggs, namely: Reids, Phillips (Huber), Bullard, Pace (Adams Park), Buzzard Roast (West Lake). (Additional resource material on this railroad was included in Harris' History of Pulaski-Bleckley County.)

### THE MACON, DUBLIN AND SAVANNAH RAILROADS
(Prepared by Mrs. Agnes Goss (H. L. D.) Hughes.)

The building of the Macon and Dublin Railroad was a dream realized by the late Dudley M. Hughes. His mother-in-law, Mrs. Hugh Lawson Dennard, said to him one day: "Dudley, why don't you move to the railroad instead of building one to your door?" He could easily have moved to the railroad, for his uncle, Seaborn J. May, left to him at his death, a beautiful Colonial home in Athens surrounded by a block of building lots in the heart of the business section of Athens. Here the Hughes family could have lived and educated their children at the popular Lucy Cobb and the University of Georgia. Mr. Hughes preferred to sell the Athens property and remain at his home in Twiggs County. Two of his children were educated there as boarding pupils: Hennilu at Lucy Cobb and Daniel G. Hughes at the University of Georgia, while Dennard, the eldest son, chose Mercer.

Dudley M. Hughes had other ideas. He knew that a railroad built through Twiggs and Laurens Counties would benefit all the farmers. Roads were unpaved at that time, and there would be passenger trains on which they could go to Macon to attend to business, buy their clothes, supplies for the farms, and above all else receive daily mail and The Macon Telegraph, and send their mail every day. Before the railroad was built, they received mail once a week and farmers alternated a weekly schedule of sending a Negro on a mule to Jeffersonville or Cochran or Buzzard's Roost for the mail.

Although no record can be found in the Macon office of the Macon, Dublin and Savannah Railroad, there are some residents of the Danville vicinity who remember Danville's first railroad agent, a starry-eyed little girl to whom prospective passengers reported at the home of her parents, the late Mr. and Mrs. Dudley M. Hughes, where they asked their little daughter, Hennilu, to flag the train for them. Hennilu, feeling as important as if she were president of the Railroad, would dash down the path through the woods to the railroad track where she climbed a tree and scanned the horizon for the first sign of smoke from the engine. On sighting the smoke, she told the prospective passengers that the train was approaching, and down from the tree she slid and flagged the train. This was her job by appointment, and she was known and loved by every engineer and conductor. All her life those trains and the men who ran the trains were dear to her, and whenever she passed trains as she drove her automobile in later years to Macon, she always graciously saluted the engineers. They knew her and always responded in a most friendly manner.

The dream of building a railroad was realized and the actual construction of the Macon and Dublin Railroad was begun August 17, 1885 and the construction was completed during July 1891. The name of the Company was changed May 31, 1890 to read, Macon, Dublin and Savannah Railroad Company, and under date of June 12, 1902, the charter of the Macon, Dublin and Savannah Railroad Company was amended, changing the home office of the Company to Macon, Bibb County, the former home office having been located at Dublin, Laurens County. This was the only railroad with home office in Macon. The extension from Dublin to Vidalia, a distance of approximately 39 miles, was commenced April, 1901 by the Illinois and Georgia Improvement Company and was completed during April, 1902, making a distance of 93 miles from Macon to Vidalia.

The actual date of the running of the first revenue train between Macon and Dublin was during December, 1891, according to records of the Macon office of the Macon and Dublin Railroad. The Macon Telegraph of July 23, 1891, carries the account of a barbecue held in Dublin on that date of the formal opening of the Macon and Dublin Railroad. All records of the Dublin office of the Railroad seem to have been lost when the transfer of the office to Macon was made.

The promoters of the Macon and Dublin Railroad were: Hon. Dudley Mays Hughes, his father, Hon. Daniel Greenwood Hughes, and Col. John M. Stubbs of Dublin. Minter Wimberly, Esq., was attorney for the Railroad.

Dudley M. Hughes was the first president of the Macon and Dublin Railroad. He was followed by James T. Wright for several years, James A. Blair, Jr., of New York, was president in 1912. During a subsequent period, S. Davis Warfield was president. Legh R. Powell, Jr. was president for 20 years, being succeeded in 1952 by John W. Smith.

Col. H. S. Morse was the first superintendent, and in 1910 R. A. Williams came to the Road as superintendent and retired in 1952, being succeeded by R. A. Walker.

The first agent of the Road at Danville was W. R. Haynes, and the Macon, Dublin and Savannah files in the Macon office give the following agents who served at Danville: Henry Carl Hodges, Norman Glisson Reeves, Frank C. Sumner, John Buford Franklin, William Lawrence Hardin, DeWitt Talmadge Mayfield, Miss Margie Nell Williams, and Mrs. Lillian Willis Wall.

The earliest records of agents in Jeffersonvile in the Macon files of the Macon, Dublin and Savannah Railroad give Robert Brown Norris, Walter Lee Hall, William Leonard Hines, Dewitt Talmadge Mayfield, Mrs. Ruth Rountree and James Maddox.

One of the leading stations along the M. D. and S. Line is Dry Branch. Through this office flows the greatest tonnage of any station along the route. Several of the known agents who served at ths office were: Jim Rogers, T. K. Horton, D. Z. Lindsey, R. L. Powell, B. Wills, a Mr. Johnson, R. N. Wood, D. T. Mayfield, F. G. Ross, O. L. McBryant, and W. L. Hardin.

Engineers from Macon records are A. J. Brundage, T. G. Reddy, R. Joiner and J. F. Heyser.

One of the first conductors on the M. D. and S. Railroad was Thomas L. Hill of Danville. R. C. Garrison was employed in 1904 and served until his death. T. E. Fowler was another old-time conductor.

From the Macon Telegraph of July 23, 1891, we quote: "To make a long story short, the Macon and Dublin has been completed and it can be said with truth and pride that not a cent of indebtedness rests on the road. The stockholders have paid

First trip of Macon and Dublin Train. Front row: Captain Dunn, Hon. Dudley M. Hughes, James T. Wright, Mrs. Dudley M. Hughes, Mrs. Dow Ripley. Second row: Merrill Callaway, Mrs. J. D. Stetson. Third row: Charlie Raleigh, Col L. D. Shannon, Dennard Hughes, Mrs J. D. Stetson, Dan G. Hughes and Miss Anne Crutchfield.
(Colored persons' names unknown.)

for construction and not a bond has been issued. The sum of $100,000 was subscribed among the large and small farmers."

An interesting feature was that during the grading of the Macon and Dublin Railroad, a rival railroad company known as the Sparks Company was grading a road on parallel lines with the Macon and Dublin Road. It was nip and tuck between the two, but the Macon and Dublin won, and succeeded in getting the charter for their railroad.

The passenger service on the M. D. and S. Railroad was discontinued on December 31, 1949, and since that time the railroad has been completely dieselized, its main line relaid with heavier rail and stone ballast and gravel applied, its physical property now being in splendid condition and handlng a good freight business.

Although the short line road was a wholly owned subsidiary of the Seaboard, the old and respected Macon and Dublin and Savannah Railroad was absorbed into the Seaboard Air Line Railroad Company on March 1, 1958.

The M. D. and S. never made it to Savannah except in its name, although the line was extended in that direction 39 miles to Vidalia.

## HIGHWAYS

The County has many miles of hard-surfaced roads including four major highways: U. S. 80, Ga. 57, U. S. 23-129—Ga. 87 and Ga. 96.

BUILDING GEORGIA HIGHWAY 87, U. S. 129. A direct route from Macon, through Twiggs County to Cochran and points south, was presented to the Georgia Highway Commission, with no material results, as early as 1923. Soon thereafter the Cochran Short Route Association was organized, with one objective, "The Short Route to Macon."

In 1925, the Association employed Captain Henry R. Collins of Cochran, an experienced road builder, to grade the road. Mr. Collins, together with certain Association Officials, went to Atlanta to meet with John N. Holder, the State Highway Chairman. The trip helped to bring about much needed aid in making the road become a reality. Mr. Holder made arrangements for the Association to use certain reconditioned machinery and provided a number of prisoners to use as laborers. Local road camps along the road route were located as follows: Tarversville, where the old Dr. Slappey home was headquarters, at Savage Creek, Belchers Branch and finally a camp near the John Denson Home. It took three years to complete the road through Twiggs.

The road was hard-surfaced with Twiggs County limestone in 1933-1936.

Highway factual data otained from the records of the State Highway Department of Georgia are as follows:
STATE ROUTE 18—Jeffersonville-Wilkinson County Line

Authorized to become part of the State System December 23, 1942, and grading and paving construction began in June, 1954, and was completed in December, 1955.
STATE ROUTE 19—Wilkinson County Line-Bibb County Line

This section of the State System is a part of the original 4,800 miles of county seat to county seat roads established in creating the State System of Roads by an Act of Legislature in 1919.

The first improvement on this state route began in April, 1921 and was completed in February, 1924; the contract was for grading and soil surfacing 9.30 miles, beginning at the Bibb County line, and extending southwestwardly toward Jeffersonville, including the construction of a bridge over a small stream near Dry Branch. That section of this state route begining at the Wilkinson County line in Danville and ending in Jeffersonville was graded, begining in April, 1924 and completed in April, 1925. This contract was 11.74 miles long.

# HISTORY OF TWIGGS COUNTY 161

The paving of State Route 19, U. S. 80 began at the Wilkinson County line in December, 1931, extending northwestwardly to the Bibb County line, and was completed in January, 1936; this construction was authorized in four contracts of 9.38 miles, 3.52 miles, 1.04 miles and 9.12 miles—a total of 23.06 miles.

STATE ROUTE 57—Jones County Line-Wilkinson County Line

Part of original 4,800 miles of the state system. The improvement of this road was authorized under two contracts, the grading started in February, 1937, and the paving completed in December, 1941.

STATE ROUTE 87—Bleckley County Line-Bibb County Line

Known as the Cochran Short Route from Macon, authorized to become part of the state system of roads October 16, 1929, by the Traylor-Neill Act.

On the contract for grading, soil surface and structures, work began in November, 1933, and the paving was completed in September, 1936. Beginning at the Bleckley County line and extending northwestwardly to the Bibb County line, consisting of 8 bridges totaling 0.21 miles, and 20.02 miles of paving, with a total length of 20.23 miles.

STATE ROUTE 112—Bleckley County Line-Wilkinson County Line.

That section of this route from the Houston County line near Westlake Station on the Southern Railroad to State Route 87 south of Tarversville became part of the state system of roads January 9, 1937, as State Route 127 in September, 1956. This section was relocated to a newly constructed road, beginning at the Houston County line and extending east to State Route 187 immediately north of Tarversville, and the State Route number changed to SR-96. This section of road was constructed under two contracts; 3.08 miles, including three bridges, beginning at the Houston County line and extending east 3.08 miles; construction began in July, 1954 and was completed in October, 1956. In December, 1954, construction began on 2.55 miles of this road, to complete the paving to SR-87. This construction was completed in October, 1956.

That section of SR-96 between Tarversville and Jeffersonville was added to the state system of roads January 9, 1937, with the grading and paving construction beginning in March, 1950, at SR-87 and completed in July, 1950, ending at SR-19 in Jeffersonville, a distance of 12.66 miles.

That section of SR-96, beginning with a junction of SR-19 in Jeffersonville and extending east to the Wilkinson County line was made part of the state system of roads on January 1, 1935; it is 3.71 miles long; a contract for grading the entire section and paving the section within the city limits of Jeffersonville was authorized in January, 1939 and construction completed in August, 1939; construction for paving that section beginning at the city limits of Jeffersonville and ending at the Wilkinson County line was started in December, 1946 and completed in August, 1947.

STATE ROUTE 112—Bleckley County Line-Wilkinson County Line

This section of road was added to the state system July 15, 1939, with the construction for paving this road beginning in February, 1950 and completed in June 1950. The bridge over Rocky Creek was in place when the road was added to the state system of roads.

## TELEPHONE SYSTEMS
## THE DRY BRANCH, GEORGIA TELEPHONE COMPANY

The indenture for establishing the Dry Branch Telephone Company was drawn up April 25, 1911. T. S. Tharpe was the authorized agent of the Company in charge of buildings, improvements, appliances, etc. The capital stock of the Company was

$1000.00 and each share of capital stock was $100.00. The principal business office was at Dry Branch in Twiggs County.

Persons recorded as having shares of capital stock in the local Company were: P. W. Martin, Cecil Morgan, T. S. Tharpe, George W. Tharpe, S. T. Burkett, George W. Burkett and B. D. Tharpe, Sr.

Today this community is served by the Macon Telephone System of which it is an integral part.

## JEFFERSONVILLE TELEPHONE COMPANY

Mr. James Jackson Wall built the original plant about the year 1905. He later traded or sold the business to a Mr. Stephens, then it went under the name of Stephen-Carey Telephone Company. The bank of Soperton foreclosed on the Stephen-Carey Company and a Mr. Thompson came in possession of the business. It was Mr. Thompson who had the Company chartered in 1919 under the name of the Jeffersonville Telephone Company. Later owners have been Charlie C. Humphries and W. G. Spears. On January 1, 1939, Mr. Spears sold the Company to O. B. Lineberger who continues to own and operate the Company.

## DANVILLE TELEPHONE COMPANY

The Danville Telephone Company began business about 1914. Mrs. Mitt Williams was the operator. In 1915, Mrs. Williams sold the Company to Dr. J. A. Hembree; in 1918, Dr. Hembree sold it to E. J. Davidson; in 1925 Mr. Davidson sold it to W. G. Spears, and in 1939 Mr. Spears sold the Danville Exchange to O. B. Lineberger of Jeffersonville who had also purchased the Jeffersonville Telephone Company. Today the citizens of both Danville and Jeffersonville enjoy the same service and are operated as one business.

Ref.: Information on both the Jeffersonville and Danville Telephone Companies was compiled by Mrs. Irene W. Gleeson.

## NEWSPAPERS

The Twiggs County New Era (Jeffersonville) is the only local newspaper published in the County. "A Warm Advertising Medium" is the way in which the New Era characterizes itself. Special editions of the paper have been published from time to time, including school issues, an FFA issue, a special Thanksgiving issue following the close of World War II in 1945.

In 1937, the publication, which appears each Thursday, won first place in the War Cry contest. Later it won a third place citation in the same competition, and it placed in the GPA "most fearless editorial" category. All editorials were written by the late C. C. McCrory, owner of the paper.

Local papers which have been published in Twiggs County include the Twiggs County Tribune (1890), The Twiggs Herald, The Twiggs County Citizen, The Middle Georgian, Twiggs County Local, The New Era, and The Twiggs County New Era. The editors include Albert Courtney Wimberly, John J. Wimberly, Samuel Lowrie, J. W. Bradshaw, J. E. Moses, H. P. Griffin, Jr., W. C. Kelly, J. H. Reese. Cowan E. Jones, A. K. Smith, R. E. White, J. A. Peacock, J. S. Abercrombie, C. C. McCrory and Mrs. Lois W. (C. C.) McCrory.

## TELEGRAPH SERVICE

Generally telegraph service is as close as a telephone. Limited public telegraph service is available through the several railroad depot offices of the County.

## U. S. MAIL SERVICE

Local mail service is generally adequate—rural deliveries as well as urban deliveries and dispatches are made daily. Post offices serving the citizens of Twiggs include: Cochran, Danville, Dry Branch, Gordon, Huber, Jeffersonville and Macon.

A special built U. S. Mail cart for Rural Free Delivery at Jeffersonville in early 1900's, Wm. Rufus Carswell, carrier.

## TELEVISION

The only television studio and broadcasting station in Middle Georgia is located in Twiggs, the WMAZ-TV Station. The station is on the Cochran Short Route, Ga. Highway No. 87, U. S. 129 near the Twiggs-Bibb County line.

The information contained in this communication chapter does not present a composite picture of the Twiggs communication scene. This is due largely to the additional advantages afforded Twiggs through urban Bibb County, as air travel, radio facilities, et cetera.

# CHAPTER XII

# ORGANIZATIONS OF TWIGGS COUNTY

## MAJOR GENERAL JOHN TWIGGS CHAPTER
## DAUGHTERS OF THE AMERICAN REVOLUTION

The Regent of Georgia State Society of the National Society, Daughters of the American Revolution, Mrs. Robert H. Humphrey, appointed J. Lanette O'Neal Faulk, Mrs. Hugh Lawson, as Organizing Regent on June 8, 1955 to make the necessary preparations for the organization of a local chapter in Twiggs County. The membership of the Twiggs ladies in the John Ball Chapter, D.A.R., had grown too numerous for the best interest of the Chapter's work.

The organizational meeting for the Twiggs Chapter was held in the home of Mrs. Hugh Lawson Faulk on August 18, 1955, with Mrs. Alton V. White, Sr., as co-hostess. At this meeting the hostesses presented a gavel as a "love gift" to the Chapter.

Mrs. Humphrey, presiding as State Installing Officer, installed the following elected officers: Regent, Mrs. Hugh Lawson Faulk; Vice Regent, Mrs. Ezekiel J. Wimberly; Recording Secretary, Mrs. J. T. Early; Corresponding Secretary, Mrs. Joseph W. Faulk, Sr..; Treasurer. Miss Ruth Chapman; Chaplain, Mrs. Kathleen J. Carswell; Registrar, Mrs. J. T. McCormick; Historian, Mrs. S. S. Jones; Librarian, Mrs. A. W. Adams.

The Chapter organized with twenty-eight charter members, namely: Mesdames Glenn Adams (A. W.); Mary W. Bailey (J. N.); Estelle J. Balcom (J. H.); Virginia H. Cadden (J. T.); Kathleen J. Carswell (W. R.); Elizabeth G. C. Chapman (O. T.); Grace T. Crawford (P. G.); Lucile W. Day (H. C.); Wilma A. Early (J. T.); Cletia A. Faulk (J. W.); J. Lanette O. Faulk (H. L.); Laura W. Faulk (H. G.); M. Austelle S. Faulk (J. W.); Ethleen H. Howell (Hugh); Agnes G. Hughes (H. L. D.); E. Opal T. Jones (S. S.); Cornelia J. McCormick (J. T.); Margaret W. O'Neal (J. T.); Clara B. Porter (C. B.); Edna T. Powell (R. L.); Inez R. Shedd (J. P.); Lizzie K. Wall (W. T.); Julia F. White (A. V., Sr.); L. Rosaline D. White (A. V., Jr.); Helen D. Wimberly (E. J.); Frances L. T. Wood (V. E.); Misses Ruth Chapman and Jennie Wimberly.

The Chapter was confirmed by National Society Board of Management on October 13, 1955 as a functioning Chapter duly organized.

The Chapter's name honors the illustrious Revolutionary hero, Major General John Twiggs, whose name was a synonym of terror to the British.

The following members have been accepted by National Society since October 13, 1955: Mesdames Patricia A. Wimberly Frazier (W. R.); L. Irene Wimberly Gleeson (C. C.); Clara Cox Miller (J. C.); Elizabeth Hendricks Pierce (V. K.); Austelle S. Faulk Singleton (C. D.); Charlotte Wimberly Smith (T. R.); Mary E. Hendricks Wilson (D. P., Jr.); Misses L. Annette Duggan; M. Jane Faulk; Neva King; Madge R. Pierce; and M. Evelyn Wimberly.

Presently there are thirty-five members. Two charter members deceased, Mrs. Laura W. Faulk, Mrs. Lizize K. Wall; lost four members by transfer to other chapters.

The objects of the Society are to perpetuate the memory and spirit of the men and women who achieved American Independence; to promote the development of enlightened public opinion and to foster patriotic citizenship.

The most outstanding project of the Chapter has been to sponsor the publication of the *History of Twiggs County*, other than marking historical sites and Revolutionary soldiers' graves in the County.

## MAJOR GENERAL JOHN TWIGGS CHAPTER, DAUGHTERS OF THE AMERICAN REVOLUTION
### CHAPTER OFFICERS 1958-1960

Mrs. Ezekiel J. Wimberly
Regent

Mrs. Clara Bradley Porter
Vice Regent

Mrs. W. Rufus Carswell
Chaplain

Mrs. Charles C. Gleeson
Recording Secretary

Mrs. H. Dennard Hughes
Corresponding Secretary

Mrs. John T. McCormick
Treasurer

Mrs. Hugh L. Faulk, Sr.
Registrar

Mrs. Joseph W. Faulk, Sr.
Historian

Mrs. V. Kendricks Pierce
Librarian

FIRST CHAPTER PROJECT AFTER THE ORGANIZATION OF THE MAJ. GEN. JOHN TWIGGS CHAPTER.—Unveiling of Revolutionary Marker, historic site of original Stone Creek Baptist Church and old church cemetery near Bibb-Twiggs Line. Sponsored by Major Gen. John Twiggs and John Ball Chapters, D. A. R., October 30, 1955. Front row, L. to R.: Mrs. Eleanor D. McSwain, Mrs. Lanette O. Faulk, Regent, Rev. R. F. Floyd, Mrs. Edna T. Powell, Mrs. Lillian T. Johnston, Mrs. Kathleen J. Carswell, Miss Ann Wood, Mrs. T. E. Bloodworth, Regent. Back row, L. to R.: Billy W. Jones, Jere A. Tharpe, Jimmy Balcom, B. D. Tharpe, Jr., and James Beck.

Float entered by Maj. Gen. John Twiggs Chapter, D. A. R., in the Twiggs County High School parade April 4, 1959 at Jeffersonville. Placed second. L. to r. Thomas H. Faulk, Raynor Early, Alton V. White, III, Mrs. A. V. White, Sr., Mrs. C. C. Gleeson. Theme—Home and Country.

## OLD MARION CHAPTER, D. A. R.

The Old Marion Chapter was organized March 21, 1922. In 1923, the chapter had twelve members, only ten of them active, and two papers in Washington. After the Chapter disbanded on February 2, 1933, several members, by invitation, joined the John Ball Chapter of Irwinton.

Since the organization of the Major General John Twiggs Chapter in 1955, some of the former members of the Old Marion Chapter have become members of this recently organized Chapter.

## THE JEFFERSONVILLE WOMAN'S CLUB

The origin of the Jeffersonville Woman's Club began in a Home Demonstration Club. It was organized October 16, 1926 by Mrs. K. J. Carswell and a group of interested women.

The Club was known as The Worthwhile Club and Mrs. J. H. Whitehurst served as its first president.

This study group prepared and presented many interesting programs on vital subjects, such as Health, Music, Art, Religions, Literature, History, Books, Home Economics, Politics, Parliamentary Law, Citizenship, and recreation for the entire family.

Fairs, flower shows, better homes and gardens as well as other various home demonstration projects were sponsored by the Club.

County Library—Mrs. E. E. Rozier, Sr. and Mrs. T. E. Methvin, Libarians.

In 1928, the Club withdrew its affiliation with the Home Demonstration Clubs and joined the State Federation of Women's Clubs, thereby changing its name to The Jeffersonville Woman's Club. Its main project has been the sponsorship of a county library which was started in the summer of 1935 and has operated since that time through the cooperation of the Twiggs County Board of Education, the Twiggs County Board of Roads and Revenue, The Jeffersonville Woman's Club and the Works Progress Administration. Mrs. Bertha D. Methvin served as its first libarian.

After the W. P. A. aid ceased, other organizations and the mining industry assisted in its financial operation.

The library began with a nucleus of four books, at the present time has 5,311, is a member of the Regional Library Association, being served monthly by the Washington Memorial Bookmobile of Macon.

A gift of $1,000 was received from Dr. W. S. Jones of Menominee, Mich., a former Twiggs Countian. The money was invested and the interest is used to purchase books by Georgia authors or books concerning Georgia.

Since its organization the Club has participated in all drives and endeavors that relate to the health and progress of the County.

In 1957, the Twiggs County High School lunch room was purchased and moved to a location on the Irwinton Highway. This building was renovated and redecorated and serves as the home of The Jeffersonville Woman's Club.

Committee:
Mrs. Bertha D. Methvin
Mrs. Ira King
Mrs. W. E. Jones, Chairman

## TOWN AND COUNTRY GARDEN CLUB

The Town and Country Garden Club of Twiggs County was organized in the home of Mrs. Kathleen J. Carswell in August, 1953.

Objectives:
1. To plant at least a dozen new bulbs each year.
2. To cooperate with the City and Civic Organizations in beautifying the town.
3. To hold at least two Flower Shows—Camellia and Daffodil—each club year.
4. To cooperate with the Jeffersonville Woman's Club in their Spring Show.
5. To start a club scrapbook and each member to keep one of the work done in her garden and in the club.
6. To sponsor yard improvement among the colored homemakers.

Officers: President, Mrs. Shines Faulk; Vice President, Mrs. D. C. Adams; Secretary, Mrs. Ira King; Treasurer, Mrs. A. T. Land, Sr.

Charter members: Mrs. A. W. Adams, Mrs. D. C. Adams, Mrs. K. J. Carswell, Mrs. Orman Daniel, Mrs. C. A. Duggan, Mrs. A. M. Gates, Sr., Mrs. Shines Faulk, Mrs. Mark B. Faulk, Mrs. Ira King, Mrs. A. T. Land, Mrs. Bruce Richardson, Mrs. G. F. Rogers, Mrs. E. E. Rozier, Sr., Mrs. Alton V. White, Sr., Mrs. Lowe Wall, Mrs. Tom Worsham, Mrs. E. J. Wimberly.

Past Presidents: Mrs. K. J. Carswell, Mrs. A. W. Adams, Mrs. C. A. Duggan.

The Club has sponsored several outstanding projects, to mention a few: Three standard daffodil flower shows, the establishment of a Roadside Park on Highway 80 near Allentown, two fall flower shows, work shops in flower arrangement, some plantings at Twiggs County High School, and sponsoring the selection of "Woman of the Year" in horticulture and arrangements.

"He that planteth a tree is a servant of God; he provideth a kindness for many generations, and faces that he hath not seen shall bless him."—Van Dyke.

Mrs. A. M. Gates, Sr.

## TWIGGS AND BRANCH GARDEN CLUB
Dry Branch, Georgia

This Club was organized at the home of Mrs. Sally J. (D.J.) Fargason, Kaolin Village, March, 1955, with seven charter members: Mesdames A. G. Bowman, D. J. Fargason, Paul Hinson, Pat Livingston, Roy Kennedy, Claude Saunders, Georgia Tice. Later members were: Mesdames W. H. Wester, B. A. Leslie, G. F. Christenbery, E. R. Dotson, Tully J. Johnston, D. F. Lewis, C. S. Welch, Thomas Wood, John Smith, and B. F. Howe. Mrs. S. C. Lyons and Mrs. Kathleen Jones Carswell were honorary members.

New members are received only by invitation and membership is limited to fifteen.

The stated purpose of the Club is, "Growth of self and community through service and knowledge." Programs alternate between the study of flower culture and the study of foreign customs and cookery.

Mrs. D. J. Fargason

## TWIGGS COUNTY DEVELOPMENT CORPORATION

The Twiggs County Development Corporation, organized August, 1952, serves as the county's Chamber of Commerce. It was chartered in October, 1952, term of Twiggs Superior Court to insure sound growth in the area. Stock was sold at $50. per share. Annual stockholder's meeting are held in July. Capital is on Savings at The Four County Bank. Interest is used to pay office expenses as members donate their services.

First Officers: D. Y. Califf, president; A. T. Land, Sr., vice president; B. W. Wright, executive vice president; E. E. Rozier, Sr., executive secretary; Miss Mary Hart Whitehurst, secretary; W. H. Martin, treasurer. First Directors: J. E. Beck, A. G. Bowman, D. Y. Califf, Mrs. K. J. Carswell, C. A. Duggan, Brady Johnson, A. T. Land, Sr., Earl Smtih, and W. V. Watson.

Other Presidents: J. E. Beck, 1954-'55; C. E. Tweedle, 1955-'56; J. T. Early, 1956-'58; D. J. Fargason, 1958-

Address: Twiggs County Development Corporation, c/o Miss Mary Hart Whitehurst, Secretary, Box 66, Jeffersonville, Ga., phone 2441.

Mary Hart Whitehurst

## HISTORY OF TWIGGS COUNTY NEWSPAPERS

The Twiggs County New Era was established in 1927 by J. S. Abercrombie, following the discontinuance of the Twiggs County Local, which was a successor to the Middle Georgian. Earlier county papers were The Twiggs County Tribune, The Twiggs Herald, Twiggs County Citizen, and The Middle Georgian.

The following have served as editors of these various papers: John J. Wimberly, Samuel Lowrie, J. W. Bradshaw, J. E. Moses, H. F. Griffin, Jr., W. C. Kelley, J. H. Reese, Cowan E. Jones, A. K. Smith, R. E. White, and J. A. Peacock. In August of 1929, Mr. and Mrs. C. C. McCrory bought the New Era from Mr. Abercrombie and it is now edited and published by Mrs. McCrory, Mr. McCrory having passed away in 1956.

During the present ownership, the New Era, though a small, four-page, six-column paper published weekly, has received some statewide, as well as national, recognition. In 1937 the Georgia Press Association awarded the Twiggs County New Era first place for having written and published the best religious editorial of the year. During other years the New Era has received honorable mention for publication of another religious editorial and the most fearless editorial by judges of the Georgia Press Association.

"Handmaiden of Sorrow," or "No Respector of Persons," written by Mr. McCrory and published in the New Era, was given national recognition when it was carried in the Union Signal, the National WCTU publication, which is printed at Evanston, Ill. and printed in The Knickerbocker Press, Albany, N. Y. The Gospel Fisherman's Team of Maine secured permission from the writer to print "No Respector of Persons" in tract form for distribution, giving the New Era credit. Rev. J. J. D. Hall of New York, otherwise known as the "Bishop of Wall Street," remarked that it was the finest and the strongest article on the subject that he had ever read. He asked permission to print and distribute the article. Mr. McCrory was an ardent prohibitionist and he never failed to let his readers understand where he stood on this subject.

The Twiggs County New Era is the official organ of Twiggs County. No other newspaper is published in the county.

Lois W. McCrory

## TWIGGS COUNTY DEPARTMENT OF PUBLIC WELFARE

The Twiggs County Department of Public Welfare began organization July 1, 1937. The Welfare Reorganization Act of 1937 provided for a State Department of Public Welfare and, for each county, a County Department of Public Welfare, composed of a Board of Welfare, consisting of five members appointed by the Board of County Commissioners, and an office staff, appointed by the Board of Welfare, each subject to approval by the State Department of Public Welfare.

Those serving on the Board of Welfare have been as follows: W. W. Wood, W. W. Johnston, W. G. Mercer, W. P. Burns, E. D. Maxwell, Jr., W. H. Lamb, D. S. McGee, and S. S. Jones.

Those currently serving on the Board of Welfare, several of whom have served many years, are: C. E. Mercer, Chairman, Mrs. H. L. Chance, O. T. Chapman, J. P. Moore, and G. F. Rogers.

Office staff has included Mrs. Louise B. Hicks, Director, and Miss Mary Evelyn Wimberly, stenographer.

The function of the agency has been to administer a welfare program of assistance and service to people meeting eligibility requirements and approved by the Board of Welfare.

Since July 1, 1937 through December 31, 1958, the Special Assistance program in Twiggs County has provided:

| | |
|---|---|
| Old Age Assistance | $1,233,539.75 |
| Aid to Blind | $ 48,608.50 |
| Aid to Dependent Children | $ 188,342.00 |
| Aid to Disabled | $ 96,193.00 |
| Total | $1,566,683.25 |

Services have been certifications or referrals for: Cancer Control Clinic, Eugene Talmadge Memorial Hospital, Macon Heart Clinic, Division of Vocational Rehabilitation, Child Welfare Foster Home Care, Adoptions, and services to other agencies.

The welfare agency has sought not only to help people in need and trouble, but also to serve a useful purpose in the community.

(Mrs.) Louise B. Hicks

## EXTENSION SERVICE IN TWIGGS COUNTY

Reports show that the Agricultural Extension Service in Georgia was inaugurated by the State College of Agriculture in 1908. The first Extension work consisted of an educational train which made a tour of every county having a railroad. Twiggs County was one of the counties visited, and many citizens met the train as it stopped at Jeffersonville. The interest was keen as the crowds came to look, talk, and listen to those in charge. So well did the train fill a need that the next legislature made an appropriation for Extension teaching of $10,000. By 1911 it had been increased to $40,000.

The Twiggs County School Superintendent, B. S. Fitzpatrick, was fully convinced that many of the needs of the county could be met by having a "demonstrator" to help the farm families help themselves. Miss Lucile Methvin (Mrs. Kirby Smith), a teacher in one of the twenty-six small schools in the county, was chosen to start the program.

During the summer of 1913 after school closed, for a period of six weeks, Miss Methvin, using her father's horse and buggy, after having purchased an "out-door" canner which included a rectangular compartment with rack for cooking with a firebox underneath using two joints of stove pipe, a capping iron and tipping steel for sealing the tin cans, began her visits to homes in the county. The flux for using the solder was made by dissolving old mason jartops in hydrocholric acid. The buggy was loaded with this equipment plus as many tin cans as possible and bulletins for canning peaches and tomatoes. She went into the homes where the women and girls requested help; generally spending a week in a community as distances were too great to go home each night. Each day with a fire going in the canner, the family gathered their products and at night tired but pleased with the cans that were ready for storage to be used that winter. For two summers this program was continued.

In 1916 and 1917, Mrs. Vernon H. Johnson (Mrs. J. Hunter Johnson) was named "Demonstrator" and served nine months of the year. To her was added the duty of encouraging girls from 12 to 14 years old to plant one-tenth acre of tomatoes and can them for home consumption. All of this was done through personal contacts and with families that desired help.

The County Board of Education, realizing that the boys were being neglected and could have a part on the program through organized Corn Clubs, particularly since the passage of the Smith-Lever Bill by Congress in 1914, making available federal funds to be matched by state funds. sponsored the project. This gave a great impetus to the Extension Work. O. D. Hall became the first County Agent in 1916. The Boys' Club for growing corn was launched. During this time the men in the county recognized the value of the training these men had and what a help they could be to their farming programs. So Mr. Hall spent much time in helping with terracing of the land and to secure pure bred hogs and cattle. No formal organizations were started, still the work was on the individual help for both boys and men.

During the year 1918, following the resignation of J. E. Thomason and J. L. Turk, County Agents, who served one year each, Miss Bertha Dunevent (Mrs. T. E. Methvin) came to work as a Home Demonstration Agent on a ten months employment basis, the months of December and January excepted. World War I brought many new problems. The state-wide slogan of "Making two blades of grass grow where one grew before" was heard on all sides, so gardening became her major project with both women and girls. In her car she carried, maybe— a soapstone, a bucket, a lard can, and some sawdust—ready to show the womenfolk how to construct a fireless cooker; or maybe a frame with cloths to show how to make a cooler; or it might be the trusted outdoor canner; or maybe it might have been school books.

For one of her duties was the teaching of the many illiterates to read and write. Schools were held for adults, utilizing farm problems for the teaching of reading, writing, arithmetic, as well as giving information about newer methods of farm activities. These meetings were held at night, generally, at the school buildings.

One day schools were held for women to learn about canning other products and to make bread. They were encouraged to raise feed for their poultry flocks. The gathering of hickory nuts, walnuts and pecan hulls was stressed; they were placed in barrels and shipped to be used in the making of gas masks for soldiers overseas.

For the first time the girls started a sewing project—an apron with an emblem on it showing a red tomato and the blue H's—Heart, Head, Hand and Health. A sewing bag and two cup towels were added to the list of sewing to be done. In the fall an exhibit was made of their work, the boys and girls were now 4-H Club members.

Next came Miss Adnah Duckworth in 1920-22 and to her was given the priviledge of starting the organization of women into clubs; Danville was the first, then Cannon next to fall into line. The Cannon Home Demonstration Club has been continuous with several of the original members still active in that club. Singing was added to the program and "Miss Duck" and her guitar were in demand, particularly among the boys and girls. In fact, some form of recreation was given at each club meeting that was held monthly at the schools and homes of the women.

In 1921, Davis S. McGee became County Agent and served two years. Added to the boys' projects were gardening, cotton and growing of sweet potatoes, as 4-H projects. Just after Mrs. Kathleen J. Carswell became the Home Demonstration Agent, following the resignation of Miss Duckworth, the first county-wide exhibit of boys and girls 4-H projects was held. The band from Gordon Institute, Barnesville came for the day, adding much to the crowd's pleasure.

From 1923 until 1929, there was no County Agent with the exception of two assistant agents, one serving a month and the other four months in 1927 and 1928.

During this time the women and girls clubs continued to grow and expand their programs. Several times during this period the women appeared before the County Board of Education and County Commissioners asking for an appropriation for the services of a County Agent. Many of the duties of a County Agent was given to Mrs. Carswell: for instance, the first farmer cooperative purchase of fertilizer was made; 30 car loads averaging 30 to 40 tons per car were purchased at a savings of $6.00 for the large orders to $9.00 for the small purchaser. Certified sweet potato plants were purchased cooperatively. The first car of poultry was sold, the train stopping in Jeffersonville and Danville. Farmers were carried to poultry meetings and pasture demonstrations.

The women formed a Home Demonstration Council in December 1932 with Miss Hennilu Hughes serving as the first County President for the nine Home Demonstration Clubs in the county.

The first two-day short course was held in New Haven Baptist Church; the second at Moore's School Building. The girls canned beans, tomatoes, corn and soup mixture. They put up peach and fig products, many of which were "Fancy packed."

The fireless cooker was still in use, but the first pressure cooker was soon brought into use, shortening the time for canning procedures. Several clubs bought a large community pressure cooker. The Home Demonstration Agent's personal cooker was used over the county. The first meat canning was done at an all-day meeting in the Grand Jury Room of the courthouse. An entire calf was canned during the day. This came about during the height of the depression of the '30's.

Many hours were spent in teaching the women to drive a car, particularly after one woman told that she would not be able to come to club meetings as there was no place to turn around under ten miles from the meeting place that was large enough for a circle.

Exhibits were sent to the Georgia State Fair, in Macon. Delegates went to state meetings in Athens, State College of Agriculure.

Dresses were made over or new ones constructed; machines overhauled; chairs were upholstered, curtains made that were stenciled with many designs. Landscaping contests were held with Mrs. Clara Porter of Danville winning the first state-wide contest. She used native shrubbery almost all together.

During the five years of W. A. Sutton's service in the county, 1929-1934, the boys' clubs increased. A pig chain started even though Mr. Sutton found one or two of the chain pigs hanging in the smoke houses instead of being kept for the offspring of the pig to go back into the chain. An egg circle was formed using Rhode Island Reds, improved strain, as the breeder stock; a few of the newer type of poultry houses were built. The boys' first camp was held. Coton growing was one of the most popular projects for the boys until the first "plow-up" program was ordered by the Federal Government.

During the depression years the county felt that the services of both the County and Home Agents were needed more than ever, so they were placed on 12-month year employment. Both Mrs. Carswell and Mr. Sutton were given additional duties besides the goal of "more food and feed produced at home." They helped with placement of W. P. A. workers; distribution of food given by the Red Cross; checking and helping with the enlistment of the C. C. C. boys; helping with the holding of Clinics for removal of tonsils and adenoids. The latter was sponsored by the

Cannon Home Demonstration Club with Macon doctors giving their services free; aiding with the purchasing of seed and food that must be bought. The first pine trees were planted on the farm of J. H. Balcom by the 4-H boys of Danville. The first work of the AAA was under the supervision of the County Agent. For the first time a clerk for the Agents was employed by the Extension Service.

Upon the resignation of Mrs. Carswell after more than 12 years of service, Mrs. Mary C. Bennett was named Home Agent and Milledge White filled Mr. Sutton's place, who also resigned, both resignations took place in 1934. They continued the programs started as the county slowly pulled out of those depression years. Once more camps and recreational meetings were held. Field demonstrations became more numerous, a few more trees were planted. The organizations were strengthened, numerically as well as in an ability to do for themselves. A poultry chain was started over the state in which 4-H members in Twiggs County took a part. Each fall saw better and more pullets brought in for sale to pay for the 100 baby chicks given out in the spring. This program has continued through the years. Now the 4-H members had from 20 to 30 projects from which to choose, with each carrying two or more. The child care and training program started under Mrs. Carswell expanded and all sorts of crafts were added to the program but keeping the basic fundamentals of feeding and clothing the family.

A week at camp was one of the highlights of each 4-H member. The women found that they could do a better homemaker's job by going away for a few days, so they, too, had a camp.

For a year, 1935-36, Miss Elizabeth Richards served the county as Home Demonstration Agent adding some special programs in the study of nutrition. During this time, a mattress making program for low income families to help use the surplus cotton and to improve family living was started and completed during the time of Miss Rodgers' service.

D. L. Moseley, T. C. Llwellyn and V. E. Lindsey each served a year as agents. During this time Rural Electrification was added in the rural areas, so much of the County and Home Agent's time was spent in helping the farm families in the purchases and learning the use of electrical equipment.

Miss Ora Kate Rodgers, Miss Kathleen Brown and Miss Elizabeth Zellner served one year each. They added to the program as outlined—"making the home a better place in which to live" by adding refinishing furniture; making slip covers; selection of pictures and other accessories for the home. Girls and women both were taking an important part in program of work for some of them were starting to give demonstrations to their neighbors.

"Slip Cover Days" were fun time as well as worthwhile for the owners of the furniture. Planning whole meals for better diets were also popular.

Mrs. Julia P. Kitchens working with Mr. Lindsey and G. D. Branch, all employed during the years of 1945 through 1950, through larger and better organizations reached more farm families; training more 4-H members to become demonstrators for their communities and taking part in state-wide contests. Exhibits at the Georgia State Fair were greatly improved. Since the use of electricity gave more time for the homemaker she utilized the time to acquire skills in the making of crafts—using wood, copper, reed for basketry, hooked and crocheted rugs; growing flowers for sale; landscaping the home grounds; more improved home poultry flocks and the freezing of home grown products were the more popular projects for the women. Among the farmers more attention was given to pastures, more corn per acre, more small grain and soil building crops, part of this was due to the smaller acreage of cotton. An increase of trees were planted; pines, mostly, while some of the boys tried their hand at growing cypress for sale as Christmas trees. Tours were made to gain knowledge as to best procedures.

Mrs. Kitchens showed a special love for the 4-H members and during the five-year period of service the 4-H Clubs responded by entering and completing more projects than ever before. She died in service in November, 1951.

H. F. Shurling, 1949 through 1955, worked with Miss Betty Hardin, Mrs. Lucy Worth Faulk, and Geraldine Ellis Morris, continued the programs by helping make the adjustments through the crop and acreage reductions as outlined by the National Government. Freezing of foods almost replaced the canning program of yesteryear.

With the coming of Dewitt Harrell and Mrs. Ora Kate Rodgers Burke as Extension Agents, in 1955-56, a new Rural Development Program began. Additional personnel were employed for the office's two assistants for the County Agents and one Assistant Home Agent and an extra clerk in the office.

In May, 1956, Twiggs became Georgia's and the Nation's first pilot county in the new United States Department of Agriculture sponsored Rural Development Program. Pilot counties were chosen throughout the country to pioneer in a new program designed to combine and intensify efforts of local people and government agencies in speeding up the rate of rural resource development. In implementing the program, Congress appropriated additional funds to be used in helping local people secure needed technical and educational assistance. In Twiggs County these additional funds were used to expand and intensify the educational and service activities of the Agricultural Extension Service, Social Security Administration, Soil Conservation Service, Farmers' Home Administration and other agencies. The Extension Service was able to expand its portion of the program by employing two new assistant agricultural agents, one assistant home demonstration agent and one additional office clerk.

Among the first and perhaps most far-reaching accomplishments of the Rural Development Program in Twiggs County was the welding together of rural and urban interests. Town and country people were encouraged to view the development of Twiggs County as a common problem rather than as discrete sets of rural problems on the other.

As a result of this understanding, people in Twiggs County were able to come together on common ground, appraise their situation and make long range plans for more fully developing and utilizing their total resources. Underlying these plans and the activities they have engendered is a deep and abiding belief that Twiggs is on the road to progress and that all Twiggs Countians stand to share in the benefits of that progress. With a Rural Development Program guided and directed by the combined, informed leadership of agriculture, business and civic interests, it is easy to visualize a Twiggs County of the future far superior to even our boldest dreams of a few years ago.

Although the Rural Development Program is new, many worthwhile accomplishments have been made in the past three years. Quoting Secretary of Agriculture Benson (Rural Development is the program initiated by the local people and Washington not calling the balls and strikes.)

The Rural Development Program is a program in its first stages. Five individual working committees were organized consisting of Agriculture, Industry, Education, Health, and Religion. Each contributing an equal proportion to Rural improvement.

The Extension Program has been of the same nature as it was before, except more fields of opportunity has been endeavored and more personnel were employed making available increased individual supervision.

Under the program drastic and important changes has taken place involving the adults and the youth programs. Some of the outstanding accomplishments has been an increase from four boys and girls attending Project Achievement Meeting in 1955 to approximately 50 boys and girls in 1959. The new method of feeding and producing swine caused pig parlors and farrowing houses to spring up in many locations of the county. County-wide recreational programs were started reaching approximately 425 boys and girls.

In an effort to increase crop production and soil fertility, 10 farmers were selected as Farm Unit Test Demonstrators, placing their entire farm under demonstration methods. They received unlimited amounts of various fertilizer materials through the Tennessee Valley Authority at a reduced price. This encouraged these 10 farms to increase fertilizer applications which has served as an educational program for other county farmers.

Three homes were established as county demonstration homes for landscaping purposes. The Extension Landscape Specialist visited the county and drew a home and lawn landscape plan on each of these to serve as county demonstration projects.

In 1959, Commissioner of Agriculture, Phil Campbell, visited the county and awarded a Bangs Free Certificate certifying all cattle in Twiggs County to be free of Bangs Disease. This was the first time an all-out program to rid the county of Bangs Disease was accomplished.

The reconditioning of furniture has played a vital part in the program. Upholstered furniture with sagging springs and damaged upholstery were completely reconditioned and new upholstery material added. This program has been quite a saving to the local people as most of them were too badly worn to use and would have to be completely replaced had they not been reconditioned. Demonstration homes have been set up for improving landscaping. Emphasis has been placed on improving landscaping. Emphasis has been placed on improving the quality of foods that are frozen or canned.

Today, the Rural Development Program has served one of the greatest needs in reaching all people in Twiggs County. It has increased beyond all expectations, and interest is still on the increase from groups and individuals in the support of the program.

By: Mrs. K. J. Carswell.

## BULLARD HOME DEMONSTRATION CLUB

The Bullard Home Demonstration Club, organized by Mrs. Kathleen Carswell at a meeting of Bullard Women at the school house in October, 1925, when this type of work was in its infancy, is one of the three oldest clubs in Twiggs County. Mrs. W. M. Laine, the first president, was assisted by a full slate of capable officers, with eighteen charter members.

The meetings were well attended as these were the days before automobiles were numerous, good roads, and local canning plants. Great interest was shown in the many new and better methods of drying, canning, pickling, and preserving the many fruits and vegetables which were grown in abundance in the home gardens. Fireless cookery was demonstrated along with many housekeeping helps. In a county-wide landscaping contest, Mrs. J. R. Cook won second place in 1929. With Mrs. Earl Haskins as nutrition chairman, the club provided food on certain days to supplement the children's lunches. Much was accomplished for the pleasure and benefit of the community.

In the Thirties, the club suffered from lack of Extension Service Leadership, but was re-organized in 1939, by Mrs. Mary Bennett, Home Demonstration Agent, assisted by Mrs. Will Mercer, County Council President. Mrs. A. S. Davis was elected President, Mrs. O. B. Fitzpatrick, Vice-President, Mrs. H. L. Faulk, Secretary-Treasurer, with many charter members in this group of twenty-three, who immediately began work to improve the school and build a lunchroom program. A kitchen and eating area were arranged, equipment secured and the first lunchroom in Twiggs County began full-scale operation. Quantities of fruits and vegetables were donated, prepared and canned, but the club needed money, so backing our president we prepared an exhibit, which won third place in the State Fair at Macon, Georgia, in 1939.

With the Club's urging, the Bullard School Board of Trustees had a deep well dug and flush toilets installed. The Club provided cabinets, wiring, screens, and paint for the lunchroom, bought shades for classrooms, stage curtains, stage furniture, erected a safety fence along highway, built a coal bin, started a library and bought playground equipment.

The Club won first place in the County Fair in 1956. Mrs. G. F. Rogers from our club served as County Council President in 1957; we also won first place on float in school beauty parade in 1958. We sponsor a recreation program for our young people. The officers now leading our work are: Mrs. L. M. Yaughn, President; Mrs. Earl Anderson, Vice President; and Mrs. J. M. Alley, Secretary-Treasurer. With Mrs. Kate Burke, our present agent, we are continuing to be greatly benefitted in work concerning our home and schools.

Mrs. L. M. Yaughn, President

## CANNON H.D. CLUB

The Cannon Home Demonstration Club was organized in 1921. It is the oldest continuous club Extension Service in the county. Charter members were: Mrs. Minnie Floyd, Mrs. C. G. Grimsley, Sr., Mrs. Mary Fowler, Mrs. R. L. Stevens, and Mrs. F. D. Carden. Miss Adnah Duckworth was the first Home Demonstration Agent to hold regular meetings with the Club.

Presidents of club through these years:

| | |
|---|---|
| Mrs. R. L. Stevens | Mrs. H. J. Waters |
| Mrs. M. H. Stevens, Sr. | Mrs. Lonnie Smith, Jr. |
| Mrs. C. G. Grimsley, Sr. | Mrs. J. C. Gregory |
| | Mrs. F. D. Carden |

Projects of the Club:

FIRST: 1925-1929—First Clinic in County for removal of children's tonsils, $7.00 a child, also, during depression years a loan closet was maintained. SECOND: Sponsored the next year toxin-anti-toxin shots for 16 children in community. THIRD: Had traveling library of 50 books kept at Mrs. Hade Stevens' home. FOURTH: During the war made bandages and kits for Red Cross, knitted scarves for soldiers, saved tin cans for defense. Members went to Macon Red Cross one day each week and made bandages. Sewed for Red Cross one day each week at school house. Secured markers for First World War soldiers' graves. Club also had nutrition classes at school taught by H. D. Agents. FIFTH: Planted shrubbery at school house and churches. In 1946, started a building program for a Clinic and Club House, and in 1948, entered Better Home and Town Contest with the Georgia Power Company. In September, 1950, deeds were drawn for the Clinic. The Committee for this was: H. L. Chance, A. T. Land, Mrs. Agnes Hughes, and Mrs. Polly Smith. The Club continues to maintain a 3-room building, this being used by the Health Nurse of the County. In 1952, Club held its first Flower Show. Club remains active in the year of 1959.

Mrs. F. D. Carden (Neva Chance Carden)<br>Mrs. M. H. Stevens, Sr. (Laura Holliday Stevens)<br>Danville, Georgia

## NEW RICHLAND HOME DEMONSTRATION CLUB

The New Richland Home Demonstration Club was first organized in the fall of 1933 under the leadership of Mrs. Kathleen J. Carswell, Home Demonstration Agent. The organization meeting was held in the home of Mrs. Norman Vaughn with eleven charter members.

The first officers of the club were: President, Mrs. Norman Vaughn; Vice President, Mrs. Georgia Roberts; Secretary and Treasurer, Mrs. Jack Vaughn.

There are only three of the charter members still active members of the club.

The early meetings of the club were devoted to learning better methods of homemaking. All day canning schools were held to teach the ladies the best methods of food preservation.

One of the first community projects was the building of the first community house in the county. A band of fifteen women set out to build this building without a penny in the treasury. Five hundred dollars in cash was raised by giving ice cream suppers, chicken and cold plate suppers. Some donations of cash were received. Lumber, logs, and brick were given by many citizens of the county.

Through the assistance of Adrian Newcomer, WPA District Supervisor, the windows, doors, roof, and labor were furnished through Federal Aid.

J. H. Vaughn gave one acre of land on the Johnson Branch road for the community building. The house is surrounded by native trees.

In the large assembly room, a six foot fireplace was built, it is finished in cement studded with small rock. A wood stove was installed in the kitchen. Here the women met and canned surplus vegetables and fruits. They were supervised by Mrs. Mary C. Bennett, Twiggs County Home Demonstration Agent.

The club has remained active through the years with 13 members enrolled at the present.

Mrs. Jack Vaughn

## STONE CREEK COMMUNITY H.D. CLUB

The Club was organized by Mrs. Julia P. Kitchens, popular Twiggs County Home Demonstration Agent, at the home of Mrs. F. J. Thomason on Riggins Mill Road, Dry Branch, Ga., in 1945. The Club met regularly in the homes of the different members until a permanent clubhouse was built across from Stone Creek Church in 1957. The money for the construction of the clubhouse was earned by the club ladies sponsoring dinners, selling wares, having rummage sales, operating bazaars, community fairs and monetary donations. Several of the local men and boys gave of their time, talents and labors in helping to erect, paint and roof the building. One of the several worthy projects undertaken to raise money for the building fund was the sale of china plates inscribed with pictures of the old and new Stone Creek Church. On the back of the plates a brief history of the church was given, it having been compiled by B. W. Jones. Presidents of the club: Mrs. F. J. Thomason, Mrs. Clara Tharpe Smith, Mrs. Robert Moseley, Mrs. G. F. Benjamin and Mrs. E. H. Johnson.

## WORTHWHILE HOME DEMONSTRATION CLUB

Several ladies near Mt. Zion and former Cannon school house had been members of the Cannon Club. But most of the Cannon Club members lived in and near Danville, so some of the members felt they needed a club in the country community, so Mrs. Julia Kitchens said if we could band together eight or more ladies, a new club would be organized. So the Worthwhile Club was organized March 4, 1946, in the home of Mrs. Burton Chance with the following ladies joining:

Mrs. Silas Chance, President; Mrs. Burton Chance, Secretary; Mrs. J. S. Fowler, Program Chairman; Mrs. Harold Reece, Reporter; Mrs. Ellen Thompson, Mrs. George Chance, Mrs. Frank Fowler, Mrs. C. L. Nobles, Mrs. Rufus Chance, Mrs. Estelle Hill, and Mrs. Ruby Fowler.

Mrs. Julia Kitchens was our Home Demonstration Agent, at that time and the name Worthwhile was selected in hope that everything done in the club work would be worthwhile. As the years passed several new members have been added. But we have lost some by death or by moving away. At present we have a membership of 22. We are all proud of our club.

## DANVILLE P.T.A.—TWIGGS-WILKINSON SCHOOL

In the early 1930's a group of interested parents, teachers, and friends of the Twiggs-Wilkinson School met regularly for the purpose of carrying out a program of school and community improvement.

On September 1, 1934, this group organized as the Parent-Teacher Association with Mrs. Lee Green as president and Mrs. M. H. Stevens, Sr. as treasurer. That year thirty membership dues were mailed to the State office. This year (1959) dues for 102 members were sent to the State office.

Because of a lack of money from other sources, our P.T.A. had to sponsor many money-making projects. As a result we have been able through the years to do much toward equipping a new school building with lights, water, desks, auditorium seats, piano, movie projector, playground equipment, an electric water cooler, a record player, and other things as needed.

In order to promote the physical welfare of our children we have helped to co-sponsor a diptheria clinic, hearing and vision test clinic, Salk vaccine clinic, and a tuberculin testing program. Each year we sponsor a pre-school clinic.

During the past twenty-five years it was felt that our organization had done much to promote the physical, mental, moral, and spiritual welfare of our children.

Within the past twelve years we have presented life memberships in the National Congress of Parents and Teachers to four deserving members: Mrs. H. L. D. Hughes, Mrs. J. C. Dickens, Mrs. Clara Porter, and Mrs. Olin Carden.

Mrs. Sanders Hall
Mrs. John Maxwell

## SMITH SCHOOL P. T. A.

The Smith School at Dry Branch, Georgia came into existence in 1921, but as to the exact date the local P.T.A. was organized is unknown. However, it was organized and functioning in 1927. Throughout its history, the Smith P.T.A. has served as an important financial arm of the school. It was through this organization that Smith received many needed aids: library books, maps, first aid supplies, shades for the classrooms, lunchroom equipment and cooking utensils, audio visual equipment and films, song books, basket ball suits, playground equipment, and instructional materials. This fine organization also sponsored the lunchroom program, built and equipped a teachers' lounge, provided janitorial service, supervised health programs and supported the wiring of the old school for electric lights.

Local presidents have been: Mrs. E. Y. Mallary, Mrs. J. D. Grace, Mrs. E. V. Adams, Mrs. Miller Bayne, Mrs. S. S. Jones, Mrs. D. S. McGee, Mrs. E. G. Dallmus, Mrs. G. F. Benjamin, Mrs. Ivan Lester, Mr. Ivan Lester, Mrs. C. R. Thomason, Mrs. C. T. Chapman, Mrs. Frank Sanders, Mrs. Roger Moye, Mrs. D. J. Fargason, and Mrs. M. J. Jones.

## TWIGGS ELEMENTARY SCHOOL PARENT-TEACHER ASSOCIATION

The Twiggs County Elementary Parent-Teacher Association was organized in September, 1956, when the Twiggs High P.T.A. divided into the Twiggs County High unit and the Twiggs Elementary unit. (The Twiggs High P.T.A. was organized in October-November, 1921.)

Officers for 1956-'57: Ralph Smith, president; Mrs. Brady Floyd, vice president; Mrs. Roger Jessup, secretary; and Mrs. Angus Hart, Jr., treasurer.

The slate for 1957-'58: Mrs. E. E. Brannen, president; Mrs. Roger Holliday, vice president; Mrs. Roger Jessup, secretary; and Mrs. Angus Hart, Jr., treasurer.

In 1958-'59, Mrs. Brannen was president until they moved in January, 1959, and

Mrs. C. L. Hodges completed the term. In February, James Hamrick was elected vice president, the position previously held by Mrs. Hodges. Mrs. Frank Elmore was secretary and Mrs. L. M. Yaughn was treasurer.

Officers for 1959-'60: Mrs. C. L. Hodges, president; Mrs. Howard Henderson, vice president; Mrs. Frank Elmore, secretary; and Mrs. J. B. Whitaker, treasurer.

Committee:
Mrs. W. M. Whitehurst
(Miss) Mary Hart Whitehurst

## TWIGGS COUNTY HIGH SCHOOL PARENT-TEACHER ASSOCIATION

When the consolidation of the schools in our county was evident in the spring of 1956, several interested people from the Smith, Twiggs-Wilkinson and Twiggs High School communities met for the purpose of organizing a County High School P.T.A. for the new school.

On April 17, 1956, the Twiggs County High School Parent-Teacher Association was organized with Mr. A. T. Wimberly, County School Superintendent, in charge of the meeting. The second Monday night in each month was designated as meeting time. Ninety-five charter members enrolled during the 1956-'57 school term. The following slate of officers was presented by the nominating committee at the May meeting and was elected for the 1956-'57 term:

President, Mrs. W. H. Wester; 1st Vice President, Mrs. J. H. Holliday; 2nd Vice President, Mrs. B. A. Leslie; 2nd Vice President, Mrs. W. H. Mercer; 2nd Vice President, Mrs. Hade Nobles; 2nd Vice President, Mrs. Frank Simpson; Secretary, Mrs. H. M. Fulbright; Treasurer, Mrs. H. H. Wimberly.

Since many things were needed for our new school the association entered into several money-making activities jointly with the Twiggs Elementary P.T.A. and co-sponsored the following projects:

Equipment for our new lunchroom, amounting to $5500.
Curtains for the stage in cafeterium.
Movie projector.
Part of salary of secretary for the school.

On November 11, 1956, the High School P. T. A. and the Twiggs Elementary P. T. A. co-sponsored Open House for the new school with the school officials and faculty. Also, the High School P. T. A. co-sponsored with the Twiggs Education Association the National Education Association Centennial Birthday Party, April 8, 1957.

During the years the P.T.A. has entered into parent-teacher consulation in an informal period held in the classrooms of teachers at the close of the P.T.A. meeting.

Committee:
H. M. Fulbright
Mrs. J. T. Early
Mrs. John Maxwell

## COOL SPRING LODGE NO. 185

Cool Spring Lodge celebrated its hundredth anniversary as a Masonic Lodge in 1954. It was originally organized under dispensation, beginning in April of 1854 and ending in October of the same year, when its warrant was granted by William S. Rockwelt, Deputy Grand Master of the Fourth Masonic District. At that meeting, the following men were appointed to offices:

Eli Sears—Worshipful Master
James R. Coombs—Senior Warden
W. W. Lee—Junior Warden
Benniah S. Carswell—Treasurer

E. Jackson Rozier—Secretary
C. B. Strickland—Senior Deacon
J. W. Summers—Junior Deacon
T. P. Smith—Tyler

The Nineteen Original Members:

| | |
|---|---|
| Ira E. Perry—Wilkinson County | John Gainey, Randolph R. J. Smith, |
| W. F. N. Browne—Wilkinson Coounty | Wm. W. Beall—Wilkinson County |
| William Allen—Pulaski County | Charles E. Taylor—Pulaski County |
| Andrew W. Arde—Wilkinson County | David Howard—Laurens County |
| Wm. A. Gainey—Twiggs County | Howard McLain—Twiggs County |
| Isaac Justice—Pulaski County | |

The original location of the lodge was at Cool Springs schoolhouse, in Wilkinson County, just out from Allentown. In 1875, it was moved to Laurens Hill, in Laurens County. At the same time, the name was changed from the Cool Springs Lodge to the Laurens Hill Lodge 185.

The lodge remained at Laurens Hill through November, 1883. Then it reverted to Cool Springs Lodge, Twiggs County Lodge at Lucy Chapel Church. In 1898, it was again moved to Danville and has remained there to this date, a building being purchased for the meeting place.

Two of the most outstanding secretaries have been J. T. Welton and John Maxwell, who served their lodge for twelve years. T. L. Hill also served the lodge faithfully for ten years as secretary and for fifteen years as Worshipful Master.

## LIBERTY HILL MASONIC LODGE NO. 308
### Dry Branch, Georgia

The Liberty Hill Lodge was chartered October 31, 1876. The present Lodge Building is the third to house the Masonic Order: the first being the second story of the old Liberty Hill Methodist Church on the east bank of Big Sandy Creek near Myrick's Mill, the second meeting hall (1913) was the second story of Antioch Baptist Church located near the west bank of Big Sandy Creek, and the third and permanent home of the Lodge was erected in 1951 about two miles west of Antioch Church on the Dry Branch-Gordon Road. Charter members were J. Balkcom, J. U. Burkett, James Bobbitt, John Cranford, E. S. Griffin, T. H. Jones, C. G. Johnson, L. A. Nash, H. Reynolds, T. M. C. Rice, K. F. Burkett, William Blackshear, Isaac Carroll, William Griffin, T. J. Joyner, J. Jessup, E. A. Nash, Wilson Pettis, D. J. Ryles, W. H. Stokes and B. J. Wood. First officers were:

| | |
|---|---|
| William Griffin—Worshipful Master | E. A. Nash—Senior Deacon |
| W. H. Stokes—Senior Warden | Daniel J. Ryles—Junior Deacon |
| Isaac Carroll—Junior Warden | E. S. Griffin—Senior Steward |
| Thomas H. Jones—Treasurer | J. N. Burkett—Junior Steward |
| T. J. Joyner—Secretary | B. J. Wood—Tyler |

by: E. C. Cranford, Sec.

## DANVILLE EASTERN STAR

Danville Eastern Star was organized in October, 1946, with Bro. R. W. Vandegriff Worthy Grand Patron of Georgia presiding.

In June, 1947, the Charter was received with Mrs. Charlotte Bowers Worthy Matron, E. L. Hill Worthy Patron, Lois Hill Associate Matron, H. B. Williams Associate Patron.

The Chapter has had sixty-eight members since organizing. The following were charter members: Mrs. Kathleen Adams, Mrs. Margaret Brown, Mrs. Mabel Brack, Mrs. Charlotte Bowers, Mrs. Lou Lee Dame, Mrs. Sallie Dickens, Miss Lois Hill, Mrs. Estelle Hill, Mrs. Ruth Hawkins, Mrs. Virginia Ham, Mrs. Elanor Luckett, Mrs. Rella

Lamb, Mrs. Grace Reece, Mrs. Georgia Waters, Mrs. Eula Bennett, G. M. Brack, Mrs. Avis Williams Taylor, Mrs. Corene Williams, E. L. Hill, C. C. Hawkins, W. R. Lamb, H. C. Melton, H. B. Williams, James C. Williams, and W. R. Bennett.

Lois Hill, Secretary

## LIBERTY HILL O. E. S. CHAPTER NO. 416
Dry Branch, Georgia

The Liberty Hill Chapter O. E. S. No. 416, Twiggs County, Dry Branch, Georgia, was organized December 28th, 1951, instituted January 11, 1952, and constituted July 3, 1952. The chapter meeting place is the Liberty Hill Masonic Lodge No. 308. The Lodge antedates the Eastern Star Chapter by almost 80 years.

It was in the new brick Masonic Lodge Hall that the Eastern Star Chapter was constituted. The Liberty Hill Chapter came into existence largely through the efforts of Mrs. Georgia Mae Mann, who was elected the first Worthy Matron.

The original Chapter officers were: Georgia Mae Mann, Worthy Matron; Roy Williams, Worthy Patron; Nell Burkett, Associate Matron; Walter Epps, Associate Patron; Doris Wimberly, Secretary; Opal Jones, Treasurer; Gladys Bowman, Conductress; Reba Kitchens, Associate Conductress.

The 39 charter members of the Liberty Hill Chapter O. E. S. No. 416: Yvonne McLain, Harriette O'Neal, Mattie Jessup, Evie Williams, Bessie Bell, Corine Johnson, Opal Jones, Myrtle Williams, Elizabeth O'Neal, Maude Kitchens, Gladys Bowman, Louell Beck, Ruth Mosley, Doris Wimberly, Keturah Kieser, Nell Burkett, Reba Kitchens, Julia Joiner, Agnes Barrentine, Frances Wood, Mary Lou Kitchens, Jewell Kitchens, Thelma Walters, Georgia Mae Mann, Bessie Tharpe, Beulah Cannon, Callie Graham, J. E. Jessup, Roy Williams, S. S. Jones, Hansel Williams, Walter Epps, Dwight Kitchens, James Beck, Grady Kitchens, J. B. Joiner, Elton Wood, Harry Bell, and W. B. Barrentine.

## THE HUBER MASONIC CLUB, INC.

The Huber Masonic Club, Inc., of Huber, Georgia, is a unit of regular Free and Accepted Masons who are employees of the J. M. Huber Corporation. It was organized February 2, 1955 to inculate love of country and faith in the ideals of which it is founded to propogate Free Masonary's great ideal "Universal Brotherhood" and to promote a closer bond of fraternal and social relations between individual members.

The club was chartered as a non-profit organization by the State of Georgia on January 14, 1959.

The membership has grown from nineteen charter members to thirty members, and represents six counties. The recently completed clubhouse is located on Sagoda Road at Marion Road. Present officers are Kenneth Cason, President; Ray Barrs, Vice President; Glenn Colwell, Secretary-Treasurer. The Board of Directors consist of Quinton Johnson, Nate Millman, J. B. Whitley and Leonard Yaughn.

Glenn Colwell, Secretary-Treasurer

## BOY SCOUTS OF AMERICA
Troop 19
Danville, Georgia

The earliest available records at the Central Georgia Council Office show 1941 as the beginning of the Troop, Troy Edwards, Scoutmaster, Roy Hill, Assistant. Early

Troop committeemen were: H. L. D. Hughes, P. H. Ward, G. M. Toney, Thomas Lee, Lonnie Smith. Members of the Troop in 1943 were: J. D. Arnold, Andrew Edwards, Jack F. Green, Francis Hill, Howard H. Hill, James Lamb, J. L. Newby, Ernest Payne, J. W. Pettis, Harold Sanders.

BOY SCOUTS OF AMERICA
Troop 15
Dry Branch, Georgia

Troop 15 was founded by Benjamin B. Shaw, local superintendent of the Georgia Kaolin Company, in 1938. The original troop committeemen were: Mr. Shaw, Chairman, S. S. Jones, Walter Epps, and A. McLain. The first Scoutmaster was R. Felix Green; the assistant, C. C. Goss, Smith High School principal. The meetings were first held at Smith School; in 1941 a scout house was built beside the small lake near Grace's Store. The charter members of Troop 15 were: Roy Casteen, Hubert Epps, Billy Joiner, Billy W. Jones, Robert J. King, Arthur Kitchens, Harold Kitchens, Jere Kitchens, Virgil Kitchens, James Lyles, Dent McGee, Keith McLain, Kirby O'Neal, H. T. Taylor. New scouts joining the Troop in 1939 were: Thomas Anderson, James Barrentine, Lawson Bostick, Jr., Quincy Casteen, Erastus Compton, John Earl Hinson, H. T. Hinson, Milton Horton, Reid Johnson, Wayne Johnson, M. J. (Jackie) Jones, C. A. Lundy, Lindy McGee, Billy Reed, and J. W. Williams.

BOY SCOUTS OF AMERICA
Troop 54—Jeffersonville, Georgia

Records at the Central Georgia Council Office at Macon give 1951 as the earliest date of this Troop. Roscoe Hammrick was the Scoutmaster in 1951; J. T. Early, D. Y. Califf, Rev. H. W. Scoats and H. F. Shurling, Troop Committeemen. Charter scouts of Troop 54 were: Pat Adams, Jr., Jerry W. Asbell, Carlton S. Faulk, John C. Faulk, Hildon Floyd, Bill Fountain, Donald Green, Jimmy Hammrick, Thomas Jones, Emory McWilliams, Frankie Maxwell, Will Methvin, Willie F. Scarbrough, William R. Sims, Doyle Stone, Jr., and Charles M. Wimberly.

(An earlier troop is reported to have preceded this one.)

FOX HUNTERS

Fox hunting is an old and honored sport in our County of Twiggs. The existence of this sport here is a valued inheritance from our English cousins as the original foxhounds in America came from England. Nature has endowed us with natural resources perfect for the plentiful supply of red and grey fox. Most prominent of the foxhounds to be found here are the Walker and the July strains, with a few Trigg hounds here and there.

The constant aim of the owners of the many packs of foxhounds to be found in Twiggs County is the improvement of the breeding of their hounds for speed and endurance in the race. One could travel but few miles in any direction without finding a pack of well-trained foxhounds in a backyard kennel.

Names to be associated with this great sport were Will Fitzpatrick, Rube Manning, Henry Myrick, Ezekiel Wimberly, George W. Faulk, R. B. Kitchens, B. D. Tharpe, Sr., and many others. Alton V. White, Sr. followed in the footsteps of his father, W. F. White of Jones County, in the breeding of the July strain of foxhound, and stimulated foxhunting among his friends. Hounds from his kennels found their way all over the United States because of their breeding characteristics for the best in hounds.

Needless to say, enduring friendships were made and sustained with hunters from far and wide who came to take advantage of the gracious hospitality of these men. The fever and excitement of a beautiful moonlight night coupled with a baying pack of hounds eager for the chase was more than the hunters could endure, unless of course, the early morning dew to follow the night gave more promise of even better hunting.

Characteristic of the sport, the hunter, horn by his side, on his prancing horse, followed the hounds chasing the cunning, agile fox over hill and dale and deep ravines. The hunter, with his heart aflame, thrilled to the mellowest music of the chase. On and on the faithful dogs pursued their cunning game, and on and on the faithful masters followed the music of their pack, dashing along the hard road-bed, leaping fences, plunging through briars and brambles, splashing mud and water, dashing on with the very madness of joy! Oh, you must have a heart kin to the heart of a hunter to know the charm and glory of the chase. The kill has been accomplished and the race is over, though only to the tired faithful dogs who now return to the casting ground alongside their masters. For again and again, will this same race be rerun and relived as told by the various members of the hunt.

Courtesy: Mrs. Alton Vestal White, Sr.

## TWIGGS COUNTY AGRICULTURAL SOCIETY

October 31, 1871 issue:

On the 28th Instant a very large number of the best and most substantial planters in Twiggs County met at the Twiggs Lodge. The most central and accessible point in the County—and permanently organized an agricultural society with the above name and elected the following officers: Dr. W. O'Daniel, President; Col. William Faulk, Vice President; Judge W. L. Solomon, Secretary-Treasurer.

Reference: The Telegraph and Messenger, Macon, Georgia.

How long this society functioned before it became defunct is not known.

## TWIGGS CHAPTER—UNITED DAUGHTERS OF THE CONFEDERACY

An organizational meeting was held at the courthouse April 26, 1909. Mrs. J. H. Johnson was elected president pro-tem and Miss Kathleen Jones, secretary pro-tem. Applicants for membership were: Mesdames O. T. Chapman, L. C. Powell, J. S. Vaughn, Ira White, Jones Mercer, J. C. Shannon, W. F. Shannon, J. E. Cowart, W. O. Johnson, R. R. Slappey, Jr., M. L. Carswell, Walter McCrary, W. H. Harrell, John Vaughn, S. C. Ward, M. H. O'Daniel, S. E. Jones, B. S. Fitzpatrick, J. H. Johnson, Misses Kathleen Jones, Nell Chapman, and Eunice Harrell.

In May, 1909, a call meeting was held at the courthouse for the purpose of selecting a name for the local chapter. The name agreed upon was the Twiggs County Chapter, U. D. C., and the number assigned this local unit was 1227.

The officers elected for a two-year term were: Mrs. L. C. Powell, President; Mrs. B. S. Fitzpatrick, Vice President; Mrs. Robert Slappey, Jr., Treasurer; Mrs. J. H. Johnson, Recording Secretary; Miss Kathleen Jones, Corresponding Secretary;

Mrs. Jones Mercer, Historian; Mrs. O. T. Chapman, Miss Eleanor Griffin, Miss Elizabeth King, Mrs. Ira White, Credential Committee.

One of the most noteworthy projects of the Chapter was the erection of the Confederate Monument at Jeffersonville. Another worthy project of the Chapter was the sending of many boxes of articles for soldiers of World War I to Army headquarters by request. These included knitted sweaters, scarves, helmets and kits for use by privates called "Housewifery kits" with needles, buttons, et cetera. Many barrels of nuts were shipped to be used in the making of gas masks.

The Chapter functioned only a few years.

Ref.: Twiggs County Citizen (Newspaper), W. C. Kelley, editor, Jeffersonville, Georgia.

## CHAPTER XIII

## DOCTORS AND NURSES

Out of the dimness of yesterdays and from a vast and nameless throng to the present come the good physicians and nurses, with their skills and kindly services and the pulsing warmth of God-given human hands, who have relieved woes and pains and set many a patient upon his way stronger and well.

In frontier homes there may have hung an old patent medicine almanac, but usually when a member of the family was beset with certain illnesses the skill of the friendly family physician was sought. The good old country doctor, wrinkled as to countenance and trousers, at times, jogging the trails and dirt roads on or behind old Dobbin, hastened—be it night or day—to bring cheer and relief to the stricken. Patients either went to the office or the doctor made home visits for nearly everything that went wrong for there were no specialists or health departments to speak of in the bygone days.

The family doctor was a leading citizen, a keen judge of human beings, had time enough to chat with the patient, a friend as well as a physician. He was almost an indispensable man toward better health and longer life for his patients.

Twiggs County has been blessed with many good country and town doctors and nurses, some were native born, others removed to the county, who have made their contribution in the art of medicine to society.

With scant records, it was impossible to determine who the first physician was to begin practice in the County. Robert Cummins, A. B. Reed, Joshua R. Wimberly and Dr. Gibson were among the earliest doctors to establish residence in the county.

Vivid memories of the "old" family doctor remain. He doesn't travel this way anymore, a new day has dawned, modern progress, and a new doctor!

The following list of doctors and nurses have numbered among those of the medical profession in the county. Mrs. Kathleen Jones Carswell submitted many of the names herein.

If any name has been omitted from this list it was not purposely done. (To include everyone who has had a part in a county's history would be almost impossible.)

### DOCTORS OF MEDICINE

A. W. Ard
A. F. Beckcom
Allen Belcher
William R. Birdsong
J. Burns
Beniah Carswell
Robert C. Carroll
George E. Chapman
Robert Cummings
E. H. Denson
Orman Daniel
C. A. Duggan, Jr.
Ira E. Dupree, Sr.
Ira E. Dupree, Jr.

C. D. Findley
J. Gallemore
O. C. Gibson
Will Gibson
J. Mitchell Hartley
James Y. Hamrick, Jr.
J. A. Hembree
J. Hulm
Boderick Jones
T. S. Jones
Tom Jones
W. S. Jones
J. N. Kennington
Arthur S. McCallum

Ezekiel McNair
R. A. Nash
R. S. Nutt
Mark H. O'Daniel
W. O. O'Daniel
S. W. Ray
A. B. Reed
T. M. C. Rice
S. L. Richardson
Holbert A. Rogers
David Rozier
John G. Slappey
J. C. Solomon

Dan H. Taylor
Dr. Thompson
Dr. Trimble
Benjamin F. Watkins, Jr.
H. S. Wimberly
J. R. Wimberly, Sr.
J. R. Wimberly, Jr.
Warren Wimberly
George W. Wimberly
Dr. Waters
A. J. Wood
Dr. Zachary

Twiggs Medical Association Organized

The Doctors of the County met July 26, 1905 at Dr. McNair's Office to organize the Medical Association of Twiggs County. Dr. M. H. O'Daniel was chosen President. Date set on August 2, to adopt a charter. Dr. Barnum of Richland, (Ga.), Counselor for this Congressional District, addressed the meeting.

D. H. Dupree, Secretary Pro-tem

Ref.: The Twiggs Herald, Friday, August 11, 1905.

## CHIROPRACTORS

James Boyd                    Howard Mercer

## DOCTORS OF DENTISTRY

M. A. Beal
S. Bond
Robert I. Butler
Paul Gates

M. D. Hembree
Robert L. Patillo
J. C. Robinson

## PHARMACISTS

Carl Holland
Wilford G. Huff
Stephen S. (Jack) Jones
W. H. McCrary

John W. Saunders
H. C. Swearinger
A. S. Williams

## REGISTERED NURSES

Bessie Fountain Austin
Louise Fountain Booth
Cora Belle Grace Brannen
Betty Stephens Birdsong
Ruby O'Neal Cullen
Laverne Fountain
Sybil Fountain
Carrie Carswell Griffin
Emmie McNair Jackson
Cornelia Cannon Harrison
Laura Reynolds Hearn
Inez Hogan

Elizabeth Mercer
Clara Cannon Moon
Idelle Kitchens Moye
Vivian Johnson Moye
Myrtle Lomax Pascell
Margaret Cannon Pennington
Virginia Slappey
Myrtle Johnson Sweeney
Myrtle Fountain Tomlin
Bessie Whitehurst
Winnie Wood

# GENERAL APPENDIX

# CENSUS AND POPULATION CHART
## UNITED STATES CENSUS OF 1810
### DISTRICT OF GEORGIA

Enumeration of Twiggs County from the 1810 Census report, page 81.

|  | Free White Males | Free White Females |
|---|---|---|
| Under 10 years of age to 10 | 588 | 540 |
| Of 10 and under 16 to 16 | 181 | 183 |
| Of 16 and under 26 to 26, including heads of families. | 248 | 285 |
| Of 26 and under 45 to 45, including heads of families. | 272 | 197 |
| Of 45 and upwards, including heads of families. | 145 | 117 |
| All other free persons except Indians not taxed |  | 7 |
| Slaves | 642 |  |
| Totals in the County |  | 3,405 |

The number of persons within my division, consisting of the State of Georgia, appears in a schedule hereto annexed, subscribed by me this eleventh day of February, A.D. 1811.

John Eppinger, Marshall.

Courtesy of Howard G. Brunsman, Chief, Population Division, Bureau of the Census of the U. S. Department of Commerce, Washington, D. C.

## U. S. CENSUS OF TWIGGS COUNTY, GEORGIA, 1830

By Peter Solomon, ass't. to the Marshall of the District of Georgia. Made Nov. 1, 1830. Witnesses: Ira E. Dupree; H. H. Tarver. Total population—8033. 2311 white males; 2180 white females; 1774 male slaves; 1733 female slaves; 17 free males of colour; 12 free females of colour; 1 alien foreigner not naturalized; 3 deaf and dumb whites; 1 deaf and dumb black; 1 blind white; 3 blind black. (Only the heads of the household in the 1830 Cenus are given. Beginning with the Census of 1850 names of the entire household and other information are recorded on the Census records.)

## U. S. CENSUS, 1830, TWIGGS COUNTY, GA.

### A
Adams, Daniel
Adams, John
Adams, John
Adams, Samuel
Adkins, Lewis
Adkins, Thomas
Adkins, William
Adkins, William
Alford, William
Alford, Wyatte
Allen, Gideon
Allen, John
Allen, William
Amons, Sarah
Anderson, Elijah
Anderson, John
Anderson, Thomas W.
Andrews, Abisha
Andrews, Joseph B.
Andrews, Robin
Angelly, Benj.
Anglin, Elijah
Anglin, Henry
Anglin, John
Ard, John
Armstrong, Wiley S.
Arnold, John
Arnuld, William
Arrington, Martha
Arrington, Rex
Asbell, Elisha
Asbell, John
Attaway, Isaiah
Averett, James
Averett, John

### B
Bablet, Thomas Sr.
Bachelor, Frederick
Baley, Peter
Baley, James
Ball, Wade H.
Ball, Sarah
Barge, Winny
Barkley, David

Barnes, John
Barnes, John Sr.
Barnes, William
Barrs, Dempsey
Barrs, James
Barton, Martha
Bass, Drewry
Basset, Thomas
Bateman, Jesse
Bateman, William
Batey, John
Batey, Rachel
Batey, William S.
Baton, William
Beacham, Sherwood H.
Beall, Spencer
Beall, Robert A.
Beckam, Ann
Beddingfield, Gideon
Bedingfield, Hardy
Beckham, William
Belcher, Robert
Berry, John
Birdsong, Rebecca
Black, John
Blackshear, Joseph
Blackshear, Isaac
Blanchet, William
Blount, Benjamin
Blount, Joseph
Blount, William
Bogs, Joseph
Bolings, John
Boman, Leonard
Bond, Benjamin
Bonds, John Peter
Boynton, Willard
Bostick, George W.
Bostick, Joshua A.
Bostick, Rhesa
Bostick, William D.
Boyt, John
Brant, Richard
Braswell, Thomas
Brecken, Andrew
Bridges, Bartlett
Bridgeman, Frances
Brooks, Mary
Brown, Daniel
Brown, Daniel
Brown, Dempsey Sr.
Brown, Dempsey Jr.
Brown, Frederick D.
Brown, Hardy

Brown, Holden
Brown, Robert
Brown, Silas
Brown, Stephen
Brown, William S.
Brown, William
Bryan, James
Bryan, James C.
Bryan, Penelope
Bryan, Thomas
Bryan, William
Bullard, Daniel
Bullard, Parthena
Bunn, Henry
Burden, William
Burkett, Hugh G.
Burkett, Uriah
Burkett, Samuel
Burnam, Lewis
Burnes, James
Burns, Joseph
Bush, Dorcas
Butler, John
Byran, Benjamin Sr.
C
Carden, Charles
Carrell, Thomas
Carswell, Alexander
Carter, William B.
Cartright, Polly
Caudle, Joseph
Chance, Edna
Chappell, Joseph Jr.
Chappell, Thomas
Chappell, Thomas S.
Childers, Malinda
Chivers, Thomas
Churchwell, Henry
Churchwell, James
Churchwell, John
Clark, Lewis H.
Clark, Silas
Clance, Wiley
Clements, Mary Ann
Cobb, Nathaniel
Cobb, Wiley
Cocks, Caleb
Coley, Dollinson
Collier, Christopher W.
Collier, Robert
Collins, James W.
Collins, Joseph
Combs, James
Cook, Barbara

Cook, William
Copra, Ira E.
Corsn, William A.
Cranford, John
Crawford, Alexander P.
Crawford, Thomas
Crawsbry, Sally
Crawsbry, Spencer
Crocker, John
Crocker, William
Cullens, Jesse
Cummins, Robert
D
Daniel, Ephriam
Daniel, Jonas
Daniel, Josiah
Darby, Isacc
Darby, Jeremiah
Davis, Abraham
Davis, Jesse
Davis, John
Davis, Moses
Davis, William
Davidson, John
Davidson, Nancy
Dawson, William
Davison, Isham
Day, Nimrod
Day, Stephen
Defore, John
Dees, Calvin
Dennard, Bird
Dennard, John E.
Dennard, Isaac
Dennard, William E.
Dennard, Shadrick
Denson, John Sr.
Denson, John Jr.
Denson, Joel
Deshazo, Richard
Deshazo, Robert
Deshazo, Rosa
Dence, Elizabeth
Dickson, John
Dickson, Mosee
Dickson, Pleasant
Dikes, John
Dobson, John
Dorman, Allen
Dowder (or Dowden),
  Jonathan
Dozier, James C.
Dozier, Lemuel
Dozier, Thomas

Dupree, Patsey
Dupree, Sterling
Durden, Jane
Durden, Johias
Durden, Richard M.
Durham, Hardy
Dye, William
Dyre, James
Dyre, Mariah
Dyre, Nancy
Dyre, Susannah
Dynnl, James

E

Easom, Messock
Eason, William
Easterlin, Shadrack
Edward, Isham
Edmunson, Hannah
Edward, James
Eldrige, William
Ellis, Ephriam
Ellis, Joseph B.
Ellis, Rhesa J. (m)
Epps, Daniel T.
Evans, Benjamin S.
Evans, Isham
Evans, John
Evans, Uriah

F

Farnum, William W.
Faulk, Mark
Fennel, Margarett
Fenrell. Susannah
Finch, Freeman
Fort, Arthur
Fitzgerald, Reuben
Fitzpatrick, John
Fitzpatrick, William
Floyd, Elijah
Foggerson, James
Ford, John
Fleming, Allen
Fort, John
Fort, Moses
Fort, Thomas
Rort, Tomlinson
Frasure (Frazier), Eilliam
Fulton, Sarah
Funderburke, Sarah
Furly, Nancy

G

Gandy. Nancy
Gafford, Fanny
Galemore, John

Ganey, John
Garrett, James
Gesetry, William
Gibbs, Howell
Gilder, Elizabeth
Gilder, Isaac
Gilbert, Bird
Glover, John
Glover, Kelly
Glover, Thomas
Golden, Benjamin
Graddy, John
Gragg, Isrial
Graham, Samuel
Granberry, Langley
Granberry, Samuel M.
Grant, Stephen
Grantham, Joshua
Grary, John M.
Gray, James
Green, John
Green, Robert
Green, William
Grier, James
Griffin, Etheldrid
Griffin, Larkin
Griffin, William
Griffin, Yancey P.
Grimes, Nathan
Grimsley, David
Grimsley, Thomas
Guardner, Harriet
Guerry, James Sr.
Guerry, James P.
Gunn, Jane

H

Hado, Nathaniel
Hagger, John
Hair, John
Hallman, George
Ham, Ichalor
Ham, John
Ham, Levi
Ham, Littleton
Ham, William
Hambrick, Hiram J.
Hamilton, William
Hammock. James
Hammond. Paschal
Harden, John
Hardiman, Joseph
Hardy, Robert
Harrell, Anna
Harrell, Cader

Harrell, Haliday H.
Harrell, John
Harrell, Samuel
Harrell, Susan
Hart, Crawford
Hart, Mamaduke
Harris, Benjamin
Harris, James
Harris, Jacob
Harrison, James
Harrison, Thomas P.
Harrison, W. C.
Hasty, Hillory
Hatcher, William
Hawhorn, Thomas
Hayden, James
Hayes, James
Hearn, John (or Jesse)
Helton (or Melton),
  Clem, Jr.
Henderson, Hannah
Henson, Caleb
Henton, Allen
Herring, Fred G.
Herring, Henry H.
Herring, Stephenson
Herring, William
Higgs, John
Hitson, Henry
Holstead, William C.
Hodges, Edmund
Hodges, Robert and John L.
Hodges, Willis
Hogan, Matthew
Holland, Daniel
Holland, Henry
Holliday, Wm.
Hollingsworth, Cornelius
Hollingsworth, Mary
Holly, Elizabeth
Holly, Isaac
Holmes, Elizabeth
Holmes, Henry
Holt, Thaddius G.
Honeycut, Seth
Hooks, Barden
Horn, Abisha
Horn, Joah
Horn, Josiah
Howell, Hiram
Hughes, Hayden
Hughes, John
Hughes, Littleberry
Humphrey, Betsey

Hunt, George
Hunt, William
Hunter, William

**J**

Jackson, Josiah
Jacobs, Nancy
Jacobs, William
James, Willis
Jameson, James
Jessop, James
Jessop, Samuel
Johnson, Abel
Johnson, Edward
Johnson, Jeremiah
Johnson, Mary
Johnson, Moses
Johnson, Nancy
Johnson, Susannah
Johnson, William
Jones, James
Jones, Jempsey
Jones, Sarah
Jones, Stephen
Jones, Thomas
Jones, William M.
Jones, Wright
Jordan, Samuel
Jordan, Wiley
Joyner, Lawrence
Joyner, Rebecca

**K**

Kays, Michael
Kelly, Benjamin U.
Kelly, Edward
Kelly, Matthew
Kent, John
Kent, Price
Kent, Thomas
King, John
King, Joseph
King, Leraney (f)
King, Mourning
King, Nathan
King, Wiley

**L**

Lamb, Arthur
Lamb, Meda
Lamb, Reuben
Land, Henry
Land, Jesse
Lane, Benjamin S.
Lassy, John G.
Laver, Mary
Lawson, Roger

Lee, Henry
Lee, Jordan W.
Leonard, Elizabeth
Lewis, Jacob
Lewis, James
Lewis, Laton
Liles, Ephraim
Lingo, John R. T.
Lindsey, Richard
Lindsey, Thomas
Linton, John
Lipsey, Amesa B.
Liston, Levi
Little, George
Little, Merrit
Littlefield, John S.
Lockland, uncan M.
Long, Nimrod W.
Lovet, Asemelalet
Lovett, Moses
Low, Caleb
Lowry, James R.
Lowery, John R.
Loyless, Henry
Lucas, Arthur
Lucas, Sena
Lunsford, James S.

**Mc**

McCant, Delathia
McCant, Valentine
McCrea, Council S.
McCrary, Isaac
McCrane, James
McCrary, John
McCullars, Hiram
McDaniel, Alexander
McKenny, Julius
McLoud, John
McMillan, Micajah
McMullin, James
McMurry, Samuel
McWilliams, Asa
McWilliams, Saly

**M**

Majors, Eleanor
Mancil, Robert
Manning, Jarvis
Marlow, John
Martin, John
Martin, Joseph
Martin, Kinchen
Martin, Robert
Martin, William
Massey, Daniel

Matthews, Sally
Maxwell, William
Melton, Seynthia
Melton, Clem Sr.
Mercer, Hymerick
Meredith, Thomas
Merritt, Uriah
Miles, Daniel
Minchew, Phillip
Minchew, Calvin
Minton, Benjamin
Mirock, Anny (Myrick?)
Mixon, Michael
Moon, John D.
Moon, William H.
Moore, Thomas
Montgomery, Mary
Morey, Alfred
Morey, James
Morgan, James
Morris, John
Monroe, Edward
Mosely, Isaiah
Moulden, Tucker
Murphey, James

**N**

Napper, Shadrick
Nash, Reuben A.
Nealy, William
Nelson, Alfred
Nelson, Alexander
Nelson, John
Nelson, William
Newberry, Nancy
Newby, Exum
Night, Elizabeth
Night, James
Nix, Washington
Nobles, Andrew
Nobles, Solomon
Nobles, William
Nunry, Henry

**O**

Oglesby, Benjamin
Oliver, James
Oliver, Luramy
Oliver, Urley
Oliver, William
O'Neal, Britain
O'Neal, James
Opsy (or Ossey), Joseph
Outlaw, John

**P**

Pace, Hardy

Pace, James
Pace, Kendred
Page, Elizabeth
Parker, Henry
Parker, Hiram
Parker, Jesse
Parker, John
Parker, Joseph Sr.
Parker, Joseph Jr.
Parish, John
Parrot, James
Passmore, Samuel
Pate, Samuel
Patton, George
Paton, Ichabor
Paul, James
Paul, John
Peacock, Henry
Pearce, Alexander
Pearce, Charlotte
Pearce, Jacob
Pearce, Jacob Jr.
Pearce, James (Jarvis)
Pearce, John
Pearce, Lazarus
Pearce, Theophilus
Pearson, James
Pearson, William
Peek, Ira
Perkins, William H.
Perry, Henry H.
Perry, Terrell
Perry, Thornton
Perry, William
Perry, Wimberley
Perryman, David B.
Perryman, Harmon
Peters, Elizabeth
Peters, William B.
Pettis, Mark
Pettis, Moses
Pettis, Stephen
Phelps, Elias
Philips, Hardy
Player, Thomas
Pope, Elijah
Powell, Enos
Pope, James
Pope, Jesse
Prescot, William

R

Rabon, Charles
Rabon, John
Radford, Balen

Radford, Robert
Rains, Alfred
Rains, John
Rains, Sarah
Raley, John
Ramey, Signal
Rawls, Joseph
Ray, Benjamin
Ray, Eda (m)
Ray, James
Regal, Wythe
Reid, Peter
Reid, William H.
Reynolds, Joseph
Reynolds, Peyton
Ricks, Patience
Richards, William L.
Robert, Harry
Roberson, George
Robinson, Matthew
Roby, Josiah
Rogers, Samuel
Roods, John F.
Roods, Lera
Rouse, Henry J.
Rouse, Mary
Royal, Vincent
Rutherford, John

S

Saffold, Daniel
Sanderfer, Thomas R.
Sapp, Abram
Sapp, Moses
Sauls, Cullen
Sauls, Reuben
Sauls, Theophilus
Sauls, Thompson
Saunders, Ambrose Sr.
Saunders, Ambrose Jr.
Sanders, Dennis D.
Saunders, Elizabeth
Saunders, Mary
Saunders, William
Sawyer, Cader
Sawyer, John
Sawyer, Joseph
Saxon, Benjamin A.
Saxon, Henry
Scarbrough, Anies (f) (Annice)
Scott, William
Self, Chappell B.
Shaw, George
Shine, Daniel W.

Shearly, James
Shicks (or Spicks), Betsy
Sikes, Akelly
Sikes, Hampton
Sledge, Hiram
Slight (or Hight), John
Simpson, David
Sims, John
Sims, Pheriba
Smith, Benjamin B.
Smith, Jacob
Smith, John
Smith, Lovett B.
Smith, Needham
Smith, Polly
Smith, Thomas
Smith, Wiley
Smith, William
Solomon, Henry
Solomon, Lazarus
Solomon, William
Souhall, William
Spears, Archibald
Spencer, Zachariah
Spullock, Solomon
Stanford, William W.
Stephens, Helman
Stephens, Richard
Stephen, William
Stephenson, Henry
Steward, David
Steward, Desin
Stafford, Joshua
Stiles, Clarissa
Stinson, Elam
Stokes, Thomas M.
Stokes, Samuel D.
Street, Richard
Streetman, Isaac L.
Streetman, Jane
Streetman, Samuel
Stone, William
Summerlane, William
Sumner, William
Surls, Raymond
Sutton, Jesse
Sutton, Peter
Swearington, Bolen
Swinney, Edward
Taber, Wesley
Tarver, Hartwell H.
Tarver, Rebecca
Tarver, Henry
Tarver, Ruffin R.

Tarver, William M.
Tatum, Nathaniel
Taylor, Cornelius
Taylor, David
Taylor, George
Taylor, Jacob
Taylor, Lemuel
Taylor, Samuel
Taylor, Thomas
Terrill, Thomas
Tharp, Charnick A.
Tharp, Jeremiah A.
Tharp, Ruth A.
Thigpen, Joshua N.
Thompson, Benjamin
Thompson, David
Thompson, Henry T.
Thompson, Howell
Thompson, John
Thompson, Mary
Thompson, Peter G.
Thompson, Sylvia
Thompson, Washington
Thompson, William
Thomison, John
Tidwell, Millen
Tilman, John
Tippen, Needham
Tison, Hiram
Tison, Sterling
Treeluck, Bryant
Treeluck, George
Treeluck, John
Treeluck, Nawiel (m)
Trull (Trues), James
Tyler, John

U
Underwood, John
V
Vann, Saunders
Veal, Burwell
Veal, William
Vickers, Nancy
Vincent, James
Vincent, Thomas
W
Wade, Jesse
Walden, Samuel
Wall, Joseph
Wall, King D.
Wall, Lydia
Wall, James G.
Wall, William E. A.
Walters, Jess Sr.
Walters, Jesse Jr.
Ward, Willis
Ware, Arthur
Ware, James
Warren, Lott
Warters, Isaac
Warters, John
Warters, William
Watkins, Alfred
Watters, William
Weatherington, John
Webb, James H.
Welch, George W.
Welch, James
Westbrook, Mary
West, Isham
West, Rena
West, Samson

Wheeler, Amy
Wheeler, John
Wheeler, Noah
Whitehead, Martha
Whitehead, Richard
Wiley, Mary Ann
Wills, Joseph L.
Wilkerson, John
Williams, Abraham
Williams, Jesse
Williams, John
Williams, Lavina
Williams, Mary
Williams, Sally
Williams, William
Williams, Winny
Wilson, John
Wimberley, Ezekiel
Wimberly, William Jr.
Wimberly, James Sr.
Wimberly, James
Wimberly, Joshua R.
Wimberly, William Sr.
Wood, David H.
Wood, Isaac
Wyatt, Elijah
Y
Yelverton, Bryant T.
Yeights, Jesse
Young, George
Young, Isaac
Young, John
Young, John Jr.
Young, Sarah
Young, W. W.

## POPULATION STATISTICS FOR TWIGGS COUNTY

In 1826 the population given in the Georgia Stateman, for Twiggs, west of the Oconee River, was 5819.

Census of 1850—total, 8,179; 1880—8918; 1900—8716 and the 1950 Census according to the United States Census for Twiggs was 8,309. (Males—4177; Females—4131); Persons employed, Males 2,216; Females, 514.

All of the available original census records from 1790 to 1880, inclusive, are on file in the National Archives and Records Service, Washington 25, D. C., where they are open for examination. Available census records for the counties of Georgia are on microfilm at the Department of Archives and History, Atlanta 9, Ga., including various years for each county.

## ABSTRACT OF TWIGGS COUNTY TAX DIGEST FOR 1818 - 1826 - 1853

Reference: Georgia Department of Archives and History, Atlanta, Georgia

Land districts were marked off into certain areas in the county where property owners lived to return their taxes. A captain for the district was selected by holding an election with the free holders voting. The free holder who received the majority vote in that area became the Captain and subsequently his name was given to the district for that year.

If persons residing in the county owned property elsewhere, under the column headed, County where land lies, they were required to declare same. (Shown in bracket.)

The tax digests give such information as: number of acres of type of land, to whom granted, adjoined, watercourse, county, aggregate value of land, polls, number of persons subject to military duty, professions, Negroes owned, stock in trade, et cetera. Each year's tax return varied in form.

Compilers' note: The names of persons and other words copied from records may be misspelled. If so, remember the old records are dim, deteriorating with age, the paper brittle and broken, and the script writing in many of the records is practically illegible to the researcher. However, the best interpretation has been given.

## TWIGGS COUNTY TAX DIGEST FOR 1818

*Captain Robert Belcher's District Number 25 and Portions of Nos. 24 and 28*

Adams, Abm.
Angelly, Ben
Angelly, Alex
Angelly, Miles
Albritton, Wm.
Anderson, Willis
Anderson, Lewis
Belcher, McCuin
Belcher, Littleton
Bozeman, Nathan
Brown, Danl.
Beckman, Wm.
Bastie, L. B.
Baldwin, Wm.
Barton, John
Bishop, John
Bell, Joseph
Black, Henry
Bullard, Wiley
Belcher, Robt.
Barrow, Francis
Collins, Thos. G.
Chivers, Larkin
Chivers, Joel
Cooper, Isaac
Crocker, Wm.
    (Practicing Atty.)
Crittendon, John
Chain, Sarah

Crumpton, David
Coon, Jas.
Coon, John
Carter, Sam'l.
Calvin, John
Chitty, Jas.
Churchwell, Henry
Caster, John C.
Connell, Thos.
Denton, Thos.
Daniel, Elijah
Daniel, Wm.
Disbazo, John
Disbazo, Robt.
Duke, John R.
Duke, John
Danner, Alben
Durham, Jas.
    (agt. for Jas. Durham, Jr.)
Dunn, Jacob
Deshazo, William
Dunn, William
    (agt. for Free Man of Colour)
Deshazo, Robert
Dorman, Allen
Denon, Wm. (?)
Dick, Saml.

Dorman, Mitchell
Elliot, John
Elliot, Susannah
Ellison, Wm.
Ethridge, Abel
Ethridge, Lewis
Elliot, Jas.
Fort, A., Jr.
    Adm.—H. Zorn, Dcd.
Fulghum, Micajah
Faulkner, Job
Faulkner, Asa
Ford, John F.
Flemming, John
    (Columbia Co.)
Flemming, Robt.
Fort, A., Sr. (Pulaski Co.)
Fleming, Jas.
Fort, Moses
Guardner, Samuel
Grimes, William
Gray, Davis
Gray, John
Grace, Matt R.
Griffin, Lewis L.
    (Bullock Co.)
and Exr. for Griffin, Wm.
Hawkins, Thos.
Hawkins, Calvin

Hammock, Wm.
Howell, Hescheah
Hargraves, Leml. P.
Hutchison, Jas.
Harrison, Jonathon
Harrison, George
Harrison, George
Harrison, Levi
Hoskins, Stephen
Heninton, John
Harris, Asa
Hayse, Alex
Howell, John
Jacobs, Wm., Sr.
Jones, Wm. P.
Jamerson, D.
Jamerson, G. T.
Lewis, Jas.
Lassiter, Amos
Lovette, Moses
Lovette, Jas.
Montgomery, Jas.
Montgomery, Jas., Sr.
Minsey, Aaron
McCoy, Chas.
McHenry, Robt.
Moffett, Gabl., Jr.
  (Practicing Atty.)
McKey, Jas.
Minsey, Nathan
Massers, John
Massers, Jacob
Moffett, Gabl., Sr.
  (Wilkinson &
  Washington)
Mabon, Wm.
Mills, A.
Minsey, Jacob, Jr.
Morgan, Joseph
Matthews, John
McIntyre, Arch'd
Murphy, Jas.
Minsey, Philip
Napier, G. M.
Nobles, Leonard
Nobles, Wm.

Pentecost, F. L.
Pearce, John, Sr.
Pearce, Jacob, Jr.
Pearce, John, Jr.
Powell, Sam'l
  (Telfair Co.)
Priddy, Robt.
Priddy, Ben
Pearce, Lazarus
Pope, Jesse
Perry, Henry H.
Patterson, John
Pearce, Jacob, Sr.
Pearce, Jas.
Palmer, George
Pitts, Martin (Telefair)
Pearce, Jacob, Sr.
Powell, Wm.
Powell, J.
Priddy, John
Parker, A.
Perry, Isaac
Perry, A. C.
  (Washington Co.)
Perry, Wm.
  (Washington Co.)
Roberts, Jas.
  (Town lot in Marion)
Robertson, Solomon
Ragan, Robertson
Rhodes, Wm.
Ray, J. W.
Rutherford, John
Robertson, Wm.
Rutlance, Whitmell
  (Tattnal and Wayne Co.)
Russell, Thos.
Robertson, Jeremiah
Robb, Robert (Jones Co.)
Solomon, Wm.
Smith, George
Smallwood, Francis
Stapeer, John
Smith, Thos.
Smith, Jas.

Smith, John
Shines, Jas. W.
Speed, Martin
Slatter, H. H.
Spullock, Jas.
Solomon, Henry
  Adm., John Land, dcd.
Summons, A. or
  (Simmons)
Summons, A. and Co.
Shellman, Robt.
Spann, James
Stafford, Joshua
  (Wilkinson Co.)
Spann, B. H.
Terrell, Henry M.
Taylor, Simmon
Thompson, Nelson
Wheeler, Noah
Whitaker, Richd
Woods, Abel
West, Hamlin
West, Isham
Weaver, Julius
Williams, Saml.
Wright, Ezekiel
Weldon, Jas.
Wimberly, Joshua R.
  (Practicing physician)
Weldon, Robert
Williams, Jacob
Youngblood, Jacob
Zorn, Sarah
Zuber, Abm.
Zuber, Caleb
Zuber, Joshua
  (Oglethorpe Co.)

*Defaulters*
Barr, John
Dorton, Wm.
Dorman, Ephriam
Dunncan, Saml.
Gorham, Willis
King, Ledler
Pender, David

## Captain Wiley Belcher's District No. 28

Alexander, Saml.
Alexander, Jas. W.
Adkinson, Robt.
Andrews, Robin
  (Pulaski Co.)

Anderson, Rueben
  guar. for W. & M.
  Anderson
Barker, John (Telefair Co.)
Barr, John

Barr, Bartlett S.
Barr, John J.
  guar. Wm. Buts' orphans
Barbree, Staucell
  (Screven Co.)

Bond, Solomon
Bowden, Wm.
Bowden, Jesse
Bowden, Wm.
Barnes, Jno.
Barker, Geo.
Brown, G. A.
Bull, Jacob
Barbee, John S.
Bryant, Ben
Bridges, John Sr.
Belcher, Wiley
Belcher, Ferrell
Busbee, Jeremiah
Braswell, Wm.
Bridges, Jno.
Burnet, Lewis
Barclay, David
Barclay, Jno.
Barclay, Gill
Burnett, Jos.
Bryant, Arthur
Casey, Jno.
Chance, Henry L.
Chance, Nancy
Cloud, Wm.
Can, Milby
Castleburg, Jno.
Cochran, Jas.
Cloud, Jno. (Jones, Laurens, Wayne, Pulaski, Baldwin Co.)
Cook, Phillip
Coon, Henry, Sr.
  Agt., Benj. Isbett
Coon, Henry L.
Cloud, Jas.
Clamput, Saml.
Clamput, Saml., Sr.
Davis, Abrm.
Davis, Jacob
Dunn, Richard
Davis, Rease
Davis, Wright
  (Laurens, Telfair Co.)
Davidson, Jno.
Durham, Benj.
Easterlin, Jas.
Ethridge, Jno.
Fennele, Robt.
Fagan, Geo.
Farener, Luke
Fortsan, Henry

Farmer, King
Farris, Saml.
Harris, Jas.
Harrell, Wm.
Hinson, Asa
Harden, Jas.
Hollandworth, Jesse
Hollandworth, Jno.
Hollandworth, Jas.
Harwell, Simon
Holley, Wm.
Hobbs, Lewis
Irwin, Wm.
Green, Hardy
Graham, Saml.
Green, Wm.
Griffin, Wm.
Goss, Matthew
Griffin, Jno.
Gorman, Jas.
Gentry, Wm.
Gatting, Major
Hayse, Lunanny
Hardan, Hall
Hidleburg, M. C.
Hardin, Mark
  (Telfair Co.)
Hidleburg, Jno.
Henderson, Daniel
Higgs, Jno.
Hunter, Hardy
Irby, Jos.
Johnston, Jacob
Joyner, Ebenezer
  Exr., Caleb McKinney
Johnston, Jeremiah
Johnston, Wm.
Jones, Jas.
  agt. for free man of colour
Jones, Jas., Sr.
Jones, Thos.
Johnston, Robt.
Knight, Jas.
Keenor, Jno.
Kelly, Thos.
Lewis, Daniel
Lewis, Laten
Lewis, Jacob
Leonard, Calvin
Littlefield, Abraham
Littleton, Jno.
Littlefield, Wm.

Lessell, Edm.
Lions, Red (Wayne Co.)
Littlefield, Haswell
McKinney, Jos.
Moore, Jas.
Magee, Laurence
Moore, Lewis
Magee, Philip
McKinzee, Jno.
Moon, H.
McDonald, Moses
Matthews, T.
  Guard., Wm. Butts orphans
O'Neal, Britton
Perminter, Jno.
Patton, Jas.
Pearson, Josiah
Powell, Wm.
Perry, Jas.
Rigdon, Stephen
Rouse, Ben P.
Ray, Benj.
  (Jones & Wilks Co.)
  Exr. Geo. Ray (Col'mb)
Reed, A. B.
  (Practicing Phy.)
Reed, Jno.
Ray, Jno.
Rogers, Jas.
Rutland, Oran B.
Smith, Thos.
Self, David
Self, Elizabeth
Smith, Jas. B.
Stanford, Wm.
Stanford, Robt.
Smith, Turner
Streetman, Wm.
Streetman, Saml.
Simmons, Amos
Smith, Powell
Saunders, Peterson
Shine, Jno.
Streetman, William
Smith, Silas
Simms, Leond
  (Washington Co.)
Streetman, Issac L.
Taylor, Robt.
Tatam, Nathl.
Truman, Jas. B.
Williams, Drury

Weahtersby, Stephen
Wilson, Geo.
Wilson, Saml.

Williams, Jno. D.
Wilkes, Reuben
Wade, Richard

Willoby, Jno., Sr.
Young, Jno.
Young, Wm.

*Capt. Bozeman's District*

Alfred, Furnsy
Alfred, Wyatt
Benson, Joseph
Bozeman, Ethld
Busbee, John
Bass, Bryant
Burn, Wm.
Burnes, Joseph
Bozeman, Elizabeth
Bozeman, David
Bridger, Joseph
Bridges, Bartlet
  (Wilks. Co.)
Barnes, John
Coward, Zach
Carter, John
Carter, Joel
Carter, Ben. J.
Carter, Stephen
Collins, Andrew
Carter, Abner
Coward, Henry
Curry, Robt.
Cone or Cox, Jas.
Durham, Stephen
Duffell, Thos.
Davis, Joseph G.
Davis, Jesse
Drew, James C.
Davis, Arthur
Ellis, Edwin
Fowler, Joseph
  (Pulaski Co.)
Funderburg, Elizah
  (Telfair Co.)
Gilder, Sinnot
Gilder, Jas.

Harvey, Ben
Holmes, Shad'k.
Holly, Borgey
Harvey, John
Hooks, Bardin
Hitty, Edwd
Hunter, William
Hunter, Charles
Holmes, Jas.
Higgs, Mary
Hooks, Harmon
Johnston, Ben
Jamerson, Joseph
Johnston, Amy
  (Telfair Co.)
King, Joseph
King, Allen (Telfair Co.)
Kirkham, Robt.
Luther, Mooreland
Little, Morris
Lasster, Brinkley
Little, George
Montgomery, Lewis
Mills, John
Pyres, Danl. (Pulaski Co.)
Parker, Micajah
Pace, Jas. (Burke Co.)
Pugh, Dorothy
Rogers, Cullen
Riddle, Henry
Railey, Gimpsy
Railey, Irsiah
Rickey, Richard
Richmond, Sam'l.
  (Washington Co.)
Stevens, Holmon

Stevens, Richard, Sr.
Stevens, William
Stevens, Richard, Jr.
Simpson, Jas.
Simpson, Jacob
Saunders, Dennis D.
Smith, Wm.
Stephens, Eslie
Sutton, Jas. W.
Sims, John
Sherrod, Elizabeth
Stevens, Jones
  (Wilkinson Co.)
Sulton, Ben
Smith, John
Saunders, Wright
Smith, John
Smith, Stephen
Shines, Dan'l. W.
Smith, Andrew
Sutton, Chas.
Taylor, Henry
Tirwin, Rebecah
Tirwin, Wm.
Wilkinson, John
Walden, Reuben
Walden, Green
Wheeler, John
Waters (Walters), Jesse
Womble, John
Willis, Zacob
Wimberly, Ezekiel
Williamson, Wm. W.
Yerty, Jacob
Yerty, Geo.
Yelverton, Bryant

*Captain Brown's District (portions of districts No. 26 and 25)*

Alsa, Thos. (?) (Burke)
Birge, Jno.
Benifield, Gideon
Brock, Jno.
Beaman, Matthew
Benefield, Meakam

Bryant, Blake (or Bryan)
Brown, Jas. (Laurens Co.)
  guar. Jas. Vasser orph.
Bozman, Mady
Collins, Elisha
Commander, Sam'l.

Crocker, Jno.
Chastin, Abin
Curry, Saml.
Carely, Jno.
Childers, Osborn
Dunn, Davis, Sr.

Dunn, David, Jr.
Dunn, Jessie
Denon, Aaron
Davis, Thos.
Dennard, Thos.
Dinon, Moses
Denon, Jas.
Dennard, Shadk
Dennard, Issac
Dennard, Jesse
Dennard, Wm. E.
Denon, Jeremiah
Dennard, Wm. E.
Denon, Jeremiah
Dunn, Jas.
Dennard, Jno. D.
Dennard, Keneda
Dennard, Jno. E.
Easterlin, Henry
Ezell, Jane
Fitzgerald, Reuben
 (Telfair Co.)
Frazner, Wm.
Fort, Thos.
Fielding, Thos.
Fox, Thos.
Guerry, Peter U.,
 Exr. for Guerry, Jno.
Guerry, Jas. Sr.
Green, Aquillan
Gibbs, Howell
Graham, David
Griffin, Jno.
Graggs, Grace
Gamper, Caden (?)
 (Pulaski Co.)
Griffin, Wm.
Griffin, Susannah
Griffin, Ethelred

Gold, Jno.
Hickey, Jos.
Hathoon, Joshua
Harrison, Jas.
 (Laurens Co.)
Harney, Thos.
Holland, Daniel S.
Holland, Jethro
Henry, Jno.
Henry, Wm.
Henry, Adm.
Henry, Shadk
Holyfield, Sian
Hayse, Davis
Hayse, Jno.
Hester, Jas.
Harris, Ben
Hayse, Jas.
Hall, Jno.
Holly, Grace
 Adm., E. Robertson,
 Orph.
Hayse, James
Holly, Issac
 (Jasper & Washington
 Co.)
Jordan, Henry
Jones, Stepgen
Jones, Thos., Sr.
 (Warren Co.)
Jones, Thos.
Kelly, Ben W.
Lovery, Jno. R.
Lane, Jas.
Matthews, Isham
McHarris, Thos.
Magee, Levin
Magee, Crawford
McKegney, Geo.

Magee, Jas.
Martin, Robt.
Miller, Andrew
 (Laurens Co.)
Nichols, Jas.
 (Wilkinson Co.)
Page, Leml.
Passmore, Saml.
Phillips, Chas.
Peacock, Robt.
Pearce, Wm.
Reynold, Robt.
 guar. E. Robertson's orph.
Robertson, Jas
Stevens, Solomon
Sledge, Collin
Sinclair, Jno.
Sinclair, Jesse
Stuart, Josiah
Spann, Richard C.
Spurlock, Mary
Smith, Britton
Stone, Wm.
Taylor, Zackr.
Tarver, Henry
Ward, Enoch
Wimberly, Frederick
Wimberly, E.
 Adm., Abm Wimberly
Wimberly, Jas.
Wimberly, Perry
Wimberly, Jas. B.
Wood, Issac
Watson, Fredk.
Watson, David
Watson, Michael
Willis, Jas. & Wm.
West, Eli
Veal, Wm.

*Captain Bullocks' District (portions of Nos. 27 and 28)*

Anderson, John
Bullock, Irwin
Barrow, Green
Busbee, Jeremiah
Bell, Susannah
 (Oglethorpe Co.)
Boyce, Christopher
Blackshear, Wm.
Bass, Drury
Bell, Jonothan

Bobbit, Thos.
Busbee, Nimrod
Barnes, Wm.
Birden, Wm.
Collins, William
Collins, Joseph
Crosby, Spencer
Crosby, Geo.
Crawford, Wm.
Cuningham, Andrew

Carr, William
Chandler, Wm.
Collins, Wilson
 (Trustee, D. Vann)
Cherry, Rebuah
Chancellor, John
Castleberry, Margaret
Davis, John
Dopson, Avonillan
Evans, Hesikiah

Evans, Phereha
Evans, Turner
Edmunson, Willis
Fagan, Benj.
Folingham, Moses
Frederick, Wm.
  (Pulaski Co.)
Filingham, Jarvis, Jr.
Filingham, Jarvis
Guardner, Jacob
Goss, Wm.
Guardner, Thos.
Griffin, Jno.
Griffin, Leroy
Guard, Elijah G. (?)
  (Jones & Wayne Co.)
Hill, Willoby
Hoskins, Bary B.
Heaton, Owen
Hood, Alex
Hollandworth, Issac
Holbourn, Geo.
Henison, John
  Adm. Howell, Thomas
Hinson, Caleb
Hinson, John
Hutchison, J. W.
  (Wilkinson Co.)
Hammock, Lewis
Horton, Hugh
Horton, Amos
Jones, Allen
James, John
Jernigan, Alex
Jordon, Wiley
Jones, Levi (Wilkinson Co.)
Jessup, Gus
Jernigan, Moody
Jamerson, D. (Burke Co.)
Jenkins, Wm. F.
Linton, Jno, Sr.
Linton, Hugh
Lisles, Sherwood
Lisles, John
Lindsey, T. Raka

McWilliams, Jas.
Matthews, Leodk
  (Wilkinson Co.)
Matthews, Barry
  (Laurens Co.)
Majors, Elrod
May, Jas.
Mayors, Thos.
Maxwell, William
Meadors, Aver (?)
Moseley, Elial
Mathews, Levi
Morgan, Edw'd.
Mixon, Merideth
Matthews, John
Martin, Wm. (Pulaski Co.)
Nelson, Alex
Nobles, Wm.
Normas, Jas.
Nixon, Wm.
Owens, Wm.
Parker, Gab'l.
Pettis, Moses
Pate, Allen
Pettis, Mark
Powell, John
Pearce, Thos.
Phillips, Jno
Perryman, Harmon
  (Boundary-Perrymans
  Mill)
Pettis, Stephen
Parker, John
Quak, Peter
  (Washington Co.)
Quak, Sam'l.
Reed, Josiah
Rowland, Jno.
Reynolds, Joseph
Raves, Philip
Raburn, Richd.
Raburn, Budd, Jr.
Rogers, John
Shows, John, Sr.

Shows, Adam
Spears, Nathl.
Stuckey, Jno.
Shackleford, Jas.
Seal, Andrew
Stiles, Jno.
Strickland, Joel
Strickland, Arch'd.
Stafford, Allen
Shows, John
Smith, Jas. (Pulaski Co.)
Stanford, Reuben
Simmons, Wm.
Tharp, Charnic
Taylor, Thos.
Tharp, Charnick, Jr.
Todd, Joshua
Thorp, Wm.
Tharp, Jer. (Wilkinson Co.)
Tharp, John A.
Vann, Edw'd.
West, Jonothan
Williams, Hodges
Whitis, Jno.
Warsworthy, Henry
Willis, Wm.
Watts, Jacob
Wilson, John
Windham, Jno.
Wood, Jno.
Williams, Jno.
Williams, David
Willis, Thos.
Williams, Berry
Watson, Jas. H.
Wilkinson, Adams
Wall, Jesse R.
Wall, Jas.
Wall, Major
Williams, Jesse
  (Hancock Co.)
Williams, Abm.
Young, Isaac
Young, Sarah

*Captain Ellis District No. 23*

Arnold, Jno. (Telfair)
Berryhill, Wm.
Berry, Jno.
Brackin, Jas.
Brown, Jas.

Berry, Jno. Sr.
  "—Adm., Simon Stinson
  (Burke)
Berry, Hasey
Berry, Matthew

Bowman, Leond
Guard. Bozeman, M. L.
  (Pulaski)
Bradshaw, Chestley
Ballard, Charles

Beaty, Thomas (Laurens)
Cartledge, Jas.
Chapman, Jno.
Conner, Jno.
Carswell, Alex
Cooper, Wm.
Clapton, Wm.
Ellis, Samuel
Ellis, Wm.
Ellis, Rheasa J.
Fowler, Simmons
Forhand, Amos
Garrett, Jas.
Graddy, Fred'k.
Galimore, Jno.
Galimore, Jas.
Grimsley, Wm.
Gates, Ben
Gilder, Isaac
Goode, Robt.
Gates, Jas.
Goza, Martin
Graddy, Jno.
Hughes, Littleberry (Telfair)
Hughes, Jno.
Henry, David
Holmes, Elijah
Holoda, Thomas

Johnston, Burwell
Johnston, Mich'l.
Joyce, Jesse
Lamb, Arthur
Lamb, Reuben
Lewis, Jacob
Leigh, Durham
Lipham, Moses (Montgomery, Laurens, Pulaski, Green, Washington)
Mock, Harmon
Mock, Jno. Sr. (Telfair & Jefferson)
Mock, Jno. Jr.
Mills, Elijah
Malant, Jas.
McMurry, Jas.
Mitchell, Mary
Mansfield, Fredk
Nicks, L. B.
Nicks, Jno.
Peters, Wm. (Oglethorpe)
Pouncey, Jno.
Padget, Luke
Quatleburn, David
Rabun, Jno.
Regan, Joseph

Smith, Jno. Sr. (Telfair)
Sapp, Henry
Spears, Sara
Sims, Isaac
Sims, Jno.
Sauls, Chard
Truluck, Jno.
Thompson, Charles
Thompson, Jno. Jr.
Thompson, Pantlock
Thompson, Jno. N.
Thompson, Henry
Thompson, Jno. H.
Tison, Joab
Tison, Littleton
Vickens, Jesse
Vickens, Jacob
Vickens, Wm.
Vickens, Young
Vickens, Drury
Vickens, Wiley
Vickens, Sarah
Vickens, Jashua
Willis, Jas.
Webb, Jas. H.
Ward, Antimus
Ward, Shadk
Williams, Mark

*Captain Hodges' District No. 25 and portions of Nos. 24 and 23*

Abbot, Abner A.
Allen, John
Anderson, Wm.
Asbell, Elisha
Asbell, John
Brackin, Isaac
Buck, Hardy
Brooks, Wiley
Bell, John
Bishop, Abner (Montgomery & Jackson)
Bishop, Wm.
Barnes, Archelius
Barnes, Jesse
Barnet, Miles
Burton, John
Buck, Wherry
Burnham, Elizah
Cornelius, Geo.
Curry, Whitmell
Chapman, Robert C.

Clark, Wm.
Cummins, Robert (Physician) (Land—Montgomery & Wayne Co's. Lots in Marion & Hartford)
Dick, Obadiah
Denson, Isaac
Denson, Jno.
Durham, Hardy
Dishroon, Wm.
Durham, John
Dennis, John
Denson, Joel
Edmonson, Bryant
Exum, Messoe
Elliot, Ben
Fred'k. Hiram
Faulk, Wm.
Faulk, Mark
Faulk, John

Finley, Thomas
Finley, David (Burke)
Finley, Jas. H.
Gilmore, John H. (Tatnall)
Gilmore, Elizabeth (Tatnall)
Goldine, Drury
Goldbie, Aaron (Pulaski)
Gregory, Matt
Hammock, Thomas
Henderson, Jno.
Holmes, Josiah
Hart, Marmaduke
Hart, Edwin
Hammock, Paschal (Pulaski & Telfair)
Hodges, Edm.
Holada, Wm.
Hodges, Robt.
Hammock, Elijah

Horn, Joab
"—Guard, Green, W.
Howell, Arthur
Hardin, John
Joyner, Ben
Jones, Wright
Jones, John
Lawson, Amos
Listan, Levi
Lawson, Davenport
Leonard, Thomas
Lawson, Roger
"—(Guard. John M. Gamble) and Agt. for Lawson, Charles M.
Lawson, Charles M.
McCullen, Matt (Wayne Co.)
Moore, Moses
McMurray, Land
Mimms, M.
Morris, Wm.
Morris, Henry
Nickez, Elijah
Nickez, Edward

Nelson, Wm. T.
Opry, Hugh
Payne, Saml.
Payne, Dan'l, Adm. for Wm. Payne
Pittman, Jno.
Pitts, Stephen
Pittman, Jesse
Pope, Soloman
Perry, Wm. (Washington)
"—(Admr J. Vasser)
Perry, Edward
Passmore, John
Perry, Thomas
Pope, Jesse
Pumphrey, Redin
Radford, Robt.
Ricks, Jas.
Ricks, Harris (Pulaski Co.)
Rouse, Henry
Rouse, Mary
Smith, Wm.
Smith, Wm. H.

Sauls, Reuben
Sangster, Peter
Sherwood, Wright
Sanders, John
Sauls, Jacob
Sauls, Thomas
Travis, John
Tirvin, George
Thompson, Wm.
Ussery, Ed. D.
Vasser, Willis
Wilkinson, Saunders
Whitehead, Charles
Wood, David
Williams, Thomas
Wheat, Moses
Warrell, Isiah
Williams, Alex
Weathers, Samie
Wood, Samuel P.
Wilson, Bythenny
Webb, Thomas
Wade, Jas.
Wimberly, Wm.
Wimberly, Mary

*Captain Jefferson's District*

Adkins, Robt.
Alston, Joshua
Averret, Jeremiah (Laurens Co.)
Adkins, Jno.
Anglin, Henry
Adkins, Thos.
Adkins, Lewis
Adkins, Wm.
Buckelew, Fredk.
Brown, Jesse
Black, Thos.
Buckelew, Jas.
Barley, Henry
Bullock, Buxwell
Bullock, Richard
Black, Elizabeth
Ball, Hiram
Blades, Isreal
Bennet, Edward
Blackshear, Enoch
Bailey, Wm.
Brown, Levin
Blackshear, Moses
Blackshear, Randse

Blackshear, Jacob
Blackshear, Issac
Bailey, Elijah
Bennet, Randal
Casleberry, Jno.
Clemans, Hugh
Coffeld, Gressum
Cortney, Ernie
Collier, Ben
Campbell, Chas.
Chappell, Thos.
Calhoun, Jas.
Childers, Nathan
Darby, Nicholas
Darby, Micajah
Dees, Jacob
Davis, Jno.
Day, Stephen
Day, Nimrod
Epps, Edward
Edwards, David
Fitzpatrick, Elizabeth
Fulton, Thos.
Fitzpatrick, Wm.
Gibson, Jas.

Glover, Kelly
Golden, Jno.
Hathorn, John
"—Guard. Hathorn, Jas.
Homes, Silas
Hare, Thos.
Hall, Jas.
Hall, Jos.
Hicky, Wm.
Herrin, Elizabeth
Hayse, Jno.
Horne, Hansell
Hunt, Wm. Jr. (Telfair Co.)
Hunt, Wm.
Hemphill, Wm.
Hall, Stanley
Herrin, Fred'k. G.
Hathorn, Jno.
Jamerson, Geo.
Jamerson, Sarah
Jamerson, Wm. L.
Jamerson, Jno.
Joyner, Benager
Johnston, Asa
Jones, Wm.

Jefferson, Jno.
Jefferson, Jas.
Kent, Price
Kent, Henry
Lanier, Jas.
Lintan, Jno.
Low, Caleb
Low, Wm.
Lane, Jos.
Lindsey, Issac
Lindsey, Jared
Lindsey, Gold
Lindsey, Chas.
Lindsey, Thos.
Melton, Wm.
McLendon, Jas.
Moore, Thos.
  (Pulaski & Wayne Co.)
McMullin, Jos.
McMullin, Wm.
Matthews, Ben
Melton, Clem
Matthews, Jno.
Matthews, Malcomb
McAhey, Wm.
McDaniel, Alex
Maseley, Wm.
Maseley, Mary
Morgan, Issac

Morgan, Jno.
Martan, Fredk.
Melton, Quin
Martin, Hiram
Mann, Hiram
Martin, Wm.
Pate, Jas.
Pate, James
Paul, Jno.
Pinson, Wm.
Powell, Elkana
Pandle, Matthew
Parker, Hiram
Parker, Jos.
Poore, Jno.
Parker, Hening
Peacock, Jonathan
  (Pulaski Co.)
Poore, Thos.
Richardson, David
  (Telfair)
Slatter, Jno.
Slatter, Wm.
Smith, Jno. D.
Smith, Jos.
Solomon, Lazarus
Scott, Wm.
Scott, Wm.

Scott, Ben
Scarboro, Noah
Tanner, Vincent
Taylor, Geo.
Taylor, Edmd.
Taylor, Edwd. Jr.
Vinson, Jas.
Wall, Ghad'k.
Wade, Henry
Wade, John
Williams, Geo.
Ware, Jas.
Ward, Nath'l. (for Ward, Elizabeth)
"—Guard. Ward, Thos.
Wood, Jos.
Wall, Ezekiel, Jr.
Wheeler, Jno.
Warren, Jno.
Wood, Jno.
Wall, David
Wall, Jesse
Weatherby, Jos.
Waters, Issac
Willis, Geo.
Wall, King D.
Young, David
Young, Geo.

### Captain Smith's District (Nos. 24 and 25th Districts)

Anderson, Stanley
Brown, Silas
"—(Guard. for Sara Brown)
Brown, Dempsey
Brown, Henry E.
Brown, Wm.
Brunson, Dave
Bateman, Jesse
Brunson, David (Pulaski)
Bunn, Henry
Bateman, Jno.
Barron, Wm.
Bateman, Simon
Bryan, Jas. C.
"—Exr. Edward Mobley
Brown, Jno.
Baker, David
Bell, Jno.
Bryan, Edward (Laurens, Oconee, R. & Jasper)

Bryan, Jas. Jr.
Bryan, Joseph (Pulaski)
Bryan, Joseph
Barron, Thomas C.
Brown, Hilby
Benson, Thomas W.
Brown, Jesse D.
Cool, Simmons
Clark, Jas (Calffrey and Robertson)
Cathright, Jas. (or "G")
Churchwell, Jas.
Churchwell, Jonothan
Cathright, Mary (Jackson, Telfair)
Cooper, Jno.
Carter, Wm. B.
Coats, Oswell
Carter, Thomas
Coats, Thomas (Jones)
Coats, Wm.

Calpprey, Lewis (or Calffrey)
"—Guard. for Edward Burton
Dishroon, Jno.
Dupry, Jereniah
Dupry, Jno.
Duprey, Wm. H.
Davis, Elbert
Driver, Jno.
Dunwoody, Mary
Daniel, Lewis
Edwards, Jno.
Finley, Jas.
Fulgham, Jesse
Genton, Wm.
Graves, Archd
Glenn, Robt. (Tatnall, Altahama)
Gliden, Jacob

Gliden, Gilbert
Graves, Jas.
  (Guard. Tobias a free
  man of color.)
Harrison, Jas.
Hodges, Ben
Homes, Thomas
Hunt, Jno.
Hamelton, Wm.
Hasty, Noel
Harris, Simon
Hunt, Ben
Hunt, Lewis
Hunt, Henry (Telfair,
  Washington)
Hunt, Thomas
Ingraham, Edward
Jordan, Ew B.
Jamenson, Robt.
Jamenson, Wm.
Kendricks, Jas.
Knight, Mary
Knight, Abel
Knight, Jas.
Lowe, Acquillan
Low, Wm.
McKinney, Rachael
McKenny, Jas.
Mills, Shadk
Mosely, Isiah
Mann, David W.
Matthews, Henry
Mims, Seaborn

Massey, Dave
  Trustee Mt. Morah
  Church (No. 24)
Mobley, E. Edward
  (Agt. for Jno. Jackson
  free man of color)
Mosley, Silas
Minsey, Jacob
O'Neeland, David
Pace, Wm.—Agt. (Burke)
Pace, Cherry
  (Burke)
Parnell, Jas.
Perry, Thornton
Pace, Hardy
Pollack, Jesse
Powers, Jas.
Railey, Charles
Raines, R., Admr.
  (Hancock)
Railey, John
Robertson, Will (Telfair)
Reynolds, Mary
Ross, Godfrey
Simpson, Jno.
Simpson, Soloman
Smith, L. B.
Stevens, Samuel
Smith, Richard, Sr.
  "—Guard. Jno McRay's
  Orphans (Burke)
Smith, Thomas
Smith, Jno. M.

Sinton, Henry
Sinton, Ben A.
Segar, Samuel
Simpson, Sirrell
Shuler, Jas. R.
Stokes, Jas.
Veazey, Ezekiel
Wiley, Edward M.
Ward, Elijah
Wyatt, Elijah
Williams, Jno.
Ward, Willis
Williams, Hull
Wilson, Samuel
Watson, Silas
Walker, Burwell
Wilkinson, Micajh
Ward, Elisha
Wheeler, Richard (Jasper)
Walker, Charlotte
  (Wilkinson)
  Defaulters
Curry, Jacob
Cunningham, Wm.
Duprey, Simon
Hamm, Obediah
Hamm, Wm.
Jobson, Francis
Kendrick, Wm.
Mabory, Jordon
Perfew, Andrew
Scott, Jno.
Simpson, Uniah

1818   TAX RETURNS TWIGGS COUNTY, GA.

Amount of Taxable Property

| | |
|---|---:|
| Captain Bozeman's dist. | $ 155.30¾ |
| Captain Robt. Belcher's dist. | 463.89¾ |
| Captain Wiley Belcher's dist. | 285.63¼ |
| Captain Bulloch's dist. | 160.53¾ |
| Captain Brown's dist. | 207.57½ |
| Captain Ellis's dist. | 146.57 |
| Captain Hodges' dist. | 238.45½ |
| Captain Jefferson's dist. | 160.53½ |
| Captain Smith's dist. | 320.90¾ |
| | $ 2139.41½ |
| Amt. assessed on Defaulters | 16.25 |
| | $ 2155.66½ |

Nov. 1, 1818
Certified by
Robert Hodges,
R.T.R.T.C.

Georgia      )
Twiggs County)

    This will certify that the Grand Jurors of the County have at the August Term 1819 allowed the Tax Collector the sum of forty-four dollars and seventy-seven cents as the amount of his insolvent list for the taxes for the year 1818 and recommends that he be credited by that sum in settlement with Treasury of this State.

                            Timothy Matthews,
                            Foreman

## TWIGGS COUNTY TAX DIGEST FOR 1826

### Capt. Pearson's District

Andrews, John H.
Andrews, Abisha
Andrews, Robins
Anderson, John
Ard, John
Bond, Solomon
Bryan, Thomas
Barnes, John
Bowman, Leonard
Bowden, Jesse
Barr, John G.
Bowers, Benjamin
Barnes, Littleton
Barbree, John L.
Collier, Jesse
Campbell, John
Crawford, Martin N.
Chance, Nancy
Cooke, Philip
Daniel, William
Durden, Josiah
Durden, Lane
Davis, Abraham
Dye, William, Jr.
Easterling, James
Ells, Nathaniel
Eaves, John
Easterling, Shadrack
Fennel, Robert
Graham, Ishmael
Graham, Samuel
Gaudy, Griffin
Granbbery, Langler
Granbery, James M.
George, William
Hydrick, Powell
Higgs, John

Harrell, Hardy
Heidlebergh, John
Harris, James T.
Harrel, Samuel
Hollingsworth, Jesse, Sr.
Hollingsworth, William
Johnson, William, Jr.
Johnson, Jeremiah
Jordan, Wiley
Jones, Thomas
Jones, John D.
Jacobs, Zackariah
Keebler, Zack
Keebler, Edward
Linsey, Rivhard
Lloyd, Nicolas
McCullers, Hirman
McCullers, Faith
Manning, Jarris
O'Neal, Brittain
Ogledby, Benjamin
Parker, Allen
Powell, William C.
Pace, Thomas
Philips, Elias
Powell, Jeremiah
Pearson, James
Perkins, Wm. H.
Reed, John
Ray, Benjamin
Ray, Benjamin L.
Ray, John
Reynolds, Robert
Rogers, Samuel
Ray, Benjamin, Jr.
Rogers, Newman

Shaw, George
Smith, Thomas, Jr.
Stanford, Robert
Self, Chapel B.
Smith, Thomas, Jr.
See, Anthony
Streetman, Samuel
Saunders, Benjamin
Saunders, Ambrose, Jr.
Saffold, Daniel
Stucky, Daniel
Self, David
Smith, Stephen
Smith, Benjamin
Thomas, Thomas
Tyler, John
Williams, Richard V.
Weathersby, Stephen
Wall, King D.
Willis, Benj F.
Wall, Joseph
Williams, Drury
Young, William
Young, John L.
Young, George
Young, John
   Defaulters
Atinson, Robert
Anderson, Elijah
Bowman, Fredk
Isham, Fennel
Culwell, Hiram
Holland, William
Jones, James
Kendrick, William
Stanford, Samuel

### Capt. Wimberly's District

Attaway, I
Also, Thomas
Arnold, John
Alford, Wyatt
Bedingfield, Hardy
Berry, John
Bryan, Thos
Cose, Caleb
Cose, Charles

Convar, Terence C.
Carswell, Alexander
Carswell, James B.
Chatman, William
Clark, Silas
Dennard, John Z.
Dyer, Nancy
Dikes, John
Ellis, Rheso J.

Fowler, Simmans
Garret, James
Gilbert, Birdd
Griffin, Allen
Grimsley, William
Grady, John
Gallimore, John
Hughs, Littlebery
Hughs, Hayden

Hammock, Paschale
Hammock, John
Hall, Furney
Herring, Delihah
Height, John
Hodges, Edward K.
Hitson, Harry
Joyce, Daniel
Johnson, Edward
Jones, Wright
Knight, James
Lewis, Jacob
Lamb, Luke
Lane, Benjamin
Lamb, Reuben
Lamb, Arthur
Lamb, Grady
Methvin, Nathan
Methvin, Joseph
Methvin, Thomas
Mansfield. Fred'k.
McCant, James
McCant, Valentine

McCarty, Authory
Moore, William
Noles, Daniel
Nicks, John
Nicks, William
Nobbles, Andrew
Nicks, Washington
Nicks, John
Oliver, William
Perkins, William
Pope, Elijah
Pope, James
Philips, Nimrod
Peters, Williams
Pagit, Luke
Perkins, Linkfield
Peters, William
Rouse, Allen
Slone, William
Sauls, Cullen
Saniford, Thos. R.
Smith. William
Sauls, Thompson

Thompson, John
Thompson, John
Truluck, George
Thompson, Mary
Trut, B. W.
Thompson, Berry
Truluck, John
Tippet, Fred'k.
Tippet, Lewis I.
Thompson, John
Vickers, Nancy
Williams, Joseph
Whittle, Micajah
Whittle, Watson
Webb, James H.H.
Wimberly, William
Wyatt, Elizah
*Defaulters*
George Jones
Hardy McKeuzie
Elizabeth McMurry
Warren Williams

*Capt. Streetman's District*

Augelly, Mills
Augelly, Benjamin
Albritton, William
Augelly, Alexander
Albritton, Matthew
Beckham, William
Bullard, Wiley
Belsked, Robert
Churchwell, Henry
Cooke, Arthur B.
Churchwell, John
Desbozo. Robert
Dosier, Thomas
Davidson, Isaac
Davidson, Ishaw
Davidson, William
Davidson, John
Desbozo, Richard
Dorman, Allen
Desbozo. William
Esow. Meshack
Eldridge, William
Fleming, Allen
Fort, Zackariah
Fort, Arthur
Gentry, William
Grover, John A.

Grimes, Nathan
Gorderman, John L.
Heidleberg, McClemnsy
Hearn, Jesse
Holmes, Oliver
Harrell, H. H.
Holmes, Henry
Howell, Francis
Howell, James
Hodo, Nathaniel
Howell, Hiram
Harris, Simon
Hunt, William
Jacobs, William
Jacobs. Joshua
Irby, Daniel
King, John
Kimsey. Thomas
Lewis, Layton
Lewis, James
Minshew, Aaron
Minshew, Jacob
Murphy, James
Minshew, Philip
O'Daniel, Daniel
Pope, Jesse

Philmon, Barbara
Pearce, Theoplius
Pearce, Thomas
Pearce, Jacob
Pearce, John
Pearce, Lazarus
Pearce, James
Pearce, Alexander
Perry, Henry H.
Pearce, Wiley
Pippin, Neslbarn B.
Perry, Arthur C.
Reynolds, Peyton
Streetman, Isgae
Stafford, Pashnal
Smallwood, Francis
Smith, Lovett B.
Wheeler, Nancy
Wheeler, Noah
Westinghouse, John
West, Hampen
West, Isham
Whitehead, Richard
Zorne, Sarah
Ziterouer, Nath'l.
Zorne, Thomas

HISTORY OF TWIGGS COUNTY 207

*Defaulters*
Marchauts, John
Abraham Adams
John Adams
Francis Adams
James Filmon
Kincheon Dawson
John Hughs
John Pate
Shadrack Jacobs
Sherwood Beckham

Cornelius Kimsey
William Brown
Hiram Waller
Nathal Minshew
Matthew Coleman
George Hunt
Harmon Robinson
Ezekiel Harris
William Hatcher
Smith Hanery

James F. Wheeler
William Powell
John Harryl
James Montgomery
Kader Harryl
Durant Green
Henry R. Rogers
Richard Street
Ashley Street
James Fulton

*Capt. Solomon's District*

Arrington, Thomas
Barton, John
Brown, George
Barty, Rachal
Botts, McAllen
Barclay, David
Barr, Arthur
Brantley, Green
Bostick, I. D.
Beall, Robert A.
Clements, Thomas
Cooke, Williams
Crocker, William
Cummings, Robert
Dowden, Jonathan
Dorman, Cullen
Evans, R. A.
Everett, John
Ellums, Charles
Fort, Owen C.
Fulton, Thomas
Farnum, William W.
Finch, Freeman
Fort, Maoses
Griffin, Larkin
Gates, Thomas I.
Glover, John
Gainer, Joseph
Goodwin, V. Hartwell
Hughs, John
Hodge, Willis

Hargrove, R. W.
Hart, Edwin W.
Hughs, James
Holt, Thaddeus
Jenkins, Lawrence
Jameson, David
Jones, Thomas
Kelly, James
Kelly, Benjamin W.
Long, Nimrod W.
Lee, Jordan W.
Lee, Henry
Lyon, James
Loyless, Henry
McIntyre, John
McCloskey, Thomas
McMurry, Nancy
McIntyre, John
McMurry, Saml F.
Moffet, Henry Z.
McBeth, James
Neal, John
Opry, Joseph
Page, Stephen
Peck, Ira
Pitman, Jesse
Russell, Leva
Rolston, V. Jones
Solomon, William
Sinclair, Robert D.
Stephens, Richard

Stephens, Jone
Solomon, Lazarus
Summerline, William
Smith, James
Solomon, James
Sawyer, John
Solomon, Henry
Thompson, Merender
Towle, Frederick
Torwin, George
White, Fredone
Wall, David
Wall, Arron
Wall, Solomon
Warren, Lott
Young, E. V. W.
*Defaulters*
Spurlock Jones
Wm. R. Jones
L. S. Griffin
John G. Lefoy
Arminde Russell
John Flemming
Creed T. Woodson
Joseph Folker
John Chivers
Rick Ricks
Evan Powell
Ramsey Newson
Philip Pitman

*Capt. Holliday's District*

Asbell, Elisha
Asbell, John
Allen, Gideon
Bridges, James
Blount, Benjamin

Blount, William
Brown, Dempsey
Barnes, John
Burnham, William
Brown, William

Barrs, James
Bryan, Redick
Bostick, Wm. P.
Blount, Joseph
Bush, Jordan

Barber, James H.
Bridges, Sampson
Bryan, Benjamin
Clements, Archibald
Chance, Silas
Evans, Uriah
Ferrell, Henry
Findley, Daniel
Faulk, Mark
(Admr. Wm. Faulk)
Faulk, Sarah
Hodges, Edward
Hodges, John
Holliday, Thomas
Holliday, Wm.
Horne, Wiley
Horne, Joan
Horne, Josiah
Horne, Abishai
Henderson, John
Hart, Marmadine
Hart, Hardy
Hammock, Charles
Hammock, Thomas
Hodge, Robert

Joyver, Lawrence
Joyver, Rebecca
Knight, Robert
Little, George
Lovatt, Hymbrech
Liston, Levi
Little, Merit
Manning, Axum
Minton, Buryo
Mobley, Daniel
Mercer, Humbuck
McCullus, Matthew
Newby, Axum
Nobles, William
Opry, Amos
Pitman, Jesse
Petts, Martin
Pitman, John
Pearson, William
Perry, William
Petts, Stephen
Pumfrey, Redin
Rouse, Redin
Rouse, Mary
Radford, Robert

Smith, William
Sauls, Theophilus
Swearingen, Bolin
Smith, Taylor
Summers, William
Thompson, William
Taylor, David
Veal, Burwell
Weaver, Wm. R.
Ware, James
Wilson, Bethena
Waters, John
Waler, Arnold J.
Weaver, John
Wetherford, Alfred
Wimberly, James
*Defaulters*
William Whigham
Hendred Pace
Harrison Henson
Hillory Newman
Stephen Walter
James Hart
Jesse Barnes
Thomas Westbrook

*Capt. Tison's District*

Anderson, Thomas W.
Adams, Herman
Adams, Samuel
Bunn, Henry
Brown, Daniel
Bateman, Jesse
Bryan, James C.
Barron, William
Bryan, James A.
Bryan, James
Bryan, Susannah
Brown, Hardy
Brazil, Solomon
Bryan, Penelope
Carter, Wm. D.
Carter, John
Cooley, Donaldson
Churchwell, James
Clark, William
Clark, Zenes
Clark, James
Dupree, Jeremiah
Dupree, Simon
Dennard, John J.
Dupree, Orrin H.

Daniel, Jonas
Dunwoodee, James
Dunwoodie, Cather
Dupree, William H.
Dickson, Macachi
Daniel Ephriam
Dupree, Ira E.
Duncan, Moses
Edwards, William
Forehand, Amos
Funderbergh, Elijah
Gathis, Edward
Gilder, Irby
Gilders, Jacob
Glenn, Robert
Hunter, William
Hunter, Charles
Hinson, Matthew
Hayden, M. B.
Hamilton, William
Hamilton, Wm. and Co.
Jobson, Francis W.
Knight, Dabney
King, Wesley
Kelly, Jesse

Knight, George
Lawson, Hugh
McCray, Gustavas
McCray, Archibald
Massey, Daniel
Oliver, James
Oliver, Wiley
Oliver, McDaniel
Oliver, Wm.
Oliver, Joseph
Perry, Thornton
Pace, James
Powers, James
Perry, Terrell
Pace, Hardy
Penney, Alfred
Pollock, Martin
Richards, Wm. L.
Rogers, Henry
Ross, Godfrey
Stephens, Samuel
Stephens, Richard
Stephen, Wm.
Sexton, Henry
Saxon, John L.

Saxon, James S.
Sauls, Reuben
Sutton, Peter
Sexon, Benj. A.
Sutton, Jesse
Tull, James

Thigpen, Joshua M.
Tarver, Hartwell H.
Vehain, James
Wiley, Wm.
Wheat, Moses
Wynne, R. W. W.

Ward, Phereby
Womble, Nancy
Wheeler, John, Jr.
Wiley, Mary
Wimberly, Joshua R.
Yates, Jesse

*Capt. King's District*

Arrington, Rix
Burnes, Joseph
Batings, John
Barkwell, John W.
Barrs, Dempsey
Bartlett, Bridges
Burnham, Lewis
Brown, Dempsey
Cobb, Wiley
Cooke, Robert
Carter, Joel
Campbell, John
Gilder, Isaac
Griffin, Yancy
Hooks, Bardin
Hasty, Hillory
Hathway and Butts
Hatway, E.
Hooks, Harmon
Kelly, Edwards
King, John
King, Charles
King, Tilfoy
King, Josepeh
King, Bell
McNaughton, James
Maulden, Tucker
Pugh, Dorothy
Roberts, Josiah

Revell, Matthew
Revell, Micajah
Stephens, Holdman
Slappey, John G.
Saunders, Wright
Sherred, Saunders
Simons, John
Smith, James
Saunders, John
Sims, Phereby
Smith, John
Stokes, Henry
Sherred, Haywood
Sherrod, Elizabeth
Shine, Daniel W.
Saunders, D. D.
Thompson, Howell
Wilkinson, John, Sr.
Wilkinson, John
Walden, Green
Walden, Saml.
Wheeler, John
Waters, Jesse, Sr.
Waters, Jesse
*Defaulters*
James Smith
John B. Lifsey
John Dickson
Archibald Hammer

Calvin Penny
Rainey, Sr.
Signal Rainey
Thompson (?)
Richard Smith
Sterling Tison
Isiah Mosely
A. B. Ridley
John Crawford
Spencer Wright
Jacob Gilder
Sameul Carter
Benj. Wyatt
Hawell Wooten
William Bird
William Bryan
William Hale
George Jarvis
Theos M. Chamberlain
Edward Monroe
Charles Raily
James Dorman
Keaton Everitt
Morris Pollock
Wm. Bateman
Willis Ward
Theophilus Booth
Daniel Hunt
Brady Carter

*Capt. Blacksher's District*

Adkins, Lewis
Anglin, Henry
Allen, John
Blackshear, Joseph
Blackshear, O.
Boggs, Joseph
Blackshear, Isaac
Brock, Daniel
Butler, Isaac, Jr.
Collier, Robert
Claudle, Ephriam (?)
Chidders, Isaac

Christopher, Levi M.
Caudle, Jospeh
Christtopher, Jane
Chappel, Thomas
Collier, Richard
Christopher, Beverly
Day, Nimrod
Day, Stephen
Dunn, James
Davis, John
Dunn, Jesse
Epps, Daniel T.

Edwards, James D.
Evans, Isham
Epps, Edward
Ellis, Ephriam
Fitzpatrick, E.
Fitzpatrick, John
Fitzpatrick, William
Fort, Thomas
Fort, John
Gilstrap, Charles
Green, Aquilla
Green, David

Green, James
Glover, Kelly
Hays, James
Hale, James
Hays, David
Herrin, Fredk
Hays, Daniel C.
Jones, Thomas
Johnson, Abel
Jkevor, Solomon (?)
Johnson, Moses
Jameson, James
Jones, Stephen
Johnson, John C.
Johnson, Joel J.
Lenton, John
Lou, Caleb
Lansford, James S.
Lane, John
Lee, Alexander
Lingo, John R. T.
Linsey, Thomas
Matthews, Wm.
McMullen, James
McDaniel, Alex'r
Murray, Barnes H.

Melton, Elbert
Matthewson, Philip
McMullen, Joseph
Mott, Levi
Morgan, James
Moore, Thomas
Melton, McKenney
Maxwell, William
Myrick, Richard
Meriwether, Alex'r.
Melton, William
Perryman, David B.
Pearce, Evans
Patton, George
Pate, Samuel
Parker, Henry
Parker, Jesse
Paul, John
Parker, Hiram
Phillips, Daniel A.
Philips, Hestor
Railey, Jospeh
Radford, John
Rutherford, John
Richardson, David
Stokes, Samuel D.

Sapp, Moses
Stevenson, John
Scott, Davis
Smith, John
Smith, Joseph
Smith, James
Sapp, Abraham
Solomon, John
Taylor, Edmund
Taylor, Lemuel
Tucker, Joseph
Taylor, Cornelius
Thomas, Edwin
Taylor, George
Vincent, James
Wells, Joseph
Wall, James, Jr.
Williams, Abraham
West, Sampson
West, Emberson
Waters, Isaac
Wood, Isaac
Warren, John
Young, George
Young, David

*Capt. Bostick's District*

Allen, John
Adams, John Sr.
Adams, John
Adams, Daniel
Adams, David
Anderson, John
Alford, Benjamin
Allston, Joshua, Sr.
Bullock, Boston
Bostick, Rhesa
Barnes, Wm.
Bedsell, Isaac
Bailey, Peter
Boss, Rowell
Bell, Spencer
Bobbett, Spencer
Bailey, Thomas
Bass, Drury
Burden, Wm.
Bass, Benjamin
Bridges, Benjamin
Bell, Samosin
Buckalew, Fred'k.
Fillingim, L. R.

Fillingham, John J.
Grantham, Joshua
Gardener, Jacob
Griffin, Moses
Griffin, John, Jr.
Griffin, James
Griffin, Leroy
Hood, Alexander
Hatcher, Dempsey
Hinson, Caleb
Hatcher, Thomas
Hill, Nancy
Honeycut, Seth
Holman, George
Hollongsworth, Isaac
Hatcherm, Hamilton
James, George
Jessup, James
Jones, Levi
Jessup, Samuel
Jenkins, Wm. F.
Jernigan, Alex'r.
Kent, John
Kent, Henry

Kent, Thomas
Kent, Price
Lebton, John
Leith, Mary
Matthews, Sam'l.
Martin, Wm.
McWilliams, Asa
McWilliams, James
Matthews, Banjamin
Majors, Eleazor
Mealy, James
Martin, Joseph
Nelson, Alexander
Norris, Green
Norman, Candace
Outlaw, Jeremiah
Odom, Mills
Outlaw, John
Parker, John
Perryman, Harmon
Pottis, Stephen
Parker, Gabriel
Pearce, Theophilus
Palmer, George

Powell, John
Pottis, Mark
Rawls, Philip
Raburn, Ichabod
Rawls, Silas
Raburn, Joel
Rabun, Charles
Rhodes, Eliakim
Rawls, Moses
Smith, B. B.
Smith, Needham
Sapp, Henry
Smith, James
Smith, Asa
Sledge, Hiram
Stewart, Desire
Tatum, Nath'l
Tharp, Wm. A.

Tarvin, William J.
Tharp, Charnick A.
Tharp, Jeremiah A.
Toler, Robert
Taylor, Thomas
Vann, Edward
Vann, Saunders
Williams, Jesse
Williams, George
Wilson, John
West, Jonathan
Wheeler, Avery
Wall, James
Williams, Jesse
Young, Isaac
Young, Sara
*Defaulters*
John Griffin, Sr.

Ruth Tharp
John Kimbrough
John Gardner
Achilles Liles
Henry Stephenson
Robert Green
Isham Stephens
William Bailey
Joseph Reynolds
Wm. Culpepper
John B. Teal
Owen O'Daniels
Jacob W. Cobb
Abraham Williams
Joseph Drawhorn
Allen Dillard
Joshua Alston, Jr.
Kinchen Martin

*Capt. Gragg's District*

Bedingfield, Gideon
Buchanon, B. B.
Bedingfield, Robert
Bridges, Joseph
Brown, William S.
Brown, William
Brown, Alexander
Brown, Alfred
Brocking, Richard
Brount, Richard
Bossman, James N.
Bostick, Davis
Crocker, John
Chasteen, Abraham
Collins, Elisha
Childers, Osborn
Chivers, Thomas
Dennard, Hugh L.
Dennard, Shadrack
Defore, John
Dennard, Bird
Dennard, Jared
Dickson, Jeremiah
Dickson, William
Dennard, Alexander
Dickson, Moses
Dickson, Pleasant
Dennard, Wm. E.
Deshazo, Wilson
Ennis, James
Everitt, Josiah
Fitzgerald, Reuben

Griffin, James
Guerry, James, Sr.
Gregg, Israel
Graham, David
Gibbs, Howell
Guerry, James P.
Green, John
Griffin, Ethelred
Granberry, George
Granberry and Robertson
Griffin, Wm.
Harrison, James
Holley, Isaac
Holland, Henry
Hare, John
Harris, Benjamin
Holland, Daniel S or L
Holland, James
Hamm, Littleton
Hamm, John
Hamilton, E.
Jackson, Timothy
Ivy, Hilson
Lawson, Roger
Lowry, James R.
Lowry, John R.
McCrary, John T.
Martin, Robert
McKenzie, William
McCrown, James
Matthews, Isham
Nunnery, Henry

Nunn, Edward
Nobles, Solomon
Powell, Lewis
Parrot, James
Paramore, John
Player, Thomas
Pasmore, Samuel
Powell, Needham
Pearce, Charlotte
Robertson, George
Richardson, Daniel
Rogers, Lucien
Renfroe, David B.
Sainney, Edmund
Gdn. of John Spivey's Orphans
Sutton, John
Sapp, Riley
Terrell, Thomas W.
Truluck, John, Jr.
Tabor, Zachariah
Taylor, Samuel
Thigpen, John M.
Thompson, Peter G.
Tabor, Hudson D.
Veal, William
Welch, George W.
Wimberly, James
Wimberly, Ezekiel
Wimberly, William
Willis, James
Weaver, John H.

Weldon, Robert
Woodward, Joseph
*Defaulters*
Orvin D. Tucker
Saml D. Jones
James T. Thompson
Henry H. Perry
Isaac Hagers

Stephen Petts
Levi Rush
James Parks
William Fraser
Isaac Dennard
Isaac Fraser
James Hayden
Lovic Green

Alston Harris
Zilphy Sledge
Meredith Hare
James Dickson
Jacob Evans
Threat Thompson
Hiram Berien

## TWIGGS COUNTY TAX DIGEST FOR 1853

*Bluff District*

No. 372 District
Georgia Militia

| Names | Polls | Acres of Land | County where the land lies |
|---|---|---|---|
| Angely, Alexander W. | 1 | 202 | Twiggs |
| Anderson, Cornelius | 1 | 80 | Cherokee |
| Adkins, Joseph | 1 | | |
| Belcher, William | 1 | | |
| Bullard, Allen B. | 1 | 400 | Twiggs |
| Barrot, Jonathan A. | 1 | 85 | Twiggs |
| Bullard, Daniel | 1 | 1200 | Twiggs |
| "—adm. est. Bullard, Canadcy, Dec. | | 202 | Twiggs |
| Belcher, Joseph | 1 | 210 | Twiggs |
| Belcher, McGuin | 1 | | |
| Belcher, Nancy | | 400 | Twiggs |
| Beckcom, Allen B. | 1 | 1248 | Twiggs |
| Beal, James L. | 1 | 202 | Twiggs |
| Beckcom, Simon N. | 1 | 1200 | Twiggs |
| "—exr. est. Beckcom, Labon, dec. | | 1060 | Twiggs and Gilman |
| "—adm. est. Brooks, Livinia N., dec. | | 405 | Twiggs |
| Brazile, John | 1 | 101 | Twiggs |
| Crocker, Dewitt E. | 1 | 202 | Twiggs |
| Davidson, Moses | 1 | | |
| Dye, Jas. M. | 1 | 101 | Twiggs |
| Davidson, Jos. | 1 | 600 | Twiggs |
| Deshazo, Robert | | 200 | Twiggs |
| "—adm. est. Deshaza, Richard, dec. | | | Pulaski |
| Davidson, Sarah | | 140 | Twiggs |
| Durden, Benj. | 1 | 112 | Twiggs |
| "—adm. est. Phillips, John F., dec. | | 66 | Twiggs |
| Everitt, John B. | 1 | | |
| Everitt, Henery E. | 1 | 515 | Twiggs |
| "—guar. Everitt, Joshua; Everitt, Sarah; Everitt, Mary | | | |
| "—Curtis, Zacharia—man of colour | | | |
| Everitt, James | 1 | | |

| | | | |
|---|---|---|---|
| Faulk, Charles R. | 1 | 1200 | Twiggs |
| "—adm. est. Faulk, Henry, dec. | | 1700 | Twiggs |
| Hudson, Nathaniel C. | 1 | | |
| Hearn, Amos J. | 1 | | |
| Hearn, Lucitta | | 300 | Twiggs |
| Hearn, Wm. | 1 | | |
| Hearn, John | 1 | | |
| Hunt, Henry | 1 | | |
| Hammond, Abner G. | 1 | 650 | Twiggs |
| Hunt, Noel | 1 | | |
| Harrell, Jonathan | 1 | | |
| Mannin, Wm. | 1 | | |
| McKinney, Wm. F. | 1 | | |
| O'Daniel, Daniel | 1 | 230 | Twiggs |
| Pitts, Jesse | 1 | | |
| Perry, David M. | 1 | | |
| Paul, John F. | 1 | 200 | Twiggs |
| Perry, Henry H. | 1 | 363 | Twiggs |
| Pearce, Alexander | 1 | 163 | Twiggs |
| "—adm. est. Vinson, Anna, dec. | | 101 | Twiggs |
| Paul, Robert | 1 | 2400 | Twiggs |
| Pace, Thomas B. | 1 | 900 | Twiggs |
| "—guar. Pace, William & Frances J. | | | |
| "—agt. Pace, Fanny | | | |
| Peacock, Dupree | 1 | | |
| Powell, John | 1 | | |
| Pearce, Theophilus | 1 | 640 | Twiggs |
| Reynolds, Charles P. | 1 | | |
| Reynolds, Peyton | 1 | 1733 | Twiggs and Lowdes |
| "—adm. est Faulk, Mark, dec. | | 2400 | Twiggs |
| "—agt. Faulk, Nancy | | 120 | Twiggs |
| Solomon, Lewis | 1 | 2332 | Irwin, Appling, Tho. |
| "—agt. Solomon, Hardy | | | |
| "—adm. est. Solomon, Carey, dec. | | 202 | Twiggs |
| Smith, Hardin F. | 1 | 405 | Twiggs |
| Whitehead, Missouri A. | | | |
| "—adm. est. Whitehead, C. C., dec. | | 401 | Twiggs |
| "—agt. Loyless, Henry M. (minor) | | | |

Defaulters
Adams, Daniel
Bullard, Charles
Bullard, Wiley
Bobbitt, Thomas
Churchwell, Henry
Deshazo, William
Hunt, James
Holley, Isaac C.
Jacobs, Wiley
Summerlin, William
Shell, William
Scott, Mack
Thompson, Alexander

*Glover's District*

No. 324 District
Georgia Militia

| Names | Polls | Acres of Land | County wher Land lies |
|---|---|---|---|
| Asbell, John | | 1200 | Twiggs |
| Asbell, Bryant | 1 | — | |
| Asbell, Andrew W. | 1 | 418 | Twiggs |
|   agt. for Martha Asbell | | | |
| Bunn, Henry | 1 | 6170 | Twiggs |
|   adm. on est. of Frederic Wimberly, dec. | | 445 | Sumter |
|   agt. for Hugh L. Bunn | | | |
| Burnes, James C. | 1 | 4400 | Twiggs and Bak. |
| Burnes, Nancy | | 600 | Twiggs |
| Churchwell, William | 1 | — | |
| Durham, Hardy | | 5300 | Twiggs |
| Defore, Etheldred | 1 | 2 | Twiggs |
| Denson, Tilman R. | 1 | 775 | Twiggs |
|   agt. for Wm. Denson, minor | | | |
|   agt. for Nancy Denson | | 300 | Twiggs |
| Faulk, John | 1 | 1100 | Twiggs |
| Glover, Thomas | 1 | — | |
| Hart, Hardy | 1 | 718 | Twiggs and Dody |
| Horne, Joel | 1 | 100 | Twiggs |
| Harris, Mary | | 160 | Twiggs |
| Hart, Mourning | | 108 | Twiggs |
| Johnson, Burrell | 1 | 50 | Twiggs |
|   agt. for Thos. H. Holida | | 50 | Twiggs |
| Johnson, Martha | | | |
|   agt. for Thos. H. Holida | | 100 | Twiggs |
| Little, John | 1 | 1 | Twiggs |
| Lee, George W. | 1 | 650 | Twiggs |
| Latson, E. B. | 1 | 126 | Twiggs |
| Moore, Stephen | 1 | | |
| McCoy, John B. | 1 | | |
| Mellen, Seth S. | 1 | | |
| Newby, Josiah | 1 | | |
| Newby, Hilliard S. | 1 | 92 | Twiggs |
|   adm. on est. of Renyard Hasty | 1 | — | |
| Pearce, John M. | 1 | — | |
| Shine, Daniel W., Sr. | | 2595 | Twiggs |
| Shine, Daniel W., Sr. | | 500 | Coweta |
| Shine, Daniel W., Jr. | 1 | — | |
| Thompson, William | 1 | 202 | Twiggs |
| Veal, Burrell | 1 | 110 | Twiggs |
| Wimberly, Henry S. | 1 | 1150 | Twiggs |
|   trustee for minors of Fred Wimberly, dec. | | 1000 | Baker |
| Ware, James | | 1826 | Twiggs |
| Ware, Britton S. | 1 | — | |

Welch, Elisha                        1        —
  Defaulters: Glovers District
Sauls, Robert C.
Thompson, James

*Higgsville District*

No. 354 District
Georgia Militia

| Names | Polls | Acres of Land | County where land lies |
|---|---|---|---|
| Arnold, Berry | 1 | 490 | Lownds |
| Arnold, Needham | 1 | 100 | Twiggs |
| Allen, John | 1 | 2473 | Twiggs and others |
| Bull, William H. | 1 | 304 | Twiggs |
| Berry, William G. | 1 | | |
| Berry, Matthew A. | 1 | | |
| Exr. of est. of Berry, John, dec. | | 450 | Twiggs |
| Bridger, Sampson | | 202 | Twiggs |
| Brown, Thomas | 1 | | |
| Bridger, James W. | 1 | 50 | Twiggs |
| Chance, Aldred | 1 | 40 | Cherokee |
| Collins, Loydia | | | |
| adm. est. of W. P. Collins, dec. | | 450 | Twiggs |
| Davis, William | 1 | | |
| Ellis, John B. | 1 | | |
| Ellis, James D. | 1 | 100 | Twiggs |
| Ellis, Matthew A. | | | |
| Floyd, Andrew | 1 | 250 | Twiggs |
| Fields, Frederic M. | 1 | | |
| Floyd, Wm. | 1 | | |
| Floyd, Nevil G. | 1 | 150 | Twiggs |
| Floyd, Wm. A. | 1 | | |
| Fowler, Matthew C. | 1 | 240 | Twiggs |
| Floyd, Charles | 1 | | |
| Ganey, John | 1 | 800 | Twiggs |
| Grantham, Thomas | 1 | | |
| Gallemore, Levi | 1 | 607 | Twiggs |
| Gallemore, John | 1 | 2353 | Twiggs, Wilkinson |
| Hughes, Daniel G. | 1 | 1550 | Twiggs |
| adm. est. of Thomas Johnson, dec. | | | |
| Hughes, Ellender | | | |
| Hughes, Andrew | 1 | 606 | Twiggs |
| Howell, Wright S. | 1 | 104 | Twiggs |
| Howell, Frederic | 1 | 101 | Twiggs |
| Howell, Daniel | | 101 | |
| Holland, Daniel | 1 | 700 | Twiggs |
| Howell, John | 1 | | |
| Horton, Madison | 1 | | |
| Howell, Wright | | 202 | Twiggs |
| Johnson, Daniel H. | 1 | | |
| guar. Green B. Johnson | | 310 | Twiggs |

| Name | Polls | Acres | County |
|---|---|---|---|
| Lamb, Henry | 1 | 555 | Twiggs |
| Lamb, Meady | 1 | 1300 | Twiggs |
| Lee, John | 1 | 202 | Twiggs |
| Mcant, James | 1 | | |
| Middleton, Owen | | 33 | Twiggs |
| McCoy, Owen G. | 1 | | |
| "—agt. Martha M. McCoy | | | |
| McCoy, Warren S. | 1 | | |
| Nobles, William | 1 | 172 | Twiggs |
| Putnal, Daniel | 1 | | |
| Pope, Elijah | | 405 | Twiggs |
| Putnal, Stephen | 1 | | |
| Pope, John | 1 | | |
| Rosar, John L. B. | 1 | | |
| Stafford, Elisha | 1 | 100 | Twiggs |
| Stokes, W. R. B. | 1 | 150 | Twiggs |
| Sauls, Bryant | 1 | | |
| Sauls, Theophilus | | 820 | Twiggs, Early |
| adm. est. of M. D. Heart | | | |
| Sauls, Seaborn Y. | 1 | | |
| Thompson, Haywood | 1 | | |
| Thompson, John | 1 | | |
| Thompson, Corder | 1 | | |
| Thompson, Bery | 1 | 102 | Twiggs |
| Vincent, Thomas | | 436 | Twiggs |
| Vaughn, Daniel | | 1381 | Twiggs |
| trustee for Martha Hargrove | | 202 | Pulaski |
| Defaulters: | | | |
| Grantham, Joshua | 1 | | |

## *Jeffersonville District*

No. 325 District
Georgia Militia

| Names | Polls | Acres of Land | County where Land lies |
|---|---|---|---|
| Bell, Charles C. | | 360 | Twiggs |
| Bell, Egbert J. | 1 | | |
| Bateman, John E. | 1 | | |
| Burkett, Thos. W. | 1 | | |
| ex. on Solomon Burkett, dec. | | 540 | Twiggs |
| Burkett, Solomon | 1 | | |
| Badger, Baldwin | 1 | | |
| Berry, Nathan | 1 | | |
| Blackshear, Ezekiel | 1 | | |
| Brazil, Green H. | 1 | 202 | Lawrence |
| agt. for wife and children | | | |
| Bryant, William | 1 | 1342 | Twiggs, Cherokee |
| exr. on est. of A. S. Bryant, dec. | | 1200 | Twiggs |
| agt. for Mary Bryant | | 1000 | Twiggs |
| Cook, John F. | 1 | | |

| | | | |
|---|---|---|---|
| Chapman, John | 1 | 2000 | Twiggs |
| Chapman, Margaret | | 500 | Twiggs |
| Chapman, John | 1 | | |
| guar. for minors of Wm. Chapman | | | |
| Chivers, Thomas | 1 | 400 | Twiggs |
| guar. for Caroline and J.W.B. Mercer | | | |
| guar. for George Ann Mercer | | | |
| Crepey, Daniel F. | 1 | | |
| Coleman, John G. | 1 | 378 | |
| agt. for James Dean, trustee for Laura H. Coleman | | | |
| Denard, James E. | 1 | | |
| Denard, Hartwell S. | 1 | | |
| Davis, John D. | 1 | | |
| Dupree, Ira E. | 1 | 689 | Twiggs |
| Danforth, J. R. | 1 | | |
| Dennard, Anna | | 50 | Twiggs |
| Fraser, Andrew F. | 1 | | |
| Faulk, William | 1 | 1650 | Twiggs |
| Faulk, William | | | |
| agt. for Robert R. Slappy | | | |
| trustee for Virginia Faulk | | | |
| Faulk, James | 1 | | |
| Gragg, Israel | | 614 | Twiggs |
| guar. for Cullen and Lacy Green | | | |
| Galloway, William | 1 | | |
| Glover, John | 1 | 1730 | Twiggs |
| guar. for persons of colour 4 Mary, Frances, Peggy, and Elizabeth Curtis | | | |
| Gragg, Samuel P. | 1 | 771 | Twiggs and Cherokee |
| adm. on est. of W. E. Dennard, dec. | | | |
| agt. for Bejamin Harris | | 80 | Cherokee |
| Hatch, Sam W. | 1 | | |
| Hughes, Haywood | 1 | 2900 | Pulaski |
| exr. of est. of Aley Hughs, dec. | | 607 | Twiggs |
| adm. of John A. Winn, dec. | | 202 | Pulaski |
| Horne, Wm. D. | 1 | | |
| agt. for Anna Higgs | | 640 | Twiggs |
| Johnson, Nathan | 1 | | |
| Johnson, Alice | 1 | | |
| Joiner, Andrew L. | 1 | 247 | Twiggs |
| Johnson, Harmon | 1 | | |
| Kite, James | 1 | | |
| Lowry, John H. | 1 | | |
| agt. for Alice Lowry | | 2200 | Twiggs |
| adm. on Frederic D. Lowry, dec. | | 692 | Pulaski |
| Long, John K. | 1 | | |
| Long, Durham | | | |
| Long, Ellis | 1 | | |
| Methvin, John | 1 | | |

| Name | Polls | Acres | County |
|---|---|---|---|
| Methvin, William | 1 | 1650 | Twiggs |
| Mercer, Garner | 1 | 372 | Twiggs |
| guar. minors of Bery F. Vincent | | | |
| McDaniel, James D. | 1 | | |
| Methvin, Samuel R. | 1 | 952 | Twiggs |
| McCallum, Archibald | 1 | 1987 | Twiggs |
| McGowin, Noah | 1 | | |
| Middleton, Jonathon | 1 | | |
| Murphy, Josiah | 1 | 932 | Twiggs |
| Murphy, Matthew R. | 1 | | |
| Morris, Lemuel | 1 | | |
| Nobles, Lewis | 1 | | |
| Nobles, Daniel | 1 | | |
| Perry, Henry M. | 1 | | |
| Read, Thomas C. | 1 | | |
| Radford, Mary | | 700 | Twiggs |
| Read, Fletcher | 1 | 52 | Twiggs |
| Sharp, Jones E. | 1 | | |
| Sinclair, Jessie | 1 | 460 | Twiggs |
| Sinclair, Miles D. | 1 | | |
| Sinclair, John L. | 1 | | |
| Stephens, Edmund | 1 | 101 | Twiggs |
| Strickland, Corden B. | 1 | | |
| Wimberly, Abraham | 1 | | |
| Ward, Maurice | 1 | 100 | Twiggs |
| Wimberly, Robt. R. | 1 | 980 | Thomas and Ware |
| agt. est. of J. J. Boynton, dec. | | 1000 | Twiggs |
| agt. for Penelope Wimberly | | 900 | Twiggs |
| Wimberly, Mary | | 1000 | Twiggs |
| exr., Ezekiel Wimberly | | | |
| Wood, Phillip J. | 1 | | |
| Wimberly, Caroline H. | | 1413 | Twiggs, Union |
| adm. on Joshua R. Wimberly | | | |
| Wilder, Milton | 1 | 837 | Twiggs, |
| guar. Jacob L., trustee for Caroline E. Bankston | | | |
| Wimberly, Robt. S. | 1 | | |
| Wynn, Elmina | | | |

Defaulters:
Barrs, John
Holstead, A. J.
Wood, James

*Marion District*

No. 423 District
Georgia Militia

| Names | Polls | Acres of Land | County where Land lies |
|---|---|---|---|
| Arrington, Thomas N. | 1 | 765 | Twiggs |
| "—Exr. Est. Averitt, James, Dec. | | 1400 | Twiggs |
| "—guar. Cook, Jona | | | |
| "—guar. for Arrington, Tho. and Robt. | | | |

| | | | |
|---|---|---|---|
| Burkett, Andrew A. | 1 | — | |
| Crocker, Evans E. | 1 | 405 | Cherokee, Twiggs, Macon |
| " | 1 | 160 | Murray |
| "Exr. Est, Crocker, William Dc'd. | | 767 | Twiggs, Gilman |
| " " | | 80 | Cherokee |
| Crocker, William H. | 1 | — | |
| Eddy, Nelson H. | 1 | — | |
| Evans, Georgia Ann | | | |
| Everitt, John | 1 | — | |
| Edmonson, James | 1 | — | |
| Finch, Delila | | 405 | Twiggs |
| Finch, Floyd A. | 1 | 80 | Twiggs |
| Finch, William C. | 1 | 112 | Twiggs |
| "—guar. for Curtis, Peggy, a woman of colour | | | |
| Faulk, Henry | 1 | 475 | Twiggs |
| Goodwin, John S. | 1 | 300 | Twiggs |
| Gentry, Pleasant | 1 | — | |
| Green, John | 1 | — | |
| Harrell, Moses | 1 | — | |
| Herring, John R. | 1 | — | |
| Harrold, Samuel | 1 | 362 | Twiggs |
| Harrold, Jesse | 1 | — | |
| Jones, Thomas S. | 1 | 1600 | Twiggs |
| Kelly, William S. | 1 | 410 | Twiggs |
| "—guar. Kelly, Leanna | | | |
| Kelly, Lucinda | | | |
| Lowe, Thomas | 1 | — | |
| Loyless, Martin H. | 1 | — | |
| Land, Henry | 1 | 820 | Twiggs |
| "—Exr. est. Land, James, dec. | | | |
| Morton, William M. | 1 | — | |
| McMillian, Littleberry | 1 | — | |
| Peacre, Elias | 1 | 60 | Twiggs |
| Pearce, Lucinda | | 810 | Twiggs |
| Peck, Ira | | 1052 | Twiggs, Dooly |
| Raley, John | 1 | 108 | Twiggs |
| Ray, Charles | 1 | — | |
| Richardson, Stephen L. | 1 | — | |
| Summerlain, Eli | 1 | — | |
| Scovill, Samuel D. | 1 | — | |
| Solomon, Frances adm. est. of Solomon, James, dec. | | 1100 | Twiggs |
| Stebbins, Thomas F. | 1 | — | |
| Solomon, Peter adm. est. of Solomon, Henry F., dec. | | 1042 | Twiggs |
| Washington, Robert B. | | 12 | Twiggs |
| Zachry, William T. | 1 | — | |

## McDonald's District

No. 356 District
Georgia Militia

| Names | Polls | Acres of Land | County where the Land lies |
|---|---|---|---|
| Angely, Mills | 1 | 150 | Twiggs |
| Anglin, Henry | 1 | | |
| "—adm. est. Averitt, Benj., dec. | | 400 | Twiggs |
| Anglin, Jasper | 1 | | |
| Blackshare, Jesse | | | |
| Cannon, James | 1 | 140 | Twiggs |
| Collier, Jesse M. | 1 | 250 | Twiggs |
| Edmondson, John | 1 | | |
| Epps, John C. | 1 | 1300 | Twiggs |
| Edmonson, William | 1 | | |
| Fitzpatrick, William | 1 | 202 | Twiggs |
| Floyd, Wiley J. | 1 | | |
| Fitzpatrick, John | 1 | 3000 | Twiggs |
| "—agt. Fort, Mary E. | | | |
| "—Fitzpatrick, Elizabeth | | | |
| "—adm. est. Davis, John, dec. | | | |
| Griffin, William | 1 | 202 | Twiggs |
| "—adm. Griffin, Wm., dec. | | 160 | Gilmer |
| Hughes, Thomas M. | 1 | | |
| Humpheries, Wm. C. | | | |
| Ives, Daniel | 1 | | |
| Jones, Nancy | | 500 | Twiggs |
| Jones, Elias | 1 | 950 | Twiggs |
| Jones, Thomas H. | 1 | 300 | Twiggs |
| Jones, Henry T. | 1 | 430 | Twiggs |
| "—agt. Jones, Mary | | 202 | Twiggs |
| "—guar. Andrews, Henry T. | | | |
| Johnson, Charles G. | 1 | 860 | Twiggs |
| Johnson, Birwill | 1 | | |
| Johnson, Oliver | 1 | | |
| Johnson, James M. | 1 | | |
| Lewis, Whitfield | 1 | | |
| Lockhart, Lemuel S. | 1 | 380 | Twiggs |
| "—guar. min. children of O'Neal, George M., dec. | | | |
| Liles, Hampton | 1 | | |
| Lee, Franklin | 1 | | Twiggs |
| Lingo, John T. | 1 | 167 | |
| Lanier, Avery | 1 | | |
| Lockhart, Thomas P. | 1 | | |
| Lingo, Elijah H. | 1 | | |
| Lavar, Robert J. | 1 | | |
| Love, Stephen | 1 | | |
| Lingo, Richard T. | 1 | 580 | Twiggs |
| Moore, Willis S. | 1 | | |
| Moore, Thomas | 1 | 1169 | Twiggs |

| Name | Polls | Acres | County |
|---|---|---|---|
| Myrick, Seth P. | | 3200 | Twiggs |
| Moore, Archibald H. | 1 | | |
| Malanney, Michael | 1 | 202 | Twiggs |
| Newberry, Levi | 1 | | |
| Nash, Reuben A. | 1 | 2652 | Twiggs and others |
| Newberry, Henry H. | 1 | | |
| Parker, Joseph | 1 | | |
| Pate, Elizabeth | | 121 | Twiggs |
| Parker, Shaba | | 136 | Twiggs |
| Parker, Jarrot | 1 | | |
| Peterson, Moses | 1 | | |
| Pate, Wm. T. | 1 | | |
| Ryles, Vincent | 1 | | |
| Rivers, Jonathan | 1 | 202 | Twiggs |
| Raley, Charles | 1 | | |
| Ryles, Wm. A. | 1 | | |
| Sapp, Moses | 1 | 150 | Twiggs |
| Stephenson, Henry | 1 | | |
| Sapp, Walton | 1 | | |
| Sapp, Selim | 1 | 100 | Twiggs |
| Taylor, Lemuel | 1 | 267 | Twiggs |
| Taylor, Sebron | 1 | | |
| Vinson, Joseph S. | | 125 | Twiggs |
| Vinson, Elizabeth | | 50 | Twiggs |
| Wood, Greenberry | 1 | 162 | Twiggs |
| Waters, Reuben A. | 1 | 300 | Twiggs |
| Waters, William | 1 | 202 | Carrol |
| Waters, Elizabeth | | 202 | Twiggs |
| Wood, Issac | | 202 | Twiggs |
| West, Henry | 1 | | |
| "—agt. West, John W. | | 160 | Twiggs |
| "—West, Alfred | | 160 | Twiggs |
| Defaulters: | | | Cherokee |
| Harrell, Henry P. | | | |
| Harrell, James L. | | | |
| Lavarr, David | | | |
| Moore, Jeptha | | | |
| Pope, Woodward | | | |

*Pearson's District*

No. 323 District
Georgia Militia

| Names | Polls | Acres of Land | County where the Land lies |
|---|---|---|---|
| Andrews, Isham G. | 1 | 855 | Twiggs |
| Ard, Daniel | 1 | | |
| "—agt. Ard, Andrew J. (minor) | | 100 | Twiggs |
| Ard, George W. | 1 | | |
| Andrews, Ivy R. | 1 | 85 | Twiggs |
| Andrews, Abisha | 1 | 991 | Twiggs |
| Andrews, John R. | 1 | 60 | Twiggs |

| | | | |
|---|---|---|---|
| Andrews, James W. | 1 | 400 | Twiggs |
| "—trust. Horne, Elizabeth H. | | | |
| "— " . Bull, Lucinda A. | | | |
| "— " . Tull, Sarah | | | |
| "— " . Jeffers, Adaline J. | | | |
| "— " . Riggins, America | | | |
| Bryan, Henry | 1 | 100 | Twiggs |
| Bates, David | 1 | | |
| Bond, Solomon J. | 1 | | |
| Bond, Warren R. | 1 | | |
| Bond, John P. | 1 | 755 | Twiggs |
| Barnes, William | 1 | 202 | Twiggs |
| Burkett, Robert | 1 | | |
| Bull, Jessie J. | 1 | 1235 | Twiggs |
| Bowden, Matthew | 1 | | |
| Barclay, John A. | 1 | 465 | Twiggs |
| Bridger, Lilas | 1 | | |
| Cowan, John W. | 1 | 395 | Twiggs |
| Clark, Sarah | | 98 | Twiggs |
| Clark, Lewis B. | 1 | | |
| Denson, Joel J. | 1 | | |
| Davidson, Issac | 1 | 100 | Twiggs |
| Davidson, James | 1 | 76 | Twiggs |
| Davidson, William | 1 | 101 | Twiggs |
| Denson, John H. | 1 | 2156 | Twiggs |
| "—agt. est. Jones, Stephen, dec. | | 202 | Twiggs |
| "— " Wester, Wm., dec. | | 100 | Twiggs |
| Davis, John | 1 | 350 | Twiggs |
| Glover, Nicholas | 1 | | |
| Hinson, Elam | 1 | 911 | Twiggs |
| "—guar. for man of colour Curtis, Thomas | | | |
| Hinson, Elam, Jun. | 1 | | |
| Harrold, Issac H. | 1 | | |
| Hinson, William | 1 | 150 | Twiggs |
| Hinson, Margaret | | | |
| Hail, James C. | 1 | 100 | Twiggs |
| Herring, Arthur A. | 1 | | |
| Johnson, Jeremiah | 1 | 707 | Twiggs |
| Jones, John | 1 | | |
| Liles, James | | | |
| Land, William | 1 | | |
| Land, Newton | 1 | | |
| Melton, Clem | 1 | | |
| "—agt. min. children | | | |
| Mannin, Gatlin | 1 | | |
| Melton, Matthew | 1 | 200 | Twiggs |
| Melton, Green M. | 1 | | Twiggs |
| Melton, Martin | 1 | 100 | Twiggs |
| Melton, William | 1 | 100 | Twiggs |
| Morea, Alfred | 1 | 250 | |
| Mannin, James | 1 | | Twiggs |

| Name | Polls | Acres | County |
|---|---|---|---|
| Melton, Elisha | 1 | 100 | Twiggs |
| Norris, Issac | 1 | 707 | Twiggs |
| " " | | 250 | Decatur |
| "—adm. est. Andrews, John H., dec. | | 202 | Twiggs |
| Newman, Elisha M. | 1 | — | |
| Nash, Acton E. | 1 | — | |
| O'Neal, John | 1 | 50 | Twiggs |
| O'Neal, Harrison | 1 | 444 | Twiggs |
| Ogletree, Nancy | | 250 | Twiggs |
| Philips, William T. | 1 | 67 | Twiggs |
| Philips, Henry H. | 1 | 67 | Twiggs |
| Pearson, James | 1 | 420 | Twiggs |
| Philips and Dorsey | | 777 | Twiggs |
| Ray, James R. | 1 | — | |
| Read, William H. | 1 | 1217 | Twiggs |
| Raburn, Richard | 1 | — | |
| Read, Franklin | 1 | — | |
| Read, Alphens L. | 1 | — | |
| Ray, Benjamin | 1 | 1218 | Twiggs |
| Ray, Benjamin T. | 1 | — | |
| Solomon, Hardy | 1 | 500 | Twiggs |
| Stewart, Larkin W. | 1 | 1000 | Twiggs |
| Sanders, Ambrose | 1 | 50 | Twiggs |
| Solomon, Ruffin A. | 1 | — | |
| Tharp, Jefferson | 1 | — | |
| Tharp, John D. | 1 | 700 | Twiggs |
| Tharp, Thaddeus | 1 | — | |
| Tull, Bennet | 1 | 202 | Twiggs |
| "—guar. Tull, Frances A. | | | |
| Tidwell, Miner | 1 | 335 | Twiggs |
| Wall, Wm. E. A. | 1 | — | |
| Wall, Dyre | 1 | — | |
| Wilks, James H. | 1 | 100 | Twiggs |
| Webster, Alletha | | 2 | Twiggs |
| Williams, B. M. J. | 1 | 54 | Twiggs |
| Wilks, Henry | 1 | — | |

Defaulters:
Durdin, Henry
Durdin, Samuel, Jr.
Glover, George, Jr.
Melton, Harrison
Razor, Edmund
Woodard, James

*Shadygrove District*

No. 326 District
Georgia Militia

| Names | Polls | Acres of Land | County where the Land lies |
|---|---|---|---|
| Arnold, James J. | 1 | 202 | Twiggs |
| Arnold, Green B. | 1 | 101 | Twiggs |
| Allen, Nancy | | 502 | Twiggs and Putnam |

| | | | |
|---|---|---|---|
| Allen, Robt. L. | | 172 | Twiggs |
| adm. on the est. of Jas. Simpson | | 202 | Pulaski |
| Arnold, John | 1 | | |
| Bozeman, Wm. W. | 1 | 300 | Twiggs |
| Bridges, Green B. | 1 | | |
| Coley, Donaldson | | 1000 | Twiggs |
| Coley, Jas. W. | 1 | | |
| Crocker, John W. | 1 | | |
| Davis, Wiley | 1 | | |
| Defore, John | | 95 | Twiggs and Cherokee |
| Defore, Wm. | 1 | | |
| Evans, Uriah | 1 | 1 | Twiggs |
| Evans, Jas. T. | 1 | | |
| Edwards, Isham G. | 1 | 725 | Twiggs and Cherokee |
| Floid, Zachariah | 1 | | |
| Grantham, Wm. A. | 1 | | |
| Grimsley, Sherwood | 1 | 100 | Twiggs |
| Grimsley, Irwin | 1 | 202 | Twiggs |
| Herring, Wm. | | 3220 | Twiggs and Thos. |
| guar. for Jos. J. Lowery | | | Twiggs |
| Jones, Francis M. | 1 | 2 | Twiggs |
| Johnston, Edwin B. | 1 | | |
| Johnston, Sarah | | 130 | |
| Kitchens, Lawrence | 1 | | |
| King, Jos. Sr. | 1 | 2515 | Twiggs, Pulaski, Lau. |
| exr. on est. of Nathan King, dec., | | | |
| guar. for min. of Nathan King, dec. | | | |
| King, Jos., Jr. | | 100 | Twiggs |
| Knight, John | 1 | | |
| Knight, Mary | | 202 | Twiggs |
| Little, Matthew | 1 | | |
| Little, John | 1 | | |
| Little, Berry | 1 | | |
| Lowry, Barbay F. | | 202 | Twiggs |
| Meadows, Isaac H. | 1 | 202 | Twiggs |
| Meadows, Issac J. | 1 | | |
| Meadows, John B. | 1 | 202 | Pulaski |
| Maulden, Council | 1 | 202 | Twiggs |
| Lamb, Willis F. | 1 | | |
| Lamb, Willis, adm. on est. of R. Lamb, dec. | | 4267 | Twiggs |
| Lamb, Floid | 1 | | |
| Newby, Robert T. | 1 | | |
| Newby, Exom | | 325 | Twiggs |
| guar. for min. of Hillary Hasty | | | |
| Padget, Josiah | 1 | 202 | Twiggs |
| Padget, Wm. | 1 | | |
| Rozar, Robert | 1 | 1078 | Twiggs |
| Sanders, John | 1 | 74 | Twiggs |
| Vaughn, William T. | 1 | 202 | Twiggs |
| Wade, Willis H. | 1 | 300 | Twiggs |
| Wilkinson, John | 1 | 910 | Twiggs |

| Names | Polls | Acres of Land | County where the Land lies |
|---|---|---|---|
| Wilkinson, Wm. W. | 1 | — | |
| Wynne, Wm. | 1 | 100 | Twiggs |
| Ware, Jas. M. | 1 | 2700 | Twiggs |
| Whitehurst, Morgan L. | 1 | 405 | Twiggs |
| Walters, Wm. | 1 | 807 | Twiggs |

Defaulters:
Barnes, Archibald
Ganey, William
Lynn, Edwin
Phillips, Anderson

*Smith's District*

No. 355 District
Georgia Militia

| Names | Polls | Acres of Land | County where the Land lies |
|---|---|---|---|
| Ashley, John | 1 | — | Twiggs |
| Adams, James | 1 | 202 | |
| Alexander, Abram. S. | 1 | 202 | Lee |
| Adkins, Franklin | 1 | — | |
| Bodwell, Enoch | 1 | 100 | Twiggs |
| Brown, Stephen W. | 1 | — | |
| Barefield, Frederick | 1 | 202 | Twiggs |
| Birdsong, John J. | 1 | — | |
| Bobbit, James | 1 | 264 | Twiggs |
| Barrentine, Silas | | 100 | Twiggs |
| Barefield, Larkin | 1 | 677 | Twiggs |
| Balkcom, James | 1 | 943 | Twiggs |
| "—agt. est. Birden, Wm., dec. | | 200 | Twiggs |
| "—guar. Nelson, Franklin | | | |
| Bragg, James F. | 1 | 464 | Twiggs |
| Balkcom, Henry | 1 | 200 | Twiggs |
| Blaylock, Zadock | 1 | 75 | Twiggs |
| Barclay, Oliver H. P. | 1 | — | |
| Birdsong, Thomas J. | 1 | — | |
| Cranford, Benjamin | 1 | 200 | Twiggs |
| Cranford, Wm., Sr. | | 600 | Twiggs |
| "—guar. Nelson, Nunan | | | |
| Cranford, John W. | 1 | — | |
| Collins, Rebecca | | 86 | Twiggs |
| "—guar. min. heirs of Collins, James, dec. | | 204 | Twiggs |
| Cranford, John, jun. | 1 | 150 | Twiggs |
| Cranford, Lewis | 1 | — | |
| Clance, Reuben | 1 | — | |
| "—trust. min. children | | 101 | Twiggs |
| Cranford, John, Sr. | | 423 | Twiggs |
| Cranford, James M. | 1 | — | |
| Croom, Rabun | 1 | 161 | Twiggs |
| Crosby, Abram S. | 1 | 202 | Twiggs |

| Name | | | |
|---|---|---|---|
| Champion, Elias S. | 1 | 202 | Twiggs |
| Cranford, William F. | 1 | — | |
| Carrell, Issac | 1 | 300 | Twiggs |
| Crosby, Tillman | 1 | 100 | Twiggs |
| Crosby, Thomas | 1 | 100 | Twiggs |
| Crosby, Asa G. | 1 | 302 | Twiggs |
| Chappell, Wm. | | — | |
| Chappell, Thos. S. | 1 | 900 | Twiggs |
| Croom, Emra | 1 | 91 | Twiggs |
| Dyre, Abraham | 1 | — | |
| Dyre, Thos. | 1 | 500 | Twiggs |
| Day, Lewis R. | 1 | — | |
| Donally, Patrick | 1 | — | |
| Davis, Moses | 1 | — | |
| Epps, Daniel T. | | 1400 | Twiggs |
| Epps, Edward C. | 1 | 202 | Twiggs |
| Epps, Thos. P. | 1 | 202 | Twiggs |
| Evans, Hezekiah | 1 | — | |
| Evans, Obediah | 1 | — | |
| Farmer, John | 1 | 102 | Twiggs |
| Farmer, Gabriel | 1 | — | |
| Griffin, E. S. | 1 | 622 | Twiggs |
| Green, Western M. | 1 | — | |
| Goldin, Benj. T. | 1 | 302 | Twiggs |
| Goldin, Bery F. | | 202 | |
| Galloway, Wilson | 1 | — | |
| Gibson, Thos. | 1 | 32 | Twiggs |
| Henderson, John | 1 | 100 | Twiggs |
| Hogan, John H. | 1 | 220 | Twiggs |
| Hollingsworth, Mary | | 202 | Twiggs |
| Hardy, James | 1 | — | |
| Hammock, James | 1 | 1662 | Twiggs |
| "—adm. on est. Wm. Nelson, dec. | | | |
| Hinson, Caleb | 1 | 202 | Twiggs |
| guar. Neptune Curtis, Betsy Curtis, Jane Curtis | | | |
| Jones, Charles | 1 | — | |
| James, Wiley | 1 | — | |
| Jones, Thos. B. | 1 | — | |
| Jordan, Jacob | 1 | 170 | Twiggs |
| Jessop, Isaiah | 1 | — | |
| Jenkins, Milly | | 66 | Twiggs |
| Jessop, James, Jr. | 1 | — | |
| Jessop, Bery F. | 1 | 100 | Twiggs |
| Jessop, James, Sr. | | 740 | Twiggs and others |
| exr. on est. of Samuel Jessop, dec. | | | |
| Liles, Thomas | 1 | 217 | Twiggs |
| Lockhart, James | 1 | — | |
| Laner, Alexander | 1 | — | |
| Liles, James | 1 | — | |
| Liles, James | 1 | — | |
| Lingo, Wm. S. | 1 | 515 | Twiggs |

| | | | |
|---|---|---|---|
| Land, Jesse | 1 | 202 | Twiggs |
| Land, John | 1 | | |
| Land, Wm. | 1 | | |
| Liles, Sherrod | 1 | | |
| Linch, Louise P. | 1 | | |
| Martin, John | 1 | 300 | Twiggs |
| Mcwilliams, Asa | 1 | 405 | Twiggs |
| Mcwilliams, Simon | | | |
| Myrick, Richard | 1 | 250 | Twiggs |
| "—guar. for min. of D. Evans | | | |
| Martin, John M. | 1 | | |
| Martin, Hiram J. | 1 | | |
| McGough, Thos. C. | 1 | 565 | Dooly |
| Mcwilliams, Asa, BT | 1 | | |
| Maxwell, Mary A. | | 410 | Twiggs |
| Mcadamis, James | 1 | 150 | Twiggs |
| Mixon, Zilpha | | 202 | Cherokee |
| Moore, Saul J. | 1 | 125 | Twiggs |
| Mixon, Michael | 1 | | |
| Martin, Wm. J. | 1 | 340 | Twiggs |
| Martin, James W. | 1 | | |
| Maxwell, William | | 202 | Twiggs |
| Maxwell, Hugh | 1 | 202 | Twiggs |
| Mcadams, Thos. | 1 | | |
| Matthews, Jordan | | 242 | Twiggs |
| guar. for Mary Jane Thomas | | | |
| Mixon, Calvin J. | 1 | | |
| McGough, James C. | 1 | | |
| Moore, Wm. H. | 1 | 50 | Twiggs |
| Nelson, John A. | 1 | 2570 | Twiggs and Cherokee |
| guar. of min. of Sanders Vann, dec. | | 202 | Muscogee |
| Nelson, Wm. W. | 1 | | |
| Nichols, Jas. | 1 | | |
| Nell, Wright | 1 | | |
| O'Kelly, Wm. | 1 | 300 | Twiggs |
| Outlaw, Nancy | | 110 | Twiggs |
| Passmore, Saml. S. | 1 | 100 | Twiggs |
| Pettis, Elijah F. | 1 | 80 | |
| Pettis, Wm. J. | 1 | | |
| Pettis, Mark | | 300 | Twiggs |
| Parker, Robt. K. | 1 | 378 | Twiggs and Cherokee |
| agt. for est. of John Parker, dec. | | 2150 | Twiggs and others |
| agt. for Venus Curtis | | | |
| Pettis, Wilson | 1 | 205 | Twiggs |
| Pettis, Issac | 1 | 202 | Twiggs |
| Paul, Jas. E. | 1 | | |
| Raines, Calvin J. | 1 | | |
| Ryle, Joshua C. | 1 | | |
| Ryle, John J. | 1 | | |
| Reynolds, Hubbard | | 607 | Twiggs |
| Reynolds, Joseph | | 50 | Twiggs |
| Reynolds, John W. | 1 | | |

| Name | Polls | Acres | County |
|---|---|---|---|
| Sanders, Jeremiah | 1 | — | |
| Street, Rhesa | 1 | — | |
|   adm. on est. of Benj. Koonce | | 202 | Twiggs |
| Smith, Benj. B. | | 405 | Muscogee |
| | | 607 | Lee |
| | | 405 | Baker |
| | | 490 | Lowdnes and in Twiggs, Gilmer, Lumpkin, Paulding, Habersham, Hall, Appling |
| Stone, Wm. H. | 1 | — | |
| Taylor, Edmund J. | 1 | — | |
| Tharp, Benj. | 1 | 180 | Twiggs |
| Taylor, James | 1 | — | |
| Tharp, Simeon | 1 | 280 | Twiggs |
| Tharp, Charnic A. | | 1125 | Twiggs |
| Tharp, Jeremiah A. | | 1848 | Twiggs and Cheroke |
|   guar. min. trus. Margaret Tharp | | | |
| Taylor, Samuel | | 2635 | Twiggs |
| Vann, Mary | | 57 | Twiggs |
| Vann, Edward | 1 | — | |
| Williams, Simon | | | |
| Williams, Mary | 1 | 40 | Cherokee |
| Williams, Martha | 1 | — | |
| Wall, Jas. B. | | 404 | |
| Williams, Abraham | 1 | 303 | Twiggs |
| Woodall, Jas. W. | | | Twiggs |
|   adm. on Wm. Smith, dec. | | | |
| Williams, Simeon | 1 | 150 | Twiggs |
|   agt. for Needham Parker | 1 | 2000 | Twiggs |
| Wall, Jas. G. | | | Twiggs |
|   guar. for Crof Curtis (man of colour) | 1 | — | |
| Williams, Jos. | 1 | 355 | |
| Williams, Jesse | 1 | — | Twiggs |
| Wood, John L. | | 353 | |
| Young, Issac | | | Twiggs |
|   Defaulters: | 1 | — | |
| Adkins, Lewis | 1 | — | |
| Bostwick, Resa | | | |

*Tarversville District*

No. 376 District
Georgia Militia

| Names | Polls | Acres of Land | County where the Land lies |
|---|---|---|---|
| Bunn, Thaddeus J. | 1 | 440 | Twiggs |
| Bryan, Jas. | 1 | 1540 | Twiggs |
| Coley, Wm. W. | 1 | — | |
| Carter, Henry | 1 | 202 | Twiggs and Cherokee |
| Carter, Jas. | 1 | — | |
| Denson, Richard | | 54 | Forsythe |
| Dean, Burton | 1 | — | |

| | | | |
|---|---|---|---|
| Forehand, Jas. N. | 1 | — | |
| Gilder, John W. | 1 | 150 | Twiggs |
| Gilder, Wm. J. | 1 | — | |
| Jones, Taliaferro | 1 | 290 | Habersham |
| Jones, Bennet | 1 | 202 | Twiggs |
| Jordan, Green H. | | 1415 | Twiggs |
| Jordan, John A. | | 1256 | Twiggs |
| Lee, Hixon C. | 1 | — | |
| Mccrea, Gustavus | 1 | 831 | Twiggs |
| Massey, Eunice | | 201 | Twiggs |
| Morris, Allen | 1 | — | |
| Opry, Josiah | 1 | — | |
| Rowell, Anthony | 1 | — | |
| Rainey, Signal | 1 | 66 | Marion |
| Slappey, Robert R. | 1 | 2000 | Twiggs |
| Saxon, Benj. A. | 1 | 500 | Twiggs |
|   agt. for Esther Dunwoody | | | |
| Scarborough, Wm. M. | 1 | — | |
| Spradley, Dillard | 1 | — | |
| Tillotson, John S. | 1 | — | |
|   agt. for est. of Jos. M. Bryant, dec. | | 954 | Twiggs |
| Tarver, Andrew J. | 1 | — | |
| Tarver, Wm. M. | 1 | 820 | Twiggs and Cherokee |
|   exr. of est. of H. H. Tarver | | 9202 | Twiggs and Stewart |
| White, Nelson C. | 1 | — | |
| Walker, Charles | | 2010 | Twiggs |
|   guar. for Daniel Walker, Jr. | | | |
| Walker, Geo., Jr. | | | |
|   guar. for Henry Wimberly, minor | | | |
| Whitaker, Tho. R. | 1 | — | |

Georgia
Twiggs County

I do hereby certify that the preceding page contains a true and just account of all the taxable property as received by me as well as those returned by default in and for said county for the year 1853.
This 29th of June 1853.

Wright Neal R. T. R.

Amt. given in    :  $4521.72 net
Amt. given in default  :  $   39.82
                          $4561.54 gross

$ 4,521.72
      6%
$271.3032    Receivers coms
                Recpt. Given 2nd Aug. 1853

## TOTAL AMOUNT OF THE TAXABLE PROPERTY OF THE CITIZENS IN THE TEN DISTRICTS

| Polls | number of acres of land | | | | |
|---|---|---|---|---|---|
| | 1st class quality | 2nd class quality | 3rd class quality | pine land | aggregate value of land |
| 579 | 3,268 | 77,411 | 46,344 | 118,814 | $1,195,083 |

## CHANGES IN MILITIA DISTRICTS

| 1818 | 1826 | 1830 | 1833 | 1853 | Present | Militia District No. |
|---|---|---|---|---|---|---|
| Robert Belcher's | Streetman's | I. L. Streetman's | Roger's | Bluff's | Bluff | 372 |
| Wiley Belcher's | Pearson's | S. Streetman's | S. Streetman's | Pearson's | Pearson | 323 |
| Brown's | Gragg's | McCroan's | Pound's | Jeffersonville | Jeffersonville | 325 |
| Bozeman's | King's | Brown's | Herring's | Shadygrove | Shadygrove | 326 |
| Ellis' | Wimberly's | Oliver's | Ellis' | Higgsville | Higgsville | 354 |
| Hodges' | Holliday's | Carden's | Prescott's | Glover's | Wares | 324 |
| Jefferson's | Solomon's | Boynton's | Harrison's | Smith's | Smith | 355 |
| Smith's | Tison's | Dean's | Stephen's | Tarversville | Tarversville | 376 |
| Bullock's | Blackshear's | Will's | {Fulgham's | McDonald's | {McDonald | 356 |
|  |  |  | {Bostick's |  | {Hammock | 1322 |
|  | Bostick's | Bostick's |  | Marion | Marion | 423 |

(The district may vary as to where the taxpayer returned his tax, because sometimes a portion of a large or small district would be cut off to add to another area. or a new district would be formed.)

Courtesy of Dixon Hollingsworth, Sylvania, Ga.

# ABSTRACT OF DEED RECORDS
# THE FIRST INDEX BOOK, 1809 - 1900
*(Clerk's Office, Twiggs Superior Court)*

(These records have been re-recorded since the fire which destroyed the Court House on February 6, 1901.)

Legend to Kind of Instrument

| | |
|---|---|
| D | Deed |
| WD | Warranty Deed |
| Adm D | Administrators Deed |
| Gft D | Gift Deed |
| Q C D or Q Cl D | Quit Claim Deed |
| Mtg D | Mortgage Deed |
| Exr D | Executors Deed |
| Pwr Atty | Power of Attorney |
| Tst D | Trustee Deed |
| Shff D | Sheriff Deed |
| BDTL | Bond Title |
| Trf D | Transfer Deed |
| Est D | Estate Deed |
| Guard D | Guardian Deed |

| Grantor | Grantee | Instrument | Date | Book | Page |
|---|---|---|---|---|---|
| Adams, H. D. | Mary C. Jones | WD | 1-22-1897 | A | 285 |
| Asbell, Bryant | Kinch Washington | WD | 5-10-1895 | A | 292 |
| Adams, James | Calvin Minshew | WD | 9-26-1834 | A | 330 |
| Averitt, Wm. N. | Timothy Sears | WD | 12-29-1827 | A | 398 |
| Arrington, Thos. N. | Elias Pearce | AdmD | 10-25-1853 | B | 27 |
| Adams, G. B. and Susan N. | Mary E. Griffin | WD | 1- 3-1876 | B | 86 |
| Arnold, W. H. | Trustees of School | WD | 1-15-1899 | B | 111 |
| Arnold, Dock and Senate, Et Al | Needham Arnold | WD | 2-14-1889 | B | 148 |
| Asbell, Sarah F. and others | Mrs. S. M. Newby | WD | 1-13-1886 | B | 206 |
| Andrews, C. G. | Abell S. M. Andrews | GftD | 1-20-1885 | B | 285 |
| Aubrey, G. H. | A. G. Butts | WD | 2-26-1890 | B | 490 |
| Attaway, Isaiah | William Chapman | WD | 1- 4-1838 | B | 545 |
| Allen, Sarah R., admx. | S. E. Moore | AdmD | 11- 6-1877 | D | 20 |
| Allen, Sarah R., admx. | Geo. O. A. Daughtry | AdmD | 4- 7-1880 | D | 21 |
| Asbell, Bryant, admr. | Thomas Glover | AdmD | 1- 4-1859 | D | 71 |
| Arnold, James J., heirs of | Elizabeth Rasier | WD | 10-22-1892 | D | 468 |
| Arnold, Jas. J., heirs of | June Phillips | D | 10-22-1892 | D | 183 |
| Asbell, E. V. | Geo. R. Asbell | D | 4-10-1897 | D | 493 |
| Andrews, C. S. M. | C. G. Andrews | Gft D | 9-18-1899 | A | 178 |
| Adams, Obadiah | Geo. Knight | WD | 4- 3-1845 | D | 511 |
| Adkins, J. H. | James Manning | D | 3- 6-1894 | F | 495 |
| Achey, Louise | George M. Coris | D | 7-14-1888 | D | 555 |
| Arnold, Sarah E. | W. C. Pope | D | 1-13-1897 | F | 522 |
| Arnold, J. W. | W. H. Arnold | WD | 1-25-1899 | G | 3 |
| Brewater, J. F. F. | New England Mtge. Co. | WD | 4-15-1897 | A | 55 |
| Burns, James C. | Fannie L. Burns | GftD | 9-22-1893 | A | 63 |
| Burke, Belle D. | Fannie L. Burns | WD | 8- 6-1897 | A | 66 |
| Burns, W. P. | Fannie L. Burns | WD | 8-17-1891 | A | 67 |
| Barclay, J. A. | Monroe Phillips | OCD | 5-23-1897 | A | 86 |
| Bozeman, L. W. | A. B. Small | WD | 1-26-1899 | A | 96 |
| Bowden, Mattie | Charles F. Pearce | WD | 4-13-1899 | A | 105 |
| Bullard, Mrs. E. | Monroe Phillips | Lease | 10-29-1898 | A | 119 |
| Barton, John | M. S. Thompson | WD | 8- 7-1863 | A | 134-134 |
| Barton, Fannie L. | L. S. Dickson | WD | 6-13-1893 | A | 141 |
| Blasingale, W. P. | W. W. Hallam | WD | 6-22-1900 | A | 139 |
| Barton, W. M., C. W. and P. S. | L. S. Dickson | WD | 6- 8-1893 | A | 141 |
| Barton, W. M., C. W. and P. S. | L. S. Dickson | Bond Title | 6- 9-1893 | A | 142 |
| Butler, Lady B. | Guarantee Co. of Ga. | WD | 10-15-1895 | A | 147 |
| Barclay, J. A. | Lucind Kennington | OCD | 12- 9-1886 | A | 161 |
| Balkcom, J. F. | Mary C. Beemis | MTgD | 7- 2-1888 | A | 199 |
| Baskins, Mrs. N. G. | W. C. Gibson | OCD | 11-19-1893 | A | 203 |
| Barnes, Archelus | Thomas Glover | WD | 10- 7-1853 | A | 236 |
| Burns, James C. | Emma E. Newby | GftD | 9-22-1893 | A | 274 |
| Bobbitt, Emma B. | A. T. Small | WD | 1-20-1899 | A | 274 |
| Brown, Ella J. | Walker Jones | WD | 11-18-1891 | A | 284 |
| Balkcom, J. F. | Louis Chapman | WD | 10-26-1881 | A | 294 |
| Barclay, J. A. | W. C. Faulk | WD | 1-15-1902 | A | 326 |
| Burnette, Samuel | Wm. Wilmott | QCD | 11-24-1845 | A | 329 |

| Grantor | Grantee | Instrument | Date | Book | Page |
|---|---|---|---|---|---|
| Boynton, Joseph | Daniel Bullard | QCD | 12- 7-1846 | A | 330 |
| Bunn, Henry | Daniel Bullard | QCD | 8-15-1854 | A | 336 |
| Belcher, Robert | Payten Reynolds | WD | 6-19-1830 | A | 336 |
| Burnett, S. B. | Daniel Bullard | WD | 1-11-1847 | A | 337 |
| Burkett, W. J. | A. B. Small | WD | 4-29-1887 | A | 344 |
| Brannan, C. M. | Lee Lewis | Bd T | 7-15-1899 | A | 347 |
| Brown, H. R. | M. T. Kitchens | WD | 1- 4-1898 | A | 363 |
| Burkett, W. J. | L. W. Burkett | WD | 9- 5-1871 | A | 490 |
| Burkett, T. W. | Louisa C. Burkett | WD | 9-12-1872 | A | 491 |
| Burgess, Mrs. Mary | Mrs. L. J. Griffin | WD | 12-22-1896 | A | 490 |
| Bowden, J. M. | Wm. J. Hearn | WD | 10-25-1900 | A | 520 |
| Balkcom, Ichabod | Cicero Reynolds | WD | 1-16-1879 | A | 531 |
| Burns, Marion | Minnie Lee Burns | GftD | 7-21 1898 | A | 590 |
| Brown, J. T., heirs of | Each other, Division | | 9-21-1895 | A | 594 |
| Brown, Eliza | James W. Vaughn | GftD | 5- 7-1888 | A | 594 |
| Burkett, Lizzie and Sol. T., guard. | Sallie E. Kitchens | QCD | 10-30-1900 | A | 620 |
| Barclay, J. A. | D. S. Faulk | WD | 10-30-1896 | A | 640 |
| Brown, Herbert R. | Sarah E. Kitchens | WD | 11-24-1880 | B | 9 |
| Bullard, Daniel | William O'Daniel | QCD | 1-16-1890 | B | 49 |
| Bullard, Allen B. | Bersheba Church | WD | 11-14-1844 | B | 61 |
| Barclay, J. A., executor | Henrietta Willis | AdmD | 6- 5-1889 | B | 70 |
| Barclay, J. A. | Phillip Willis, & Et Al | WD | 11-20-1900 | B | 71 |
| Bunn, Henry | O. W. Whitaker | WD | 12-23-1873 | B | 80 |
| Bryan, Geo. W. | Jas. H. R. Washington | WD | 12-26-1862 | B | 81 |
| Burns, Fannie L. | R. E. L. Burns | GftD | 5-31-1898 | B | 119 |
| Brown, F. M. | Reubin Lowe | WD | 8-12-1898 | B | 131 |
| Bullard, Mrs. E. and others | Mrs. S. M. Newby | QCD | 11-20-1896 | B | 200 |
| Butler, T. J. | L. C. Burkett | WD | 11-15-1891 | B | 226 |
| Blalock, Isaac | M. L. Clance & B. F. Blalock | WD | 11- 6-1888 | B | 260 |
| Bunn, Henry | R. R. Slappey | AdmD | 12- 1-1857 | B | 268 |
| Burns, James C. | Fannie B. Burns | GftD | 9-22-1893 | B | 303 |
| Burns, R. E. L. | Mary L. Burns | WD | 2-22-1896 | B | 352 |
| Banks, John R. | Henry Carter | QCD | 11-14-1860 | B | 367 |
| Baker, James | Mrs. Ruth Bryant | WD | 10-25-1876 | B | 371 |
| Brown, H. R. | Shorter Crawford | WD | 7-31-1896 | B | 380 |
| Barclay, J. A. | A. F. Martin | QCD | 5-13-1897 | B | 432 |
| Barksdale, John | John Chapman | AdmD | 1-21-1849 | B | 546 |
| Bryant, William | Bennet Jones & D. G. Hughes | WD | 11-16-1861 | B | 554 |
| Bond, Amamnda & Nancy Sims | R. W. Bond, S. J. & J. T. Bond | WD | 3- 4-1890 | B | 586 |
| Bull, W. H. & Wife | S. J. and J. T. Bond | WD | 7-23-1874 | B | 588 |
| Bond, Joel H. | John T. Bond | WD | 12-18-1866 | B | 590 |
| Bond, Ruffin W. | S. J. Bond & Heirs | WD | 7- 9-1880 | B | 589 |
| Brewster, J. F. F. | New England Mtge. Security Co. | WD | 12-11-1895 | D | 8 |
| Best, E. F. | M. A. Williams | WD | 12-14-1879 | D | 58 |
| Best, E. F. | E. F. Hammock | WD | 12- 4-1879 | D | 88 |
| Beckom, Ella J. | Dr. G. L. Johnson, Guard. | | 2- 1-1874 | D | 99 |

| Grantor | Grantee | Instrument | Date | Book | Page |
|---|---|---|---|---|---|
| Bull, Jacob | | Will | 7-25-1822 | N | 119 |
| Bozeman, L. F. | B. F. Carden | GftD | 10- 2-1897 | S | 219 |
| Bunn, Henry | Frederick D. Wimberly | WD | 5- 7-1863 | S | 222 |
| Bignon, Joseph | Isaac H. Meadows | WD | 1-13-1894 | D | 303 |
| Burkett, J. H. | Louisa M. Burkett | WD | 12-26-1873 | D | 381 |
| Barker, E. N. | Joel TL Deese | WD | 7- 9-1898 | D | 409 |
| Bryan, M. L. | Matthew E. Slappey | D | 1860 | D | 512 |
| Bryan, Jas. | Joseph Bryan | D | 11- 7-1850 | D | 521 |
| Barnes, William, Barnes, James & Sarah E. Barnes, Mary C. Barnes, John Barnes | John Barnes | WD | 1-19-1895 | F | 17 |
| Sugar Smith | Benjamin Barnes | WD | 7-30-1897 | F | 19 |
| Benford, Mrs. Mary E. | I. M. McCrary & Children | WD | 1- 7-1887 | F | 20 |
| Benford, Mary A. by Admr. | Mrs. Mary E. Benford | D | 7- 6-1887 | F | 425 |
| Barclay, J. A. | Uzail Sherman | D | 10-31-1882 | F | 465 |
| Bullard, A. B. | Chas. B. Rynolds | D | 7-13-1858 | F | 482 |
| Bullard, Chas. & Et Al | Chas. B. Reynolds | D | 9-13-1858 | F | 485 |
| Benford, James R. | R. M. Benford | D | 11-10-1886 | F | 483 |
| Bozeman, Chas. F. | Chas. G. Arnold | D | 11-22-1894 | F | 484 |
| Balkcom, M. C. & Et Al | J. J. Taylor | QCD | 1-30-1889 | F | 499 |
| Bollinger, Solomon E. | James Lewis Spears | WD | 3- 9-1896 | G | 4 |
| Bollinger, John F. | James Lewis Spears | WD | 3- 9-1896 | G | 5 |
| Chapman, Lucy C. | British and American Mtge. Co. | WD | 2-18-1899 | A | 14 |
| Chapman, Geo. E. | C. Y. Johnston | WD | 4-12-1897 | A | 37 |
| Coombs, J. W. | W. L. Link Pr. of Atty. | | 4-26-1892 | A | 153 |
| Coombs, J. W. | James H. Tallman | WD | 8-24-1892 | A | 154 |
| Collins, A. F. | Mrs. Sarah Atkins | WD | 8-17-1889 | A | 170 |
| Cowels, Geo. Heirs of | James B. Moore | QCD | 1-15-1898 | A | 181 |
| Cannon, John T. | Georgiann Cannon | WD | 8-15-1899 | A | 321 |
| Chapman, Wm. T. | Louis Chapman | WD | 11-16-1887 | A | 324 |
| Cumming, Ridley Exr. | James Spring | ExrD | 3-25-1836 | A | 328 |
| Cook, J. T. | J. R. Cook | WD | 1-24-1900 | A | 333 |
| Cooper, Jas. W. | Day and Butts | WD | 3-14-1831 | A | 336 |
| Crocker, Wm. H. | W. E. Carswell | WD | 5- 8-1877 | A | 387 |
| Chairs, Green H. | Wm. N. and Abner Averit | AdmD | 7- 5-1827 | A | 403 |
| Callahan, Laura E. Exr. | Cicero Goodwin | ExrD | 7- 6-1900 | A | 421 |
| Chance, Alfred | John T. Fowler | WD | 3-22-1879 | A | 481 |
| Chance, Wm. | John T. Fowler | AdmD | 12- 8-1887 | A | 482 |
| Chambers, F. Guard. | Willie A. Harrison | QCD | 11-24-1899 | A | 542 |
| Chapman, John | Mary E. Chapman | WD | 7-10-1890 | A | 566 |
| Chapman, Mary E. | Lucy C. Chapman | WD | 11-30-1898 | A | 566 |
| Chapman, P. H. | Lucy C. Chapman | WD | 11-30-1898 | A | 566 |

| Grantor | Grantee | Instrument | Date | Book | Page |
|---|---|---|---|---|---|
| Commissioners of Ordinary | B. S. Fitzpatrick | Heirs Part | 10- 1-1883 | A | 581 |
| Coombs, Jas. R. | Willie Nobles | WD | 12- 7-1872 | A | 586 |
| Chance, Wm. C. | H. H. Chance & others | GftD | 9- 2-1895 | A | 620 |
| Coombs, A. B. | Mary S. Wimberly | WD | 5-12-1891 | B | 15 |
| Coley, Charlotte T. | Mary S. Wimberly | WD | 5-12-1891 | B | 16 |
| Cannon, W. F. | Mrs. Willie A. Harrison | WD | 1-17-1887 | B | 39 |
| Champion, Martha M. | William O' Daniel | WD | 1-11-1880 | B | 47 |
| Coley, Wm. H. | James A. R. Washington | QCD | 5-22-1886 | B | 80 |
| Carroll, J. B. | A. B. Small | WD | 12-12-1898 | B | 81 |
| Chance, Wm. | Reubin Lowe | WD | 8-25-1891 | B | 131 |
| Collins, Ellen & Et Al | John Arnold, Jr. | WD | 10-25-1898 | B | 147 |
| Corder, Newitt, admr. | H. S. Newby | AdmD | 12-26-1889 | B | 204 |
| Crosby, Avarilla | R. A. Denning | GrdD | 1-16-1901 | B | 212 |
| Clance, M. L. and others | J. W. Bryant, Trustee | TstD | 8- -1900 | B | 262 |
| Carter, Mrs. M. E. | John F. Carter | GftD | 11- 2-1883 | B | 366 |
| Cranford, J. W. | Shorter Crawford | WD | 11-16-1891 | B | 381 |
| Carswell, Alexander | Wm. Oliver | AdmD | 9- 7-1824 | B | 540 |
| Carswell, G. L. | J. R. Wimberly | WD | 3- 7-1899 | B | 420 |
| Crawford, Julia J. | Thomas G. Hill | WD | 3- 1-1872 | B | 493 |
| Coleman & Newsom | S. J. & J. T. Bond | WD | 9-10-1878 | B | 585 |
| Christian, J. M. W. | S. J. & J. T. Bond | WD | 1- 4-1890 | B | 586 |
| Coleman, Martha A. and Et Al | B. M. Latson | QCD | 11-25-1878 | D | 33 |
| Coleman. Martha A. and Et Al | Anna Latson | QCD | 11-25-1878 | D | 45 |
| Carroll, Cordelia | Mary E & Sallie P. Carroll | QCD | 7- 8-1893 | D | 165 |
| Carroll, W. F. | Mary E. & Sallie P. Carroll | WD | 3-16-1894 | D | 166 |
| Chance, W. C. | Dony Carter | GftD | 11-16-1892 | D | 211 |
| Cabaniss, J. W. | W. Custis Nottingham | QCD | 1-28-1889 | D | 322 |
| Crosby, A. G. | I. F. Crosby | WD | 1-24-1868 | D | 356 |
| Crosby, I. F. | Sisaly Crosby | WD | 12-18-1877 | D | 357 |
| Carter, Henry | M. E. Slappey | D | 10-29-1859 | D | 516 |
| Cobb, Mary Ann by Admr. | Lamar Cobb | AdmD | 10-17-1892 | F | 487 |
| Denson, Mrs. J. H. | W. A. Denson | WD | 12- 7-1892 | A | 74 |
| Denson, M. L. | Emma J. Phillips | WD | 2-23-1899 | A | 84 |
| Durden, Georgia A. | J. T. Pearce | QCL | 1-10-1900 | A | 105 |
| Dickson, L. S. | W. P. Blasingale | WD | 10-31-1896 | A | 138 |
| Denson, Mrs. M. L. | E. J. Denson, Jr. | AdmD | 10-31-1900 | A | 246 |
| Dupree, Ira E. | Mrs. Lelia Nutting | WD | 11-24-1882 | A | 289 |
| Doss, A. & H. | Phillips & Dorsey | WD | 3- 7-1854 | A | 569 |
| Dunn, Wm. M. | A. B. & Andrew Small | WD | 12- 5-1868 | A | 616 |
| Denson, E. J. (Deacon) | Wm. O'Daniel | WD | 11-11-1872 | B | 62 |
| Defore, Martha & Et Al | F. M. Smith | WD | 1-17-1891 | B | 236 |
| Demers, Albert F. | Frances A. Fales | QCD | 3- 9-1895 | B | 532 |
| Daughtry, Geo. O. A. | Ira E. Dupree | WD | 1-10-1883 | D | 21 |
| Denson, Tilmon R. | I. F. Crosby | WD | 2- 2-1844 | D | 356 |

| Grantor | Grantee | Instrument | Date | Book | Page |
|---|---|---|---|---|---|
| Dupree, Ira E. | H. A. Snelling | TfrD | 12-31-1888 | D | 356 |
| Deese, Lizzie | W. N. Fleetwood | WD | 6-17-1891 | D | 408 |
| Davidson, Joseph | John A. Barclay | D | 12-10-1856 | D | 487 |
| Davis, W. A. & Et Al | J. J. Laylas | QCD | 1-30-1889 | F | 499 |
| Davis, Peninah, by Agt. | J. R. Wimberly | ShfD | 6- 1-1886 | F | 510 |
| Davis, W. A. | R. A. Nash, Trustee | GCD | 6- 1-1889 | F | 510 |
| Evans, J. T., Sheriff | Henry J. Newby | ShfD | 6- 4-1876 | A | 111 |
| Evans, J. T., Admr. | Henry J. Newby | AdmD | 4- 4-1876 | A | 112 |
| Epps, James | W. J. Harrison | WD | 12-13-1882 | A | 311 |
| Evans, J. T., Sheriff | W. E. Carswell | ShfD | 4-13-1874 | A | 388 |
| Evans, J. T., Sheriff | I. N. Maxwell | ShfD | 4- 4-1874 | A | 406 |
| Everett, Henry E. | John A. Barclay | WD | 9-26-1854 | A | 562 |
| Ellis, Martha E. | James T. Glover | WD | 1-29-1874 | A | 598 |
| Edmonson, B. M. & J. R. | Wm. S. Edmonson | WD | 1-20-1895 | A | 653 |
| Ely, Julia A. | T. S. Tharp | WD | 1-18-1900 | B | 3 |
| Epps, Wm. V. | Loula L. Epps | GftD | 9- 1-1891 | B | 21 |
| Epps, Mrs. M. L., Heirs of | Loula L. Epps | QCD | 2- 6-1892 | B | 21 |
| Everett, John | Johnathan Dowden | WD | 11-28-1828 | B | 37 |
| Epps, Loula L. | Dr. J. C. Solomon | WD | 11-15-1898 | B | 76 |
| Epps, D. T. | Martha L. Epps | GftD | 2- 2-1868 | B | 116 |
| Evans, J. T., Sheriff | Cordelia E. McDonald | ShfD | 2- 1-1876 | B | 180 |
| Easterlin, Eula A. & others | John Day | BdTl | 12- 1-1900 | B | 193 |
| Early, Eleazer & Jane | John Forsyth | WD | 2-27-1812 | B | 489 |
| Everett, Henry E. | James Everett | WD | 2- 6-1849 | D | 34 |
| Elsie Fruit Land Co. | Daniel G. Hughes | WD | 12- 3-1897 | D | 84 |
| Epps, D. T. | E. D. Epps | GftD | 3-10-1867 | D | 145 |
| Epps, E. D. | A. B. Small | WD | 12-16-1880 | D | 145 |
| Evans, Mary F. | George Lucas | WD | 1-27-1892 | D | 181 |
| Epps, Martha, Et Al | Emma J. Pearce | WD | 9-20-1884 | D | 185 |
| Edge, P. W. | W. H. Andrews | WD | 2-21-1880 | D | 377 |
| Evans, J. T., Shff. & Haywood Hughes | Mrs. Elmina Hughes | ShfD | 12-28-1876 | D | 392 |
| Everett, J. B. & Chas. Bullard | Chas. P. Reynolds | WD | 8-13-1858 | F | 482 |
| Fuller & Jocelyn | A. J. Thompson | WD | 11-19-1895 | A | 223 |
| Floyd, Fannie B. | Geo. E. Chapman | WD | 4- 8-1897 | A | 33 |
| Faulk, D. S. | Fannie L. Burns | BdTl | 2- 3-1896 | A | 69 |
| Fitzpatrick, W. H., Shff. | P. T. Murphy | ShfD | 7- 4-1893 | A | 126 |
| Fitzpatrick, W. H., Shff. | Asa L. Strong | ShfD | 1- 7-1892 | A | 144 |
| Fitzpatrick, W. H., Shff. | J. W. Coombs | ShfD | 7- 5-1892 | A | 152 |
| Fitzpatrick, Thulia E. | Jas. H. Tallman | WD | 3-21-1894 | A | 171 |
| Fitzgerald, Phillip | E. B. Robertson | WD | 1-18-1882 | A | 177 |
| Floyd, N. G. | Sarah A. E. Grimsley | GftD | 4-16-1895 | A | 262 |
| Flint, Charles L. | New England Mtg. & Co. | WD | 4- 9-1887 | A | 264 |
| Floyd, N. G. | Martha J. Chance | WD | 4-16-1895 | A | 298 |
| Floyd, N. G. | Joseph H. Floyd | GftD | 4-16-1895 | A | 302 |
| Faulk, Mary A. | Allie L. Slappey | WD | 10- 2-1895 | A | 358 |
| Fuller & Jocelyn | Interstate Land & Improvement Co. | QCD | 3-10-1898 | A | 364 |
| Fort, Tomlinson | Green H. Chairs | AdmD | 12- 8-1826 | A | 403 |

| Grantor | Grantee | Instrument | Date | Book | Page |
|---|---|---|---|---|---|
| Fitzpatrick, Elizabeth G | Mrs. A. E. Solomon | AdmD | 3-21-1869 | A | 470 |
| Fowler, Elva A., Heirs of | J. T. Glover | WD | 1-25-1894 | A | 481 |
| Finney, Ella V. | H. A. Jones | WD | 1-11-1884 | A | 525 |
| Fitzpatrick, B. S. | Board of Education | GftD | 3- 2-1897 | A | 578 |
| Fitzpatrick, B. S. | M. F. Fitzpatrick | WD | 12-10-1894 | A | 583 |
| Fuller & Jocelyn | E. A. King | WD | 3-10-1892 | A | 595 |
| Frazier, Z. H. | Mary S. Wimberly | WD | 5-12-1891 | B | 14 |
| Faulk, George W. | Georgia A. Glover | WD | 3-15-1888 | B | 24 |
| Faulk, James G. | Henry Land | QCD | 2-17-1845 | B | 33 |
| Faulk, W. C. | J. W. Coombs | MtgD | 9- 1-1890 | B | 286 |
| Finch, Mary A. | Sallie D. Pettis | GftD | 1-22-1883 | B | 342 |
| Faulk, Mrs. Mary A. | Tarversville Baptist Church | GftD | 1- 5-1912 | D | 427 |
| Fitzpatrick, John | Thomas H. Jones | WD | 4-15-1856 | B | 343 |
| Fitzpatrick, J. H. | Newton Sanders | WD | 1- 5-1897 | B | 474 |
| Fales, Frances A. | Andrew Fales & Kate Sumner | QCD | 5-19-1897 | B | 537 |
| Flint, Chas. L. | J. F. F. Brewster | QCD | 12-28-1888 | D | 7 |
| Finch, Mary A. | W. F. Finch | WD | 2- 8-1885 | D | 52 |
| Fuller & Jocelyn | Isaac Taylor | WD | 11-17-1892 | D | 74 |
| Flint, Chas. L. | John R. Wimberly | WD | 12-14-1886 | D | 114 |
| Faulk, Geo. W., Jr. | R. R. Glover | WD | 6-  -1892 | D | 187 |
| Finch, B. F. | W. F. Finch | WD | 5-24-1899 | D | 221 |
| Flanders, B. & Son | Wilson Bobbitt | WD | 10-16-1883 | D | 318 |
| Floyd, J. C. | Fannie B. Floyd | WD | 12- 4-1900 | D | 325 |
| Faulk, G. W., Jr. | Mary A. Faulk | WD | 3-16-1892 | D | 380 |
| Fleetwood, Mrs. S. J. & Et Al | W. N. Fleetwood | WD | 6-17-1891 | D | 408 |
| Fleetwood, W. N. | A. L. Richardson | WD | 6-22-1891 | D | 409 |
| Fleetwood, W. N. | Joel T. Deese | TrfD | 9-26-1892 | D | 412 |
| Fowler, D. B. | Morcilla Fowler | GftD | 10-17-1899 | D | 426 |
| Flanders, David, Estate of | D. J. Baer | D | 12- 2-1890 | D | 578 |
| Fuller, Wm. A., Et Al | Will R. Haynes | D | 3-10-1892 | F | 405 |
| Fowler, D. B. | Ellen E. Yopp | WD | 2-10-1896 | F | 512 |
| Fowler, Erasmus | Ellen E. Yopp | WD | 2-10-1896 | F | 513 |
| Fowler, Allie & Et Al | W. E. Pope | D | 1- 8-1900 | F | 515 |
|  | Elizabeth Arnold | QCD | 1- 8-1900 | F | 516 |
|  | H. T. Pope | QCD | 1- 8-1900 | F | 517 |
|  | Smickly Lucas | QCD | 1- 8-1900 | F | 518 |
|  | J. L. Shears | QCD | 1- 8-1900 | F | 519 |
| Griffin, Mary E. | Mrs. A. M. Griffin | WD | 2-16-1887 | A | 6 |
| Griffin, A. M. and Griffin, H. F., Griffin, W. Y. | Mrs. Elanor Griffin | WD | 6-25-1894 | A | 7 |
| Gordon, W. M., Admr. | W. H. McCreary | Admr. | 10-26-1900 | A | 8 |
| Glover, James T. | British-American Mtg. Co. |  | 12- 1-1898 | A | 10 |
| Griffin, A. M. | Mary J. Wimberly | WD | 12- 3-1891 | A | 13 |
| Glover, Geo. Z, Executor | Mayer & Wats | Exr.D | 2- 8-1900 | A | 24 |
| Glover, Mrs. H. Clifford | Mrs. H. A. Gunn & L. D. Moore | WD | 12- 7-1900 | A | 26 |
| Griffin, Mrs. A. M. | W. Y. Griffin | WD | 4-20-1892 | A | 27 |

| Grantor | Grantee | Instrument | Date | Book | Page |
|---|---|---|---|---|---|
| Glover, Georgia A. | Fannie L. Burns. | Adm.D | 12-14-1881 | A | 63 |
| Graham, Benj. | Winnie Marcus | WD | 12-24-1900 | A | 128 |
| Griffin, H. F., Sheriff | James B. Moore | Shff.D | 11- 6-1894 | A | 146 |
| Guarantee Co. of Ga. | Alijah Catlin | WD | 3-31-1896 | A | 148 |
| Graham, Benj. | Tom Solomon | Agreement | 1-22-1901 | A | 167 |
| Griffin, H. F., Sheriff | J. T. Robertson | Shff.D | 1- 2-1894 | A | 176 |
| Guarantee Co. of Ga. | James H. Tallman | WD | 4- 1-1896 | A | 187 |
| Gibson, O. C., Admr. | W. C. Gibson | Adm.D | 12-20-1889 | A | 195 |
| Gibson, Jas. S. | W. C. Gibson, | QCL.D | 10-24-1893 | A | 203 |
| Gibson, Thos., Jr. | W. C. Gibson, | QCL.D | 11- -1893 | A | 204 |
| Glover, E. C., Et Al | Mayer & Watts | WD | 12-21-1900 | A | 216 |
| Gallemore, Geo. L. | Jno. L. Gallemore | WD | 12-13-1899 | A | 222 |
| Gallemore, G. R. and S. M. Gallemore & Et Al | Jno. L. Gallemore | QCD | 11-16-1893 | A | 223 |
| Gallemore, Mattie M. | Jno. L. Gallemore | QCD | 12-20-1893 | A | 224 |
| Gallemore, G. R. and J. L. Gallemore & Et Al | S. M. Gallemore | QCD | 11-16-1893 | A | 224 |
| Gallemore, M. J., Admr. | Sam M. Gallemore | Adm.D | 8- 6-1894 | A | 225 |
| Griffin, Mrs. A. D. | Deacon's Baptist Church (Colored) Jeffersonville | WD | 10- 6-1881 | A | 226 |
| Graham, Benj. | Ava Ashley | WD | 12-24-1900 | A | 228 |
| Gordon, J. W. | Robert R. Slappey | WD | 10-29-1847 | A | 239 |
| Gray, M. A. | Wm. Chance | WD | 10-27-1890 | A | 296 |
| Gallemore, Levi | Martha J. Gallemore | QCD | 8- 2-1881 | A | 303 |
| Gallemore, G. R., J. L. & Et Al | Martha J. Gallemore Guardian | QCD | 11-16-1893 | A | 305 |
| Gallemore, Geo. R. | Geo. L. Gallemore | Gft.D | 3-18-1899 | A | 323 |
| Gallemore, Geo. R. | Mrs. S. A. Methvin | QCD | 5-11-1899 | A | 346 |
| Griffin, A. M. | H. H. Jones | WD | 11- 9-1878 | A | 390 |
| Griffin, A. S. | Mrs. L. J. Griffin | WD | 12-14-1895 | A | 496 |
| Gamble, T. E. & Et Al | Thomas Lowe | WD | 5-12-1897 | A | 368 |
| Gibson, Thos. | Minnie G. Gibson | Gft.D | 7-24-1897 | A | 552 |
| Guarantee Co. of Ga. | Howard M. Smith | WD | 2- 7-1896 | A | 557 |
| Gibson, Wm. C. | Thos. Gibson | WD | 10-30-1890 | A | 552 |
| Griffin, W. & S. E. | D. S. Faulk | Mtg.D | 10-20-1899 | B | 76 |
| Griffin, H. F., Shff. | Benj. Graham | Shff.D | 1- 1-1895 | A | 621 |
| Griffin, H. F., Shff. | O .T. Chapman | Shff.D | 4- 3-1894 | A | 653 |
| Griffin, R. S. | Mrs. Dony Griffin | Gft.D | 11-30-1894 | B | 11 |
| Glover, Georgia A. | Jas. T. Glover | WD | 3-10-1890 | B | 23 |
| Glover, Reese R. | Georgia A. Glover | WD | 10- 1-1895 | B | 28 |
| Glover, Georgia A. | J. T. Glover | WD | 1- 5-1895 | B | 32 |
| Gallemore, Jno. L. | Reuben Lowe | WD | 8- 5-1897 | B | 133 |
| Glover, Harriett C. | Mrs. S. M. Newby | WD | 8-24-1889 | B | 205 |
| Glover, Harriet C. | M. T. Fannin & Ellie W. West | WD | 6- 2-1894 | B | 228 |
| Glover, F. W., Admr. | Miss S. Z. Solomon, | Adm. D | 1- 6-1885 | B | 228 |
| Griffin, H. F., Shff. | J. R. Wimberly Ordinary | Shff.D | 4- 3-1894 | B | 349 |
| Gordon, Mrs. L. F. | John Lowe | WD | 12-30-1896 | B | 363 |
| Griffin, Mary E. | D. G. Lee | Adm.D | 3-17-1881 | B | 416 |

| Grantor | Grantee | Instrument | Date | Book | Page |
|---|---|---|---|---|---|
| Griffin, Mary C. | Willie O. Sanders | WD | 10-28-1897 | B | 475 |
| Guarantee Co. of Ga. | R. R. Slappey, Sr. | QCD | 7- 1-1890 | B | 561 |
| Guarantee Co. of Ga. | Margaret F. Demers | WD | 11-16-1895 | B | 562 |
| Griffin, Mrs. L. J. | Jennie L. Methvin | WD | 10-26-1897 | D | 65 |
| Glover, Thomas | Bryant Asbell | QCD | 1- 4-1859 | D | 72 |
| Gallemore, Levi, Admr. | Nedham S. Lee | Adm.D | 12- 2-1874 | D | 119 |
| Glover, John T. | Cordelia Carrole | QCD | 10-24-1879 | D | 165 |
| Gordon, W. M. | J. W. Cabaniss | WD | 1-22-1898 | D | 322 |
| Gordon, J. W. | James Bryan | WD | 10-29-1847 | D | 518 |
| Green, Myles | Zachariah Lamar | WD | 10-16-1821 | F | 487 |
| Harrison, Willie A. | Albert L. Richardson | Mtg.D | 3-25-1891 | A | 9 |
| Hill, Thos. G. | Ella Brown | WD | 12-21-1879 | A | 49 |
| Hill, Thomas G. | Jackson Shiver | WD | 2-28-1879 | A | 54 |
| Hill, Mrs. I. D. | P. K. Dederick | Mtg.D | 12-31-1900 | A | 59 |
| Horne, Mary R. | Mollie & Minnie Hughes | WD | 5-14-1898 | A | 68 |
| Hearn, Wm. | J. T. & R. W. Bond | WD | 10-25-1900 | A | 101 |
| Haddock, Wm. | L. L. Minshew | WD | 3-28-1885 | A | 76 |
| Hearn, Jessie | C. F. Pearce | WD | 5-11-1899 | A | 107 |
| Hill, T. L. | Wm. W. Howell | WD | 2-23-1891 | A | 156 |
| Hill, Robt. A. | Egbert A. Hill | WD | 1- 1-1879 | A | 164 |
| Hall, J. H. | George Cowles | WD | 11-15-1890 | A | 180 |
| Hughes, Hayden | Daniel G. Hughes | WD | 6- 3-1853 | D | 78 |
| Hughes, Daniel G. | Chas. J. Pretzman Et Al | WD | 12-13-1892 | D | 82 |
| Hammock, E. F. | E. F. Crosby | WD | 6-25-1884 | D | 88 |
| Harrison, W. J. | E. F. Crosby | WD | 3-10-1884 | D | 89 |
| Hill, Thos. L. | N. S. Lee | WD | 1-25-1890 | D | 120 |
|  |  |  | 11- 2-1893 | D | 120 |
| Hinson, Elam | Mrs. Anna Read | Gft.D | 12-10-1871 | D | 140 |
| Howington, Jno. C. | Mrs. Anna Read | WD | 12-12-1874 | D | 140 |
| Harrell, Isabelle | Hattie L. Cochran | WD | 12- 3-1899 | D | 175 |
| Harrell, Mrs. J. L. | Mrs. A. E. Dennard | WD | 5- 3-1899 | D | 141 |
| Hughes, D. G. | R. A. Hill | WD | 11-22-1873 | D | 182 |
| Heirs of Jas. J. Arnold | Jane Phillips | WD | 10-22-1892 | D | 183 |
| Hughes, Wm. J. | R. R. Slappey | WD | 12- 8-1880 | D | 197 |
| Hinson, Elam | Martha Herring | Gft.D | 2-14-1868 | D | 237 |
| Hatcher, Nannie E. | James A. McCallum | WD | 6-12-1897 | C | 86 |
| Hollingsworth, C., Shff. | Tillman R. Denson | D | 8- 1-1843 | D | 357 |
| Hughes, Haywood | Mrs. Elmina Hughes, Shff. | D | 10-28-1876 | D | 392 |
| Hughes, Elmina | W. T. Reynolds, Guard. | WD | 10-28-1891 | D | 392 |
| Hughes, E. W. | E. McNair | WD | 11-14-1885 | D | 451 |
| Hammond, Abner G. | John A. Barclay | D | 9-26-1854 | F | 467 |
| Hill, Ellen C. | Lettie J., Thos. D. Tidwell | D | 12- 2-1895 | F | 485 |
| Hearn, M. A. C. | by Shff. J. M. Bowden | Shff.D | 4- 4-1893 | F | 492 |
| Hughes, Haywood | Elizabeth Hammock | D | 11-18-1856 | F | 513 |
| Hogg, Mrs. Mollie | James Lewis Spears | D | 3- 9-1896 | F | 516 |
| Interstate Land and Improvement Co. | W. R. Haynes | WD | 2-27-1901 | A | 70 |
| Ivey, F. P. | Jack and Amanda Shiver | WD | 11-14-1899 | A | 244 |

| Grantor | Grantee | Instrument | Date | Book | Page |
|---|---|---|---|---|---|
| Jones, Mary R., Admr. | Mary R. Horne | Admr.D | 12- 5-1876 | A | 459 |
| Johnson, H. V., Gov. | Clayborn Doss Plat & Grant | | 12-17-1808 | A | 573 |
| Johnson, Francis S., Admr. | W. R. Phillips | Admr. D | 12-12-1856 | A | 574 |
| Jessup, Elizabeth | Board of Education Smith Dist. Twiggs Co. | GftD | 4-29-1899 | A | 577 |
| Jessup, A. M. | W. A. Kitchens, | Power of Atty. | 8-20-1897 | A | 626 |
| Jones, Thos. H., Admr. | J. P. Mercer | Admr. D | 3- 6-1879 | A | 648 |
| Jones, John C. | Ella W. Wood | WD | 10- 7-1891 | A | 649 |
| Jones, S. E. | W. H. Califf, Jr. | WD | 2-23-1899 | A | 650 |
| Jones, Mary C. | Chesley Parker | Q Cl D | 10-15-1895 | A | 69 |
| Jones, S. E., Shff. | Mary C. Jones | Shff. D | 3- 2-1895 | A | 68 |
| Johnson, C. G. | M. W. Sapp | Guard. D | 12-30-1880 | A | 135 |
| Jones, S. E., Shff. | J. R. Wimberly Ordinary | Shff. D | 5- 4-1897 | B | 154 |
| Johnston, C. Y. | T. A. McMims | WD | 11-18-1896 | B | 162 |
| Jones, M. A., L. M., H. M. and Et Al | Thos. J. Jones | WD | 5-18-1899 | B | 217 |
| Jackson, Nathan & others | Wade Jackson | QClD | 9-18-1899 | B | 258 |
| Jones, Ben L. | John & Lucind Lowe | WD | 12-10-1897 | B | 320 |
| Jones, Elias | M. L. Pettis | WD | 12-10-1886 | B | 340 |
| Johnston, F. M., Admr. | A. F. Martin | Admr. D | 12-22-1890 | B | 431 |
| Jones, Martha A. | Thos. H. Mercer | WD | 11- 6-1900 | B | 512 |
| Jones, Martha A. | Edna C. Mercer | WD | 1-10-1900 | B | 513 |
| Jones, Henry M. | Edna C. Mercer | WD | 4- 1-1899 | B | 513 |
| Jones, A. B. & Wife | Bennet Jones, Sr. | WD | 12-10-1877 | B | 547 |
| Jones, Bennet | Mrs. Fannie Jones | WD | 11-12-1887 | B | 549 |
| Jones, Bennet | R. R. Slappey | WD | 9- 4-1862 | B | 555 |
| Jones, S. E., Shff. | Minter Wimberly | Shff D | 12-16-1898 | D | 47 |
| Jones, Martha A. | Thos. H. Mercer | WD | 11- 6-1900 | B | 512 |
| Jones, Martha A. | Edna C. Mercer | WD | 1-10-1900 | B | 513 |
| Jones, Henry M. | Edna C. Mercer | WD | 4- 1-1899 | B | 513 |
| Jones, A. B. and Wife | Bennet Jones, Sr. | WD | 12-10-1877 | B | 547 |
| Jones, Bennet | Mrs. Fannie Jones | WD | 11-12-1887 | B | 549 |
| Jones, Bennett | R. R. Slappey | WD | 9- 4-1862 | B | 555 |
| Jones, S. E., Shff. | Minter Wimberly | Shff D | 12-16-1898 | D | 47 |
| Johnson, John S. | Henry Lucas | WD | 1- 8-1889 | D | 156 |
| Jones, S. E., Shff. re Ida Reynolds | W. T. Reynolds Guard. | Shff.D | 2-12-1896 | D | 393 |
| Jordan Betsey | Sevelia Fleetwood | WD | 3-29-1876 | D | 408 |
| Jocelyn, Franklin, Et Al | Will R. Haynes | WD | 3-10-1892 | F | 405 |
| | | | 4-11-1895 | F | 406 |
| Kendrick, H. C. | John Barton | WD | 12-27-1850 | A | 136 |
| King, John P. | Danile Bullard | WD | 3- 6-1843 | A | 329 |
| Kitchens, Carrie E. | Sarah Ann Kitchens | WD | 12-10-1895 | A | 500 |
| Kitchens, Effie | J. M. Kitchens | WD | 3-13-1900 | A | 501 |
| Kennington, Nancy V. | J. H. Jessup, Power of Atty. | | 9- 4-1897 | A | 626 |
| Kitchens, Perry M. | W. S. Edmonson | WD | 10-26-1897 | A | 653 |

| Grantor | Grantee | Instrument | Date | Book | Page |
|---|---|---|---|---|---|
| Kelly, M. A. E. | James T. Glover | WD | 1-17-1872 | B | 30 |
| Kelly, M. A. E. | James T. Glover | WD | 1- 6-1873 | B | 31 |
| Kelly, M. A. E. | James T. Glover | WD | 2- 4-1867 | B | 34 |
| King, A. D. | James L. Harrell | WD | 7- 2-1858 | D | 141 |
| Knight, George | Wilson Hendrick | WD | 9-22-1848 | D | 515 |
| Knight, George | Joseph M. Bryan | WD | 1-10-1850 | D | 519 |
| Lingo, T. A. | B. C. Tharp | WD | 12- 5-1889 | A | 20 |
| Lyles, Amond V. | John T. Pearce | QCD | 2-18-1898 | A | 104 |
| Lyles, Nora | C. F. Pearce | QCD | 11-19-1898 | A | 104 |
| Lamb, Henry F. | W. H. Howell | WD | 9- 5-1895 | A | 157 |
| Lowe, John | Mayer and Watts | WD | 10-12-1900 | A | 207 |
| Lee, Needham S. | Elafair G. Sauls | WD | 6- 1-1895 | A | 232 |
| Lamb, Arthur B. | John G. Sanders | WD | 9-20-1883 | A | 266 |
| Lamb, H. F. | Allie J. Sanders | WD | 6-15-1895 | A | 281 |
| | | | 11-27-1888 | A | 283 |
| Lamb, D. T. | J. N. Nobles | WD | 10-11-1879 | A | 272 |
| Lamb, Ben Hill | Henry Howell | WD | 11-18-1884 | A | 310 |
| Laylip, Henry | James Spring | WD | 1-15-1836 | A | 336 |
| Lowe, Thomas | John M. Lowe | QCD | 12-27-1898 | A | 368 |
| Land, John C., Heir of | A. J. Land | QCD | 1-13-1890 | A | 423 |
| Lee, W. H. | James M. Kitchens | WD | 3-14-1890 | A | 501 |
| Lockett, Moses | Macon Mining Co. | Lease | 12- 7-1900 | A | 636 |
| Land, James | Henry Land | WD | 2-17-1845 | B | 26 |
| Land, Rebecca J. | James T. Glover | WD | 1-14-1860 | B | 31 |
| Land, James and Lucretia | Henry Land | WD | 10-25-1847 | B | 35 |
| Loyless, H. M., Admr. | James T. Glover | Admr D | 12- 6-1859 | B | 36 |
| Lowe, Thomas | William O'Daniel | WD | 1- 2-1873 | B | 59 |
| Lowe, Reuben | F. M. Brown | WD | 12-13-1898 | B | 122 |
| Lamb, E. V. & John H. | Charles Larned | Deed to Secure debt | 7-20-1883 | D | 5 |
| Lamar, L. M., U.S. Marshall | Charles Larned | WD | 1-14-1887 | D | 6 |
| Larned, Charles | Charles L. Flint | QCD | 4-13-1887 | D | 7 |
| Latson, E. B., Heirs of | Martha A. Coleman Et Al | Ag'mt. | 11-25-1878 | D | 33 |
| Latson, W. T. & Sallie Latson | B. M. Latson | | 1- 7-1898 | D | 33 |
| Locke, R. D., U.S. Marshall | John R. Wimberly | Shff D | 4-12-1884 | D | 112 |
| Lamar, L. M., U.S. Marshall | J. F. Brewster | Shff D | 3- 2-1887 | D | 115 |
| Lamb, Henry | Henry Howell | WD | 8-19-1874 | D | 143 |
| Lamb, Henry | Cool Spring Church | WD | 11- 3-1876 | D | 171 |
| Land, F. H. | Wm. J. Hughes | WD | 1-31-1872 | D | 197 |
| Larned, Charles | John E. Kimball | WD | 9-15-1894 | C | 102 |
| Latson, Simon P. | Abner G. Hammock | WD | 10- 1-1853 | D | 485 |
| Lang, Adam A. | John A. Smith | D | 12- 9-1880 | D | 553 |
| Lucas, Smithy | Ellen E. Yopp | D | 1- 8-1900 | F | 512 |
| Lucas, Smithy, Et Al | W. E. Pope Elizabeth Arnold H. T. Pope J. L. Spears | QCD | 1- 8-1900 | F | 515-519 |
| Lucas, George | Mrs. Ellen E. Yopp | D | 2-28-1899 | F | 521 |
| Lucas, Henry | Mrs. Ellen E. Yopp | WD | 1-10-1900 | F | 524 |

| Grantor | Grantee | Instrument | Date | Book | Page |
|---|---|---|---|---|---|
| Melton, William | Timothy Sears | WD | 3-11-1829 | A | 400 |
| Melton, Clem & Wm. | Sally Williams | Admr. D | 12- 7-1830 | A | 404 |
| Meredith, Wyatt, Admr. | Timothy Sears | Admr. D | 1- -1848 | A | 399 |
| Montgomery, Edward | James Spring, Et Al | WD | 4- 3-1833 | A | 399 |
| Minshew, Calvin | James Spring | WD | 1836 | A | 339 |
| Montgomery, Edward | James Adams | WD | 1-11-1834 | A | 329 |
| Mayer & Watts | H. A. Gunn & L. D. Moore | | 12- 7-1900 | A | 25 |
| Miller, Mollie S. | John T. Pearce | QCD | 2- 4-1898 | A | 103 |
| Miller, David R. | Samuel J. Paulding | WD | 4- 5-1890 | A | 247 |
| Mayer & Watts | J. Walker Jones | QCD | 12-30-1898 | A | 279 |
| Martin, A. F. | Ben L. Jones | WD | 11-22-1895 | A | 318 |
| Murphy, P. F. | Ophelia R. Phillips | WD | 5-26-1894 | A | 367 |
| Methvin, S. R., Exect. | D. G. Hughes | Admr. D | 7- 2-1861 | A | 405 |
| Miller, Mollie E. | James H. Tallman | Mtg. D | 1- 1-1885 | A | 472 |
| Methvin, Jennie | L. J. Griffin | WD | 12- 1-1896 | A | 497 |
| Martin, Sallie L. | Willie A. Harrison | WD | 6-20-1893 | A | 532 |
| Martin, James W. | Wm. J. Martin | WD | 1-29-1842 | A | 537 |
| Martin, John M. | Wm. J. Martin | WD | 2- 6-1846 | A | 537 |
| Martin, Hiram J. | Wm. J. Martin | WD | 1- 3-1851 | A | 538 |
| Martin, A. F. | Mrs. Willie A. Harrison | WD | 11-12-1885 | A | 539 |
| | | Admr. D | 4- 6-1894 | A | 543 |
| Miller, E. B. | P. W. Edge | Mtg. D | 11-14-1883 | A | 544 |
| Massengale, A. M. | W. R. Phillips | WD | 5-11-1857 | A | 567 |
| Massengale, A. M. | Joseph Smith | Pwr. Atty. | 5- 4-1857 | A | 568 |
| Mercer, J. P. | John C. Jones | WD | 3- 1-1880 | A | 648 |
| Methvin, Samantha | Daniel Bullard | Mtg. D | 6- 5-1886 | B | 57 |
| Miller, David R. | Samuel J. Paulding | WD | 6- 3-1890 | B | 67 |
| Maxwell, A. L. | E. F. Pettis, Trustee | D | 4-13-1872 | B | 159 |
| Maxwell, A. L. | Leonard Skeits | WD | 2- 4-1873 | B | 186 |
| Maxwell, I. N. | Pauline Maxwell | WD | 11-16-1895 | B | 304 |
| Minshew, Lewis L. | B. A. Gilman | WD | 7- 1-1892 | B | 548 |
| Martin, Robert | William Walters | WD | 11- 1-1834 | B | 541 |
| Moore, Stephen E. | Dudley M. Hughes | WD | 2-16-1883 | D | 20 |
| Mercer, J. P. | M. S. Epps | Admr. D | 4-15-1876 | D | 30 |
| Miles, J. R. & A. F. Becom, Admr. | F. L. Carswell | Admr. D | 11-17-1893 | D | 47 |
| Meadows, Paul, Exr. | W. B. Watts | D | 12- 3-1878 | D | 304 |
| Melton, Rebecca | Nettie C., E. N., J. T. & Wm. B. Melton | D | 3-27-1890 | D | 525 |
| Melton, Mrs. L. S. | J. A. Barclay | QCD | 12- 9-1900 | F | 477 |
| Manning, Mrs. Julia, Admr. | J. H. Adkins | Admr. D | 3- 6-1894 | F | 496 |
| McHenry, W. F. & O. L. Co. | W. A. Roush & G. W. Hubbell | Lease | 12- 9-1898 | A | 121 |
| McCreary, M. J. | Grace C. Jones | WD | 3-13-1893 | A | 251 |
| McCoy, J. T. | D. S. Faulk | Mtg. D | 12- 5-1899 | L | 380 |
| McCaw, James N. | Macon Mining Co. | WD | 5-22-1900 | A | 635 |
| McMillen, Mary Ann | George Lucas | WD | 11- 7-1887 | D | 182 |
| McCrary, I. N. and Children by Trustee | Henry S. Parks | D | 2-27-1891 | F | 21 |
| McCrea Josephine A. | Chas. Larned | D | 12- 2-1884 | F | 445 |

| Grantor | Grantee | Instrument | Date | Book | Page |
|---|---|---|---|---|---|
| McIntosh, Geo. | Wm. H. Crocker | D | 1- 3-1878 | F | 486 |
| Nash, E. A., Exr. | Susan E. Tharp | Exr. D | 12-17-1883 | A | 18 |
| Nash, A. E. | Mazie M. Tharp | WD | 1-18-1882 | A | 21 |
| Nash, A. E. | Benj. G. Tharp | WD | 12-15-1890 | A | 22 |
| Nottingham, Rosa M. | P. K. Dederick | WD | 10- 1-1900 | A | 64 |
| Newby, Sarah M. | V. C. Alte | WD | 1- 4-1899 | A | 73 |
| Nisbett, Jas. A. | R. R. Menshew | Admr. D | 9-29-1856 | A | 75 |
| Newby, S. M. | J. C. Newby | WD | 1-18-1895 | A | 235 |
| Newby, Jas. C. | Phillip W. Hand | WD | 9-19-1896 | A | 236 |
| Nobles, Harriett J. | Jackson Nobles | WD | 8-30-1875 | A | 271 |
| Nutting, Leila J. | H. C. Glover | WD | 9- 3-1900 | A | 287 |
| Newby, S. M., Admr. | J. S. Vaughn | Admr. D | 6- 5-1894 | A | 321 |
| Nelson, John A. | Martha F. and F. M. C. Rice | WD | 12- 4-1874 | A | 333 |
| Nottingham, W. D., Admr. | E. H. Beckley | Admr. D | 3-24-1899 | A | 381 |
| Nourse, F. E. | A. J. Phillips | WD | 7-31-1900 | A | 420 |
| Nutting, Leila J. & E. Jones | J. D. Jones | WD | 7-24-1886 | A | 418 |
| Nobles, Elizabeth | Sarah R. Kitchens | GftD | 6-28-1895 | A | 499 |
| Nelson, John A. | W. J. Burkett | WD | 7-24-1866 | A | 490 |
| Nobles, Wm., Heirs of | Willis Nobles | QCD | 12-15-1875 | A | 586 |
| Nelson, E. J. | W. R. Rogers, Jr. | WD | 5-19-1899 | A | 628 |
| Nelson, E. J. | James N. McCaw | WD | 3- 1-1900 | A | 629 |
| Nelson, W. J. | James N. McCaw | WD | 2- 7-1900 | A | 630 |
| Newby, S. M. | Bryant Asbell | WD | 4-15-1897 | B | 201 |
| Newby, Henry J. | Mrs. S. M. Newby | GftD | 3- 1-1876 | B | 207 |
| Newby, Mrs. S. M. | Mrs. Sarah M. Glover | WD | 3-28-1900 | B | 208 |
| Nottingham, Rosa M. | L. J. Griffin | WD | 10-15-1900 | B | 302 |
| Nelson, B. S. | A. A. Nelson | WD | 5- 9-1881 | B | 403 |
| Nutting, Leila J. | A. F. Martin | WD | 5-15-1897 | B | 433 |
| Newby, H. J. | W. T. Vaughn | QCD | 4-13-1875 | D | 9 |
| Nelson, Geo. W. | Joe Peacock | Admr. D | 7- 3-1894 | D | 60 |
| Newby, S. M. | E. F. Newby | WD | 12-22-1897 | D | 203 |
| Nelson, J. R. | Johnson & Harris | WD | 2-18-1887 | D | 323 |
| Nelson, Jack | Mattie Crawford | D | 3- 5-1897 | F | 463 |
| Nelson, E. J. | Antioch Colored Church | D | 10-29-1888 | F | 497 |
| O'Neal, Harrison | J. I. O'Neal | WD | 1-31-1890 | A | 649 |
| Oliver, Wm. | Joel Hamiter | WD | 8-28-1834 | B | 543 |
| O'Neal, John | Sallie M. O'Neal | WD | 5-16-1899 | B | 582 |
| O'Neal, John | Thomas O'Neal | WD | 11-15-1880 | D | 339 |
| Pettis, M. L. | Sallie D. Pettis | GftD | 1-17-1887 | A | 44 |
| Pettis, Sallie D. | Henry J. Pettis | WD | 4-18-1887 | A | 45 |
| Phillips, L. S. | Emma J. Phillips | WD | 8-28-1899 | A | 82 |
| Phillips, J. B. | Emma J. Phillips | WD | 3- 3-1899 | A | 83 |
| Phillips, Emma J. | E. A. Hallman | WD | 2-26-1900 | A | 85 |
| Phillips, Monroe | E. A. Hallman | WD | 3-12-1900 | A | 87 |
| Phillips, John | W. A. Denson | WD | 2-20-1897 | A | 89 |
| Phillips, W. R. | Standard Lumber Co. | Lease | 11- 7-1898 | A | 95 |
| Pearce, W. R. | Ben L. Jones | WD | 1 3-1896 | A | 100 |
| Pearce, Laura A. | Chas. F. Pearce | WD | 9-11-1900 | A | 100 |
| Pearce, J. T. | C. F. Pearce | WD | 9-11-1900 | A | 106 |

| Grantor | Grantee | Instrument | Date | Book | Page |
|---|---|---|---|---|---|
| Phillips, Ophelia R. | E. A. Hallman | Lease | 10-21-1899 | A | 115 |
| Pettis, E. F., Shff. | J. A. Barclay | Shff D | 4- 6-1886 | A | 160 |
| Pettis, E. F., Shff. | J. H. Hall | Shff D | 7- 1-1890 | A | 179 |
| Phillips, Ophelia R. | P. T. Murphy | WD | 7- 7-1894 | A | 183 |
| Peck, Ira | Samuel Burnett | QCD | 10-16-1845 | A | 330 |
| Parson, L. E., Exr. | J. R. Cook | Exr. D | 1-16-1900 | A | 332 |
| Peck, Ira | Daniel Bullard | WD | 6-16-1845 | A | 338 |
| Phillips, Haywood H. | Dellia, Roxie & Lorena Phillips | Will | 11-14-1882 | A | 341 |
| Pettis, E. F., Shff. | Nancy L. Bobbitt | Shff. D | 6- 1-1886 | A | 363 |
| Phillips, A. J. | Guarantee Co. of Ga. | WD | 10-30-1897 | A | 528 |
| Preston, Geo. C. | Equitable S. Co. | WD | 2-17-1898 | A | 529 |
| Phillips, Emma J. | J. T. Bond & R. W. Bond | WD | 12-21-1900 | A | 557 |
| Phillips, W. R. | R. L. Henry | Mtg. D | 3-19-1898 | 1 | 279 |
| Pridgett, John M., Et Al | Elmina H. Winburn | WD | 12- 6-1894 | A | 610 |
| Payne, Geo. F. | E. J. Nelson | WD | 7-29-1825 | A | 631 |
| Pettis, Joannah | Mattie J. McCrary | WD | 5-17-1892 | B | 22 |
| Perry, David M. | Wm. O'Daniel | WD | 1-13-1884 | B | 45 |
| Pearce, Alexander | Wm. O'Daniel | WD | 2-23-1870 | B | 46 |
| Paul, Robert | Wm. O'Daniel | WD | 10-12-1877 | B | 51 |
| Paul, Robert | Samantha Methvin | WD | 1- 8-1876 | B | 59 |
| Padgett, Wm. W. | Heirs of Wm. B. Padgett | WD | 9-15-1885 | B | 74 |
| Padgett, Mary A. E. | L. J. Carroll | Gtf. D | 9-10-1892 | B | 90 |
| Pettis, E. F. | Joannah Pettis & Children | WD | 9- -1886 | B | 160 |
| Padgett, Mary A. E. | Julia A. Taylor | WD | 9- 9-1892 | B | 209 |
| Pope, H. F., W. E. & others | Mrs. Allie Fowler | WD | 1- 8-1900 | B | 229 |
| Pettis, E. F., Shff. | L. Smith | Shff. D | 1- 6-1891 | B | 390 |
| Phillips, Jane and others | Nancy Ann Phillips | Agreement | 10-22-1892 | B | 469 |
| Pearce, John M. | Bennet Jones, Sr. | Admr. D | 4- 2-1872 | B | 547 |
| Payne, Wm. S., Atty. | Ben Hand | WD | 1-31-1890 | B | 569 |
| Paul, Mrs. E. M. | Deacons, Green Grove Baptist Colored Church 25th Dist., Public Rd. from Bullard to Marion) | WD | 4- 1-1893 | D | 5 |
| Peck, Ira., Admr. | James Everett | Admr. D | 1- 4-1848 | D | 34 |
| Pretzman, Chas. J., Et Al | Elsie Fruit Land Co. | WD | 6-21-1893 | D | 83 |
| Phillips, Lorah H. & Roxie | Ophelia R. Phillips | WD | 5- 1-1884 | D | 159 |
| Price, Mary Ann | George Lucas | WD | 4-17-1884 | D | 181 |
| Pope, John | Wm. T. Vaughn & Et Al | D | 10- 6-1860 | D | 321 |
| Parker, Chesley | Wesley Hooker & Barcus Nelson, Deacons of Stone Creek Colored Church | WD | 5- 4-1887 | D | 346 |
| Peacock, S. E. | Mrs. M. C. Jones | QCLD | 11-29-1881 | D | 366 |
| Peacock, E. M. | F. A. & G. W. Cannon | WD | 11-30-1888 | D | 384 |

| Grantor | Grantee | Instrument | Date | Book | Page |
|---|---|---|---|---|---|
| Peacock, Elmina | Turner Peacock | WD | 9-21-1898 | D | 488 |
| Phillips, Wm. T. & Henry H. | John Davis | WD | 10-25-1856 | D | 526 |
| Parker, Chesley, by Shff. | David Flanders | Est. Bond | 1- 7-1890 | D | 575 |
| Pace, Thomas B. | Abner Hammond | WD | 3- 8-1850 | F | 478 |
| Pearce, Theophilus | Joseph Davidson | WD | 2-28-1852 | F | 478 |
| Pace, Thomas B. | Hartwell L. Solomon | D | 1- 3-1861 | F | 479 |
| Pope, H. T. & Et Al | W. E. Pope | D | 1- 8-1900 | F | 518-515 |
| Pope, W. E. | George Lucas | WD | 2-23-1899 | F | 522 |
| Pettis, E. F. | Joannah Pettis | Est. D | 1-27-1892 | I | 574 |
| | | | | (Minute Bk) | |
| Q no names | | | | | |
| Read, Mary J. | Monroe Phillips | WD | 1-19-1899 | A | 90 |
| Read, Mary J. | E. A. Hallman | WD | 1- 1-1900 | A | 92 |
| Roush, W. A. & G. W. Hubble | E. A. Hallman | Lease D | 7-22-1899 | A | 115 |
| Richardson, A. L. | Willie A. Harrison | Agreement | 3- 9-1891 | A | 166 |
| Rice, Ira A. | Wm. C. Gibson | WD | 2-11-1896 | A | 202 |
| Rogers, Geo. T. & Sons | Mayer & Watts | WD | 12-29-1897 | A | 288 |
| Read, Wm. H. | Daniel B. Melton | GftD | 3- 3-1869 | A | 353 |
| Rogers, Josiah | Timothy Sears | WD | 12-12-1814 | A | 393 |
| | (Land Grant to H. Scott) | | | | |
| Ray, Ben T., Jr. H. H. Ray & Et Al | A. J. Land | WD | 10-19-1895 | A | 425 |
| Ray, B. T. | Heirs of John C. Land | QClD | 11-22-1889 | A | 422 |
| Reynolds, Hubbard | Ichabod Balckom | WD | 2-24-1868 | A | 530 |
| Reynolds, Cicero | Wm. T. Reynolds | WD | 9-21-1881 | A | 531 |
| Reynolds, Moses | Harrison & Martin | WD | 6- 2-1891 | A | 533 |
| Reynolds, Moses H. | Willie A. Harrison | QClD | 2-27-1894 | A | 535 |
| Robertson, F. J., Shff. | Mrs. J. J. Kitchens | Shff D | 8- 5-1884 | A | 551 |
| Roberts, Mary Jane and others | E. F. Cranford | WD | 10- 2-1899 | A | 558 |
| Rice, Mrs. M. F. | James N. McCaw | WD | 2-27-1900 | A | 631 |
| Rice, Mrs. M. F. | Geo. F. Payne | WD | 5- 6-1895 | A | 637 |
| Ray, B. F. | John Cribb | WD | 11- 6-1886 | B | 6 |
| Rowell, Nat J. | James B. Moore | QClD | 1- 3-1900 | B | 163 |
| Ryle, B. F. | G. B. Ward | WD | 12-19-1892 | B | 520 |
| Rawls, Joseph | Wm. Walters | WD | 10-31-1834 | B | 542 |
| Radfords, Henry, Exr. | Daniel G. Hughes | Admr. D | 12- 2-1867 | D | 78 |
| Read, R. F. | Mary J. Read | WD | 4- 2-1875 | D | 91 |
| Read, Wm. H. | Ellen Read, Julia Denson & others | WD | 3- 3-1869 | D | 106 |
| Read, Ellen & John Phillips | Geo. M. Read | WD | 12-18-1870 | D | 107 |
| Read, Ben F. | Rupell F. Read | WD | 12-11-1869 | D | 154 |
| Read, Willis A. & G. M. | R. F. Read | WD | 8-30-1887 | D | 154 |
| Reynolds, Ida C. by Shff | W. T. Reynolds | Guard. D | 2-12-1896 | D | 393 |
| Richardson, A. L. | Joel T. Deese | WD | 6- 8-1898 | D | 410 |
| Reynolds, L. B. | E. McNair | WD | 11-14-1885 | D | 450 |

| Grantor | Grantee | Instrument | Date | Book | Page |
|---|---|---|---|---|---|
| Reynolds, Chas. P. | John A. Barclay | D | 6- 8-1880 | F | 483 |
| Raupcan, James | Myles Green | WD | 5- 6-1819 | F | 488 |

(Now in Twiggs, formerly in Baldwin County, lot No. 154 in the 7th District of Baldwin, adjoining the Ocmulgee River.)

| Grantor | Grantee | Instrument | Date | Book | Page |
|---|---|---|---|---|---|
| Solomon, Mrs. J. L. B. | J. J. Wall | WD | 6-21-1888 | A | 43 |
| Solomon, M. E., Exr. | J. J. Wall | WD | 12-24-1894 | A | 47 |
| Shiver, Jack and Amanda | C. Y. Johnston | WD | 11-14-1899 | A | 56 |
| Story, Thos. M. & Julia | J. B. Thompson | Exr. D | 10- 7-1897 | A | 73 |
| Small, A. B., Agt | E. A. Hallman | Cont'ct | 6- 1-1899 | A | 93 |
| Small, A. B. | L. W. Bozeman | QClD | 7-31-1899 | A | 97 |
| Slappey, Allie L. | J. E. McDonald | Lease | 4-30-1897 | A | 98 |
| Sanders, Allie J. | C. Y. Johnston | WD | 10-15-1895 | A | 157 |
| Smith, Howard M. | Wm. C. Gibson | WD | 2-15-1896 | A | 200 |
| Slappey, A. L. | Mayer & Watts | WD | 12- 7-1899 | A | 208 |
| Slappey, J. G., Guard. | Mayer & Watts | Admr.D | 2- 6-1900 | A | 215 |
| Stokes, W. H., Shff | Mrs. M. D. Johnson, | Shff D | 7- 1-1879 | A | 257 |
| Sauls, Bryant | Martha Ann Sauls | GftD | 10-26-1893 | A | 261 |
| Sanders, John R. | John G. Sanders | WD | 12-13-1899 | A | 268 |
| Smith, Virginia, and Ed. | Louis Chapman | WD | 12-20-1892 | A | 525 |
| Spring, James | Daniel Bullard | WD | 1-28-1837 | A | 328 |
| State of Georgia | Akiles Liles | Grant | 1-24-1824 | A | 331 |
| Streetman, B., Admr. | Daniel Bullard | AdmrD | 11- 3-1846 | A | 338 |
| Sims, Allen M. | Daniel Bullard | WD | 11-14-1849 | A | 340 |
| Solomon, Hardy | Nancy Ann Solomon | GftD | 5-20-1875 | A | 342 |
| Solomon, Hardy | H. L. Solomon & J. Hammock | Gft. D | 6-20-1892 | A | 343 |
| Solomon, N. M. & W. G., Exrs. | Hardy Solomon | QClD | 3-22-1884 | A | 343 |
| Slappey, R. R. | F. W. & M. F. Slappey | WD | 1- 9-1877 | A | 357 |
| Stokes, W. H., Shff | Elizabeth Denson | ShffD | 4- 2-1879 | A | 360 |
| Sanders, Mary Ann | Mary Elizabeth Bloodworth | WD | 1- 5-1899 | A | 362 |
| Stokes, W. H., Shff | H. H. Jones | ShffD | 9- -1877 | A | 391 |
| State of Georgia | West Vincent | Grant | 5- 1-1811 | A | 393 |
| State of Georgia | Harriett Scott | Grant | 9-14-1814 | A | 395 |
| State of Georgia | James Reeves | Grant | 2-14-1811 | A | 396 |
| Sears, Wilson C. | Timothy Sears | WD | 9-24-1835 | A | 400 |
| Stokes, F. M. | S. J. & L. C. Stokes | WD | 11-17-1890 | A | 410 |
| Stokes, W. R. B. | S. J. & L. C. Stokes | WD | 12-15-1892 | A | 411 |
| Stokes, Mary N. | Heirs of Elva A. Fowler | WD | 1-25-1894 | A | 479 |
| Smith, Howard M. | Guarantee Co. of Ga. | QClD | 10- 3-1897 | A | 529 |
| Sanders, Jeremiah, Admr. | John Kitchens | AdmrD | 11- 2-1870 | A | 549 |
| Smith, Joseph | W. R. Phillips | WD | 5-11-1857 | A | 470 |
| Small, A. B. | Board of Education | GftD | 8-31-1900 | A | 579 |
| Stokes, J. A. | Board of Education | GftD | 2-24-1899 | A | 579 |
| Shannon, J. C. | W. H. Harrell | WD | 3-25-1893 | A | 589 |
| Slappey, Mrs. J. F. | Frank Lowe | WD | 3-12-1898 | A | 591 |
| Solomon, Averilla E. | Josie Solomon | WD | 2-10-1898 | A | 599 |
| Sherwood, J. K. O. | American Mtg Co. | QClD | 2- 2-1884 | A | 602 |
| Shannon, L. D. | A. E. Vickers | WD | 11-13-1879 | A | 602 |
| Small, Andrew E. | A. B. Small | WD | 12-13-1873 | A | 617 |

| Grantor | Grantee | Instrument | Date | Book | Page |
|---|---|---|---|---|---|
| Small, Augustus B. | Anna T. Small & Children | GftD | 4- 4-1876 | A | 617 |
| Stokes, W. H., Shff | R. L. Harrison | ShffD | 4- 6-1880 | A | 651 |
| Singleton, Wm. B. | Sarah E. Kitchens | WD | 2- 4-1871 | B | 9 |
| Stokes, W. H., Shff | James T. Glover | ShffD | 7- 1-1862 | B | 25 |
| Solomon, Jas. B & Va. | Wm O'Daniel | WD | 2-24-1880 | B | 44 |
| Solomon, C. A. | Wm O'Daniel | WD | 1-28-1880 | B | 48 |
| Solomon, Va. & I. B. | Wm. O'Daniel | QClD | 2-24-1880 | B | 50 |
| Solomon, Louis | Wm O' Daniel | WD | 2- 9-1868 | B | 51 |
| Solomon, Virginia & Et Al | Wm O' Daniel | WD | 10-26-1881 | B | 54 |
| Solomon, Mary E. | Jas. C. Solomon | WD | 1-24-1885 | B | 77 |
| Stokes, W. R. B. | F. M. Stokes | GftD | 12-15-1892 | B | 112 |
| Sapp, Moses W. | Henrietta Sapp | Guard D | 1-12-1883 | B | 136 |
| Stokes, J. E., N. P. Ex. Off J. P. | Heirs of John Pope | Division | 5-10-1883 | B | 147 |
| Saulsbury Respass & Co. | Louisa C. Burkett | WD | 11-12-1881 | B | 153 |
| Shines, Sarah C. | J. E. McDonald | WD | 1-17-1876 | B | 182 |
| Sheriff, S. E. Jones | A. B. Small | ShffD | 6- 7-1898 | B | 264 |
| Solomon, Sarah F. | Her Heirs | Will | 9-21-1898 | B | 272 |
| Solomon, S. Z. | Lucy A. Solomon | WD | 6-22-1896 | B | 289 |
| Shff, W. E. Jones | Mary C. Jones | ShffD | 4- 2-1895 | B | 297 |
| Slappey, Allie L. | Mrs. S. E. Jones | WD | 11- -1900 | B | 323 |
| Solomon, S. F. & Heirs | Betty Asbell | WD | 3-18-1896 | B | 328 |
| Stokes, W. R. B. | Wm I. Stokes | D of Gft | 12-15-1892 | B | 478 |
| Sheriff, H. F. Griffin | J. R. Wimberly Ordinary | ShffD | 4- 3-1894 | B | 349 |
| Slappey, Dr. J. G. | John F. Carter | WD | 10-22-1896 | B | 366 |
| Stokes, Mary A. | S. P. Wall | WD | 1-31-1900 | B | 376 |
| Smith, H. T. | Uzail Shermon | WD | 11-24-1877 | B | 383 |
| Shermon, Uzail | W. H. Harrell | WD | 11- 8-1882 | B | 384 |
| Sheriff, E. F. Pettis | L. Smith | ShffD | 1- 6-1891 | B | 390 |
| Sumner, Kate E., Ex. | D. S. Faulk | Admr.D | 12-27-1900 | B | 391 |
| Sheriff, S. E. Jones | Geo C. Preston | ShffD | 1- 4-1898 | B | 414 |
| Sanders, Newton | Willie O. Sanders | GftD | 10-22-1897 | B | 476 |
| Slappey, Robert R. | F. W. & M. F. Slappey | WD | 10- 2-1873 | B | 556 |
| Slappey, Robert R. | Robert R. Slappey, Jr. | WD | 10- 2-1873 | B | 557 |
| Solomon, John W. | Solomon J. Bond | WD | 11- 3-1869 | B | 589 |
| Smith, Robert & Eugenia | S. E. Moore | WD | 2-19-1872 | D | 19 |
| Shannon, J. C. | J. S. Burke | WD | 11-16-1894 | D | 54 |
| Stokes, W. H., Shff | E. F. Best | ShffD | 5- 7-1879 | D | 58 |
| Slappey, Jenette . | John G. Slappey | WD | 2- 8-1894 | D | 139 |
| Stokes, H. F. & other Heirs | J. A. Stokes | WD | 3- 9-1897 | D | 152 |
| Stokes, Margaret E. | J. A. Stokes | WD | 3- 9-1897 | D | 153 |
| Stokes, W. H., Shff | W. F. Carroll | ShffD | 7- 1-1879 | D | 164 |
| Stokes, W. H., Shff | L. D. Shannon | D | 6- 7-1881 | D | 365 |
| Shannon, L. D. | Ira E. Dupree | Transfer | 8-29-1881 | D | 365 |
| Stokes, W. H., Shff | Mrs. S. E. Peacock | D | 3- 2-1880 | D | 366 |
| Snelling, H. A. | Mrs. M. E. Hatcher | WD | 12-31-1888 | D | 365 |
| Small, A. B. | Mrs. H. L. Cochran | WD | 11-27-1900 | D | 379 |
| Streetman, Samuel | Joseph Davidson | WD | 8- 1-1836 | D | 485 |
| Saxon, Henry & John L. | David Thompson | WD | 9-26-1829 | D | 513 |

| Grantor | Grantee | Instrument | Date | Book | Page |
|---|---|---|---|---|---|
| Smith, Jno A. | Louise Achey | D | 4-10-1888 | D | 553 |
| Smith, S. & Et Al | Benj. Barnes | WD | 7-30-1897 | F | 19 |
| Slappey, M. R., M. F., and J. G. | Henry G. Slappey | D | 10-14-1885 | F | 448 |
| Slappey, Henry, Exr. | Virginia A. Slappey | Exr.D | 11- 1-1898 | F | 448 |
| Slappey, R. R. | F. Wand & M. F. Slappey | D | 10- 2-1873 | F | 449 |
| Stokes, W. P., Guard. | Erasmus & D. B. Fuller | WD | 2- 4-1896 | F | 512 |
| Spears, J. L. | Mrs. Ellen E. Yopp | D | 1- 9-1900 | F | 523 |
| Tharp, Susan E. | Benj. C. Tharp | WD | 11-13-1886 | A | 19 |
| Throut, W. P. | J. J. Wall | WD | 11-19-1890 | A | 48 |
| Thompson, F. F. & M. E. Whitaker | Wirt H. Hallman | WD | 12-15-1899 | A | 135 |
| Thayman, Susan | Georgia Ann Wright | GftD | 3-19-1892 | A | 204 |
| Tharp, Alex C. & Fannie M. | Mitchell Day | WD | 3-12-1883 | A | 301 |
| Thompson, J. B. | Itter Thompson | WD | 3- 1-1888 | A | 370 |
| Tarver, W. B. | J. D. Jones | WD | 1- -1875 | A | 391 |
| Thomas, Ellott | Timothy Sears | WD | 1- 4-1825 | A | 398 |
| Tharp, Alex C. | Fannie M. Tharp | WD | 6- 1-1897 | A | 414 |
| Tharp, Joseph | John Herring | WD | 2-12-1872 | A | 484 |
| Tripp, E. D. | Willie Nobles | WD | 12-16-1875 | A | 587 |
| Tharp, Fannie M. | Sallie M. O'Neal | WD | 7-14-1899 | B | 581 |
| Thompson, David | George Knight | WD | 7-31-1843 | D | 515 |
| Vaughn, Wm. T. | C. A. Vaughn | TrustD | 9-12-1877 | A | 129 |
| Vaughn, Wm. T. | Clayton A. Vaughn | GftD | 12-29-1896 | A | 130 |
| Vaughn, W. T. & Elizabeth | Robt. A. Hill | WD | 12-26-1877 | A | 165 |
| Vaughn, Wm. T. | Wiley J. Floyd | WD | 11-14-1865 | A | 234 |
| Vickers, A. E. | Thos. H. Holliday | WD | 8-28-1866 | A | 243 |
| Vaughn, J. S. | Mrs. S. M. Newby | QClD | 6- 5-1894 | A | 322 |
| Vanvaulkenburg, J. E., (receiver) | Chas. T. Lathrop | Admr.D | 11- 1-1889 | A | 332 |
| Vaughn, Wm. T. | Elizabeth J. Asbell | GftD | 3-25-1872 | A | 342 |
| Vickers, A. E. | J. K. O. Sherwood | MtgD | 2- 2-1884 | A | 600 |
| Vickers, A. E. | Dudley M. Hughes | WD | 11-26-1885 | A | 600 |
| Vaughn, Nancy P. | J. R. Vaughn | GftD | 12-11-1897 | B | 8 |
| Vaughn, W. T. & Elizabeth | Julia C. Burns | GftD | 11- 6-1888 | B | 19 |
| Vaughn, Wm. T. | Minnie J. Asbell | GftD | 10-27-1896 | B | 207 |
| Vann, Mary & Nancy | James A. Bush | WD | 12-10-1880 | B | 257 |
| Vaughn, Wm. T. | James C. Burns | QClD | 5- 4-1875 | D | 10 |
| Vaughn, Wm. T. | Daniel G. Hughes | WD | 12-23-1869 | D | 183 |
| Vaughn, W. T. | C. A. Vaughn | GftD | 4-11-1900 | A | 625 |
| Watts, W. B. | Mayer & Samuel Power of Atty | Pwr. Atty | 10-26-1897 | A | 23 |
| Ward, James E. | C. B. Lamb | WD | 12- 2-1899 | A | 35 |
| Ward, James E. | C. Y. Johnston | MtgD | 3-25-1899 | A | 57 |
| Wimberly, Henry S. | Esther L. Wimberly | GftD | 8-29-1873 | A | 132 |
| Washington, Kinch (Col.) | Georgia Ann Wright | GftD | 3-19-1892 | A | 205 |
| Witt, W. C. | Charlotte Witt | Agreement | 11- 5-1891 | A | 210 |
| Witt, Charlotte | W. C. Gibson | Transfer | 8- 9-1895 | A | 212 |
| Williams, M. A. | H. J. & M. E. Williams | GftD | 2- 5-1883 | A | 245 |
| Whitaker, O. W. & Harriett | David R. Miller | WD | 5-17-1890 | A | 249 |

| Grantor | Grantee | Instrument | Date | Book | Page |
|---|---|---|---|---|---|
| Washington, Nancy | Kinch Washington (Col.) | WD | 2- 4-1892 | A | 292 |
| Washington, Berry (Col.) | Kinch Washington | WD | 11- 6-1890 | A | 292 |
| White, Ashley M. | Levi Gallemore | WD | 8-17-1882 | A | 304 |
| Ward, Maurice | Abb E. Lewis | WD | 1- 3-1871 | A | 317 |
| Wimberly, Jos. W. (Admr. Receiver) | W. E. Carswell | AdmrD | 12-15-1886 | A | 388 |
| Wilkinson, John | Timothy Sears | WD | 1-22-1819 | A | 397 |
| Williams, Sarah | John W. Allen | WD | 2- 7-1845 | A | 401 |
| Wimberly, Esther L. | S. J. & L. C. Stokes | WD | 2-13-1900 | A | 410 |
| Whitehurst, Allie L. | J. D. Jones | QClD | 8-15-1888 | A | 419 |
| Wimberly, Henry S. | J. D. Jones | WD | 6- 5-1880 | A | 417 |
| Wimberly, J. W. | E. T. Wimberly | WD | 11- 3-1892 | A | 498 |
| Wilson, Fannie R., & Et Al | Willie A. Harrison | QClD | 11-24-1899 | A | 535 |
| Wiley, C. M., Ordinary | M. M. Edge & Children | Distb'tion | 12- -1898 | A | 546 |
| Wolcott, Robt. R. | B. S. Fitzpatrick | AdmrD | 1-16-1900 | A | 580 |
| Walker, Mrs. W. D. | Ellen M. Williams | WD | 10-10-1892 | A | 590 |
| Williams, Ellie M. | Marion Burns | WD | 7-23-1896 | A | 590 |
| Wimberly, Sarah E. & Et Al | Loula A. Kitchens | WD | -1897 | A | 627 |
| Wimberly, J. J. | J. A. Barclay | WD | 3-18-1886 | A | 640 |
| Wimberly, J. R., Ordinary | Harriett Epps | QClD | 3-29-1887 | A | 646 |
| Wood, Ella E. | J. T. Wood | WD | 7- 6-1897 | A | 647 |
| Wimberly, Henry S. | Mary M. Stokes | WD | 11-26-1894 | B | 12 |
| Wimberly, Henry S. | James E. Stokes | WD | 10-31-1895 | B | 12 |
| Whitehead, Missouri A. | Wm O'Daniel | WD | 8- 3-1868 | B | 58 |
| Whitaker, O. W. & H. E. | David R. Miller | WD | 3-27-1890 | B | 64 |
| Wilkinson, John | Marietta M. Wilkinson | WD | 3-13-1872 | B | 72 |
| Wilkinson, John | A. L. Wilkinson | WD | 12-15-1873 | B | 72 |
| Wilkinson, Harriett | John Wilkinson | GftD | 6- 1-1876 | B | 73 |
| Wilkinson, John | A. L. Wilkinson | WD | 6- 1-1876 | B | 73 |
| Washington, Mary Ann | O. W. Whitaker | WD | 11-13-1879 | B | 82 |
| Winburne, E. H. | J. C. Bozeman | WD | 8- 9-1893 | B | 113 |
| Winburne, E. H. | Elizabeth F. Newby | WD | 3-10-1894 | B | 121 |
| Wimberly, J. R., Ordinary | Mrs. E. L. Epps | QClD | 10-11-1897 | B | 155 |
| Williams, Martha D. & Others | W. B. Johnson | WD | 12-10-1895 | B | 196 |
| Williams, Mrs. M. A., | W. J. Harrison | WD | 1-16-1882 | B | 224 |
| J. R. Wimberly, Ordinary | Mrs. Narcissa Myrick | QClD | 5-11-1896 | B | 348 |
| Washington, Kinch | His Children | GftD | 10- 1-1896 | B | 395 |
| Woodall, J. W. F. | Palmira Woodall | GftD | 10-28-1889 | B | 411 |
| Wimberly, Henry S. | Thomas G. Hill | WD | 12-24-1875 | B | 495 |
| Waterer, William | Josiah Attaway | WD | 3-19-1836 | B | 543 |
| Waterer, William | Isiah Attaway | WD | 2-19-1836 | B | 544 |
| Willinghan, E. M. | Wm S. Payne | Pwr Atty | 1- 5-1887 | B | 568 |
| Willingham, E. P. | Ben Hand | WD | 1- 2-1892 | B | 570 |
| Whitehurst, Burke | Josie R. Solomon | QClD | 2-13-1900 | D | 68 |
| Wimberly, Dr. H. S. | B. C. Flannagan & Son | WD | 1-25-1873 | D | 111 |
| Wimberly, John R. | Charles L. Flint | WD | 4- 5-1884 | D | 113 |

| Grantor | Grantee | Instrument | Date | Book | Page |
|---|---|---|---|---|---|
| Willingham, E. Pringle | Augustus Powell | WD | 1-19-1892 | D | 336 |
| Woodward, Baldwin & Co. | Wm E. Jackson | Pwr Atty | 1- 5-1884 | D | 462 |
| Woodward, Baldwin & Co. | Shelton Napier | WD | 2-26-1884 | D | 463 |
| Winn, Chas S. | M. E. Slappey | D | 12- 7-1864 | D | 510 |
| Wimberly, J. R., Ordinary | Nettie, Emmett & Willie B. Melton | D | 12-29-1893 | D | 523 |
| Willingham, E. P. | Fred King | WD | 1-16-1891 | F | 87 |
| Wimberly, F. D., Jr. Admr. | Mrs. Mary A. Beuford | WD | 5-24-1879 | F | 424 |
| Wimberly, J. R. | I. N. McCrary | QClD | 5-24-1898 | F | 427 |
| Watts, Kate C. | W. B. Watts | GftD | 1-28-1893 | F | 481 |
| Winburne, Elmina H. | Wm H. Arnold | D | 12- 6-1894 | F | 484 |
| Winburne, Elmina H. | Chas H. Bozeman | D | 11-22-1894 | F | 484 |
| Wimberly, J. R. | W. A. Davis | QClD | 8-29-1888 | F | 510 |
| Watts, John B. | Robert A. Hill | D | 11- 3-1863 | F | 514 |
| Wade, Dock | R. A. Hill | D | 7-31-1866 | F | 514 |
| Zorn, Thomas | Isham West | WD | 7-26-1827 | A | 336 |
| Zorn, Thomas | Edward Montgomery | WD | 2-14-1832 | A | 337 |
| Yopp, S. W., Shff | Wirt H. Hallman | ShffD | 7- 3-1900 | A | 88 |
| Yopp, Mrs. Ellen E. | J. Louis Spears | Bond for Title | 2-22-1897 | A | 524 |
| Yopp, Mrs. Ellen E. | Smithy Lucas | WD | 1-10-1900 | D | 156 |
| Yopp, Mrs. Ellen E. | George Lucas | WD | 2-28-1899 | D | 181 |

EXCERPT OF LAND GRANT

STATE OF GEORGIA

By his Excellency, David B. Mitchell, Governor and Commander in Chief of Army and Navy of this State and of the Militia—That in pursuance of the Act of the General Assembly of the State, passed on the 26th of June 1806 for making distribution of the land in the Counties of Wilkinson and Baldwin. I have given granted and by these presents in the name and behalf of the State, do give and grant unto West Vincent of Thomas District, Hancock County, Georgia, 202½ acres, 23rd District Wilkinson, Number 95.

## Abstract of Deeds from other Index Books to 1901

| Grantor | Grantee | Date of Instrument | Kind of Instrument | Book | Page |
|---|---|---|---|---|---|
| Arnold, Benjamin & Rebecca | James E. Stokes | 12-17-1874 | Deed | G | 431 |
| Arnold, Julia, et al | Elie King | 9-28-1894 | Deed | I | 495 |
| Arnold, Mark | Joseph J. Arnold | 10-22-1892 | W Deed | J | 566 |
| Adkins, F. H. | James Epps | 11- 5-1873 | Deed | J | 350 |
| Askew, Willie | Harden T. Smith | 8-15-1864 | Deed | G | 408 |
| Anderson, John | James Hammock | 8-23-1849 | Deed | G | 346 |
| Andrews, Isham | Wm. Andrews | 9- 6-1875 | D Gift | N | 76 |
| Andrews, I. G. & J. B. | Robin Andrews | 3- 5-1884 | Adm. D | N | 78 |
| Andrews, I. G. & J. B. | Isaac Norris Estate | 4- 5-1844 | Deed | N | 80 |
| Andrews, Abisha | Wm. A. Andrews | 12- 6-1858 | Trust D | N | 912 |
| | Joseph H. Bull | 3-10-1869 | W Deed | N | 114 |
| | Isham G. Andrews | 1-10-1857 | W Deed | N | 118 |
| Ard, Andrew J., et al | Susan J. Hall | 2-21-1893 | Deed | J | 127 |
| | Annie Lee Ard | 11-12-1895 | Deeds | J | 127 |
| Ard, Andrew J. | Louisa K. Lyles | 2- 7-1893 | Deed | J | 313 |
| Ard, Andrew J. | Elizabeth J. Battox | 2- 7-1893 | Deed | J | 313 |
| Angelley, Alex W. | Henry Bunn | 11-11-1853 | Deed | I | 146 |
| Averett, James S. Pate. admr | Silas Barrentine Thomas Dye | 7-24-1850 | Deed | I | 386 |
| Bull, Mary M. | Jesse J. Bull Estate | 10-   -1857 | Deed | N | 80-81 |
| Bull, Joseph | Last Will & Testament | 7-25-1822 | Will | N | 119-20 |
| Barclay, J. A. | Mrs. Will J. Newby and children | 4-25-1885 | Deed | I | 142 |
| Bryant, Z. W. | John H. and Mrs. M. B. Reynolds | 11-21-1899 | Settlement | J | 395 |
| Bryant, Wm. | Charles R. Faulk | 3-31-1870 | Deed | L | 385 |
| Burkett, J. W. | James Hammock | 10-21-1873 | Deed | G | 338 |
| Burket, Louisa | C. M. Hornsby | 4-11-1896 | Deed | G | 581 |
| Burkett, E. S. | Macon & Dublin R. R. Co. | 10-18-1890 | Deed | I | 203 |
| Burkett, Lizzie M. | John H. & Mrs. M. B. Reynolds | 11-21-1899 | Deed | J | 395 |
| Burkett, Thos W. Exr. Solomon Estate | Wm. Faulk | 2-10-1855 | Exr.D | J | 540 |
| Brown, Wm. | Labon Beckcom | 2-13-1847 | Deed | G | 412 |
| Blalock, Fannie — Julia | Ichabod Balkcom | 12-23-1877 | W Deed | J | 408 |
| Bozeman, James State Grant | Polly Brown | 10- 3-1808 | Grant | G | 428 |
| Bozeman, L. W. | Joslia Horton | 7-31-1899 | Deed | I | 39 |
| Bozeman, Addie | J. T. Vaughn | 2-10-1894 | Deed | I | 337 |
| Bozeman, Charles H. | W. T. Arnold | 3-16-1893 | Deed | I | 494 |
| Bozeman, Charles H., et al | Eli King | 9-28-1894 | Deed | I | 495 |
| Bozeman, Fannie M. | Eli King | 11-18-1881 | Deed | I | 494 |
| Bozeman, L. E. | W. J. T. Carden | 10- 2-1897 | Deed | 3 | 490 |
| Bell, Mary T. | S. J. & J. T. Bond | 10-   -1896 | Deed | I | 232 |
| Bozeman, W. W., Dep. Shff. | Alislea Andrews | 12- 1-1857 | Shff.D | N | 91 |

| Grantor | Grantee | Date of Instrument | Kind of Instrument | Book | Page |
|---|---|---|---|---|---|
| Bowden, J. M. | L. Lyles | 12- 4-1897 | QCD | G | 368 |
| Bowden, A. E., et al | Martha Coleman | 11-25-1878 | Deed | I | 428 |
| Bowden, Jerry M. | Lucinda I. Bowden | 8-22-1888 | Deed | J | 131-132 |
| Bowden, John J. | Lucinda J. Bowden | 9- 4-1889 | Deed | J | 132 |
| Bryan, Benjamin | Wm. Faulk | 6- 1-1853 | Deed | J | 17 |
| Bond, Thomas W. | J. W. W. Christian | 10- 6-1883 | Deed | J | 86 |
| Bateman, John E., admr. of Estate of Wm. Batemen | Henry Bunn | 2- 4-1851 | Adm D | I | 145 |
| Bunn, Hugh L. | Wm. B. Tarver, B. M. Tarver, F. D. Wimberly | 11- 1-1866 | Deed | I | 148 |
| Barrentine, Jas & Wilson | Rebecca Evans | 6-12-1866 | Adm.D | I | 384 |
| Blount, Joseph | James G. Faulk | 9-22-1839 | Deed | J | 543 |
| Chapman, Lewis | Macon & Dublin R. R. Co. | 4-16-1886 | Deed | I | 210 |
| Chapman, Wm. T. | Macon & Dublin R. R. Co. | 4-16-1886 | Deed | I | 209 |
| Chapman, W. B., Guard. | G. W. Tharpe | 5- 4-1898 | Deed | I | 287-288 |
| Chapman, Wm. T. | Mrs. A. E. Solomon & Mrs. M. I. Whitehurst | 12-26-1892 | Deed | I | 217 |
| Campbell, Martha | Lucinda Bowden | 9-10-1889 | Deed | J | 133 |
| Carswell, Benaiah S. | Macon & Dublin R. R. Co. | 4-27-1886 | Deed | I | 208 |
| Carswell, Elizabeth by J. H. Napier, adm. | Eugenia S. Napier | 12-29-1897 | Adm.D | I | 214-215 |
| Carswell, B. as trustee, et al | Mrs. J. V. Harrell | 3-18-1891 | Deed | J | 359 |
| Carswell, DeWitt | Mrs. Mariln Carswell | 12-18-1900 | Deed | L | 585 |
| Collins, Mrs. A. F. | Lucy A. Solomon | 12-24-1888 | Deed | G | 471 |
| Collins, E. J. & L. M. | R. A. Hill | 1-18-1778 | Deed | N | 245 |
| Chambers, Franklin | Elmina Chambers | 3-19-1883 | Deed | G | 318 |
| Chambers, F. gdn. | John H. & Mrs. M. B. Reynolds | 11-21-1899 | Deed | J | 395 |
| Cook, J. A. | J. L. Harrell | 12- 2-1893 | Deed | I | 75 |
| Carroll, Mary Ella | Sallie B. Carroll | 2-25-1898 | Deed | H | 309 |
| Cranford, Harriett | Shorter Cranford | 7- 3-1899 | Deed | F | 379 |
| Cranford, John as trustee for Mary Jane Roberts and children | Mary Jane Roberts and children | 1-17-1877 | Tst.D | L | 422 |
| Coley, Turner | Labon Beckcom | 1-19-1832 | Deed | J | 415 |
| Cribb, John | W. F. Carroll | 4-30-1879 | Deed | G | 477 |
| Cowan, W. A. | John C. Epps | 6-15-1850 | Deed | G | 521 |
| Cummins, Ridley W., exec. | Berry Hendrick | 3-25-1836 | Ex-Deed | L | 18 |
| Crosby, Isiah | Elijah Pettes | 2- 6-1858 | Deed | I | 88 |
| Defore, Narcessa L. | L. C. Bowden | 2- 7-1893 | Deed | J | 313 |
| Denson, M. L. | L. C. Bowden | 4-19-1899 | Deed | I | 361 |
| Dupree, Ira E. & Jacob M. | George Smith & Iwen Faulk | 8-20-1880 | Deed | I | 181 |

| Grantor | Grantee | Date of Instrument | Kind of Instrument | Book | Page |
|---|---|---|---|---|---|
| Durden, Sara S. | Malissa Durden | 8-29-1889 | Deed | I | 531 |
| Dyer, G. C., et al | Gillie C. Dyer | 12-21-1882 | Deed | I | 185-186 |
| Daren, Jacob Van | Stephen Jones | 12- 5-1876 | Deed | J | 245 |
| Davis, Caroline, et al | Eliza A. Lore | 9- 3-1887 | Deed | I | NoPage |
| Davis, Henry B. | John W. Quackenbush | 12-29-1877 | Deed | L | 466 |
| Davis, John, adm. | Estate of Jessie J. Bull | 10-   -1857 | Adm Deed | N | 180-181 |
| Epps, Willie E., adm. | H. V. Epps | 1- 6-1883 | Adm Deed | G | 522 |
| Epps, Martha L., et al | Heneritta Epps | 9-20-1884 | Deed | G | 524 |
| Epps, Rufus J. | Macon & Dublin R. R. Co. | 4-24-1886 | Deed | I | 206 |
| Epps, Mollie | Victoria Henderson | 11- 8-1897 | Deed | L | 322 |
| Early, Peter, Gov. by Anthony Peters | Thomas Taylor | 8- 7-1815 | Grant | I | 425 |
| Evans, John | Richard L. Rogers | 2- 8-1837 | Deed | N | 79 |
| Eve, Wm. F., adm., et al | John Forsyth | 11-12-1847 | Deed | I | 149-150 |
| Edge, R. W. | Mary T. Bell | 1-20-1877 | Deed | I | 235 |
| Ellis, Ephriam | Samuel Pate | 1-22-1839 | Deed | I | 385 |
| Floyd, Fannie B. | George E. Chapman | 3- 4-1896 | Deed | I | 135 |
| Floyd, M. G. | M. J. Floyd | 4-16-1895 | Deed | I | 410 |
| Fitzpatrick, W. H., Sheriff | J. M. Bowden | 4- 4-1893 | Deed | G | 366 |
| Fitzpatrick, J. J. | B. S. Fitzpatrick | 12- 1-1883 | Deed | I | 164 |
| Finch, Wm. C. | Floyd A. Finch | 12-15-1850 | Deed | I | 83 |
| Finch, Mary A. | T. S. Marcy | 12-17-1880 | Deed | I | 83 |
| Faulk, Mrs. C. R. | Mrs. W. C. Faulk | 1-22-1886 | Deed | G | 445 |
| Faulk, D. S. | Mrs. Ada Birdsong | 7-25-1895 | Deed | I | 141 |
| Faulk, Alice P. | Macon & Dublin R. R. Co. | 4-24-1886 | Deed | I | 207-208 |
| Faulk, Mary A. | H. G. Faulk | 10-30-1896 | Deed | J | 465 |
| Fline, Charles L. | John F. F. Brewster | 1-14-1889 | Deed | I | 146 |
| Fort, Moses by C. C. Whitehead, atty | Benjamin Koonce | 1- 8-1840 | Deed | I | 147 |
| Fuller, Wm. A., et al | H. J. Paul | 11-17-1892 | Deed | I | 438 |
| Griffin, Mrs. S. E. | S. E. Jones | 6-24-1898 | Deed | L | 351 |
| Gibson, Wm. C. | Betsyan Cicers Chain | 10-18-1890 | Deed | F | 289 |
| Glover, Thos. | Evelyn C. Glover | 1- 8-1876 | Deed | I | 139 |
| Glover, Georgia | Laura Faulk | 6-   -1883 | Deed | J | 272 |
| Gallemore, Levi | Macon & Dublin R. R. Co. | 4-16-1886 | Deed | I | 210-211 |
| Gone, R. B. | Macon & Dublin R. R. Co. | 8-19-1890 | Deed | I | 201 |
| Harrison, Willie A. | F. E. Wimberly | 3-23-1892 | Deed | I | 312 |
| Hinson, Cintha | Lucinda E. Melton | 9- 9-1893 | Deed | J | 519 |
| Hughes, Haywood | Franklin Chambers | 3- 6-1876 | Deed | F | 308 |
| Hughes, Elmina | M. E. Burney | 10-16-1891 | Deed | G | 319 |
| Hughes, Gaul G. | F. N. Maxwell | 6-16-1891 | Deed | G | 587-588 |
| Hammock, James Jr. | Ichabod Balkcom | 10-16-1875 | Deed | F | 335 |
| Holliday, Thomas H. | M. J. Floyd | 12-19-1885 | Deed | I | 411 |

| Grantor | Grantee | Date of Instrument | Kind of Instrument | Book | Page |
|---|---|---|---|---|---|
| Howell, Daniel | Wm. J. Bozeman | 1-22-1851 | Deed | G | 386 |
| Howell, Wright | Daniel Howell | 7-22-1848 | Deed | G | 385 |
| Howell, Henry | Reuben Lamb | 9- 3-1887 | Deed | I | No Page |
| Harrell, Mrs. Dora | Shedrick Flagg | 12-19-1895 | Deed | G | 422 |
| Harrell, J. L. | J. R. Cook | 12- 2-1893 | Deed | I | 33 |
| Harrell, Isabella | S. E. Marcy | 9-25-1894 | Deed | I | 82 |
| Harrell, W. H. | John R. Reynolds | 12- 5-1898 | Deed | N | 99 |
| Hornsby, C. M. | J. C. Solomon | 12-29-1896 | Deed | G | 580 |
| Hall, J. H. | Julia A. Ely | 7- 2-1890 | Deed | I | 107 |
| Hall, Susan J. | Clara Ard | 1-19-1897 | Deed | J | 127-128 |
| Hall, William B. | Thadero A. Lingo | 3-24-1884 | Deed | J | 471-472 |
| Hall, John H. | Union Savings Bank and Trust Co. | 4-14-1899 | Deed | L | 70 |
| Hendrick, Berry | Jas. G. Faulk | 12-27-1838 | Deed | L | 18 |
| Hester, Mrs. Pauline | G. W. Tharpe | 4-14-1898 | Deed | I | 288 |
| Horne, Isaac | Isham Andrews | 11- 6-1883 | Deed | N | 77 |
| Herring, John R. | John A. Herring | 1- 8-1883 | Deed | J | 246 |
| Herring, Martha A. | John L. Wall | 12-20-1880 | Deed | L | 509-510 |
| Jones, J. Walker | J. T. Day | 12- 2-1893 | Deed | F | 374 |
| Jones, Stephen | C. A. Solomon | 7-11-1881 | Deed | G | 486 |
| Jones, F. M. | J. P. Mercer | 6-17-1876 | Deed | G | 296 |
| Jones, Thomas H. | John Fitzpatrick | 9- 5-1883 | Deed | I | 164 |
| Jones, Bennet | Thomas Dier | 2-15-1879 | Deed | I | 177 |
| Jones, T. S. | Mrs. Alice P. Faulk | 8-22-1885 | Deed | J | 410 |
| Jones, John | Wm. Manghram & Manning Bowling | 10-31-1807 | Deed | N | 81 |
| Jeter, Pauline | Mrs. Pauline Hester, Arthur & B. W. Chapman | 4-16-1898 | Deed | I | 288-289 |
| Johnson, Robert | Jacob Bull | 10- 2-1816 | Deed | N | 823 |
| Jessup, J. H. & A. M. | Mrs. Lula A. Kitchens | 8-  -1897 | Deed | G | 479 |
| Irvin, Jared Gov. | Joseph Richey | 5-30-1807 | Land Grant | N | 87 |
| Johnston, John B. | J. S. Johnston | 7- 9-1891 | Receipt | I | 237 |
| Jewell, Wm. H. | Wm. H. Baleliun | 1- 2-1884 | Deed | I | 21 |
| Johnston, John S. | Sarah A. Pettes | 7- 9-1891 | Deed | I | 327 |
| Jewell, D. A. & Mary A. | Woodard Baleliun Company | 1-17-1878 | Deed | I | 20-21 |
| Ives, Mary | James Leslie | 1-27-1900 | Deed | I | 54 |
| Ives, Elizabeth | Mary Jane Ryles | 3- 2-1882 | Deed | I | 185 |
| Ives, Lizzie | Dollie Dyer | 12-21-1881 | Deed | I | 197-198 |
| Joselyn, Franklin C. | H. J. Paul | 11-17-1892 | Deed | I | 438 |
| Kitchens, Nancy | D. W. Kitchens | 10-30-1868 | Deed | L | 386 |
| Kitchens, Oran W. | Howard Donan | 11-22-1889 | Deed | M | 22 |
| Kennington, Mrs. Nancy V. | J. H. Jessup | 9- 4-1897 | Deed | G | 478 |
| Kennington, W. G. | Joseph Williams | 3-15-1889 | Deed | I | 108-109 |
| Lyles, Lenorah | James H. Bull | 12- 6-1897 | Deed | I | 367 |
| Lyles, Sarah & Thomas | John Gardner | 1- 7-1857 | Deed | I | 199 |
| Lowe, George H. | Thomas W. Bond | 10-27-1882 | Deed | J | 85 |
| Lowe, John H. | James B. Wall | 2-13-1858 | Deed | L | 511 |

| Grantor | Grantee | Date of Instrument | Kind of Instrument | Book | Page |
|---|---|---|---|---|---|
| Lamb, Henry | Felix A. Johnston | 7- 8-1871 | Deed | I | 131 |
| Lamb, Reuben R. | Allie J. Sanders | 7-17-1878 | Deed | I | 329 |
| Lamb, H. F. | Francis M. Sanders | 1-10-1881 | Deed | I | 328 |
| Lamb, H. C. | W. H. Lamb | 3-25-1893 | Deed | L | 548 |
| Lucas, George | W. E. Pope | 2-23-1889 | Deed | J | 239 |
| Lynn, Richard | Jacob Bull | 3-17-1820 | Deed | G | 427 |
| Lord, Harriett | B. S. Fitzpatrick | 1-16-1900 | Deed | I | 164-165 |
| Lingo, T. A. | L. A. Wash | 1-31-1893 | Deed | J | 444 |
| Lingo, R. W. | Thadeus A. Lingo | 3-24-1884 | Deed | J | 471-472 |
| Land, Margaret | Mary M. Ray | 3-11-1891 | Deed | N | 77 |
| Lockhart, Mallie | Fannie Leslie | 12-10-1891 | Deed | I | 54 |
| Little, Martha | Joseph J. Arnold | 10-22-1892 | Deed | J | 566 |
| Lindsey, John F. | Wm. C. Finch | 12-11-1850 | Deed | I | 84 |
| Latson, E. C., B. M., W. T., & A. S. | Amanda Bowdon | 11-25-1878 | Deed | N | 43 |
| Methvin, Samuel R. | Wm. Faulk | 11-24-1851 | Deed | J | 536 |
| Miller, Mollie E. | Heneritta V. Epps | 9-20-1884 | Deed | J | 524 |
| Martin, F. M. & J. T. | John D. Dyre | 1-27-1886 | Deed | I | 201 |
| Mayer, Sam | W. H. Bryan | 11-20-1890 | Deed | K | 27 |
| Mercer, Mary | Ella Floyd | 4- 7-1897 | Deed | I | 151 |
| Meadows, Isaac H. | Isaac J. Meadows | 11-22-1850 | Deed | G | 349 |
| Mills, J. R. | Mrs. Ella J. Beckcom | 11-17-1893 | Deed | G | 408 |
| Melton, Emma J. | Martha D. Williams | 12-10-1888 | Deed | I | 2 |
| Melton, Stephen H. | John P. Bond | 1- 2-1862 | Deed | J | 85 |
| Maddox, Elizabeth F. | Louisa K. Lyles | 2- 7-1893 | Deed | J | 313 |
| Marcy, T. S. | J. W. Marcy | 1- 1-1884 | Deed | I | 82-83 |
| Methodist Episcopal Church | Mrs. J. V. Harrell | 3-18-1891 | Deed | J | 359 |
| Murray, Joseph E. | S. H. Bayerton | 12-23-1868 | Deed | L | 385 |
| Massey, Daniel | Henry Carter | 12- 1-1868 | Deed | I | 166 |
| Mayer & Watts | W. H. Bryan | 12-27-1889 | Deed | L | 26 |
| Marine and Fire Insurance Bank | James G. Faulk | 1- 7-1845 | Deed | J | 539- 40 |
| Malanay, Michael | Isaac Newell | 7- 2-1857 | Deed | I | 384- 85 |
| Moree, Alfred | Wm. H. Bull | 7-29-1854 | Deed | I | 412- 13 |
| Owens, Henry | George Williams | 1-19-1811 | Deed | N | 82 |
| Nash, A. E. | Jas. Barrentine | 1-18-1872 | Deed | I | 383 |
| Norris, Isaac | Benjamin Ray | 1- 6-1847 | Deed | N | 78 |
| Newby, S. M. | J. S. Vaughn | 7-10-1894 | Deed | I | 141 |
| Newby, James E. | Phillip W. Harrell | 9-19-1896 | Deed | I | 231- 32 |
| Nutting, Lelia J. | W. P. Burns | 11- 4-1890 | Deed | F | 382 |
| Nelson, D. K. | Missouri Williams | 8- 7-1876 | Deed | I | 9 |
| Nelson, G. W. | Macon & Dublin R. R. Co. | | Deed | I | 202 |
| Nelson, A. A. | George W. Tharpe | 11-22-1899 | Deed | I | 290 |
| Napier, J. H. | Eugenia C. Napier | 12-29-1897 | Deed | I | 214- 15 |
| O'Neal, John | J. H. Ray | 9-12-1886 | Deed | J | 126- 27 |

| Grantor | Grantee | Date of Instrument | Kind of Instrument | Book | Page |
|---|---|---|---|---|---|
| Nowell, Isaac | Silas Barrentine | 1-26-1858 | Deed | I | 383- 4 |
| Orr, Lige | G. E. Ray | 4- 8-1846 | Deed | 57 | 107- 8 |
| Pearce, Addie | Friendship Church Elias J. Denson & Deacons | 3- 3-1872 | Deed | G | 273- 74 |
| Pearce, Emma J., et al | Henritta V. Epps | 9-20-1884 | Deed | G | 524 |
| Pearce, Mrs. Emma J. | C. M. Hornsby | 5-12-1894 | Deed | G | 581- 82 |
| Pearce, Alex, adm. | Susan N. Beckcum | 1- 6-1853 | Deed | I | 32 |
| Pearce, Jacob | Simon Tharpe | 5- 6-1850 | Deed | I | 107 |
| Pearce, R. A., H. T., J. T. & W. R. | P. W. Edge | 12- 7-1885 | Deed | I | 233 |
| Pearce, Chas. F. | P. W. Edge | 2-19-1886 | Deed | I | 233 |
| Pearce, Laura A. | J. W. Paul | 1- 3-1896 | Deed | H | 338 |
| Powell, John S. | Benjamin Bryan | 8-10-1821 | Deed | L | 384 |
| Pettis, Mark | I. F. Crosby | 5-11-1857 | Deed | I | 87- 88 |
| Pettis, Elijah F. | I. F. Crosby | 2- 6-1858 | Deed | I | 88 |
| Pettis, Elijah F. | J. H. Hall | 7- 1-1890 | Deed | I | 107- 08 |
| Pettis, Sara A. | J. S. Johnston | 7- 9-1891 | Receipt | I | 237 |
| Peacock, Joseph | Macon & Dublin R. R. Co. | 9-20-1890 | Deed | I | 202- 03 |
| Peacock, Elizabeth M. | Macon & Dublin R. R. Co. | 5- 3-1886 | Deed | I | 211 |
| Porter, Anthony | Thomas Tayler | 8- 7-1815 | Grant | G | 425 |
| Pearson, James | Wm. H. Andrews | 8- 2-1875 | Deed | N | 76 |
| Paul, J. W. Sr. | J. W. Paul Jr. | 3- 9-1897 | Deed | H | 337 |
| Paul, H. J. | Leila J. Paul | 12- 6-1894 | Deed | I | 438 |
| Poe, Robt. F., admr., et al | John Forsyth | 11-12-1847 | Deed | I | 149- 50 |
| Pickles, M. E., et al | Ella Floyd | 4- 7-1897 | Deed | I | 151 |
| Pope, H. T. | Henry L. Lucas | 1-18-1897 | Deed | I | 504 |
| Roberts, Henry | Narcissa Cranford | 3-21-1877 | Deed | L | 423 |
| Rozier, Reubin & Lizzie | W. B. Padgett | 11- 8-1894 | Deed | F | 311 |
| Ray, Mary A. D. | B. T. & J. H. Ray | 9- 3-1864 | Settlement | 30 | 76 |
| Reynolds, Hubbard | A. J. Bryant | 10-13-1884 | Deed | I | 144 |
| Reynolds, Hubbard | J. W. Bryant | 10-13-1884 | Deed | I | 144 |
| Reynolds, L. B. | Macon & Dublin R. R. Co. | 4-17-1886 | Deed | I | 209 |
| Read, Benjamin F. | J. H. Ray | 3-26-1870 | Deed | I | 397 |
| Read, W. H. | B. F. Read | 2-17-1869 | Deed | N | 70-1 |
| Richey, Joseph | Henry Owens | 12-27-1809 | Deed | N | 85 |
| Rasberry, Georgiam S. | Wm. T. Vaughn | 1- 3-1871 | Deed | I | 140 |
| Ryle, Mary, et al | Gillie C. Dyer | 12-21-1892 | Deed | I | 185 |
| Ryle, Mary Jane | Dallase Dyer | 12-22-1886 | Deed | I | 199 |
| Ryle, Mary Jane | John D. Dyer | 3- 2-1882 | Deed | I | 197 |
| Ryle, Mary Jane | Thomas Dyer | 3- 2-1882 | Deed | I | 197 |
| Ryle, B. F. | W. W. Mixson | 5- 3-1890 | Deed | L | 388 |
| Renfroe, A. F. | Macon & Dublin R. R. Co. | 4-15-1886 | Deed | I | 208-09 |
| Rice, Mrs. M. F. | Macon & Dublin R. R. Co. | 8-11-1890 | Deed | I | 203 |

| Grantor | Grantee | Date of Instrument | Kind of Instrument | Book | Page |
|---|---|---|---|---|---|
| Rice, Mrs. M. F. et al | Mrs. Pauline Hester Arthur & B. W. Chapman | 3-16-1898 | Deed | I | 288-90 |
| Smith, Harden T. | Simeon Tharpe | 1-19-1858 | Deed | I | 109 |
| Smith, John A. | Macon & Dublin R. R. Co. | 4-16-1886 | Deed | I | 211 |
| Smith, Jas T. | J. B. A. Norris | 12- 5-1884 | Deed | I | 303 |
| Smith, J. A. & H. E. | W. P. Williams | 12-21-1880 | Deed | J | 279 |
| Smith, Sarah E. | Ichabod Balkcom | 12-23-1887 | Deed | I | 408 |
| Sanders, Lizzie M. | John S. Vaughn | 11-21-1885 | Deed | G | 293 |
| Sanders, Jeremiah, admr. | Missouria Williams | 8- 7-1876 | Deed | I | 9 |
| Sanders, Allie J., Francis M. | John S. Johnston | 12- 8-1883 | Deed | I | 328 |
| Sanders, Allie J. Mary E., et al | Reuben Lamb | 9- 3-1877 | Deed | I | 328 |
| Sanders, F. M. | J. S. Vaughn | 2-19-1894 | Deed | I | 337 |
| Sanders, Allie J. | William H. Bryan | 12- 2-1886 | Deed | L | 28 |
| Sanders, Allie J. | Mayes & Watts | 11-27-1888 | Deed | L | 27 |
| Stokes, J. E. | Thomas G. Hill | 12-21-1874 | Deed | G | 432 |
| Stokes, W. H., Shff | Geo. W. Tharpe | 3- 1-1881 | Shff. Deed | I | 106 |
| Stokes, W. R. B. | M. J. Floyd | 11- 4-1895 | Deed | I | 409 |
| Stokes, Jinnett R., (W. R. S., et al | M. J. Floyd | 12-19-1885 | Deed | I | 409-10 |
| Solomon, James C. | Macon & Dublin R. R. Co. | 4-24-1886 | Deed | I | 206 |
| Solomon, Sarah F. | Macon & Dublin R. R. Co. | 4-28-1886 | Deed | I | 209 |
| Solomon, Peter, exect. of est. of Henry Solomon | Wm. Faulk | 12-16-1856 | Deed | J | 537 |
| Solomon, Henry | Jas. G. Faulk | 12-10-1845 | Deed | J | 540-41 |
| Sauls, K. T. | I. S. Floyd | 1-17-1887 | Deed | I | 158 |
| Sauls, Mary F. | Jas. W. Vaughn | 5- 7-1888 | Deed | G | 498 |
| Sauls, Mary M., et al | M. J. Floyd | 12-19-1885 | Deed | I | 409-410 |
| State of Georgia | Polly Brown | 5-13-1807 | Grant | G | 429 |
| State of Georgia | Thomas Taylor | 8- 7-1815 | Grant | G | 426 |
| Sawyer, Amanda by S. E. Jones, Shff. | Victoria Henderson, Mollie Epps, Minnie Baker | 5- 4-1897 | Deed | L | 321 |
| Stroup, Sarah V. | Mary M. Ray | 2-19-1878 | Deed | N | 80 |
| Tharpe, Geo. W. | Mrs. Nancy Tharpe | 2-28-1885 | Deed | I | 106 |
| Tharpe, Mary E. | Jas. H. Evans | 1-29-1898 | Deed | I | 155-56 |
| Tharpe, J. D. | J. H. Ray | 3- 8-1886 | Deed | J | 126 |
| Tharpe, Joseph | John Herring | 1- 8-1874 | Deed | J | 246 |
| Tarver, Mrs. Annie P. | Mrs. I. M. Wimberly | 11-21-1896 | Deed | N | 66-67 |
| Vaughn, John S. | Geo. R. Vaughn | 12- 9-1885 | Deed | G | 394 |
| Vaughn, Wm. T. | John S. Johnston | 12-16-1871 | Deed | I | 130 |
| Vaughn, Elizabeth & W. T. | Sanders Rasberry | 1-16-1870 | Deed | I | 142 |
| Vaughn, J. S. | Susie E. Vaughn and children of J. S. Vaughn | 10-16-1894 | Deed | I | 315-16 |
| Vandiver, Martha | Labon Beckcom | 3- 3-1840 | Deed | G | 416 |

| Grantor | Grantee | Date of Instrument | Kind of Instrument | Book | Page |
|---|---|---|---|---|---|
| Vincent, Jas T. | Mrs. Mary M. Sauls | 5-10-1865 | Deed | I | 410 |
| Wood, A. J., G. B., J. T., I. W., et al | Ella Floyd | 4- 7-1897 | Deed | I | 151 |
| Wall, J. G. | Nancy Tharp | 3- 3-1868 | Deed | I | 108 |
| Wall, Mrs. R. A. by J. T. admr. | V. A. Peacock | 6- -1895 | Deed | I | 335 |
| Wimberly, Sara E., et al | Mrs. Lula A. Kitchens | 1897 | Deed | G | 479 |
| Wimberly, H. S. | Wilson Barrentine | 2- 1-1870 | Deed | I | 178 |
| Wimberly, J. A. | Macon & Dublin R. R. Co. | 4-15-1886 | Deed | I | 208 |
| Wimberly, H. S., Trustees, et al | Mrs. J. V. Harrell | 3-18-1891 | Deed | J | 359 |
| Wimberly, R. R. | Wm. Faulk | 9-16-1859 | Deed | L | 16 |
| Williams, M. A., et al | Wm. J. Nelson | 12- 7-1897 | Deed | I | 200-201 |
| Williams, Dewey | Jacob Bull | 8-17-1821 | Deed | N | 75 |
| White, Freedom | Labon Beckcom | 12- 4-1832 | Deed | G | 411 |
| Whitehead, C. C. | S. N. Beckcom | 1- 5-1848 | Deed | I | 32 |
| Wolcott, R. R., admr. Harriett Lord | B. S. Fitzpatrick | 1-16-1900 | Deed | I | 164-165 |
| Willingham, I. H. Jr. | J. S. Vaughn | 12- -1886 | Deed | L | 98 |
| Willis, Jas. T. | J. J. Bull | 11- 2-1846 | Deed | N | 79 |
| Wilson, Fannie R. | Mrs. M. B. & J. H. Reynolds | 11-21-1899 | Deed | J | 395 |
| Winborn, Elmina H., et al | Eli King | 9-28-1894 | Deed | I | 495 |
| Yopp, Samuel & W. & Ellen E. | Mrs. Mary A. Faulk | 2-16-1891 | Deed | N | 23-24 |

## LETTERS TESTAMENTARY

The following records are from an old Letters Testamentary record book which gives the names of the persons who made a Last Will and Testament, the executor, and/or executrix, the date witnessed, and the name of the ordinary.

Book listed as book "B" is on file in the office of the Clerk of Superior Court of Twiggs County, Jeffersonville, Georgia. In prior years, someone placed this old record book on file in the clerk's office.

The dates which appear in this record show that such person's Last Will and Testament which was probated in Twiggs County ante-date the fire which destroyed the Twiggs County Court House February 6, 1901. Therefore, copies of the original Last Will and Testament of the persons named will not be found on file in the Twiggs County Ordinary's Office unless some member of a family had a copy of the will and testament re-recorded after the fire.

GEORGIA         TWIGGS         COUNTY

LETTERS TESTAMENTARY    (NO. 14)    COMMON FORM

BY THE HONORABLE ORDINARY OF SAID COUNTY

| Name | Executor and/or Executrix | Ordinary | Date Witnessed |
|---|---|---|---|
| Eunice Massey | Henry Carter | John T. Glover | 6th Nov. 1866 |
| A. Lanier | Lavinia B. Lanier | John T. Glover | 6th Nov. 1866 |
| Silas Barrentine | Jas. Barrentine & Wilson Barrentine | John T. Glover | 2nd July 1866 |
| Asa McWilliams | William Griffin | John T. Glover | 4th Mar. 1867 |
| Wm. M. Varnum | Susan L. Varnum | John T. Glover | 3rd June 1867 |
| Elijah E. Crocker | Ezekiel W. Crocker & Wm. H. Crocker | John T. Glover | 7th Oct. 1867 |
| Daniel O'Daniel | Wm. O'Daniel | W. S. Kelly | 5th Oct. 1868 |
| Wm. Methvin | Martha Methvin | W. S. Kelly | 2nd Nov. 1868 |
| Daniel W. Shine | Jas. T. Glover | W. S. Kelly | 9th Nov 1868 |
| C. A. Tharp | Jos. & Simeon Tharp | W. S. Kelly | 9th Nov. 1868 |
| Meadows, Issac H. | Paul Meadows | W. S. Kelly | 7th Dec. 1868 |
| Jas. G. Wall | Thos. W. Burkett | W. S. Kelly | 11th Jan. 1869 |
| Ira E. Dupree | Matthew J. Carswell | W. S. Kelly | 5th Apr. 1869 |
| Gustavas McCrea (solemn form) | Jno. A. McCrea & Wm. W. McCrea | Jno. F. Shine | 6th Sept. 1869 |
| Wm. Methvin (solemn) | Wm. D. Horne | Jno. F. Shine | 6th Sept. 1869 |
| Reuben A. Nash (solemn form) | Acton E. Nash & Mary A. Nash | Jno. F. Shine | 1st Nov. 1869 |
| Matthew C. Fowler | Willis Allen Wm. A. Gainey and Elvy Ann Fowler | Jno. F. Shine | 6th June 1870 |
| Jeremiah A. Tharp | Alex C. Tharp & Vincent W. Tharp | Jno. F. Shine | 11th July 1870 |

| Name | Executor and/or Executrix | Ordinary | Date Witnessed |
|---|---|---|---|
| Lemuel Taylor | Mary Taylor | Jno. F. Shine | 3rd Oct. 1870 |
| Sarah Johnston (Solemn Form) | Jno. S. Johnston | Jno. F. Shine | 10th Oct. 1870 |
| Lewis Solomon | M. E. & C. A. Solomon | J. M. Burkett | 6th Feb. 1872 |
| Geo. Epps | Simeon Tharp | J. M. Burkett | 3rd June 1872 |
| Piety Steely | Joshua R. Wimberly | J. M. Burkett | 3rd June 1872 |
| Mary A. Maxwell | Martha Kennington | C. A. Solomon | 5th May 1873 |
| Henry Carter | Mrs. M. E. Carter | C. A. Solomon | 12th May 1873 |
| Sampson Bridgers | Levi Gallemore | C. A. Solomon | 1st Sept. 1873 |
| Mrs. Mary A. Faulk | W. A. Wiggins | C. A. Solomon | 5th April 1875 |
| Exum Newby | R. T. Newby | C. A. Solomon | 3rd May 1875 |
| Elam Hinson | John C. Howington | C. A. Solomon | 4th Oct. 1875 |
| Archibald McCallum | Emserly E. McCallum | C. A. Solomon | 6th Nov. 1876 |
| Henry Lamb | Doctor T. Lamb | C. A. Solomon | 2nd July 1877 |
| John Sanders | Jane Sanders | C. A. Solomon | 6th Aug. 1877 |
| Ezekiel Wimberly (Dated 3rd July, 1843) | J. J., Polly, E. A. and R. R. Wimberly | C. A. Solomon | 4th Sept. 1878 |
| C. A. Bunn | Pulaski S. Holt (County of Bibb) | C. A. Solomon | 1st Mar. 1880 |
| Mrs. C. A. Bunn | Pulaski S. Holt | C. A. Solomon | 5th Apr. 1880 |
| Mary R. Jones | J. D. Jones | C. A. Solomon | 5th Apr. 1880 |
| Nancy Outlaw | Gather Kennington | C. A. Solomon | 4th Oct. 1889 |
| Robt. A. Hill | Thos. G. Hill | C. A. Solomon | 6th Dec. 1880 |
| John Glover | Saml. R. Methvin | J. E. McDonald | 6th Mar. 1865 |
| Martha Johnson | Thos. H. Holliday | C. A. Solomon | 1st Aug. 1881 |
| I. E. Peacock | Thos. S. Jones | C. A. Solomon | 8th Mar. 1882 |
| Jos. Sinclair | Sophia Sinclair | C. A. Solomon | 9th Sept. 1882 |
| Haywood Phillips (solemn form) | Monroe Phillips | C. A. Solomon | 6th Mar. 1883 |
| Cordelia Tharp | Mary Elizabeth Tharp | C. A. Solomon | 4th Jun. 1883 |
| Mrs. C. H. Wimberly | Dr. J. R. Wimberly | Wm. Griffin | 7th Jan. 1884 |
| C. A. Solomon | Sarah F. Solomon & M. E. Solomon | Wm. Griffin | 8th Jan. 1884 |
| Robt. Paul (solemn form) | Elizabeth M. Paul | J. R. Wimberly | 3rd Mar. 1885 |
| Thos. G. Hill | Dudley M. Hughes | J. R. Wimberly | 14th May 1885 |
| Thos. W. Burkett | Nancy Jane Burkett | J. R. Wimberly | 6th July 1885 |
| Ezekiel Wimberly (1843) | J. W. Wimberly | J. R. Wimberly | 2nd May 1887 |
| H. S. Newby (solemn form) | Mrs. Sarah M. Newby & R. R. Newby | J. R. Wimberly | 5th May 1890 |
| Bennet Jones | J. W. Jones | J. R. Wimberly | 18th Jun. 1890 |
| J. D. Jones | Mrs. Eloise Jones | H. F. Carswell of Wilkinson County, Ga. for J. R. Wimberly, Ordinary of Twiggs County, Disqualified by relationship. | 7th May 1891 |
| Euphanie Jessup | John Jessup | J. R. Wimberly | 13th Oct. 1891 |
| R. T. Newby | Mrs. Elvina H. Winbourne | J. R. Wimberly | 3rd Feb. 1892 |

| Name | Executor and/or Executrix | | |
|---|---|---|---|
| Mrs. Ida C. Reynolds | F. Chambers | J. R. Wimberly | 4th July 1892 |
| John Chapman | G. E. Chapman | J. R. Wimberly | 4th Jan. 1893 |
| Mrs. J. B. L. Solomon | M. E. Solomon | J. R. Wimberly | 16th Oct. 1893 |
| J. C. Burns | Mrs. Ellen Burns | J. R. Wimberly | 5th Feb. 1894 |
| M. J. Whitehurst | Mrs. J. F. Solomon | J. R. Wimberly | 5th Feb. 1894 |
| Daniel Bullard | Walter B. Hill & Mrs. Elizabeth Bullard | J. R. Wimberly | 15th Sept. 1894 |
| W. L. Solomon | Mrs. A. E. Solomon, Jas. C., and W. W. Solomon | J. R. Wimberly | 23rd May 1895 |
| B. S. Carswell | Dewitt Carswell | J. R. Wimberly | 1st July 1895 |
| N. S. Lee | Mrs. Sarah Jane and W. H. Lee | J. R. Wimberly | 22nd Jun. 1895 |
| Elizabeth Denson | E. J. Denson | J. R. Wimberly | 7th Sept. 1896 |
| Mrs. Sarah F. Solomon | Mrs. Lucy A. Solomon | J. R. Wimberly | 5th Feb. 1900 |
| H. S. Wimberly | W. F. Wimberly | J. R. Wimberly | 3rd May 1897 |
| H. H. Slappey | R. R. Slappey | J. R. Wimberly | 5th Sept. 1898 |
| Mrs. N. E. Hatcher (solemn) | W. T. Wall | J. R. Wimberly | 3rd July 1899 |
| Isabella W. Macy | W. J. Macy | J. R. Wimberly | 3rd July 1899 |

I, W. H. Martin, Clerk Superior Court of Twiggs County, do hereby certify that I have compared the foregoing copy for Mrs. Hugh L. Faulk of:

Book listed as book "B" Letters Testamentary that were filed in this office. This certificate is given to help protect the originals records of this Twiggs County.

Signed: W. H. Martin, Clerk Superior Court Twiggs County

## "PICKIN'S FROM THE PRESS"

Ad in THE STATESMAN AND PATRIOT, Monday, July 16, 1827
Stephen F. Miller
Attorney-At-Law. Has located himself in Marion, Twiggs County, Georgia. His professional services are respectfully tendered to the community and his strict attention and industrious experiences will be given to all business confided to his management.
Marion    7/2/1827           79 St.

DAILY MACON TELEGRAPH, Macon, Georgia
Friday Evening, August 4, 1832
Married—
on Wedneday evening last, in Twiggs County, by James Hammock, Esq., Mr. John Keith, a Revolutionary Veteran soldier, aged 87 years, to Miss Nancy West, aged 16 years.

GEORGIA MESSENGER, Macon. Georgia
1826 to 1828
Stage fare from Macon to Savannah $17.00, March 24, 1828 Issue.
A Post Office has been established at Raines Store, (presently Jeffersonville) Twiggs County and is now regularly supplied with mail. Nov. 1, 1827.

FEDERAL UNION, Milledgeville, Ga.
Tuesday morning, Jan. 24, 1860
Notice appearing in the paper—
Administration on estates—Celinda Hodges Faulk on estate of Henry Faulk, Jan. 10, 1860.
    signed at Marion by Lewis Solomon, Ord'y; John S. Goodwin, Jan. 10, 1860.

GEORGIA MESSENGER, Macon, Georgia
Wednesday, Feb. 18, 1824,    Vol. A.  No. 48
Academy
Pleasant Mount Academy is now open for the reception of pupils, in which will be taught Orthography, Reading, Writing, English, Grammar, Arithmetic, Geography, Book-keeping, Geometry, etc. It is situated near the junction of the roads leading from Fort Hawkins and Stone Creek Meeting House to Marion, Twiggs Co.
The situation is high and pleasant, with a never-failing spring of water. Good board can be had in respectable families homes in the immediate neighborhood, on reasonable terms. Terms of Tuition moderate.
                William Johnson, Teacher

    A 1910 Professional Directory included in the Twiggs Paper
Dr. A. J. Hembree, physician and surgeon, Danville
H. F. Griffin, Jr., Attorney-At-Law, Jeffersonville
Hal. B. Wimberly, Attorney-At-Law, Dublin
R. V. Hardeman, Attorney-At-Law, Jeffersonville
Minter Wimberly, Attorney-At-Law, Macon
Dr. R. I. Butler, Dentist
Mark H. O'Daniel, M.D.
Dr. J. G. Slappey
M. J. Carswell, Attorney-At-Law
Richard A. Harrison, Attorney-At-Law
James D. Shannon, Attorney-At-Law

FEDERAL UNION, Milledgeville, Ga., Saturday morning, December 14, 1861 Tax Collectors were appointed for "War Tax". Appointments were confirmed by the Secretary of Treasury—Tax Collectors of "War Tax" in the District composed of counties in Georgia—Twiggs and Wilkinson Counties—T. H. Jones.

GEORGIA MESSENGER, Macon, Georgia

April 21, 1824
St. John's Lodge    No. 13
Marion, Twiggs County, Georgia
April 2,    AL—5824
Imposter appearing at this lodge.
Robert L. Perryman, Sec.
June 4, 1824,    In Marion, Twiggs County, on Thursday evening last, Henry Bunn, Esq. married Mr. S. H. Clarke to Elizabeth Barton.

GEORGIA MESSENGER, Macon, Ga., Saturday, May 12, 1832

The preliminary Convention for amending the Constitution of the State met at Milledgeville, on Monday last, and adjourned on Tuesday evening. General David B. Mitchell was elected Chairman, and P. C. Gulen, Secretary. 27 Counties were represented. Twiggs County by George W. Welch, Esq.

GEORGIA MESSENGER, Saturday, April 21, 1832, Macon, Ga.

Married—
In Twiggs County, on Thursday evening, 19th inst., by the Reverend Charles Hardy, Mr. Archibald M. Campbell of Macon, Georgia, to Miss Mary W. Willis, of the former place.

GEORGIA MESSENGER, Macon, Ga., Saturday, May 19, 1832

Married—
At the residence of George W. Welch, Esq., in Twiggs County, on the 10th inst., Dr. Joshua R. Wimberly, to Miss Caroline Starr.

GEORGIA MESSENGER, Macon, Ga., Thursday, June 28, 1832

Died—
At Montpelier Springs in Monroe County, on the 2nd Inst., Mrs. Nancy Cook, consort of Major Phillip Cook, of Twiggs County, after a distressing illness of more than ten months, in the 38th year of her age.

Excerpts of items which appeared in the GEORGIA MESSENGER, Macon, Georgia.

May 14, 1831—BOAT NEWS—Arrived from Darien, Boat William Penn, Mr. Blair of Twiggs County, owner, with full cargo of salt to B. S. Griffin.

June 18, 1831—Notice—CAMP MEETINGS of the Methodist Churches in this and neighboring counties . . . In Twiggs County commencing on the 14th of July.

July 30, 1831—Died, in Twiggs County, on the 24th instant, Mr. James Guerry.

FEDERAL UNION, Tuesday, March 6, 1860

Twiggs County, Georgia
John Glover, letter of Administrator with will annexed on Dr. William M. Morton, of said County, deceased.
Jan. 30, 1860
                    Marion, Lewis Solomon, Ord'y.

TWIGGS HERALD, May 29, 1903
Auburn Institute

The work of Auburn Institute will close on June 9th—exercises will be held at the school, evenings of June 11th and 12th.

J. C. McEachin, Principal

Teachers elected—
Monday night City Council elected teachers for Auburn Institute for the session of 1903-1904, Prof. J. C. McEachin, Principal, Miss Mary Y. Griffin, Assistant.
Sept. 18, 1903 in society column, Jeffersonville
Prof. J. C. McEachin returned to Helena Tuesday to rest until opening of school, October 5, 1903.

TWIGGS HERALD, Sept. 18, 1903
Twiggs High School

The fall term of Twiggs High School will begin Monday, October 5th. Matriculation fee $1.50 to town and county students alike. Tickets secured from J. C. Shannon before pupils will be admitted.

T. S. Jones, Mayor
J. C. Shannon, Sec.-Treas.

TWIGGS HERALD, Friday, May 20, 1904
Twiggs High School
Close of spring term, June 17th

I would like to say that this has been a successful year's work.

While I have given the people whom I have served for the past two years my very best efforts as a teacher, they have shown their appreciation of such efforts by kind words rendered doubly strong by their smiles and approval. The attendance and interest of the pupils have constantly increased since I accepted the principalship of the school, then as Auburn Institute, now Twiggs High School.

I would be derelict to my duty, however, were I not to make personal mention of my assistant, Miss Griffin. I have never been associated with a truer type of noble womanhood.

J. C. McEachin, Principal

TWIGGS COUNTY CITIZEN, June, 1909
Lt. A. C. Wimberly, U. S. A.
Fort Robinson, Neb. is now in Yosemite Valley of California.

TWIGGS COUNTY CITIZEN, June 10, 1909
Dr. Geo. W. Wimberly came from California to Jeffersonville about a year ago. Later located at Dublin. Appointed by the Interior Department at Washington as resident physician on an Indian reservation in Wisconsin.

TWIGGS COUNTY CITIZEN, Nov. 27, 1909
Farmers' Union of Twiggs County addressed by Dr. Ben F. Watkins, November 13th at Bullards.

TWIGGS HERALD, Nov. 17, 1905
Application for a Bank Charter at Jeffersonville

GEORGIA JOURNAL and MESSENGER, Macon, Georgia
Wednesday, July 28, 1858
Marriage notice—

On the evening of the 22nd inst., by Rev. Lewis Solomon, William L. Solomon, Esq., to Miss Avarila Fitzpatrick, daughter of Colonel John Fitzpatrick, all of the County of Twiggs, Georgia.

FEDERAL UNION, Milledgeville, Georgia
Tuesday, March 6, 1869     Number 41
Georgia, Twiggs County
Whereas, Green W. Bateman, Administrator on the estate of Jesse Bateman, late of said County, deceased, applies for letter of dismission from said administratorship, fully executed.
                          Marion, Lewis Solomon, Ord'y.

FEDERAL UNION, Milledgeville, Georgia
Tuesday morning, July 27, 1858
Twiggs Lodge No. 164, F. A. M.
Held at Marion, Georgia, a tribute to a deceased member, Theophilus Pearce.
                  Committee:   William H. Crocker
                                  George R. McCall
                                  Henry Faulk
W. Neel, Secretary
Georgia, Twiggs County

Elisha Davis, guardian of person and property of John H. Bull and Mary M. Bull, minor orphans of Jesse J. Bull, applies to be discharged from this duty, John Davis applies for letters of guardianship.
    Marion, July 13, 1858
                        Lewis Solomon, Ord'y.

THE MACON NEWS, December 29, 1954
"J. F. Hinsons of Dry Branch observe Golden Anniversary"

SOUTHERN RECORDER, December 23, 1851
Richland Academy commences Tuesday, January 7th. "The mode of instruction will, as far as possible, be vigorously, analytical."
                      J. E. Crosland, Principal

THE MACON TELEGRAPH AND NEWS, Sunday, February 23, 1941
B. S. Fitzpatrick superintendent of schools for 46 years. "Friends honor Twiggs Educational Pioneer, still going strong at 86."

TWIGGS COUNTY NEW ERA, November 15, 1940
"Captain George W. Methvin of the Twiggs County Defense Corps has selected five defense corps members to act as advisers to draftees in filling out their — questionairs: — S. S. Jones, Dry Branch and Georgia Kaolin section; G. F. Benjamin, Huber; E. C. Finney, Jeffersonville and Fitzpatrick; H. W. Mercer, Jeffersonville and Myricks Mill; and Troy Edwards, Danville."

TWIGGS COUNTY NEW ERA, November 15, 1935
"Twiggs sand used in paving. The sand used in the paving on the entire distance of Route 80 from Danville to Dry Branch, in Twiggs County, was purchased from C. C. Humphries and came off his land at Myricks Mill."

TWIGGS COUNTY NEW ERA, January 12, 1953
"Twiggs Landmark is being razed. Hotel being moved . . ."

MACON NEWS, July 11, 1955
"Twiggs County revamps $900,000 school plan"

TWIGGS COUNTY NEW ERA, July 5, 1940
"Oil drilling in Twiggs will soon begin, according to Dr. J. M. Boyd"

THE CHRISTIAN INDEX, March 24, 1955
"One of the Georgia Historical Markers identifying the Stone Creek Baptist Church in Twiggs County, has been unveiled by the Church. Established in 1808, the church is the oldest in the County."

TWIGGS COUNTY NEW ERA, May 28, 1953
"A Marker will be unveiled on Sunday afternoon, May 31, at 3:30 on the grave of John Wimberly, revolutionary soldier, by the John Ball Chapter of the D. A. R."

ATLANTA JOURNAL, 1954 (Around Town by Hugh Park)
"Waterproof Methodist compete with Dry Branch Baptist—in the rural church- of-the-year contest" (Stone Creek Church placed third in Georgia.)

TWIGGS COUNTY NEW ERA, June 7, 1940
"Home Coming Day at historic Richland Church—between 400 and 500 people were present."

TWIGGS COUNTY NEW ERA, May 14, 1953
"Macon groups bring aid to Twiggs tornado victims."

MACON TELEGRAPH AND NEWS, Sunday, June 8, 1958
"The Twiggs County D. A. R. Chapter will unveil a roadside marker near Dry Branch, Ga. on U.S. Highway 80 at 4 p.m. today, commemorating the oldest house in Twiggs County."

THE MACON NEWS, April 25, 1955
"Marker unveiled at Magnolia Plantation—"to" pay tribute to the memory of the late Congressman Dudley Hughes."

TWIGGS HERALD, July 4, 1902
Cut of Architects drawing of new Court House. . . .

TWIGGS HERALD, Nov. 2, 1902
Article on mad dog bite, child of J. I. Newby, use of Mad-Stone owned by Wimberly brothers and sister.

TWIGGS HERALD, Feb. 5, 1904
Obituary of Dr. Wimberly and of Wm. Faulk.

TWIGGS HERALD, July 31, 1903
Dr. W. A. O'Daniel made the first deposit in new bank that opened in Jeffersonville. (Twiggs Co. Bank).

MACON TELEGRAPH, Dec. 31, 1864
Yesterday afternoon, about 2:00 o'clock the up passenger train on the M & B RR, met with a serious accident. The trestle work over Savage Creek, about 20 miles from here, gave way, percipitating the engine into the creek, killing the engineer and fireman instantly. We learn that the engineer was the son of Jonathan Collins, Esq., one of our most respected citizens.

GEORGIA JOURNAL, Milledgeville, Tuesday, Jan. 9, 1821
John G. Bird, attorney-at-law, has opened an office in Marion, Twiggs County, Ga.

THE TWIGGS HERALD, March 27, 1903
Old Uncle Ezekiel Blackshear celebrated his 90th birthday on the 15th. 40 present to honor one whom God gave length of days.

MACON TELEGRAPH, Monday, April 2, 1827

Agreeable to an order of the Inferior Courts of Twiggs County—A Negro woman, by the name of Amy "will be" sold as the property of Josiah Rogers, deceased, for the benefit of the heirs and creditors. Terms cash.

John Neal, Adm'r.

GEORGIA JOURNAL, Milledgeville, Aug. 31, 1824
"TEN DOLLARS REWARD." Runaway from the subscriber on Sunday the 11 inst. a Negro man by the name of Ben. If any person will apprehend said Negro and lodge him in any jail, so that I get him again, shall receive the above reward and all reasonable expenses paid. Ben is about 5 feet 7 or 8 inches high, 21 or 22 years old, dark complected, lively, active and quick spoken, and . . .

David Ingreham
Marion, Twiggs County

GEORGIA JOURNAL, Milledgeville, Tuesday, May 4, 1824
A GOOD BARGAIN. The subscriber has for sale on accommodating terms, (a credit from one to four years) 2,000 acres of good land, lying in Twiggs County, near the Ocmulgee River, two miles from Buzzard Roost Ferry, whence at all times the river is navigable to Darien. The lands all join, and have excellent creeks for mills, and small streams well suited to the convenience of the panter. There are three well improved places, 200 acres of cleared land on each, two miles distant from each other; together with orchards sufficient to make two thousand gallons of brandy. The soil in point of fertility and durability is equal to any in the state. All the lands free from incumbrance, with grants and deeds to the present owner regularly in possession. Young Negroes, bank stock, or notes, payable in any of the chartered banks in the State, will be received in payment. Those who wish to settle themselves convenient to trade, would do well to view the premises they being situated midway between Macon and Hartford.

James C. Bryan

GEORGIA STATESMAN, Milledgeville, Georgia
Tueday, July 18, 1826
Volume I, Page 123

## FOURTH OF JULY IN TWIGGS COUNTY

At a meeting of the citizens of this county at the "Oakmulgee" Academy on the 3rd ult. it was Resolved, that the fiftieth Anniversary of American Independence be celebrated in a style suitable to the commemoration of with lustrious epoch. The meeting after having called Robert Glenn, Esq. to the Chair, and appointed Mr. Stephen F. Miller Secretary then proceeded to select Committees to make suitable and preparatory measures for the celebration of the day. Whereupon D. D. Shannon, Henry Bunn, Francis Jobson, Ichabod Davis, John G. Slappey, J. R. Wimberly, John V. Blackwell, Hugh Lawson, James Bryan, and Robert Glenn, Esq., a committee to prepare Toasts. And Drs. Ira E. Dupree, J. G. Slappey, J. R. Wimberly, J. W. Backwell and Hugh Lawson, a committee to procure the Orator and Reader of the Day. The Committee reported that Mr. Joseph D. Thompson would deliver an Oration, and Mr. S. F. Miller read the Declaration of Independence.

At 11:00 o'clock, on the fourth instant, the day consecrated to the laudable feelings of patriotism and gratitude, a large assemblage of citizens convened at the Methodist Church from various parts of the County to offer at the Shrine of National Liberty, the rich testamonies of devotion and reverence.

The Clerical duties of the day were discharged with great ability by the Reverend Mr. Dupree, who during his discourse, adverted in very impressive language to the horrors of the Revolution. The Declaration of Independence was then read, preceded by a concise, but annimated exordium, by Mr. S. F. Miller;—Mr. Joseph D. Thompson then delivered an able and patriotic Oration. After which citizens formed the procession on the left of the LaFayette Volunteers, and marched in front of the Ocmulgee Academy, where a sumptious dinner prepared. Mr. William H. Dupree acted as President of the Day, and Mr. Hartwell H. Tarver, as Vice President.

Much good feeling and harmony prevaded the company, and at six o'clock, after having our bodies and spirits refreshed by the entertainment, we separated each returning to his respectative home reviewing inmelicieus contemplation, the agreeable exercises of the day. Previous to our dispersion, the following toasts were drunk, accompanied with music and the discharge of musketry, from the LaFayette Volunteers:

1. The day we celebrate. May each succeeding return find us of Home! Sweet Home! (6 Cheers)
2. George Washington, contrasted with Heroes, Statesman, and Patriots, the Sun, in the centre of revolving planets. (8 Cheers)
3. America, Liberty's second birthplace, Religion's security, and Science's theatre. (4 Cheers)
4. Thomas Jefferson and the Declaration of Independence—"All men were created equal", Mr. Randolph's mutilated analysis of this phrase to the contrary notwithstanding; looks like detraction and savours of sacrilege. (8 Cheers)
5. Negro Slavery. We concede with the many Philantropists that it is the unwelcome patrimony, and debasing legacy of our ancestors, but its total abolition must rest and remain with their posterity alone, and not with the anatical pretenders of emancipation of the North .(10 Cheers)
6. Our Country. Union, firmness, and consistency in our government, instead of so much whim, detraction and party malignity. (10 Cheers)
7. Education. The grand palladium and chief corner stone in a republican form of government. (3 Cheers) Song—*American Star.*
8. The Georgia Patriot, and Georgia Statesman. The genuine Republicans, the true federalists, and the real friends to justice and humanity, and the confirmed union of these United States.
9. Death to the Monster Partyism and a sincere repentance to its phrenzied votaries, whose motto is darkness before light, and Party angrandizement in preference to public good.
10. The Star of the Altar of '76. May it beam with unquenchable fire to atone for the blood shed by our forefathers. (10 Cheers)
11. Gen. Andrew Jackson. The favorite his country. May the civic wreath adorn the hero's brow.
12. A free Press, unshackled by demagouges and unpolluted by calumnies and sophestry. A free Commerce, unshackled by defrauding merchants and tariff laws. A free Navigation, unshackled by European despots, and carried on by generous and brave tears of America. With all these heavenly blessings, the industrious citizens will reap a full reward for all his toil in the grand field of science and agriculture.
13. The Ladies. Our arms shall protect them in war, and encircle them in peace. (10 Cheers)

### VOLUNTEERS

By the President. George M. Troup, we believe he fears no responsibilities,
By the Vice-President. The District System. The Republican principle pursued by the Republican States.
By John Shine, a revolutionist. May the sons and daughters of America, never forget their forefathers' legacy, which was, and is, Liberty, Union, and the Constitution. (10 Cheers).

By Joseph D. Thompson. The United States. The Garden of Liberty and Independence. The Seat of Learning and Eloquence, the mistress of the Arts and Science—and the centre of uninterrupted Religion and generous Government. May they never fall prey to that "ambitious and selfish faction supported by corruption", which proved an overthrow to the Republic of Greece, Carthage, and Rome. (24 Cheers).
By George W. Welch. May the Argus, yes, and Herculean strength of democracy be ever ready to watch and defend against the encroachments of Aristocracy. (10 Cheers).
By James W. Bryan. The people of Georgia. May they ever stand in readiness to shed their blood in the cause of their rights when they are trampled upon.
By Robert Glenn, Esq. Maj. Gen. Andrew Jackson. The hero of the South; he defeated Packingham at New Orleans, the rads in Georgia, though beaten by John the Second, may he triumph in 1829. (6 Cheers).
By Young Johnson of Macon. We are here convened for the purpose of commemorating the day on which our Independence was declared—whilst we are unanimous in the eulogies of our fathers, let us not prove ourselves the degenerate sons of those fathers whom we so sincerely revere, by sacrificing to party spirit, that freedom which was achieved at the expense of the best blood of our ancestors and may the free sons of America ever love to hate tyrantys.
By James A. Bryan. Governor Troup. To his country, a friend, and Instructor, to his profession an Ornament, to mankind a benefactor.
By Robert F. Glenn, Jr. G. M. Troup. He is as brave as Gen. Gates, as magnamious as Falstaff, and as uncertain as Arnold.
By Sterling Tison. G. M. Troup. His motto is—God and his Country.
By John D. Dennard. John Q. Adams. Although the troopers winked at his election to the Presidential seat, and rather give him the staff than Old Hickory, he has now broken their heads with it.—They now execrate and abuse him, whilst the righteous people of these United States say "well done thou good and faithful servant," enjoy thy preferment.
By John Wheeler, Jr. John Q. Adams. His is the first Administration that has openly run the principle of Patronage against that of Patriotism.
By Henry Bunn, Esq. The villany of Crowell, the duplicity of Gaines and the political profligacy of Andrews, have justly called forth the public indignation of Georgia. (6 Cheers)
By Signal Rainey. May the time speedily arrive, when party spirit, with its pernicious tendencies, shall be buried in oblivion, and one general principle of democracy reign pre-dominant in the bosom of every American.
By Stuting Dupree. John Crowell. A villian at heart politically, a rascal in the affairs of the government, his friends are afraid to own him, his enemies hate and detest his policy; esco procul profani is the salutation of Republicans to him and John Clark.
By James Swearingen. The Republicans of Georgia and friends of the Union, are content with the majority that go for the land, if it is under the New Treaty.
By Joshua Thigpen. Col. Benton of the U. S. Senate. A star of the first magnitude, having liberty for the centre of its orbit illuminates the Republican world. (8 Cheers).
By John L. Hodges. Georgia. May she always be foremost in opposing federal usurpation of State Rights.
By Jared Tomlinson. Gen. Andrew Jackson. Though in the minority of '25, broken bones to those who would ride into office on him in '26.
By James Hayden. The Gordian knot of Turkish despotism. May the sword of Republican Greece guided by the light of true liberty, speedily cut it into atoms.
By James Oliver. He who enters into compromise for the sake of political advancement dishonors himself, and is unworthy of the support of wise and virtuous free men.

By David Glenn of Washington County. Peace remain with the State of Georgia. May she rest in peace, and submit to all righteous and just decisions of her twelve twin, and eleven younger sisters; and may all disorganizers be blasted in their attempt to disturb her tranquility. (6 Cheers).

By Theophilus L. Parker. The District System. A son of federalism, engendered by partyism, and cherished by those who wish to curtail; the suffrage of the people.

By Dr. Slappey. National Anniversaries. May they ever be encouraged as the source of patriotic and lofty sentiment, and not as the arena of party strife, or personal animosities.

By David Graham, Esq. The Union of the two great Empires, Monroe and Elbert. The republics of the earth tremble for the result and hope that they will permit the United States to retain their present form of Government a little longer. "Angry fools are very harmless things."

By Dr. Dupree. The Congress at Panama. Odious frightful and speculative; a measure the most impolite, calculated to compromit the neutrality of this republic and thereby destroy the wisest and most prominent feature in the provision of its Constitution.

By William H. Exum. The State of Georgia. May her patriotic friends be found in readiness to repel any invasion from any part of the United States, when it may be well known that she has yielded to her rights and respects that union.

By Wade H. Ball. 'Tis high time for the enemies of the old treaty to quit their cowheel war, and turn to making corn.

By Hugh Lawson. The memory of Captain Ezekiel Wimberly. The worthy President of our last celebration—

> Tho' no civic wreath adorns his brow,
> Nor sculptered stone bespeaks him now,
> He was an honest man.

(Drank standing, in profound silence.)

By William W. Tarver. "The Father of His Country." May his virtues be remembered, and may that emulation which he diffused among the soldiers of the revolution, kindle in the breast of every American when their rights are invaded. (10 Cheers).

By Frederick D. Wimberly. The Legislature of 1825. The majority of which lost sight of their country's good to satiate their fanatic spleen and ambition, and were aiming at the root of our republic; if they proceed in mad career, too soon will we have it to say, "troga fuit."

By Richard Stephens. The Legislature of '25. The Republicans who composed that body, firm as a planter, and as frightful to the Troupers as a Mississippi Sawyer; they are the true friends of Old Hickory, and the admiration of every Republican of Georgia.

By William D. Glenn. Gen. Andrew Jackson. He is loved by his friends, respected by his enemies, the favorite of his Country, and the admiration of the world. (6 Cheers).

By Stephen F. Miller. The Congress of the United States. The grand bulwark of our National Safety. (6 Cheers).

By Henry S. Wimberly. Georgia. Peace throughout the Union, but her rights to a fractional part now or never.

By Councell S. Bryan of Macon. The Orator of the Day. Possessed of genius and integrity; may this country know and appreciate his worth.

By William Clark. To the Editors of the Patriot and Statesman. Like the Chimberazo among the Andes, how reared the summit of their height, far above all other Editors of the State, from whence in every direction with interpid capacity, they hurl the bolts that prostrate aspiring tyranical demagogues, and extend the flashes of correction to all.

By William Stephens. The first day of September next—The day of the Troopers wrath;—and shall Crowell, Andrews, Gaines, John Q. Adams, the Secretary of War, the Hostile Delegation, (so called), and the large majority in Congress "be able to stand?"

By Council Clark. The Georgia Patriot. A fixed Star, that imparts light and heat to the Journal and Recorder. (16 Cheers).

By Samuel Stephens. Friend of the Old Treaty. I hear good news from the North; there is a large supply of cogwheel gun-flints, wooden nutmegs and merino sheep, such as the Yankey peddlers sold; coming on for us to defend the Old Treaty and our hundred and twenty surveyors with.

By Dr. Joshua R. Wimberly. Party spirit should be moderately tolerated as a necessary ingredient, but is like every other good, subject to abuse. (3 Cheers).

By Josiah Daniel. The Fair - Oh Woman! in hours of ease uncertain, coy and hard to please, when fortune frowns and friends grow scarce. A devil incarnate thou.

By Dr. Ira Dupree. The LaFayette Volunteers and their commander, John G. Slappey. May they always be found in the ranks of Republicanism, ready to defend the country's rights. (8 Cheers).

By H. Lawson. The President and Vice President of the Day.

# LEGISLATIVE ACTS RELATING TO TWIGGS COUNTY

Excerpts of Laws passed, 1809 - 1870, by the Georgia Legislature relating to Twiggs County, Georgia. (Not a complete listing)

(The Act to create the County of Twiggs and a few other Acts appear in other chapters).

GEORGIA LAWS     1810     Pages 40, 42

An Act. To establish and make permanent the site of the public buildings in the County of Twiggs.

By the Senate and House of Representatives of the State of Georgia, in General Assembly.

1. That the Court House and other public buildings for the County of Twiggs shall be erected at or near Joiner's Spring above Savage Creek, on Lot Number 73 in the twenty-fifth district, late Wilkinson, now Twiggs County.

2. That John Harden, Jacob Ricks, William Davis, Lovet B. Smith, and James McCormick be, and they are hereby appointed commissioners of the Court House and Jail of the said County of Twiggs, and they or a majority of them are hereby authorized to purchase as a site for the public buildings not less than 75 nor more than 200 acres of the said lot number 73 above described; and they or a majority of them are hereby authorized to contract for and superintend the building of the Court House and Jail for the said County of Twiggs at the place mentioned in the first section of this Act, after giving at least thirty days previous notice in one or more of the public Gazettes in the Ocmulgee District.

3. And further enacted, That the said Commissioners be and they are hereby authorized to lay off on such Land as may be so purchased as aforesaid, such number of lots as they or a majority of them may think proper, and the same expose to public sale, after giving thirty days' notice as above, on credit, at four equal installments, the purchaser giving bond with approved security to the said Commissioners and their successors in the Office for the amount of such sales—The proceeds of said sales to be applied to the erection of the public buildings in said County and for other county purposes.

4. And further enacted by the authority aforesaid, That all acts and parts of acts militating against this Act be and the same are hereby repealed.

                     Benjamin Whitaker
                     Speaker of the House of Representatives
                     Jared Irwin
                     President of the Senate

Executive Department of Georgia
Assented to 8th Dec. 1810
David B. Mitchell, Governor

GEORGIA LAWS     1810     Pages 44-45

An Act, amendatory to an act for laying out the County of Twiggs passed 14th Dec. 1809, and also to enable the Justices of the Inferior Courts, to draw Grand and Petit Jurors.

1. Be it enacted, That the Inferior Courts for the County of Twiggs shall be holden on the first Monday in February and October in each year.

2. That the Justices of the Inferior Court for the County of Twiggs or a majority of them, together with the Clerk of the Superior Court and Sheriff of said County be, and they are hereby authorized on the first Monday in January in every two years thereafter, or at any other time that to them shall be convenient, being at least sixty days previous to the time pointed out for holding the said Superior and Inferior

Courts in the said County of Twiggs, to break the seal or seals of the Jury box of the County aforesaid, and to draw from thence a sufficient number of persons to serve as Grand and Petit Jurors in the Superior Court of said County, as also a Petit Jury for the Inferior Courts; and the Jurors being drawn, the said Jury box again to seal and deliver together with the key or keys to the proper officer or officers, as pointed out by law.
4. That the true construction of the fifth section of the Act to which this act is amendatory is that all officers shall hold their respective appointments in the County in which they respectively resided at the passage of said Act, and not otherwise.
Assented to Dec. 13, 1810.

GEORGIA LAWS    1810    Page 72
Twiggs
An Act, To make valid the proceedings of the late Clerk of the Superior Court of Twiggs County and to point out the places of holding County Elections—
Section 1. That all the acts and proceedings of Archibald McIntier, lately acting as Clerk of the Superior Court of Twiggs County, so as such acts and proceedings were consistent with the duties and powers of a Clerk of a Superior Court, shall from henceforth be deemed, held and taken as lawful, legal and valid to all intents and purposes.
Section 2. From passage of this act the Superior and Inferior Courts of said County of Twiggs, and all County elections shall be held at the house of John Harden in said County, until a Court House shall be erected at the site pointed out by law for holding Courts.
Section 3. That it shall be the duty of the Justices of the Inferior Court of Twiggs County to advertise for and hold an election for a Clerk of the Superior Court of said County, on the third Monday in February next, they giving thirty days notice thereof at three or more of the most public places in said County.
Section 4. That the lot of land in the Twenty-fifth District, Wilkinson, now Twiggs, known by number 25, granted to _____ Dunn, and by him conveyed to the late Commissioners appointed for the purpose of fixing on a suitable and convenient place for the erection of the public blildings in said Twiggs is hereby declared to be re-invested in the said _____ Dunn, his heirs and assigns, upon his re-funding to the present Commissioners, so much of the conideration money as he may have received and cancelling such obligations as may have been given him for such purposes.
Section 5. Purchases of lots may cancel their obligations—
Assented to Dec. 15, 1810.

GEORGIA LAWS    1810    Page 72
An Act, To apportion the Representatives among counties in this State according to the third enumeration in conformity to the Seventh Section of the first Article of the Constitution.
Twiggs, two.
Assented to Dec. 15, 1810.

--- --- ---

Resolutions, originated in the House of Representatives,    Page 152.
Thursday, 29th Nov. 1810.
Resolved, That Jacob Ricks be, and he is hereby appointed a Justice of the Inferior Court, for the County of Twiggs, in lieu of Robert Glenn, Esquire, resigned.

--- --- ---

In the Senate    20th Nov. 1810.    Page 165
Academies, Commissioners of, in several counties that are new, Twiggs County, Jacob Ricks, James McCormick, James Johnston, Thomas Daniel, Abraham Wood.

GEORGIA HOUSE JOURNAL, 1811, page 4, House of Representatives list the members—Twiggs County, Willis Anderson, Ezekiel Wimberly, Esquires.
Page 36,   A bill to regulate the town of Marion, Mon. 18th Nov., 1811.

GEORGIA LAWS    1811    Page 223
In the House of Representatives, Thursday, 5 Dec. 1811.
Resolved, That Henry Gragg be, and he is hereby appointed a Commissioner of the Academy of Twiggs County, in lieu of James Johnston, resigned.

GEORGIA LAWS    1811 - 1819    Page 939
No. 614    Marion.
An Act to regulate the town of Marion, in Twiggs County.
Section 1. Be it enacted by the Senate and House of Representatives of the State of Georgia, in the General Assembly met—enacted by authority of the same,   That Robert Cummins, James Spann, Thomas W. Harris, Martin Kolb and Henry Loyless, Esquires, be and they are hereby appointed commissioners of the said town of Marion, and they and their successors in office shall have full power and authority to make and ordain all such by-laws and regulations, which they deem necessary and proper for the government of said town, keeping in repair the streets and preservation of the public springs; provided such by-laws shall not be repugnant to the laws and Constitution of this State; and that no penalty thereby imposed shall extend to life, or limb, or corporal punishment of any white person, and provided also, that said Commissioners shall not impose any poll tax upon the citizens of said town, which shall exceed one dollar on each poll, within the term of one year.
Section 2. And be further enacted,   That said commissioners shall continue in office until the first Monday in Jan. 1813, at which time, and on the first Monday in every year thereafter, all free white male citizens of said town, who have given in taxable property and are entitled to vote for members of the General Assembly, shall convene at the Court House in said town, and proceed to elect by ballot who shall continue in office for the term of one year; at which election any two justices of the Inferior Court, or justices of the peace of said County, who are not candidates, may preside.

Robt. Iverson, Speaker of the House of Rep.
Matthew Talbot, Pres. Senate.
Executive Dept., Ga.
Assented to 13, Dec. 1811
D. B. Mitchell, Governor

GEORGIA LAWS    Page 940    1811 - 1819
No. 615    To incorporate the town of Marion, in the County of Twiggs, and vest certain powers in the Commissioners thereof,
Section 1. That Henry M. Terrell, John Flemming, Martin Pitts, Lemuel P. Hargrave, and Moses Fort, be, and are hereby appointed Commissioners of said town; and they and their successors in office, or a majority of them shall have full power to pass all by-laws and regulations which they may deem necessary, for the improvement and repair of roads and streets within limits of the corporation, and for the preservation of good order, and all other corporate acts, which may be necessary for the comfort and convenience of the citizens of said town.
Section 2.   Continuance of commissioners and future elections—
Section 3. And be further enacted, That the said incorporation shall extend to and include all the tract of land originally purchased by the Commissioners of Twiggs County, for a site for public buildings, together wth all the land lying within four hundred yards of the Court House in said town.
Section 4.   Commissioners may appoint officers they deem necessary for carrying

the aforesaid powers into effect and fill vacancies that may happen by death, resignation, or otherwise, in their body.

                      Benj. Whitaker
                      Speaker of the House of Rep.
                      Wm. Rabun
                      Pres. of Senate

Assented to Dec. 12, 1816
D. B. Mitchell, Gov.

    GEORGIA LAWS    1812    Page 155
Twiggs County    Justices of the Inferior Court appointed,
In the House of Representatives, Saturday, 7th Nov. 1812,
Resolved, That the Executive appointment of Samuel Alexander and Jeremiah Dupree as Justices of the Inferior Court for the County of Twiggs be, and the same is hereby confirmed.

    GEORGIA LAWS    1813    Page 85
In the House of Representatives, 9th Nov. 1813
Resolved, That Miles Gathwright and James Ware, be appointed Commissioners of the public buildings for the County of Twiggs, in the place of John Hardin and Lovey B. Smith, resigned.

    GEORGIA LAWS    1815    Page 113
In the Senate, 29th November, 1815
Resolved, That James Hutchinson be, and he is hereby appointed a Commissioner of the public buildings of the County of Twiggs, in the place of Miles Gathwright, deceased.

    Page 115
In the Senate    11th December, 1815
Resolved, That Willis Anderson be, and he is hereby appointed a Commissioner of the public buildings in the County of Twiggs, in the place of William Davis, resigned.

    PAGE 11    JOURNAL OF GEORGIA
House of Representatives of Georgia    1816
Mr. Roger Lawson gave notice that he would move for the appointment of a Committee to prepare and report a bill to appoint Trustees for Twiggs County Academy and incorporate the same and for other purposes.    (bill read three times in the House)

    GEORGIA LAWS    1816    Page 104
An Act to appoint Trustees for Twiggs County Academy and to incorporate the same, and for other purposes.
Whereas, by the promotion of literary information, it is believed that the public is benefitted, and as it comports with the genius of our government to promote and encourage all literary institutions, and as some private subscriptions have been raised by the citizens of Twiggs County for the purpose of effecting the foregoing object; Be it enacted by the Senate and House of Representatives of the State of Georgia, in General Assembly met, and it is hereby enacted by the authority of the same, that Archibald McIntyre, Moses Fort, Samuel Dick, Dr. Robert Cummins, and William Crocker, and their successors in Office, be and they are hereby appointed trustees of the Academy of Twiggs County, to be known by the said trustees be a body politic and corporate by the name and style of the trustees of the Marion Academy, - - - -

    GEORGIA LAWS    1816    PAGE 210    In the Senate, Nov. 13, 1816
Resolved, That Arthur C. Perry and William Dunn be and are hereby appointed as Commissioners of Public Buildings of the County of Twiggs, in the place of Jacob Ricks, deceased, and James Ware, resigned.

In the Senate, Nov. 2, 1816
Resolved, That Moses Wheat be, and he is hereby appointed a Commissioner of Public Buildings of the County of Twiggs, in the place of James McCormick, resigned.

GEORGIA LAWS     1817     Page 51
An Act to authorize the Inferior Court of Twiggs County to transcribe the records of the Court of Ordinary of said County into a bound book or books, and t confirm the same in Courts of record.

Benjamin Williams
Speaker of the House of Representatives
Mathew Talbot
President of the Senate

Assented to 18th Dec. 1817
William Rabun, Governor

GEORGIA LAWS     1811 - 1819
No. 157    An Act    Nov. 27, 1817
An Act to make permanent the site of public buildings in County of Twiggs.
Section 1. The Commissioners of the Court House and Jail of Twiggs County are required to transfer all monies, etc. in their hands to the Justices of the Inferior Court. Said justices of the Inferior Court are vested with the same powers that said Commissioners possessed.
Section 3. Said justices of the Inferior Court after paying debts contracted for by the Commissioners may appropriate the remainder of the funds arising from sale of lots to the use of Marion Academy. May sell lots in the town not already disposed of and use for academy and to the best interest of the County, as said Court may deem necessary.

GEORGIA LAWS     1821     Page 5.     An Act. Assented to 3rd Dec. 1821
Public lands belonging to County of Twiggs under control of the Justices of the Inferior Court, and lands of the said Robert Cummins, are divided by a creek, the course of the bed of which may be changed to the advantage of both parties, and shall be the dividing line.

Resolutions    Page 133    In the Senate, 26th Nov. 1821
Resolved, That Zachariah B. Hargroves be and he is hereby appointed a Notary Public for the County of Twiggs.

GEORGIA LAWS     1822     In the House of Representatives
Resolved, That John McIntyre and Larkin Griffin be appointed Notaries Public for the County of Twiggs and the town of Marion.
Approved, Nov. 18, 1822.

GEORGIA LAWS     1828     Page 17
An Act to incorporate Jefferson Academy in Twiggs County, and appoint Trustees for the same.
To be established near Raine's store in Twiggs County, an Academy to be known by the name of Jefferson Academy and that Thomas W. Terrell, John R. Lowry, James Guerry, Sr., James Willis, and John E. Denhard and their successors in office be and etc. declared to be a body politic and corporate, by the name and style of the trustees of Jefferson Academy.

Irby Hudson, Speaker House of Rep.
Thomas Stocks, Pres. of Senate

Assented to Dec. 17, 1828
John Forsyth, Governor

## TWIGGS COUNTY

Legislative acts show how changes took place from time to time in elections and districts. Elections to be held at the Court House; at James Garrett's or the Justices' court in Captain Oliver's district; at John Anglin's or the place of Justices' courts in Captain Strutman's district; at Hartwell H. Tarver's or the place of Justices' courts in Dean's district; and at the house of Benjamin B. Smith or the place of Justices' courts in Captain Bostick's district, 1829. Vol. IV 180—The foregoing act repealed, 1830, pam. 110—Elections to be held at Marion; at the house of H. H. Tarver; at the house of Benjamin B. Smith; and at the house of S. Granberry, 1831, pam. 125.

Ref.: Prince's Digest of Georgia Laws 1837, page 968.
Dawson's Compilation of the Laws of the State of Georgia
Published in 1831     Page 180.

An Act to establish Election Districts in the County of Twiggs.—6 sections to this act—

Warren Jordan
Speaker of the House of Representatives
Thomas Stocks
President of the Senate

Assented to 22nd Dec., 1829
George R. Gilmer, Governor

GEORGIA LAWS     1834     Page 20

An Act to alter Act passed 26th Dec. 1831 that names of William A. Tharp, Jeremiah A. Tharp, and James Pearson be inserted in lieu of William A. Sharpe, Jeremiah A. Sharp and William Davis, Trustees of Stone Creek Academy.
General Assembly of Georgia     1851 - 1852
Title 1   Academies and Free Schools
An Act to provide for the Education of the Poor, approved, Jan. 22, 1852, page 1, there are 22 sections to this Act which relate to such as, funds, distribution of funds, Commissioners, duties, power, Constitution and by-laws, gifts, and bequests, officers, trustee power, pledge to teach, appropriations, boards and such.
Page 335 of Georgia Laws 1851-1852 (No. 209)   An act was approved on Jan. 15, 1852 relating to the education for the poor, so far as Twiggs County is concerned—
Treasurer to be selected in each Militia District,
Bond, Commission
Duty of Inferior Court
Duty of Treasurer and the repealing clause.

GEORGIA LAWS     1853-54, 1855-56, 1857     Page 162

Twiggs Lodge Incorporated, Number 164 of Free and Accepted Masons.
Section V, # 18,  Be it further enacted that John Glover, W. M.; E. A. Wimberly, S. W.; J. U. Burkett, J. W.; Hardy Solomon, Treas.; Wright Neel, Sec'y.; S. Methvin, J. D.; W. H. Crocker, S. D.; James Evans, Tyler; the officers of the Twiggs Lodge # 164 of Free and Accepted Masons, situated in Marion, Twiggs County, and their successors in office, be and they are hereby declared capable in law and in equity of suing and being sued of purchasing and holding real and personal property, of giving and receiving titles for the same, to use a common seal, and to do all other things which corporate bodies may in law do, connected with the objects of their association.

Assented to 22nd Dec., 1857

GEORGIA HOUSE JOURNAL     1858     Page 187
Friday, Nov. 26, 1858

The House met pursuant to adjournment—
Hon. Henry Faulk of Twiggs County.
Mr. Faulk of Twiggs reported a bill to be entitled an act to establish a Board of Education in the County of Twiggs, and to confer certain specified powers upon them; also, to determine what teachers shall be entitled to draw upon the Poor School Fund of said County.
Wednesday, 1st Dec., 1858     Page 217
Mr. Faulk reported a bill for the suppression of the sale of a published debate between the Rev. W. G. Brownlow and the Rev. A. Payne, entitled "Ought American Slavery to be Perpetuated?"

GEORGIA LAWS     1858     Page 49 to 51
Education No. 40
An act to provide for the education of the children of this State between certain ages, and to provide an annual sinking fund for the extinguishment of the public debt.
Assented to Dec. 11, 1858
Now as this act looks toward a common school education system of the State it is headed Education. Previous legislation under the head of Academies and Free Schools. See Cobb, N. D., pages 1 to 7; Acts of 1851 and 5, pages 1 to 4; Acts of 1853 and 4, pages 7 and 8; Acts of 1855 and 6, page 11; and Acts of 1857, pages 9 to 12.

GEORGIA LAWS     1859     Pages 28, 29, 30, 31
Article Three     Common Schools     (No. 24)
(An act to alter and amend an Act, entitled to provide for the education of children of this State, between certain ages, and to provide for an annual sinking fund, etc.)
Section 1. How Educational Fund is to be drawn when Ordinary fails to give bond as Treasurer.
Section 2. Ordinary of Worth County
Section 3. Ordinary of all counties in the State to pay for teaching poor children.
Section 4. Expenditure of Educational Fund of the State.
Section 5. Children between 6 and 18 entitled to fund.
Section 6. The word Elementary Branches wherever occurring in the Act of which this amendatory shall be construed to mean Spelling, Reading, writing and Arithmetic; but children entitled to the benefits of Public School funds, shall not be debarred from pursuing the studies of English Grammar and Geography, the tuition of which shall be paid for out of said funds, provided said tuition shall not exceed the rates of sixteen dollars per annum.
Section 7. Board of Education.
Section 8. Educational fund how disbursed, Examination of teachers.
Section 9. Ordinary to be Treasurer, his duties.
Section 11. Treasurer in default shall pay a percentage.
Section 10. Treasurer refusing to pay out fund, how dealt with.
Section 12. Repealing clause.

Sec. IV. Be ot further enacted, That in each County of this State, there shall be a Board of Education, which Board shall consist of the Justices of the Inferior Court, the Ordinary, and some other person to be selected by said Justices of the Inferior Court and Ordinary, having reference to his proficiency in the "Elementary Branches" upon which teachers are now or shall be required to be examined; majority of Board shall constitute a quorum for transaction of business.

GEORGIA LAWS     1860     Page 211
See Act No. 219. "To prevent the peddling of spirituous liquors in the Counties herein named . . . Twiggs - - -

An Act assented to the 11th day of Dec., 1861
No. 68. Act to allow all slaves and Free Persons of color who may leave this State in the service of any person in or connected with the military services, may return to the State of Georgia, and shall not be held liable to pains or penalties of any law now existing prohibiting their leaving or returning to Georgia.

Public Laws,   1865
Education No. 30, Page 50
An Act to increase per diem pay of teachers entitled to the benefit of the Poor School funds of this State of Georgia.

GEORGIA LAWS    1862 - 1866    Page 44    No. 84
An Act to provide for citizens of Twiggs County to settle the question of the removal of the County site from Marion, its present location, to Jeffersonville in said County . . . Election to be ordered by Justices of Inferior Court.
Approved 10th Dec. 1866.

GEORGIA LAWS    1866    Page 39
No. 70. An Act to consolidate the Offices of the Clerk of the Superior Court and the Inferior Court in Counties of . . . Twiggs . . . (Henry, Dougherty, Clayton) . . . the reason for this act . . . in consequences of small fees . . .

GEORGIA LAWS    1869    Page 21
Twiggs County, Criminal Court in, . . . Organize Criminal Court . . .
Approved March 9, 1869.

GEORGIA LAWS    1870    Pages 49 to 61 inclusive
An Act to Establish a System of Public Instruction
An Act was passed to constitute the Georgia State Board of Education with officers and duties, County Boards, Trustees, Teachers, and Ambulatory Schools, all setting the duties . . .
There are 51 sections to this act.
Approved 28th day of July 1870.
For the laws heretofore regulating "common schools" and "school funds" see Irwin's Revised Code, sections from 1269 to 1302 inclusive. The system being entirely changed from the former, was complicated.

# REVOLUTIONARY WAR RECORDS

"For what avail the plough or sail
Or land or life if freedom fail?"  —Emerson

Few Revolutionary Records for Twiggs County are available but the following data was copied from various sources.

## REVOLUTIONARY SOLDIERS OF TWIGGS

List I. Reference: Knight, Lucian Lamar, *Georgia Roster of the Revolution*. Atlanta: Index Printing Company, 1920. (Lottery 1820 and 1827)

John Barker
Dempsey Brown
Grisham Cofield
Joseph Collins
Joseph Crittendon
Andrew Cunningham
Thomas Fulton
Thomas Hatcher
John Hawthorne
Isaac Hollinsworth
George Holmon
David Jameson
Henry Kent
Aquila Lowe
Samuel Pate

Edward Penny
Harmon Perryman
Charles Railey
Rehum Redding
Henry Sapp
John Simpson
William Smith
Lazarus Solomon
Richard Stephens
John Stiles
John A. Tharpe
Thomas Thombey
Henry Wall
William Wheeler

List II. Reference: Hitz, Alex M., *Authentic List of All Land Lottery Grants Made to Veterans of the Revolutionary War*: Atlanta, State of Georgia, 1955.

(Residing in Twiggs County)

Angelly, Alexander
Barber, Stancill
Bird, William
Brown, Dempsey
Buckelew, Frederick
Bullock, Daniel
Carter, Samuel
Cofield, Gresham
Collins, Joseph
Crafford, John
Crawford, John
Cunningham, Andrew
Darby, Nicholas
Dunn, Sr., Benjamin
Durden, Benjamin
Easterling, James
Falkner, Asa
Fowler, Sr., Joseph
Fulton, Thomas
Gilder, Isaac
Gilder, Robert
Goodwin, Lewis
Griffin, Peter

Hatcher, Thomas
Hawthorn, John
Henderson, John
Holliday, William
Holman, George
Jamison, Sr., David
Johnson, Jacob
Jones, Thomas
Kent, Henry
Liles, Ephriam
Linton, Sr., John
Low, Acquilla
Mahon, William
Matthews, John B.
Pate, Sr., Samuel
Penny, Edward
Perryman, Harmon
Peters, Quilliam
Railey, Charles
Ray, Benjamin
Redding, Rehum
Rogers, James

Simpson, Jacob
Simpson, Sr., John
Smith, William
Solomon, Lazarus
Stanford, Robert
Stephens, Sr., Richard
Stiles, John
Tharpe, Sr., John A.

Tyler, Needham
Wall, Henry
Wells, Julius
Wheeler, William
Wickers, Allen
Williams, David
Williby, John

List III.  Reference: Miller, Stephen F., *The Bench and Bar of Georgia*, Philadelphia: J. B. Lippincott and Co., 1858.  (Vol. I, page 249)
William Duffel, Charles Raley and John Shine.

List IV.  Reference: Smith, James F., *The Cherokee Land Lottery*. Harper Bros., 1838.  (Page 325)  (Soldiers & Widows)

Lewis Goodman
William Holliday
Ephraim Liles

Mary Nichols
Mary Phillips
Ditha Williams

List V.  Reference: White, George, *Historical Collections of Georgia*. New York: Pudney and Russell, 1854.

Arthur Fort
John Lawson

Henry Sapp
John Shine

List VI.  Reference: Davis, Eleanor Pearl, *Notes on the Allentharp and Tharp Families*: Jeffersonville, Ga.: A. K. Smith Press: (private printing, limited 100 copies) published by B. D. Tharpe, Sr., 1944.
Vincent T. A. Tharp
John A. Tharp

List VII.  Reference: Houston, Martha Lou, 600 *Revolutionary Soldiers and Widows of Revolutionary Soldiers Living in Georgia*: Washington, D. C., 1932.

Lewis Goodwin
Sara Harvey
William Holliday
John Kent
Martha Kent

Ephraim Liles
Mary Nicholas
Mary Phillips
Elvilah Slatter
Ditha Williams

List VIII.  Revolutionary Soldiers' Graves Marked by local chapters, Daughters of the American Revolution.

John Jones
John Shine
Vincent A. Tharp

Lazarus Solomon
John Wimberly

List IX.  Some known Revolutionary Soldiers' Graves which have not been marked with patriotic grave markers.

Edward Bryan
Isaac Gilder
Evans Long

John Stiles
Henry Sapp

## THE LAFAYETTE VOLUNTEERS

General Lafayette, although a Frenchman by birth, had spent several years in the service of the Colonial American Forces who were fighting for their independence against the British. It was not until after the successful completion of the American Revolution that General Lafayette became a national hero. In 1825 General Lafayette, then in his sixty-eighth year of life, made an official state visit to many of the states of America, one of the states being Georgia. The Lafayette Volunteers, a group of about 80 Twiggs County men, went to pay their respects to General Lafayette at the State Capitol in Milledgeville. Stephen F. Miller, in his *Bench and Bar of Georgia*, gives this vivid account of the Lafayette Volunteers.

In March, 1825, while General Lafayette was making his triumphal tour through the Southern States, a company was formed, called the "Layafette Volunteers," of which John G. Slappey was elected captain, Theophilus M. Chamberlain first, Hamilton R. Dupree second, and Francis W. Jobson third lieutenant, and Stephen F. Miller, orderly-sergeant. This corps adopted a cheap uniform, and, with drum and fife, and a beautifully-painted white silk flag, presented by the ladies, it took up the line of march for Milledgeville, having as a much-venerated charge three Revolutionary soldiers, Fathers William Duffel, John Shine, and Charles Raley, in a conveyance provided for the occasion. When the troops reached Marion from Tarversville, they halted an hour or two, in which time the orderly-sergeant availed himself of the courtesy of a friend (John L. Jones) to obtain a sword to render him more worthy of respect in his official character. That sword belonged to Major William Crocker . . . The Lafayette Volunteers had reached a hill near Fishing Creek, within sight of Milledgeville, when the roar of cannon announced the arrival of Gen. Lafayette. An express was sent to tender our command to the marshal in the ceremonies of reception. The reply was that the great reception and review would be the next day, at 10 o'clock, when our presence would be very acceptable. This was in the afternoon. Wishing to show ourselves, and to get a glimpse of the "Nation's Guest," we marched into the town and halted opposite the Government House, where General Lafayette was quartered. Our captain went in and was introduced by Gov. Troup; then the captain introduced the three Revolutionary veterans to Gen. Lafayette, who, on seeing Father Duffel, cordially embraced him, saying, 'I remember you— I remember you well. You were one of my bodyguards, and helped carry me from the field when I was wounded at Brandywine. I am happy to see you—very glad to see you.' or words to that effect. The grateful meeting over, the company returned to camp, first conducting our aged friends to the boarding house of Captain Solomon Betton, where they and the officers took lodging.

Early the next morning all was life and motion. Before the appointed hour, some eight or ten military companies, from Wilkinson, Hancock, Jones and the adjoining counties, were to be seen marching to the review ground. The Lafayette Volunteers, from Twiggs, had paraded two or three principal streets with music and banner, when the intendant, Peter F. Jaillette, Esq., came out of the house and saluted our flag. We halted and returned the proper civilities. He expressed his admiration of our beautiful flag and bade us welcome to the city.

. . . A splendid military ball was given in the Capitol, in honor of Gen. Lafayette. The Representative and Senate Chambers were stripped of all furniture and formed into dancing saloons. The company was indeed gorgeous. Epaulettes, swords, sashes, and other war-trappings looked terribly beautiful. And then the matchless array of ladies, skimming in the dance like fairies—many of them. There was a full band of music in the gallery of each hall. Everything had a classic air, particularly the generals and sergeants—the latter claiming equality, at least for a few hours, in the republic of amusement formed by a junction of France and the United States for a limited period. That republic of social enjoyment was plain enough to interest great minds, and yet so magnificent that the feeble were astonished.

Capt. Slappey, accosting the orderly in the ballroom, dispatched him to headquarters with a polite request to the first lieutenant to send the flag of the company, to be displayed as the Committee of Arrangements might direct, they having expressed a desire to have it for the occasion. The flag was of pure white silk, very ample in its dimensions, with an eagle tastefully painted on one side, with the arrows and olive-branch in his talens, like other patriotic eagles, and a scroll in his beak inscribed "The Nation's Guest," and below this bird of Love, "Welcome Lafayette." On the reverse side was a pile of cannon balls, guarded by a large rattlesnake in coil, with uplifted head, flaming eyes, and darting tongue. The picture looked dangerous indeed. But, to relieve the mind of the beholder, the word "Liberty" appeared in blazing characters above the snake. With such protection, all knew that "liberty" was safe. And then, to make it doubly secure, the name of the company was painted below the balls and the serpent:—"Lafayette Volunteers, Twiggs County, 1825". Such was the flag. (See next page for a picture of the flag).

. . . On marching homeward, the company was supplied with refreshments as they passed Dr. Williamson's splendid mansion (formerly Robert Rutherford's) within a mile or two of Milledgeville; and again, a few miles farther, when opposite Gen. Clark's residence, another favor of the same kind was experienced: Gen. Clark himself came to the road and conversed familiarly with the officers and men, (about eighty in all) most of whom received a personal introduction to him. . . .

Nothing special occurred until the company reached Meriwether's Store, within four miles of Marion. There they saw a large collection of persons, many of whom were intoxicated and disposed to quarrel. Robert L. Perryman, the lawyer, had just been seriously stabbed in the abdomen, and was lying in a room near the store. While Ensign Walton was in the act of mounting his horse, with the standard of colors in his hand, the horse took fright; and, holding on to the standard, the ensign became entangled in it, was thrown, and had his under lip and chin severely gashed. Doctor Slappey, (our captain) an excellent surgeon, sewed up the wound, put on straps of adhesive plaster, and we continued our march, the ensign along with us. As we passed the house of Archibald McIntyre, Esq., (the old clerk of the Superior Court) a signal gun was fired from his piazza, and soon he was in our midst, talking in his lively Scotch style, praising our soldierly appearance, and treating us to very substantial refreshments. A mile farther, the sword was returned to Major Crocker, with many thanks.

# WORLD WAR I

"They were summon'd from the hillside,
They were call'd in from the glen,
And the Country found them ready at the
stirring call for men."
—L. G. Ford

Official Service Records World War I (1917-1919)
Twiggs County Vol. I Army, Navy and Marine Corps
Twiggs County Clerk's Office and Georgia Veterans Service Office

Aaron, Casandra, Pvt.—3,583,327 Col.
Anderson, David, Pvt.—3,583,329 Col.
Anderson, Howard—220,808 Col.
Anderson, James Allen, Pvt.— Col.
Anderson, Tom, Pvt. 1,934,376 Col.
Anderson, Wiley, Pvt.—3,583,328 Col.
Andrews, Heyward, Pvt.—3,491,434 Col.
Anthony, Richard, Pvt.—230,238 Col.
Arnold, John D., Cpl. 3,033,573 White
Asbell, George E., Pvt.—
  3,995,531 White
Ashely, Adolphus U., Pvt. 1—
  3,580,312 Col.
Ashley, Frank, Pvt. 1—1,927,741 White
Ashley, Henry W., Pvt. 1—
  1,344,318 White
Ashley, Orpheus Jr., Pvt.—
  5,066,299 Col.
Ashley, Richard, cook—2,649,327 Col.
Ashley, Wm. S., Pvt. 1—2,654,327 Col.
Atkins, Thomas C., Pvt. 1—
  2,346,445 Col.
Balcom, Frank C., Cpl.—707,559 White
Barswell, Dock, Pvt.—3,493,111 Col.
Barswell, Joe, Pvt.—2,656,005 Col.
Bazley, Frank—Pvt.—3,502,929 Col.
Bell, Harvey, Pvt.—3,583,332 Col.
Bell, John H., Pvt.—4,009,485 Col.
Bell, Wilson, Pvt.—3,654,313 Col.
Benford, John M., Pvt.—283,016 Col.
Blanton, Alonzo, Pvt.—
  4,431,432 White
Blount, Wm. C., Pvt.—4,559,520 White
Bowden, Charlie S., Pvt.—
  4,559,851 White
Bozeman, James C., Pvt.
  1,159,809 White
Bragg, John J., Pvt.—1,343,418 White
Bromon, Gus, Pvt.—2,654,330 Col.
Brooks, Fred, Pvt.—2,345,769 Col.
Brooks, Jim, Pvt.—3,580,314 Col.
Brown, Grady, Pvt.—232,443 White
Brown, Will, Pvt.—3,492,977 Col.
Brown, Willie, Pvt.—3,502,646 Col.
Broyles, Lem, Pvt.—3,583,194 Col.
Bryant, Elbert, Pvt.—4,009,487 Col.
Bryant, Herbert, Pvt. 1—1,934,360 Col.
Buckner, Wm. F., Pvt. 1—
  633,040 White
Burkett, Robert, Pvt.—5,066,296 Col.
Burnett, Jordan, Pvt.—3,583,334 Col.
Burns, Ephraim Jr., Pvt.—3,580,313 Col.
Butler, Aaron, Pvt.—3,581,909 Col.
Butler, Clarence G., Pvt.— White
Califf, David Yancey, Pvt.—
  1,365,864 White
Cannon, Freeman L., Pvt.—
  3,995,532 White
Cannon, James E., Pvt.—
  2,597,144 White
Carden, Frank D., Pvt. 1—
  1,359,693 White
Carden, John, Pvt. 1—1,342,281 White
Carson, Lambert, Pvt.—3,417,920 White
Carswell, John—Pvt. 1—2,654,329 Col.
Carswell, Robert B., Sgt. 1—
  1,340,052 White
Carter, Henry W., Pvt. 1—
  4,305,173 White
Chambliss, Claud, Pvt.—3,491,332 Col.
Chance, Homer L., Pvt.—
  2,597,146 White
Chapman, Colton, Pvt. 1—
  2,345,798 Col.
Chapman, Glover, Pvt. 1—
  3,580,318 Col.
Chapman, John S., Pvt.—3,583,336 Col.
Clemmons, Charlie, Pvt.—4,009,488 Col.
Coates, George Jr., Pvt.—5,066,303 Col.
Cobb, Alex, Pvt.—4,009,489 Col.
Cobb, F. S., Pvt.—2,656,018 Col.
Cobb, Joe, Pvt. 1—230,273 Col.

Coley, Herbert, Pvt. 1—2, 652,832 Col.
Coley, James, Pvt.—3,588,335   Col.
Collier, John Grant, Pvt.—
  2,653,193   White
Collins, Charlie, Pvt. 1—230,399   Col.
Combs, Will, Pvt.—4,008,673   Col.
Cook, Benjamin S., Pvt.—
  4,559,521   White
Crawford, Willie L., Pvt. 1—
  3,583,339   Col.
Crosby, Dick S., Pvt. 1—1,342806 White
Culver, Will, Pvt.—3,586,859   White
Curtis, Will, Pvt.—4,009,493   Col.
Dalton, Will, Pvt. 1—3,492,871   Col.
Darity, Chapman C., Pvt.—
  4,007,977   White
Davis, Grady, Pvt. 1—2,382,739   White
Dawson, Gartrell, Pvt.—2,649,317 Col.
Dal, James L., Pvt.—1,354,216   White
Defore, Wm. A., Pvt.—2,597,147   White
Dennard, Roy Johnston, Pvt.—
  4,462,333   White
Denson, Homer L., Cpl.—3,490,978 Col.
Denson, Jerry T., Cpl.—2,650,102 Col.
DeWit, Kizzie, Pvt.—4,884,381   Col.
Dillard, Dilman, Pvt.—4,009,496   Col.
Dillard, John, Pvt.—3,993,989   Col.
Dixon, Homer, Pvt.—3,991,197   Col.
Dixon, Walter S., Pvt. 1—
  2,587,504   White
Doty, James C., Pvt.—2,924,628   White
Draper, John, Pvt.—3,638,123   Col.
Dupree, Henry T., Pvt.—
  2,365,269   White
Dupree, James, Pvt. 1—3,499,201 White
Durham, Aaron, Pvt.—3,580,316   Col.
Edwards, Fred Pritchard, Pvt.—
  3,580,985   Col.
Edward, Irvie, Pvt.—3,491,373   Col.
Ellen, Ezral, Pvt.—1,928,148   Col.
Elliott, Walter H., Sgt.—
  1,197,301   White
Epps, Andrew R., Cpl.—
  1,930,993   White
Everett, Taylor L., Sgt.—
  2,133,727   White
Findley, Sidney, Pvt. 1—3,580,319 Col.
Finney, Charlie L., Pvt.—3,491,372 Col.
Finney, Eugene G., Pvt.—
  1,003,843   White
Fitzpatrick, John, Pvt.—5,068,302 Col.
Floyd, Arthe, Pvt.—3,583,342   Col.
Floyd, Clarence, Pvt.—4,884,182   White

Floyd, George, Pvt.—3,580,318   Col.
Floyd, Irwin, Pvt. 1—227,964   Col.
Fowler, Harvery, Pvt.—3,499,221 White
Freeman, Plato Spurgeon, Pvt.—
  1,546,764   White
Freeman, William G.—3,417,928 White
Friday, Charlie, Pvt.—3,491,326   Col.
Gallemore, Reese, Pvt.—3,583,346 Col.
Glover, Eddie, Pvt.—2,654,335   Col.
Glover, Wm., Pvt.—5,066,309   Col.
Gray, Robert, Pvt.—3,583,345   Col.
Green, Joe B., Sgt. 1—1,113,316 White
Green, John Jr.—3fi583,344   Col.
Gresham, Bailey, Pvt. 1—
  3,499,298   White
Gresham, Ellis L., Pvt.—
  3,499,239   White
Griggs, John Lawson, Pvt.—
  3,584,799   White
Hammock, Claud L.—2,653,182   White
Hammock, Robert, Pvt.—5,006,306 Col.
Hand, Benjamin, Pvt.—3,583,365   Col.
Hand, Benjamin H.—3,580,321   Col.
Hand, Gordon, Pvt.—3,583,350   Col.
Hand, Vine Allen Jr., Pvt.—
  3,005,897   Col.
Harden, Griffin David, Pvt.—
  3,499,299   White
Harrell, Claude, Sgt.—3,499,287 White
Harrell, Daniel B., Cpl. 4,559,526 White
Harrell, Emory Speer, Pvt.—
  2,653,195   White
Harris, Robert, Pvt.—2,654,337   Col.
Harrison, Richard—3,580,326   Col.
Hart, Alex Jackson—1,928,201   Col.
Harvey, Frank, Pvt.—3,491,320   Col.
Harvey, Joe, Pvt.—3,580,325   Col.
Hasty, Gerald, Sgt.—1,931,093   White
Hattaway, Jack, Pvt.—3,499,220 White
Hattaway, Richard D.,Pvt.—
  4,008,001   White
Hester, Hubert, Cpl.—801,756   White
Hill, Tracy (Whithead) Act. Sgt.—
  4,462,320   White
Hollimon, Nathan, Pvt.—1,927,138 Col.
Horne, David, Pvt. 1—2,654,319   Col.
Howell, Wright, Pvt. 1—
  3,498,157   White
Hughes, Eddie L., Pvt.—
  4,009,496   Col.
Hughes, General Washington, Pvt.—
  3,581,924   White
Hughes, Lee, Pvt.—2,650,099   Col.

Hughes, Raymond L., Pvt. 3,581,923 Col.
Hughes, Sam, Pvt.—3,488,780 Col.
Hughes, Samuel, Pvt.—2,650,094 Col.
Hughes, Spurgeon, Pvt.—3,581,925 Col.
Hughes, Willie, Pvt.—3,580,320 Col.
Humpheries, Medie, Pvt.— 5,066,297 Col.
Humpheries, Perry A., Pvt.— 2,924, 659 White
Irvin, Eddie L. J., Pvt.— 3,491,057 Col.
Jackson, Ben, Pvt.—1,934,656 Col.
Jackson, Colemen—2,650,085 Col.
Jackson, Irvin F., Pvt.—4,561,022 White
Jackson, John, Pvt—XX Col.
Jackson, Will, Pvt.—3,491,323 Col.
James, Benjamin, Pvt. 1—2,654,339 Col.
James, Courtney, Pvt.—4,009,490 Col.
James, Henry, Pvt.—4,571,278 Col.
James, Jessie, Pvt.—5,066,298 Col.
Jefferson, Marion—3,583,352 Col.
Johnson, Eddie, Pvt.—1,934,366 Col.
Johnson, Henry Grady, Pvt.— 5,066,308 Col.
Johnson, James, Pvt. 1—3,503,560 Col.
Johnson, Joel Jackson, Pvt.— 1,354,237 White
Johnston, Francis M., Pvt.— 114,159 White
Johnston, Joseph P., Pvt.— 1,345,271 White
Jones, George E., Pvt.—2,920,356 White
Jones, Jere C., Pvt.—3,995,391 White
Jones, Stephen S., Sgt.—751,405 White
Jones, Willie E., Sgt.—20,361 White
Jordon, Moses, Pvt.—2,650,514 Col.
King, Dan, Pvt.—3,580,328 Col.
Kizzie, Dewitt, Pvt.—4,884,381 Col.
Lawson, Newt.— Col.
Ledbetter, Hubert, Pvt.— 3,499,341 White
Ledbetter, Olin, Pvt.—3,244,397 White
Lee, Terrell J. Pvt.—3,995,392 White
Lewis, John—4,133,939 Col.
Lewis, Oscar, Pvt. 1—3,491,380 Col.
Little, Claude H., Pvt.—1,931,234 Col.
Lucas, John W., Pvt.—3,029,664 White
Mallory, Juit, Pvt.—1,927,144 Col.
Manson, Charlie, Pvt.—3,993,088 Col.
Manson, Clinton, Pvt.—3,583,353 Col.
Marcus, Samuel C., Pvt. 3,503,629 Col.
Marcus, Walter M., Cpl.—4,009,500 Col.

May, George Washington, Cpl.— 3.580,995 Col.
McCallum, Arthur S., Pvt.— 5,592,204 White
McKinley, George, Pvt.—4,009,499 Col.
Methvin, Ernest H., Pvt. 1— 1,077,417 Col.
Methvin, Merrill Elmo, Pvt.— 4,462,390 White
Methvin, Richard E.—2,924,688 White
Middleton, Buster, Pvt.—3,491,336 Col.
Miller, Jack, Pvt.—2,650,083 Col.
Mims, Horace, Pvt.—5,066,295 Col.
Nesbitt, Sam E., Pvt.—3,996,754 Col.
Newby, Arthur M., Pvt.—745,602 White
Newby, Jerome L(ee), Pvt.— 1,356,437 White
Oenton, Arthur, Pvt.—5,066,304 Col.
O'Neal, George H., Pvt.— 2,654,942 White
Orr, Elbert, Pvt.—4,009,501 Col.
Padgett, Tom G., Pvt.—3,499,090 White
Parker, McKinley, Pvt.—3,491,431 Col.
Parker, Robert, Pvt. 1—3,580,334 Col.
Paul, Oscar, Pvt.—4,559,529 White
Paul, Wiley P., Pvt.—172,729 White
Pettis, Tommie, Sgt.—1,020,970 White
Phillips, Robert H., Cpl.— 1,342,967 White
Phillips, Ross F., Sgt.— 1,342,951 White
Phillips, Wm., Pvt.—3,580,333 Col.
Pipkins, Taylor, Pvt.—3,580,331 Col.
Powell, Robert, Pvt.—2,654,312 Col.
Price, Louis, Pvt.—722,086 White
Putnam, Anthony C., Sgt.— 2,653,187 White
Rainey, Allen, Pvt.—5,065,349 Col.
Redd, Junior, Sgt.—3,583,356 Col.
Rice, Charlie, Pvt. 1—3,580,335 Col.
Ringwood, Wm., Pvt.—221,047 Col.
Robertson, Mark, Pvt.—3,492,649 White
Rogers, Dan, Pvt.—221,046 Col.
Rooks, Leaman C., Pvt.— 3,029,665 White
Rouse, James H., Pvt.—2,650,089 Col.
Rouse, Frank, Pvt.—3,580,323 Col.
Rouse, Jessie, Pvt.—2,650,103 Col.
Rozer, Emmett D., Pvt.— 3,995,385 White
Rozier, Cephus, Pvt.—2,650,622 Col.
Rozier, Willis, Pvt.—4,503,625 Col.

Ryle, Charles E., Pvt. 1—
3,029,666 White
Ryle, Dallas M., Pvt. 1—
3,033,540 White
Sams, Lee, Pvt.—950,615 Col.
Sams, Sherman Theodore, Pvt.—
5,066,307 Col.
Sanders, Mark A., Pvt.—
2,902,586 White
Sanford, Willie Harvey, Pvt. 1—
3,580,341 Col.
Sauls, Herman, Pvt.—3,995,388 White
Savier, Ulysses, Pvt.—3,580,336 Col.
Saviour, Lonnie, Pvt.—4,133,953 Col.
Shedrick, Irvin L., Pvt.—2,650,518 Col.
Shines, Joe Jr., Pvt.—3,583,358 Col.
Simmons, John, Pvt.—4,009,503 Col.
Simmons, Rufus, Pvt.—3,583,359 Col.
Sinclair, Grant, Pvt. 1—3,580,337 Col
Slade, Paul, Pvt.—1,934,342 Col.
Smith, Carl C.—2,385,589 Col.
Smith, George, Pvt. 1—1,637,209 White
Smith, Robert C., Sgt. 1—964,727 White
Solomon, Henry D. C., Pvt.—
5,592,219 White
Solomon, Paul L., Pvt.—
4,458,632 White
Stanley, Allen, Pvt.—4,007,621 Col.
Stephen, William, Pvt.—3,580,340 Col.
Stephens, William H., Pvt.—
4,009,505 Col.
Stinson, Jimmie, Pvt.—3,582,198 Col.
Stokes, Davis L., Pvt. 1—
2,654,222 White
Stone, Patrick, Pvt.—1,354,890 White
Stubbs, Wm. E., Pvt.—2,653,174 White
Swiney, Rich, Pvt.—4,562,840 Col.
Thornton, Howard C., 1st Sgt.—
728,832 White
Todd, Lee, Pvt. 1—1,928,621 Col.
Terry, Tom, Pct 1—3,491,200 Col.
Tharpe, Archie, Pvt.— Col.
Thomas, Felix L., Cpl.—3,491,371 Col.
Thomas, George, Pvt.—3,492,736 Col.
Thomas, John Fate, Pvt.—
5,066,331 Col.
Thomas, Tom, Pvt.—2,649,320 Col.
Thompson, Ollie, Pvt.—3,583,360 Col.
Thompson, Tommie, Pvt.—
3,029, 668 White
Thompson Wm. C., Pvt. 1—
2,651,257 White

Thompson, Wm. J., Pvt.—
1,343,535 White
Underwood, Dewitt, Pvt.—3,581,947 Col
Vickers, Andrew, Pvt.—221,060 Col.
Vinson, Emmett, Pvt.—2,654,320 Col.
Walker, Arthur, Pvt.—221,064 Col.
Walker, Douglas, Pvt.—1,927,971 Col.
Walker, Lucius, Pvt. 1—
3,524,892 Col.
Walker, Rufus, Pvt.—3,583,364 Col.
Wall, Wm. Jackson, Pvt.—
4,456,230 White
Washburn, Fred R., Sgt.—
1,359,341 White
Washington, Horace, Pvt.—
4,009,774 Col.
Washington, Mathew, Pvt.—
2,654,308 Col.
Washington, Napoleon, Pvt.—
3,491,421 Col.
Washington, Postell, Pvt. 1—
3,580,344 Col.
Waters, Emmett, Pvt.—3,492,684 Col.
Watkins, Ellsworth B., Pvt.—
2,900,616 White
Wheeler, Joe, Pvt. 1—3,491,371 Col.
Whipple, Daniel B., Pvt.—
3,497,262 Col.
Whipple, Henry, Pvt—3,492,646 Col.
White, Lucien, Pvt. 1— 1,365,112 White
White, Ornie B., Pvt.—750,236 White
Williams, Orange, Pvt.—1,934,347 Col.
Wimberly, Berry, Pvt.—5,066,300 Col.
Wimberly, Clinton, Pvt. 1—
3,580,345 Col.
Wood, Edward G., Pvt.—
871,639 White
Wood, Ernest W., Pvt.
4,559,532 White
Woodford, Elijah Jr., Pvt 1—
3,580,342 White
Wright, Jack, Pvt.—1,931.307 Col.
Wright, William, Pvt.—2,650,109 Col.
Yopp, Robert H., Pvt.—
1,349,599 White

*Died while enlisted*

Bailey, Flemnon, Pvt.—3,491,322 Col.
Beal, Zack, Pvt.—3,583,331 Col.
Carter, Plural, Pvt.—3,499,363 White
Durham, Matt, Pvt.—1,934,355 Col.
Edwards, Robert H., Pvt.—
2,653,169 White
Floyd, Frank, Pvt.—3,995,387 White

Floyd, Rabon, Pvt.—4,559,523   White
Harris, Frank, Pvt.—3,580,327   Col.
Humpheries, Abe, Pvt.—3,583,347 Col.
Lucas, Tom, Pvt.—3,995,534   White
Mathis Oliver L., Pvt.—2,649,321  Col.
Methvin, Charlie E., Pvt.—
  3,995,535                   White
Rouse, Mose, Pvt.—            Col.
Stubbs, Prince Jr., Pvt.—4,009,771 Col.
Wimberly, Sherman, Pvt.—
  3,580,343                   Col.

Official Service Navy Records World War—1917-1919

Bozeman, Shield, Loid
  Fireman 1st Class            112-82-70
Everett, John Ester—
  Machinist Mate 1st Class     140-88-99
Everett, Thomas Russell—
  Machinist Mate 1st Class     140-89-51
Hill, Charles Winder—
  Ship's Cook 4th Class        172-89-48
Johnston, Rabun Eugene—
  Carpenter's Mate 2 C. Av.    154-87-60
Johnston, Thomas Felix—
  Seaman 2nd Class             154-86-99
Jones, Cowan Everette—
  Chief Pharmacists Mate       154-94-30
Jones Henry Grady—
  Seaman 2nd Class             154-99-88
Jones, John L.—
  Seaman 2nd Class             114-38-65
Lamb, Byron Surry—
  Landsman Quartermaster—
  Aviation                     184-83-90
McCallum, James Ware—
  Boatswain Mate 1st Class     132-66-27
Sanders, Nellie Jane—
  Landsman for Yoeman          174-80-92
Self, Lonnie Oscar—
  Fireman 1st Class            191-48-94
Solomon, Paul Lee—Midshipman
Smith, Cap C.—
  Seaman 2nd Class             192-78-84
Fort, James Lynn—Major        White
Ray, Smith W.—Captain         White
Slappey, Eugene Nelson— 1st Lt. White

Additional names of World War I Veterans not appearing in the above list, but were found in other references:

Brown, J. R.
Cannon, W. E.
Coventry, E. E.
Crosby, Ivey
Davidson, George E.
Die, Z. E.
Everett, J. E.
Freeman, McDuffie
Fitzpatrick, Mark W.
Hammock, W. J.
Hartley, J. M. (M.D.)
Hall, Richard D.
Kitchens, E. P.
Kitchens, E. W.
Kitchens, H. L.
Kitchens, I. V.
Leslie, R. D.
Mallory, E. Y. Jr.
Martin, T. J.
Meeks, B. A.
Methvin, G. W.
Methvin, L. S.
Monroe Price
Shannon, D. H.
Simmons, Gerald
Stringfield, J. W.
Stripling, W. C.
Stroup, I. E.
Thomas, Robert
Upshaw, Rufus
Wade, P. J.
Wall, G. D.
Ward, Charlie
Wells, Marion

## WORLD WAR II

Every possible effort was made by the compilers to obtain a complete list of World War II veterans, however, no list, by counties, was available for release at that time. A temporary World War II Honor List of Dead and Missing was prepared by the War Department* in 1946, and the following names were shown as being from Twiggs County, Georgia in a letter addressed to B. W. Jones and signed by Pete Wheeler, State Director, Department of Veterans Service:

| | |
|---|---|
| Collins, Herman N. | 34 087 613 |
| Moseley, Davis L. | 0- 315 247 |
| Nobles, General J., Jr. | 0- 1307 659 |
| Shaw, Archie L. | 34 063 890 |
| Shy, Newton B. | 34 570 548 |

\* *The Dept. of the Navy prepared a similar list, but did not break it down by counties.*

Listed below is an unofficial roster of World War II servicemen who were inducted or enlisted from Twiggs County prior to June, 1942.

(*W*—White; *N*—Negro)

| | | | |
|---|---|---|---|
| Johnnie Aaron | N | Armour Floyd | N |
| Liston Victor Adams | W | Harry Floyd | W |
| Edward Lynell Anderson | N | Patrick Floyd | W |
| James Orman Arnold | W | William Homer Floyd | W |
| Charles Elton Asbell | W | Joe Brown Ford | W |
| James H. Baggarly | W | Marshall Fowler | W |
| John Dallas Barrentine | W | John William Francis | W |
| Wm. Edgar Barrentine | W | William James Gallemore | W |
| Andrew Jackson Beall | W | Matthew Glover, Jr. | N |
| Sherman Bell | N | Robert Grady, Jr. | N |
| Robert Hughes Bethune | W | Hugh Bert Hamrick | W |
| Aubrey Carson Birdsong | W | Benjamin Hand | N |
| Jessie Clarence Bloodworth | W | Earnest Eugene Hardy | W |
| Griffin Willie Bond | N | Richard Lewis Harrison | W |
| James Williard Bone | W | Earnest Hudson Hataway | W |
| Jule Felton Brooks | W | James Irwin Hendricks | W |
| Dave Brown | N | Woodrow Wilson Hill | W |
| James F. Brown | W | Willie James Hubbord | N |
| Sylvester Brown | N | Maynard Ives | W |
| Thomas Herbert Brown | W | John Norman Jobson | W |
| Jerone Royal Chapman | W | Ralph Cecil Land | W |
| Earl Wilburn Collins | W | James Cleveland Long | W |
| Henry S. Collins | W | Mark Marcus | N |
| Herman Norwood Collins | W | Curtis McLendis | N |
| James Curry | N | Frank Parham | W |
| Lewis Dunforth | N | Elgin Washington Peck | N |
| David Dennard | N | Betrice Pettigrew | N |
| Mack Griffin Dennard | N | Eddie Pettis | W |
| Albert Alonzo Duncan | W | James Hunter Roberts | W |
| Woodrow Wilson Dupree | N | George Robertson | N |
| Reuben Williams Edwards | W | Bobbie Lee Rozier | N |
| George Watkins Faulk | W | William McKinley Sapp | W |
| William Thomas Faulk | W | John Willie Sanders | N |

| | | | |
|---|---|---|---|
| Homer Clyde Sauls | W | Jere Alex Tharpe | W |
| Raymond Earl Sims | W | Robert Tharpe | N |
| John Pruett Slappey | W | Sandy Wilson Turner | N |
| J. C. Smith | N | James Buford Whitaker | W |
| Nathaniel Stephens | N | Arthur Junior Williams | N |
| Elmer Curtis Symonds | W | Linton H. Wood | W |
| Billie Dunn Tharpe, Jr. | W | | |

## CEMETERIES IN TWIGGS COUNTY

"Blessed are the dead which die in the Lord from henceforth Yea, saith the Spirit, that they may rest from their labours; and their works do follow them."— Revelation 14:13.

---

Compilers' note: It will be noted that many of the cemetery records in this volume were copied by friends. If you have ever tried to copy inscriptions from old tombstones surely you realize just how difficult it was to correctly read the dates and oftentimes the name. While every effort was made to copy accurately, when possible a recheck was made in order to eliminate mistakes. Yet, the compilers cannot vouch for complete accuracy. The most pertinent data was copied. It was impossible to include all of the epitaph which appeared on some of the tombstones.

Many of the early families had their dead buried near their homes, because the few morticians were not always available to rural areas, roads were almost impassable at times, grave robbers, and the convenience afforded for visiting and cleaning. It was supposed that the graves would be safer on their own property. A few private burial grounds were inclosed by stone walls, others by wrought iron fences and wooden pickets.

Some of the old burial grounds and graves have passed into oblivion for different reasons: markers were not durable, fallen stones covered by erosion, sometime abandoned, after the family sold the land, and a few have been destroyed.

The cemeteries recorded herein are only a few of the white cemeteries which are located in the county.

### ANTIOCH BAPTIST CHURCH CEMETERY
(near Dry Branch, Ga.)
(Marked Graves)

Annie L. Cranford
March 3, 1907 - Nov. 28, 1944
Mrs. Ben H. Cannon
1904 - 1958
Shirley Fellows
1954 - 1955
Ida C. Brown
1891 - 1958
Lizzie Balkcom
Wife of S. T. Burkett
Feb. 13, 1876 - June 5, 1948
Solomon T. Burkett
June 28, 1867 - Dec. 28, 1957
Thomas R. Smith
Infant - 1949
N. S. Sapp
1886 - 1929
M. L. Sapp
Died 1942 - 84 years old
Mrs. D. Sapp
Age 89 - Died Nov. 29, 1943
K. Wimberly
May 27, 1919 - July 11, 1931

J. W. Sapp
Dec. 25, 1889 - April 21, 1944
Bobby R. Mickler
June 4, 1932 - August 25, 1945
T. E. Williams (C.S.A.)
Dec. 15, 1848 - Feb. 12, 1933
Mrs. Rebecca Birdsong Williams
June 15, 1860 - April 13, 1940
Walter Epps, Jr.
Infant - 1944
Mrs. J. A. Lyles
May 12, 1873 - April 19, 1949
Gillie A. Crosby
Wife of J. W. Crosby
Feb. 20, 1887 - Dec. 5, 1930
Jerry Crosby
1949 - 1952
W. J. Jones
Nov. 24, 1852 - Feb. 13, 1938
Susan Jones
May 6, 1850 - Feb. 20, 1936
William L. Jones
Dec. 26, 1885 - July 27, 1949

Homer Jones
April 10, 1893 - March 14, 1939
John Thomas Wood
Jan. 3, 1858 - Oct. 3, 1932
Ella Evanda Wood
Jan. 23, 1866 - Nov. 25, 1944
Nell C. Cumbess
1913 - 1958
Clyde R. Cannon
1893 - 1958
Freeman L. Cannon, Jr.
Infant - 1926
Henry I. Clance
1887 - 1949
J. N. Reid
Dec. 10, 1854 - May 31, 1924
Sara F. Myrick
Wife of J. N. Reid
1854 - 1934
H. Griffin Atkins
March 15, 1882 - Oct. 12, 1933
Mary Ruth Atkins
March 8, 1910 - Sept. 26, 1917
Infant son of H. G. & Anna Atkins
Sept. 10, 1911
Nancy Ann Atkins
1849 - 1937
Ira L. Wimberly
March 12, 1917 - Aug. 21, 1944 (U.S.N.)
Pierce E. Compton
Died April 24, 1943 (Soldier)
A. S. Compton
Dec. 28, 1888 - Oct. 17, 1929
Alma Sapp
Infant - 1939
Dora Sapp
William G. Kitchens
Aug. 2, 1868 - Nov. 14, 1934
Della K. Kitchens
Nov. 28, 1872 - Oct. 6, 1944
Dr. J. N. Kennington
Sept. 17, 1867 - Jan. 28, 1933
Betty Joyce Bostick
1936 - 1939
Mary Lizzie Bass
Oct. 14, 1859 - March 1, 1933
Narcissae Cranford
Aug. 29, 1841 - Feb. 14, 1920
Fannie Myrick Griffin
July 21, 1856 - May 11, 1921
Henry D. Myrick
Dec. 14, 1898 - March 25, 1932

Ernest L. Myrick
1900 - 1958
Richard T. Myrick
Nov. 27, 1862 - Dec. 29, 1943
Elizabeth Leslie Myrick
Aug. 21, 1875 - March 11, 1953
William Henry Myrick
March 17, 1870 - Nov. 14, 1947
Infant Daughter - J. S. & L. D. Bacon
1907
William Epps
Died 1920
Mrs. W. T. Epps
Died 1912
John S. Epps
March 10, 1887 - April 23, 1937
Charles T. Epps
March 16, 1882 - July 20, 1950
Mazie Nash
Dec. 27, 1839 - July 26, 1922
Lynton A. Nash
Dec. 24, 1838 - July 17, 1919
Mrs. C. B. Barrentine
1889 - 1955
Gus Barrentine
1885 - 1958
John Clance (C.S.A.)
Dosia Clance
1900 - 1924
Addie Clance Lyles
June 26, 1884 - March 25, 1936
Nathan Henderson Lyles
Oct. 12, 1858 - May 28, 1928
Joseph Snow
Infant - 1939
N. C. Crosby
1932 - 1946
James W. Crosby
Infant - 1950
Mary L. Crosby
Infant - 1928
Annie Crosby
Infant - 1924
S. A. Adkins
Sept. 13, 1877 - Jan. 21, 1946
Sidney Adkins
Oct. 27, 1913 - Apr. 21, 1953
Lucille Adkins
May 25, 1932 - June 27, 1957
Virginia J. Evans
Sept. 14, 1868 - Oct. 17, 1932
Mrs. Irene Epps
1913 - 1932

Jack Cumbess
1856 - 1929
Homer J. Cumbess
May 5, 1909 - Feb. 8, 1936
Mrs. Sudie Cumbess
1877 - 1932

Johnnie W. Sapp
Sept. 1, 1894 - Jan. 28, 1934

Copied By:
Mr. & Mrs. B. W. Jones &
Donald H. Lindsey

## BOND CEMETERY

John P. Bond
Jan. 17, 1806 - April 26, 1879
S. J. Bond
June 14, 1828 - Dec. 18, 1896
Julia E. Melton
June 22, 1868 - May 4, 1914
John T. Bond
Dec. 8, 1839 - Nov. 3, 1920
Ruffin W. Bond
Sept. 3, 1849 - Oct. 19, 1935
W. R. Bond
July 19, 1830 - Feb. 17, 1906
G. S. Bond
Dec. 11, 1868 - Nov. 19, 1891
M. Theo. Rice
Feb. 12, 1875 - Feb. 21, 1935
John B. Bond
July 5, 1865 - Jan. 4, 1942

Elizabeth Bond
Oct. 21, 1810 - June 2, 1885
Nancy L. Sims
Jan. 8, 1838 - March 12, 1904
Julia V. Bond Johnson-Shepherd
Aug. 30, 1866 - May 12, 1944
Amanda M. Bond
May 15, 1836 - March 18, 1908
Sarah Jane Ray Bond
May 15, 1833 - Nov. 2, 1857
Robert Bond
July 22, 1861 - May 1, 1863
G. A. Brown
Sept. 22, 1915 - Age 55
Lucia Rice Bond
Dec. 3, 1869 - July 22, 1939
Margarett Anderson
Died March 10, 1910, Aged 58 years

Copied by:
Mrs. John Cantrell

## BURKETT CEMETERY

Louisa C. Epps
Wife of Washington J. Burkett
Sept. 8, 1847 - Nov. 30, 1914
Washington J. Burkett
April 11, 1840 - Oct. 14, 1907
Mamie R. Burkett
1879 - 1934
Homer A. Burkett
1869 - 1937
W. L. Burkett
Age 42 yrs. - Died June 4, 1912
Thomas R. Burkett
Nov. 25, 1858 - Dec. 8, 1884
H. Clifton Burkett
Aug. 8, 1878 - Oct. 25, 1881
Joseph U. Burkett
Feb. 28, 1883 - Nov. 24, 1888

Eliz S. Burkett
April 11, 1837 - Dec. 16, 1912
K. F. Burkett
March 25, 1838 - June 8, 1887
Louisa M. Burkett
June 18, 1841 - Nov. 19, 1909
Lady Belle Butler
Dec. 11, 1869 - March 22, 1943
Thomas Jefferson Burkett
May 31, 1858 - April 28, 1943
Mattie L. Burkett
Dec. 30, 1864 - June 21, 1895, Age 31
Married J. O. Marcy, Nov. 15, 1882
After his death married E. L. Brown

Copied by:
Mr. & Mrs. B. W. Jones

The Burkett Cemetery is located in Smith's Militia District, about a mile from Dry Branch, Georgia, a few yards off U. S. Highway No. 80.

## BEECH SPRING M. E. CHURCH CEMETERY

Reese Ramey
Died Sept. 7, 1914 - Age 76 yrs.
David Franklin Phillips
Willie Fox Phillips
Ruby Phillips Richards
Ross F. Phillips, Jr.
George W. Christian
Mamie Martin Christian
Inela Christian Cranford
John H. Cranford
Janet Yaughn
Aug. 18, 1939 - Aug. 29, 1939
C. J. Richardson, Jr.
1928 - 1942
Mary Frances Smith
July 19, 1948 - Nov. 24, 1949
Mrs. Tessie King
Mr. Andrew J. Cribb
Mrs. Andrew J. Cribb
Mary Cribb
James R. Edmonson, Jr.
Feb. 4, 1910 - Nov. 5, 1943
Dollie Edmonson
May 7, 1885 - June 29, 1927
Edmonson Infant
1955
Ray Irby
July 16, 1900 - Jan. 31, 1941
Jimmie Hopkins
April 1, 1944 - Mar. 18, 1947
R. W. Edwards
1874 - 1953
Mrs. R. W. Edwards
1874 - 1955
Ellis L. Gresham
Georgia Pvt. 157 Depot Brig.
Nov. 3, 1895 - May 28, 1932
William Wiley Millirons
Sept. 16, 1875 - Oct. 5, 1906
Lucinda Millirons Bloodworth
Mary Crosby Bloodworth
Sarah Ann Johnson Roland
In memory of Kennedy, husbands of Susan Bullard, Son of Wiley and Perthena Bullard
Aug. 1, 1819 - June 28, 1852
Columbus Augustus
Son of Kennedy and Susan Bullard
May 20, 1850 - Dec. 10, 1850
Emma,
Daughter of A. B. & M. A. Bullard
July 26, 1852 - Oct. 2, 1856
Mrs. M. W. Wood
Unmarked
Daniel Bullard and Wife
Mr. W. H. MacLease
Unmarked
Mr. Lucas
Unmarked
Beneath this stone lie the remains of Capt. S. Goodwin, born in England Dec. 25, 1795 - Died in Marion, Twiggs County, Apr. 20, 1857 aged 61 yrs., 4 mos. & 20 days.
"In all the relations of life he sustained himself with dignity and honor." Erected by his friend H. Faulk.
William O. Johnson
Mar. 28, 1873 - Apr. 15, 1914
Mrs. Dollie C. Johnson
July 30, 1870 - July 7, 1938
Nellie J. Ellis
March 16, 1905 - April 18, 1934
Edward Ellis
April 18, 1934 - March 26, 1935
Clayton Johnson
Feb. 3, 1897 - Sept. 14, 1914
Mildred Woodson
Oct. 28, 1920 - Nov. 5, 1920
Julian R. Cook
May 5, 1847 - Jan. 4, 1910
Minnie N. Cook
Nov. 14, 1850 - June 2, 1922
Laura Elvira
wife of Julian R. Cook
Daughter of Thomas S. & Mary C. Jones
June 16, 1847 - June 25, 1880
Julian R.
son of J. R. & L. E. Cook
Died Sept. 11, 1879 - age 8 mos.
Berta
Daughter of J. R. & L. E. Cook
Mar. 18, 1875 - Aug. 25, 1896
Cornelius E.
Son of J. R. & L. E. Cook
Aug. 15, 1868 - Nov. 16, 1886
Minnie Korrinne Cook
Dec. 26, 1886 - June 6, 1888
Edith Land
Aug. 3, 1879 - aged 4 years
Woodruff Infant
Parents—
Leroy O. & Lulie Cook Woodruff

## LOWE - JOHNSTON LOT

Cornelia Ann Mims
wife of Thomas Lowe
July 26, 1829 - Aug. 31, 1911
Thomas Lowe
Co. I, 5th Ga. Regt. C. S. A.
Dec. 26, 1826 - Jan. 17, 1880
E. Martin Lowe
Feb. 26, 1858 - Oct. 1, 1885
John Lowe
Sept. 2, 1862 - Oct. 17, 1869
Cornelia Elizabeth Lowe
Dec. 1, 1866 - July 26, 1882

William Warren Johnston
March 20, 1868 - June 18, 1951
Thomas Felix Johnston
Seaman 2 Cl. U.S.N.R.F.
Dec. 23, 1896 - Aug. 23, 1921
Ruby Alleine Johnston
Oct. 31, 1893 - Oct. 9, 1894
Edgar R. Zachary
Mar. 25, 1905 - May 4, 1938
May Methvin Hutchins
Parents:
James S. & Mary Methvin Hutchins

Mrs. W. W. Johnston, an elderly member of Beech Springs, M. E. Church, stated that the following Confederate Veterans were buried in unmarked graves in the church cemetery: Joseph Adkins, Moses Franklin Harrell, Thomas Lowe, James Carey Paul, and John Wood.
Mr. & Mrs. Harrell lie in unmarked graves, parents of John, Bill & Frank Harrell.
Copied by Mrs. Cornelia Johnston McCormick
Located on Bullard-Jeffersonville Road, east from Bullard.
(There are other graves which are sunken and unmarked.)

## BECKHAM - FORT

Mrs. Lavinia Brooks
wife of William P. Brooks
Born in South Carolina Feb. 20, 1801
Died Twiggs County March 23, 1853

Wilson Brooks
Son of William P. & Lavenia N. Brooks
Departed, 17th Jan. 1846
Aged 15 yrs. 1 Mo. 25 days.

Copied by Hugh L. Faulk, July 22, 1958 from the broken grave slabs piled in a gully back of colored Calvary Baptist Church on U. S. Highway No. 23-127. The other stones were not legible for copy. The cemetery was located on property formerly owned by Beckham. The burial plot was destroyed by the landlord about 1942.

## BRYAN CEMETERY

Edward Bryan
Jan. 4, 1764 - Nov. 8, 1825
A Patriot of the Revolution
He bore arms at the age of 16 years
in defending his country
Mrs. Temperance Bryan
Jan. 24, 1812 - Oct. 12, 1842
Elijah B. Bryan
Son of Blackshear & Temperance Bryan
May 25, 1830 - Sept. 16, 1857

Harriett F.
Wife of Alex Everett
Daughter of Ed and Penelope Bryan
Ex 4th, March 1859 - Age 40
Penelope Bryan
April 13, 1773 - Aug. 19, 1839
Blackshear Bryan
Died in 46th year of his age.
Joseph M. Bryan
Son of Blackshear & Temperance Bryan
Aug. 15, 1828 - Nov. 20, 1857

The Bryan Cemetery is located in Twiggs County, Ga., near the Southern Rail road in the western part of Twiggs, west of Crooked Creek, on property formerly owned by Bryan, land lot numbers 269, 264, 241. Northeast from the Railroad about one mile, straight line. Graves are enclosed in a brick wall in a field of pine trees.

Copied by Hugh Lawson Faulk, July 8, 1957

## CONCORD CHURCH CEMETERY MARKED GRAVES

Burke, J. N.
Sept. 24, 1858 - Jan. 28, 1910
Burke, Mary White
Jan. 21, 1868 - July 21, 1902
Burke, Florence
Sept. 26, 1895 - Nov. 17, 1905
Chapman, Ann W.
Died Oct. 28, 1845
Chapman, William
Jan. 9, 1789 - Feb. 10, 1828
Gallemore, Samuel M.
Apr. 13, 1871 - Sept. 9, 1936
Gallemore, Mary Luna
Mar. 19, 1899 - July 16, 1915
Gallemore, Lilla J.
Nov. 2, 1863 - Feb. 4, 1897
Gallemore, John L.
Dec. 19, 1865 - May 1, 1910
Gallemore, Infant
Died Aug. 29, 1900
Gallemore, Infant
Died June 4, 1904
Gallemore, Elliot
Aug. 30, 1894 - Oct. 1, 1924
Gallemore, Levi
Oct. 16, 1824 - June 8, 1890
Gallemore, Martha
Nov. 13, 1840 - Apr. 14, 1910
Gallemore, William J.
Age 35 yrs. - Died Dec. 3, 1869
Gallemore, Hannah
Age 70 yrs. - Died Dec. 22, 1908
Gallemore, Eliazabeth
Dec. 6, 1832 - July 24, 1853
Gallemore, John A.
Sept. 6, 1852 - Sept. 24, 1853

Hamiter, George
3 yrs. 3 months - Died Sept. 14, 1838
Hamiter, Mary
2 yrs. - Died Dec. 20, 1836
McNair, Jane
Nov. 30, 1839 - May 25, 1858
McNair, Sarah
Nov. 12, 1815 - Oct. 30, 1850
Sanders, Walter
Feb. 15, 1900 - Nov. 20, 1910
Sanders, Mary
Aug. 16, 1868 - Feb. 9, 1900
Smith, Sarah
Oct. 28, 1848 - Jan. 19, 1907
Wade, H. G.
Dec. 14, 1888 - Apr. 9, 1930
White, Anna L.
Aug. 3, 1871 - Aug. 9, 1908
White A. M.
July 24, 1842 - Aug. 25, 1892
White, Susan Cordelia
Aug. 6, 1850 - Apr. 14, 1889
White, Jim B.
Died Dec., 1926
Williams, Mary
Apr. 2, 1836 - June 13, 1906
Williams, W. P.
June 24, 1824 - Mar. 27, 1893
Williams, Maud A.
Aug. 1, 1875 - Sept. 8, 1895
Williams, J. L.
Apr. 27, 1861 - Mar. 31, 1925
Williams, Ernest
Dec. 6, 1872 - May 8, 1898

## COOMBS LOT
### MARKED GRAVES AT THE SITE OF
### OLD RICHLAND CREEK CHURCH CEMETERY

Zilpha Coombs
Daughter of
James and Susannah H. Coombs
Died in Jones Co., N. C., Sept. 1817
Alfred Hargett Coombs
Son of
James and Susannah H. Coombs
Born July 30, 1823
Died Aug. 21, 1826
Susannah Coombs
Daughter of

James and Susannah H. Coombs
Born Aug. 30, 1825, Jones Co., N. C.
Died March 20, 1829
Mrs. Susannah Coombs
Wife of James Coombs
Died May 1, 1835
Ann E. Coombs
Wife of D. H. Coombs
Died in Laurens Co., Ga. Dec. 29, 1866
Age 41 years, 2 mo., 23 days

James Coombs
Died Feb. 15, 1846
Mary Ann Elizabeth Glover
Wife of James Tharp Glover
Daughter of
James and Susannah H. Coombs
Born July 16, 1829
Died Oct. 1, 1849
Richard Henry
Son of D. H. and A. E. Coombs
Died in Petersburg, from a wound
received while in Confederate Service.
June 23, 1864.
William Henry Coombs
Son of
James and Susannah H. Coombs
Fell in battle at Oulusfi, near Ocean
Pond Florida. A Lieut. of Co. I, 6th Reg.
Ga. Volunteers, C. S. A.
Born March 23, 1832
Died Feb. 20, 1864

(The old Church site is near James R. Wimberly's home, on Richland Creek.)

## CROCKER CEMETERY

Major William Crocker
Sept. 1, 1777 - June 22, 1835
Mary E. Crocker
Wife of William Crocker
April 25, 1783 - Oct. 20, 1872
Martha Margaret Crocker
Feb. 6, 1813 - Oct. 14, 1825
Martha Howard Crocker
Wife of S. S. Mellon and
Daughter of E. E. and Betsey Crocker
April 3, 1833 - July 27, 1853
Allen Belcher
Died Twiggs County, Ga.
1799 - April 14, 1830
David E. Crocker
Son of
Major Wm. and Mary E. Crocker
March 9, 1818 - March 30, 1862
Henry Peter F. Solomon
Feb. 1, 1842 - Oct. 27, 1842
Col. Elijah Evans Crocker
March 20, 1803 - Sept. 24, 1867
Frances E. Crocker
Wife of David E. Crocker
Daughter of Hardy and Frances Pace
Jan. 9, 1819 - Jan. 3, 1850
James Solomon
Oct. 17, 1800 - March 7, 1842
Henry Solomon
Son of Lazarus Solomon
March 22, 1791 - Jan. 16, 1847
Judge W. L. Solomon
A Mason
Jan. 31, 1834 - May 4, 1895
Avarilla E.
Wife of W. L. Solomon
Born Twiggs County, Ga.
Jan. 20, 1831 - Jan. 1, 1910
Mary E. Solomon
Wife of Shedrick E. Jones
Daughter of
W. L. and Avarilla Solomon
Feb. 7, 1863 - Nov. 10, 1891
Louisa Frances
Second daughter of
Allen and Mary E. Belcher
Jan. 2, 1830 - Oct. 3, 1830
Frances
Second daughter of
Nimrod and Catherine Long
Jan. 15, 1850 - Nov. 22, 1850
Charles Reynolds Faulk
Son of Mark and Nancy Reynolds Faulk
Jan. 24, 1831 - Sept. 23, 1881
Josephine Solomon
Wife of Charles Reynolds Faulk
Daughter of
James and Frances Crocker Solomon
Dec. 29, 1837 - Feb. 23, 1903
Our children:
Chas. Henry Faulk
March 12, 1861 - Aug. 15,
Frances Reynolds Faulk
Jan. 5, 1858 - Aug. 18, 1866
James Mark Faulk
Oct. 4, 1865 - Nov. 20, 1867
Mary Janett Faulk
Aug. 12, 1856 - Dec. 25, 1870

Located west of Jeffersonville about one mile north from the site of Marion Church for Colored.

Copied by Mrs. Kathleen J. Carswell

## DURHAM - WIMBERLY CEMETERY
(Located on State Highway No. 96—3 miles west of Jeffersonville)

Hardy Durham
Sept. 8, 1786 - July 26, 1860
In his 74th year
Sabra Lawson
Wife of Hardy Durham
Died 1871, age 74
  (grave unmarked)
Henry Slappey Wimberly, M.D.
March 26, 1812 - March, 1896
  (grave unmarked)
Caroline Durham
Wife of H. S. Wimberly
July 22, 1817 - Died, 1864
  (grave unmarked)
Durham Ezekiel Wimberly
Son of H. S. and C. Wimberly
Oct. 28, 1834 - Nov. 4, 1835
Polly A.,
Daughter of H. S. and C. Wimberly
July 21, 1852 - April 10, 1859
Durham Ezekiel
Son of H. S. and C. Wimberly
Nov. 8, 1837 - Died 1854
Carrie D.,
Wife of J. D. Jones
Daughter of H. S. and C. Wimberly
Feb. 24, 1850 - March 21, 1874
Charlotte W.
Daughter of J. B. and A. L. W. Taylor
Aged 6 years and 7 months
Alice Lowry Wimberly Taylor
March 28, 1851 - Jan. 18, 1876
  (Data on the unmarked graves was furnished in 1956 by the great granddaughter of Hardy Durham, Mrs. Laura T. Wimberly (Henry G.) Faulk. Copied by Mrs. John Wimberly Faulk).

## DYE CEMETERY

Located in Twiggs County, Georgia, on property now owned by Leonard M. Yaughn, U. S. Highway #129 and 23. The burying ground is out in an open field surrounded by trees. There are other unmarked graves.
Tombstone inscription
James Albert Dye        Born Feb. 10, 1849        Died Dec. 26, 1899
                                        Copied by James Yaughn

## EPPS-CHAMPION CEMETERY

Located across the road from New Haven Church—Bodies reinterred from the original cemetery near Antioch Church due to mining operation.

Hartwell A. Epps
Aug. 16, 1833 - Nov. 21, 1859
Ellis F. Champion
Dec. 25, 1826 - Nov. 22, 1864
Thomas P. Epps
Died Nov. 21, 1859
Age 30 years, 3 months and 24 days
James Thomas
Son of
E. E. and M. A. Champion
Nov. 18, 1856 - Oct. 29, 1858
Copied by:
  Will Hammock &
  B. W. Jones

## FAULK CEMETERY

Mark Faulk, Sen.
1779 - Feb. 3, 1836
Age 56 years
James G. Faulk
March 2, 1814 - March 30, 1847
Age 33 years
Mark Faulk, Jr.
1815 - Jan. 1, 1837
Age 21 years
Henry Faulk
March 19, 1827 - Nov. 7, 1852
Dr. Abraham Garber
Born in Montgomery Co., Penn.
Died in Charleston, S. C.
March 9, 1815 - Aug. 21, 1849
James G.
Son of William and V. Faulk
March 8, 1853 - June 9, 1854

Located on farm of W. T. Faulk on what is known as "Denson Level", ten miles west of Jeffersonville, Old Richland Church road.

## FAULK CEMETERY, "SUNNYSIDE"

George W. Faulk, Sr.
Jan. 31, 1833 - Oct. 19, 1893
Mary Shine Faulk
Wife of George W. Faulk, Sr.
July 23, 1837 - Feb. 18, 1915
Nancy G.
Daughter of G. W. & Mary A. Faulk
March 4, 1862 - Oct. 20, 1870
Sallie V. Faulk
Wife of John T. Land
Daughter of G. W. & Mary A. Faulk
Died March 6, 1877
Age 20 yrs., 5 mos., 19 days
Janette V.
Daughter of G. W. & Mary A. Faulk
Oct. 21, 1881 - July 11, 1882
George W. Faulk, Jr.
Dec. 29, 1863 - Aug. 9, 1911
Ida E.
Wife of G. W. Faulk, Jr.
Dec. 8, 1875 - July 4, 1917

Lottie
Wife of M. S. Faulk
Dec. 4, 1870 - Sept. 23, 1893
Mark Jr.
Son of Mark & Mary Faulk
June 13, 1910 - Feb. 19, 1912
George Watkins
Son of H. G. & L. T. Faulk
May 25, 1902 - Sept. 25, 1907
Henry Glenn
Son of H. G. & L. T. Faulk
July 25, 1904 - Dec. 29, 1905
Laura T. Wimberly
D. A. R. Marker
Wife of Henry G. Faulk
March 26, 1873 - Feb. 9, 1957
Sarah L. Faulk
May 27, 1878 - May 23, 1957
Mary Ella
Wife of J. H. Solomon
Aug. 23, 1869 - Aug. 18, 1895

Cemetery located on old RiRchland Church road about 11 miles west of Jeffersonville, Twiggs County.

Copied by William T. Faulk

## FINCH CEMETERY
(Near Fitzpatrick, Ga.)

John T. Finch
Died, Dec. 19, 1817
Aged 19 years
Infant of
Wm. C. and Louisa Finch
Louisa Finch
Consort of Wm. C. Finch
Died, Oct. 19, 1848
Aged 22 yrs., 8 mos.

Freeman Finch
Died, Jan. 2, 1848
Aged 19 yrs., 11 Mos.
William C. Finch
Died, Feb. 17, 1857
Aged 35 yrs., 10 Mos.
William F. Finch
Died, Sept. 2, 1855
Aged 3 yrs.

Copied by: B. W. Jones

## FITZPATRICK CEMETERY
(Fitzpatrick, Ga.)

Benjamin Smith Fitzpatrick
Feb. 18, 1855 - April 15, 1944
Fleeta Butler Fitzpatrick
Dec. 19, 1860 - May 24, 1936
Infant Son of B. S. and F. B. Fitzpatrick
Oct. 20, 1899 - March 9, 1900
Epsie Lee Miller
Daughter of W. D. and M. E. Miller

Dec. 8, 1888 - Aug. 20, 1900
Infant Son
A. J. and D. H. Epps 1900
Martha L. Epps
Wife of J. C. Epps
July 15, 1827 - Aug. 20, 1891
John C. Epps
Oct. 19, 1812 - Oct. 28, 1865

Alice Jane Davis
1937 - 1944
Willie Bell
Daughter of W. D. and M. E. Miller
Infant, 1901
Mrs. Henrietta Hunnicut
Feb. 16, 1855 - Sept. 18, 1889
Married, Nov. 21, 1886
John Fitzpatrick (Unmarked)
(Statement Geo. Fitzpatrick)

Elizabeth H. Fitzpatrick (Unmarked)
(Statement Geo. Fitzpatrick)
Washington Fitzpatrick (Unmarked)
(Statement Geo. Fitzpatrick)
Henrietta F. Epps
Died March 8, 1811 - Aged 22 years
Lillian Epps
Died Oct. 20, 1851 - Aged 2 yrs., 8 Mos.
Copied by:
    George Fitzpatrick &
    B. W. Jones

## HAMMOCK CEMETERY
(Hammock G.M.D.—near New Haven ChCurch—and the old Hammock Homestead)

James Hammock (Unmarked)
(Statement by Will Hammock)
E. F. Hammock
Mar. 26, 1849 - Sept. 3, 1914
Mary Elizabeth
Daughter of T. E. and W. A. William
   Nov. 28, 1868 - June 8, 1885
Manda L. Hammock
Jan. 30, 1902 - Aug. 3, 1902
John Ivey Kitchens
Feb. 4, 1899 - June 10, 1899
J. H. Combess
1867 - 1890

Mary, wife of E. F. Hammock
Died Oct., 1889—Age 31 years
Mary A. Hammock
July 22, 1893 - Apr. 16, 1925
Lizzie Hammock (Infant)
1904
Andrew Hammock
Mar. 4, 1895 - July 23, 1898
Annie Eurham Kitchens
Oct. 30, 1897 - July 5, 1898
Copies by: Will Hammock and B. W. Jones

## HARRISON FAMILY CEMETERY
(Near New Haven Church)
(McDonald G.M.D.)

Georgia A.
Wife of W. J. Harrison
Nov. 6, 1846 - Feb. 9, 1906

William J. Harrison (C.S.A.)
Co. C, 4 Ga. Inf.
Jan. 17, 1841 - Sept. 6, 1907
Copied by B. W. Jones

## HERRING CEMETERY
Riggins Mill Road, Dry Branch, Georgia

Benjamin Grady Herring
Oct. 28, 1894 - March 10, 1896
Mary Ellen Herring
Nov. 13, 1861 - Sept. 12, 1899
Twin Infants of
J. A. and Mary Ellen Herring
Born July 10, 1899,
Both died the same year
Arthur L. Herring
March 20, 1884 - Jan. 25, 1952

John R. Herring
1822 - Aug. 13, 1904
Mary P. Herring
Died Nov. 11, 1908
John Arthur Herring
Oct. 26, 1861 - May 18, 1927
Lula Martin Herring
April 19, 1876 - April 16, 1947
John Henderson Treadwell
Dec. 14, 1918 - June 25, 1919
Copied by W. R. Herring

## HINSON CEMETERY
(Two miles south of Stone Creek Church)

Elam Hinson, Sr.
1801 - 1875
Elizabeth H. Hinson
1813 - 1892
Maragret Hinson
1766 - 1867
Caleb Hinson
Soldier - War of 1812
1764 - 1845
Charles S. Bowden
Died 1937
Joe L. Simmons
1894 - 1945
George T. Land
1875 - 1952
B. F. Land
1852 - 1938
Mary S. Land
1873 - 1940
Jessie Land
1845 - 1933
J. D. Land
1900 - 1942
Nettie L. Harper
1883 - 1957
Mandy Lyles
1858 - 1931
Aaron Martin (CSA)
1847 - 1928
James E. Mitchum
1870 - 1936
Florence Edna Mitchum
1899 - 1907
Francis Reed
1838 - 1885
Mrs. S. E. Mullis
1840 - 1910
Mrs. Anna Hinson Read
1849 - 1932
Fannie Batts
L. M. Sapp
Billy Manning
1930 - 1938
Paul W. Manning
1906 - 1937

Mary H. Lyles
Died 1912
Laura J. Simmons
1890 - 1957
P. A. Simmons
Ernest Simmons
1924 - 1958
D. W. Simmons
1893 - 1944
Thelma Barnes
W. H. Simmons
1890 - 1958
Ruth Simmons
Thomas Simmons
Gladys Simmons
Ethel M. Hendry
1899 - 1948
Molly W. Ethridge
1892 - 1958
Mary E. Hinson
1860 - 1945
W. C. Bobbitt
1856 - 1936
Emma Hinson Bobbitt
1855 - 1938
A. J. Land, Sr.
1864 - 1953
Mrs. A. J. Land, Sr.
Will D. Durden
Lucrecia H. Simmons
1860 - 1951
J. W. Simmons
1861 - 1938
James F. Hinson
1881 - 1958
Mrs. James F. Hinson
1890 - 1955
James Oscar Bobbitt
(Statement: Mrs. J. B. Reed)
Rosa Raines (unmarked)
Martha Wall (unmarked
Fannie Wall (unmarked)
Copied by:
    Mrs. Bernice L. Jones

## JEFFERSONVILLE CEMETERY, JEFFERSONVILLE, GA.

Mrs. Annie Solomon Adams
Oct. 11, 1873 - Sept. 12, 1944
F. H. Adkins

John Adkins
Ralph David Anderson
Oct. 11, 1917 - Sept. 10, 1958

Will Balcom
Nov. 18, 1881 - Nov. 3, 1904
J. F. Balcom
No date on slab.
Bible date furnished
Feb. 19, 1845 - Dec. 23, 1921
Frank C. Balcom
Oct. 19, 1886 - Oct. 8, 1938
James Heyward Balcom
Jan. 15, 1880 - Feb. 19, 1959
Herschel Balcom
Mrs. Ellen Hughes Balcom
Date from Bible
Feb. 16, 1856 - Jan. 19, 1936
Charlie Bennett
Sept. 5, 1887 - Dec. 11, 1946
Lem Burkett
Mary Lizzie-Mercer Burnes
Jan 18, 1869 - July 12, 1907
R. E. L. Burns
May 8, 1869 - July 29, 1926
James Beall
May 9, 1870 - July 19, 1949
Mollie Brown (J. T.) Beall
June 10, 1848 - June 1, 1935
Clyde H. Bridges
Jan. 4, 1900 - Sept. 5, 1945
Cornelia Methvin Baker
July 30, 1886 - Jan. 17, 1952
John Solomon Baker
Oct. 31, 1870 - March 13, 1950
Mrs. Lucy Solomon Coombs
July 10, 1864 - Feb. 3, 1941
Nannie Storey Chappell
Sept. 20, 1860 - Apr. 13, 1939
Thomas William Chappell
Aug. 28, 1858 - Oct. 22, 1939
Harry E. Califf
May 28, 1908 - Aug. 5, 1957
J. P. Califf
Myrtice Califf
May 7, 1903 - July 10, 1904
A. M. Cranford
1874 - 1952
Arthur Emmett Cochran
April 7, 1884 - Dec. 7, 1884
Clara Maud Cochran
Sept. 27, 1885 - Dec. 27, 1885
Thomas Chivers
April 20, 1802 - July 9, 1874
Mary Ann Califf
June 25, 1844 - Jan 25, 1925

William H. Califf
March 2, 1839 - Aug. 23, 1903
Robert Luther Califf
Aug. 13, 1872 - Dec. 14, 1897
David E. Califf
July 20, 1863 - March 16, 1882
William H. Califf
Sept. 30, 1866 - June 9, 1930
William E. Califf
Aug. 10, 1909 - Feb. 27, 1929
W. H. Califf, III
Sept. 15, 1903 - May 6, 1904
Edith Califf Sanders
Born and Died Sept. 12, 1941
Ava Califf Wall
April 25, 1928 - July 1, 1929
Sarah C. Wall
Jan. 14, 1901 - Feb. 5, 1933
William Jackson Wall
Aug. 2, 1897 - March 26, 1941
W. R. Carswell
Nov. 26, 1881 - Nov. 26, 1911
Anna T. Chapman Carswell
Wife of W. E. Carswell
Oct. 27, 1846 - Oct. 27, 1899
William E. Carswell
Nov. 6, 1836 - Dec. 17, 1901
William E. Carswell
Infant
S. E. Jones
Feb. 7, 1857 - July 27, 1930
Anna Mitt Carswell Jones
July 30, 1873 - Aug. 22, 1944
Laura Carswell Powell
Jan. 13, 1867 - Feb. 3, 1934
James Powell
W. T. Chapman
July 20, 1850 - Sept. 18, 1902
Louisa K. Sinquifield Chapman
(Mrs. W. T. Chapman)
Oct. 23, 1852 - Oct. 7, 1890
John Chapman
Oct. 1, 1888 - Sept. 15, 1893
Anna C. Chapman
Oct. 10, 1834 - June 29, 1868
John Chapman
Jan. 6, 1820 - Oct. 8, 1892
Mary C. Chapman
April 7, 1837 - March 31, 1908
William H. Fitzpatrick
Feb. 22, 1847 - Oct. 14, 1893
Irwin Fitzpatrick
Oct. 2, 1871 - April 18, 1955

Elizabeth M. Fitzpatrick
Jan. 23, 1850 - Oct. 25, 1929
Willie E. Fitzpatrick
Nov. 14, 1893 - Nov. 20, 1893
Icie M. Fitzpatrick
April 5, 1879 - Dec. 5, 1910
Clare B. Fitzpatrick
March 31, 1876 - July 2, 1939
Claudia F. Hendricks
April 13, 1878 - June 8, 1950
Faulk, W. C.
Jan. 12, 1855 - Mar. 7, 1922
Faulk, Alice Jones (Mrs. W. C.)
May 2, 1859 - Apr. 7, 1940
Faulk, Thomas J.
Mar. 9, 1886 - Dec. 23, 1943
Faulk, Shedrick J.
Nov. 8, 1892 - Mar. 27, 1938
Finch, Mary Ann (Mrs. Floyd A.)
Sept. 12. 1829 - Dec. 22, 1897
Finch, William Freeman
July 3, 1862 - Sept. 27, 1910
Finch, Mary Augusta (Mrs. B. F.)
July 13, 1876 - Sept. 24, 1910
Ford, R. M.
1872 - 1936
Ford, Alice (Mrs. R. M.)
1870 - 1936
Gates, Mary Lou (Mrs. J. G.)
Apr. 2, 1841 - Sept 25, 1907
Gates, John G.
Feb. 4, 1828 - Sept. 25, 1905
Gates, J. G.
July 23, 1870 - Dec. 20, 1874
Gallemore, William J.
June 29, 1875 - July 13, 1950
Gates, Albert Martin, Sr.
May 15, 1882 - July 4, 1956
Gates, Willie
Feb. 6, 1860 - Oct. 14, 1879
Gettys, William B.
Nov. 23, 1863 - Jan. 18, 1926
Gettys, Annette Blanton
Nov. 21, 1871 - June 23, 1932
Griffin, L. L.
Feb. 20, 1870 - Oct. 24, 1941
Griffin, Gillie Myrick
Nov. 4, 1872 - June 9, 1948
Griffin, William
Jan. 8, 1825 - Nov. 23, 1884
Griffin, Mary A.
Nov. 26, 1832 - Jan. 11, 1910

Griffin, Eli Shorter, Jr.
Dec. 8, 1878 - Dec. 14, 1897
Griffin, Avarilla M.
May 28, 1877 - Aug. 21, 1879
Griffin, Ardella Jones
1854 - June 15, 1895
Griffin, Eli Shorter
1852 - Nov. 1880
Griffin, Albert Spalding
Mar. 15, 1869 - Dec. 1918
Griffin, Eli Shorter
1829 - 1891
Griffin, Avarila Nash
1831 - 1905
Griffin, J. L., Sr.
_____ - _____
Griffin, J. L., Jr.
_____ - _____
Griffin, W. Louis
Feb. 7, 1887 - Nov. 26, 1918
Griffin, Henry Faulk
Mar. 7, 1919 - Mar. 24, 1953
    Cpl. At. Co., 121st Infantry
Glover, Mary A.
Mar. 12, 1840 - Feb. 17, 1884
Glover, John
Feb. 10, 1801 - Feb. 10, 1865
Hamrick, Claude F.
1893 - 1950
Harrell, J. L.
Sept. 25, 1820 - May 10, 1893
Harrison, Richard Augustus
Oct. 25, 1886 - Feb. 20, 1956
Hamrick, Mary Etta
March 28, 1889 - Dec. 10, 1947
Huff, Wilford G., Dr.
Nov. 30, 1880 - Aug. 21, 1941
Horne, Will F.

Higgs, Anna
_____ - Age 68
Huckabee, Jewette W.
_____ - _____
Huckabee, Stella M.
_____ - _____
Hudgins, Mrs. Minnie L.
_____ - _____
Hudgins, H. B.
_____ - _____
Hatcher, John Will, Jr.
June 27, 1922 - July 9, 1924
Hatcher, John Will, Sr.
June 26, 1886 - Dec. 16, 1922

Hatcher, Linton
Nov. 22, 1855 - Mar. 18, 1934
Hunt, O. S.

Hughes, Mrs. Heyward

Latson, Elva Jean Cowart
_____ - 1916
Libby, Nancy A.

Libby, Charlie

Latimer, Hugh M. (Infant)

Larsen, Margaret VanDyke
Mar. 27, 1883 - Apr. 3, 1956
Lyles, Mrs. Belle Crosby

Martin, Augustus, Franklin, Sr.
May 19, 1852 - Feb. 25, 1926
Martin, Mrs. Mollie Denson
Aug. 5, 1867 - Sept 1, 1887
Martin, John Denson
Sept. 22, 1886 - Aug. 30, 1906
Martin, A. F., Jr.
Mar. 6, 1885 - Nov. 24, 1932
Martin, Mrs. Sallie Reynolds
July 27, 1862 - June 18, 1946
Martin, Louise (Infant)
Oct. 19, 1913 - June 15, 1914
Martin, Lucia (Infant)
1896 - 1896
Martin, Herman R.
1890 - 1892
Martin, William Reynolds
1899 - 1899
Martin, Will

Norris, Corris Van Diviere (Mrs. R.B.)
June 17, 1866 - Oct. 31, 1930
Norris, Robert Brown
Feb. 27, 1859 - Aug. 10, 1947
Oxford, Thelma Pickett
Aug. 3, 1907 - June 16, 1955
Pettis, Dr. M. L.
Apr. 17, 1852 - May 17, 1889
Pettis, E. F.
May 8, 1847 - June 29, 1905
Pettis, Joannah Neal
Dec. 18, 1842 - Mar. 26, 1917
Jones, Elias
  (Unmarked—Statement Mrs. Estelte J. Balcom)

Jones, Mary
  Unmarked—(Statement of Mrs. Estelle J. Balcom)

Jones, Edwin
  Unmarked—(Statement of Mrs. Estelle Jones Balcom)
Jones, Stephen
Aug. 29, 1841 - Dec. 6, 1911
Jones, Belle Cook
Apr. 16, 1849 - Jan. 15, 1925
Jones, Clarence
Apr. 6, 1872 - Jan. 14, 1897
Jones, Mattie Dee
Apr. 7, 1877 - Oct. 20, 1905
Jackson, Irvin F., Sr.
June 10, 1895 - Sept. 9, 1952
Jackson, William Mark
May 19, 1886 - July 8, 1953
Jackson, Lois Eloise
Oct. 28, 1895 - Nov. 15, 1940
Jackson, Hugh V.
Oct. 6, 1883 - Oct. 4, 1948
Jackson, Sarah C.
Aug. 6, 1916 - June 6, 1917
Jackson, Randall A.
Feb. 20, 1860 - Feb. 9, 1927
Johnston, Francis M.
1862 - 1892
Johnston, Cordelia Alvod
1869 - 1915
Johnston, Mary L. Hunter
Aug. 4, 1860 - Apr. 15, 1933
Johnston, C. Y.
Nov. 8, 1859 - Nov. 4, 1931
One infant grave in Johnston Lot
Johnson, Mollie
Nov. 24, 1871 - Sept. 25, 1903
Johnson, Mollie Jewel
Nov. 24, 1900 - Aug. 20, 1903
Johnson, J. H.
(Unmarked)
Johnson, Mrs. (Mother of Mollie
  Johnson) Unmarked
McCallum, Carrie
_____ - Mar. 20, 1933
McCallum, James Archibald
Nov. 28, 1871 - June 10, 1949
McCallum, Kate Storey
Mar. 14, 1869 - Aug. 29, 1955
Infant son of

McCallum, H. A. & Mary Faulk
Dec. 3, 1934 - Dec. 3, 1934
McWilliams, James A.
Apr. 1, 1889 - July 6, 1954
McInnis, James, his wife Delpria
  Chives
Jan. 23, 1802 - Feb. 14, 1877
McCoy, Mary Ann Mercer
Oct. 13, 1850 - Nov. 27, 1912
McCoy, James Thomas
Dec. 6, 1838 - Mar. 24, 1912
Methvin, Leland S.
July 27, 1894 - Sept. 16, 1947
Methvin, Florine Whitehurst
Sept. 20, 1896 - Mar. 30, 1948
Methvin, Thomas Eugene
Aug. 27, 1888 - Apr. 9, 1947
Methvin, William Horne
Feb. 8, 1900 - Nov. 6, 1954
Methvin, Paul
Aug. 16, 1908 - July 11, 1958
Smith, Allen Kirby
June 4, 1892 - Dec. 8, 1953
Solomon, Cicero A.
June 22, 1835 - Nov. 23, 1883
Sarah F. Zachry
  Wife of C. A. Solomon
June 9, 1831 - Jan. 27, 1900
Jehue O. Marcy
Aug. 2, 1861 - Sept. 16, 1890
Ira Dupree Jones, Infant son of
  John H. & Mattie C. Jones
Apr. 26, 1877, age 6 yrs., 4 mos.
Reynolds, W. T.
(Unmarked)

———— - ————

Reynolds, Laura Hughes
(Unmarked)

———— - ————

Reynolds, Mrs. Ida Hughes
Dec. 8, 1858 - May 7, 1892
Singquifield, Amanda J. Parker
Feb. 18, 1824 - Mar. 3, 1900
Solomon, John Henry
June 17, 1864 - Jan. 2, 1929
Solomon, Miss Jack
May 11, 1860 - Aug. 6, 1919
Solomon, John H.
(Unmarked)

———— - ————

Solomon, W. M.
(Unmarked)

———— - ————

Solomon, Miss Pearl
(Unmarked)

———— - ————

Solomon, Mrs. Josie Whitehurst
(Unmarked)

———— - ————

Smith, Amy E.
1868 - Mar. 6, 1919
Slappey, Robert R., Sr.
1877 - 1931
Slappey, Lucy Locke
1881 - 1939
Slappey, Robert R., Jr.
  WW I, Ga. Sgt. Army Air Force
May 17, 1903 - Sept. 9, 1956
Stevens, Josiah
(Unmarked)

———— - ————

Shannon, John Carey, Sr.
July 22, 1857 - Dec. 3, 1929
Shannon, Mary Lou Faulk (wife
  J. C. Shannon)
June 20, 1858 - Feb. 13, 1937
Shannon, Bertha Wall
May 26, 1886 - Feb. 13, 1935
Shannon, William Faulk
Apr. 4, 1886 - July 17, 1937
Shannon, James Douglas, Atty.
June, 1889 - July 27, 1959
(Rev.) Steeley, W. R.
1818 - Oct. 13, 1890 (age 72)
Toney, L. M.
1873 - 1928
Thomas, J. G.
Aug. 10, 1851 - Mar. 22, 1918
Thomas, Mrs. J. G. & Son
(Unmarked)

———— - ————

  (Double Grave—killed by
  Lightning)
Varner, Mrs. Annie E. Killebrew
  (Forest G. Varner)
Dec. 29, 1872 - Nov. 6, 1917
Vaughn, Jack S, Sr.
———— - Feb. 24, 1924
Vaughn, Susan Johnston
Jan. 11, 1864 - Jan. 17, 1954
Vaughn, John H.
Jan. 26, 1878 - Dec. 18, 1950
Vaughn, Mary Lou Harrell
July 31, 1882 - Dec. 21, 1954
Vaughn, Harry
(Unmarked)

Whitehurst, W. M.
1875 - 1944
Whitehurst, Elizabeth Miss
(Unmarked)

———— - ————

Whitehurst, James H.
Feb. 25, 1877 - Apr. 21, 1951
Whitehurst, Joe

———— - ————

Whitehurst, Mrs. Mamie Balcom

———— - ————

Wester, John Henry
Mar. 27, 1876 - July 14, 1917
Wimberly, Gus
(Unmarked)

———— - ————

Beckcom, Ella Gena
———— - Jan. 14, 1954
Beckcom, Allen Franklin
Dec. 23, 1837 - June 21, 1910
Johnson, Lee Clifford
May 14, 1860 - Jan. 6, 1896
Johnson, Ella Wiggins
May 27, 1840 - Oct. 11, 1911
Berry, Walter S.
Oct. 8, 1863 - Oct. 9, 1864
Berry, J. F., Rev.
Sept. 6, 1837 - Sept. 5, 1866
  (Killed by Lightning)
Bell, Mrs. Janie
(Unmarked)

———— - ————

Dupree, Elliott Moore
8 yrs., 6 mos.
Dupree, Ira E.
Apr. 23, 1800 - Mar. 17, 1869
Dupree, Fannie Bryan, wife of Ira
  E. Dupree
Nov. 18, 1815 - June 19, 1885
Dupree, Sarah T.
Died June 23, 1853 (Age 15 yrs.)
Joyner, Andrew L.
May 10, 1816 - Nov. 21, 1854
Love, George O.
July 20, 1893 - Dec. 30, 1947
Horne, Emily
Mar. 14, 1840 - Dec. 13, 1866
Goins, Lillie B.
    (J. C. & A. E. Goins)
    2 Adult Graves
(Unmarked)
Raleigh, Mrs. Belle Harrell
(Unmarked)

Jones, Dr. Thomas S.
Aug. 21, 1864 - Feb. 16, 1926
Jones, Mrs. Grace C. (wife, T. S. Jones)
Aug. 20, 1869 - Feb. 15, 1952
Jones, Georgia Burns
  (Wife, T. S. Jones)
Apr. 5, 1872 - Sept. 4, 1891
Jones, Eunice Harrell
Apr. 13, 1886 - July 28, 1941
Jones, Stephen Harrell
Jan. 5, 1912 - Jan. 20, 1930
Harrell, W. H., Sr.
Dec. 25, 1856 - Jan. 6, 1918
Harrell, Josephine V. Everett
Dec. 14, 1854 - Sept. 23, 1933
Harrell, Cleo Belle
———— - Aug. 1, 1896
Vaughn, Bill Snookey
Nov. 10, 1913 - July 25, 1921
Methvin, Ernest H.
———— - Mar. 17, 1939
Methvin, Charlie E.
1890 - 1916
Methvin, Eugenia Carswell
Oct. 10, 1864 - July 25, 1916
Methvin, Thomas Eugene
Dec. 8, 1862 - Jan. 25, 1916
  (4 Infants' Graves)
Mims, Mamie Cornelius
July 13, 1870 - Mar. 27, 1957
Carswell, Mary Lou Carswell Slappey
Aug. 24, 1866 - Dec. 11, 1948
Carswell, Willie Eliz. Mims
July 10, 1865 - Oct. 25, 1896
Carswell, Dewitt
Jan. 26, 1866 - Apr. 11, 1906
Carswell, Mattie R.
Aug. 4, 1851 - June 11, 1914
Carswell, Dr. E. S.
Nov. 20, 1830 - June 2, 1895
Mrs. Dykes
(Unmarked)
Everett, Leila Carswell
1826 - 1912
Mrs. Blizzard

———— - ————

Clance, Mrs. Ed.

———— - ————

Griffin, William Louis
Feb. 7, 1887 - Nov. 26, 1918
Griffin, Sarah Estelle Glover
Mar. 7, 1864 - Jan. 29, 1935

Griffin, Henry Faulk
Jan. 6, 1859 - Nov. 9, 1926
Griffin, Henry Faulk, Jr.
Aug. 13, 1884 - Mar. 19, 1954
Glover, Henry Grady
Mar. 1, 1888 - Nov. 10, 1896
Glover, A. John
Apr. 6, 1860 - Aug. 2, 1892
Hunt, O. S.
1883 - 1957
Methvin, Will
Nov. 14, 1868 - Mar. 11, 1936
Methvin, Jennie Griffin
Oct. 21, 1871 - July 12, 1955
Methvin, Jimmy
Mar. 9, 1940 - Mar. 15, 1940
Methvin, William
July 13, 1804 - July 30, 1869
Methvin, Emily Minnie
July 25, 1863 - Sept. 1, 1868
Watson, Norma Jean
May 14, 1956 - Feb. 6, 1958
Lindsey, Martha A.
Sept. 30, 1846 - Jan. 28, 1924
Lindsey, Green J.
Oct. 17, 1840 - Dec. 12, 1920
McDonald, Cordelie E. Jones
    Wife of J. E. McDonald
Oct. 20, 1848 - Aug. 12, 1926
Sims, Annie Bowen
Apr. 10, 1844 - July 25, 1928
Sims, Orphelia
Jan. 21, 1894 - Feb. 11, 1900
McCrary, H. W.
Mar. 23, 1858 - Mar. 22, 1915
McCrary, Walter H.
Oct. 17, 1880 - Apr. 17, 1939
McCrary, Mattie Jane
Sept. 21, 1852 - Jan. 26, 1918
McCrary, Mary Yancey Griffin
Mar. 18, 1882 - June 6, 1909
Marchman, Will
(Unmarked)

---

Thornton, Lucile McCrary
Feb. 23, 1886 - Feb. 25, 1942
McDonald, Cordelia Laney
1847 - 1872
McDonald, James D.
Apr. 4, 1818 - Aug. 20, 1870
McDonald, Laney Field
    (Wife of J. D. McDonald)
Feb. 20, 1816 - Aug. 10, 1886

Patterson, Lucy Mildred
Dec. 15, 1898 - June 3, 1900
Nelson, Ruth Rose Wheeler
    Wife of Theodore Nelson, Chicago, Ill. & daughter of Grattan H. Wheeler, Steven Co., N. Y.
Apr. 5, 1831 - Nov. 24, 1891
Nichols, Lula C. Martin
1883 - 1950
Renfore, Thomas J.
Sept. 15, 1853 - Nov. 17, 1885
Thornton, P. J.
1860 - 1944
Thornton, Willie Harrell
1876 - 1956
Rooks, Green P., Co. K., 11 Ga.
    Inf., C. S. A.
George, Edwin Henry
1910 - 1947
Snow, Fla Tau
May 14, 1906 - Jan. 18, 1915
Snow, Geo. F.
1867 - 1938
Slappey, Mrs. Mary Coffee
Apr. 10, 1867 - July 17, 1951
Slappey, J. G. (M.D.)
Feb. 26, 1853 - June 27, 1932
Slappey, Nancy Exom
Mar. 3, 1905 - Nov. 11, 1923
Slappey, Peter Harrison
Dec. 12, 1907 - Jan. 12, 1908
Self, E. L.
Nov. 22, 1865 - Jan. 12, 1941
Self, Nancy Jane
Dec. 9, 1879 - Oct. 26, 1958
Self, L. J.
Feb. 18, 1919 - Jan. 9, 1942
    (War Service—Battle-lost at sea)
Shannon, John Carey
Apr. 1, 1880 - Feb. 13, 1948
Slappey, Fred
(Unmarked)

---

Slappey, Mrs. Fred
(Unmarked)

---

Whitehurst, Mamie Balkcom
June 14, 1877 - July 18, 1953
Whitehurst, Joel
Jan. 6, 1873 - Apr. 4, 1922
Garner, Ida Parrott
1891 - 1947

Parrott, L. W., Rev.
Oct. 5, 1853 - Oct. 13, 1908
  Dates furnished by dau., Mrs. J. C. Shannon)
Wimberly, Ezekiel Turner
Sept. 2, 1863 - June 17, 1946
Wimberly, Jennie King
June 13, 1876 - Nov. 12, 1957
Wimberly, Ezekiel Jenkins
Mar. 29, 1904 - Dec. 11, 1951
Walker, W. H.
White, James I., Jr.
Jan. 17, 1900 - Mar. 24, 1944
White, John Gates
Aug. 19, 1896 - _____
White, Mamie Gates
Sept. 6, 1873 - Jan. 15, 1920
White, James Ira
May 14, 1872 - July 26, 1920
Walters, Henry M.
July 15, 1932 - Nov. 22, 1959

Walters, Mary Nell
Mar. 25, 1918 - Mar. 21, 1931
Wood, Addie Hatcher
Aug. 21, 1881 - Feb. 20, 1958
Wood, William Walker
July 23, 1882 - Sept. 21, 1946
Wood, Linton Hatcher
Aug. 31, 1917 - Dec. 10, 1948
McNair, Josephine Pope
Sept. 10, 1841 - Feb. 17, 1926
McNair, Dr. Ezekiel
Aug. 14, 1849 - Sept. 16, 1913
Jackson, Emily McNair
Apr. 11, 1884 - July 5, 1952
Jackson, George W.
Feb. 22, 1880 - Jan. 5, 1934
McNair, Idus Lafayette
Jan. 26, 1874 - Feb. 13, 1953
McNair, Julia Hinton
Apr. 13, 1868 - Jan. 4, 1956

Cemetery record copied by Miss Clyde Martin and Mrs. Irene Martin Rockmore.

## JONES-DENSON CEMETERY
(U. S. Hwy. 80 at Ripley)

John Jones, Revolutionary Soldier
1753 - 1800 (D.A.R. marker)
John Walker Jones
Jan. 23, 1866 - Nov. 23, 1933
Laura Leone Jones
April 12, 1900 - Sept. 17, 1900
John Walker Jones, Jr.
March 15, 1895 - Oct. 5, 1895
Mattie Clyde Jones
July 24, 1891 - Sept. 8, 1895
Claude Leone Jones
    Wife of John Walker Jones
July 12, 1870 - April 30, 1900
Mary, wife of Maj. Thomas S. Jones,
    Daughter of Wm. A. Cowan
Dec .18, 1822 - Nov .23, 1910
Maj. Thomas S. Jones
Dec. 10, 1818 - Aug. 27, 1872
Stephen Jones
Jan. 22, 1849 - aged 65 yrs.
Infant T. S. J.
Stephen, son of Maj. T. S. & Mary C.
    Jones—Died Sept. 20, 1852
Bennie, son of Maj. T. S. & Mary C.
    Jones—Died Jan. 8, 1871
William, son of Maj. T. S. & Mary C.
    Jones—Died Mar. 23, 1873

John Faulk Land
Sept. 1, 1877 - Dec. 27, 1880
Henry Solomon Denson
Mar. 5, 1871 - Mar. 10, 1939
Florence Rogers Denson
Died June 12, 1932
N. Amelia—Consort of Wm. J. Henry
    Dau. J. H. & E. Denson
Nov., 1825 - Sept. 10, 1851
Margaret Stuckey Denson
Mar. 22, 1865 - Aug. 5, 1891
Dr. Elias Jones Denson
Sept. 21, 1843 - Aug. 17, 1927
Melissa Read Denson
Oct. 13, 1846 - July 26, 1878
John H. Denson
June 14, 1806 - Oct. 24, 1893
Elizabeth Denson
Dec. 10, 1810 - Jan. 17, 1896
John Horne Denson
Nov. 20, 1887 - July 6, 1943
Hazel Elizabeth
    Dau. W. A. & M. L. Denson
1891 - 1896
William A. Denson
Sept. 4, 1856 - June 11, 1897

Martha Leila Denson
Aug. 27, 1860 - Feb. 2, 1932
William A., son, W. A. & M. L. Denson
1897 - 1898
Ella Durden Day
1862 - 1954
John J. Day (Infant)
1906 - 1907

John Day
Aug., 1869 - Mar., 1936
Infant daughter, John & M. Day
Apr. 7, 1903
Stephen Duanne, son of John &
   Carolyn Simmons
1956

Copied by: Mrs. Kathleen J. Carswell and Mrs. Bernice L. Jones.

## JONES-PEARCE CEMETERY
(Hwy. 80—5 mi. South Dry Branch)

Note: An old deed held by R. M. Wood, Sr. refers to this cemetery as the Jones Cemetery, but no visual markings are Jones. Indications of several unmarked graves are evident.

Emma Jane Epps
Wife of W. R. Pearce
Nov. 10, 1857
Oscar Pearce (Unmarked)
(Statement of R. M. Wood, Sr.)
Mattie Tharpe Jones (Unmarked)
(Statement of C. E. Mercer)

Tom Jones (Unmarked)
(Statement of C. E. Mercer)
Charles R. Wrights
Died May 22, 1849
John Pearce (Unmarked)
(Statement of R. M. Wood, Sr.)
Viola Epps Jones (Unmarked)
(Statement of C. E. Mercer)

Copied by: B. W. Jones and Mrs. Kathleen J. Carswell.

## LIBERTY HILL METHODIST CHURCH CEMETERY

Levi Mathis
1818 - 1901
Sarah E. Mathis
1829 - 1882
William F. Bryant
Jan. 27, 1887 - Apr. 27, 1957
John Birdsong
Mar. 31, 1857 - Jan. 2, 1909
Mary M. Birdsong
Aug. 19, 1855 - Feb. 2, 1930
C. Walker Birdsong
Nov. 17, 1890 - Aug. 8, 1939
Jim T. Cannon
Born 1877
Susie B. Cannon
1878 - 1948
John Henry Martin
1905 - 1959
Mary Ellen Martin, infant
1949
Dudley M. Griffin
Son of L. L. & C. E. Griffin
1908 - 1909
James R. Kelley
Co. B, 14 Ga. Inf., CSA
L. C. Griffin
1932 - 1933

Edgar W. Griffin
1898 - 1901
Robert S. Griffin
Dec. 4, 1860 - Jan. 10, 1937
Vera Griffin Cannon
Mar. 4, 1898 - Apr. 17, 1921
Emma G. Shepherd
Aug. 20, 1894 - Nov. 14, 1956
Mrs. Carl Balkcom
1925 - 1951
Newton Sanders
8 Ga. Mil., CSA
Children of B. A. & M. B. Reddick
Died 1905 - and died 1906
Georgia S. Cannon
Nov. 20, 1854 - Nov. 6, 1938
John F. Cannon
Sept. 7, 1854 - Apr. 24, 1926
E. S. Sapp
Mrs. A. A. Brantley
1910 - 1939
Mary E. Griffin
Oct. 26, 1911 - Mar. 7. 1927
James Barrentine
Co. I, 26th Ga. Inf., CSA

Wilson Barrington
Co. I, 26th Ga. Inf., CSA
Sarah Sanders
Wife of Wilson Barrington
Feb. 19, 1845 - Apr. 3, 1929
Henry F. Barrentine
Died Oct. 10, 1920, age 2 yrs.
Horace E. Hammock
Nov. 9, 1896 - Jan. 7, 1940
Virginia Barrentine
Wife of Marcus L. Hammock
Sept. 10, 1866 - Oct. 5, 1944
George Frank Cannon
Apr. 28, 1875 - Dec. 19, 1942
Leila Holland Cannon
July 20, 1877 - Mar. 17, 1946
Inft. Dau. G. F. & Leila Cannon
Mar. 4, 1926
Henry L. Griffin
1856 - 1888
Benjamin Parker
Co. G, 48th Ga. Inf., CSA

Will P. Parker
1872 - 1955
Mrs. Mollie Parker
Died Feb. 10, 1926
J. H. Parker
1872 - 1953
Sidney Birdsong
1894 - 1931
Willie Jones
1925 - 1927
William Jones (infant)
1933
Bertha Jones
1931 - 1935
William B. Jones
July 27, 1887 - Dec. 24, 1945
Mary P. Jones
1895 - 1958
Infant of
Mr. and Mrs. G. M. Dewberry
Infant of
Mr. and Mrs. J. Wood
    Copied by: Mrs. Bernice L. Jones

## MARION CEMETERY

Peter LaBree
October 14, 1822
Brentwood, N. H.

Died aged 36 years
He leaves a wife and three children
to mourn his death.

Copied by Mrs. Ethel Shannon Butler.
(Located at site of Marion, former county seat.)

## MERCER CEMETERY
(Near Myricks Mill)

Thomas Moore
July 18, 1779 - Feb. 18, 1861
Alma Ward Mercer
1878 - 1937
Jones Ira Mercer
1880 - 1939
Mary Wood Mercer
2nd Wife John P. Mercer
Died Jan., 1935, Age 77
(Statement C. E. Mercer)
Ella Mercer
Dau. J. P. & M. E. Mercer
(Statement C. E. Mercer)
Clarence Mercer
Child, J. P. & M. E. Mercer
(Statement C. E. Mercer)
Lucile Sanders Mercer

Apr. 1, 1889 - March 31, 1958
William Garner Mercer
Sept. 4, 1875 - Aug. 24, 1943
Inf. Dau. C. C. & Martha Mercer
(Statement C. E. Mercer)
John Pink Mercer (C.S.A.)
Dec. 16, 1844 - June 25, 1911
Mary Eliza Mercer
Feb. 24, 1850 - Feb. 24, 1890
Lula Mercer
Dau. J. P. & M. E. Mercer
(Statement C. E. Mercer)
Charlie Callaway
Wife of Thomas H. Mercer
Nov. 11, 1876 - June 12, 1942
Thomas H. Mercer
Aug. 17, 1873 - Oct. 15, 1916

    Copied by: C. E. Mercer and B. W. Jones

## MT. ZION BAPTIST CHURCH CEMETERY
(Near Danville, Georgia)

J. S. Fowler, Jr.
Oct. 3, 1918 - Sept. 20, 1920
H. L. Lucas
Jan. 7, 1850 - Sept. 4, 1935
Smithie Pope Lucas
———— - June 5, 1923
William H. Moore
1888 - 1954
Sandra Baggarly
Jan. 7, 1945 - Feb. 2, 1945
Lizzie Viola Joiner
1875 - 1945
William Daniel Fowler
———— - Apr. 14, 1952
Infant son of Mr. and Mrs. J. H. Lee
———— - ————
Mrs. J. H. Lee
Feb. 1, 1896 - Mar. 20, 1946
George Lucas, Jr.
A. H. Arnold
Mar 6, 1889 - Feb. 2, 1940
John L. Lucas
———— - June 17, 1921
Lillie May Pettis
Nov. 6, 1894 - Aug. 14, 1931
Mrs. Terrel V. Pettis
June 23, 1877 - June 26, 1958
Terrell V. Pettis
1885 - 1956
Mildred Florine Brown
Sept. 29, 1929 - Sept 30, 1931
Lee R. Morgan
May 7, 1910 - Oct. 13, 1958
J. W. Pettis
———— - May 1, 1946
Infant son of Mr. & Mrs. Dempsey Lynn
Oct. 29, 1954 - Oct. 29, 1954
Jack Lynn
Feb. 23, 1944 - Mar. 26, 1945
Dempsey Lynn
May 15, 1920 - Oct. 31, 1954
Clarence O. Asbell
May 1, 1881 - Feb. 19, 1958
Georgia Ann Davis Asbell
Feb. 27, 1860 - Jan 2, 1940
Emmett V. Asbell
1871 - 1948
Mack C. Arnold
1871 - 1951

Joseph Jefferson Arnold
Nov. 18, 1867 - Oct. 9, 1929
Andrew Hobson Arnold
Aug. 3, 1898 - Apr. 28, 1918
Fannie Lee Phillips
July 11, 1895 - Nov. 29, 1950
Jim J. Phillips
Mar. 30, 1891 - Jan 4, 1957
Velma Phillips Little
Feb. 9, 1916 - Dec. 4, 1956
J. Lewis Spears
Nov. 24, 1852 - July 5, 1905
Margarete Spears
Apr. 30, 1851 - July 21, 1924
John E. Spears
Sept. 28, 1876 - Apr. 7, 1903
Shelton Spears
Sept. 11, 1885 - Apr. 5, 1904
Carroll Spears
Oct., 1888 - Mar., 1905
Robert Sanders Stevens
May 16, 1947 - May 27, 1947
Infant son of Mr. and Mrs. J. J. Lee
———— - Jan., 1910
Julian S. Lee
Oct. 7, 1877 - Feb. 3, 1949
Julian Lee
Apr. 17, 1938 - Apr. 19, 1938
Gurnith Smith Lee
Nov. 13, 1909 - June 27, 1942
Robert Olin Carroll
Aug. 20, 1901 - Apr. 22, 1907
Molly Raley Carroll
Aug. 20, 1874 - Sept. 15, 1948
R. E. Carroll
Sept. 15, 1875 - Dec. 19, 1911
Thelma Florine Phillips
Sept. 7, 1926 - Aug. 13, 1932
Earl Spears
Nov. 26, 1896 - June 9, 1928
Eula C. Spears
July 22, 1886 - Apr. 7, 1920
Reuben G. Sanders
Aug. 2, 1886 - May 20, 1949
George B. Newby
July 19, 1908 - June 18, 1957
David F. Brown
Feb. 1, 1867 - Jan. 4, 1945
Della W. Brown
1876 - 1958

Carrie Stevens Ham
May 18, 1884 - Jan. 3, 1944
Infant son of Mr. & Mrs. H. H. Newby
June 8, 1934 - June 8, 1934
Infant of Mr. & Mrs. H. H. Newby
Sept. 19, 1937 - Sept. 20, 1937
Annie Lou Little
Aug. 3, 1880 - Nov. 26, 1940
Walter J. Smith
Apr. 22, 1904 - Aug. 10, 1948
Joseph Stanley Arnold
July 2, 1913 - Aug. 13, 1914
Flois Evelyn Smith
1931 - 1932
H. J. Chance, Sr.
May 5, 1900 - Jan. 4, 1953
J. C. Chance
1852 - 1940
Margie Reynolds Chance
Mar. 15, 1858 - Apr. 28, 1935
Averett Union Ham
1877 - 1955
Patricia Ann Carter
Oct. 6, 1950 - Oct. 6, 1950
W. H. Carter
Oct. 3, 1936 - 1936
Infant son of Mr. & Mrs. L. F. Brewer
Oct. 1, 1945 - Jan. 1, 1946
Mrs. Sallie Fowler
1875 - 1955
Dudley Carter
1899 - 1955
Romie Carter Pope
Sept. 12, 1888 - Sept. 1945
John Pope
_____ - _____
Donnie Chance Carter
_____ - 1916
John B. Carter
1892 - 1948
Plural Carter
_____ - Oct. 1, 1918
Twin daughters of Mr. & Mrs. Edison Dominey
_____ - Oct. 5, 1955
Moscus Eugene Snipes
Nov. 13, 1934 - Nov. 16, 1934
Cora Lee Edge Carter
Oct. 7, 1900 - Oct. 23, 1950
Ruthie Carter
Oct. 16, 1922 - Sept 10, 1926
Willie Carter
Jan. 19, 1925 - Sept. 3, 1929

Lillie B. Lucas Carter
1901 - 1945
Leo Davis, Jr.
Died Aug. 18, 1938
Ethel D. Fowler
Oct. 29, 1911 - Jan. 26, 1953
Lois Fowler
Jan. 9, 1919 - June 30, 1951
Mary Lee Fowler
Mar., 1929 - June, 1930
Summerday Infant
_____ - Aug. 26, 1954
F. F. Fowler
Apr. 26, 1878 - Jan. 11, 1944
Annie Mae Fowler
July 17, 1928 - Feb. 13, 1936
Allie Fowler
Jan. 2, 1855 - Nov. 13, 1910
William H. Fowler
Nov. 30, 1853 - June 9, 1936
Fannie William Fowler
Oct. 7, 1863 - May 29, 1918
Henry Franklin Fowler
June 22, 1932 - Jan. 27, 1934
Blanche Hill Carswell
Sept. 7, 1883 - July 27, 1913
J. T. Hill
Mar. 24, 1879 - Aug. 13, 1930
Egbert W. Hill
Apr. 4, 1847 - Nov. 28, 1900
India Iola Lee
May 27, 1886 - Feb. 23, 1932
C. H. Lee
Mar. 16, 1883 - Oct. 26, 1918
W. H. Lee
Oct., 1904 - Feb., 1936
Vance Lee
June, 1906 - Apr., 1937
Edgar Lee Hill
Sept. 1, 1875 - Sept. 3, 1953
Carrie Jane Hill
Oct. 5, 1873 - Dec. 9, 1942
Minnie L. Hill
Jan. 1, 1864 - Sept. 7, 1937
Robert H. Yopp
Feb. 29, 1892 - June 10, 1944
Nellie White
May 19, 1887 - Feb. 20, 1913
Sam W. Yopp
May 12, 1854 - Aug. 4, 1913
Ellen Yopp
Mar. 30, 1864 - May 23, 1926

S. T. Hill
Aug. 10, 1836 - Feb. 21, 1875
Robert A. Hill
Nov. 11, 1821 - Aug. 28, 1880
Thomas G. Hill
Oct. 30, 1827 - May 3, 1885
Olive E. Tindall
May 3, 1858 - May 12, 1937
Lettie J. Tindall
Aug. 5, 1817 - Mar. 19, 1892
Thomas D. Tindall
May 25, 1856 - Sept. 28, 1915
Hennie H. Tindall
Mar. 24, 1893 - June 10, 1894
Charlie S. Tindall
Feb. 21, 1892 - Mar 26, 1892
Myrtle Yopp
June 6, 1892 - Aug. 19, 1894
Ellen A. White
Dec. 1, 1907 - Aug. 22, 1908
Louisa Shenod
Dec. 27, 1809 - Dec. 24, 1893

Charity Maxwell
Feb. 14, 1845 - Apr. 29, 1902
J. B. Johnston, Jr.
Aug. 27, 1903 - Jan. 14, 1904
Leona Johnston
Aug. 18, 1870 - July 11, 1899
Bonnie Leone Johnston
July 4, 1899 - Sept. 11, 1899
William C. Chance
_____ - 1918
Carrie Lee Chance
_____ - _____
Zilphia Floyd Chance
June 16, 1874 - Jan. 22, 1938
Sadie M. Hasty
Mar. 6, 1874 - Nov. 18, 1958
C. H. Hasty
_____ - Dec. 26, 1937
Mary Missouri Hasty
1832 - Feb. 8, 1910
Daniel Alfred Hasty
Mar. 4, 1876 - Nov. 18, 1891
Grave of Phillip Bryant, slave of William C. Chance

## NELSON CEMETERY
(Near Dry Branch, Ga.)

Willie C. Tharp
Son of W. D. & M. M. Tharpe
Sept. 12, 1883 - Sept. 5, 1909
Augustus F.
Son of B. C. & M. M. Tharp
June 12, 1897 - Jan. 24, 1898
Julius E. Rice
Nov. 27, 1866 - Apr. 19, 1927
Martha F. Nelson
Wife of Dr. T. M. C. Rice
Apr. 21, 1843 - May 22, 1915
S. L. Nelson
Jan. 25, 1837 - May 25, 1882
Lena R.
Daughter of B. C. & M. M. Tharp
Sept. 28, 1895 - June 9, 1896
Wilbur J. Nelson
Apr. 25, 1863 - Mar. 5, 1883
Bertha J. Rice
Feb. 18, 1883 - July 26, 1887
Infant son Rice
Dec. 30, 1869 - Dec. 30, 1869
Mary Emma Rice
Feb. 10, 1869 - Feb. 17, 1869

T. M. C. Rice, M. D.
Sept. 10, 1836 - Mar. 26, 1890
Sally Fanny Rice
June 4, 1860 - Aug. 29, 1884
Lavinia Chappell
Who departed this life
April 14, 1851—aged 83 yrs, 6 mo.
J. M. Nelson
May 16, 1838 - July 1, 1862
Franklin C. Nelson
Feb. 9, 1832 - Nov. 9, 1870
Hartwell A. Nelson
Aug. 6, 1883 - May 9, 1896
Nancy H. S. Nelson
Jan. 18, 1822 - Sept. 14, 1887
Elbert S. Chappell
Jan. 7, 1834 - Sept. 15, 1856
Ida E. Patterson
Feb. 12, 1866 - June 4, 1900
Joseph W. Chappell
Jan. 3, 1833 - Jan. 23, 1833
Edward A. Nelson
Oct. 28, 1830 - Nov. 13, 1892
John R. Nelson
May 8, 1849 - Jan. 4, 1888

Lou Nelson
(dates illegible)
Ben Nelson
(dates not legible)
Ben F. Nelson
Jan. 21, 1829 - Nov. 30, 1835
John A. Nelson
April 3, 1807 - May 9, 1886
John T. Chappell
June 18, 1843 - July 21, 1844
Martha F. Chappell
Oct. 21, 1838 - Sept. 16, 1846
Jeremiah
son of S. & N. Tharp
Nov. 27, 1858 - Nov. 27, 1858
Martha F. Nelson
Died Mar. 20, 1839
Aged 26 yrs., 6 mos., 29 days
Ella Clifford
Daughter of Simeon & Nancy Tharp
Dec. 28, 1853 - Mar. 14, 1861
Emily Tharp
Daughter of S. & N. Tharp
Sept. 17, 1861 - Sept. 17, 1861
William D. Tharp
Mar. 7, 1856 - Nov. 28, 1883
Rev. Simeon Tharpe
Nov. 15, 1827 - Apr. 3, 1896
Wm. Chappell
Died Jan. 12, 1859
Aged 31 years & 2 mos.
(A Masonic Emblem on this marker)
Joseph B. Tharp
Son of S. & N. Tharp
Dec. 21, 1859 - Aug. 18, 1860
Nancy Tharpe
Dec. 24, 1830 - May 6, 1908
A. E. Nash
1829 - 1893
Ruth Chappell
Wife of Thom. S. Chappell
Nov. 7, 1802 - May 27, 1874
Thomas S. Chappell
June 24, 1801 - July 29, 1861
Roxie A.
Wife of A. E. Nash
Aug. 20, 1836 - April 2, 1873
Married April 21, 1857
    Copied by: Mrs. Eleanor Davis McSwain

## NEW HAVEN BAPTIST CHURCH CEMETERY

John B. Barrentine
Mar. 3, 1868 - July 13, 1949
Edna Barrentine
Feb. 18, 1919—Age 6 yrs.
Mary A. Barrentine
1842 - 1916
John Durham Collins
Co. C, 4th Ga. Inf., C.S.A.
W. T. Williams
Della Martin Williams
Aug. 26, 1891 - Mar. 15, 1930
Thomas J. Martin
Nov. 20, 1889 - May 20, 1931
William F. Martin
Mar. 26, 1865 - Feb. 9, 1930
Ida Martin
Aug. 13, 1855 - Feb. 18, 1932
George C. Martin
Jan. 12, 1887 - Apr. 28, 1897
Joseph W. Wrye
July 4, 1856 - June 26, 1922
James Bud Wrye
Feb. 7, 1900 - Dec. 24, 1951
Minnie Wrye
Nov. 11, 1866 - Dec. 15, 1952
Elizabeth W. Smith
Feb. 4, 1897 - Feb. 22, 1956
Marshall Blackshear
1916 - 1952
Lillie Crosby
Wife of James F. Hamm
Feb. 20, 1887 - Dec. 12, 1948
James Franklin Hamm
Sept. 5, 1879 - Apr. 25, 1954
Lillie M. Hamm, Inft.
1917
I. M. Hamm
1907 - 1908—Inft.
E. L. Hamm
1906 - 1907
Mrs. W. C. Hamm
1859 - 1956
W. C. Hamm
Dec. 1, 1852 - Mar. 12, 1910
Mrs. W. C. Hamm
July, 1853 - Mar. 20, 1901
James H. Hammock
World War II, USNR
Aug. 20, 1917 - Oct. 5, 1958
Olin Hammock, Sr.
1907 - 1945

Annie H. Ethridge
Sept. 22, 1912 - Feb. 7, 1942
Mrs. Mary Williams
Dec. 6, 1855 - Feb. 8, 1932
J. S. Williams
Died Feb. 16, 1901—Age 51 yrs.
J. B. Williams
1884 - 1934
Mrs. J. I. Dykes
Died 1898 (1st grave in cemetery)
T. M. Birdsong
1865 - 1937
Mahala M. Holland
June 24, 1851 - June 21, 1930
James J. Holland
Sept. 11, 1850 - Jan. 25, 1899
Lillian Leslie
Wife of W. I. Cumbess
Nov. 14, 1909 - Aug. 24, 1954
Johnny Dupree
Inft.—1949
Jimmie T. Dupree, Jr.
1895 - 1953
Betty Epps
Feb. 28, 1871 - Nov. 28, 1936
Ernest L. Epps
Oct. 20, 1911 - Mar. 15, 1934
Ruben G. Epps
1876 - 1947
Ada Sapp Epps
1883 - 1919
Alma Epps
May 6, 1885 - May 31, 1912
James Epps
Nov. 14, 1848 - Apr. 24, 1899
Harriet Epps
Jan. 17, 1850 - Jan. 29, 1899
Mrs. Avie Williams Crosby
1876 - 1952
Elijah Hamm
1880 - 1907
Mrs. Roxie Hamm
Cicero S. Denning
1874 - 1947
Cary M. Nichols
Feb. 13, 1883 - Jan. 23, 1955
Arrie Wrye Shouse
1903 - 1959
Mary Ann Martin
Wife of R. E. Thompson
Dec. 4, 1858 - June 28, 1931
Mrs. E. Birdsong
April, 1837 - Nov., 1922

John Cribb
Co. C, 49th Ga. Inf., C.S.A.
Fannie C. Etheridge
Wife of J. T. Dupree
Died Dec. 23, 1930—Age 53 yrs.
Morgan Dupree
Mar. 15, 1908 - Sept. 18, 1936
John R. Dupree
1931 - 1934
Minnie Lee Carpenter
1877 - 1939
Samuel J. Wise
1897 - 1948
Carolyn N. Brown
1952—Inft.
W. R. Wimberly
1877 - 1952
J. C. Wimberly
Inft.
Carline Wimberly
Died Feb. 24, 1906
J. A. Wimberly
Died Feb. 24, 1924
Mrs. Katie Adkins
Died Apr. 25, 1956
Jim Sanders Collins
Dec. 23, 1857 - June 7, 1932
Sallie Fann Collins
Mar. 26, 1884 - Jan. 4, 1952
Inft. Son L. B. & Beulah Birdsong
1917
Leila W. Kitchens
1886 - 1945
Ellam Barrentine
Died Feb. 27, 1929—Age 62 yrs.
George Barrentine
William Day
Co. C, 4th Ga. Inf., C.S.A.
1841 - 1928
Lillie M. Barrentine
Died Nov. 11, 1930
George Martin
Co. E, 26th Ga. Inf., C.S.A.
Mrs. G. W. Martin
R. E. Birdsong
June 23, 1911 - Apr. 14, 1930
Monroe Birdsong
Oct. 3, 1889 - July 25, 1956
Ida C. Martin
Dec. 2, 1891 - Mar. 11, 1959
Abe S. Martin
Jan. 18, 1853 - Oct. 16, 1931

Laura
Wife of A. S. Martin
Oct. 10, 1863 - May 2, 1925
Annie L. Martin
1901 - 1904
Charlie R. Ives
1870 - 1944
J. D. Ives
1904 - 1937
Corine Crosby
Dec. 1, 1917 - July 6, 1922
William R. Epps
1907 - 1908
Augustus H. Epps
Oct. 16, 1869 - Apr. 28, 1933
Elizabeth Ives Epps
June 22, 1878 - Aug. 16, 1957
Roxie H. Holland
Nov. 10, 1856 - July 1, 1932
Walker F. Holland
May 31, 1931 - Apr. 20, 1941
Elijah F. Crosby
1850 - 1931
Richard L. Harrison
Aug. 5, 1851 - July 18, 1926
Willie A. Martin
Wife of Richard L. Harrison
Aug. 26, 1855 - Apr. 17, 1939
J. W. Cannon
June 8, 1866 - Feb. 16, 1934
Alice Bernice Smith
Wife of Osie W. Balkcom
Feb. 2, 1893 - June 24, 1955
Osie Bernard Balkcom
Oct. 24, 1910 - Sept. 7, 1957
Birdie Crosby
1916 - 1958
N. C. Crosby
1890 - 1953
Mrs. N. C. Crosby
1894 - 1952
George Moore
1882 - 1956
George W. "Jack" Moore
World War II
Jan. 18, 1925 - Apr. 28, 1956

Ivy Lyles
1909 - 1955
Mary S. Bledsoe
1871 - 1957
Ens. Margaret E. Chapman
U. S. N. C.
June 2, 1924 - Oct. 11, 1950
Floyd Cranford
World War II, USNR
1916 - 1956
Doris V. Dupree
Wife of Kelly Vinson
1924 - 1952
Diane Vinson
1952 - 1959
Perry Moore
1883 - 1937
Mrs. W. R. Sapp
1882 - 1949
Mazie Jane Dyer
Wife of Will H. Cannon
Mar. 31, 1878 - June 14, 1948
Will H. Cannon
1872 - 1942
John Bell Barrentine
1898 - 1935
Virginia Dyer Barrentine
1867 - 1946
James Leonard Barrentine
1914 - 1951
G. W. Shepard
1855 - 1935
George F. Leslie
1872 - 1959
Mrs. A. J. Champion
1881 - 1949
W. F. Champion
1910 - 1946
Pearl Champion
Mrs. Horrace O. Holder
1882 - 1950
James Robert Gordon
World War II
1921 - 1952
O. Z. Crosby
1884 - 1955

Copied by: Mr. and Mrs. B. W. Jones

## O'DANIEL FAMILY CEMETERY

William O'Daniel
May 2, 1838 - May 22, 1900
Elizabeth M. O'Daniel
Sept. 29, 1841 - Dec. 11, 1911

Stephen Richardson O'Daniel
Nov. 17, 1869 - Sept. 26, 1884
Mary Cordelia O'Daniel
Dec. 7, 1862 - Oct. 1, 1882

W. A. O'Daniel
Oct. 31, 1865 - Aug. 7, 1906
Christopher C. Smith
July 31, 1853 - March 29, 1902
Mattie O'Daniel
Wife of C. C. Smith
March 19, 1868 - Feb. 10, 1942
Mrs. Louisa O'Daniel
Sept. 1, 1807 - Sept. 13, 1872

Daniel O'Daniel
1806 - Aug. 26, 1868
Paul C.
Son of H. F. & M. A. Land
Mar. 8, 1876 - Dec. 7, 1880
Clara Crisp Smith
Dau. of C. C. & Mattie O'Daniel Smith
Nov. 2, 1895 - Feb. 3, 1896
Ethel Lawrence
No dates

Copied by Cornelia Johnston McCormick, Mrs. J. T. (Located midway between Bullard and Old Marion.)

## PACE CEMETERY

Hardy Pace
Husband of Fanny Pace and
Son of Thos. & Cebell Pace
May 11, 1784 - Nov. 17, 1836
Wm. H.
Son of Hardy and Fanny Pace
Jan. 8, 1834 - May 22, 1834
Rebecca Barton
Consort of Wm. Barton and
Dau. of Hardy and Fanny Pace
Jan. 9, 1814 - Oct. 29, 1836
Lizzie B.
Dau. of T. G. and M. Holder

Jan. 9, 1858 - Oct. 11, 1858
James T. Pace
Husband of Laura Pace and
Son of Hardy & Fanny Pace
Jan. 4, 1821 - Nov. 26, 1849
Martha E.
Daughter of Hardy and Fanny Pace
Sept. 6, 1829 - Mar. 17, 1848
Cebell F. Holder
Consort of Troy G. Holder and
Daughter of Hardy and Fanny Pace
Apr. 21, 1827 - Oct. 8, 1853

The Pace Family Cemetery is located a few hundred yards off a dirt road which begins at a gully on the Cochran Short Route, State Highway 87, about three miles south of Bullard. The road leads west to Adams Park, Twiggs County.

Copied July 22, 1957 by Hugh L. Faulk.

## PEARCE CEMETERY

A Masonic Insigna on the Tombstone
Theophilus Pearce    Died July 8, A.D. 1858    Aged 53 yrs, 7 mos., 22 days
Located in Twiggs County, Georgia, Bluff Militia District, about three miles from Friendship Baptist Church on a dirt road east of the church.

Copied by: H. L. Faulk

## HENRY H. PHILLIP'S CEMETERY
(About 13 miles S. of Macon on Cochran Highway)

Henry Heywood Phillips
Co. C, 22nd Battalion,
Ga. Cavalry, C.S.A.
By Mrs. Francis G. Clark

Martha Catherine Durden Phillips
1828 - 1890

## W. H. READ CEMETERY
(One mile east of Read's Station on Southern Railroad)

William Humphrey Read
Born Mar. 23, 1799 in N. C.
Russell Floyd Read
1844 - 1904
Co. G, 48th Ga. Regiment, C.S.A.
Mary Jane Read
Wife of R. F. Read
1851 - 1930

William Hamilton Read
1833 - 1864
Co. G, 48th Ga. Regiment, C.S.A.
Benamin Franklin Read
Lockett's Co., Ga. Cavalry, C.S.A.
Joseph Read
  (Statement of Mrs. J. B. Read)
  By Mrs. Francis G. Clark

## RICHLAND BAPTIST CHURCH CEMETERY

Amanda M. Beckom
Wife of S. L. Richardson
Apr. 3, 1833 - Jan. 17, 1859
Nancy Bunn
Wife of Rev. Henry Bunn
Died Sept. 22, 1853
Age 55 yrs., 11 mos., 1 day
Freddie Wimberly (Infant)
Warren Weaver Wimberly
May 31, 1866 - Apr. 27, 1908
Harriet Maria Bunn Wimberly Tarver
Jan. 24, 1816 - Sept., 1879
Frederick Davis Wimberly
Mar. 23, 1840 - July 16, 1893
William A., Martha A. and Porcia P.
Children of Henry and Nancy Bunn
Clara Joan Minter
Jan. 28, 1838 - Aug. 14, 1907
John Osborn
Judson Shine Bunn
Born July 11, 1840
Mrs. Catherine A. Anderson
Sept. 23, 1794 - Oct. 6, 1836
Sarah G. Ezell
Died Apr. 2, 1842—Aged 23 yrs.
Son of J. B. Gordon & Mrs. Gordon
Mrs. Sophia Asbell
Wife of Bryant Asbell
Nov. 1, 1814 - Jan. 19, 1859
James Ware
Feb. 26, 1785 - June 6, 1856
Mrs. Mary Ware
Apr. 14, 1789 - Sept. 17, 1855
Sarah McCallum
Jan. 31, 1812 - Feb. 26, 1848
Maria
Wife of Robert Paul, Sr.
Dec. 6, 1860
Aged 50 years, 11 mos. & 18 days

Rev. Henry Bunn
Born Nash Co., N. C.
Dec. 18, 1795 - Sept. 3, 1878
Henry H. Bunn
Sept. 5, 1852—Age 24
Florence Weaver (Infant)
William Minter Wimberly
Jan. 6, 1861 - Dec. 25, 1919
Isolene Minter Wimberly
May 23, 1841 - Dec. 31, 1898
Lucy Cary Hughes
Dau., Daniel & Henrietta Hughes
June 3, 1864 - July 5, 1885
Henrietta Cary Moore
Wife of Daniel Greenwood Hughes
May 5, 1830 - Oct. 1, 1880
John B. Gordon
Apr. 7, 1879 - Jan. 4, 1934
John Asbell
Nov. 3, 1781 - Apr. 12, 1858
Ann E. Wimberly
Wife of E. A. Wimberly
Apr. 3, 1825 - July 18, 1853
James Monroe Ware
Aug. 22, 1815 - Jan. 1, 1862
John Hodges
Son of Archibald & Sarah McCallum
Apr. 4, 1839 - Mar. 9, 1848
Henry Monroe
Jan. 5, 1838 - July 13, 1845
Sarah Jane
Feb. 19, \_\_\_\_\_ - Apr. 22, 1844
James Monroe
Sept. 13, 1840 - Nov. 17, 1843
James William
Dec. 19, 1830 - Nov. 26, 1838
Robert Augustus
Son of Thomas & Elizabeth Glover
June 7, 1829 - Nov. 9, 1831

B. S. Newby
June 12, 1872 - July 29, 1910
Major George W. Welch
Died Nov. 6, 1838—Aged 47 yrs.
Sarah Elizabeth
Dau. of Thomas & Elizabeth Glover
May 25, 1827 - Feb. 19, 1846

Frances Caroline
Dau. of Thomas and Elizabeth Glover
Oct. 18, 1833 - May 13, 1836
Robert Radford
Died Feb. 16, 1851—Aged 70 yrs.
Henry B. Radford
Jan. 9, 1856 - Nov. 7, 1857

Located six miles west of Jeffersonville on the historic Richland Baptist Church road.

Copied by: William T. Faulk

## SOLOMON-FAULK CEMETERY

William Faulk
Son of Mark and Nancy Faulk
Aug. 1, 1822 - Jan. 19, 1904
Nancy Reynolds Faulk
Dau. of Charles Reynolds
Wife of Mark Faulk, Sr.
1802 - 1866
John Faulk
Son of Mark and Nancy Faulk
Oct. 21, 1830 - Dec. 12, 1894
Va. Shannon
Wife of John Faulk
Dau. of James and Frances Shannon
July 14, 1847 - May 2, 1888
Henry Faulk
June 30, 1822 - Jan. 4, 1860
A Representative in Ga. Legislature from Twiggs Co. four years. Judge of the Inferior Court 11 years. Member of Richland Baptist Church.

Laura Janette
Dau. of Wm. and Virginia Faulk
Oct. 24, 1850 - July 22, 1886
Va. A. Faulk
Wife of William Faulk
Dau. of Henry Solomon
Jan. 9, 1828 - June 17, 1862
Virginia S.
Dau. of W. and V. Faulk
Wife of J. C. Shannon
Mar. 14, 1857 - Mar. 11, 1896
Victoria A. Solomon
Wife of John Faulk
May 27, 1837 - Mar. 4, 1870
Henrietta Ellen
Dau. of Henry & Celina Hodges Faulk
Oct. 23, 1853 - Jan. 11, 1857
Henry Solomon
Mar. 22, 1791 - Jan. 16, 1847
MOTHER
Aug. 20, 1805 - Nov. 7, 1857

Cemetery located a few miles west from Ripley on a county dirt road on the place commonly known as the "Billy Solomon Place." Owned by the Shannon Family.

Copied by: H. L. Faulk

## STONE CREEK BAPTIST CHURCH CEMETERY II

(Note: The original church cemetery is located near the Bibb-Twiggs county line where the first church-site was located. Several of the old graves are marked, among them being that of Rev. Vincent A. Tharp, Revolutionary soldier.)

George Washington Burkett
March 17, 1872 - Oct. 11, 1943
George Alton O'Neal
June 19, 1885 - Aug. 25, 1953
Jerry Chappell Miller, Sr.
1884 - 1955
Jerry Chappell Miller, Jr.
Oct. 13, 1928 - Jan. 26, 1959
G. L. Edwards (Infant)
July 5, 1948

L. R. Edwards
Jan. 30, 1939 - Mar. 12, 1941
Charlie R. Thomason
World War II Veteran
Nov. 11, 1914 - July 21, 1952
Ross P. Thomason
Feb. 25, 1886 - Apr. 18, 1958
Mrs. George H. Wimberly
1883 - 1947

Jessie Mae DeFore
July 16, 1908 - Mar. 21, 1957
LaGail Jordan
1954 - 1955
James H. Cannon, Jr.
June 3, 1920 - June 1, 1947
James H. Cannon, Sr.
Jan. 3, 1892 - Apr. 24, 1959
William Edd Cannon
Aug. 15, 1890 - Mar. 26, 1956
Louise Miller Wardlaw
1894 - 1952
Frank Simmons
July 23, 1900 - Nov. 18, 1935
Mrs. Belle DeFore
Feb. 10, 1876 - Nov. 25, 1941
Mrs. Dora Belle DeFore
Oct. 6, 1920 - Dec. 15, 1937
L. A. Simmons
Died Mar. 27, 1937
Mrs. L. A. Simmons
1878 - 1957
Homer T. Taylor
  W.W. I veteran
May 10, 1895 - Dec. 24, 1949
Fannie M. Hinson
Wife of A. C. Tharpe
Sept. 3, 1847 - Nov. 18, 1938
Bill Dunn Tharpe
Sept. 25, 1879 - June 24, 1946
Thomas S. Tharpe
Nov. 2, 1868 - Nov. 27, 1939
Clara A. Tharpe
Wife of Mack B. Smith
Feb. 2, 1892 - Nov. 17, 1955
Dr. Andrew J. Wood
June 30, 1854 - July 16, 1938
J. A. Lyles
Feb. 15, 1871 - Aug. 20, 1941
Robert M. Kitchens
1936 - 1945
Manie A. Kitchens
1915 - 1945
Mrs. G. C. Land
1892 - 1947
Jean Barrentine (Infant)
1949
Julia Hinson Symonds
1888 - 1949
Charles Earl Barrentine, Jr.
1948 - 1953 (tornado victim)
J. E. Bunch
Died 1944

Marvin D. Simmons
Oct. 13, 1936 - Sept. 8, 1952
James W. Barrentine, Jr.
Aug. 28, 1938 - Aug. 2, 1940
Mrs. J. W. Manspile
Died July 20, 1944
J. W. Manspile
Died Sept. 25, 1943
Ross L. Kitchens, Sr.
Apr. 14, 1878 - July 5, 1939
Mattie E. Wilson
Aug. 18, 1861 - Oct. 22, 1937
Hubert Barnes
Jan. 29, 1922 - Aug. 25, 1938
Ben Frank Barnes
May 18, 1915 - Aug. 23, 1946
Ben Barnes
E. F. Dorsey
Mar. 10, 1858 - Sept. 19, 1937
Hugh M. Dorsey
Nov. 27, 1915 - June 1, 1941
Mosely Infant
1946
Henry T. Hinson
Sept. 21, 1883 - Feb. 10, 1952
Minnie Sapp Hinson
Apr. 14, 1888 - Feb. 22, 1956
Patricia Ward (Infant)
1950
Buster Brown
Dec. 25, 1910 - Oct. 14, 1954
Miriam Simmons (Infant)
1953
Infant of Jerry Hinson
1957
Mrs. Lois S. Hinson
May 19, 1902 - June 24, 1951
Eva Bond Etheridge
Aug. 27, 1888 - Feb. 26, 1952
Joseph A. Etheridge
Jan. 30, 1877 - Feb. 21, 1950
Leslie Comer Kimberly
World War II Veteran
Oct. 31, 1919 - Aug. 8, 1957
Walter L. Lyles
1884 - 1952
Mary Jones (Infant)
Dau. Claud Jones
1950
James F. Flewellyn
Korean Veteran
Sept. 23, 1930 - Jan. 9, 1957

Anna Lee Mixon
Wife of Griffin Atkins
Sept. 9, 1887 - Mar. 2, 1950
Worthy R. Bennett
Dec. 28, 1903 - Dec. 5, 1956

F. H. Treadwell
1886 - 1945
William A. Treadwell
World War II Veteran
Sept. 20, 1913 - Oct. 27, 1952
Copied by: Mr. & Mrs. B. W. Jones

## JEREMIAH A. THARP CEMETERY NO. 1
(Off Riggins Mill Road, Dry Branch Ga.—near first homesite of J. A. Tharp)

Ider
Dau. of V. W. and E. Tharp
1860 - Sept., 1861
Louisa A.
Consort of Thos. Pace
Oct. 11, 1821 - Mar. 28, 1848
Louise M.
Dau. of T. B. and L. A. Pace
Dec. 5, 1847 - May 25, 1848

Jane A.
Consort of J. A. Tharp
Mar. 7, 1799 - Oct. 16, 1845
Sephine
Dau. of T. B. and L. A. Pace
Dec., 1841 - Feb. 20, 1842
Jane A.
Dau. of J. A. and Jane A. Tharp
Mar. 2, 1825 - Sept., 1843
Copied by: Mrs. Eleanor Davis McSwain

## JEREMIAH A. THARP CEMETERY NO. 2
(Riggins Mill Road, Dry Branch, Ga.)

J. A. Tharp
1793 - 1870
T. A. Tharp
Oct. 11, 1830 - Sept. 1, 1855
Jerry
Son of F. C. and E. J. Nelson
Aug., 1858 - Feb. 26, 1859
William A. Tharp
Died Sept. 25, 1841—Aged 52 yrs.

A. C. Tharp
1832 - 1897
Thadeus A.
Son of T. A. and E. S. Tharp
Nov. 9, 1854 - Nov. 10, 1855
Margaret
Wife of J. A. Tharp
Oct. 1, 1793 - Dec. 23, 1836
Copied by: Mrs. Eleanor Davis McSwain

## VAUGHN CEMETERY
(Near Mount Zion Baptist Church)

Daniel Vaughn
Oct. 9, 1780 - Feb. 19, 1854
Age 73 yrs, 4 mos.

Sarah Vaughn
May 5, 1782 - Oct. 21, 1853
Age 71 yrs., 5 mos.

## W. T. VAUGHN CEMETERY
(Near John Shine Vaughn's old home)

William Thomas Vaughn            May 6, 1821 - Mar. 28, 1901
  (Other graves marked but of more recent date.)
  By: Mrs. Francis G. Clark

## WATERS-WOOD-LANIER CEMETERY
(Near Fitzpatrick, Ga.)

Isaac Waters Wood
Mar. 30, 1845 - Mar. 9, 1925
Mary S. Wood
Wife of Isaac W. Wood
Oct. 15, 1854 - Aug. 7, 1917

W. J. Waters
Billy Lanier Kitchens
Son of B. M. & A. L. Kitchens
Mar. 14, 1925 - Oct. 31, 1925

Winnie B. Wood
Sept. 10, 1906 - Sept. 8, 1937
Infant Son of E. G. & Ela Floyd
Aug. 29, 1901 - Sept 1, 1901
Ida Day Wood
1885 - Apr., 1922
Green Berry Wood, Sr.
Mar. 16, 1815 - Apr., 1896
Catheryne Waters Wood
Feb. 17, 1827 - 1885—Age 58
Mary Jane Waters (Unmarked)
Died 1907—Age 72
(Statement of Mrs. Alma L. Kitchens)
William "Billy" Waters (Unmarked)
Died 1898
(Statement of Mrs. Alma L. Kitchens)
Eva Rosaline
Dau. of Davis and Nora McGee
Oct. 10, 1919 - Oct. 23, 1921
Phillip J. Wood

Co. G, 48 Ga. Inf., C.S.A.
W. A. Lanier
Dec. 26, 1856 - Sept. 28, 1940
Infant of W. G. & Mary Cannon
Edith E. Wood
Nov. 24, 1917 - Aug. 15, 1941
Green Berry Wood, Jr.
Nov. 30, 1870 - Oct. 7, 1921
Jennie Wood
Mar. 21, 1851 - Sept., 1881
William Calder Lanier (Unmarked)
Son of W. A. and E. F. Lanier
Age 13
(Statement of Mrs. Alma L. Kitchens)
Virginia Lanier (Unmarked)
Dau. of W. A. & E. F. Lanier
Age 19
(Statement of Mrs. Alma L. Kitchens)
Margaret Waters Wood (Unmarked)
(Statement of Mrs. W. T. Christian)

Copied by: M. V. Davidson and B. W. Jones

## EZEKIEL WIMBERLY CEMETERY

William Evans Wimberly
Son of E. A. & Louisa H. Wimberly
Dec. 18, 1866 - Nov. 23, 1940
Ezekiel A. Wimberly
Apr. 7, 1820 - June 2, 1885
Ezekiel Wimberly
Born North Carolina
Sept. 1, 1783 - May 5, 1843
Sheriff, Legislator, Presidential Elector,
Maj. Gen. Ga. Militia in the late war
with Great Britain
John Wimberly
1755 - 1835
Son of Ezekiel
and Mary Davis Wimberly

Revolutionary Soldier
D. A. R. Marker
Louisa A. Wimberly
Feb. 1, 1836 - Oct. 13, 1900
Henry E. Wimberly
July 31, 1826 - Aug. 10, 1848
Polly Bryan Wimberly
Born North Carolina
Oct. 12, 1787 - Oct. 22, 1875
Two Brick Vaults (Unmarked)
Emily Tucker
Dau. of Orin D. Tucker & Lucinda
1825 - 1826
Evans Long
Son of Reuben Long & Mary Harrison

Located on U. S. Highway 80, two miles north of Jeffersonville, Ga., east of the M. D. & S. Railroad tracks.

Copied by L. O. Faulk

## DR. JOSHUA RHODES WIMBERLY CEMETERY

Dr. Joshua R. Wimberly
   - Jan. 24, 1844—at 48 yrs.
Caroline H. Starr
1805 - After 1870
Wife of Dr. J. R. Wimberly, Sr.
(Unmarked—Statement of Mrs. L.
Irene Wimberly Gleeson)

George Wimberly
C. S. A.
(Unmarked—Statement of Mrs. L.
Irene W. Gleeson)
Henry T. Wimberly
May 27, 1954—at 19 yrs., 5 mos.

Dr. J. R. Wimberly II
Nov. 26, 1843 - Jan. 10, 1904
Adelaide A.
Wife of J. R. Wimberly
Nov. 16, 1848 - Oct. 6, 1890
Frederick Ezekiel Wimberly
Nov. 25, 1868 - Aug. 12, 1932
John Lowry Wimberly
Jan. 24, 1841 - Sept. 28, 1908
Mary Jane Wimberly
May 31, 1849 - Dec. 16, 1909
Lily Carolyn
Dau. of J. J. & L. C. Wall
Sept. 7, 1892 - Feb. 8, 1896
Edwin Eugene
Son of Samuel & Melinda M. Hatch
    - Aug. 2, 1851—Age 3 mos.
Samuel Wesley Hatch
1822 - 1864
James Jackson Wall
Dec. 31, 1884 - Jan. 22, 1923
Eight Infants (Unmarked)
Jennie
Dau. of D. S. and Carrie W. Faulk
    - Aug. 3, 1911—Age 8 mos.

Daniel Shine Faulk
Aug. 25, 1860 - June 19, 1948
Carrie Wimberly Faulk
Sept. 1, 1876 - Dec. 26, 1940
Charles C. Gleeson
Dec. 2, 1897 - Aug. 27, 1950
New Jersey, Cox, USNRF—W.W. I
Cox. USNRF—World War I
Joshua Rhodes Wimberly III
July 19, 1871 - July 19, 1924
Bessie Leonora Wimberly
Oct. 25, 1873 - Aug. 29, 1910
Matthew James Carswell
Jan. 15, 1873 - Aug. 18, 1929
Son of Matthew James and
Ellen H. (Dupree) Carswell
Mary Adelaide
Wife of M. J. Carswell
Dau. of Joshua R. and
Adelaide A. (Steely) Wimberly
Ellen Huff Carswell
Feb. 12, 1906 - May 25, 1958

Copied by: Mrs. C. C. Gleeson

## LAND LOTTERY

A perusal of the history of Georgia during the Revolutionary period and succeeding days that followed give horrible accounts of the struggles of the early settlers in this new territory. In spite of these hazards, the fertile land and favorable climate lured settlers from other territories into these Georgia counties. Therefore, it was necessary to move inland to claim land wherewith to create new counties. In the due course of time the original counties which covered such vast territory, were subdivided and have become the parent county of smaller counties.

The rush of settlers who kept coming into Georgia quickly took up all available lands east of the Oconee River and there was clamor for more land. The abundant resources seen by the settlers stretching beyond their boundary and of necessity for livelihood led them to trespass on these lands. Then complaints came from the Indian inhabitants and of course there were bloody uprisings among the redmen and whitemen for land.

Some action had to be taken to protect the citizens and obtain more land. The State Government had to act—by an Act of the Georgia Legislature on February 17, 1783 Headright grants were provided as the means of distribution of land to the early settlers for various services rendered their country. It was about the turn of the nineteenth century that the United States government began negotiating terms with the Creek Indians to cede more land in Georgia. Finally, treaties were negotiated in 1802, 1804, 1805 and in subsequent years with the Indians ceding land between the main streams in Georgia at intervals, still continuously pushing westward until the boundary line extended to the Chattahoochee River. Due to frauds in the early grants of land, the Legislature changed the law to distribution by Land Lottery. Surveys were made, tickets provided, some had numbers, others blanks, classifications set for eligibility in drawing. Records of these grants may be reviewed at the Georgia Department of Archives and History. An interesting history of GEORGIA BOUNTY LAND GRANTS has been compiled by Alex M. Hitz, Officer in Charge, State Surveyor General Department.

## LAND LOTTERY GRANTS 1805 and 1807
## FIRST LAND LOTTERY
## ALSO KNOWN AS THE 1805 LOTTERY

| | | |
|---|---|---|
| AUTHORITY | Act of May 11, 1803 | |
| YEAR OF DRAWING | 1805 | |
| COUNTIES | Baldwin | 5 Districts (1 thru 5) |
| | Wayne | 3 Districts (1 thru 3) |
| | Wilkinson | 5 Districts (1 thru 5) |
| SIZE OF LAND LOTS | Baldwin 202½ acres | 2970 feet square |
| | Wayne 490 acres | 4620 feet square |
| | Wilkinson 202½ acres | 2970 feet square |
| GRANT FEE | $ 8.10 per 202½ acre Land Lot | |
| | 19.60 per 490 acre Land Lot | |

PERSONS ENTITLED
    TO DRAW

| | |
|---|---|
| Bachelor, 21 years or over, one-year residence in Georgia, citizen of United States | 1 draw |
| Married man, with wife and/or child, one-year residence in Georgia, citizen of United States | 2 draws |
| Widow with minor child, one-year residence in Georgia | 2 draws |
| Minor orphan, or family of minor orphans, with father dead and mother dead or remarried | 1 draw |

## SECOND LAND LOTTERY
## ALSO KNOWN AS THE 1807 LOTTERY

| | | | |
|---|---|---|---|
| AUTHORITY | Act of June 26, 1806 | | |
| YEAR OF DRAWING | 1807 | | |
| COUNTIES | Baldwin | 15 Districts (6 thru 20) | |
| | Wilkinson | 23 Districts (6 thru 28) | |
| SIZE OF LAND LOTS | Baldwin | 202½ acres | 2970 feet square |
| | Wilkinson | 202½ acres | 2970 feet square |
| GRANT FEE | $12.15 per 202½ acre Lot | | |

PERSONS ENTITLED
   TO DRAW

| | |
|---|---|
| Bachelor, 21 years or over, three-year residence in Georgia, citizen of United States | 1 draw |
| Married man, with wife and/or minor child three-year residence in Georgia, citizen of United States | 2 draws |
| Widow, three-year residence in Georgia | 1 draw |
| Spinister, 21 years or over, three-year residence in Georgia | 1 draw |
| Minor orphan, father and mother dead, three-year residence in Georgia | 1 draw |
| Family of minor orphans, father and mother dead, three-year residence in Georgia | 2 draws |
| Minor orphan, father dead, mother living, three-year residence in Georgia | 1 draw |
| Family of minor orphans, father dead, mother living, three-year residence in Georgia | 1 draw |

PERSONS EXCLUDED   Any fortunate drawer in the previous Land Lottery

NOTE   The ORAL oath to be made by a married man, bachelor, widow, spinster or guardian of orphans did not require a detailed statement as to kinship, ancestry or descent. If, by chance, any such oath may have been written or transcribed, it could be found only in the Minutes of the Inferior Court of the County where made.

                                                                                              AMH

STATE OF GEORGIA, LAND LOTTERY GRANTS OF ORIGINALLY WILKINSON COUNTY, NOW TWIGGS, INDEX 1805, DISTRICTS 23 THROUGH 28. REFERENCE: LAND OFFICE RECORDS—REEL 193

By courtesy of Mrs. Edna Earle Todd Sterrett (R. W.)

800 East Avenue, Park Ridge, Illinois.

Microfilm on file in the Department of Archives and History, Atlanta, Georgia.

    Note: Any names that may be misspelled will in all probability be due to interpretation of the handwriting from the records; it is almost impossible to read the records correctly.

## 23 DISTRICT WILKINSON COUNTY 1805
*(Now Twiggs County)*

| NAME | DISTRICT | RESIDENCE | DATE |
|---|---|---|---|
| John Parks (Col.) | Parks | Wilkes | 21 Nov. 1807 |
| Willey House (S. W.) | Smith's | Oglethorpe | 8 Mar. 1808 |
| Archelus Pope | Hatchett's | Oglethorpe | 21 Nov. 1807 |
| Jos Patterson | Roebuck's | Elbert | 7 Sept. 1809 |
| Wm. McDade | | Richmond | 6 June 1808 |
| Wm. Barksdale | Heath's | Warren | 5 May 1808 |
| Hugh McNeely | Tarver's | Jefferson | 27 Nov. 1811 |
| John. Waller | 2nd | Baldwin | 10 Nov. 1814 |
| Benj. Parker | Holt's | Hancock | 29 Oct. 1807 |
| Silvery Pollard | Clark's | Elbert | 31 Dec. 1807 |
| Robert Rogers | 4th | Baldwin | 15 Nov. 1810 |
| Francis Durrence | McDonald's | Tatnall | 8 Dec. 1807 |
| Eli Rushen | W. Renfroe's | Washington | 17 Dec. 1807 |
| Nancy Mason (widow) | Sidwell's | Wilkes | 19 Sept. 1808 |
| John Kennedy Sr. | Tarver's | Jefferson | 21 Sept. 1809 |
| Arris Cox | Everette's | Franklin | 14 Dec. 1808 |
| Lewis Reynolds | Martin's | Burke | 21 Oct. 1807 |
| John Burton | Gordon's | Burke | 12 May 1808 |
| Jos. C. Thrasher | Butler's | Greene | 3 Nov. 1814 |
| John Desmukes Jr. | 1st | Baldwin | 28 June 1809 |
| Hugh Cravy Jr. | Spains | Burke | 13 Sept. 1808 |
| John Trueluck | | Jefferson | 22 Sept. 1809 |
| Daniel Vaughn | 10th | Columbia | 6 Dec. 1810 |
| Ransom Cooper | 2nd | Baldwin | 27 Feb. 1808 |
| Margaret Strength | 2nd | Baldwin | 10 Feb. 1815 |
| Thos. Bacon Jr. | | Liberty | 15 Nov. 1808 |
| Wm. Chapman | Birdsong's | Hancock | 1 Jan. 1808 |
| John Mitchell's orphans | Beasley's | Oglethorpe | 26 Nov. 1807 |
| Jac. Stewart's orphans | 7th | Columbia | 23 Feb. 1809 |
| George Farmer | Moore's | Oglethorpe | 9 Dec. 1808 |
| John Upton | | Columbia | 11 Aug. 1810 |
| Issac J. Barrett | Barrett's | Elbert | 28 Aug. 1809 |
| Ezekiel Bowman | Johnson's Bat. | Jackson | 25 Nov. 1807 |
| John Davis | Martin's | Burke | 20 Dec. 1808 |
| Saml. Slocum | Bostick's | Jefferson | 16 Dec. 1808 |
| Larken Clark | Clark's | Elbert | 12 Nov. 1808 |
| Thos. Jarrell | Milner's | Wilkes | 17 Nov. 1808 |
| Hamp. McIntosh | | McIntosh | 29 Apr. 1808 |
| Braddock McDaniel | Henderson's Bat. | Jackson | 20 Oct. 1807 |
| Nancy Bally (orp.) | Johnson's Bat. | Jackson | 7 Nov. 1809 |
| Spear Bletch | | Effingham | 4 May 1808 |
| John Strainger | Hudson's | Oglethorpe | 23 Feb. 1808 |
| Lenus Parker | Bussey's | Lincoln | 9 Nov. 1808 |
| Sarah Edwards | Moore's | Greene | 6 Apr. 1808 |
| Thompson Curry | Chiver's | Washington | 24 Apr. 1810 |
| Edward Sutton | 4th | Baldwin | 25 Aug. 1808 |
| John W. Jackson | Jones | Warren | 5 Nov. 1812 |
| William King, Dr. | Dawson's | Greene | 21 Sept. 1813 |
| Susannah D. Morarity | | Richmond | 19 Nov. 1807 |
| Wm. Dixon's orphans | Pace's | Washington | 30 Sept. 1813 |

| | | | |
|---|---|---|---|
| Jos. Fitzpatrick | Jenkin's | Greene | 1 Dec. 1807 |
| Francis Gartrell Esq. | Wellburn's | Wilkes | 30 Aug. 1808 |
| Fanny Tennel widow | | Wilkinson | 19 Nov. 1807 |
| John Murphey | Wellburn's | Wilkes | 8 July 1808 |
| Allen J. Bridges | Hattchett's | Oglethorpe | 18 Feb. 1809 |
| John Buis | Gumm's | Hancock | 27 Oct. 1807 |
| Patten Wise | Smith's | Oglethorpe | 29 Jan. 1808 |
| Daniel McIntosh | Flournoy's | Greene | 12 Sept. 1808 |
| Wm. Todd | Cooper's | Wilkes | 3 Jan. 1810 |
| Elijah Kersey | 57th | Montgomery | 20 Oct. 1807 |
| Sarah Taylor | 54th | Montgomery | 28 Oct. 1807 |
| Daniel Dougherty | Hall's | Tatnall | 16 Dec. 1808 |
| Wm. Chapton | 7th | Columbia | 3 Dec. 1808 |
| Frances C. Wilkinson (widow) | | Liberty | 27 Nov. 1807 |
| Edward Young Sr. | Mulkey's | Burke | 6 Dec. 1808 |
| Robt. Taylor Sr. | Faulkner's | Elbert | 25 Mar. 1811 |
| Pleasant Bryant | Henderson's Bat. | Jackson | 23 Oct. 1807 |
| Thos. Fuzzell | Garrett's | Washington | 15 Jan. 1811 |
| Henry Garrett's orphans | Coffee's | Hancock | 19 Sept. 1808 |
| Asa Lincecum | 3rd | Baldwin | 28 Oct. 1807 |
| Aaron Dudley's orphans | | Liberty | 12 May 1808 |
| Jonathon Glaze | | Richmond | 6 Sept. 1808 |
| Thos. Robertson | Pemberton's | Chatham | 29 July 1808 |
| Moses Pamell | Bryant's | Franklin | 8 Oct. 1810 |
| Saml. Willson Jr. | 2nd | Baldwin | 29 Mar. 1808 |
| Ezekiel Underwood | Blackwell's | Elbert | 2 Dec. 1807 |
| Ellis Jameson | Sidwell's | Wilkes | 14 Dec. 1810 |
| John Hall | | Liberty | 8 Dec. 1807 |
| Absalom Farrer | 4th | Columbia | 14 Nov. 1808 |
| J. H. Harrison | | McIntosh | 10 May 1808 |
| Chas. M. Govlesby | | Effingham | 9 Sept. 1808 |
| Sally Copeland | Bell's | Oglethorpe | 16 Aug. 1809 |
| Isaac Fells | Neyle's | Chatham | 8 Sept. 1809 |
| . . . . . . Cosby (widow) | Thompson's | Elbert | 15 Dec. 1808 |
| Lewis Bickers | Carlton's | Greene | 6 Jan. 1815 |
| Conrad Liverman | Williams | Bullock | 28 Feb. 1809 |
| Rachel Taylor | Godfrey's | Bullock | 20 Oct. 1807 |
| George Cagle | Robinson's | Clarke | 10 Feb. 1808 |
| Jas. McCant | Forth's | Burke | 12 Nov. 1808 |
| Enoch Pearson | Moon's | Elbert | 11 Aug. 1808 |
| Robt. McNeely | 2nd | Baldwin | 30 Jan. 1808 |
| Haskey Thurmon | Butler's | Greene | 12 Feb. 1808 |
| John Nixson | Everette's | Franklin | 7 Sept. 1808 |
| David Sims | Brown's | Clarke | 18 Apr. 1808 |
| West Vinson | Thomas | Hancock | 1 May 1811 |
| Leveon Stanford | Willson's | Warren | 28 Nov. 1808 |
| Wm. Young's orphans | Kendrick's | Washington | 28 Mar. 1810 |
| Abram. Peavy | Heath's | Warren | 22 Oct. 1807 |
| John Reeves orphans | Dixon's | Franklin | 30 Sept. 1812 |
| Jas. Green | Smith's | Hancock | 25 Nov. 1807 |
| Hugh Ector | Hartsfield's | Oglethorpe | 1 Feb. 1808 |
| Harriett Scott | Carter's | Warren | 24 Sept. 1814 |
| Jas. Reeves | Milner's | Wilkes | 14 Dec. 1811 |
| John Bledsoe | Hatchett's | Oglethorpe | 29 Nov. 1810 |

| Name | Unit | County | Date |
|---|---|---|---|
| John Ratcliff | | Liberty | 29 Nov. 1809 |
| Paschal Traylor's orphans | Smith's | Oglethorpe | 10 May 1808 |
| Jas. Willson | McLean's | Chatham | 24 Oct. 1808 |
| David Beety | Moore's | Oglethorpe | 17 July 1810 |
| Abrm. Strobhart | Pettybone's | Chatham | 29 July 1808 |
| John Brannan | Williamson | Screven | 3 Feb. 1808 |
| Wm. P. Dearmond orph. | | Richmond | 8 Oct. 1808 |
| John Chapman | Willborn's | Wilkes | 26 Oct. 1807 |
| Saml. Collins | Wright's Bat. | Jackson | 28 Nov. 1807 |
| Martin Deadwiler | Faulkner's | Elbert | 3 Oct. 1809 |
| Thos. Decheneaux | Pemberton's | Chatham | 22 Dec. 1807 |
| Clayton Huskey | Hill's | Warren | 1 Jan. 1808 |
| Henry Gilly | 51st | Montgomery | 5 Dec. 1809 |
| John Ashley | Ashley's | Camden | 6 Apr. 1808 |
| Elender Giler | Coleman's | Jefferson | 13 Apr. 1808 |
| Penelope Newdigate (widow) | Pettybone's | Chatham | 3 Dec. 1807 |
| Jas. Griffin | Blackshear's | Washington | 23 Nov. 1808 |
| Wm. Miles | 10th | Columbia | 25 Oct. 1808 |
| Larry Larry | Flournoy's | Warren | 19 May 1810 |
| Wm. Ray | Anderson's | Washington | 18 Apr. 1808 |
| Benj. Duncan | Johnson's Bat. | Jackson | 28 Apr. 1808 |
| Wm. Price | Collins | Washington | 27 July 1808 |
| Cyrus Gildersleeve | | Liberty | 9 Dec. 1807 |
| Moses Brome | Pinkston's | Hancock | 21 Oct. 1808 |
| Jane Walker | Thomas | Hancock | 1 Feb. 1810 |
| David Holmes | Cockran's Bat. | Jackson | 24 Nov. 1807 |
| Matthias Gray | Devereaux | Warren | 12 Apr. 1808 |
| Benj. Brown | Blackwells' | Elbert | 10 Oct. 1809 |
| Arthur Youngblood | Holt's | Hancock | 14 Jan. 1812 |
| Jane Burk | Herb's | Chatham | 22 Jan. 1808 |
| Hugh Powell | Huff's | Hancock | 23 Dec. 1808 |
| Lee Allen Harris | | Glynn | 12 May 1808 |
| Assenah Eason (widow) | Watkins | Oglethorpe | 12 Nov. 1808 |
| Wiley Blount | Burney's | Washington | 20 Feb. 1811 |
| Jesse Burson | 1st | Baldwin | 24 Oct. 1807 |
| Clayborn Maddox | Cockran's Bat. | Jackson | 24 Oct. 1807 |
| Gottheilf Israel Nees | | Effingham | 17 Nov. 1808 |
| Richardson Perry | Martin's | Clarke | 13 Nov. 1809 |
| Jos. B. Jones | Crowder's | Hancock | 30 Sept. 1813 |
| Jos. Herndon | Brown's | Clarke | 7 Sept. 1810 |
| Richard Raburn | Neal's | Warren | 22 Apr. 1808 |
| Wm. Owen | Hudson's | Oglethorpe | 13 Oct. 1808 |
| Wm. Casey | 5th | Baldwin | 8 Apr. 1811 |
| Dread Thomton | Smith's | Oglethorpe | 5 Jan. 1808 |
| Ezekiel Wimberly Sr. | Renfroe's | Washington | 16 May 1808 |
| Christian C. Millirons | 7th | Columbia | 2 Nov. 1810 |
| Wm. Mikell | Williams | Bullock | 12 Nov. 1808 |
| Jas. Lambert | Blount's | Burke | 23 Jan. 1808 |
| Ludnell Armstrong | Martin's | Clarke | 18 Dec. 1809 |
| Jas. Joice | Armstrong's | Tatnall | 23 Nov. 1808 |
| John Harris | | McIntosh | 2 May 1810 |
| Jas. Wade Jr. | Sheet's | Wilkes | 17 Nov. 1808 |
| Joshua Jackson | Milner's | Wilkes | 15 Nov. 1808 |
| Emory Lassiter | Sandiford's | Burke | 19 May 1808 |

| | | | |
|---|---|---|---|
| Peter Goza | Newson's | Warren | 13 Jan. 1808 |
| Moses Westberry | Stafford's | Tatnall | 15 Nov. 1810 |
| Issac Holly | Willis | Washington | 24 Feb. 1808 |
| Sally Penn | Oliver's | Elbert | 9 Nov. 1812 |
| Jas. Smith | 7th | Columbia | 23 Feb. 1808 |
| Issac Fuller | Holt's | Washington | 5 Oct. 1808 |
| Peggy Curry (widow) | | Lincoln | 30 Jan. 1815 |
| Solomon Mobley | Armstrong's | Tatnall | 5 Mar. 1808 |
| Wm. Pittman | 5th | Baldwin | 13 Jan. 1808 |
| Henry Hurley | Malone's | Wilkes | 10 Jan. 1810 |
| Jeremiah Teedwell | Stewart's | Clarke | 9 Jan. 1808 |
| Richard Reynolds' orph. | Rorey's | Wilkes | 3 Dec. 1808 |
| Lucy Waumick (widow) | Pettybone's | Chatham | 28 Mar. 1808 |
| Delila Smith | Moon's | Elbert | 14 May 1812 |
| Aaron Gardner | 56th | Montgomery | 5 Sept. 1814 |
| Robt. McGowan | Mitchell's | Clarke | 16 May 1808 |
| Thos. Owens | Hartfield's | Oglethorpe | 21 Dec. 1810 |
| Ann Hudson | | Richmond | 3 Apr. 1812 |
| Joshua Ballard | Wellborn's | Wilkes | 14 Nov. 1809 |
| Lachariah Arnold | Watkins' | Oglethorpe | 27 Nov. 1809 |
| Lunsford Low | Montgomery's | Burke | 14 Oct. 1808 |
| Wm. Kilgore | Shivers | Hancock | 1 Sept. 1808 |
| Henry McDawdy | Heard's | Wilkes | 19 Nov. 1807 |
| Robt. Holton | | Wilkinson | 13 Mar. 1810 |
| Danl. Jenkins' orphans | White's | Chatham | 17 Nov. 1828 |
| Wm. Wright | | Effingham | 13 Jan. 1808 |
| Elizabeth Vallotton (widow) | Pettybone's | Chatham | 23 Jan. 1809 |
| Hugh Hancrow | McGuire's | Elbert | 17 Dec. 1810 |
| Jesse Barefield | | Wilkinson | 3 Nov. 1814 |
| Wm. Glass | Heard's | Wilkes | 3 Dec. 1807 |
| Wm. Brooks (son of Peter) | Milner's | Wilkes | 16 Dec. 1808 |
| Wm. Downs | | Effingham | 1 July 1808 |
| Jas. Freeze's orphans | Jones' | Lincoln | 23 Nov. 1818 |
| Chas. McCardell Devereux's | Devereux's | Warren | 29 Oct. 1814 |
| Jas. Murphey | | Richmond | 18 Dec. 1810 |
| Young Gresham (colonel) | Greer's | Greene | 30 Dec. 1808 |
| Elijah Lunsdale | 4th | Baldwin | 15 Oct. 1810 |
| Wm. Dawson | Hewell's | Oglethorpe | 2 Mar. 1808 |
| Robt. H. Mapp | Hudson's | Hancock | 23 Oct. 1807 |
| Burrell Roberts' orphans | Sharp's | Burke | 28 Sept. 1814 |
| Geo. Martin | 7th | Columbia | 16 Nov. 1808 |
| Jas. Hunt | Carswell's | Burke | 15 Dec. 1807 |
| Judith Green (widow) | Cooper's | Wilkes | 15 Nov. 1808 |
| Benj. Temple | Pinkston's | Hancock | 27 Sept. 1813 |
| Jac. Shankle | Christians' | Franklin | 10 June 1809 |
| Wm. McDonald | | McIntosh | 11 Nov. 1809 |
| Rachel Powell | 7th | Columbia | 21 Nov. 1810 |
| Wm. Heard | Greer's | Greene | 2 Aug. 1815 |
| Cecelia Van Allen (widow) | Cooper's | Wilkes | 25 Oct. 1814 |
| David Bazemore | 2nd | Baldwin | 7 Aug. 1815 |
| Jos. Peign | | Wilkinson | 19 July 1808 |
| Rhodum Griggs | Barnes | Hancock | 3 May 1810 |
| John Evers | | Jefferson | 14 Nov. 1808 |
| Penelope Inlow | Carter's | Warren | 6 June 1809 |

| | | | |
|---|---|---|---|
| John Lawson | Blackshear's | Washington | 4 Oct. 1808 |
| Francis Biggam | Barnes' | Hancock | 9 Nov. 1808 |
| Jos. Whitlock's orph. | Baxter's | Greene | 7 Jan. 1829 |
| Gibson Clark | | Lincoln | 13 Nov. 1809 |
| Saml. Bailey | Blackwell's | Elbert | 22 Sept. 1813 |
| John Hailes | Hitchcock's | Oglethorpe | 3 Nov. 1807 |
| Wm. Godbee | Mulkey's | Burke | 1 Oct. 1808 |
| Edwd., Mary, & Sarah McFarlin (orphans) | | Richmond | 6 Sept. 1808 |
| John Evans | Everett's | Franklin | 11 May 1808 |
| Brown's orphans | Cockran's Bat. | Jackson | 7 Nov. 1812 |
| Jas. Hatcher | Hillyer's | Elbert | 16 Dec. 1808 |
| Abram. Waters | | McIntosh | 2 Dec. 1807 |
| Reubin McCoy | Oliver's | Elbert | 7 Nov. 1808 |
| Alex. Patterson | Roebuck's | Elbert | 13 Nov. 1808 |
| C. F. Triebner | White's | Chatham | 31 May 1808 |
| Barnett Meadows | Wems' | Franklin | 6 Dec. 1809 |
| John Dukes | Duke's | Clarke | 23 Apr. 1808 |
| Jas. Childs | Week's | Hancock | 28 Sept. 1808 |
| Jane Morrison | Morrison's | Elbert | 28 Dec. 1809 |
| Wm. Jones | 5th | Columbia | 23 July 1808 |
| John Caldwell | 2nd | Columbia | 27 Nov. 1812 |
| Jas. McDonald's orph. | 10th | Columbia | 30 Aug. 1813 |
| Mary Armour | Charlton's | Greene | 28 Nov. 1811 |
| Mary Mayfield (widow) | Henderson's Bat. | Jackson | 25 Nov. 1807 |
| Henry Wanderwedel | Candler's | Hancock | 29 Oct. 1807 |
| Thos. Lockett | Baker's | Warren | 22 Nov. 1808 |
| Gay S. Roberts | 50th | Montgomery | 31 Oct. 1814 |
| Arthur Fort Jr. | Devereux's | Warren | 9 Dec. 1807 |
| Jas. O'Berry | 1st | Baldwin | 15 Mar. 1808 |
| Wm. Evans Jr. | Malone's | Wilkes | 14 Nov. 1808 |
| Jas. Montfort | Rony's | Wilkes | 21 Nov. 1807 |
| Thos. Warner | Coleman's | Jefferson | 7 Dec. 1807 |
| Jennett McNair | 7th | Columbia | 7 Nov. 1808 |
| John Murphey | Wilborns' | Wilkes | 8 July 1808 |
| Geo. Williams | 2nd | Baldwin | 21 May 1808 |
| John Stubblefield's orph. | Cockran's Bat. | Jackson | 26 Feb. 1808 |
| Jeremiah Mathews | Gumms | Hancock | 22 Oct. 1808 |
| Thos. Green | Gartrell's | Lincoln | 4 Jan. 1809 |
| Polly Smallwood | Hendrix's | Wilkes | 25 Feb. 1811 |
| Mary Davis | Clark's | Elbert | 17 Dec. 1811 |
| Adam Simmons Sr. | Hewell's | Oglethorpe | 30 Nov. 1807 |
| Saml. Perkins | 59th | Montgomery | 25 Feb. 1811 |
| Issac Hancock | Hooper's | Franklin | 11 May 1808 |
| Stephen Tredwell | Hopkin's | Clarke | 22 Nov. 1808 |
| Phillip Jenkin's orph. | Field's | Burke | 26 Nov. 1810 |
| Wm. Baxter White | Sharpe's | Burke | 20 May 1808 |
| John Lamar's orph. | 5th | Columbia | 24 Oct. 1807 |
| Saml. Barnett | Henderson's Bat. | Jackson | 16 Apr. 1808 |
| Eliz. Belger (widow) | Devereux | Warren | 21 Oct. 1807 |
| Edw. Burke | | Richmond | 17 Oct. 1808 |
| Jas. Russell | King's | Lincoln | 11 Nov. 1809 |
| Jeremiah Morris | Candler's | Hancock | 14 Aug. 1809 |
| Farish Carter | 1st | Baldwin | 18 Apr. 1808 |

| Wm. Gains | Blounts | Burke | 3 Dec. 1808 |
| Edw. Oneal | 3rd | Columbia | 17 Dec. 1808 |
| David Daniel | Ballard's | Burke | 15 Nov. 1808 |

## 24 DISTRICT WILKINSON COUNTY 1805
*(Now Twiggs County)*

| NAME | DISTRICT | RESIDENCE | DATE |
|---|---|---|---|
| William Wiley | 8th Dist. | Columbia | 29 Sept. 1813 |
| James B. Govlesby | Smith's | Oglethorpe | 30 Nov. 1807 |
| Hezekiah Blankinship | Crowder's | Hancock | 19 Nov. 1808 |
| Benjamin Purkins | Cockrans Bat. | Jackson | 4 Jan. 1808 |
| Joshua Harris | Jones | Lincoln | 15 Nov. 1808 |
| John Crumbly | | Wilkinson | 4 June 1808 |
| Chaney Duke (widow) | Sharp's | Burke | 9 Nov. 1809 |
| David Hay | Stovall's | Wilkes | 7 Dec. 1807 |
| George Micklejohn | Montgomery's | Burke | 15 Jan. 1810 |
| Watson Allison | Cockran's Bat. | Jackson | 6 Nov. 1812 |
| Jesse Boran's Orphans | Huff's | Hancock (D. B. Perryman) | 12 Nov. 1828 |
| Daniel Loyd | Kendrick's | Washington | 12 Nov. 1808 |
| Isaac D. Manley | Bryan's | Franklin | 16 Nov. 1811 |
| Jesse Boswell | Malone's | Wilkes | 28 Jan. 1808 |
| Lewis Pitts (Orphan) | Jones | Warren | 21 Nov. 1807 |
| Joseph Harrison | Wright's Bat. | Jackson | 5 Jan. 1808 |
| (Granted to Josephine Harrison) | | | |
| James Knight | Spains | Burke | 13 Sept. 1808 |
| Simon Fraser | | Liberty | 1 Oct. 1808 |
| John Robertson | Barne's | Hancock | 19 Nov. 1807 |
| John Kidd, Senr. | Hatchett's | Oglethorpe | 19 May 1808 |
| Arthur Knight | Heard's | Wilkes | 23 Jan. 1808 |
| Henry Shackleford, Jr. | Clark's | Elbert | 18 Aug. 1810 |
| Baldwin Fluker | Willis | Washington | 22 Jan. 1809 |
| Wingate Hall | Candler's | Hancock | 27 Mar. 1815 |
| Shadrack Moore, Senr. | Burney's | Washington | 30 Sept. 1813 |
| Jane Dobbins | Tramell's | Clarke | 21 Nov. 1807 |
| Benjn. Harvey | | Wilkinson | 28 Sept. 1810 |
| Wm. Booles, Senr. | Greer's | Greene | 23 Nov. 1808 |
| Mary Ray (S.W.) | Seliman's | Clarke | 18 Jan. 1808 |
| Winnefred Raines (widow) | | Wilkinson | 6 July 1808 |
| Thomas Byne | Carswell's | Burke | 12 May 1808 |
| John Simmons | Butler's | Clarke | 24 Nov. 1809 |
| Wm. Kelly | Hudson's | Hancock | 13 Nov. 1809 |
| Henry Sadler | Smith's | Camden | 7 Jan. 1808 |
| John Sams | Beasley's | Oglethorpe | 25 Nov. 1807 |
| James Nunn's orphans | Chiver's | Washington | 4 Nov. 1814 |
| Henry Pope's orphans | Norman's | Wilkes | 8 July 1809 |
| John Cody | Wright's Bat. | Jackson | 24 Oct. 1807 |
| George Elliott | Howell's | Oglethorpe | 7 Jan. 1809 |
| Lott Harton | Week's | Hancock | 5 Nov. 1810 |
| George Barnett | Hatchett's | Oglethorpe | 27 Nov. 1809 |
| Daniel Jackson | 2nd | Baldwin | 30 Apr. 1808 |

| Name | Unit | County | Date |
|---|---|---|---|
| Elijah Phillips | Malcom's | Wilkes | 28 Jan. 1808 |
| Benjn. Hargraves' orphans | Carswell's | Burke | 30 Sept. 1810 |
| Randal Henderson | Sherrard's | Tattnall | 19 Sept. 1809 |
| Frederick Knight | | Jefferson | 29 Mar. 1808 |
| Parr Hutchinson | Winslett's | Hancock | 12 Dec. 1807 |
| Charles Huckely | Barkesdale's | Hancock | 6 Jan. 1808 |
| Drury Mims | 1st | Baldwin | 10 Nov. 1808 |
| Thomas Dukes, Jr. | Smith's | Oglethorpe | 16 Nov. 1810 |
| William Walton | Gordon's | Burke | 19 Dec. 1808 |
| Bernard Bignon | | Richmond | 6 July 1808 |
| Ebenezer Stark | Herb's | Chatham | 29 Feb. 1808 |
| Robert Wicker | 1st | Baldwin | 13 Sept. 1808 |
| William Pitts | Mtichell's | Clarke | 17 Dec. 1808 |
| John Fielder | 5th | Baldwin | 4 Nov. 1808 |
| Joseph Sessions | Hendricks | Washington | 26 Nov. 1808 |
| Robert Flournoy | Fulton's | Jefferson | 5 Dec. 1807 |
| Charity Walker | 4th | Baldwin | 30 Sept. 1813 |
| Henry Nicholls | | Effingham | 16 Nov. 1811 |
| Gibson Joiner | 52nd | Montgomery | 23 July 1810 |
| Sarah Beaty | 59th | Montgomery | 23 Oct. 1807 |
| David Travis | Henderson's | Jackson | 16 May 1808 |
| Whitson Young's orphans | Montgomery's | Burke | 12 Nov. 1828 (E. M. Pearce) |
| Joseph Benson | Kennon's | Lincoln | 18 Nov. 1809 |
| Laird W. Harris | Huff's | Hancock | 2 Dec. 1807 |
| Simon Brewer | Week's | Hancock | 22 Dec. 1807 |
| Jeremiah Miller | Martin's | Burke | 21 June 1808 |
| James McClain | Thompson's | Franklin | 19 Nov. 1807 |
| Charles Finch | Pope's | Oglethorpe | 25 Feb. 1808 |
| Elizabeth Steptoe (orphan) | Sandiford's | Burke | 13 Feb. 1808 |
| John Germany, Jr. | 3rd | Columbia | 5 Mar. 1808 |
| Loamia Granberry | | Jefferson | 12 Dec. 1807 |
| Jermiah Dean's orphans | Cochran's Bat. | Jackson | 1 Mar. 1813 |
| John Royal, Senr. | Morrison's | Elbert | 17 Sept. 1808 |
| John Kimbro | 3rd | Baldwin | 21 Nov. 1807 |
| Edmund Warren | Pettybone's | Chatham | 1 Dec. 1810 |
| Isham Gunter | Morrison's | Elbert | 30 May 1808 |
| Wm. Johnson | Cooper's | Wilkes | 12 Apr. 1808 |
| Jane Kennon | Tidell's | Wilkes | 22 Nov. 1809 |
| Mary McNair | 7th | Columbia | 19 Nov. 1807 |
| James Manning | Hillyer's | Elbert | 5 Nov. 1807 |
| William Coram | 9th | Columbia | 10 May 1808 |
| William Chapman | Pettybone's | Chatham | 13 Nov. 1807 |
| John Ivie | Weem's | Franklin | 11 June 1808 |
| Thomas Moreman | Wellborn's | Wilkes | 22 Aug. 1808 |
| Hezekiah Bussey's | Bussey's | Lincoln | 24 Sept. 1813 |
| John Britt, Senr. | Burney's | Washington | 20 Dec. 1809 |
| Wm. Smith, Jr. | Martin's | Clarke | 20 Oct. 1807 |
| Olympia Muse Morton (orphan) | Hooper's | Franklin | 11 Nov. 1809 |
| William Robertson | Martindale's | Clarke | 15 Nov. 1808 |
| Charles Loyd | Robinson's | Clarke | 18 Nov. 1808 |
| Luke Bozeman | 56th | Montgomery | 1 July 1809 |
| John Ball | Wright's Bat. | Jackson | 21 Nov. 1807 |
| Salathiel Holton | W. Rebfroe's | Washington | 5 Mar. 1808 |

| | | | |
|---|---|---|---|
| Sarah Turner (orphan) | Garrett's | Washington | 9 Dec. 1816 |
| Wm. Harris' orphans | Levi's | Greene | 14 Sept. 1810 |
| William Stinson | 2nd | Baldwin | 21 Jan. 1808 |
| Thomas Ingram | Bussey's | Lincoln | 14 Jan. 1808 |
| Lemuel Page | Anderson's | Washington | 3 Dec. 1808 |
| Jacob Ammons | Jones' | Lincoln | 15 Dec. 1808 |
| James Lamkin (orphans of Jeremiah) | 3rd. | Columbia | 25 May 1808 |
| James Carter | Willson's | Warren | 21 Oct. 1807 |
| Nicholas Baggett | | Jefferson | 3 Dec. 1807 |
| Polly Locker | Shiver's | Hancock | 24 Aug. 1808 |
| Leonard Sims | Byne's | Burke | 16 Nov. 1811 |
| Thomas Duffill | Wiggins | Washington | 30 Sept. 1813 |
| Lemuel Green | Watson's | Greene | 12 Dec. 1807 |
| Samuel Graham | 1st | Baldwin | 15 Dec. 1808 |
| Travis Thigpen | 53rd | Montgomery | 4 Dec. 1813 |
| James Mercer | Dixon's | Franklin | 22 Sept. 1813 |
| Jesse Baker | Barkesdale's | Hancock | 29 Jan. 1808 |
| Jonas Daniel | Kendricks | Washington | 14 Sept. 1808 |
| William Beard | Johnson's Bat. | Jackson | 25 Nov. 1807 |
| David Love's orphans | Stewarts | Greene | 25 Oct. 1807 |
| Daniel Highsmith | Halls | Tattnall | 22 June 1810 |
| Hugh Montgomery | Bosticks | Jefferson | 2 Feb. 1808 |
| Joseph Adcock | May's | Lincoln | 20 May 1808 |
| Robert Tripp | Barne's | Hancock | 24 Jan. 1811 |
| Benjn. Daniel | 50th | Montgomery | 5 Oct. 1809 |
| David Pinkerton | 5th | Baldwin | 3 Oct. 1809 |
| Verity Farmer | Byne's | Burke | 15 Dec. 1808 |
| Adam Cope | Pettybone's | Chatham | 7 Dec. 1807 |
| George Earnest Sr. | Pinkston's | Hancock | 8 Jan. 1808 |
| James Leak (orphan) | Robertson's | Clarke | 9 Nov. 1810 |
| Robert Hammock | Young's | Wilkes (Hardens Creek) | 10 Nov. 1807 |
| Aaron Aldridge | Neal's | Warren | 22 Jan. 1808 |
| Benjn. Humphrey | Cook's | Clarke | 24 Oct. 1807 |
| Lydia Meadows | Moore's | Greene | 8 Feb. 1808 |
| John Linzy | Godfrey's | Bullock | 9 Feb. 1807 |
| Lewis Braddy | Devereux's | Warren | 18 Jan. 1808 |
| Henry Fletcher | Parish's | Bullock | 10 May 1808 |
| Benjn. Jones | | Liberty | 8 Jan. 1808 |
| James Fulcher | McDonald's | Tattnall | 15 Dec. 1808 |
| William Martin | Hitchcock's | Oglethorpe | 3 Nov. 1807 |
| Leonard Keeling | Keeling's | Elbert | 27 Nov. 1809 |
| Richard Whitefield | Neyle's | Chatham | 29 Dec. 1807 |
| Nathaniel Parkhard | | Screven | 10 May 1808 |
| Polly Willis | Willis' | Washington | 2 Aug. 1813 |
| Stafford Selman | Cleghorn's | Franklin | 12 May 1808 |
| Wm. Sally & Felix Elon | Pemberton's | Chatham | 29 July 1808 |
| Samuel Jourdan | Cockran's Bat. | Jackson | 6 Mar. 1809 |
| Thomas Gilham | Beasley's | Oglethorpe | 11 May 1808 |
| William Flournoy | Smith's | Hancock | 16 Aug. 1811 |
| Reubin McLean | Beasley's | Oglethorpe | 30 Oct. 1807 |
| John Jones | Crews' | Camden | 24 Feb. 1808 |

| Name | Company | County | Date |
|---|---|---|---|
| William Greene | 1st | Baldwin | 26 Nov. 1807 |
| Adam Cope | Pettybone's | Chatham | 7 Dec. 1807 |
| Robert Smith | Keeling's | Elbert | 20 July 1808 |
| Daniel Brown | Dye's | Elbert | 31 Dec. 1807 |
| George Shaw | Newsom's | Warren | 9 Jan. 1808 |
| George Cawley | 54th | Montgomery | 12 Dec. 1807 (Granted to Geo. Crawley) |
| Sophia Seales | Thomas' | Hancock | 5 Dec. 1807 |
| John Oliffs' orphans | Williams | Bullock | 19 May 1808 |
| Walker Lewis | Love's | Greene | 25 July 1808 |
| Randall Sorrow | Hewell's | Oglethorpe | 9 Aug. 1808 |
| Edmund Cody | Neal's | Warren | 1 Dec. 1807 |
| Thomas Angle | Smith's | Oglethorpe | 5 Jan. 1808 |
| David King | Burney's | Washington | 23 Oct. 1807 |
| William Thompson | Henderson's | Jackson | 9 Jan. 1808 |
| Elizabeth Walters | Conner's | Franklin | 16 Nov. 1808 |
| John Martin | Chiver's | Washington | 13 Jan. 1808 |
| Charles Brooks | Flourney's | Warren | 26 Nov. 1807 |
| Valentine Mooney | Cockran's Bat. | Jackson | 13 Nov. 1814 |
| James, John, Elizabeth, Clary & Mary Ware, orphans | | Richmond | 9 Nov. 1814 |
| Nathaniel Camp | Wright's Bat. | Jackson | 24 Nov. 1807 |
| Timothy C. Dunaway | Norman's | Wilkes | 10 Dec. 1810 |
| Anthony Minter | Renfroe's | Washington | 7 Nov. 1808 |
| William Purvis | Hendley's | Bulloch | 20 Oct. 1807 |
| Elizabeth M. Kidd | Clark's | Elbert | 12 Apr. 1808 |
| William Willson | McDowell's | Franklin | 14 Jan. 1811 |
| John Snider | | Richmond | 5 May 1808 |
| James McFarland | Carter's | Warren | 22 Dec. 1809 |
| Edward Kelly | Renfroe's | Washington | 6 Feb. 1808 |
| John McDaniel | 2nd | Wayne | 26 Dec. 1809 |
| Washington Wems | Bryant's | Franklin | 5 Nov. 1807 |
| Isaac Parker | Coffee's | Hancock | 11 Jan. 1808 |
| Edward Mobley | Holt's | Hancock | 23 Aug. 1809 |
| John Miller | Henderson's Bat. | Jackson | 20 May 1808 |
| Sarah Griner | William's | Bullock | 3 Dec. 1807 |
| Nathan Chaffin | Malone's | Wilkes | 5 Feb. 1810 |
| Isaac Edmundson | Parish's | Bullock | 19 Nov. 1807 |
| Joseph Cowen | 1st | Baldwin | 31 Dec. 1807 |
| Thomas Spencer | Howard's | Washington | 30 Nov. 1809 |
| James Jordan | Roebuck's | Elbert | 18 Aug. 1810 |
| James Sanders | 3rd | Baldwin | 23 Mar. 1808 |
| Mark Rawlings | 3rd | Baldwin | 17 Dec. 1807 |
| James McCullough | | Liberty | 21 Nov. 1807 |
| Collier Barksdale | Cooper's | Hancock | 10 July 1809 |
| Isaac Tredwell | Hopkin's | Clarke | 14 Jan. 1808 |
| Allen Bullard | Morrison's | Elbert | 22 Oct. 1807 |
| Pickett Shiflet | Roebuck's | Elbert | 13 Apr. 1810 |
| John Lewis | Sandiford's | Burke | 29 Oct. 1807 |
| Joseph Carter | Carter's | Warren | 6 May 1809 |
| George Daniel | Harper's | Clarke | 7 Nov. 1808 |
| Jane Findley | Greer's | Greene | 10 May 1808 |
| John Bassett | | McIntosh | 1 Dec. 1807 |

| | | | |
|---|---|---|---|
| John Moss, Jr. | King's | Lincoln | 13 July 1809 |
| Samuel King | Neyle's | Chatham | 20 May 1808 |
| Nancy Neyland | Kendrck's | Washington | 21 May 1808 |
| Mary Burnett | Williams | Bullock | 22 Oct. 1807 |
| James Sheperson | Hutchison's | Screven | 6 Jan. 1808 |
| Burrell Rose | | Screven | 21 Nov. 1807 |
| Joseph Jones | Moore's | Oglethorpe | 21 Nov. 1807 |
| Maulden Amos | 10th | Columbia | 19 Nov. 1812 |
| James Parnell | 4th | Baldwin | 6 Mar. 1810 |
| Nicholas Dickson | Hudson's | Hancock | 29 Apr. 1808 |
| William Bland's orphans | Mulkey's | Burke | 16 Nov. 1808 |
| Reddick Watson | | Wilkinson | 6 July 1808 |
| Joseph Neel | Keelings | Elbert | 24 Nov. 1807 |
| Wm. & Mary Thornhill (orphans) | Forth's | Burke | 15 Dec. 1809 |
| Lewis Smith | 3rd | Baldwin | 2 Nov. 1807 |
| Levi Phillips | Hitchcok's | Oglethorpe | 21 Nov. 1807 |
| Thomas Jordan | Garrett's | Washington | 9 Jan. 1808 |
| Robert Craig | 57th | Montgomery | 30 Sep. 1813 |
| John Frazer | Jones' | Lincoln | 3 Feb. 1808 |
| Mary Deens (widow) | Burney's | Washington | 20 Jan. 1808 |
| William Barker | Milner's | Wilkes | 9 Feb. 1808 |
| Nancy Little | Collins' | Washington | 10 Nov. 1808 |
| Elias Bailey | Thompson's | Burke | 17 Dec. 1807 |
| Wm. Dredden | | Wilkinson | 10 May 1808 |
| John Patrick | 1st | Columbia | 7 Dec. 1808 |
| William Burford | Rea's | Greene | 28 Sept. 1813 |
| Samuel Horton | Gumm's | Hancock | 31 Oct. 1807 |
| Thomas Gordon | Baine's | Hancock | 31 Dec. 1807 |
| Thomas Spalding | | McIntosh | 31 Nov. 1807 |
| Henry Ezzell | Birdsong's | Hancock | 30 Oct. 1807 |
| Labon Kent | | Effingham | 10 May 1808 |
| James Colley | Watkin's | Oglethorpe | 5 Oct. 1809 |
| Jesse Smith's orphans | Collins | Washington | 23 Mar. 1814 |
| Benjamin Jones, Sr. | Cockran's Bat. | Jackson | 22 Dec. 1814 |
| Redden Stringer | 50th | Montgomery | 23 Nov. 1808 |
| Joel Early | Watt's | Greene | 19 Nov. 1807 |
| Rebecca Stanton | Winslett's | Hancock | 30 Jan. 1808 |
| Silas Grigg | Edge's | Wilkes | 4 June 1808 |
| David Tilley | Sandiford's | Burke | 31 Oct. 1807 |
| Thomas Landrum | Hatchett's | Oglethorpe | 31 Dec. 1808 |
| James Blackstone | 6th | Columbia | 29 Nov. 1808 |
| Thomas B. Miller | | Liberty | 30 Oct. 1807 |
| Thomas Fontain | Jones' | Warren | 16 June 1808 |
| Mary Harnage (widow) | | Liberty | 22 July 1808 |
| Jacob Lamb | Gorden's | Burke | 30 Jan. 1808 |
| Charles Tuggle | Grove's | Elbert | 28 Oct. 1807 |
| Jermiah Peters | Cooper's | Wilkes | 30 Nov. 1810 |
| John Lewis, Jr. (M) | Hudson's | Hancock | 30 Sept. 1812 |
| Keziah McCardell (widow) | Bussey's | Lincoln | 1 Mar. 1808 |
| James Shackleford | Roebuck's | Elbert | 22 Nov. 1809 |
| James Burditt | Cooper's | Wilkes | 5 Nov. 1810 |
| Mary Gray | Ballard's | Burke | 18 May 1808 |
| John Laws | Jenkins' | Greene | 14 Nov. 1808 |
| William Smith | Robinson's | Clarke | 25 July 1808 |

| Name | Company | County | Date |
|---|---|---|---|
| John Pierce | Sharp's | Burke | 7 Nov. 1807 |
| Adam Loving | Heard's | Wilkes | 12 Dec. 1807 |
| Anna Dewberry (widow) | Heath's | Warren | 24 Aug. 1808 |
| Nathaniel Coates, Sr. | Rony's | Wilkes | 6 Oct. 1808 |
| Zachariah Lewis Fryar, Sr. | Gordon's | Burke | 12 Nov. 1808 |
| William York | Everett's | Franklin | 25 Apr. 1808 |
| Joshua Hodges, Jr. | Williams' | Bulloch | 11 Jan. 1808 |
| Phebe Dixon | Willis' | Washington | 20 May 1808 |
| Samuel Foster's orphans | Week's | Hancock | 2 May 1814 |
| Henry Taylor | Selman's | Clarke | 2 Jan. 1809 |
| Samuel Boggs | Hendrick's | Wilkes | 1 June 1808 |
| Joel Grizzell | Thompson's | Elbert | 20 Apr. 1808 |
| William Anderson | Spain's | Burke | 7 Nov. 1807 |
| John Brinkley | 3rd | Baldwin | 21 Oct. 1807 |
| Edward Cox | 3rd | Baldwin | 8 July 1808 |
| William Slaughter | Alford's | Greene | 24 Nov. 1807 |
| John Cone | Garrett's | Washington | 25 June 1809 |
| William Lyon | | Richmond | 18 Oct. 1808 |
| Jonas Stephens | Hardwick's | Jefferson | 23 Oct. 1809 |
| William Swain | | Glynn | 5 Dec. 1807 |
| Jacob Rogers | Denmark's | Bulloch | 8 Jan. 1808 |
| Nathaniel Howell | Owsley's | Grene | 12 Oct. 1810 |
| Charles Lawther | | Screven | 30 Nov. 1807 |
| Elizabeth Wynne (widow) | Forth's | Burke | 16 July 1810 |
| Simon Bardin | Hardwick's | Jefferson | 14 May 1808 |
| John Olive | 7th | Columbia | 12 Nov. 1808 |
| John Walraven | Everett's | Franklin | 1 Mar. 1808 |
| Dempsey Wood | Sherrard's | Tattnall | 10 May 1808 |
| Benjamin Finney | 6th | Columbia | 28 Oct. 1807 |
| Charles Sawyer | Butler's | Clarke | 21 Nov. 1807 |
| Timothy McGuire | Cockran's Bat. | Jackson | 16 Jan. 1809 |
| Thomas Franklin | | Wilkinson | 31 Aug. 1808 |
| John Bonnell, Sr. | | Screven | 29 Dec. 1807 |
| James Carter | 1st | Baldwin | 11 Apr. 1808 |
| Francis Cook | Dye's | Elbert | 20 Nov. 1807 |
| Christopher Lowry | McDowell's | Franklin | 15 Nov. 1809 |
| William Riley | Henderson's | Wilkes | 18 Dec. 1807 |
| Elijah Betsell (orphans of Isaac) | Cooper's | Wilkes | 7 Nov. 1807 |
| Francis Poythress' orphans | Coffee's | Hancock | 20 Nov. 1809 |
| Clara Rogers (Miss) | Baker's | Warren | 24 May 1808 |
| John Raiford | | Jefferson | 15 Apr. 1808 |
| John Stepp | Stewart's | Oglethorpe | 22 Mar. 1808 |
| Thomas King's orphans | | Liberty | 9 Dec. 1816 |
| David Hart | Bostick's | Jefferson | 30 Nov. 1808 |
| Absalom Davis, Sr. | Thomspon's | Elbert | 5 Oct. 1809 |
| William Curry | Carlton's | Greene | 7 Dec. 1807 |
| Benjamin Ansley | | Chatham | 22 Jan. 1808 |
| Henry Jordan | 1st | Baldwin | 15 Jan. 1810 |
| Dempsey Taylor | | Wilkinson | 28 May 1808 |
| Isaac Pennington | Wright's Bat. | Jackson | 3 Mar. 1808 |
| Jesse Weathers, Sr. | Armor's | Greene | 26 Nov. 1807 |
| Ambrose Murphey | Collin's | Washington | 29 Sept. 1808 |
| Thomas Grant's orphans | Henderson's | Wilkes | 12 Oct. 1810 |
| David Huckeby | Barksdale's | Hancock | 15 Mar. 1809 |

| Name | District | County | Date |
|---|---|---|---|
| Thomas Atkinson | Wellborn's | Wilkes | 19 Nov. 1807 |
| David Walker, Sr. | 6th | Columbia | 16 Dec. 1808 |
| William B. Maxwell | Abraham's | Chatham | 25 Jan. 1808 |
| Charles Stovall | May's | Lincoln | 1 Apr. 1808 |
| John Wingfield | Hatchett's | Oglethorpe | 12 Jan. 1808 |
| William Loyd | Robinson's | Clarke | 3 Aug. 1808 |
| Wm. Baker, Sr. orphans | | Liberty | 14 Oct. 1808 |
| James Clayton | Johnson's Bat. | Jackson | 24 Oct. 1807 |
| Reubin Barrow | Devereux's | Warren | 1 Feb. 1808 |
| Jonathan Hogue | Bell's | Oglethorpe | 8 Feb. 1811 |
| Alexander Campbell | 3rd | Columbia | 3 Nov. 1807 |
| Peter Strozer, Sr. | Henderson's | Wilkes | 5 Dec. 1807 |
| Stephen Tredwell | Hopkin's | Clarke | 22 Nov. 1808 |
| John Carrell | 4th | Baldwin | 12 Dec. 1808 |
| John Jackson | Rorey's | Wilkes | 25 May 1809 |
| Robert Ratliff's orphans | Jones' | Lincoln | 29 Mar. 1808 |
| William Garr | Clark's | Elbert | 16 Jan. 1809 |
| John Alley | Abraham's | Chatham | 25 Feb. 1808 |
| Willis Wall | Clark's | Elbert | 19 Dec. 1808 |
| John McDonald's orphans | Spain's | Burke | 19 Dec. 1808 |
| Samuel Johnson | Owsley's | Grene | 25 Jan. 1808 |
| Rebecca Cleghorn | Cleghorn's | Franklin | 15 Mar. 1809 |
| Stephen Daniel | 3rd Dist. | Baldwin | 10 Nov. 1808 |
| John Alston | | Effingham | 6 Mar. 1810 |
| Alexander S. Roe | White's | Chatham | 17 Dec. 1808 |
| lexander Scroggins | Moore's | Oglethorpe | 22 Nov. 1808 |
| Lewis Lee | Bostick's | Jefferson | 25 Aug. 1808 |
| Cecileus Camp | Brown's | Clarke | 25 Aug. 1808 |
| Robert McEver | Cockran's Bat. | Jackson | 1 Feb. 1808 |
| Edmund, Peter, Samuel, Susannah & Thomas Jefferson Bugg orphans | | Richmond | 5 Apr. 1808 |
| Benjamin Salmons | Coleman's | Jefferson | 24 July 1808 |
| Peter Goolesby, Sr. | Smith's | Oglethorpe | 10 Dec. 1807 |
| John Burkhalter, Sr. | Neal's | Warren | 8 Jan. 1808 |
| Daniel Yarnell, Sr. | Hudson's | Hancock | 3 Nov. 1807 |
| John Wyall, Sr. | 5th Dist. | Baldwin | 17 Nov. 1807 |
| Mary Dye | Neal's | Warren | 31 Oct. 1807 |
| Randall Cornett | Montgomery's | Burke | 18 Jan. 1808 |

## 25 DISTRICT WILKINSON COUNTY 1805
*(Now Twiggs County)*

| NAMES | DISTRICT | RESIDENCE | DATE |
|---|---|---|---|
| Christian D. & Ephriam Keiffer (orphans) | | Effingham | 16 Dec. 1811 |
| Charles Sheppard | Chiver's | Washington | 17 Dec. 1808 |
| Julian Bailey | Blackwell's | Elbert | 20 Mar. 1810 |
| Abram Crowley | Hatchett's | Oglethorpe | 15 Nov. 1808 |
| Phillip Miller's orphans | Mulkey's | Burke | 7 Dec. 1808 |
| Milly Dean (S. W.) | Hitchcock's | Clarke | 16 Feb. 1808 |
| Molton Gray | Week's | Hancock | 6 Dec. 1808 |
| Wm. Duncan | Keeling's | Elbert | 22 Jan. 1808 |
| Peter Guerard | Abraham's | Chatham | 22 Jan. 1808 |
| Wm. Russell | Spain's | Burke | 25 Nov. 1807 |
| Stephen Stanford's orphans | 9th | Columbia | 25 Sept. 1813 |
| John M. Lee | Mulkey's | Burke | 2 Jan. 1808 |
| Martha Wood | Montgomery's | Burke | 4 May 1808 |
| Allen Arnold | Bell's | Oglethorpe | 28 July 1808 |
| Green Reeves | Howard's | Washington | 1 Dec. 1808 |
| Jeremiah Connell | Love's | Greene | 6 Aug. 1808 |
| Sophia Densler | White's | Chatham | 25 Oct. 1808 |
| Henry Holcombe | Pettybone's | Chatham | 17 Feb. 1808 |
| Elijah Williams | Neal's | Warren | 7 Mar. 1808 |
| Wm. Drane | 7th | Columbia | 21 Nov. 1807 |
| Wm. Burt | Bryan's | Franklin | 4 Dec. 1808 |
| Dickerson Culpepper | Jones' | Warren | 31 May 1808 |
| Henry Thompson | Busey's | Lincoln | 22 Sept. 1813 |
| Jas. Gollcher | Heard's | Wilkes | 24 Nov. 1807 |
| Henry Hunt | Flounoy's | Greene | 2 Oct. 1809 |
| Page Talley | Tarver's | Jefferson | 24 July 1809 |
| Thos. Scott | Hudson's | Hancock | 1 Aug. 1815 |
| Elias Jernigan | William's | Bulloch | 24 Nov. 1808 |
| Josiah Erwin | Sidwell's | Wilkes | 11 Aug. 1810 |
| Henry Howell | Sharp's | Burke | 10 Dec. 1810 |
| Wm. Whigham | Fulton's | Jefferson | 11 May 1808 |
| Mary McBride | Tarver's | Jefferson | 14 Sept. 1808 |
| Mary Slaten | Wright's Bat. | Jackson | 12 Nov. 1808 |
| John Neely | Thomas' Dist. | Jefferson | 12 Nov. 1808 |
| John Muckeroy's orph. | Smith's | Oglethorpe | 15 Aug. 1809 |
| Eli Shankle | Johnson's Bat. | Jackson | 10 June 1809 |
| Randolph Traylor | Martin's Dist. | Clarke | 29 Sept. 1808 |
| French Strother | Hatchett's | Oglethorpe | 21 Feb. 1809 |
| Jac. Flournoy's orph. | Flounoy's | Warren | 7 Nov. 1814 |
| Stephen Sawyer | 1st | Baldwin | 25 Oct 1811 |
| John Jones | Wright's | Jefferson | 30 Sept. 1809 |
| Hartwell Moore | 1st | Baldwin | 21 Nov. 1807 |
| Elizabeth Duncan (widow) | Williamson's | Screven | 24 Apr. 1809 |
| Wm. Roland | Newsom's | Warren | 28 Nov. 1808 |
| Burwell Cannon | Henderson's | Wilkes | 5 Dec. 1807 |
| Amos Wright | Hill's | Warren | 8 Mar. 1808 |
| Robt. McGrady | Christian's | Franklin | 8 Dec. 1810 |
| Joel Phillips | 5th | Baldwin | 9 Nov. 1812 |
| Wm. Brumbly | Burney's | Washington | 8 Oct. 1808 |

| | | | |
|---|---|---|---|
| Wm. Brown | Baine's | Hancock | 19 Dec. 1807 |
| John Beard | Pettybone's | Chatham | 10 Nov. 1810 |
| Wm. Donaldson | Pettybone's | Chatham | 21 May 1808 |
| Jac. Lamb | Gordon's | Burke | 30 Jan. 1808 |
| Roland Williams, Jr. | Henderson's | Wilkes | 6 Dec. 1809 |
| Isaac Phillips | Butler's | Clarke | 27 Apr. 1808 |
| Asa Dennis | Wilson's | Warren | 23 Mar. 1808 |
| Thos. Parsons | | Glynn | 16 Dec. 1808 |
| Thos. Miles | Holt's | Washington | 13 Jan. 1809 |
| Jerusha Barefield | Martin's | Burke | 20 July 1808 |
| Jas. Pace | | Richmond | 6 Sept. 1811 |
| Leorard Abercrombie | 2nd | Baldwin | 13 Jan. 1810 |
| John Rowsey, Sr. | Oliver's | Elbert | 10 Mar. 1808 |
| Elizabeth Whitehead | Cockran's Bat. | Jackson | 24 Aug. 1810 |
| Wm. Hudgins | Gartrell's Dist. | Lincoln | 24 Oct. 1810 |
| Susannah Parrot (widow) | Blackshear's | Washington | 4 Oct. 1808 |
| John Ashurst | Smith's | Hancock | 22 May 1810 |
| Robt. Thompson | Davenport's | Greene | 22 Oct. 1807 |
| Chas. Webb | Abraham's | Chatham | 6 Nov. 1809 |
| Isaac Pevey's orph. | | Screven | 25 Aug. 1808 |
| Elizabeth Harris | Jones' | Lincoln | 18 Dec. 1810 |
| David Sloan | McLean's | Chatham | 24 Oct. 1808 |
| Sally Wiggins | Carswell's | Burke | 24 Sept. 1810 |
| John Yarbrough | Williams | Bullock | 2 May 1808 |
| Wm. Landers | 4th | Columbia | 13 Dec. 1808 |
| John Slater | Pettybone's | Chatham | 22 Oct. 1808 |
| John Childers | Jno. Smith's | Oglethorpe | 1 Aug. 1808 |
| Geo. Ozborn | Flournoy's | Warren | 21 July 1808 |
| Anthony Story | Williford's | Elbert | 24 Nov. 1807 |
| Wm. Greer | Hudson's | Oglethorpe | 17 Aug. 1808 |
| Jesse Dunford | Spain's | Burke | 10 Oct. 1808 |
| Jos. Hobbs | Beasley's | Oglethorpe | 20 Oct. 1807 |
| Wm. Barnes | | Glynn | 23 Apr. 1808 |
| Belinda Slade (Miss) | Baker's | Warren | 15 Sept. 1808 |
| Robt. D. Martin | Carlton's | Greene | 28 Nov. 1808 |
| John Perryman | 10th | Columbia | 22 May 1809 |
| Ann McCullough | | Richmond | 12 Nov. 1808 |
| Jesse Johnson | J. Henderson's | Wilkes | 21 Sept. 1813 |
| Delila Guice (widow) | Jones' | Lincoln | 14 Dec. 1808 |
| Francis Loyal's orph. | Hitchcock's | Clarke | 11 Dec. 1810 |
| Drury Stovall | May's | Lincoln | 29 Mar. 1808 |
| Henry Jackson | Heard's | Wilkes | 7 Nov. 1814 |
| Robt. Nixon | 3rd | Baldwin | 30 Oct. 1810 |
| John Farrell | Rony's | Wilkes | 5 Dec. 1807 |
| Wm. Way | | Richmond | 7 Dec. 1808 |
| Thos. Edwards | Moore's | Greene | 6 Apr. 1808 |
| Wm. Nelson Jr. | 52nd | Montgomery | 19 July 1810 |
| Hugh Montgomery | Wright's | Jackson | 7 Nov. 1807 |
| John Tompkins | Ashley's | Camden | 24 Feb. 1808 |
| Willm. McCracken | Dixon's | Franklin | 14 Nov. 1808 |
| John Waddel | Tramell's | Clarke | 24 Nov. 1807 |
| Alexander Angelly | | Jefferson | 30 Nov. 1810 |
| Jas. McMullen's orph. | Montgomery's | Burke | 8 Nov. 1815 |
| John Oliver. Sr. | Oliver's | Screven | 15 Dec. 1808 |

| | | | |
|---|---|---|---|
| Perrin Farrow | Cockran's Bat. | Jackson | 1 Sept. 1813 |
| Solomon Willson | Martin's Dist. | Burke | 13 Sept. 1808 |
| Tilman Nibblet | Barker's | Warren | 29 Jan. 1811 |
| Moses Fillinger | Dawson's | Greene | 6 Sept. 1813 |
| Wm. Gray | Martin's | Burke | 11 Sept. 1808 |
| Pleasant Turner | Wellborns | Wilkes | 29 Sept. 1808 |
| Isaac Muckleroy | Moore's | Oglethorpe | 8 Nov. 1808 |
| David Beaty | Moore's | Oglethorpe | 21 Feb. 1810 |
| John Barnett | Hudson's | Oglethorpe | 9 Nov. 1812 |
| Absalom Barrow | 51st | Montgomery | 22 Dec. 1808 |
| Geo. Woodruff | Pemberton's | Chatham | 3 Dec. 1807 |
| Richd. Hubbard | Thompson's | Elbert | 11 Jan. 1808 |
| Joel Denson | | Wilkinson | 7 Nov. 1807 |
| Elisha Pullen | Sheet's | Wilkes | 5 Mar. 1808 |
| Jane Hubbard | Clarke's | Elbert | 17 Sept. 1810 |
| Sterling Heath | Barnes | Hancock | 2 Nov. 1810 |
| Wm. Starks | 10th | Columbia | 21 May 1808 |
| Thos. Findley | Blount's | Burke | 28 Oct. 1808 |
| Fereby Griffin | Carswell's | Burke | 1 Nov. 1810 |
| John Casey | Henderson's | Jackson | 15 Nov. 1808 |
| Geo. King's orph. | 4th | Columbia | 5 Feb. 1810 |
| Chas. Buckner | Shiver's | Hancock | 18 Dec. 1807 |
| Margaret Quinn | 10th | Columbia | 8 Dec. 1808 |
| Thos. B. Scott | Mobley's | Elbert | 4 Apr. 1809 |
| John Heath | Renfroe's | Washington | 31 Oct. 1808 |
| Absalom Eakin | Keeling's | Elbert | 15 Nov. 1808 |
| John G. Underwood | | Liberty | 8 Dec. 1807 |
| Wm. Andrews | Birdsong's | Hancock | 27 Nov. 1807 |
| Williby Fenn | Robinson's | Clarke | 21 Dec. 1810 |
| Ayres Cartledge | 4th | Columbia | 2 Dec. 1807 |
| Wm. Badula's orph. | Sandiford's | Burke | 21 Nov. 1807 |
| John Henneda | Busey's | Lincoln | 4 Nov. 1807 |
| Saml. McGehee | Thompson's | Elbert | 11 Jan. 1808 |
| Wm. Daniel (maj.) | Watt's | Greene | 21 Feb. 1810 |
| Edm'd. Byne's orph. | Byne's | Burke | 29 Nov. 1811 |
| Jas. Benley's orph. | Martin's | Burke | 14 Dec. 1808 |
| Wm. Hill | Gumm's | Hancock | 12 Mar. 1808 |
| Frances Burge (widow) | Carter's | Warren | 1 Feb. 1808 |
| Jas. Hall, Sr. | | Jefferson | 28 Jan. 1808 |
| Richd. S. Footman's orph. | Austin's | Bryan | 21 Jan. 1808 |
| Aaron Goolesby | Smith's | Oglethorpe | 21 Jan. 1808 |
| Robt. Garrard | Sidwell's | Wilkes | 3 Feb. 1810 |
| Wm. Cope | Cockran's Bat. | Jackson | 20 Oct. 1807 |
| Polly Lamar (orph.) | | Richmond | 16 May 1808 |
| Nathaniel Bridges | 1st Dist. | Baldwin | 17 Sept. 1808 |
| Wm. Gibson | Smith's | Camden | 22 June 1808 |
| Job Jackson | Barksdale's | Hancock | 29 Dec. 1810 |
| Geo. Cliffton | Cook's | Clarke | 29 July 1808 |
| Eirie Perkins' orph. | Wright's | Jefferson | 10 Mar. 1808 |
| Jac. Hensler | | Effingham | 5 Dec. 1807 |
| Wm. Yarbrough | Hitchcock's | Clarke | 1 Apr. 1809 |
| Peter Hughes | Moore's | Oglethorpe | 19 Nov. 1807 |
| Edward Ross | 8th | Columbia | 23 May 1811 |
| Samuel Williams | | Richmond | 12 Nov. 1808 |

| | | | |
|---|---|---|---|
| Richd. Smith | Rea's | Greene | 2 Sept. 1811 |
| John Brooks | Wright's Bat. | Jackson | 31 Dec. 1811 |
| Campbell Marrable | Hudson's Dist. | Oglethorpe | 16 Nov. 1809 |
| Wm. P. Hardwick | Hardwick's | Jefferson | 10 Dec. 1807 |
| Caleb Bazer | 3rd | Baldwin | 28 Mar. 1808 |
| Jas. Pye, Sr. | Jno. Smith's | Oglethorpe | 12 Nov. 1808 |
| Thos. Wood's orph. | 2nd | Baldwin | 15 Nov. 1816 |
| Haywood Harper | Harper's | Clarke | 11 Apr. 1808 |
| Jas. Stewart | Mitchell's | Clarke | 7 Aug. 1815 |
| Thos. Reed, Jr. | 10th | Columbia | 10 July 1809 |
| Matthew Carter, Jr. | Denmark's | Bullock | 9 May 1808 |
| Harriett Carpenter | Pettybone's | Chatham | 4 Feb. 1808 |
| John Perkins' orph. | Holt's | Hancock | 27 Dec. 1810 |
| Jane Kennedy | Tarver's | Jefferson | 21 Sept. 1809 |
| Jos. Key | Carlton's | Greene | 10 Nov. 1810 |
| Jos. Christler | Clark's | Elbert | 22 Dec. 1808 |
| Jas. Green, Sr. | 1st | Baldwin | 25 July 1808 |
| Robt. Strickland | 2nd | Baldwin | 20 Dec. 1808 |
| John Patterson, Sr. | Blount's | Burke | 11 Oct. 1810 |
| Robt. Lucas | Cooper's | Hancock | 19 Oct. 1808 |
| John McTire | | Richmond | 25 Nov. 1808 |
| Keriah Kemp | Delk's | Washington | 27 July 1808 |
| John Jeter | 2nd | Baldwin | 12 Dec. 1808 |
| Christian Williamson | Pace's | Washington | 2 June 1809 |
| Daniel Chitwood | Griffith's | Franklin | 21 Dec. 1810 |
| Francis Jones | | Screven | 25 Aug. 1808 |
| John Dukes | Duke's | Clarke | 11 May 1810 |
| Benj. Wilkinson | Heard's | Wilkes | 24 Jan. 1812 |
| Thos. Carter | 2nd | Baldwin | 7 Feb. 1808 |
| David Bailey | Chiver's | Washington | 30 Aug. 1814 |
| Gotthelf Sherrans | | Effingham | 22 Apr. 1808 |
| Elizabeth Belcher | Forth's | Burke | 20 Dec. 1808 |
| John Vickers | Silman's | Clarke | 4 May 1812 |
| Jesse Davidson | Carter's | Warren | 5 Feb. 1810 |
| Polly Yarborough (Miss) | Heath's | Warren | 8 Feb. 1811 |
| John Green, Sr. | Brown's | Clarke | 28 Dec. 1807 |
| John Pearre, Sr. | 5th | Columbia | 23 Nov. 1808 |
| Thos. Studstill | Brown's | Camden | 12 Sept. 1812 |
| Chas. Wheeler | 6th | Columbia | 3 Feb. 1810 |
| Tamerlane Jones | Crowder's | Hancock | 21 Mar. 1815 |
| Curtis King | Dawson's | Greene | 9 Nov. 1812 |
| Acton Nash | Henderson's | Wilkes | 22 Jan. 1808 |
| Lachariah Knowles, Sr. | Fields' | Burke | 1 Aug. 1808 |
| Thos. Murray's orph. | Hartsfield's | Oglethorpe | 20 Sept. 1809 |
| Asa Crabb | 4th | Columbia | 27 Nov. 1811 |
| John Allen | Devereux's | Warren | 31 Dec. 1807 |
| Saml. Whitaker | | Richmond | 21 June 1810 |
| John Ragan | 2nd | Baldwin | 17 Dec. 1811 |
| Wm. Haynie | Martin's | Burke | 31 May 1813 |
| John Gemiany, Sr. | 3rd | Columbia | 21 Dec. 1808 |
| Jas. Wade, Sr. | Sheets' | Wilkes | 17 Nov. 1808 |
| Rebecca Baker (orphan) | Thomas' | Jefferson | 2 Feb. 1808 |
| Jas. Jenkins | Baker's | Warren | 15 Feb. 1809 |
| Jas. K. Jones | 10th | Columbia | 25 Mar. 1808 |

| | | | |
|---|---|---|---|
| Jas. Smylie | | Liberty | 27 Dec. 1808 |
| Philip Ihley | Harden's | Chatham | 8 Dec. 1807 |
| Danl. Playle | Oliver's | Screven | 26 Aug. 1808 |
| Sarah Harris | Renfroe's | Washington | 30 Sep. 1813 |
| Susannah Monfort | Carlton's | Greene | 27 Dec. 1808 |
| David Patterson | | Richmond | 19 Jan. 1809 |
| Epps Brown | Barne's | Hancock | 2 Dec. 1808 |
| Wm. Smith | Coleman's | Jefferson | 28 Sept. 1809 |
| Sally Bentley | Grove's | Elbert | 15 Nov. 1808 |
| Frizzle, Elizabeth, Fanny & Daniel Etherington (orphans) | | Richmond | 25 July 1809 |
| Jas. Blanchard | 3rd | Columbia | 12 Dec. 1808 |
| Henry Matthews | | Wilkinson | 4 June 1810 |
| Thos. Morgan | | Effingham | 10 May 1808 |
| Thos. S. Slaughter | Holt's | Hancock | 24 May 1811 |
| Chas. Groom | Holt's | Washington | 30 June 1810 |
| Peter Sudor | White's | Chatham | 22 Dec. 1807 |
| Thos. Pearson | | Liberty | 13 Oct. 1808 |
| Boaz Stanaland | Denmark's | Bullock | 9 Jan. 1808 |
| Shimy Drakes' orphans | Coffe's | Hancocvk | 12 Nov. 1828 |
| Mary Back (widow) | Jno. Smith's | Oglethorpe | 9 Sept. 1808 |
| Joachim D. Swinney | Huff's | Hancock | 16 Dec. 1808 |
| Thos. Smith | Moore's | Oglethorpe | 24 Aug. 1808 |
| Benj. Hampton | Cockran's Bat. | Jackson | 30 Sept. 1813 |
| Henry McNair's orphans | Neal's Dist. | Warren | 30 Sept. 1813 |
| Andrew Townsen | 5th | Baldwin | 5 June 1808 |
| Susannah Fry | Watkin's | Oglethorpe | 12 Aug. 1808 |
| Jas. Diell | Cockran's Bat. | Jackson | 24 Nov. 1807 |
| Reddick Smith | Greer's Dist. | Greene | 30 Sept. 1813 |
| Peter Durouzuex | | Jefferson | 25 Aug. 1808 |
| John Howell | 2nd | Baldwin | 2 Dec. 1807 |
| John Stanton | Heard's | Wilkes | 29 Mar. 1811 |
| David Irwin | 1st | Baldwin | 28 Jan. 1808 |
| Nathaniel Venable | Wright's | Jackson | 3 Feb. 1808 |
| Jas. Finch | Hudson's | Hancock | 11 Dec. 1810 |
| Simon Bexsley | Harb's | Chatham | 5 Nov. 1808 |
| John Morris | Cockran's Bat. | Jackson | 6 Apr. 1808 |
| Polly Parish | Love's Dist. | Greene | 28 Nov. 1809 |
| Philip D. Woolhopter | White's | Chatham | 18 Apr. 1808 |
| Jas. Boyt | Gordon's | Burke | 25 Nov. 1807 |
| Jer. Holliday's orphans | Wright's Bat. | Jackson | 5 Nov. 1812 |
| Absalom Harris | Cornelius Dist. | Franklin | 20 Jan. 1812 |
| Oney Copland | Bell's | Oglethorpe | 16 Aug. 1809 |
| Hannah Walker | Wright's Bat. | Jackson | 30 Nov. 1807 |
| Josiah Norris | Moore's Dist. | Oglethorpe | 28 Sept. 1813 |
| Isaac Collier | Beasley's | Oglethorpe | 26 Nov. 1807 |
| Chas. Smith | Henderson's Bat. | Jackson | 21 Nov. 1808 |
| Elizabeth Price (widow) | White's Dist. | Chatham | 2 Dec. 1807 |
| Elizabeth Hudson (widow) | Sims' | Clarke | 24 Nov. 1810 |
| Bray Warren | Newsom's | Warren | 22 Dec. 1809 |
| Edmund Lyon | King's | Lincoln | 5 Nov. 1808 |
| Edward Burke | | Richmond | 17 Oct. 1808 |

## 26 DISTRICT WILKINSON COUNTY 1805
*(Now Twiggs County)*

| NAMES | DISTRICT | RESIDENCE | DATE |
|---|---|---|---|
| Alex. Gordon | Fulton's | Jefferson | 29 Jan. 1808 |
| Jas. Marsh | Montgomery's | Burke | 23 Sept. 1808 |
| Timothy S. Barham | 1st | Columbia | 12 Nov. 1808 |
| Danl. Roberds | Baxter's | Greene | 12 Dec. 1807 |
| Jese Brown | Thomas' | Jefferson | 17 Oct. 1808 |
| Wm. Jeffries | Moore's | Greene | 6 Nov. 1811 |
| Obedience Bugg | | Richmond | 9 Nov. 1812 |
| Jas. Watson | 5th | Baldwin | 15 Jan. 1808 |
| Benj. Blitch | | Effingham | 18 Jan. 1808 |
| David Mims | Hall's | Tatnall | 5 Feb. 1808 |
| Susannah Petee | Cooper's | Wilkes | 5 Dec. 1809 |
| John Jones' orphans | Byne's | Burke | 12 Nov. 1808 |
| Thos. Dallis | Jones' | Lincoln | 3 Feb. 1808 |
| Jared Handley | Forth's | Burke | 26 Oct. 1808 |
| Jos. Thompson | Cockran's Bat. | Jackson | 13 Oct. 1808 |
| Jas. Salter | Collin's Dist. | Washington | 24 July 1809 |
| Christian Gugel | Pettybone's | Chatham | 7 Dec. 1807 |
| Saml. Strong | Jno. Smith's | Oglethorpe | 19 Dec. 1810 |
| Hardy Newsom | Willson's | Warren | 16 Feb. 1808 |
| Jinckes Perkins | McLean's | Chatham | 14 Dec. 1808 |
| Jas. Lyon | 3rd | Baldwin | 15 Oct. 1810 |
| Geo. Wheeler | Roebuck's | Elbert | 19 Nov. 1807 |
| Vachal Gater | Flemming's | Lincoln | 24 Nov. 1810 |
| John Tatom | Newsom's | Lincoln | 10 May 1808 |
| Aaron Wood | | Jackson | 5 Apr. 1809 |
| Alex. Steel | Mitchell's | Clarke | 26 Oct. 1807 |
| Jeremiah Terrell | Roebuck's | Elbert | 31 Dec. 1807 |
| Archalus Fluellen Esq. | Jones' | Warren | 5 Dec. 1807 |
| John Baker | Martin's | Clarke | 11 Nov. 1809 |
| Wm. Shockley | Henderson's Bat. | Jackson | 12 Apr. 1808 |
| David Hurley | Godfrey's Dist. | Bullock | 15 Jan. 1810 |
| Jesse Morris' orphans | 7th | Columbia | 25 Jan. 1808 |
| Wm. B. Peacock | | Liberty | 20 Nov. 1809 |
| Catherine Jarvey Goff (orphan) | Wright's | Jefferson | 31 Dec. 1807 |
| Bathsheba Jones | Hall's | Tatnall | 17 Aug. 1808 |
| Thos. Hutchens | Edge's | Wilkes | 1 Jan. 1808 |
| David McCormack | Duke's | Clarke | 19 Nov. 1810 |
| Stephen Knight | Williamson's | Screven | 29 Feb. 1808 |
| Lewis McElroy | Johnson's Bat. | Jackson | 23 Feb. 1808 |
| Abram Gibson's orphans | 5th Dist. | Columbia | 26 Oct. 1812 |
| Mary Gordon (widow) | Rony's | Wilkes | 12 May 1808 |
| Priscilla Dillard | Pace's | Washington | 10 Dec. 1807 |
| Wm. Sikes | | Richmond | 25 Nov. 1808 |
| Peter Brooks, Senr. | Johnson's Bat. | Jackson | 13 Apr. 1808 |
| Abram Christler | Johnson's Bat. | Jackson | 19 Nov. 1807 |
| Daniel Gunn, Sr. | Henderson's Dist. | Wilkes | 27 Nov. 1807 |
| Polly Jones | Waller's | Hancock | 2 Aug. 1808 |
| John Burk | Martin's | Burke | 3 Dec. 1808 |
| Michael Dixon | | Screven | 8 Jan. 1810 |
| Charity Hargrove (widow) | | Montgomery | 6 July 1811 |

| | | | |
|---|---|---|---|
| Josiah Ellington | Hendrick's | Wilkes | 7 Oct. 1808 |
| John Malone | Hitchcock's | Clarke | 2 Dec. 1808 |
| Francis Durrence | McDonald's | Tatnall | 2 Oct. 1809 |
| Thos. Morris orphans | Hutchinson's | Screven | 10 Dec. 1808 |
| Jos. Talbott | Henderson's | Wilkes | 3 Apr. 1813 |
| John C. Patrick | Jenkin's | Greene | 14 Jan. 1808 |
| E. Wyly's orphans | Oliver's | Screven | 25 Aug. 1818 |
| John Cartlidge's orphans | 3rd | Columbia | 12 Dec. 1808 |
| Chas. Garner | Duke's | Clarke | 20 July 1808 |
| Levi Horn | Johnson's Bat. | Jackson | 19 Jan. 1808 |
| Roger Harkins | 8th Dist. | Columbia | 20 May 1813 |
| Jas. Butler, Sr. | Cockran's Bat. | Jackson | 10 Feb. 1808 |
| Jesse Gunn | Ballard's Dist. | Burke | 26 Oct. 1810 |
| Peter Oliver | Flournoy's | Warren | 11 July 1810 |
| Thos. Jenkins, Jr. | Hooper's | Franklin | 25 May 1809 |
| Wm. Phillips | Butler's | Greene | 17 Nov. 1810 |
| Joel Jones | Barksdale's | Hancock | 31 Dec. 1807 |
| Matthew Phillips | Watt's | Greene | 22 Dec. 1807 |
| Benj. Walker | Neal's | Warren | 19 Nov. 1807 |
| Hugh Blair, Sr. | 11th | Columbia | 21 May 1808 |
| Urshla Doss (widow) | Johnson's Bat. | Jackson | 17 Dec. 1808 |
| Wm. Johnson | Hendley's Dist. | Bullock | 11 Dec. 1807 |
| Herman Crum | | Effingham | 13 Nov. 1809 |
| Robt. Walker | Rea's | Greene | 25 Sept. 1813 |
| Drury Towns | Thompson's | Elbert | 30 Nov. 1810 |
| John Orr | Henderson's Bat. | Jackson | 7 Jan. 1808 |
| Thos. Harris' orphans | Hitchcock's Dist. | Clarke | 28 July 1810 |
| Jos. Smith | 1st | Baldwin | 28 Nov. 1809 |
| Micah Calhoon | | Jefferson | 7 Aug. 1815 |
| Samuel Olive | Moore's | Oglethorpe | 6 Feb. 1810 |
| Wm. Blackwell, Sr. | Allen's | Franklin | 12 Nov. 1808 |
| Jac. Chivers | Renfroe's | Washington | 17 May 1809 |
| Sarah Morrel (widow) | 54th | Montgomery | 11 Jan. 1808 |
| Dorothy Langham (widow) | Henderson's | Wilkes | 30 Nov. 1809 |
| Anna Craige | Gordon's | Burke | 2 Mar. 1809 |
| Wm. Kennedy | | Richmond | 2 Dec. 1807 |
| Edward Ryan | Field's | Burke | 1 July 1810 |
| Permenns English | Stewart's | Oglethorpe | 25 Nov. 1807 |
| Joshua Baker, Sr. | Harper's | Clarke | 18 Mar. 1811 |
| Nancy Redding | Griffith's | Franklin | 22 Oct. 1807 |
| Jas. Kennedy | | Glynn | 4 May 1808 |
| Wm. Holley | 50th | Montgomery | 6 July 1808 |
| Edmund Tarvis | Herb's | Chatham | 30 Nov. 1808 |
| Elizabeth Cornelius | Harden's | Chatham | 15 Dec. 1809 |
| Solomon Perkins | Hendrix's | Wilkes | 2 Aug. 1810 |
| Thos. Bell's orphans | Barne's | Hancock | 24 June 1808 |
| Wm. Hall | Hall's | Tatnall | 26 July 1810 |
| Thos. L. Edwards | Howard's | Washington | 30 July 1810 |
| Hartwell Moore | 1st | Baldwin | 22 Oct. 1808 |
| Sally Eads (orphan) | Jno. Smith's | Oglethorpe | (no date listed) |
| Murrel Thomas | Silman's | Clarke | 21 Nov. 1807 |
| Jas. Bennett | Montgomery's | Burke | 29 Mar. 1808 |
| Ann Mary Zipperer (widow) | | Effingham | 16 Jan. 1809 |

| | | | |
|---|---|---|---|
| John Haynes | Hitchcock's | Clarke | 2 Dec. 1808 |
| Jos. Young | Love's | Greene | 12 July 1808 |
| Baldwin Fluker | Willis' | Washington | 26 Dec. 1808 |
| Jas. Nicholls, Jr. | Blount's | Burke | 25 Nov. 1808 |
| Josiah Hatcher | Ballard's | Burke | 23 Dec. 1808 |
| Eliza Johnson (L. J.) | Pemberton's | Chatham | 1 Nov. 1814 |
| Uriah Amoson | Garrett's | Washington | 26 Mar. 1808 |
| Thos. Phelps | Silman's | Clarke | 8 Dec. 1807 |
| Joshua Draper | Wilson's | Warren | 12 May 1810 |
| Jas. Hancock | McDonald's | Tatnall | 13 Nov. 1809 |
| John Turner | Thomas' | Jefferson | 16 Dec. 1808 |
| Richard Hill | Baker's | Warren | 7 July 1809 |
| Michael Bailey's orphans | Sheet's | Wilkes | 21 Oct. 1812 |
| John Boston, Jr. | | Effingham | 9 Nov. 1808 |
| John Goza | Holt's | Washington | 22 Mar. 1808 |
| John Horn | Delk's | Washington | 15 Feb. 1808 |
| Aaron Greer | Dawson's | Greene | 25 Oct. 1814 |
| Tyra Swift | Hooper's | Franklin | 25 Nov. 1808 |
| John Lane, Jr. | Cornelius | Franklin | 19 Nov. 1810 |
| T. Poole (Miss) | Baker's | Warren | 15 Nov. 1808 |
| Leonard Nobles | | Richmond | 14 Sept. 1809 |
| David Speer | Rea's | Greene | 6 June 1809 |
| Benj. Bevin | 11th | Columbia | 30 Nov. 1807 |
| Nathan Bostick | Bostick's | Jefferson | 15 Nov. 1808 |
| Penelope Ridgdell | Neal's | Warren | 7 Mar. 1808 |
| Jac. Reed | Hitchcock's | Oglethorpe | 10 Dec. 1807 |
| Sally Kerson | Hill's | Warren | 24 Sept. 1812 |
| John Pinkston, Jr. | Renfroe's | Washington | 27 Dec. 1808 |
| Wm. Gilliland | Barksdale's | Hancock | 9 Nov. 1812 |
| Benj. Brantley, Jr. | Holt's | Hancock | 26 Apr. 1809 |
| John Cowart | | Jefferson | 12 Nov. 1808 |
| Thos. Thompson, Sr. | Bird's | Bryan | 20 June 1808 |
| Wm. Page | | Glynn | 12 Dec. 1808 |
| John Green, Jr. | Tarver's | Jefferson | 2 Aug. 1815 |
| Benj. Tidd | | Chatham | 19 Dec. 1808 |
| Asenath Bowling (orph.) | Blount's | Burke | 8 Dec. 1810 |
| Hezekiah Cartwright | Greer's | Greene | 7 Aug. 1815 |
| Reddock Rogers | Martin's | Burke | 15 Sept. 1814 |
| John Barker's orphans | Malone's | Wilkes | 25 July 1808 |
| Ephriam Fennell's orphans | | Wilkinson | 15 Oct. 1810 |
| John Grimes | 8th | Columbia | 23 Feb. 1808 |
| Keziah Dukes | Coffee's | Hancock | 7 July 1814 |
| Francis Settle | Johnson's | Camden | 25 May 1814 |
| Robt. Bird | Hendrix's | Wilkes | 6 Apr. 1808 |
| Wm. N. Way | | Liberty | 12 Nov. 1808 |
| David Betteson | Harden's | Chatham | 17 Feb. 1808 |
| Jos. Mayo | | Jefferson | 10 Dec. 1807 |
| Richd. Boyd | Martindale's | Clarke | 19 Nov. 1807 |
| Eliza Vivion | | Jefferson | 30 Nov. 1808 |
| Jas. Churchill | | Richmond | 10 Oct. 1809 |
| Cammel Tyson | | Effingham | 1 June 1812 |
| Alex. Johnson | Cook's | Clarke | 27 Sept. 1813 |
| John Knox's orphans | Willborn's | Wilkes | 30 Apr. 1808 |
| Saml. Harrison | | Wilkinson | 3 Oct. 1815 |

| Name | District | County | Date |
|---|---|---|---|
| John Evans | Cockran's Bat. | Jackson | 2 Mar. 1813 |
| Mary Marshall (W) | Gumm's Dist. | Hancock | 11 Mar. 1811 |
| Chas. Doughtry | Hitchcock's | Clarke | 11 Dec. 1810 |
| Amos Daniel | Waller's | Hancock | 13 Aug. 1814 |
| Paul H. Wilkins | | Liberty | 27 Nov. 1807 |
| Jas. Jeffers | | Screven | 7 Aug. 1815 |
| Jos. Smith | 4th | Baldwin | 21 June 1811 |
| Donald McDonald, Jr. | McGuire's | Elbert | 23 Sept. 1811 |
| Herod Bowan | Howard's | Washington | 26 Jan. 1811 |
| Jesse Cobbs | Stewart's | Clarke | 1 Jan. 1808 |
| Wm. Taylor | | Wilkinson | 22 Aug. 1808 |
| Wiley Espey | 4th | Columbia | 3 May 1810 |
| Francis McCall | William's | Bullock | 26 July 1815 |
| Polly Johnson | Hatchett's | Oglethorpe | 18 Dec. 1810 |
| John Trimble | Butler's | Greene | 2 Dec. 1807 |
| Joel Reese | Barne's | Hancock | 27 Sept. 1813 |
| Matthew Matthews | Smith's | Hancock | 7 Jan. 1811 |
| Isaac Martin | Silman's | Clarke | 25 May 1810 |
| Goodrich Jones | Butler's | Clarke | 30 July 1810 |
| Wm. Aaron | Griffith's | Franklin | 16 Nov. 1811 |
| Job Bird | Hendrix's | Wilkes | 11 Dec. 1809 |
| Jas. Willis | Devereux | Warren | 18 Jan. 1810 |
| John Whaley | Stewart's | Greene | 1 Mar. 1813 |
| John Brooker | | Glynn | 12 Dec. 1807 |
| Archd. Warren | Sharp's | Burke | 2 Nov. 1808 |
| Elkana Loftin | | Wilkinson | 5 Sept. 1815 |
| John Hannon | 5th | Columbia | 14 Dec. 1811 |
| Jacob Linder, Jr. | | Glynn | 11 July 1808 |
| Abram D. Lyon | Pemberton's | Chatham | 4 Jan. 1812 |
| Saml. Walters | Pope's | Oglethorpe | 19 Nov. 1807 |
| Henry V. Rowell | Wright's | Jefferson | 4 Dec. 1809 |
| Wm. Davis | Faulkner's | Elbert | 12 Nov. 1808 |
| Andrew White | Robinson's | Clarke | 29 Dec. 1810 |
| John Paulk | 6th | Columbia | 23 Sept. 1808 |
| Alcie Brown | Gordon's | Burke | 2 Feb. 1811 |
| Wm. Freeman | | Screven | 7 Nov. 1809 |
| Polly Baker | Love's | Greene | 6 Feb. 1810 |
| John Dyess | | Liberty | 1 Dec. 1807 |
| Frances Sheftall (widow) | Pemberton's | Chatham | 3 Dec. 1807 |
| Polly Ellison | Cornelius | Franklin | 9 Jan. 1812 |
| Wiley Childers | Thompson's | Elbert | 13 Mar. 1809 |
| Moses Ayres, Jr. | Thompson's | Franklin | 3 Sept. 1814 |
| Sally Ridgeway | Faulkner's | Elbert | 1 Dec. 1812 |
| Wm. Wilder | | Effingham | 31 May 1808 |
| Solomon Stephens | Wim's | Franklin | 25 Oct. 1808 |
| Thos. Brookins | Kendrick's | Washington | 4 Oct. 1815 |
| John Dial | Cleghorn's | Franklin | 15 July 1808 |
| John Peters | Davenport's | Greene | 28 Mar. 1815 |
| Edmond Harper | Clarke's | Elbert | 14 Oct. 1808 |
| Scarlett Allen | Carter's | Warren | 12 Dec. 1808 |
| Henry Taylor | Silman's | Clarke | 6 Feb. 1808 |
| Archelus Moon | Moon's | Elbert | 25 Oct. 1807 |
| Jas K. P. Jack | Willborn's | Wilkes | 14 Dec. 1810 |
| Wm. Prewett | Roebuck's | Elbert | 23 Jan. 1808 |

| | | | |
|---|---|---|---|
| Chas. Mitchell's orphans | Wright's Bat. | Jackson | 27 Nov. 1828 |
| Thos. Holder | 9th Dist. | Columbia | 26 Oct. 1808 |
| Jacob Hershman | Pettybone's | Chatham | 8 Nov. 1808 |
| Sarah Joseph (widow) | Heard's | Wilkes | 7 Aug. 1815 |
| Jos. Newton | 1st | Baldwin | 18 Jan. 1810 |
| Jonathan Thomas | 2nd | Baldwin | 20 Jan. 1808 |
| David Peeples | Watt's | Greene | 26 Oct. 1830 |
| Hezekiah Gates, Jr. | Wright's | Jefferson | 13 Mar. 1809 |
| Nelly Wingate | Devereux | Warren | 14 May 1808 |
| John Beggars | Sidwell's | Wilkes | 10 Mar. 1814 |
| Wm. Henderson | Stovall's | Wilkes | 20 Nov. 1810 |
| Wm. Harrison | Holt's | Washington | 27 July 1811 |
| Jas. Phelps | Faulkner's | Elbert | 7 Dec. 1809 |
| Geo. Cubbage | Austin's | Bryan | 16 Oct. 1810 |
| Roland Jackson | Love's | Greene | 1 Jan. 1810 |
| Edward Carter | Hartsfield's | Oglethorpe | 31 Mar. 1815 |
| Wm. Niblack | Crew's | Camden | 17 Aug. 1814 |
| Vardiman Rooks | | Screven | 16 Dec. 1808 |
| John Hodge | | Screven | 21 Nov. 1807 |
| Ann L. Mabrey | Crew's | Camden | 26 June 1808 |
| Horatio, Wm. & Christopher Bowen orphans | Mobley's | Elbert | 24 Nov. 1807 |

## 27 DISTRICT WILKINSON COUNTY 1805
*(Now Twiggs County)*

| NAME | DISTRICT | RESIDENCE | DATE |
|---|---|---|---|
| John Bigham | Fulon's | Jefferson | 2 Mar. 1809 |
| Alexander McDaniel | Owsely's | Greene | 17 Dec. 1811 |
| Sarah Gray | Heard's | Wilkes | 20 Sept. 1813 |
| John P. Dwight | 1st | Baldwin | 19 Nov. 1807 |
| Wm. Henry & Mary Bowen | Pettybone's | Chatham | 24 Oct. 1808 |
| Luke Sapp, Sr. | Thompson's | Burke | 19 Nov. 1810 |
| Thomas McCoy | Duke's | Clarke | 13 Mar. 1808 |
| James S. Lyner | Hooper's | Franklin | 28 Nov. 1807 |
| Reubin Kent | Hutchison's | Screven | 27 Apr. 1808 |
| John Allen | Wright's Bat. | Jackson | 10 Dec. 1811 |
| John Gray | Smith's | Hancock | 27 Sept. 1813 |
| Peggy McCann | Carswell's | Burke | 10 Dec. 1814 |
| Roderick Harper | McGuire's | Elbert | 14 May 1808 |
| James McCluskey | Henderson's Bat. | Jackson | 30 Mar. 1813 |
| Henry Evans (orphan) | Blount's | Burke | 31 Oct. 1814 |
| William Crawford | | Glynn | 16 Dec. 1808 |
| Evan Price | Malone's | Wilkes | 23 Sept. 1813 |
| Samuel Sanders | | Liberty | 15 Oct. 1808 |
| James Studdard | 5th Dist. | Baldwin | 9 June 1813 |
| John Pryor (an orphan) | 1st Dist. | Baldwin | 13 Aug. 1811 |
| Clement Wynne | Carter's | Warren | 1 Dec. 1810 |
| Alexander Pope | Hillyer's | Elbert | 19 Nov. 1807 |
| Celia Stringer (widow) | Martin's | Burke | 29 Sept. 1809 |
| James Bolton | Mulkey's | Burke | 31 Oct. 1810 |
| Obadiah Jones | McDowell's | Franklin | 14 Apr. 1814 |
| Robert Ellison, Sr. | Cockran's Bat. | Jackson | 5 June 1815 |
| Nathan Hodges | McDonald's | Tattnall | 24 Mar. 1809 |
| Rice Webb | | Jefferson | 4 Dec. 1813 |
| James Bird | King's | Lincoln | 23 Nov. 1808 |
| Jeremiah Thrower | 3rd Dist. | Baldwin | 12 Jan. 1813 |
| Alexander Rozer | 8th Dist. | Columbia | 29 Aug. 1810 |
| Asa Lathrop | Smith's | Camden | 28 Nov. 1808 |
| John Course | | Richmond | 12 May 1808 |
| William Carr | William's | Bullock | 9 Nov. 1814 |
| William Norris | 2nd Dist. | Baldwin | 12 Sept. 1812 |
| John Vickers | Spain's | Burke | 9 Dec. 1807 |
| Lewis Pike | Wright's Bat. | Jackson | 4 Dec. 1809 |
| John Roberts | Greer's | Greene | 28 June 1809 |
| Ephraim Bullock | | Jefferson | 8 Nov. 1809 |
| Felix Megee | Tilman's | Clarke | 2 Aug. 1813 |
| Thomas Ray | Tilman's | Clarke | 8 Mar. 1815 |
| John Bradford, Sr. | Sheet's | Wilkes | 1 Nov. 1815 |
| John Golden, Sr. | May's | Lincoln | 2 Oct. 1810 |
| Solomon Right | McLean's | Chatham | 29 July 1808 |
| Lot House | King's | Lincoln | 6 Nov. 1810 |
| James Moore | Cockran's | Jackson | 12 Nov. 1808 |
| John Moore | Love's | Greene | 26 Oct. 1807 |
| Geo. W. Hardwick | Tarver's | Jefferson | 12 Jan. 1809 |
| William Cahill | Neal's | Chatham | 16 Dec. 1808 |

| | | | |
|---|---|---|---|
| Milly Dunn (widow) | Thompson's | Burke | 26 Sept. 1810 |
| Green Cato | Huff's | Hancock | 5 Apr. 1810 |
| Solomon Page | Burney's | Washington | 10 Feb. 1808 |
| Absalim Evans | Moore's | Greene | 30 Nov. 1809 |
| George Easter | Sherrard's | Tattnall | 17 Sept. 1813 |
| William Greene | Hillard's | Burke | 14 Nov. 1808 |
| Anselin Anthony | Heard's | Wilkes | 15 Nov. 1808 |
| Edward Robinson's orphans | Howard's | Washington | 5 Jan. 1819 |
| William Whigham | Fulton's | Jefferson | 12 May 1808 |
| William Murray | Cooper's | Wilkes | 19 Nov. 1807 |
| Peter Prevatt | Brown's | Camden | 24 Feb. 1808 |
| Jesse Legrand | Keeling's | Elbert | 30 Sept. 1813 |
| Thomas Flournoy | | Richmond | 10 Dec. 1807 |
| Jane Patterson | Carlton's | Greene | 7 Dec. 1807 |
| Pearson Duncan | Keeling's | Elbert | 22 Jan. 1808 |
| Joseph D. W. Luke | 2nd Dist. | Columbia | 2 Aug. 1815 |
| Robert Dixon | | Screven | 7 Nov. 1807 |
| Shadrack Floyd | Clark's | Elbert | 5 Dec. 1810 |
| Spencer Maddux | Bussey's | Lincoln | 15 Sept. 1814 |
| Moses Alexander | Baker's | Warren | 12 May 1810 |
| Benjamin Stanford | Willson's | Warren | 9 Nov. 1814 |
| John Sylvester | | Screven | 20 Mar. 1811 |
| Jeremiah Gilstrap (an orphan) | Martin's | Burke | 29 Nov. 1810 |
| Sarah Harper | Butler's | Greene | 24 Aug. 1812 |
| James McCartney | Johnson's Bat. | Jackson | 5 Jan. 1808 |
| Daniel Green | 1st Dist. | Baldwin | 7 Nov. 1814 |
| Polly Sturdivant | 2nd Dist. | Baldwin | 29 Sept. 1815 |
| Elijah Carney | Hardin's | Camden | 7 Aug. 1815 |
| Nathan Brassel | Coleman's | Jefferson | 3 Nov. 1808 |
| James Erwin | Henderson's Bat. | Jackson | 2 Aug. 1813 |
| John Randle's orphans | Cooper's | Hancock | 12 Nov. 1828 |
| William Taylor | Petybone's | Chatham | 22 Jan. 1808 |
| Richard Beasley | Norman's | Wilkes | 2 Aug. 1815 |
| John Morse, Sr. | King's | Lincoln | 13 Aug. 1814 |
| William Binion | 4th Dist. | Columbia | 20 May 1811 |
| Abner Jinkes | Moore's | Oglethorpe | 5 Sept. 1815 |
| Elizabeth Box | White's | Chatham | 2 Aug. 1815 |
| Owen Baldwin | 10th Dist. | Columbia | 26 Nov. 1808 |
| John Barron | Wright's Bat. | Jackson | 19 Oct. 1808 |
| Mary Cockran | Grove's | Elbert | 7 Oct. 1808 |
| Lott Ivie | Wem's | Franklin | 5 Nov. 1814 |
| Moses Fleming | Blackwell's | Elbert | 6 Dec. 1808 |
| John Hardman | Howell's | Oglethorpe | 30 Sept. 1813 |
| Lewis W. Saxon | Thompson's | Elbert | 31 Oct. 1814 |
| Mauris Cain | Park's | Wilkes | 3 Nov. 1814 |
| Edward Prater | 7th Dist. | Columbia | 10 Dec. 1811 |
| John Pettybone | Pettybone's | Chatham | 15 Jan. 1808 |
| Sarah Robinson | Armor's | Greene | 24 Aug. 1815 |
| Philip Waters | Bussey's | Lincoln | 16 Dec. 1807 |
| Luke Willson | | Effingham | 7 Aug. 1815 |
| Ralph Penrose | Montgomery's | Burke | 23 Sept. 1808 |
| Milly Smith | Dixon's | Franklin | 4 Oct. 1815 |
| Andrew Weldon | 4th Dist. | Columbia | 13 Dec. 1810 |
| Anthony Garnett | 3rd Dist. | Columbia | 3 Oct. 1815 |

| | | | |
|---|---|---|---|
| Jesse Lee | Pope's | Oglethorpe | 7 Aug. 1815 |
| John Smith | Yowell's | Franklin | 7 May 1808 |
| John Marshall | Bussey's | Lincoln | 20 Sept. 1811 |
| Abner Wheeless | Huff's | Hancock | 9 Oct. 1809 |
| Henry Shackleford, Sr. | Clarke's | Elbert | 30 Sept. 1813 |
| Polly Horton | Barkesdale's | Hancock | 23 Sept. 1813 |
| Wylie Saxon | Edge's | Wilkes | 14 Oct. 1811 |
| John Beland | Stewart's | Oglethorpe | 11 May 1808 |
| Thompson Ragland | Thompson's | Elbert | 9 Dec. 1808 |
| William Alexander | Cockran's Bat. | Jackson | 10 Nov. 1814 |
| Nathan Bond, Jr. | Blackwell's | Elbert | 14 Nov. 1808 |
| Nancy Carrell | William's | Bullock | 24 Nov. 1808 |
| John N. Simpson | Cooper's | Wilkes | 15 Nov. 1808 |
| Benjamin Crowley, Sr. | Hatchett's | Oglethorpe | 27 Mar. 1813 |
| Solomon Oberry | | McIntosh | 29 July 1808 |
| John Saxon | Forth's | Burke | 3 Sept. 1810 |
| William Watson | Watt's | Greene | 3 Oct. 1815 |
| Burrel Williams | Johnson's Bat. | Jackson | 30 Sept. 1813 |
| Elizabeth Hart | Wem's | Franklin | 9 Oct. 1815 |
| Wm. Ballard's orphans | Dawson's | Greene | 18 Apr. 1822 |
| Samuel Gorman | William's | Bullock | 7 Aug. 1815 |
| John Cooper | Pettybone's | Chatham | 18 Aug. 1808 |
| Timothy McGuire | Cockran's Bat. | Jackson | 3 Oct. 1815 |
| Thomas Pate | 5th Dist. | Baldwin | 30 Sept. 1813 |
| Charles Ulmer | | Effingham | 17 Dec. 1807 |
| James Edwards | Rorey's | Wilkes | 19 Nov. 1807 |
| Edmund Allums | Delk's | Washington | 8 Nov. 1810 |
| Mary, Joseph & Samuel Pool, orphans | Bostick's | Jefferson | 20 July 1813 |
| Hugh McCain | Mitchell's | Clarke | 1 Nov. 1808 |
| Peter Bradshaw | Hatchett's | Oglethorpe | 29 Sept. 1815 |
| John E. Hartridge | Pettybone's | Chatham | 17 May 1808 |
| William Baker, Jr. | | Liberty | 2 June 1815 |
| Eli Selman | Cleghorn's | Franklin | 12 Nov. 1808 |
| Edward Carrell | Cornelius | Franklin | 16 Nov. 1811 |
| Jacob Jackson's orphans | | Liberty | 4 Oct. 1815 |
| Robert Coughron | | Screven | 27 Nov. 1807 |
| Pherbe Ronell | Sandiford's | Burke | 26 Sept. 1810 |
| James Morrell | Pemberton's | Chatham | 26 Feb. 1808 |
| Absalom Frauthain | McDowell's | Franklin | 20 Oct. 1812 |
| Robert Martin | Cockran's Bat. | Jackson | 26 Feb. 1808 |
| Nancy Middeton (widow) | Greer's | Greene | 25 Nov. 1807 |
| Epps Chatham | McDowell's | Franklin | 25 Aug. 1812 |
| Robert Thompson | Hillyer's | Elbert | 5 Nov. 1807 |
| John Green | Cockran's Bat. | Jackson | 13 Jan. 18__ |
| Sarah & John Gilbert | Pettybone's | Chatham | 6 Apr. 18__ |
| Aaron Wood | | Jackson | 1 Mar. 1810 |
| Shadrack Reach | 57th Dist. | Montgomery | 4 Nov. 1807 |
| William Williamson's orphans | McDowell's | Franklin | 21 Sept. 1813 |
| Asa Cox's orphans | 4th Dist. | Baldwin | 3 Sept. 1812 |
| Spencer Shropshire | Stewart's | Oglethorpe | 28 Sept. 1813 |
| John Nicholson | Hudson's | Oglethorpe | 2 June 1815 |
| Sally Greer | Wiggin's | Washington | 19 May 1810 |
| Francis Pugh | Hendley's | Bulloch | 6 Dec. 1809 |

| | | | |
|---|---|---|---|
| James Tate (orphan) | Thompson's | Elbert | 28 Aug. 1810 |
| Goodwin Brantley | Shiver's | Hancock | 18 Dec. 1815 |
| William Reynolds | Martin's | Burke | 2 Nov. 1807 |
| Samuel Lively | Henderson's Bat. | Jackson | 23 May 1811 |
| Nathaniel Front | Johnson's Bat. | Jackson | 30 Sept. 1813 |
| Robert Roebuck, Jr. | Roebuck's | Elbert | 6 Dec. 1808 |
| John King | Henderson's Bat. | Jackson | 30 Sept. 1813 |
| William C. Wylly | | Effingham | 2 Dec. 1809 |
| Price Connelly | Brown's | Clarke | 28 Apr. 1815 |
| Reben Underwood | Pace's | Washington | 26 Nov. 1811 |
| John McDaniel | Holt's | Washington | 2 Oct. 1815 |
| Thomas Hughes | McLean's | Chatham | 2 Oct. 1815 |
| Sarah Kindrick | 10th Dist. | Columbia | 15 Sept. 1808 |
| Snoden Kirkland | Cooper's | Wilkes | 20 Dec. 1808 |
| William Warmack | 54th Dist. | Montgomery | 5 July 1813 |
| William Dingler | Thompson's | Elbert | 25 Nov. 1808 |
| Micajah Hendry | Garrett's | Lincoln | 7 Mar. 1808 |
| Dickerson Holliday | Wellborn's | Wilkes | 18 Oct. 1810 |
| Enock Embry | Hartsfield's | Oglethorpe | 30 Nov. 1808 |
| John Oaks | Hatchett's | Oglethorpe | 12 Nov. 1808 |
| Darling Glover | | Jefferson | 17 July 1808 |
| Michael Daugherty | 7th Dist. | Columbia | 6 Dec. 1809 |
| Benjamin M. Williams | Waller's | Hancock | 2 June 1815 |
| John Rutledge | Johnson's Bat. | Jackson | 21 Mar. 1808 |
| John Hammock | Robinson's | Clarke | 2 Aug. 1815 |
| Archibald Tanner | Cockran's | Jackson | 24 July 1813 |
| Batt Jones | Spain's | Burke | 13 Sept. 1808 |
| William Osborn | Mobley's | Elbert | 4 Nov. 1807 |
| Elizabeth Riden | Baxter's | Greene | 1 Aug. 1808 |
| Jonathan Jones, Jr. | Kendrick's | Washington | 20 Aug. 1808 |
| Joseph Norman | Johnson's Bat. | Jackson | 30 Dec. 1807 |
| Jane Mitchell (widow) | Stewart's | Clarke | 5 Nov. 1814 |
| Nancy Chambers | Thomas' | Jefferson | 11 Aug. 1810 |
| John Wall | Harper's | Clarke | 25 Nov. 1807 |
| Joseph Griffin | Dye's | Elbert | 18 Nov. 1808 |
| John McMurrin | Flournoy's | Warren | 8 Feb. 1810 |
| David Ridgesdill | Oliver's | Elbert | 8 Feb. 1808 |
| Henry Brook | Watson's | Greene | 3 Nov. 1814 |
| Wm. Hammock | Wellborn's | Wilkes | 14 Mar. 1814 |
| Peter Rockmore | Newsom's | Warren | 20 Jan. 1808 |
| Seth Kennedy | Wingslett's | Hancock | 4 Nov. 1811 |
| Joshua Betts | Wright's Bat. | Jackson | 20 Mar. 1810 |
| Abner Turner | Armor's | Greene | 28 June 1809 |
| Abigail Atkinson (widow) | Wright's Bat. | Jackson | 2 May 1808 |
| John Darden | Thompson's Dist. | Elbert | 4 Dec. 1809 |
| John Harper | Milner's | Wilkes | 13 Dec. 1810 |
| Julan Neil | Hopkin's | Clarke | 9 Nov. 1812 |
| Gresham Herrin | Mitchell's | Clarke | 5 Dec. 1812 |
| Lewis McLendon | Harris' | Wilkes | 2 Oct. 1815 |

## 28 DISTRICT WILKINSON COUNTY 1805
*(Now Twiggs County)*

| NAME | DISTRICT | RESIDENCE | DATE |
|---|---|---|---|
| Betsy Wheeler | Newsom's | Warren | 16 Sept. 1812 |
| Moses Blackshear | Collin's | Washington | 14 Nov. 1811 |
| William Dukes, Sr. | Hopkin's | Clarke | 29 Feb. 1808 |
| Jesse Hammock | | Jefferson | 26 Sept. 1808 |
| Stephen Timmons | | Liberty | 29 July 1808 |
| Nancy Bell | Burk's | Burke | 4 Nov. 1807 |
| Uriah G. Mitchell | Anderson's | Washington | 31 Dec. 1807 |
| Green Williamson | Smith's | Hancock | 28 Jan. 1808 |
| Theodore Carlton | Pettybone's | Chatham | 11 July 1809 |
| Benjamin Christopher's orphans | Moore's | Greene | 9 Sept. 1811 |
| Edmund Taylor | Hutchinson's | Screven | 15 Dec. 1808 |
| Donald McDonald, Sr. | McGuire's | Elbert | 28 Sept. 1811 |
| Harmon Perryman | Jones' | Warren | 2 Dec. 1809 |
| John Chappell, Jr. | Huff's | Hancock | 28 Nov. 1810 |
| Martha Dees | Armstrong's | Tattnall | 28 May 1809 |
| Jack Wright | Jones' | Lincoln | 19 Nov. 1807 |
| Thomas Neel | 56th Dist. | Montgomery | 21 Nov. 1808 |
| John Williams | White's | Chatham | 15 Apr. 1808 |
| John Spain's orphans | Spain's | Burke | 26 Sept. 1808 |
| Thomas Martin | Howard's | Washington | 28 Oct. 1808 |
| George D. L. Schmidt | McLean's | Chatham | 27 Sept. 1809 |
| Elisha Poore | Malone's | Wilkes | 17 Sept. 1811 |
| Nancy Ross (orphan of Hamon Ross) | 59th Dist. | Montgomery | 27 Feb. 1815 |
| Owen Griffin's orphans | Heard's | Wilkes | 17 Aug. 1812 |
| Rubin Medders | 1st Dist. | Baldwin | 1 Jan. 1810 |
| John Turner Brown | | Screven | 4 Mar. 1808 |
| Bernard Kelly | Rorey's | Wilkes | 19 Nov. 1808 |
| Thomas Irwell | Wiggin's | Washington | 19 Jan. 1809 |
| Harris Gresham | Bell's | Oglethorpe | 21 Nov. 1807 |
| Lucy Hill | Cockran's Bat. | Jackson | 28 Oct. 1808 |
| Lewis Miller | Wiggin's | Washington | 25 Apr. 1809 |
| Sarah Head, orphans of Richard Head | 59th Dist. | Montgomery | 12 July 1808 |
| Lazarus Solomon | 53rd Dist. | Montgomery | 16 Aug. 1810 |
| Ann Willson | 1st Dist. | Baldwin | 10 Feb. 1808 |
| Henry Farrow | Pope's | Oglethorpe | 6 Feb. 1810 |
| William Dennard | | Wilkinson | 13 Mar. 1810 |
| Alexander Johnson | Davenport's | Greene | 17 May 1808 |
| Thomas Wynne, Sr. | Week's | Hancock | 20 Sept. 1808 |
| Richard Scott | 2nd | Baldwin | 22 Oct. 1807 |
| Henry Wall | Hardwick's | Jefferson | 10 Aug. 1808 |
| Elizabeth Summon (widow) | Hopkin's | Clarke | 12 Aug. 1808 |
| Elijah Kersy | 57th | Montgomery | 21 Oct. 1807 |
| Thompson Hemphill | Carlton's | Greene | 27 Jan. 1808 |
| Jane Russell (widow) | Stewart's | Oglethorpe | 1 Dec. 1808 |
| David Cox | Jones' | Warren | 1 Jan. 1810 |
| Fanny Red (S) | Week's | Hancock | 6 Jan. 1808 |
| Elizabeth Jones (widow of Tom) | Newsom's | Warren | 22 Jan. 1808 |

| | | | |
|---|---|---|---|
| Robert Fairchild | | Wilkinson | 29 Jan. 1808 |
| Anna Stanton | Park's | Wilkes | 10 May 1808 |
| Thomas Feagin | Barkesdale's | Hancock | 3 Dec. 1807 |
| Joseph Bailey | Bell's | Oglethorpe | 7 Dec. 1807 |
| Ansel Hudgins | 2nd Dist. | Baldwin | 26 Oct. 1807 |
| James Childers | Thompson's | Elbert | 2 Aug. 1808 |
| James Rachel | Garrett's | Washington | 12 Aug. 1808 |
| John Seales, Jr. | Barrett's | Elbert | 30 Sept. 1813 |
| Hosea Carlisle | Wright's | Jackson | 8 Nov. 1809 |
| Cader Carter | Alford's | Greene | 5 Dec. 1808 |
| Josias Boswell | 2nd Dist. | Columbia | 30 Sept. 1813 |
| Archibald Pryor | Moore's | Elbert | 9 May 1809 |
| Joseph Phillips | Wright's Bat. | Jackson | 21 Nov. 1808 |
| Lewis Powell | Gordon's | Burke | 11 May 1812 |
| Henry Harris | Neal's | Warren | 7 Aug. 1815 |
| William Potts | Henderson's | Jackson | 11 Nov. 1809 |
| Hannah Weeks | Johnson's Bat. | Jackson | 16 Nov. 1811 |
| Jenny Cozart | Barne's | Hancock | 11 Apr. 1808 |
| Alexander Irwin's orphans | Pace's | Washington | 16 Sep. 1816 |
| Jonas Stevens | Hardwick's | Jefferson | 23 Oct. 1809 |
| Henry Hart | Crew's | Camden | 31 Dec. 1810 |
| Henry Gignilliatt | | McIntosh | 2 Dec. 1807 |
| William Pearson | Kendrick's | Washington | 3 Dec. 1808 |
| William Digby | 1st Dist. | Baldwin | 23 Feb. 1808 |
| Rebecca House (widow) | Hartsfield's | Oglethorpe | 31 Aug. 1810 |
| Abram Barrow | 50th Dist. | Montgomery | 14 Nov. 1809 |
| John Cawthon | Thompson's | Franklin | 16 Sept. 1811 |
| Benjamin Canafax | Owsley's | Greene | 15 Dec. 1808 |
| John Watts | Carlton's | Greene | 5 Nov. 1812 |
| Edward Doss | Henderson's Bat. | Jackson | 22 May 1811 |
| Abi Burgeron | Mulkey's | Burke | 6 Mar. 1810 |
| David Daniel | Ballard's | Burke | 12 Dec. 1810 |
| Absalom Hamby | Cockran's Bat. | Jackson | 11 Nov. 1809 |
| Richard Martin | Anderson's | Washington | 2 Mar. 1808 |
| Morris Moore | Blackshear's | Washington | 21 July 1810 |
| Nancy Ellison | Cockran's Bat. | Jackson | 19 July 1812 |
| John Mock, Jr. | Bostick's | Jefferson | 2 July 1808 |
| William Moon, Sr. | Moon's | Elbert | 10 July 1809 |
| Absalom Autry | Greer's | Greene | 2 Dec. 1811 |
| Thomas Knapen | | Richmond | 5 May 1808 |
| John Reckell | Hatchett's | Oglethorpe | 8 Dec. 1808 |
| Edmund Carlisle | 4th Dist. | Baldwin | 9 Nov. 1812 |
| Bartlett Wootten, Sr. | Tramell's | Clarke | 2 Aug. 1815 |
| Edmund Shackleford, Sr. | Faulkner's | Elbert | 16 Oct. 1810 |
| Samuel Stenitchen's orphans | Tarver's | Jefferson | 26 Sept. 1814 |
| Richard Gideon | Henderson's Bat. | Jackson | 7 Aug. 1815 |
| Hubbard Glass | 4th Dist. | Baldwin | 11 Nov. 1812 |
| James Ponder | | Screven | 20 June 1808 |
| John Price | 50th Dist. | Montgomery | 17 Dec. 1810 |
| James Kirkpatrick | Wright's Bat. | Jackson | 15 May 1810 |
| Sarah N. Williams (daughter of James) | 6th Dist. | Columbia | 26 Apr. 1808 |
| General Lee | Williams | Bulloch | 28 Nov. 1811 |
| Sally Sayers (young woman) | Watt's | Greene | 7 Apr. 1815 |

| | | | |
|---|---|---|---|
| William Upton | 11th Dist. | Columbia | 30 May 1811 |
| James Kirkpatrick | Wright's Bat. | Jackson | 7 Aug. 1815 |
| John Major | Herb's | Chatham | 26 Feb. 1808 |
| Benjamin F. Duyckinck | | Richmond | 2 Dec. 1809 |
| James Sims | Harden's | Chatham | 2 Dec. 1809 |
| George Millen | White's | Chatham | 16 Dec. 1809 |
| Solomon Hagen | Williams' | Bulloch | 25 Jan. 1808 |
| Philip P. Colbert | Hitchcock's | Oglethorpe | 12 Nov. 1808 |
| William H. Waller | 2nd Dist. | Baldwin | 17 Oct. 1814 |
| William Sanford | Barne's | Hancock | 25 Oct. 1808 |
| Mary Cobourn (widow) | Byne's | Burke | 18 Dec. 1809 |
| Thomas Landrum | Hatchett's | Oglethorpe | 27 Sept. 1812 |
| Thomas Dean | Williford's | Elbert | 30 Sept. 1813 |
| Jesse Evans | 5th Dist. | Baldwin | 7 Aug. 1815 |
| Thomas Melville | | Liberty | 7 Aug. 1815 |
| John Watkins | Stewart's | Oglethorpe | 7 Aug. 1815 |
| Abel Randall | Wem's | Franklin | 21 Oct. 1807 |
| Samuel Hudson | | Screven | 4 Dec. 1810 |
| James Jones | Roebuck's | Elbert | 3 May 1811 |
| Robert Ivey | Devereux's | Warren | 23 Apr. 1811 |
| Stith Evans | Huff's | Hancock | 24 Aug. 1808 |
| Charlotte Shelton | Neal's | Warren | 4 Dec. 1813 |
| John Davis | 5th Dist. | Baldwin | 7 Aug. 1815 |
| Polly Brown | Candler's | Hancock | 3 Nov. 1808 |
| Daniel Evans | 5th Dist. | Baldwin | 5 Nov. 1812 |
| Absalom Pyor | Thomas | Jefferson | 23 Mar. 1809 |
| James Briggs | 57th Dist. | Montgomery | 20 Nov. 1810 |
| Esther Jones (widow) | Forth's | Burke | 2 Nov. 1810 |
| Samuel Caldhoon | Coleman's | Jefferson | 5 Sept. 1815 |
| Geo. Waggoner, Jr. | Hill's | Warren | 26 Aug. 1811 |
| Jesse Malphures | Stafford's | Tattnall | 24 Jan. 1811 |
| Henry Conn | Johnson's Bat. | Jackson | 8 Dec. 1807 |
| Elizabeth Baker (orphan) | 3rd Dist. | Baldwin | 8 Dec. 1814 |
| William Stephens | Grove's | Elbert | 27 Nov. 1807 |
| William I. Minton (son of John) | Rorey's | Wilkes | 24 May 1812 |
| Pheneas Holmes | Stewart's | Clarke | 6 Dec. 1810 |
| Abraham Smith | 2nd Dist. | Baldwin | 11 Aug. 1817 |
| James Crozier | Burk's | Burke | 21 Dec. 1810 |
| William Arnold | Clark's | Elbert | 5 Dec. 1810 |
| Stephen Williford | Williford's | Elbert | 29 Sept. 1812 |
| James Clemmons | Edge's | Wilkes | 20 Aug. 1810 |
| Allen Rawls | Stafford's | Tattnall | 18 Nov. 1808 |
| Joseph Riche | Cockran's Bat. | Jackson | 20 Jan. 1809 |
| Wm. Morgan's orphans | 8th Dist. | Columbia | 3 Nov. 1807 |
| John Jones | Cooper's | Hancock | 21 Oct. 1807 |
| Stephen Witmire | Henderson's Bat. | Jackson | 5 Nov. 1810 |
| Jane McCune (widow) | Roebuck's | Elbert | 19 Oct. 1809 |
| James McCanell | 4th Dist. | Baldwin | 3 Nov. 1814 |
| John Gaston | Armor's | Greene | 21 Oct. 1808 |
| Samuel Thornton | Smith's | Hancock | 31 Oct. 1807 |
| Abraham Cobb | 6th Dist. | Columbia | 3 Aug. 1815 |
| Stephen Crow | Brown's | Clarke | 3 Apr. 1810 |
| Jesse, Sinsey & Wm, Figgs (orphans) | Hilyer's | Elbert | 17 Nov. 1808 |

| | | | |
|---|---|---|---|
| Alexander Duvall | Henderson's Bat. | Jackson | 7 Aug. 1815 |
| Jesse Powell | Blackshear's | Washington | 30 Apr. 1810 |
| John Conyers, Jr. | Williamson's | Screven | 14 Dec. 1810 |
| John Allen, Sr. | Davenport's | Greene | 31 Oct. 1812 |
| William White | Field's | Burke | 12 Mar. 1811 |
| Sarah Raines | Everett's | Franklin | 14 July 1815 |
| Jeremiah Tilman | 58th Dist. | Montgomery | 31 Aug 1809 |
| Jarrel Beasley | Watson's | Greene | 15 Aug. 1808 |
| Thomas Laurence | Alford's | Greene | 17 Dec. 1808 |
| David Scarborough | | Glynn | 21 Oct. 1807 |
| Nancy Wallace (widow) | Rea's | Greene | 30 June 1810 |
| Willson Johnson | Delk's | Washington | 13 Dec. 1810 |
| John Townsen | Hudson's | Oglethorpe | 13 Sept. 1808 |
| James Lindsey | Harris' | Wilkes | 25 Nov. 1807 |
| Christopher Hendrickson | Abraham's | Chatham | 5 Jan. 1808 |
| Obadiah Pryor | Tramell's | Clarke | 26 Oct. 1807 |
| Willis Anderson | | Wilkinson | 8 Jan. 1808 |
| Stephen Bishop | Butler's | Greene | 7 Jan. 1808 |
| Young Clerk's orphans | 9th Dist. | Columbia | 7 Nov. 1816 |
| Wm. R. Jones | Young's | Wilkes | 1 June 1808 |
| Henry Fleman | Hartsfield's | Oglethorpe | 18 Jan. 1808 |
| Thomas Delk | | Wilkinson | 25 Jan. 1808 |
| John Darby | Coleman's | Jefferson | 30 Sept. 1813 |
| Richard Wheeler | | Wilkinson | 23 Oct. 1809 |
| Thomas Murphy's orphans | Sharp's | Burke | 5 July 1810 |
| Milly Perry (widow) | Willis' | Washington | 4 Jan. 1808 |
| Jacob Keener | | Richmond | 3 Dec. 1807 |
| Job. Jackson | Cockran's Bat. | Jackson | 30 July 1808 |
| William Peacock's orphans | | Liberty | 21 May 1810 |
| Rice Ellington | Morrison's | Elbert | 4 July 1811 |
| William Cawthon | | Wilkinson | 9 Aug. 1815 |
| | | (to Philip Cook) | |
| John Stroud | Robinson's | Clarke | 21 Nov. 1807 |
| John Sappington | Henderson's | Wilkes | 15 Dec. 1808 |
| Samuel Johnson | Forth's | Burke | 27 Aug. 1814 |
| Joshua Patrick | Carlton's | Greene | 10 Nov. 1810 |
| Mary A. Bishop | | McIntosh | 19 July 1808 |
| William Irvin | Williams | Bulloch | 1 Oct. 1810 |
| Rebin Turner | | Liberty | 30 Nov. 1808 |
| Daniel Lewis | 1st Dist. | Baldwin | 16 Jan. 1808 |
| William Bramlett | Henderson's | Wilkes | 9 Nov. 1808 |
| John Young | | Screven | 25 Jan. 1808 |
| Eleazar Comens, Jr. | Collin's | Washington | 25 Nov. 1808 |
| Wm. Streetman | Johnson's Bat. | Jackson | 27 Sept. 1808 |
| William Simmons | Candler's | Hancock | 27 June 1809 |
| Mary Sorrells | Brown's | Clarke | 10 Nov. 1808 |
| John T. Baker's orphan | | Liberty | 4 Sept. 1809 |
| Clayton Doss | Johnson's Bat. | Jackson | 17 Dec. 1808 |
| Daniel Dill | | Richmond | 3 Nov. 1814 |
| Solomon Kellet | Wright's Bat. | Jackson | 10 June 1809 |
| David Robinson (J I C) | Sandifor's | Burke | 31 Aug. 1808 |
| Christopher Burt | McDonald's | Tattnall | 7 Dec. 1808 |
| Wm. A. Grant | | Chatham | 17 Aug. 1808 |
| Martin Harden | Thompson's | Franklin | 7 Jan. 1808 |

| | | | |
|---|---|---|---|
| Nathaniel Barnett | Mobley's | Elbert | 1 Nov. 1814 |
| Robert Larrimore | Keeling's | Elbert | 27 Aug. 1814 |
| George Alor | Jones' | Lincoln | 21 Nov. 1808 |
| Thomas Moore | Forth's | Burke | 3 Sept. 1808 |
| Charles Taylor | Cornelius' | Franklin | 26 May 1808 |
| Samuel Sneed | Alford's | Greene | 29 Mar. 1808 |
| Joseph Woodall | Blackwell's | Elbert | 9 Jan. 1808 |
| John Clarke | Martin's | Burke | 9 May 1810 |
| Thomas Stephens (Captain) | 2nd Dist. | Baldwin | 31 Aug. 1808 |
| Mary Waggoner (widow) | Hill's | Warren | 6 Aug. 1808 |
| Peter Strozer, Jr. | Henderson's | Wilkes | 28 Nov. 1808 |

# GENEALOGICAL APPENDIX

# BIOGRAPHICAL SKETCHES
## OF SOME FAMILIES OF TWIGGS COUNTY

"From our virtues comes our honor,
But from our ancestors our names."
—Selected.

*Note About Sketches*

The compilers and the Maj. Gen. John Twiggs Chapter, Daughters of the American Revolution, can not assume responsibility for any discrepancy that may be in any genealogical sketch. Every possible effort was made to prevent errors. However, unavoidably typographical errors might occur. The majority of the sketches were signed by the person or persons who submitted same. References were furnished from such records as: Bible, court house, census, cemetery, church, military, civil service, and to such published volumes as Knight, *Memoirs of Georgia*; Miller, *Bench and Bar of Georgia*; White's, *History of Georgia*; Smith, *The Story of Georgia*; County Histories; D.A.R. collections filed at the Georgia Department of Archives and History.

To list a bibliography of all references with each sketch would be almost prohibitive due to the large number furnished which would require more space than can be used within the limited budget. A fee was charged for the sketches and pictures, but no charge for references.

## THE ANDREWS FAMILY

Robin Andrews was a pioneer settler in Twiggs County, Georgia, having come from Elbert County in 1806. He and his family lived near the present Twiggs-Bibb County line. Robin was born December 7, 1771; married Elizabeth Goss October 24, 1796, and died January 7, 1843. Elizabeth Goss was born January 14, 1780, and died April 17, 1839. She was the daughter of Benjamin Goss, who immigrated from Germany in 1760, and Elizabeth Hamilton. Benjamin Goss served in the Colonial Wars and the Revolutionary War. He died in Elbert County, Georgia in 1813. Children born to Elizabeth and Robin Andrews were: Abisha, Nancy, Sarah Robinson, Martha, Elizabeth Hamilton, Ruth, Joseph Benjamin, Isham Goss, John Hamilton, and Isaac Robin. Robin was very active in Twiggs County affairs having served on that County's first Grand Jury, as Justice of the Peace, and as County Surveyor.

Abisha, the eldest of Robin and Elizabeth's children, was born November 2, 1798, and died September 17, 1861. He and his wife Lucinda were married about 1830 and had eight children, the oldest being William Abisha. William was born September 19, 1833; died December 23, 1889. On October 7, 1856 William married Winifred Mortimer Joyner of Sumter County, Georgia. Children born to this union were: Sarah M. (O'Neal), Julia W. (Andrews), Carrie Lou (Bond) and George Lunceford.

George L. Andrews was born June 19, 1868, married first to Sara Helen "Sallie" Burkette Glover, a widow of A. J. Glover of Jeffersonville, and died January 8, 1941. He lived all his life in the Andrews Home on Old Marion Road in Bibb County which was built by his grandfather, Abisha. In an Eulogy, which was read following his death in the Stone Creek Baptist Church, was mentioned the fact that he was born and died in the same room, in a bed placed in the same corner. Children born to the union of George and "Sallie" Andrews were: Ardis George, Joseph William, Louise, and Grace.

Ardis G. Andrews, the eldest child of George and Sallie Andrews, was born November 14, 1898; married to Gladys Lucille Snipes in 1925; died June 5, 1958. They had one daughter, Helen Adair, who was married to Clayton Jackson McCommon December 11, 1953. The McCommon's have three children: Clayton Jackson, Jr., born February 14, 1955; Cary Adair, born July 1, 1956; and Sara Helen, born July 19, 1959. They now reside in Macon, Georgia.

The Andrews Family were large land owners and farmers, and were very faithful to their beloved House-Of-Worship, Stone Creek Baptist Church. Here Abisha (1845), Isham (1845), and William (1883) served as Deacons, and J. E. (1870) as clerk. On Abisha's death a Tribute Of Respect was recorded in the minutes of the Church and also published in the Christian Index.

By: The C. J. McCommon Family

## REVEREND FRANCIS BARTOW ASBELL

Francis Bartow Asbell, whose life bears testimony of a close walk with his Heavenly Father, was a well known personality among the Baptist circles in middle Georgia. He was the grandson of John and Abigail Asbell, an early settler in Twiggs County, Georgia.

John Asbell and his brother, Elisha, moved to Twiggs County, Georgia from South Carolina in the early part of the nineteenth century, within the first five years after the county was created, according to records. Reference to historic Richland Baptist Church minutes show that Elisha and Celia Asbell joined the church by letter on May 5, 1818, and on April 26, 1817, John and his wife, Abigail Asbell, came into Church fellowship by letter. At Church conference on May 24, 1817 John Asbell with four other members was appointed as a Church Committee to lay off a certain parcel of land for the purpose of building a meeting house. Being willing to serve in God's work, John was appointed by the Church with four other members at Church conference on October 23, 1819 at regular conference to serve as a committee to superintend the building of a new meeting house near Duke Hart's spring. The names of John and Elisha appear on the 1818 Tax Digest as freeholders in the County.

After some few years residence here Elisha had a yearning to return to his native state, South Carolina. John purchased his property which was located near Richland Church.

Bryant Asbell, son of John and Abigail Asbell, built a colonial home, long since destroyed by fire, on his large plantation, which was located in the vicinity of the Church, and here he reared his family in the spiritual atmosphere of Richland. He was a man of integrity and of deep religious convictions.

Bryant Asbell joined Richland Church by profession of faith on May 13, 1835, was baptised and received into Church fellowship. In 1842 he was commissioned a Justice of the Peace. Born into the family circle by his first wife were three sons, John, George, and Stephen. His second marriage was to the widow, Sara Andrews Hunter. To this union was born: Clayton, Francis Bartow, Bryant, Jr., and Andrew. Bryant Asbell, Sr., died shortly after the War Between the States. His remains were interred in Richland Cemetery as were those of his parents when they were summoned to their reward. His widow married Hilliard Newby.

Francis Bartow Asbell was born March 30, 1864 in the old home near the Church which is standing at the present. He joined the Church in November, 1885, being baptized in the pool at the foot of the hill back of the Church, and was received into full fellowship. He passed to his rest on August 18, 1950 at his home in Cochran, Georgia.

In 1881 Bartow entered the school taught by Professor C. M. Wynne at Cochran. In 1888 he entered Mercer University to prepare himself for God's ministry. He was married to Carrie Rebecca Todd _____, 1891, at Macon, Georgia. She was born March 14, 1866, Wilkinson County, Georgia, died December 6, 1934 at Cochran. Mrs. Asbell served several years as President of the Woman's Missionary Society, was a member of the W. C. T. U., the Cochran Woman's Club and was active in her Church, Cochran Baptist, until she passed to her reward.

Bartow began teaching school near Cochran in the fall of 1891 and it was during this term 1891-92, although his membership was at Richland, that he was ordained to the ministry at the Cochran Baptist Church. His first pastorate was at Corinth. During his sixty years in the ministry he served many other churches, among these being Richland, Midway, Evergreen, Bethany, Union Hill, churches at Frazier, Dexter, Chester, Empire and Warthen.

He was Superintendent of Pulaski County Public Schools from 1912 through 1916. In 1917 he returned to Cochran and served in the following capacities: Bleckley County Federal Food Administrator Clerk and Treasurer of City of Cochran, 1918 to 1922; two terms as Bleckley County Tax Receiver, 1933-1941; Clerk of Bleckley County Selective Service Board, World War II; 1915-1916 Worshipful Master of Hawkinsville Lodge, F. A. M.; Worshipful Master of Cochran Lodge, F. A. M. and served the Lodge thirty years as Chaplain.

Children born to Bartow and Carrie Rebecca Asbell: Carl; Harvey; J. Emory B., married Elizabeth Fokes on March 25, 1925; Lucile; Homer; and Sara.

By: J. E. B. Asbell, Palmetto, Florida

## GIDEON BEDDINGFIELD

Gideon Beddingfield, his wife Henrietta Anne Ball Beddingfield, lived in Twiggs County in the early 19th century, buried in family cemetery, Twiggs County. Their children were: Henrietta, married Malancton Johnson, born Cambridge, N. Y. Both buried in Twiggs County, two sons, Malancton B., Jr., M.D., born Cambridge, educated college, Philadelphia, Penn. Practiced medicine Dooly County. Served Confederate Army as physician and surgeon. Buried Dooly County. Wm. S. Johnson, M. D., born Twiggs County, educated Nashville, Tenn., practiced medicine Pulaski and Dooly Counties. Buried Pulaski.

_____ Beddingfield daughter married Wm. Barton, buried Twiggs County, one daughter, Eveline.

Second wife of Wm. Barton was Melissa Beddingfield, born Twiggs County, moved to Wilcox County. Children: Anne, Martha, John, all buried in Wilcox.

Jane A. Beddingfield, born Twiggs County June 17, 1813, died Dooly County November 16, 1896, married 1837 Shemuel N. Lasseter, Educator, born Edgefield County, S. C., Dec. 28, 1814, died Dooly County March 11, 1867. Their children born Twiggs County: Henrietta March, 1838, Gideon I, 1st Lt. C. S. A., April 24, 1840, died August 23, 1896. Clifford, May 1841, Joanna Emily, February 26, 1843, Myra Belle, September 4, 1844, Isaac Shelby, Pvt. C. S. A. Jan. 10, 1846, died December 4, 1912, Mary Jane, April 6, 1847, all buried Family Cemetery, Vienna, Georgia, except Mary Jane buried Byromville, Georgia. Family moved to Vienna, Dooly County, Georgia, 1849. Three sons born in Dooly, Zadok W. and John C., twins, February 25, 1850, Shemuel P., April 1, 1853.

Harmon Beddingfield, Pvt., C. S. A., born Twiggs County, married Martha Fuller, Wilkinson County, moved to Dooly County. Children: Jessie, Anne, Leora, Kate, William H., all buried in or near Unadila, Georgia, except Anne, buried Edison, Georgia.

Submitted by: Mrs. J. M. Wooten, Vienna, Georgia

## WILEY BULLARD

Came to Georgia about 1800.

    Wiley Bullard, born before 1775 in North Carolina—died between 1826-1830 in Twiggs County.

    Parthena Bullard, born 1779-1780 in Georgia—died between June 1, 1860, June 1, 1870 in Twiggs Co., Ga.

    Daniel Bullard, born 1800-1805 in Georgia;

    1st wife born 1800-1805—name not given.

    2nd wife, Caroline Bullard, born 1800-1810—died between 1855-1860 in Twiggs Co., Ga. Had son born in 1856-57.

    3rd wife, Elizabeth, born 1829-30 in Georgia—died after June 1, 1870

4th wife, Elizabeth Barton, born_____, died after 1910,

    Children: Dora; Cora and Victoria (twins); and Daniel, born 12-25-1873. Daniel Bullard's first children born between 1805-1857 compiled from census records 1850-1860. Children born after 1857 not listed:

1. Wiley Bullard, born 1828-29
2. Charles Bullard, born 1831-32
3. Mary Bullard, born 1834-35
4. Elizabeth Bullard, born April 18, 1837
5. Henry H. Bullard, born 1839-40
6. Ira Bullard, born 1842-44
7. Madison Bullard 1847-1852

8. Monroe Bullard 1850-53
9. William Bullard. born 1856-57

Bullards who served and died in Civil War:
Wiley Bullard, born 1828-29
Enlisted, Twiggs County Guards
May 7, 1862—died of disease in 1862.
Charles Bullard, born 1831-32
Enlisted May 7, 1862
Discharged, disability June 10, 1862.
Henry H. Bullard, born 1830-40
Enlisted May 27, 1862—appointed 4th Sergeant
Wounded Cold Harbor, Va. June 27, 1862
Wounded and captured at Sharpsburg, Md. Sept. 17, 1862
Died of wounds in Sharpsburg, Md.
Ira Bullard, born 1842-44
Enlisted May 27, 1862—wounded at Cold Harbor, Va. June 27, 1862
Killed at Bentonville, N. C. 3-18-1865.

Record copied page 818—Roster of the Confercdate Soldier of Georgia, 1861-1865
Submitted by: Mrs. T. L. Everett, Sr., Waycross, Ga.

## THE BULL FAMILY

Jacob Bennett Bull was born in North Carolina. He moved to Wilkes County, Georgia, and from thence moved to Twiggs County, Georgia, and married a widow by the name of Judith Willis, who was the granddaughter of Mark Hardin, and her maiden name was Hardin. She had by her first husband (Benjamin F. Willis) two children, Benjamin F. Willis, born February 5, 1805, and Mary P. Willis, born April 25, 1813. By marriage to Jacob Bennett Bull there was born two children, James H. Bull, born May 25, 1815, and Jesse Jared Bull, born December 13, 1818.

James H. Bull left Georgia when a young man and nothing was ever heard of him.

Jesse Jared Bull married Mary Neil February 26, 1845. Four children born to this union, John Hardin Bull, born April 26, 1846; Mary Mildred Bull, born July 24, 1847; Sarah Salome Bull, born May 8, 1849, and died July 7, 1852; Jacob Bennett Bull, born November 14, 1851, and died October 28, 1853.

Jesse Jared Bull married a second time to Mary E. Carter and by this marriage there was one son, Jesse Jared Bull, Jr., born May 1, 1855. Jesse Jared Bull, Sr., died April 1, 1857 in Twiggs County, Ga., then his widow (Mary Elizabeth Bull) moved to Talbotton, Ga. in 1859, and died August 15, 1862.

John Hardin Bull lived in Twiggs County, Georgia, and married Annetta Davis, in 1865. They had born to them three children, John Jared Bull, born September 27, 1866; William Hardin Bull, born March 31, 1869; Leila Judith Bull, born September 6, 1871. John Hardin Bull's second wife was Mildred A. Bull, and they were married in March, 1881. By this marriage there was one child, Mary Lou Bull, born April 13, 1885.

Mary Mildred Bull married Joseph Hamilton Ray November 1, 1864. They had three children, Frank Jared Ray, born July 21, 1868; John Benjamin Ray, born November 23, 1870; George Edward Ray, born March 30, 1875.

Jesse Jared Bull, Jr., married Sallie E. Baldwin, February 26, 1879. They had two children, one died an infant and the other lives in Oglethorpe, Georgia.

Submitted by Mrs. Mary Johnston Ray as compiled by her late husband, George Edward Ray, Route 4, Macon, Georgia.

## WILLIAM HANSEL CALIFF

William H. Califf came to Twiggs County following the War-Between-the-States, Jones County being his earlier home. He settled at Jeffersonville where he ran a successful mercantile business.

On January 26, 1896 he was married to Avarilla Griffin, daughter of Ardella Jones and Eli Shorter Griffin, granddaughter of Col. Shorter Griffin of the Confederate States of America and Avarilla Nash, of Twiggs County. The marriage of William H. Califf and Avarilla Griffin was blessed with these children: David Yancey, Glynn, Sarah, W. H., Ruth, Marguerite, William E., and Edith.

Sarah Califf married William Jackson Wall of Jeffersonville, Georgia, February 2, 1919, and to this union were born Margaret, Barbara, Ava, Caroline, and Lillie Helen. Margaret married James Edward Beck of Gordon, Georgia, October 1, 1939 and they have two children: Sarah Eolyne and James Edward, Jr. The Becks own and operate the J. E. Beck Furniture Company at Jeffersonville.

Submitted by: The J. E. Beck Family, Jeffersonville, Ga.

## GEORGE ELLIOTT CHAPMAN

George E. Chapman, M.D.     Mrs. Minnie L. Pettey (G. E.) Chapman
(1865-1942)     (1875-1955)

Dr. George Elliot Chapman, the youngest son of John and Anne Carleton Chapman, was born December 25, 1865 at the Ante-bellum Colonial Home built by his father, located one mile northeast of Jeffersonville on the Irwinton Road. He was educated at Jeffersonville High School and Louisville Medical College, Louisville, Kentucky, where he received an M.D. degree in 1886.

Dr. Chapman was married to Minnie Lee Pettey, daughter of William and Emma Heath Pettey of Pulaski, Ga., where her father owned and operated a large plantation. Minnie Pettey was born in Macon and attended Gresham High School. At the time of her marriage she was postmistress at Pulaski, Ga., where Dr. Chapman practiced medicine six years. They moved to Danville in 1898. Their house with a six gable roof and sixteen foot ceilings, built in 1902, located in Danville on Highway 80, is still standing and occupied by their daughter, Ruth.

Dr. Chapman bought large tracts of land in Twiggs and Wilkinson Counties where he practiced medicine forty-five years. He was Physician and Surgeon for the M.D. & S. R. R. and a steward in the Danville Methodist Church forty years.

Dr. and Mrs. Chapman were the parents of ten children, three of whom died in infancy. Six daughters and a son that lived to be grown are: Anne Carleton Chapman, born 1893, B.M. graduate in piano at Wesleyan College, 1913, married 1920 Ramsey Emmett Snell, farmer and livestock dealer, Murfreesboro, Tenn. Their children are: Jane Chapman Snell, graduate of Tenn. State College; married 1943 William Hamilton Woods of Murfreesboro, Tenn., now a lawyer in Nashville, Tenn. Their children are: William Ramsey Woods, born 1950 and Robert Hamilton Woods, born 1951. Anne Carleton Snell, second daughter of Mr. and Mrs. Ramsey Snell, born 1928; graduate of Vanderbilt College 1949; married 1952 Elmer Monroe Boykin, Jr., of Laurel, Miss., now Rector of Episcopal Church, Johnson City, Tenn. Their children are: Elmer Monroe Boykin III, born 1954 and Sarah Jane Boykin, born 1956. Sarah Ramsey Snell, the youngest child of Mr. and Mrs. Ramsey E. Snell, born 1939, is a junior at University of Tennessee. Minnie Lee Chapman, born 1895, graduated from G. N. & I. C. (now G.S.C.W.) 1914 and was a student at Gordon School of Theology, Boston, Mass. at the time of her death, 1926. She taught school ten years. Mary Lillian Chapman, born 1897, B.M. graduate in Violin at Wesleyan College 1921, taught piano and violin in Florida Schools twelve years. She married 1930 Dr. Chapman Q. Dykes, Carrabelle, Fla., who died with the rank of major at Camp Davis, N. C., 1944. Mrs. Chapman Dykes died in 1947. Ruth Chapman, born in 1900, A.B. graduate of Wesleyan 1920, did graduate work at Univ. of Ga. and Emory Univ. Library School. She was teacher-librarian in Florida public schools twenty-five years. George Elliot Chapman, Jr., born 1903, graduate of Emory Univ. 1924, has been employed by the Dept. of Labor, Washington, D. C. thirty years. He is a steward and president of the Men's Bible Class at Mount Vernon Place Methodist Church. In 1935 he married Mildred Mullikin of Washington, D. C., an instructor in piano and a church organist. Their daughter, Emily Mullikin Chapman, born 1941, is a student at Lynchburg College, Lynchburg, Va. Eloise Chapman, born 1910, A.B. graduate Univ. of Ga., 1931 and M.A. graduate of Florida State Univ., 1952, is teaching in Jacksonville, Fla. She married Bill Harris of Bonifay, Fla., 1939. Their son, Carleton George Harris, born 1941, is a sophomore at Univ. of Ga. Martha Elizabeth Chapman, born 1917, graduate of Univ. of Ga. 1937, is teaching at Rome, Ga. She married Clyde Lydel Hunt of Rockmart, Ga. 1938. Their children are Elliot Lydel Hunt, born 1939, is a junior at Univ. of Ga.; Wanda Merilyn Hunt, born 1944; and Bobby Lawrence Hunt, born 1949, attend Rome public schools.

Submitted by: Miss Ruth Chapman, Danville, Ga.

## JOHN CHAPMAN

"John Chapman, son of John Williams Chapman and grandson of William Chapman of England, a centenarian soldier of the Revolutionary War, and of Edmund Burke, an emigrant from Ireland, was born in Twiggs Co., Ga., January 6, 1820. He was among the most prosperous and successful planters in his county, both before and subsequent to the Civil War, as well as one of her most useful and esteemed citizens. Perhaps not one was more esteemed for energy, industry and integrity of character by business men with whom he had dealings. His home was one of culture and refinement, the mothers of his children (for he was married four times) showing the deepest and most active maternal interest in the education and training of their children, for which they were nobly fitted. John Chapman was the father of nine children, to the most of whom he gave a college education.

Those surviving are: William T. Chapman of Whigham, Ga.; Mrs. W. E. Carswell and Mrs. C. B. Chapman, principal of Lanier High School, Macon, Georgia; Dr. G. E. Chapman of Pulaski, Ga., Paul Herbert Chapman and Lucy Carleton Chapman who reside with their widowed mother at the old homestead." (Ref.: *Memoirs of Georgia*, 1895).

Mrs. Lucy Carleton Chapman Gilbert, the only surviving member of the John Chapman family, lives in Dublin, Georgia, where she has been a popular, successful piano and voice instructor for fifty-five years. After attending Wesleyan College, she graduated at New England Conservatory, Boston, Mass. Her children are: Carleton G. Gilbert of Cleveland, Mass., John Gilbert and Orlene Gilbert of Dublin, Ga.

By: (Miss) Ruth Chapman, Danville, Ga.

## CHAPMAN

Oscar T. Chapman      Elizabeth Gilbert Carswell
(Mrs. O. T. Chapman)

December 26, 1958 was the fifty-first wedding anniversary of the Chapman's.

"Chap" is the son of Katherine Sinquefield and William T. Chapman. He began his business career as a general merchant, later adding life insurance and farming.

For fifty years or more he has served the Jeffersonville Methodist Church in many capacities—as Steward, Sunday School Superintendent, and as a planner, leader and worker in the various phases of church life; contributing generously in time, talent and money.

"Miss Lizize" is the daughter of Anna Tallulah Chapman and Captain William Edward Carswell. A graduate of Brenau College, Gainesville, Georgia, she taught piano for many years and served as pianist for the Jeffersonville Methodist Church. Her interest in young people made her home a gathering place for them for many years. She is a charter member of the Major General John Twiggs Chapter D.A.R. She served as Regent of the John Ball Chapter before the organization of the Chapter in Twiggs County, also acting in many other offices of both Chapters.

Submitted by: Mrs. K. J. Carswell, Jeffersonville

## COLLINS-GILDER

My great-grandfather, William Pinkney Collins, born March 28, 1816, died September 18, 1848, was an early resident of Twiggs County.

According to family legend, "his father came to America from Ireland, was Scotch-Irish; had only two children, the above named son, William P., and a daughter whose traditional name was Sophi Ann Caroline I; both children married into Twiggs County families."

The surname Collins is of Scotch origin.

When I was a little boy my paternal grandmother, Mrs. Siddie Blount Collins, gave me a small trunk, small enough to slip under the bed where it was kept. According to her, it had been given to my grandfather, Ivey F. Colins I, when he was a little boy. His father, William P., had owned it before him. On the underside of the trunk lid, hand painted in large, faded-brown letters, were the Gaelic initials E.b.C. The English equivalent is E.B.C. There is certainly a co-relation between this Gaelic (Irish) writing and the Irish legend of the family.—(Ref.: I reproduced the inscription for Library of Congress and the Secretary of the Embassy of Ireland, both of Washington, D. C., and they identified same as Gaelic.)

William P. Collins had several children, among them a son, "Elisha" P. Collins, 1842-1924.

In the Land Lottery of 1820, Elisha Collins, living in Captain Brown's Militia District, Twiggs County, drew Land Lot No. 242 of the 26th District, Early County, reverted. To participate in the lottery required a previous three-year residence in the state, making him a resident of the State of Georgia since 1817, or before.

In the Cherokee Lottery of 1832, Elisha Collins of Twiggs County drew Land Lot No. 15 of the 20th Land District, 3rd Section of originally Cherokee County, date of grant October 14, 1836. (Ga. Dept. of Archives and History.)

Elisha Collins is listed in the 1818 and 1826 Twiggs County Tax Digest.

Many of the early documentary records of Twiggs County have been lost in the flight of the years. The court house burned in 1901. But from the foregoing evidence, I feel confident that the Scotch-Irish progenitor of the family was Elisha Collins, or Elisha B. Collins, of Twiggs County. Perhaps he bought his personal belongings from Ireland in the inscribed trunk previously mentioned. My home at Cochran, Ga., RFD 2, burned December 26, 1946, and I lost the trunk along with many other heirlooms.

William P. Collins, son of the immigrant, was an extensive land and slave owner of ante-bellum Twiggs. He was one of the few men to own and operate a cotton gin in that era. His plantation was above Danville, near old Concord Methodist Church. The Collins' were members of Concord Church in the 1840-1850 period. William P. Collins is buried at old Concord Cemetery and by his side is buried a small son, Henry Rufus Collins, born December 7, 1844; died October 5, 1846.

Old Concord Cemetery is no longer used and the church building has long since disappeared. This historic site is on Gallemore's Mill Road about two miles east of its intersection with Highway 80, the intersection being between Danville and Jeffersonville, near Higgsville (Negro) Church.

Judge William P. Collins was commissioned Justice of the Peace, 354 (Higgsville) District, Twiggs County on February 6, 1847.

William P. Collins married Lydia Gilder in January, 1838. She was born October 12, 1805, the daughter of Isaac Gilder, Irish patriot in the Revolutionary War and pioneer settler of Twiggs County.

The 1790 census shows Isaac Gilder as a resident of Newberry County, South Carolina. Geo. L. Summer's "Newberry County, South Carolina, Historical and Geneological" published 1950, refers to: Gilder's Creek Cemetery; "Gilder's Crest", the old Nance house; Dr. James L., Dr. James K., Bessie L., and P. Fant Gilder. There is a Gilder Street in Newberry.

During the Revolutionary War, Isaac Gilder was a drummer and fifer in Captain John Ingles' Company, 2nd N. C. Regiment, commanded by Col. John Patton. He enlisted for three years, and his name appears on the muster roll for Jan., 1778, dated Feb. 6, 1778. (Adj. Gen.'s Office). He is also listed in Dr. L. L. Knight's book, "Georgia Roster of the Revolution," pages 353 and 382, and in "Hall of History," Raleigh, N. C. He served from Hyde County, N. C. In the Georgia Secretary of State's office, Atlanta, it is recorded that Isaac Gilder of Twiggs County drew Land Lot No. 392 in the 16th District of originally Early County in the lottery of 1820 for Revolutionary services, date of grant, August 23, 1839.

Isaac Gilder is found in the 1818 and 1826 Twiggs County Tax Digest.

Isaac Gilder died just prior to 1840. There is traditional evidence that he was living in 1838, at the time of his daughter Lydia's marriage. He is last listed in the 1830 Twiggs County census and as between 60 and 70 years of age. He is buried at Prospect Methodist Church cemetery in the Gilder Row, Twiggs County.

Mrs. Lydia Collins, administrator, Wm. P. Collins, deceased, is carried on the 1853 Twiggs County Digest from the 354th District.

On September 23, 1858, Mrs. Lydia Gilder Collins of Twiggs County bought a plantation in Pulaski County about two miles east of Hawkinsville on the Empire Highway. She and her children, Sophia Ann Caroline, William Rasmus, Charlotte Ellen, Elisha Pinkney, Iverson (Ivey) Fhadias and Ferdinand (Ferdy) Rufus, moved to Pulaski County, where the family has left its impress upon the community. The Twiggs County farm was kept for several years after the removal of the family. Mrs. Lydia Gilder Collins died in Pulaski County July 31, 1889. On April 17, 1932 the Hawkinsville Chapter, D.A.R. unveiled a bronze grave marker to her, the only daughter of a Revolutionary soldier buried in the Cochran cemetery.

An exhaustive history of the Collins family may be found in Mrs. Virginia Speer Harris' *History of Pulaski and Bleckley Counties, Georgia.*

This present sketch is published by courtesy of Wilbur M. Collins, President, Canada Dry International, Inc., New York City.

> Submitted by: Ivey F. Collins, II, Cochran, Georgia. (A member of Georgia Society, Sons of the American Revolution.)

## JULIAN ROSWELL COOK

Julian Roswell Cook settled in Twiggs County, Georgia shortly after the Civil War. He entered the Confederate Army in 1863, at the age of sixteen, under the command of Lt. Col. C. D. Findley, Fifth Georgia Reserve, Company "D". He was discharged from service in April, 1865 at Greensborough, N. C.

He was the son of William Arnold Cook and wife, Ann Walker. Their other children were, namely, Belle, who married Stephen Jones; Sallie married D. W. Brown; Lulie married Chancy Wright; Samuel and Nathan died young.

Julian Roswell Cook, born May 5, 1847, died January 4, 1910, married first, Laura Jones, born June 11, 1855, died June 25, 1880. Their children: Cornelius, Thomas Jones, Berta and Julian H.

Thomas Jones Cook, born January 2, 1873, died May 24, 1944, married Lula Shearose, born February 24, 1870, died Nov. 29, 1937. Children born to this union: William Arnold, married Frances McBride Jackson; Laura Belle married Terrell Albert Goodwyne; Thomas Jones, Jr., married Flora Mae McGruder.

Laura Belle Cook, born July 7, 1901, married Terrell Albert Mitchell, on Nov. 19, 1921. Children: Terrell Abert, Jr., married Eizabeth Koch; Carolyn, married George Wilson Williams; Winifred, married Reverend George Stephen Ingram;

Judith, student at Emory University, born Oct. 26, 1941.

Carolyn, born Aug. 11, 1928, married George Williams, Sept. 12, 1948. Children: George, Jr.; Laura Ellen; Cynthia Ann; Winifred, born Jan. 14, 1930, married Reverend George Stephen Ingram on March 25, 1953. Child: Chreyl Lynn Ingram.

By:  Laura Cook Mitchell, Mrs. T. A., 909 Seiler Ave., Savannah. Ga.

## COOK FAMILY

The Cook(e) family played an important part in the early history of Twiggs County and of America. William Cooke, Sr., first member of this family to live in America, was the grandson of Richard Cooke of St. Augustine Parish, Bristol, County Gloucester, England.

Richard (1) had five children by his first wife: John, 1577; Anne, 1580; William, 1582; Thomas, 1585; and Philip, 1589—all baptised at St. Augustine's Parish. The only child following his marriage to Catherine Rawley was Richard, baptised 1598.

Phillip (2) likewise married twice; William was born in 1613, Anne in 1614. Daughters by his second wife were Lucie, Mary, and Martha. All were baptised at St. Augustine's Parish.

William (3) married Mary Blackborne of Bristol, England, in 1632. William Jr. was born circa 1633; Philip was baptised in 1636 at St. Augustine's Parish. The family came to America where William Sr. was a landowner and in 1667 had 800 acres of land surveyed on the second branch of Blackwater River, Virginia. He was buried in Surry County, Va., about 1677.

William Jr. (4) married three times. The children of his second wife, Joane Roper, were Job, circa 1655, William, Reuben, Thomas, and also perhaps Robert and Henry. A Power of Attorney: Isle of Wight, Va., (Bk. 1, 1662-1715, p. 32) was recorded 9 April 1665.

John (5) married three times, the last time to Avis Killingsworth (widow). Their children were Henry, circa 1690, John, and Joanna. His will, W. B. 5 (1709-14) p. 60, Surry County, Va., dated 10 April 1711, was probated 20 June 1711. His wife's will of 9 June 1711 was probated August 15, 1711.

Henry Cook (6) changed his name by droping the last letter. His first wife was Elizabeth; his second was Mary Clarke (circa 1732); his third wife was also named Elizabeth; and his fourth wife was Elizabeth Price, to whom he had made an Article of Agreement to marry. His children were Sarah, Mary, Anne, Betty, Henry, Jane, Drury (1736), John (1738), and Ben. He was a planter and died at the age of 84 (Brunswick Co., W. B. 4, p. 241, dated November 13, 1772. Probated July 23, 1774). John served as captain at Ancrum's and in Col. Washington's Legion of Cavalry in the American Revolution.

The sons of Drury (7) were Nathan, John, and Jim. Nathan (8) married Sarah Atkinson. Nathan's children were William Arnold, Ben (Behn), Thomas Abnew, Mary, Elizabeth, and Louraine.

William Arnold Cook (9) was the first of this long family line to reside in Georgia. He married Anne Walker. Their children were Julian Roswell (Sr.), born at Baldwin County, Nathan (killed in the War Between the States), and Sam. He was a farmer.

Julian Roswell Cook Sr. (10) enlisted in Co. D, Cumming's Regiment, 5th Georgia Reserves, in July, 1864, and was a member of Camp Smith No. 484, United Confederate Veterans, Macon, Georgia. After the war he returned to Twiggs County. He first married Laura, daughter of Thomas and Mary (Cowan) Jones; their children were Cornelius, Thomas Jones, and Berta. After Laura died, he married

Minnie Jones Land, Laura's sister. Their children were Sara Louise (Lulie), born December 26, 1883, and Julian Roswell Jr., born July 20, 1889. He was operaor and owner of Elmwood Farm, Bullards, Georgia, and an active member at Beech Springs Church, Bullards, where he was interred January 4, 1910.

Julian Roswell Cook Jr. (11) attended Gordon Military Academy at Barnesville where he met and on June 20, 1910, married Martha Kate Porch, daughter of John Collier Porch and Kate (Swatts) Porch Watkins. He continued the operation of Elmwood Farm, was active in founding and improving Bullards High School, interested in public affairs, an active member of Beech Springs Church, and a Mason. His children were Sara Elizabeth, born 1912, who later married Alfred M. Bush; Dorothy Kate, 1913, who married Loyal Norman; Martha Roswell, 1916, who married Thomas F. Dooley; Helen, 1918, who married J. Ralph Roberts; and Julian Porch Cooke, 1921, who married Adah Louise Staph of San Antonio, Texas. All of his children attended Bullards High School, later attended Gordon High School, and other schools and colleges after the family moved to Barnesville, Georgia, in 1932. He became an active member of the First Methodist Church of Barnesville. He operated a photographic studio at 41 Market Street until his death January 5, 1959. Burial was at Greenwood Cemetery, Barnesville.

Julian Porch Cooke (12), a college teacher in San Antonio, Texas, served in the Army Medical Corps in Germany in World War II and in the Korean conflict. Elizabeth Cook Bush was a member of the WAVES in World War II.

Submitted by: Julian Porch Cooke, 236 West Mandalay, San Antonio, Texas.

## CLARK - WILKINSON

Bryan Clark, born October 17, 1804, came to Twiggs County as a young man and in 1833 married Susannah Adkin Wilkinson, born May 2, 1815 in Twiggs County. She was the daughter of John Lawrence Wilkinson, born September 2, 1762 in Virginia, and his wife, Christiana Luter Wilkinson. They came from North Carolina to Twiggs County about 1809. John Lawrence Wilkinson died in 1841 and is buried near the old homesite which was on the Longstreet Road near the present Twiggs-Bleckley line.

In 1834 Bryan and Susannah Wilkinson Clark moved to Sumter County, Georgia, where he died in 1845. One of their children, Adoniram Judson Clark (1839-1915), joined the Sumpter Light Guards, 4th Georgia Regiment, Doles Brigade. He was wounded at the Battle of Malvern Hill. On October 5, 1865, he married Abi Morris (1850-1907) of Russell County, Alabama.

Their son, Edgar Holt Clark, a Baptist minister, born at Hurtsboro, Alabama, May 31, 1873, married January 1, 1894, Lillie Poyner Gaulding (1873-1950) of Crawford. Oglethorpe County, Georgia.

Their children: Edgar Holt, Jr., Atlanta; Mildred, Mrs. Walter McElmurray, Augusta; and Francis Gaulding Clark (married Bessie Vaughn), Macon, Georgia. Their child: Francis Clark, Jr.

Submitted by: Mrs. Francis G. Clark, 2170 Old Holton Road, Macon, Ga.

## KATHLEEN JONES CARSWELL

Mrs. Kathleen J. (W. R.) Carswell

Kathleen Jones was born Jan. 8, 1889, to Shedrick E. Jones and Mary Solomon Jones on their farm just west of Ripley. When she was six the family residence was moved to Jeffersonville, where she grew to womanhood.

Upon her graduation from Jeffersonville schools she attended and was graduated from Lucy Cobb Institute in Athens. She taught in the public schools of Jeffersonville until her marriage to William Rufus Carswell, son of Anna T. Chapman and Captain William E. Carswell. Widowed at the age of 23, "Miss Kathleen", as she became affectionately known, supported herself and her two sons, Shedrick Jones, born in 1910, and William Rufus, Jr., born in 1912, first with a millinery shop and later with a boarding house, where most of the teachers lived, and a farm which she bought and operated. She became interested in bettering the local schools and took an active part in promoting a consolidated school for Twiggs County. She was a member of the building committee when Twiggs High School was organized and constructed in 1911 and was the first woman to serve on the school board of trustees. She served for a term as president of the Parent-Teacher Association while her sons were in school.

In 1922 she was selected as Twiggs County Home Demonstration Agent, beginning a career of service to the rural families of the state which lasted until her retirement in 1951. At the same time she worked for and received a B.S.H.E. degree in 1931, graduating from the University of Georgia just a short time before her two sons. She took post graduate work at the University of Iowa in 1936.

In 1926 she organized Jeffersonville's first woman's club, known as the Worthwhile Club, which later changed its name to the Jeffersonville Woman's Club, with a county library as its long-time objective. Upon her return to Jeffersonville to live she renewed her active membership and served as its president during 1958 and 1959.

She moved to Dodge County as home demonstration agent in 1936, introducing this work to that county. After eight years she moved to Decatur as agent for DeKalb County.

During her career as a home demonstration agent she was active in the Georgia Home Demonstration Agents' Association and won a number of state and national honors. While president of the state association in 1937 she was instrumental in getting the State of Georgia to set up a retirement plan for county and home demonstration agents which has served as a model for other states. In 1938 she was winner of the Atlanta Constitution award for Georgia agents in the "Plant to Prosper" contest. In 1939 she was selected to speak on women's part in the National Extension Service before Secretary of Agriculture Wallace in Washington, D. C. That same year she won the H. G. Hastings Company award for the best gardening project.

In 1945 she won the Distinguished Service Award of the Georgia Home Demonstration Agents' Association. In 1946 she was presented the Distinguished Service Award of the National Extension Service in Chicago.

She is a member of the Epsilon Sigma Phi National Fraternity and is now serving that organization as state historian.

Her interest in improved living standards for farm families led naturally to gardening, and in 1939 she became one of the first sixteen accredited flower show judges in Georgia. In 1959 she was elected first vice president of the Middle Georgia Flower Show Judges' Council.

She has been a member of the Red Cross for forty-five years, acting as Home Service Chairman during the panic period of the depression in 1932 and again in 1954 following the Warner Robins tornado disaster.

In 1948 the Georgia Extension Service asked her to help introduce home demonstration work to counties not already having it. Her first organizing job was in Henry County, which she liked so well she stayed on as its first agent until her retirement.

She has always been active in the Baptist Church and began teaching an adult Sunday School class at the age of seventeen. She is a charter member of the Major General John Twiggs Chapter of the Daughters of the American Revolution.

In 1951 she returned to the house in Jeffersonville where she had originally started housekeeping and which she had kept as her legal residence through the years, maintaining her interest in local affairs and voting in Jeffersonville. She continues her many creative hobbies and is in demand as a speaker and flower show judge, while her original designs in hooked rugs and handpainted china are treasured by her friends.

Submitted by Shedrick J. Carswell, Thomaston, Ga.

## CHILDERS

Osborne Childers was born in Washington County, Georgia, October 5, 1790, the eldest son of Richard Childers and Martha (Spann) Childers. He was married to Malinda Burton, the daughter of Thomas Burton, Jr., and Nancy (Nunnallee) Burton in Elbert County, Georgia, June 28, 1815. On January 24, 1814, Osborne Childers was commissioned Twiggs County Surveyor and served in that capacity until January 3, 1816. He served as a captain of the Twiggs County District Militia in 1815. He died in Twiggs County 1826-1830. Malinda (Burton) Childers later married the Rev. Fred Griffith. She died after 1832. Osborne Childers and Malinda

(Burton) Childers had three children: Dr. Erasmus Ripley Childers, M.D., Virgil Childers and one other son. Virgil Childers died in Albany, Georgia, about 1870.

Dr. Erasmus Ripley Childers was born in Twiggs County, September 6, 1819. He was graduated from the University of Pennsylvania Medical College in Philadelphia in 1840 with an M.D. degree. He then came to Summerfield, Dallas County, Alabama, and was married there on November 9, 1841, to Amanda Melvina F. Pinson, daughter of Col. Joab Pinson and Caroline Matilda (Dunn) Pinson. Dr. Childers died in Summerfield February 10, 1857. Col. Joab Pinson was the son of Isaac Pinson of Washington County, Georgia. Caroline Matilda (Dunn) Pinson was the daughter of Nehemiah Dunn of Jones County, Georgia.

Thomas Burton, Jr., was soldier in Georgia during the Revolutionary War under Gen. Elijah Clarke and a member of the Provincial Congress in Georgia. He was the son of Thomas Burton, Sr., and Sarah (Thompson) Burton of Chesterfield County, Virginia, and Elbert County, Georgia. Nancy (Nunnalle) Burton was the daughter of William Womack Nunnallee and Ann (Franklin) Nunnallee.

Richard Childers, the father of Osborne Childers, was born in Virginia about 1756, and died in Washington County. Georgia, in 1830. He was a Revolutionary soldier in Georgia; an Ensign, Eight Company, Washington County Regiment of Militia on March 29, 1793; member of Georgia House of Representatives, Washington County, 1807-08, Extra 1809; Jusice of the Peace, Washington County, commissioned July 9, 1802, and a planter. In the 1830 Census of Washington County, he is listed under the schedule of persons allotted to L. A. Jernigan as having 50 slaves.

The other children of Richard Childers and Martha (Spann) Childers were:

Sarah S. Childers, born October 15, 1788, married Henry Jordan of Twiggs County, and died in Summerfield, Dallas County, Alabama, October 17, 1845.

George E. Childers, born September 28, 1792, in Washington County, Georgia, married first Elizabeth Wimberly, daughter of Lewis Wimberly of Jones County, Georgia, the mother of his children, married secondly in Summerfield, Dallas County, Alabama, Mrs. Emily Wingfield (Sims) Woolsey Heard. He died in Mobile, Alabama, January 24, 1853, and is buried in Childers Chapel Cemetery near Summerfield. After his death, his widow married as her fourth husband, Bishop James Osgood Andrew of the Methodist Episcopal Church, South.

Elizabeth Childers, born October 12, 1794, in Washington County, Georgia, married Abner Wimberly.

John Spann Childers, born in Washington County, Georgia, February 24, 1799. married first Pamelia Burton, sister of Malinda (Burton) Childers. His only child by his first wife was Martha Ann Childers who married Benjamin Franklin Ross of Macon, Georgia. The second wife of John Spann Childers was named Mary. He was a prominent citizen in the early history of Macon, Georgia, and a member of the Georgia legislature from Bibb County. He moved to Pleasant Hill, Louisiana and died there in 1858.

Martha Spann Childers, born in Washington County, Georgia, February 17, 1801, married George Walker.

Nancy Osborne Childers, born in Washington County, Georgia, September 29, 1803, married Henry Wimberly.

Submitted by: B. M. Miller Childers, 900 Alabama Ave., Selma, Ala.

## THE WILLIAM HENRY CHANCE FAMILY

William Henry Chance was born November 30, 1876, one of nine children, to William C. Chance—one of the four organizers of the Mt. Zion Missionary Baptist Church near Danville, and a private in the Confederate Army—and Carrie Lee Chance, of Twiggs County. His brothers and sisters were: Donnie, who married Will Carter;

Haden, who married Katie Simpson; John Solomon, who married Zilphia Floyd; Mary, who married G. Grimsley and, later, W. H. "Bud" Grimsley; Annie Lou, who married Will "Boy" Little; Hannah, who married Benjamin F. Helton; Bessie, who married Ben Grimsley and Joshua H., who married Amanda Howell.

"Henry", as he was generally known in the county, was married to the former Lula Jane Sauls on July 30, 1879. Three sons and a daughter were born to the couple before his death in November, 1910, at the age of 34.

Homer Lee Chance, eldest of the four children, was born August 22, 1897. He served as Twiggs County Representative in the Georgia Legislature for three consecutive terms, from 1943-1947, and as Senator of the Fifty-first District—which included Twiggs, Houston, and Bibb Counties—for the years 1955 and 1956. In 1959, he was reelected to complete the unexpired term of Jere C. Miller, as Representative of Twiggs County in the Georgia Legislature. He was married to the former Everette Hamrick; and, following her death, to the former Minnie L. Griffin, a well known school teacher of Twiggs County. He was a member and deacon of the Mt. Zion Baptist Church and a member of the Cool Springs Masonic Lodge No. 185 F&AM, in Danville.

Henry Julian Chance, second eldest of the four, was born May 5, 1900. He was married to the former Georgia Elizabeth Arnold, of Twiggs County, and was a farmer and country store operator in Twiggs County until his untimely death on January 4, 1953, following an automobile accident in which he was fatally burned. He was the father of three children, as follows:

Henry Julian Chance, Jr., eldest, was born July 18, 1923. He was married to the former Sara Kimball Harvey, of Laurens County. A graduate of the Danville High School in 1941, he was employed in the mercantile business with his uncle, H. L. Chance, until accepting a position with the Baker-Maddox Company, in Macon. He later went into business for himself in Danville and was former Acting Postmaster of the town, a former town Councilman and a member of the Cool Springs Masonic Lodge No. 185, F&AM, in Danville. He was a member of the Huber Masonic Club, Huber, Georgia, former Consul Commander of Woodmen of the World Camp No. 1303, in Danville and the father of two sons, Henry Douglas and Randall Lee. In 1953, he became associated with the J. M. Huber Corporation as technician in the control laboratory, later transferring to Production, Sales and Service Department with the company.

Martha Opal Chance, second eldest, was born February 24, 1927. A first honor graduate of the Danville High School, she was a graduate of Business Training Institute, Macon, Georgia, completing the Executive Secretarial Course, as well as special work in tax accounting. She attended evening classes at Mercer University and completed a number of courses offered by the American Institute of Banking. Employed at Warner Robins Air Materiel Command, during World War II, she resigned to accept a teaching position with a private business college in Macon. Later, she was employed by the Allentown Warehouse Company and The Four County Bank, Allentown, Georgia. A member of the Supreme Forest Woodmen Circle, Grove No. 23, Macon, Georgia, she filled various offices in that grove as well as serving as Second State Auditor and Middle Georgia District President of the organization. She served as Secretary and Vice President of the Tau Phi Lambda Sorority and was a charter member, as well as the first Secretary of Court 1602, Women of Woodcraft, in Danville, Georgia.

Miss Molly Lou Chance, youngest of the three children, was born

March 13, 1929. A graduate of the Danville High School, she was the recipient of the "I Dare You" award for leadership ability. She was later employed at Robins Air Force Base and the H. L. Green Company, Macon. In 1946, she became associated with Smith Oil Company, in Danville. A member of the Supreme Forest Woodmen Circle, Grove No. 23, Macon, Georgia, she served as Middle Georgia District Attendant in that organization, as well as a number of offices in Grove No. 23 and in the Tau Phi Lambda Sorority. She was a charter member and the first Empress of Court 1602, Women of Woodcraft, in Danville, Georgia.

The third and only daughter of William Henry and Lula Sauls Chance was Elsie Jane. Born March 2, 1904, she married Jule K. Carden of Twiggs County, July 27, 1920; and to this union were born two children as follows:

Benjamin Henry, the son, was born October 17, 1922. He attended the Danville High School and married the former Sara Parker, of Danville. He was a farmer in the county and employed by Fickling and Walker in Macon, Georgia. He was a member of Camp 1303, Danville, Georgia, and the father of two children, Benjamin Henry, Jr. and David Bruce.

Edith Gretchen, younger of the two children, was born November 29, 1924. A graduate of the Danville High School, she was married to Hoyt Morgan Sanders, Jr., who was a life-long resident and prominent farmer in Twiggs County. To this union were born three children—Hoyt Morgan Sanders, III, Barbara Jewel, and Cynthia Ann.

William Clayton Chance, youngest of the four children of the William Henry Chances and namesake of his grandfather, William C. Chance, was born October 25, 1908. He was a member of Camp 1303, Woodmen of the World, Danville, Georgia, and was a resident of and farmer in Twiggs County throughout his entire life.  —Submitted by M. Opal Chance

## CHAPPELL FAMILY

The Chappells of Twiggs County are descendants of early Scotch-Irish and English settlers in this country. The original John Chappell came from England and received a grant of land from the King of England along the lower James River in Virginia. From there, one branch moved to Edgefield County, South Carolina, and eventually to Georgia.

Thomas Simmons Chappell, born 1801, lived near Dry Branch, Georgia, and owned land in what is now Twiggs and Bibb Counties. He died July 29, 1861. He is buried in the family cemetery near Dry Branch.

One of his sons, William Chappell, born October 12, 1827, died January 12, 1859. He, also, is buried in the family cemetery. On June 6, 1855, William married Mary Elizabeth McCallum of Scotch ancestry. Her father, Archibald McCallum, was the son of Angus McCallum and Mary McBride, both of whom came from Scotland. He was a wealthy planter who gave the land on which the Jeffersonville Baptist Church now stands. Mary McCallum, is, also, a descendant of Henry Ware, born December 16, 1756 in Maryland. He moved to Georgia and died November 22, 1807, and Henry's son, James Ware, who was born February 26, 1785, was married to Polly Mims. He is buried in the Old Richland Church cemetery. Both William Chappell and his wife, Mary, attended college. Mary graduated from the LaGrange Female College.

To William Chappell and Mary Elizabeth McCallum Chappell there were born two sons, William Thomas Chappell, Sr., born August 28, 1858, and Archibald McCallum Chappell, born March 8, 1857. Mary, after the death of her husband, moved with her two small children to a house built for her by her father near Jeffersonville, where she spent the remainder of her life, and where her two sons lived the remainder of their lives.

William Chappell's estate, consisting of land, livestock, and slaves, was sold for Confederate money during the Civil War. Mary McCallum Chappell died on January 22, 1910. Archibald McCallum Chappell, a bachelor, died in 1913.

William Thomas Chappell, Sr. was a deacon in the Jeffersonville Baptist Church, treasurer of the Ebenezer Baptist Association for 35 years, and Justice of the Peace for upward to 40 years. He married Nannie Julia Storey on June 6, 1894. She was a descendant from the Storey, King, and Ball families of Wilkinson County. She was the daughter of Richard Lawson Storey, born in Jackson County, Georgia, February 1, 1823, died Wilkinson County, Georgia, June 19, 1892. He moved to Texas with his parents in 1844, but returned to Georgia shortly thereafter. He served as Lt. Colonel in the Confederate Army during the Civil War. He, also, was secretary to a Governor of Georgia and served in the Georgia Senate. He married Sarah King, who lived from October 7, 1832 to April 17, 1918. Sarah King was a descendant of John Ball for whom the John Ball Chapter of Daughters of American Revolution was named.

William Thomas Chappell, Jr. was born March 25, 1896. He is employed by Central of Georgia Railroad and raises cattle on the old homeplace near Jeffersonville. He was married first June 5, 1924, to Alma Bennett. Their children are Evelyn Chappell, born May 19, 1926, and married March 7, 1946, to William Joseph Blizzard of Indiana, now residing in Baltimore, Maryland. They have one child, William Joseph Blizzard, Jr., born November 29, 1947. William Joseph Blizzard, Sr., is an Electronics Engineer.

William Thomas Chappell, III was born April 1, 1928, and is married to Jean Garrard of Gainesville. He is manager of Royal Brothers Poultry Processing Plant at Camilla, Georgia. He graduated from Georgia Southwestern College in Americus.

Carolyn Chappell, born June 13, 1930, attended Brenau College and is employed by Rich's Department Store in Atlanta.

William Thomas Chappell, Jr. married second on October 21, 1944, Minnie Jewel Taylor, public school teacher in Macon, who holds A.B. and M.A. degrees.

The second child of William Thomas and Nannie Chappell was Ruth Electa, born March 21, 1898. She married March 17, 1923, Herschel Victor Davis, formerly Mayor of Richland, Georgia. Ruth holds A.B. degree from Georgia State College for Women, and M.A. degree from University of Georgia. She taught for many years in public schools in Georgia and at the Georgia Southwestern College.

The third child of William Thomas and Nannie Chappell is Sarah Ellie who was born May 30, 1900, attended G. S. C. W. and taught in public schools in South Carolina and Georgia. She married May 29, 1924, George Willard Adams, who was born January 11, 1901, in Washington, Georgia. He is General Superintendent of the Macon Division of the Atlanta Gas Light Company. He graduated in Mechanical Engineering at Georgia Tech where he was a member of Sigma Chi. He has served as President of the Macon Exchange Club, having been voted the Outstanding Exchangite in 1946. He has, also, served on the Georgia State Fair Board for 17 years, and on the Board of Directros of the Macon Y.M.C.A. for many years. Their adopted daughters, nieces of George, are Mary Evelyn Adams, born October 3, 1932, and Jacqueline Chappell Adams, born February 17, 1936, married Bobbie Lee Smith, automobile dealer in Macon, on February 11, 1955. Their two children are Bobbie Lee Smith, Jr., born November 13, 1956, and Mark Adams Smith, born September 18, 1958. Mary Evelyn holds B.S. degree from Georgia State College for Women and teaches home economics in the Glynn Academy, Brunswick, Georgia.

The fourth child of William and Nannie Chappell is Richard Archibald

"Archie" Chappell, born December 23, 1901, married October 7, 1934, to Annette Richardson of Macon, who was born October 7, 1907. She graduated from Wesleyan College. Their children are Mariann, born August 8, 1935, married September 8, 1956, to Fred William Evans. They have one child, Margaret Elizabeth, born March 4, 1959. Mariann attended Randolph Macon College where she was a member of Kappa Alpha Theta, Emory University, and graduated from Mercer University with an A.B. in 1957. Fred was a member of Kappa Alpha and graduated from Mercer University with A.B. degree. He is employed by the Georgia Vocational Rehabilitation Division and is a captain in the U. S. Army Reserve.

Nancy Elizabeth Chappell, born May 15, 1939, is attending Wesleyan College, specializing in art.

"Archie" Chappell graduated from Mercer University where he belonged to Sigma Pi. He attended law school at Mercer, Emory, Georgetown and George Washington. He received an honorary Doctor of Laws degree from Mercer in 1953. He entered the service of the United States Government in 1928 and retired from that service in 1954 to enter the practice of law in Macon. He was Chief of the United States Probation System, Adminstrative Office, U. S. Courts, and a member of the United States Parole Board, Department of Justice. He lived for 17 years in Washington, D. C. He was editor of Federal Probation Magazine, served as Commander in the United States Navy during World War II, and received the Secretary of Navy Commendation Ribbon. His biography is shown in Volume 29 of the 1956-1957 edition of Who's Who in America.

Submitted by: R. A. Chappell, 2765 Hilandale Circle, Macon, Ga.

## TAYLOR LAMAR EVERETT, SR.

### TAYLOR LAMAR EVERETT, SR.

Born January 2, 1896

Educator

Great Grandson of

### JOHN EVERETT

Born 1780-1790—Died 1840-1850

John Everett, born 1780-1790, died 1840-1850, as stated in the early records of Georgia, which are filed in the Library of the University of Georgia, Athens, Georgia, was one of the prominent early settlers of Twiggs County, coming to that section in the early 1800's from the section around Edgcombe County, North Carolina.

The family to which he belongs is one of the oldest and most distinguished in America. His branch of the family had lived in Maryland, and was a descendant of Charles and his wife, both English born, who came from near London between 1632 and 1636 and made their home in Williamsburg, Virginia.

According to records filed in Twiggs County and in Washington, D. C., John Everett, born 1780-1790, owned a large plantation in Twiggs County, Georgia and properties in Marion, the first County Seat.

John Everett's children and their birthdays according to Federal census were:
1. Henry E. Everett, born 1825-26
2. John Barrett Everett, born May 30, 1827, died October 7, 1889
3. James Everett, born 1830-31
4. Joshua Everett, born 1833-34
5. Sara Everett, born 1836-37
6. Mary Ann Everett, born 1839-40

John Everett and his wife died between 1840-1850. Henry E. Everett, oldest son of John Everett, was made guardian of the four youngest children after his father's death. John sold his father's property and moved away from Twiggs County. He sold a large tract of his father's plantation to John A. Barclay in 1854—other property he sold to James Everett and Daniel Bullard 1849.

Among the Everett names (brothers and cousins of John Everett) and counties in North Carolina from which they came, found in early Federal Census of Twiggs County, filed in Washington, D. C., are:
Benjamine Everett, Onslow Co., North Carolina
Jerisiah Everett, Tyrell Co., North Carolina
Thomas Everett, Anson Co., North Carolina
Beny Everett, Richmond Co., North Carolina
Joshua Everett, Martin Co., North Carolina
Henry Everett, Anson Co., North Carolina
John Everett, Anson Co., North Carolina
Thomas Everett, Beaufort Co., North Carolina
James Everett, Beaufort Co., North Carolina
John Everett, Martin Co., North Carolina
James Everett, Martin Co., North Carolina
Thomas Everett, Martin Co., North Carolina

All of the Everetts moved away from Twiggs County except John Barrett Everett, born May 3, 1827, died October 7, 1889. He married Elizabeth Bullard, born April 18, 1837, died July 11, 1905, who was the daughter of Daniel and Caroline Bullard. She was the granddaughter of Wiley, born before 1775 in North Carolina, and Parthena Bullard, who came to Twiggs County about 1809. Wiley Bullard was of English descent and a prominent early settler of Twiggs County. His son, Daniel Bullard, became one of the largest landowners and wealthiest men of that section.

John Barrett and Elizabeth Bullard Everett's children and their birthdays according to Bible records were:
Josephine Virginia Everett, born December 14, 1854
Henry Daniel Everett, born July 21, 1857
James Charles Everett, born December 14, 1859
John Walter Everett, born August 13, 1862, died September 29, 1883
Thomas Francis Everett, born May 17, 1868
Mary Lee Everett, born October 11, 1865

Lillie Bell Everett, born March 24, 1871
William Edward Everett, born January 28, 1874

John Barrett Everett served in the Civil War with the Twiggs County unit 1862-1864. He was badly wounded in battle in 1864, Petersburg, Va., July 30.

Thomas Francis Everett, born May 7, 1868, died, 1920, the son of John Barrett Everett, followed in his father's and grandfather's footsteps. He became one of Georgia's prominent farmers. He acquired 2,000 acres of rich farm land in Twiggs County. This acreage included the original land owned by his grandfather, John Everett, born 1780-1790.

Thomas Francis Everett's interest in education and improved methods of farming was recognized throughout the state. He furnished land, labor and money for many new experiments in farming and his beautiful plantation was a proving ground for many methods of farming that are used successfully today.

Thomas Francis Everett was untiring in his effort, generous with time and money and left no stone unturned to provide a good education for his children, as well as all other children in the Everett and Bullard Community. The Everett School, which he established, was one of the first public rural schools in Georgia to have a nine months' school term.

Thomas Francis Everett was a popular and prominent citizen. He held many offices in Twiggs County, both public and fraternal. He was married to Eola Pensive Lamb, born in Twiggs Co., on January 10, 1872, died, 1924. Their children and birthdays are:

>   John Estes Everett, born October 13, 1893, World War I Veteran
>   Taylor Lamar Everett, born January 2, 1896, World War I Veteran
>   Thomas Russell Everett, born December 14, 1897, World War I Veteran
>   Harry Walton Everett, born January 18, 1900, World War I Veteran
>   Mary Frances Everett, born May 23, 1906

Thomas Frances Everett's interest in education was rewarded. All of his children were graduated from the University of Georgia or Georgia Tech.

Taylor Lamar Everett, second son of Thomas Frances and Eola Pensive Lamb Everett, was graduated from the University of Georgia with a Bachelor of Science degree in Agriculture and a Masters degree in School Administration and Supervision. For eight years he taught and served as President of the Agricultural and Mechanical School at Cochran, Georgia. Under his administration, the beautiful administration building was erected. The enrollment of students greatly increased and through his personal effort hundreds of farm boys and girls received an education and had a richer, fuller life.

In 1931, Taylor Lamar Everett became Superintendent of the Schools of Ware County. At the present time he is the oldest County School Superintendent in Georgia, in the point of service.

Taylor Lamar Everett, Sr. married Elizabeth Brown, born January 4, 1900, in Jefferson County, Georgia. Their children and grandchildren are:

>   Reaunette Everett, born December 15, 1924
>   > Married—A. Guinn Vaughn, Conyers, Georgia
>   Patricia Clara Vaughn, born March 23, 1957
>   Taylor Lamar Everett, Jr., born April 29, 1928, World War II Veteran,
>   > Japan—married Carol Carter, Lakeland, Georgia

Reaunette Everett, prominent Georgia artist, was graduated with a Master's degree in Art from the University of Georgia.

Taylor Lamar Everett, Jr., teacher and administrator, received a Masters degree in Science and a Masters degree in School Administration and Supervision, from Peabody College for Teachers, Nashville, Tennessee.

>   Submitted by:   Elizabeth Brown Everett (Mrs. T. L.), Waycross, Ga.

## ABOUT THE CO-COMPILER

J. Lanette O'Neal Faulk, daughter of the late James Thomas O'Neal and Margaret "Maggie" Wimberly, was born in Twiggs County and spent her childhood days in the Dry Branch community. In 1924 her parents moved to Macon, Georgia, where her father was employed as general superintendent of the General Reduction Company for twenty-five years.

She completed her high school course of study at the Practice School of Georgia Normal and Industrial College, graduated from Georgia State College for Women with a Bachelor of Science degree in Education and attended Mercer University. She has taught twenty-one years in the public school system of Georgia. She was principal several years at Meriwether and Bullard elementary schools and is presently employed as sixth grade teacher at Twiggs Elementary School.

Mrs. Faulk was Organizing Regent and Regent of the Major General John Twiggs Chapter, Daughters of the American Revolution, a past Regent of the John Ball Chapter, D. A. R. She is also a member of the following organizations: Major Philip Cook Chapter, United States Daughters of 1812; Colonel Thomas Hardeman Chapter, United Daughters of the Confederacy; Georgia Society, Dames of the Court of Honor; Georgia Division of National Society Daughters of Founders and Patriots of America; Georgia Branch of National Society of Sons and Daughters of the Pilgrims; Delta Chapter, Delta Kappa Gamma; Macon Chapter No. 345, Order of the Eastern Star; Minuteman for Rural Electrification; Twiggs Education Association, having served as local Unit president, Georgia and National Education Associations, and Cross Keys Baptist Church. She compiled HISTORICAL COLLECTIONS OF RICHLAND CHURCH.

Lanette was married to Hugh Lawson Faulk on May 5, 1935 by Reverend S. B. Wingfield at Macon, Georgia. Issue: two sons, Hugh Lawson Faulk, Jr., and Thomas Henry Faulk.

By Hugh L. and Thomas

## MARK FAULK FAMILY

The Faulk family, according to tradition, came from Europe (a province on the River Rhine which lay between Germany and France), settling first in this country in North Carolina; later sons of the family emigrated southward and located in Georgia.

Mark Faulk, Sr., was born in Georgia in the year 1799 (Reference 1880 Census information furnished by his children), and died Feb. 3, 1836, in Twiggs County. He was buried in the old Faulk cemetery located on what is commonly known as the "Denson Level", approximately eight miles west of Jeffersonville, on property now owned by W. T. Faulk, a great grandson. Mark Faulk, Sr., was a pioneer settler of Twiggs County. He was a successful planter and acquired a sizeable plantation, owning many slaves. (Reference: 1818-1826 and 1830 Twiggs County Tax Digest). In addition to his farming interests he operated a freight line consisting of a train of six wagons, six horses each, with a slave in charge, traveling from Savannah to Marion, and other points over the old Northern Stage Road. His is one of the few pioneer families who have descendants that have remained continuously in the county holding the old estate he left intact to the present day.

Mark Faulk, Sr., married first Milberry Phillips and three children were born to them: James G., born March 22, 1814, died March 20, 1847; Mark, Jr., born October 4, 1815, died January 1, 1837, and Lucretia, born September 1, 1817, died February 6, 1848. She married James Land.

## MARK FAULK FAMILY

Mrs. Mark Faulk, Sr.
(Nancy Reynolds)

### FAULK BROTHERS

L. to r. George W., Charles R., William. Standing, John.

Mark Faulk, Sr., married second Nancy Reynolds, born 1802, died 1868 (her parents were Charles Reynolds and Mary Dismuke), and eight children were born to this marriage: (Mark and Nancy were married on March 7, 1820.)

I. Mary, born September 7, 1821, died March 23, 1881, married R. R. Slappey.

11. William, born August 1, 1822. In early life he joined Richland Baptist Church where later he became a deacon. He was a member of the Masonic Order, a Democrat and represented his county in the legislature. On July 20, 1847 he was married to Virginia Arabella Solomon, born January 9, 1828 (daughter of Henry Solomon, born March 22, 1791, died January 16, 1847). This union was blessed with four children: Laura Jenett, born October 24, 1850, died July 22, 1886, never married; James George, born March 8, 1853, died June 9, 1854; Virginia Solomon, born March 14, 1857, died March 11, 1896, married December 1, 1878 John Carey Shannon; and Mary Lucretia, born June 20, 1858, died December 15, 1933, married March 3, 1898 John Carey Shannon.

Mr. Faulk's beautiful home, "Laurel Hill", at Marion was noted for its hospitality and many social gatherings.

Having material aid he rendered service to the Confederate States and helped to outfit the Faulk Invincibles of the 26th Georgia Regiment, commanded by Captain Eli S. Griffin, consisting of seventy-one men who volunteered on July 22, 1861, and who were in need of arms and accoutrements.

In 1891, he moved to Jeffersonville and made his home with Virginia and Carey Shannon. It was here that he passed away January 19, 1904. He was buried at his old home place near Marion. The following quotation is from his obituary: "This kind-hearted man always envinced the keenest interest in the welfare of his former slaves. His former slaves were sorrowing visitors at his bedside and mingled their tears with their white friends at his grave". (Obituary is in the possession of his granddaughter, Mrs. Laurie Shannon Boyd).

III. Jenett, born April 24, 1824, died (after 1880), married first Dr. Abraham Garber. She married second Ashley Vickers.

IV. Henry, born March 19, 1827, died November 7, 1852, married Amanda Beckom.

V. Charles Reynolds, born January 24, 1829, died September 23, 1881, married on June 13, 1853 Josephene M. Solomon. (Issue: sons and daughters).

VI. John, born October 21, 1830, died December 12, 1894 at Forsyth, Ga. He married first December 5, 1852 Augusta Victoria Solomon. Children: Victoria and James J. Victoria married J. J. Cater of Forsyth, Ga.

VII. George W., Sr., born January 31, 1833, died October 19, 1893, buried in the Faulk cemetery at his old home place, "Sunnyside", approximately nine miles west of Jeffersonville. He was married October 30, 1855, by Rev. George R. McCall, to Mary Ann Shine (daughter of Daniel W. Shine and Nancy Ann Glenn, and granddaughter of the Revolutionary soldier John Shine of North Carolina). They had eleven children:

1. Sarah Virginia, born September 16, 1856, died March 6, 1877, buried Faulk cemetery "Sunnyside". She married October 20, 1874 John T. Land.

2. Henry Glenn, born July 15, 1858, died October 29, 1947. He was married February 6, 1896, at "Gleesom Hall" in Twiggs County, by Rev. F. Bartow Asbell, to Laura Tarver Wimberly, born March 26, 1873, died Feb. 9, 1957, (daughter of Henry Slappey Wimberly, Jr., and Mary Susan Coombs). Both were members of Richland Baptist Church and among the last surviving members. They are buried in the Faulk cemetery at their old home, "Sunnyside". Six children:

(1) Mary Shine, born May 22, 1897, married June 3, 1917 Richard Augustus Harrison, born October 25, 1886, died February 20, 1956. Children: Henry Faulk, born September 23, 1918, married first April 30, 1941, Era Ellen Copeland. They had

two children: Era Sue, born February 7, 1942, and Henry Faulk, Jr., born March 27, 1943, died Nov. 6, 1957. Married second May 10, 1958 Helen E. Dew. Richard Augustus, Jr., born August 27, 1920, married first Helen Ash. Born of this marriage, a daughter, Virginia. Married second Bronzie Lois Lee and to this marriage was born a son, Richard A., III., October 15, 1946. Mary Esther, born December 18, 1923, married June 1, 1941 James Earl Tumblin, born November 15, 1907. He entered U. S. Army in 1927 and retired in 1953. Their children: Mary Wimberly, born November 26, 1942 and Richard Earl, born December 18, 1951.

(2) Hallie Wimberly, born January 30, 1900, married first October 26, 1924 Thomas Jones Faulk. She married second Dr. Waldo Ingle. Married third Jack B. Lee.

(3) George Watkins, born May 25, 1902, died September 25, 1907, buried at "Sunnyside".

(4) Henry Glenn, Jr., born July 25, 1904, died December 29, 1905, buried at "Sunnyside".

(5) Hugh Lawson, born August 29, 1907, married on May 5, 1935 J. Lanette O'Neal, born May 23, 1905. Two children: Hugh Lawson II ( Junior), born November 9, 1937, married July 26, 1959 to Doris June Barden, and Thomas Henry, born September 18, 1941. Hugh L. and Thomas enlisted in U. S. Armed Forces.

(6) Hardy Durham, born October 8, 1915, married August 20, 1943 Eulilla B. Baker, born August 29, 1921. One child: Hardy Durham, Jr., born July 15, 1957.

3. Daniel Shine Faulk, Sr., born August 25, 1860, died June 19, 1948. He was born at "Sunnyside", his family home. In 1892 he moved to Jeffersonville, where he was active in politics, serving as clerk of the court from January 1, 1893 to December 30, 1898, and as sheriff of Twiggs County from January 1, 1899 to December 30, 1902. About 1905 he went into business for himself as a cotton warehouseman, later becoming a prominent farmer of Twiggs County. In 1904 he purchased the Hardy Durham plantation, and later acquiring in 1918 the Henry Wimberly home, "Gleesom Hall", where he spent his latter years. He was a deacon of the Jeffersonville Baptist Church and served on the building committee of the new church building when it was constructed in 1917, his name being on the corner stone of the building. He married Caroline Griffin Wimberly January 19, 1902, the ceremony being performed by Rev. H. B. Wimberly. She was born September 1, 1876 and died December 26, 1940. (See Wimberly genealogy). Five children were born to this union:

(1) George W., born November 29, 1902, married May 31, 1932 Mozella Grissom, born August 13, 1906. They have one daughter: June, born June 12, 1934, married July 8, 1957 to L. R. Giordano, and they have a son: Joseph Faulk, born May 27, 1958.

(2) John Wimberly, born July 5, 1905, married August 8, 1933 Marion Austelle Sanders, born December 7, 1910. Three children: Austelle Sanders, born June 9, 1935, married June 2, 1956 Charles Donald Singleton. John Gordan, born February 16, 1937, and Beverly Rabun, born August 11, 1942.

(3) Henry Gordan, born April 12, 1908, married August 23, 1936 Mary Frances Lamb, born November 20, 1916. Four children: Carlton Shine, born May 31, 1937; Henry Daniel, born July 3, 1945; John Robert, born October 20, 1951, and Suzanne, born July 26, 1955.

(4) Jennie, born December 1, 1910, died August 3, 1911.

(5) Daniel Shine, Jr., born May 12, 1914, married Emma Woody. Two children: Alice Ruth, born July 10, 1943, and Mary Jane, born June 4, 1954.

(6) Mary Jane, born February 15, 1922.

4. Nancy G., born March 4, 1862, died October 22, 1870, buried Faulk cemetery "Sunnyside".

5. George Watkins Faulk, Jr., born December 29, 1863, died August 9, 1911.

married first October 2, 1891 Mary Belle Glover (daughter of James and Georgia B. Glover), born July 7, 1872, died November 26, 1891. He married second December 15, 1896, by Rev. J. C. Solomon (Baptist minister), Ida Elmina Balkcom (daughter of James Franklin Balkcom and Ira Ellen Hughes). Four children:

(1) Ellen Hughes, born February 8, 1898, married first Jasper McArthur Wall. Two children: Elmina Graves, born April 23, 1918, Jasper McArthur, Jr., born August 19, 1922, married Sara Adams. She (Ellen Hughes) married second David Yancey Califf, born January 21, 1897.

(2) Jeanette Vickers, born February 8, 1900, married September 16, 1919 William Heyward Harrell, born January 30, 1898. Two children: Billie Faulk, born January 3, 1921, married December 6, 1958 W. Joseph Jones. Ida Virginia, born July 11, 1922, married April 9, 1944 Joseph T. Cadden. Children: Jan, born March 20, 1945, and Ellen Hughes, born November 12, 1946.

(3) Wilhelmina, born September 9, 1905, married July 18, 1927 Rupert Clyde Hobbs, born September 17, 1907. Children: Infant son born September 10, 1928, died same date, buried North View Cemetery, Dublin, Ga. Daughter, Ellen Wilhelmina, born December 14, 1933, married September 1, 1957 Billy J. Calloway, Rome, Ga. They have a son, David Scott, born December 30, 1958.

(4) William Thomas, born September 9, 1905. Voluntarily enlisted in the United States Marine Corps February 9, 1923 and, after more than thirty-one years active service, retired June 30, 1954, with the rank of Chief Warrant Officer. He married August 31, 1929 at St. Augustine, Florida, Dorothy Edith Stokes, born June 29, 1908. Two children: Nancy Reynolds, born August 31, 1951, and Robin Terese, born August 6, 1954.

6. Mark S., Sr., born July 8, 1866, died June 2, 1944, buried New Richland Baptist Church cemetery. He married first October 19, 1892 Lottie Burke, born December 4, 1870, died September 23, 1893, buried in Faulk cemetery, "Sunnyside". He married second December 20, 1901, by Rev. H. B. Wimberly, Mary Coley Walters, born August 18, 1879. Seven children:

(1) Daniel Shine, born February 5, 1903, married May 31, 1926 Gladys Burke, born October 1, 1907. Two children: Mark S., III, born April 16, 1927, died April 24, 1927. Mark Burke, born January 11, 1929, married November 15, 1953 Lucy Worth. He entered U. S. Army September 26, 1950 and was honorably discharged September 6, 1952. They have a daughter, Monica, born November 27, 1954.

(2) Joe Walters, Sr., born August 18, 1904, married December 15, 1923 Cletia Armstrong, born August 16, 1898. Four children: Joe Walters, Jr., born February 26, 1926, married June 16, 1950 Elizabeth Park Tuten, born June 12, 1927, and they have four children: Joseph Walters, III, born April 13, 1951; May Elizabeth, born September 15, 1952; James White, born June 29, 1954, and Mary Susan, born January 15, 1958. Clayton Vaughn, born March 1, 1930. He served in U. S. Army October 28, 1952 to October 25, 1954. Vance, born January 7, 1934, enlisted in U. S. Marine Corps July 20, 1953 and was discharged July 19, 1955. He married Peggy Ann Cauley, born September 25, 1935. They have a son, Samuel Darrell, born May 9, 1957. Henry Gordon, born August 14, 1935, married May 31, 1959 Edith Hornsby, born June 19, 1941.

(3) Julia, born August 2, 1906, married February 21, 1924 Alton Vestal White, born September 7, 1892, died March 24, 1954. Two children: Mary Walters, born November 17, 1924, married September 15, 1946 Joseph N. Bailey, born March 30, 1915. No children. Alton Vestal, Jr., born September 1, 1928, married October 19, 1947 Rosaline Denson, born February 21, 1923. Two children: Rose Lane, born September 23, 1948, and Alton Vestal, III, born July 7, 1952.

(4) Mark S., Jr., born June 13, 1910, died February 19, 1911, buried Faulk cemetery, "Sunnyside".

(5) Mark S., Jr., born May 3, 1914, married December 22, 1939 Rosa Harkins Israel, born August 12, 1916. She died December 2, 1958 and was buried at New Richland Baptist Church cemetery. Two children: Mark Ann, born November 30, 1947, and Nancy Julia, born January 6, 1954.

(6) George Watkins, born November 30, 1916, married March 2, 1946 Opal Hale, born November 30, 1921. He voluntarily enlisted in the U. S. Marine Corps October 30, 1940 and was honorably discharged November 13, 1946, a Staff Sergeant.

(7) Charles Reynolds, born July 21, 1919.

7. Mary Ella, born August 23, 1867, died August 18, 1895, married October 31, 1894 J. Henry Solomon.

8. Imogene ("Gena") born February 5, 1871; never married.

9. Charles Reynolds, Sr., born April 26, 1873, died September 6, 1949, married February 12, 1895, by Rev. R. C. Sanders, to Elvenia Delegal Carswell, born October 15, 1869, died November 19, 1939. Both are buried New Richland Baptist Church cemetery. Six children:

(1) Elvenia Ironela, born October 23, 1898. Never married.

(2) Rosa Lee, born February 12, 1901, married November 2, 1919 John G. Slappey, Jr., born September 18, 1888. Three children: Fred Faulk, born July 30, 1920, married March 7, 1948 Thelma Bryant. He served in U. S. Army August 1, 1942 to November 12, 1945. Anne Nancy, born October 8, 1924, married October 4, 1941 Robert Arthur Schultz. Three children: Robert Arthur, Jr., born December 2, 1942, Anniston, Ala.; Fred Slappey, born October 5, 1944, Camp Wheeler, Ga.; and Cherlyl Anne, born January 16, 1952, Macon, Ga. William, born March 9, 1938, died March 9, 1938.

(3) Mark Henry, born October 13, 1902, married November 26, 1936 Myrtle Lee Holliday, born July 19, 1911. Four children: Mary Elvenia, born July 10, 1937, married Lloyd E. Lee. Myrtle, born August 27, 1941; Bunyan, born August 8, 1949, and Charlotte Reba, born December 20, 1952.

(4) Charles Reynolds, Jr., born August 27, 1904, married December 26, 1929 Marguerite Dupree Newby. Four children: Lawrence Newby, born January 2, 1931 married June 9, 1956 Evelyn Butler. One child: Karen Cheryl, born June 22, 1957. Sarah Marguerite, born February 25, 1932, married November 21, 1952 Clarence C. Miley. They have a son, Michael Calmore, born December 4, 1957. Rose Marie, born August 20, 1933. Carolyn Rogers, born February 17, 1935.

(5) John Slappey, born February 19, 1907, married August 16, 1936 Ruby Lee Pope. Four children: John Charles, born March 25, 1937, married July 25, 1958 Joyce Bailey. Dorothy Lee, born August 24, 1939; Imogene, born January 21, 1942, and Ruby Aileen, born July 27, 1944.

(6) George Carswell, born November 14, 1912, married first November 18, 1935 Mary Ella Holliday. He married second July 11, 1952 Virginia Edmundson Short. Three children: Georgia Virginia, born April 8, 1953; Dollie Elvenia, born September 25, 1954, and Rose Ann, born July 18, 1957.

10. Sarah Land, born May 27, 1879, died May 23, 1957, buried at "Sunnyside". Never married.

11. Jeanette Vickers, born October 21, 1881, died young. July 11, 1882, buried at "Sunnyside".

VIII. Mark Ann, born October 15, 1836, married April 20, 1854 Henry J. Slappey. She died March 9, 1928, in her 90th year, at the home of her granddaughter, Mrs. Mary Muse (J. W.) Gillespie, Albany, Ga.

William Thomas Faulk

## JUDGE WILLIAM CHARLES FAULK

William Charles Faulk was born January 12, 1855, the son of Charles Reynolds Faulk and Josephine Soloman Faulk. He was born at Old Marion and lived there continuously until January 1, 1893. At this time he and his family moved to Jeffersonville, Georgia.

Bill Charles, as he was best known, farmed with his father until 1881 at which time his father died. After the death of his father, he operated the farm for his mother, Josephine Soloman Faulk. He continued to operate these farms in connection with his mother until January, 1882 when he married Alice Pauline Jones. She was the daughter of Major Thomas S. Jones and Mary Cowan Jones. Unto this union five children were born. They were Charles R. Faulk, Mary Cowan Jones Faulk, Thomas J. Faulk, William Faulk, and Shedrick Jones Faulk.

William Charles Faulk was a deacon in the Old Richand Baptist Church until January, 1893 at which time he moved his membership to the Jeffersonville Baptist Church and continued to act as a deacon. He also taught a Sunday School class in the Jeffersonville Baptist Church for many years. He was a member of the building committee when the new church at Jeffersonville was constructed. He made liberal contributions toward the building of the church and the pastorium.

Shortly after moving to Jeffersonville he was elected tax collector. He served several terms in this office after which he was elected ordinary of Twiggs County. He served continuously in this office until his death in March, 1922.

Bill Charles Faulk spent his entire life in Twiggs County, Georgia and farmed continuously from young manhood until his death.

Submitted by: C. R. Faulk

## FITZPATRICK FAMILY SKETCH

Mark W. Fitzpatrick Home
Tarversville

The earliest known history of the Fitzpatrick family begins with Joseph Fitzpatrick, born 1720 in Goochland County, Virginia and died in Fluvana County, Virginia, 1781. Joseph married Mary Perrin Woodsen, who was born 1727 in Goochland County, Virginia. Their son, Booth, born about 1755, was married to Elizabeth Brown, also of Virginia, this couple later coming to Green County, Georgia.

John Brown Fitzpatrick (born February 9, 1807) was the son of this union and who along with the family moved to Twiggs County about 1820. On February 18, 1830 he married Elizabeth Goodwin Hart of Tallahassee, Florida, whose father—Edwin Hart—had served as the first Clerk of the Inferior Court in the newly formed Twiggs County. John brought his bride from Tallahassee in a road cart and established a home in the hill section of the county at a sight which was later to be known as Fitzpatrick. This spacious home, magnificent in its day and in a remarkable state of preservation, still stands and is owned and occupied by descendants of the Fitzpatrick family. As the first Fitzpatrick to enter Twiggs County, John became a most successful planter, acquiring vast acreage and owning many slaves. He reared a large family of children, all of whom contributed greatly to the culture, wealth and development of their county.

One of the sons of John Brown and Elizabeth Hart Fitzpatrick was William Hart Fitzpatrick, (born February 23, 1847). Will (Wm. Hart) Fitzpatrick was married to Lizzie (Thulia Elizabeth) Massey on February 18, 1869. Lizzie was born January 23, 1850 and was graduated from Wesleyan College during the War-Between-the-States. Children of this union:

    Irwin Fitzpatrick (born October 2, 1871) married Icie Ulrica McCann of Clarksburg, W. Va., October 3, 1902. John W. Davis, the 1924 Democratic candidate for President, was an usher at this wedding.

    Inez Goodwin Fitzpatrick, born January 16, 1874, married Leon Smith Fernald, June 26, 1902.

    George Clare Brown Fitzpatrick, born March 31, 1876, married Ora Bell Travis, July 10, 1918.

    Stella Claudia Fitzpatrick, born April 13, 1878, married William Columbus Hendricks, April 30, 1906.

    Lucile Hart Fitzpatrick, born August 15, 1880.

    Nellie Massey Fitzpatrick, born September 13, 1882, married Thomas Jefferson Lattimere February 24, 1914.

    Caroline Madge Fitzpatrick, born July 13, 1885, married Xillo Yeamer McCann, December 22, 1909.

    Mark Fitzpatrick, born December 12, 1889, married Jane Lippincott Duross, Jenkintown, Pennsylvania, June 22, 1933.

    Willie Elizabeth.

In 1896, three years after the death of Will Fitzpatrick, the family moved to Tarversville—the old home-place of General Hartwell Tarver. In the following years under the wise counsel of Lizzie Massey Fitzpatrick and with hard work and good management by her sons, Irvin and Mark, about the largest cotton farm in the County was established, ginning a total of 1100 bales of cotton in one season. Also contributing to the success of this venture was partner and son-in-law Xillo Yeamer McCann.

After the death of Lizzie Fitzpatrick in 1929, her daughter Lucile became Chatelaine of the house and has maintained the old home in grand style as a meeting place for children, grandchildren and great-grandchildren of Will and Lizzie Fitzpatrick.

Mark Fitzpatrick, the youngest son of Will and Lizzie Fitzpatrick, attended school at Gordon Institute in Barnesville, Georgia, and was graduated with a degree in Civil Engineering from the University of Georgia. He served with distinction in

World War I, receiving both the Purple Heart and a citation. He is presently serving his third term as Tax Commissioner in his home county.

The children of Mark and Jane Fitzpatrick are:

Duross Fitzpatrick, born October 19, 1934, was graduated from Cochran, Georgia High School. He spent one year at The University of The South at Sewanee, Tennessee, then joined the Marines for three years and is now completing his Forestry Course at the University of Georgia.

Jane Lippincott Fitzpatrick, born October 26, 1938, finished Cochran High School and entered Randolph-Macon College at Lynchburg, Virginia. She transferred to Emory University in Atlanta, Georgia.

Loxley Childs Fitzpatrick, born April 28, 1949.

Barry Kelly Fitzpatrick, born September 26, 1952.

Submitted by: The Mark Fitzpatrick Family

## GALLEMORE FAMILY

One of the pioneer citizens of Twiggs County was John Gallemore who came from North Carolina. A large farm operator and builder of Gallemore's Mill on Turkey Creek between Jeffersonville and Danville. Gallemore's Mill was operated by the family for a number of years, serving the community in grinding corn for meal and feed, also furnished a place of recreation for fishermen and picnickers.

When the M.D. & S. Railroad was built a station was established there. In the height of the picnic season the railroad would run excursions from Macon to Gallemore's Mill. Later the mill property was sold to a Mr. Deason of Wilkinson County and finally abandoned. The pond was rebuilt in 1950 by O. D. Snow who came in possession.

John Gallemore was the father of three sons, being married twice, the first wife being Betsy Joiner, the mother of William Joiner Gallemore, who died December 3, 1869, at the age of thirty-five.

William Joiner Gallemore, whose wife was named Hannah, died December 22, 1908 at the age of seventy years, was the father of two daughters. Mary Ellafair, who married Charlie Williams, of the community, and Dora R., who married A. Long of Warren County.

The children of Charlie and Mary Ellafair Williams were Augustus, whose fish pond was a model one in the county; Bessie, who married Mr. Lanz; William C., who practiced medicine for forty-seven years before retiring, and Lelia, who married Harvey Hill Maxwell.

Lelia and Harvey Maxwells' family were connected with the Danville postoffice and farming interests in Twiggs County. Their children, two daughters, Mary who married Willis Adams, and Annie, who married Hembree Carroll; their sons, Harvey Hill, who married Mrs. Ruby Cunard; Dudley; Charles; Augustus; Alton; Elliot, and John T., who married Mamie Dell Overton.

Dora R. Gallemore, daughter of William Joiner and Hannah Gallemore, who married Long, have four children, Alfred and Arthur, who practiced law in Atlanta; Earl, who worked with Gulf Corp. until retirement; Mary, who married William James Gallemore.

John Gallemore's second wife was a Miss Gainy. They had two sons, John who went to Texas to live, and Levi.

Levi Gallemore, born October 16, 1824, died June 8, 1890, whose home still stands back in a grove off the road that leads from Gallemore's Mill to Jeffersonville. Close to where Concord Methodist Church was and whose home was opened to those that came to worship with them on meeting day. He married first Elizabeth McNair, born December 6, 1832, died July 24, 1853, daughter of William and

Sarah McNair. They had one son, George Randolph Gallemore, who marriend Henrietta Methvin December 13, 1873, born May 1, 1849, died November 27, 1888. He served as a Twiggs County surveyor and taught school at Prospect school in the county. During an epidemic of hemorrhagic fever three children were lost, two sons, George, Jr. and Ruphbert grew to maturity.

Levi Gallemore's second wife was Martha Methvin, born November 13, 1840 and died April 14, 1910, daughter of Samuel Methvin, born February 22, 1817, died June 3, 1876, and Sarah Ann Sears Methvin, born February 17, 1824, died December 8, 1907. They had three sons, John Levi, born December 19, 1865, died May 1, 1910. His first wife was Lilla Smith, born November 11, 1863, died February 4, 1897. They had two sons, Levi L., born June 24,_____, died November, 1954. His wife was Nora Adams of Dodge County. Elliot Gallemore, born August 30, 1894, died October 1, 1924 in auto accident in Alabama. Lilla, the daughter of John Levi and Lilla Smith Gallemore, was born April 16, 1896. She married Homer Wade of Bleckley County, who was born December 14, 1888, died April 9, 1930. They had a son and daughter, the son, Major Guy Lamar Wade, born July 24,_____, married Gloria Hollis at the U. S. Naval Chapel, Washington, D. C., November 23, 1954. The daughter, Martha, born September 14, _____, employed Robins A. F. B.

John Levi Gallemore's second wife was Clara Horton, born October 31, 1880, daughter of Ira and Linnie Horton of Wilkinson County. They had four children, two dying as infants. A daughter Ruth, born February 15, 1902, who married Charles B. Wall, Ford auto dealer of Jeffersonville. He died in August, 1941. John L. II, born June 26, 1910, attended medical college serving as intern at Macon Hospital. marrying Eloise Graham, born October 10, 1912, daughter of the John W. Grahams of Macon, serving as health officer of Dodge County for a year. He then went to Perry, Georgia to practice medicine and established a clinic. They have been hosts to the Gallemore family and friends at a barbecue once a year on their spacious lawn. They are the parents of three sons: John Levi, III, born July 30, 1940; Graham, born February 14, 1944, and Warren, born August 28, 1949.

Samuel Methvin Gallemore I was born April 13, 1871, died September 9, 1936, his first wife being Mary Luna White, born March 19, 1899, died July 16, 1915, daughter of Jim B. and Susan Cordelia White. He served as Twiggs County tax collector for two terms, operated farms, and at the close of the horse and buggy era operated a livery stable, renting horses and buggies in the brick building now used as a casket factory in Jeffersonville. The oldest son, Iverson, born August 24, 1902, after completing business course in Macon, went to Greenville, S. C., marrying Georgia Mae Jolly of Union, S. C. They had four children: Martha Amelia, the oldest daughter; Jason, the oldest son, married Janelle Lester June 19, 1955, shortly after completing Medical College, University of South Carolina, was killed in auto accident June 23, 1956. His wife survived. David, another son, plans to enter ministerial work upon completion of education. Virginia Lucille married Howard Barnwell, they being the parents of a son, Timothy, and a daughter. James Parker Gallemore, born April 4, 1904, died Jan. 15, 1942, the son of Samuel Methvin Gallemore I and Mary Luna White Gallemore, married Fannie Mae Van Landingham, a native of Johnson County, having a son, James Parker, Jr., born February 24, 1925, who gave his life in the service of his country November 30, 1944. The daughter, Patricia Claire, born February 16, 1936, married James Mueller April 17, 1957.

Mabel Cordelia Gallemore, born July 1, 1906, employed at Burden Smith and Co. of Macon, Ga. at the time of her marriage to John Hugh Grayson, a native of Florida, born February 22, 1905. She was the oldest daughter of Samuel Methvin I and Mary Luna White Gallemore. Another daughter Sarah Martha, born December 28, 1907, served as telephone operator in Jeffersonville before going to Macon, being employed by W. T. Grant for a quarter of a century. The youngest daughter,

Mary Lois, born December 10, 1914, was carried to the home of an uncle and aunt, Ira and Mamie White, when her mother died the following July. After the death of her uncle and aunt when she was at the age of six, she returned to the home of her father. She married Walter E. Jordan in 1937, making their home in Lorain, Ohio. The youngest son of Samuel Methvin I and Mary Luna White Gallemore, Samuel Methvin Gallemore II, born August 31, 1912, married Frances Lois Floyd, born August 21, 1919, daughter of Zack and Hattie Sauls Floyd. Besides farming, he was also employed at Robins A. F. B. He served as church clerk and treasurer of Mt. Zion Baptist Church of Twiggs County, and treasurer of Ebenezer Baptist Association.

The second wife of Samuel Methvin Gallemore I was Evie Lowe of the Mt. Zion community, daughter of Rubin and Laura Lowe. She died in July of 1918, along with an infant.

The third wife of Samuel Methvin Gallemore I was Dora Sauls of the Prospect community, daughter of Cullen and Fannie Sauls.

William James Gallemore, son of Levi and Martha Methvin Gallemore, born June 28, 1875, died July 13, 1950, married Mary Long, born March 6, 1884. They had one son, William James Gallemore, Jr., born August 30, 1910. He continued to to operate the W. J. Gallemore store established by his father in Jeffersonville.

One daughter of Levi and Martha Methvin Gallemore died a young girl after being stung by red ants.

Mattie, the daughter of Levi and Martha Methvin Gallemore, taught school at Prospect School in Twiggs County before marrying Tom Holliman of Wilkinson County, going there to make their home. They have two sons, Julian and Roy. Roy married Myrtle Phillips of Macon where he made his home. The four daughters of the Holliman family, Opal and Myrtle make their home together in Dublin; Gladys married Al Hall of Laurens County, having one son, Edwin; Ethel married Ed Jerningan and make their home in Florida.

S. M. Gallemore
Jeffersonville, Ga.

## GATES

John G. Gates, s. of William and Malindy (White) Gates of Surry Co., N. C., was born February 4, 1828, died September 26, 1906. Came to Twiggs Co., Ga. before the Civil War, after serving four years in the war, returned to Twiggs Co. m. Mary Louise Chapman, d. of William and Martha Carswell Chapman. Mary Louise Chapman Gates b. April 12, 1841, died September 25, 1907. c.: (1) William R. Gates, b. Feb. 6, 1869, died Oct. 14, 1879. (2) John G. Gates, b. July 25, 1870, died Dec. 29, 1874. (3) Mary Louise (Mamie) Gates, b. Sept. 6, 1873, died Jan. 15, 1920. Five children died in infancy. (9) Albert Martin Gates, b. May 15, 1882, died July 4. 1956. Mary Louise (Mamie) Gates m. James Ira White, to this union 4 c. were born. (1) John Gates White, b. Aug. 19, 1896, died Feb. 22, 1918. (2) Cordelia Louise White. (3) James Ira White, Jr., b. Jan. 17, 1900, died March 26, 1944 (4) Helen Amanda White, m. John Marshall Gettys, s. (1) William Bryson Gettys. Albert Martin Gates m. Annette Rycroft, 4 c. were born to them. (1) Mary Louise Gates m. Dr. Robert Henry DeJarnette. c. Robert Henry DeJarnette, Jr. (2) Camella Rycroft Gates m. Dr. Oliver Coleman Whipple, c. Alice Annette Whipple. (3) Edith Annette Gates m. William Sidney Smith, Jr., c .Frances Gates Smith, William Sidney Smith III. (4) Albert Martin Gates, Jr., m. Bobbie Smith, c. Peggy Smith Gates. Albert Martin Gates, Sr., Ed. Twiggs Co. Schools, Mercer U., Macon, Ga. 1902-05, B.S. Mercer, LLD Mercer 1939. Taught Twiggs Co., Coffee Co., Mercer U., Brewton Parker Jr. College, Ailey-Mt. Vernon. Ga.. 1905-12. Private business 1913-14. Supt.

of Public Schools, Jeffersonville, Ga. 1915-16. Supt. Schools Twiggs Co. 1916-21. Pres. Brewton Parker Jr. College. Ailey-Mt. Vernon, 1922-41. Pres. Georgia Teachers College, Statesboro, 1941-43. Member Baptist Church, served as deacon 41 years. Returned to family home Twiggs Co. 1943. Supt. Schools Twiggs Co. 1949-53.

Written by: Mrs. Albert Martin Gates, Sr.
Jeffersonville, Ga.

## GETTYS

William Bryson Gettys, born November 23, 1863 at Rutherford County, North Carolina, died January 18, 1926, buried in Jeffersonville Cemetery, Jeffersonville, George. His wife, Nancy Annette (Antoinette) Blanton, born November 21, 1871 at Cherokee County, South Carolina, died June 23, 1932. She, too, is buried in the Jeffersonville Cemetery. They were married on July 4, 1900 at Limestone Springs, South Carolina. He was the son of John Gettys, born November 16, 1817, died July 15, 1886, and Alpha An Toney, born May 30, 1842, died December 21, 1877. His wife was the daughter of Jonas C. Blanton, born September 6, 1849, died July 10, 1925, and Sarah E. Whelchel, born April 2, 1849, died June 3, 1906.

His schooling was received at the Duncan's Creek Schools in North Carolina and he attended the College of the Pacific at College Park, California. Here he helped pay his expenses by his work in timber. Frugal in habits, he saved much of his pay— all of it in gold. When he returned to North Carolina he carried his gold in his cravat and a money belt. This training in the California timberlands enabled him to later start his own timber projects. However, his first job was that of Revenue Agent for the Federal Government and he was known locally as a "Brandy Gauger".

In December, 1915, William Bryson Gettys and his family moved from Zebulon, North Carolina, where he was engaged in timber operations to Jeffersonville, Twiggs County, Georgia, where he successfully pioneered the lumber industry. Coming as an experienced lumberman, he started an extensive lumbering operation, both in saw milling and operation of two large planing mills in the county. Many families, knowing of his capabilities, came from North Carolina to work with him in these enterprises.

Realizing that better schools make better citizens, Mr. Gettys, in his quiet and unassuming manner, gave to his chosen community an eleven acre tract of land, one mile east from Court House for the proposed county high school. Here a modern brick building was erected. This land has continued to be a part of the high school campus. His interest in the education of the youth of the county was one of his major community activities.

In 1920 he purchased "Hollywood", the former Chapman estate and engaged in extensive farming. His daughter, Mrs. C. A. Duggan, and her husband occupy the home now and operate one of the larger dairy farms in middle Georgia.

Their children:

I. John Marshall Gettys, born May 8, 1901, in Rutherford County, North Carolina, attended Locust Grove Institute, Locust Grove, Georgia. Married on July 19, 1921 to Helen Amanda White (see Gates Genealogy), born December 17, 1902.

A. William Bryson Gettys, born January 27, 1927, attended Riverside Military Academy, Gainesville, Georgia, graduated from G. M. C. at Milledgeville, Georgia, and attended University of Georgia, Athens, Georgia. Served in the U. S. Navy 1944 and 1945. Married on June 30, 1951 to Rose Crockett, born August 27, 1927.

II. Lois (Elois) Gettys, born May 27, 1904, in Lattimore, North Carolina, attended Fassifern in Hendersonville, North Carolina, and Lucy Cobb Institute in Athens, Georgia. Married on February 6, 1931 to Charles Anderson Duggan (see Hart's History of Laurens, County, Georgia—Duggan and Stanley Genealogy), born

July 24, 1905.

A. Charles Anderson Duggan, Jr., M.D., born January 19, 1933, graduate of Emory University and Emory University School of Medicine, Emory University, Georgia. Entered U. S. Navy in July, 1959 as a lieutenant in the Medical Corps. Married on August 14, 1954 to Charlotte Gail Hollingsworth, born January 25, 1935.

1. Charles Anderson Duggan, III, born, October 18, 1958.

B. Lois Annette Duggan, born November 5, 1934, A. B. degree from University of Florida, Gainesville, Florida.

III. William Carl Gettys, born March 15, 1910, in Lattimore, North Carolina, attended Riverside Military Academy, Gainesville, Georgia, and Mercer University, Macon, Georgia. Married on December 4, 1930 to Louise Williams, born July 13, 1910.

A. William Carl Gettys, Jr., born May 31, 1933, attended Georgia Institute of Technology, Atlanta, Georgia, and University of Georgia, Athens, Georgia. Married on February 13, 1952 to Gwen Barker, born July 19, 1934.

1. William Carl Gettys, III, born January 31, 1954.
2. John Barker Gettys, born June 25, 1957.

By Mrs. C. A. Duggan

## LUTHER LAWRENCE GRIFFIN

Luther L. Griffin
1870-1941

Luther Lawrence Griffin was born in 'Big Sandy Community' of Twiggs County, Georgia on February 20, 1870. He was the son of Rev. William Griffin (1821-84), a Methodist minister, and comrade of the Rev. Charlie Johnson, who together constituted twelve Methodist churches in middle Georgia. Rev. William Griffin was senator from the 21st district 1868-1870, a delegate to the Constitutional Convention in 1868, a member of House of Representatives 1873-74, and Ordinary of Twiggs County at the time of his death. Mary Elizabeth Lingo (1827-1907), wife of the

Rev. William Griffin, was the daughter of Capt. Richard and Nora Lingo. Luther Lawrence Griffin attended school in Jeffersonville, married Gillie Myrick, daughter of Jonah Myrick (1849-1903) and Mary Vinson Myrick (1852-1944) of Wilkinson County, Georgia. He was a Methodist, Mason, Democrat, farmer, and postmaster of 'Soloman' in Marion District of Twiggs County. He served as Tax Receiver of Twiggs County 1913-17, 1921-25, and member of the House of Representatives 1925-26, and 1927-28. Luther Lawrence Griffin was named for his great-uncle, General Lewis Lawrence Griffin, who settled Griffin, Georgia in 1840, and for whom it was named.

Born to this couple (Luther Lawrence Griffin-Gillie Myrick Griffin) were, Mary Elizabeth, Minnie Leola, William Henry, Reba Alice, Elva Agnes, Johnnie Eugenia, Robert Shorter, Dudley M., Luther Jackson, and Gillie Marie.

Mary Elizabeth, born in Laurens County, Georgia in 1894, attended Twiggs County schools, University of Georgia and taught in Georgia schools. She married Jack Johnson of Bullards, now retired from Robins Air Force Base. They have two daughters, Grace, married to George Underwood of Milledgeville, Georgia. They have two children, George Jr., and Dorothy. Edith, married to Ben Porubin of Pittsburgh, Pa. They have two children, Mary Sue and Patsy.

Minnie Leola, born in Wilkinson County, Georgia in 1896, attended schools of Twiggs County, University of Georgia, Mercer University, and G. S. C. W. She taught in Georgia schools fifteen years. She married Homer L. Chance of Danville, Georgia, a merchant, farmer, banker, and member of the House of Representatives from Twiggs County 1943-48 and Senator 1955-56. Is now serving in the House of Representatives. They have no children.

William Henry Griffin, born in Wilkinson County, Georgia in 1898, attended Twiggs County schools, is now a lumberman, farmer, banker, and civic leader in Cochran, Georgia. He married Sarah Alexander of Harrisburg, Pa. They have five children: Beatrice Marie, married to Thomas Waters, Jr., of Savannah, Georgia, they have two children, Thomas Jr. and Mary Emma; William Henry II, married Rose Mills of Hazelhurst, Georgia, they now live in Cordele, Georgia and have two children, William Henry III and Betsy; Sara Jane, married to Joe Bradley of Fairfax, Virginia, live in Macon and have two children, Bradley and Sarah Douglas; Peggy, married to Robert Muldrow of Florence, S. C., have three children, Kay, Jane, and Susan; Shirley, married to Everett Hixon of Chattanooga, Tenn., have two children, Sara Elaine and Everett Jr.

Reba Alice was born in 1900 in Twiggs County. She attended Twiggs County schools and G. S. C. W., taught school and married Clarence Thompson, a farmer of Toomsboro, Georgia. They have six children; Wilbur, married Elizabeth Tompkins of Oconee, Georgia. They have two children, Dianne and Dennie; Ray married Virginia Folsom of Cairo, Georgia, they now live in Atlanta, and have no children; Griffin, a Methodist minister, married Elizabeth Bussell of Warthen, Georgia, they have two children, Scott and Jane; Jack married Mary Ivey Dominsy of Toomsboro, they have one child, Ronald; Reba Joyce married Charles Miller of Toomsboro. They now live in Cordele and have two children, Pamela and Charles Jr.; Guy is band director of Wilco High School and is not married.

Elva Agnes, born in Twiggs County in 1902. She attended Twiggs County schools, Ashville, N. C., University of Georgia, and Mercer University. She taught school, married J. H. (Rip) Holmes of McRae, Georgia, a farmer, merchant and livestock dealer. They have one son, Jerry H. Jr. He is married to Janet Pace of Clinton, Tenn. They have one child, Renee.

Johnnie Eugenia, born in Twiggs County in 1904. She also attended Twiggs County schools and University of Georgia. She taught in Twiggs County schools, and married Eugene Sanders (deceased) of Danville, Georgia. She is now employed as clerk, City of Jeffersonville and clerk, Twiggs County Commissioners. They had two daughters, Edna, married to Joe Venable of Gainesville, Georgia, and they have two children, Joey and Gene; Betty married to Herman Clark of Warner Robins, Georgia, they have two sons, Russell and Herman Scott.

Robert Shorter, born in Twiggs County in 1906, also attended schools of Twiggs County. He is a lumberman and civic leader in Cordele, Georgia. He married Geneva Harrelson of Macon, Georgia. They have no children.

Luther Jackson was born in Twiggs County in 1910. He attended Twiggs County schools, and is now a lumberman in Cordele, Georgia. He served in the U. S. Air Force during World War II. He married Eunice Fortner of Aurora, Mo., and they have no children.

Gillie Marie, married to Fred Coleman of Winterhaven, Fla., now living in Madison, Ind. They have one daughter, Carol Marie, now attending Ball State Teacher's College in Muncie, Ind.

Brothers and sisters of Luther Lawrence Griffin, to whom married and place of death are as follows: Laura, married John Floyd, buried in Dudley, Georgia; Josephine, married Joe Vinson, buried in Dexter, Georgia; Henry Llewellyn, married Fannie Myrick, buried at Antioch in Twiggs County; Robert Slappey, married Dona Vinson, buried at Liberty Hill Church in Twiggs County; Ella, married Dock Edmonson, buried in Cordele, Georgia; Minnie, married Newton Hudson, buried in Ocilla, Georgia; Eli Shorter, married Lula Vinson, buried in Ocilla, Georgia; Mattie, married Ben Reddick, and is buried at Liberty Hill. Luther Lawrence Griffin died October 24, 1941, and is buried in Jeffersonville City Cemetery in plot with wife, Gillie Myrick Griffin and his father and mother, the Rev. William and Mary Griffin.

Mrs. H. L. Chance, Danville, Georgia<br>Mrs. Johnnie Sanders, Jeffersonville, Georgia

## THE HENDRICKS FAMILY

Mrs. Claudia F. (W. C.) Hendricks

Claudia Fitzpatrick Hendricks, daughter of William Hart and Elizabeth Fitzpatrick, was born April 13, 1878. She was graduated from Brenau College in 1898 and attended Georgia State Normal College in Athens, Georgia. After her graduation, she taught school in Talbot County where she met and married William Columbus Hendricks on April 3, 1906. After making their home in Talbot County for eight years, they moved to Twiggs County where Mr. Hendricks became engaged in farming and his wife taught school. Mrs. Hendricks was always deeply interested in all movements affecting the welfare of Twiggs Co. She took an enthusiastic part in all educational activities and civic affairs. Mrs. Hendricks was a member of the Richland Restoration League and contributed generously of her time and knowledge to the restoration of Old Richland Church. She died June 8, 1950 and is interred in the cemetery in Jeffersonville. Mr. Hendricks now makes his home with his daughter, Mrs. Pierce, and his sister-in-law, Miss Lucille Fitzpatrick, at Tarversville.

Millard William Hendricks, eldest son of William C. and Claudia Hendricks, was born in Woodland, Georgia on November 23, 1907 and was graduated from high school at McRae, Georgia and later attended the University of Georgia in Athens. He was a member of the Sigma Chi Fraternity. He married Mary Elizabeth Duross, daughter of Mr. and Mrs. John Andrews Duross of Jenkintown, Pa., on March 28, 1935. She attended William and Mary College in Williamsburg, Virginia. Millard Hendricks is now engaged in farming. Mr. and Mrs. Millard Hendricks are the parents of three children: Mary Elizabeth, born January 13, 1936 in Macon, Georgia; Jean Barry, born on March 27, 1943 in Macon; and Millard Claudius, born December 26, 1950 in Macon. Mary Elizabeth was graduated from Bay Haven Academy in Miami, Florida and received her Bachelor of Arts degree from Florida State University in Tallahassee Florida. From there she went to Radcliffe Graduate School in Boston for further study. On December 22, 1956, she married Desmond Porter Wilson, son of Colonel and Mrs. Desmond Porter Wilson of Hutchinson, Kansas. Mr. Wilson graduated from the University of the South at Sewanee, Tennessee; received his Masters degree from Emory University in Atlanta; and has been awarded a scholarship to Massachusetts Institute of Technology in Cambrigde, Mass., where he will work on his Ph. D. He was a recipient of a Fulbright award to Calcutta, India in 1958, where their daughter, Mary Elizabeth Beck was born on October 24, 1958.

Elizabeth Hendricks Pierce, daughter of William and Claudia Hendricks, was born at Woodland, Georgia on October 27, 1910. She was graduated from high school in Tarpon Springs, Florida in 1928 and attended Wesleyan College in Macon, Georgia. After graduating from the Georgia State Teachers College in Athens, Mrs. Pierce taught school in Jesup, Georgia for four years. She married Vinson Kendrick Pierce of Tatum, Texas on April 21, 1935. Mr. Pierce was connected with the Firestone Tire and Rubber Company. Mr. and Mrs. Pierce made their home in Texas with their two children until Mr. Pierce's death in 1941 at which time they returned to Twiggs County. During World War II, Mrs. Pierce worked as personnel counselor at the J. A. Jones Shipyard in Brunswick, Georgia. Following the war, she returned to Twiggs County, where she taught school at Bullards and Jeffersonville. Mrs. Pierce is presently teaching in Cochran, Georgia. 1—William Kendrick Pierce, son of Mr. and Mrs. V. K. Pierce, was born March 7, 1937 in Baton Rouge, Louisiana, and was graduated from Cochran High School in 1953 then entered the Marine Corps. He married Pauline Connelly, daughter of Mrs. James William Connelly and the late J. W. Connelly, on September 14, 1957, issue: Sara Kimberly, born December 1, 1958. 2—Madge Rebecca, daughter of Mr. and Mrs. Pierce, born April 29, 1940, Texarkana, Texas, graduated from Cochran High School, 1958, presently attending Sophie Newcomb College, New Orleans, Louisiana, where she is a member of Alpha Delta Pi sorority.

James Irvin Hendricks, son of Mr. and Mrs. William C. Hendricks, born December 10, 1916, graduated from Bullard High School, attended Louisiana State University at Baton Rouge, La., served in the Navy with the Seabees during World War II; married to Jewel Collins, daughter of Alfred Eugene Collins and wife, Cora Scwilian Cook, on June 27, 1941. He is presently employed with the Georgia State Highway Dept., residence, Yatesville, Georgia, issue: James Irwin, born March 3, 1948.

Millard W. Hendricks and Mrs. V. K. Pierce,
Jeffersonville, Georgia

## HOLLIDAY

William Holliday, a Revolutionary soldier, was granted a tract of land for his services as soldier by the State of Georgia; this grant being made December 2, 1835. It was located about six miles southwest of Jeffersonville on what is now State Highway No. 96.

He married Martha Hasty and settled here. One child was born to this couple, a son, Thomas Hartwell Holliday, in 1840.

Thomas H. Holliday married Laura Floyd, daughter of Andrew Floyd of Big Sandy Community. Their children were: Nancy Ella, born March 29, 1867; she was married to Benjamin F. Cranford; Heyward Hartwell, born January 1, 1871, married Emma Hughes; John Thomas Barkley Holliday, born July 18, 1872, married Mary Viola Sauls, daughter of Theophalaus Sauls, Jr. and Martha Jane Floyd Sauls; William Holliday, born 1874, died at the age of 4 in 1878; Andrew Hilliard Holliday, born September 3, 1876, married Mary Locke; Nancy Ella Holliday and her husband, B. F. Cranford, settled in Dodge County, Georgia; H. H. Holliday and wife settled in Laurens County, Georgia; Andrew Hillard Holliday and wife settled in Macon County, Georgia; John T. Holliday and wife, Mary Viola Sauls, settled on the Thomas H. Holliday home place in Twiggs County, Georgia, living there until their death; John T. Holliday died December 26, 1946, and Mary Viola Holliday died March 17, 1947. They were married on November 23, 1893, and lived more than 50 years together. Their children were: Laura Jane, born October 19, 1894; John Early, born August 20, 1896, died August 20, 1896; Bunyan Thomas Holliday, born August 13, 1897, died 1948; Miss Alva Holliday, born June 24, 1900; Marion Vinson Holliday, born January 2, 1902; Theodore Holliday, born October, 1903; Mozelle Holliday, born May 26, 1905, died September 22, 1906; Andrew Ben Holliday, born February 22, 1907, died March 22, 1907; Joe Brown Holliday, born May 28, 1908, died April, 1912; Mary Annie Holliday, born May 30, 1910; Myrtle Lee Holliday, born July 19, 1911; Irene and Iris Holliday, born January 13, 1913, died May, 1913; John Henry Holliday, born September 1, 1914; Mary Ella Holliday, born June 6, 1916.

William Holliday, the original settler and his wife were buried under the cedars near their old homesite, about 6 miles S.W. of Jeffersonville, on State Highway 96. Their son, Thomas H. Holliday and his wife, are buried in Prospect Church Cemetery and his grave is marked by a Confederate Army stone, he having served under Capt. John Barkley in the Confederate Army.

Compiled by: John H. Holliday, Jeffersonville, Georgia

## REVEREND WILLIAM D. HORNE

William D. Horne was born in Bertie County, North Carolina, June 26, 1813, son of Turner and Margaret (Cross) Horne, died at his Twiggs County home on October 31, 1882.

He came to Twiggs County as a young man in 1833, at the request of his widowed aunt, Mrs. Anna Horne Higgs, his father's sister, who had owned a large plantation in the county from the County's early constitution. Mrs. Higgs had no children and being in poor health made this energetic young nephew a co-business partner.

In 1832 William D. Horne was baptized by Reverend James Delk, the pastor, and received into fellowship of Sandy Run Baptist Church, near Roxobel, North Carolina, which was within the bounds of the Chowan Association. His father served as clerk of this church for several years and his grandfather, Joseph Horne, was a deacon.

On April 25, 1835 he was received by letter into fellowship of Stone Creek Baptist Church of Twiggs County. By order of this Church he was set apart to the Gospel Ministry on June 8, 1840, the Reverends C. A. Tharp, Thomas Curtis, and Austin Ellis officiating as the Presbytery. From this time on as long as he lived and his health permitted, he never ceased to minister in God's great Kingdom and served several churches in Twiggs County as pastor, among these being New Hope, Stone Creek, Jeffersonville, Antioch, Richland, Friendship, also churches in Houston County and in Laurens County. He was active in the Ebenezer Baptist Association, serving as clerk from 1851 through 1858, 1867 through 1878 and preached the Doctrinal and Missionary Sermons at many Associational Meetings.

William won the hand of fair maiden, Leanna, daughter of Charnick A. Tharp and Elizabeth Jefferson, sister of John Jefferson for whom the town Jeffersonville, was named. She was born on June 7, 1817, Twiggs County, died November 25, 1887, married on September 8, 1836. Leanna was baptized into fellowship of Stone Creek Baptist Church on November 21, 1835. Her father was pastor of this Church for many years. Their home was blessed with several children:

1—Cornelia Ann, who married first, William Methvin, had issue; being left a widow by each husband, she married second Lemuel Burkett, had issue; then third, married Joseph Bullock, issue, a son.

2—Emily, died young;

3—Margaret, married Alexander Dawson, issue; Cornelia (Mrs. Sam Hape); Leanna; Belle (Mrs. C. P. Malaier) all of Atlanta.

4—Joseph Turner "Joe," born July 1, 1848, and died January 4, 1923. He served as clerk in the Twiggs County Ordinary's office for a number of years. He later moved to Vidalia, in Toombs County, and served there as Justice of the Peace for several years until his health failed. He and his wife passed to their rest in Vidalia. He married Mary "Mollie" R. Jones, daughter of Elias and Mary (Denson) Jones, on November 27, 1873. To this union was born:

A.—Emmie, married to Robert Witherington, isue:

B.—Annie Mary, married A. P. Darby, issue;

C.—William Howard, a bachelor

D.—Joseph Norman married Mattie Groce. In 1952, after 40 years of service with the Charleston and Western Carolina Railway as a clerk, he retired. He passed to his reward at his home in Greenville, South Carolina on October 31, 1958.

E.—Ethleen married on December 26, 1914 to Hugh H. Howell, a lawyer and business executive of Atlanta. Children: Jean, Hugh, Jr., Carolyn, and Ann.

5.—William Franklin "Willie", the youngest child, a bachelor, lived until his death on the Horne home place.

Ethleen Horne Howell, Mrs. Hugh H.
40 Park Lane, N.E., Atlanta 9, Georgia

## DUDLEY MAYS AND MARY DENNARD HUGHES

Dudley M. Hughes

Mrs. Dudley M. Hughes

The lives of Mr. and Mrs. Dudley M. Hughes, two former citiezns of Twiggs County, are recorded in one biographical sketch because of the wonderful life they lived together for 54 years.

Mr. Hughes, only son of Daniel Greenwood Hughes and Henrietta Cary Moore, was born in Jeffersonville, October 10, 1848. In his youth he attended the famous Crossland Academy of Twiggs County—the old building still standing at Danville—and later attended the State University from which he graduated in 1871. Immediately Mr. Hughes engaged in the vocation of farming on the extensive lands of his father and grandfather, Hayden Hughes, of Laurens County.

As a young man of vision, energy, determination, character, and delightful personality, he succeeded admirably in his chosen profession, but there was something woefully lacking in his life until December, 1872, when he met and completely fell in love with the charming, lovely, vivacious, Mary Frances Dennard, only daughter of Captain Hugh Lawson Dennard and Sarah Anne Frances Crocker of Perry. This young woman was enjoying a dance in Macon during her Christmas holidays from a small select boarding school at Petapsco, Maryland, 10 miles out from Baltimore, when her future husband met her. The romance of the evening soon culminated in marriage, November 25, 1873.

Life was a great and wonderful adventure for "Marse Dud" and "Miss Mary", as they were affectionately known. Their main objective was to be useful to God and Man—leaving this world a better place for having lived in it.

Gracious hospitality was extended to all at their home, Magnolia Plantation, at Danville. A son, Hugh Lawson Dennard, and a daughter, Henrietta Louise (Hennilu), and a daughter-in-law, Mrs. Agnes Goss Hughes, occupy the old family home filled with heirlooms and an atmosphere of the old South pervading the high ceilinged rooms. A second son, Daniel G. Hughes II, died in 1916 during his term as Assistant Commisioner of Agriculture of Georgia.

Mr. and Mrs. Hughes settled in Twiggs County twenty miles from a railroad when there were no paved roads; no rural phones; no radios, or TV's; no electricity;—when neighbors lived far apart and frequently made spend-the-day visits; when doctors and trained nurses were scarce and undertakers rare and expensive. Mrs. Hughes, as a very young matron, rendered great service in responding to calls of illness and did not hesitate to prepare bodies for burial. The old timers referred to her as the "Little Angel of Mercy." During these days farm laborers were paid 50¢ per day, along with other compensation, and worked from daylight to dark, but a spirit of happiness and contentment prevailed throughout this section with white and colored. These were great days, pioneer days, that called for the best in everyone. Mr. and Mrs. Hughes considered it a real privilege to have had a part in the building of a substantial foundation for our great Country.

This young couple with vision and interest and the willingness to give of their all—especially financial assistance—projected the idea of building a railroad from Macon to Dublin. Easier thought and talked than put into effect. People with less love and foresight and desire to enlighten and improve this section would have retired in failure when a competitive group from Macon had succeeded in surveying, and even grading, a road bed, a distance of 35 miles from Macon towards Dublin, but leaving Jeffersonville and the section in which Mr. and Mrs. Hughes resided quite a distance from the Sparks road. This fired the Hughes group to a more energetic effort and, as a result, the Macon and Dublin Railroad was completed in 1891. This railroad marvelously developed an isolated section of country and Mr. and Mrs. Hughes had no regrets over having invested perhaps $50,000 in this progressive movement. That which disturbed them most was that friends and neighbors lost their money also. Their consolation came as the country developed and access to the outside world was brought about. All of which meant better schools.

increased value of property, improved roads—progress.

During these years of living in Twiggs County Mr. and Mrs. Hughes had organized and led a Sunday School at Mt. Zion (this must have been about 1880) Baptist Church in an old log building with the sun shining through wide cracks in summer, and wind whistling through in winter; and uncomfortable benches, the back of which struck one midway with little possibility of relaxing for a moment. Regardless of this discomfort there was sound sleeping often on the part of the deacons and others as the once-a-month sermon, of an hour and a half or longer, was brought by Rev. W. H. Steely. One day as Col. Dan Hughes and his beloved little namesake, Dan Hughes, sat together in an Amen corner Rev. Steely, pulling his spectacles down on his nose, looked out and observed deacons and laymen oblivious of what he had been saying. He determined to make a change in the situation, so he clapped his hands and stamped his foot and yelled "Wake up all you that sleepeth." Col. Hughes shook the little boy saying, "Son, wake up!" The loud reply was, "Twuz *you, you, you, you*—pa dat wuz sleep!" Needless to say the entire congregation remained attentive ever after to Rev. Steely's discourses regardless of length.

Ere long, Mrs. Hughes began the movement for a new church, a comfortable house in which God would be honored. This meant "Begging" as some referred to gentle coercion; it meant entertainment, such as, home talent plays, ice cream festivals with Japanese lanterns hanging from porches and trees; it meant all of the ladies making delicious boiled custard and turning the handle of freezers until one's arms were nearly paralyzed; it meant games and fun and everybody co-operating. In order to further the cause of money-raising there were barbecues, fish frys, and oyster suppers with all taking part in the Virginia Reel, Marching 'Round the Level,' and the young men anxious to win the prize as best "buck dancer."

Those were the days! Everyone anxious to use his or her talent for the building of the church. Mt. Zion Church was built strong and beautiful, of the best material, the pride and joy of the membership. Completed in 1890, it immediately became one of the strongest churches in the Ebenezer Association and has so remained. It seems the dear Lord smiled His approval at the simple, clean fun these dear Christians had as they labored together for His Honor and Glory.

During these years Mr. Hughes was advancing along the lines of public service. He served as State Senator; President of the Georgia State Agricultural Society; Fruit Growers Association of Georgia; Commissioner General of Georgia at the World's Fair, St. Louis; Trustee of the Danville High School; the State Normal Institute; the University of Georgia; the State Agricultural College; was elected to 61st., 62nd., 63rd., and 64th. Congresses, but the honor he appreciated above all honors was serving as Superintendent of Mt. Zion Sunday School and Deacon of his beloved church for about 40 years.

Don't think for one moment that "Miss Mary" was failing to keep step with her distinguished husband. She graciouly presided with him in the Georgia Building at St. Louis; she attended meetings and fairs of the Agricultural Society and assisted in arranging exhibits at the fairs (no decorators were available as is now possible). As evidence of her constructive work, Mrs. Hughes was presented a beautiful silver pitcher appropriately inscribed at a meeting of the National Agricultural Society. At the same time Mr. Hughes was given a gold headed cane expressing appreciation of his effective service—Mrs. Hughes served as "Lady Visitor" (trustee) to Georgia Normal and Industrial College. She also enjoyed and considered it a privilege to serve as organist and Sunday School teacher at Mt. Zion as long as she was able to do so. But the honor she appreciated above all others is the Mary Dennard Hughes Scholarship at Mercer, presented in her name by the Woman's Missionary Union of Ebenezer Association. She felt this scholarship had great possibilities for the young people to become missionaries. One must have dedicated herself or himself for Christian service before being eligible for this Loan Scholarship. Mrs. Hughes led in the planning and building of the Danville Baptist Church. "Go Ye, therefore and teach all Nations" was deeply implanted in her heart, who as a girl, joined the Baptist Church in Perry, a place for which she held the deepest affection.

Mr. Hughes was leader of much constructive Legislation during his terms of service in Congress—especially was he alert where farm and education came before this body of lawmakers. He recognized, through his interest and study and practical experience, an opportunity to fit rural boys and girls for better farms, homes, and for training in other practical vocations in rural high schools. As a result of his leadership the United States Congress passed the great and useful Smith-Hughes Vocational Education Bill, February 23, 1917. Senator Hoke Smith was Chairman of Education in the Senate, but it was necessary for the vocational bill to be accepted by the House of Representatives before its presentation to the Senate. Mr. Hughes worked valiantly and diplomatically to win the favor of Republicans as well as Democrats in the passage of his bill, and his efforts and achievements were recognized by the ovation given him by the House when the Smith-Hughes Bill became a law. A few quotations from Mr. Hughes' associates indicate the love and appreciation and understanding felt for this modest, capable, far-seeing Christian gentleman. Mr. Horace Towner, later Governor of Puerto Rico, said at the close of his high tribute—"One of my asociates speaking in private conversation today said, 'Mr. Hughes is the highest type Southern Gentleman' and I answered, "I would amend that statement by saying he is the hightest type American Gentleman." Congressman Mann, leader in the House, expressed his high regard for Mr. Hughes, thus, "He understands this great piece of legislation as no one else understands it and because of his personality, tolerance, kindness, and modesty, he has won friends for himself and built a monument to himself in this his crowning achievements."

Do you think "Miss Mary", during these active, strenuous years, had retired to oblivion or perhaps filled her time with the delightful social life in Washington, D. C. accorded Representatives, Senators, and their families? If so, you are badly mistaken. She studied with her husband the possibilities, the complications, the opposition, in the formulation of the Vocational Bill, offering practical suggestions such as, "Don't forget the girls because they are the homemakers!" And the girls have not been forgotten all through these fruitful years. Mrs. Hughes was made an honorary member of the National Homemakers of America in recognition of her part in having the girls included as homemakers. We quote from a section of the citation presented to Mrs. Hughes near her 99th. birthday. "Homemaking arts have always been first with her, but she found time to be a good citizen too; going to the polls to vote every year until she was 96. Her charming home has been opened on numerous occasions to the Future Homemakers of Danville, Georgia. We honor ourselves, the Future Homemakers, in presenting this Honorary Membership to Mrs. Hughes."

The life of Mrs. Hughes was filled with interesting experience—wonderful activities. She personally knew nine United States Presidents, Grant, McKinley, Theodore Roosevelt, Taft, Wilson, Hoover, Coolidge, Harding, and Franklin D. Roosevelt. (These names may not be consecutively recorded, but the names are correct.) She and her mother attended a brilliant reception at the fashionable Saratoga Springs in the long ago during a pleasure trip of Capt. and Mrs. Dennard and their young daughter, Mary. President Grant was the honoree. Capt. Dennard refused to accompany his wife and daughter to the reception but Mrs. Dennard was not to be disappointed, so she and young Mary put on their best and stepped out with friends. As Mother and daughter left the distinguished gathering, the daughter observed her mother removing her gloves and throwing them into some nearby shrubbery with the remark, "So much for Grant!" (It's always been a mystery why my red-blooded grandmother attended that reception. Well, so much for Grant!)

This charming and gifted woman, Mrs. Hughes, developed many skills. She was an expert horsewoman, an accomplished singer as well as a pianist and organist, learned to do fine French embroidery and drawn work. She became an artist, did beautiful wood carving. Throughout the home at Magnolia Plantation, so loved and cherished by the family, are her beautiful paintings made more distinctive because of handcarved frames.

Today young people seem to require excitement, useless activity, rock 'n roll and the like, but 83 years ago Mrs. Hughes was happily and busily occupied in creating a home of beauty and Christianity—something that money will not buy—a place where the Hughes family was always eager to return, because the foundation of this home was love and understanding and consideration and deep abiding love of God. Nothing can take the place of treasured memories that Mr. and Mrs. Hughes gave their children. A big hickory fire before which the family of five gathered daily for the reading of the Bible and prayers after which the children listened with keen interest and excitement to wonderful experiences through which these great pioneer builders had passed. There was the time "Mammy Mahalie", (Grandma Dennard's faithful housekeeper), a small black, wirey little woman—gentle most of the time, but asserting her authority whenever necessary with the children, the cook, maid, yardman who also served as coachman. (A great woman who was loved and well cared for as long as she lived.) One day Mammy heard the "Yankees are coming". Consternation in the household, but Mammy quietly went about gathering silver without consulting anyone and buried the treasures in a spot she thought safe and secure. Do you know that Yankee Captain encamped right over Mammy's beloved silver, and his tent pole made dents in a treasured silver pitcher, but the silver was not discovered? Mammy's nerves did not quite snap, the big house and negro quarters survived the torch, and I am here to tell the story. Then there was the story of the time brave, courageous General Robert Toombs spent several days in "utmost seclusion" at the home of my grandfather, Col. Daniel G. Hughes. Yankee soldiers came to this home, searched for Gen. Toombs, left without him who wanted to come out of hiding and tell those soldiers and all Yankees where to go! There were thrilling stories of the Ku Klux Klan, an organization of the highest type at that time that saved Southern women from horrors unspeakable. There were horse back rides for special fun and entertainment. Each member of the family owning a horse or pony. There were spend-the-days at the beautiful home of Uncle Bill Faulk, grandfather of the Shannons; Uncle William Solomon, grandfather of present generation of Solomons and Mrs. Kathleen Carswell; Col. Ashley Vickers, who lived in a mansion near the present site of Montrose and other hospitable homes. These were great visiting days! There were trips to Grandpa and Grandma Dennard living in Perry, a distance of 40 miles from us. To reach there in one day we would rise early, real early, leave home just as the sun was rising—driving a wonderfully matched pair of spirited horses. When we reached "Buzzard's Roost", about 20 miles distance from Magnolia Plantation, the children would receive a special treat of stick candy—perhaps 15 sticks for five cents. Then Father would drive down to the river, blow a mournful sounding horn for the ferryman, and Father would say gentle words and with the touch of a long straight whip encourage his fiery steed to walk, usually quivering with fright, on to that old flat resting on the muddy Ocmulgee. I expected at any moment to see my father, the horses, carriage, and luggage disappear into the river. This, I'm thankful to say, did not happen, but on one of our trips the horses did go out of sight and everyone got wet as the horses had to swim to get themselves and us through a swollen lagoon. Now we have a paved highway and bstantial bridges across the Ocmulgee and its tributaries. Great and wonderful changes, yes, more money everywhere, but is there as much genuine happiness, as much satisfaction in accomplishing those things that proved love for humanity? Are we too occupied and concerned over increasing our bank account?

My Mother was never happier than when she had the buggy filled with long, light green, thin-skinned, juicy watermelons from her patch and delivered them to her neighbors. She would do the same with luscious peaches brought over from her Houston County orchard or beautiful flowers from her garden. These kind neighborly deeds endeared her to the people of the community in which she lived for so many years. Her love of God was evident as she went about doing good.

The Dudley M. Hughes Vocational School in Macon is a tribute of appreciation of my Father's successful achievement, regarding the Smith-Hughes Vocational Bill; a Liberty Ship was named for this distinguished Georgian in 1943. He was appointed Chairman of various important committees such as, visiting the Panama Canal to determine plans for protecting the Canal. When Mr. Flagler completed his Railroad across the keys to Key West my Father was appointed a member of the Committee to cross the Keys on the first train. He was asked to serve as President of an important Insurance Company upon his retirement from Congress—also offered a lecture engagement on a Chautauqua Platform, and other positions were opened to him but he preferred retiring to his home at Danville.

And so, hand in hand these two noble souls, my parents, sowed seed here on earth that are bringing forth an abundant harvest in Eternity.

Of my Mother I say, "Give her of the fruit of her hands and let her own works praise her in the gates."—Proverbs 31:31.

Of my Father I say, "The fear of the Lord is the instruction of Wisdom; and before Honor is Humility."—Proverbs 15:33.

Father passed to the Great Beyond—January 26th., 1927, at the age of 79.

Mother entered Eternity—September 28th., 1954, at the age of 100.

Side by side their mortal remains rest in the old cemetery at Perry, Georgia, a place dear to their hearts.

It is with a feeling of deep humility and gratitude and appreciation and affection I have written this sketch.

    Submitted by Henrietta Louise (Hennilu) Hughes
    Danville, Georgia

## HUGH LAWSON DENNARD HUGHES

Hugh Lawson Dennard Hughes, the Congressman's son, was born in Perry, Georgia, September 6, 1874, and was educated at Mercer, the class of 1897. He was graduated with honors from Eastman Business College at Poughkeepsie, N. Y. in 1900.

Entering at once into business, he located at Danville, and was for twenty-four years a member of the Twiggs County Board of Education, and for eleven years its chairman; mayor of Danville, president of the Bank of Danville, and a member of Governor Candler's Staff, later also of Governor Terrell's Staff, and in 1923 became a State senator from the 21st District.

The secretary of the Danville School Board of Trustees lost his minutes through a fire, but it is believed that Mr. Hughes has been a trustee of the Danville High School, later named the Twiggs-Wilkinson High School, and recently, the Danville Elementary School, since 1901 and chairman of the Board of Trustees of the Danville School for twenty-four years. He was also a trustee of the Middle Georgia College at Cochran. He married on June 26, 1919 at Athens, Agnes Clifton Goss, daughter of Dr. I. H. Goss.

Colonel Hughes is a Mason, and a member of Phi Delta Theta fraternity. In social life, he is widely popular and by all classes in the community is held in the highest esteem.

Sketch was written by the late Dr. J. C. Solomon and sent through courtesy of Miss Margaret Solomon

## JOHNSTON FAMILY OF TWIGGS COUNTY

The name of Johnston is of Scotch origin and means the man from Johnston (John's Manor) in Dumfriesshire. Our Coat of Arms bears the inscription nvnovam non aratvz (Never unperpared). Thomas Johnston was first of this line locating in Georgia. He was born in South Carolina in 1760, married in 1780 and died in Columbia County, Georgia in 1825. He was a patriot of the American Revolution, proof of service being found in Revolutionary Records of Georgia, by Allan Candler. Documents show a grant signed by the governor and dated June 27, 1784 of 287½ A. of land in Washington County. The will of Thomas Johnston is found on page 113 Will Book "W", Columbia County, Georgia, bequeathing to his wife Winnifred, land, slaves, etc. for life or widowhood, to be divided at her death among all heirs, the land to go to sons, Thomas, John, Frederick, including one tract in Early County. Son, Green Berry Johnston and Daniel Vaughn, Executors.

Green Berry Johnston, son of Thomas Johnston moved to Warren County, Georgia, from there to Twiggs County (adjoining Wilkinson County.) He was the first of five generations of this family to live in Twiggs. He owned the plantation, later known as the George Asbell place and now the property of D. S. Faulk. The family cemetery is to be found back from the present highway, near where the old homestead stood. Green Berry Johnston was born July 21, 1796, was married to Sarah Vaughn October 25, 1821 and died January 23, 1837. Their children were: Felix Andrew, Edwin B., Daniel F., Jane T., Martha W., Francis Marion, Joel G., John S., and Joshua S., the last two being twins.

Felix Andrew Johnston, our grandfather, was born June 19, 1823 and was twice married. While a young man, he went to Houston County and was closely associated with the Rumph family of Marshallville. While there he was married to Susan Elizabeth Jones, of Houston. Their children were Mary (Mrs. D. T. Lamb), Sarah (Mrs. Clayton Vaughn), Cicero Young, John G., Susan E. (Mrs. J. S. Vaughn), Francis Marion. His second wife was Louisa Adeline Law of Oglethorpe, born October 15, 1841, daughter of George Washington and Charlotte Vose Law. After the death of his first wife and his marriage to Louisa Law, he moved his family back to Twiggs. Here were born Martha A., William Warren, Edwin Bruce, George Flournoy, Josie L., Clara A., and Felix Eugene. This large family he reared at the old homestead near Danville. Their home was known as one of the most hospitable to be found and was a haven for both friend and stranger. They were of the old school and were of strict Methodist faith. Lucy Chapel, which has long been a beacon light to that community, was founded through the efforts of Felix Johnston and others. In late life he built a home in Danville and it was there that he died October 21, 1904 and was the first person to be interred in the Danville Cemetery. Our grandmother lived until October 27, 1908 and was known to be one of the saints of earth. Her former pastor and close friend of the family, Rev. I. C. G. Rabun, wrote of her in her obituary, "In her make-up there were beautifully blended the Christian characteristics of both Mary and Martha; of Mary to sit at Jesus' feet and learn of him; of Martha to rise up, look well after her household, prepare for and entertain royally preachers, church-goers, friends and strangers. Hers was a busy life, for their home was the preachers' home, their children's joy, their friends' delight, and the strangers' resting place." The children in our family always called her "Little Grandma" to distinguish between her and our maternal grandmother Lowe, who was a woman of large stature.

WILLIAM WARREN JOHNSTON

MARY JONES LOWE, Wife of W. W. Johnston

William Warren Johnston, our father, was born March 20, 1868, wedded to Mary Jones Lowe November 5, 1891. She was the youngest child of Thomas and Cornelia Ann Mims Lowe of Bullard. After they married they came to live with the bride's mother and it was here that they reared their fourteen children, thirteen who reached maturity, one dying at the age of one year. The home continues to be occupied by our mother and a daughter (the writer of this sketch) and husband.

Our father was a man of high intellect and a scholar by instinct and application and was recognized as one of the best informed in the county. His great desire was that his children take advantage of every opportunity to improve themselves, stressing the fact that one is never too old to learn. He spent practically all his life's earnings educating his thirteen children, most of them attending college. While a young man he taught schools in Laurens, Pulaski and Bullard (Pine Grove School). After this he was depot agent for the Southern Railway at Bullard. He was Justice of Peace of Bluff District for many years, and was one of the first rural Letter Carriers in this area, carrying mail from Bullard Post Office during horse and buggy days. In later years this office was discontinued, consolidation of routes took place and he was carrier of Route 2, Dry Branch until his retirement at the age of sixty-five. At that time he laughingly said that he "still felt like one of the boys, but postal rules must be obeyed." Following his retirement he continued to be active in the affairs of his county, serving as trustee, secretary and treasurer of Bullard High School when operated on local tax, member of County Board of Education. At the time of his death, June 18, 1951, he was Democratic Executive Committeeman and Chairman of Twiggs County Board of Welfare.

He was a charter member of Cool Spring Masonic Lodge and after leaving his home church, Lucy Chapel, he took his place at Beech Spring, the church of his wife's family, serving at various times as secretary, steward, trustee, always present at its services. His joy and pride were seeing that the church grounds be kept clean and inviting, as well as the "Spring." He attributed his health and that of his family to drinking Beech Spring water. All of his children united with this Church and remain active Methodists.

Resolutions sent our family after his death give a graphic description of his character:

Whereas, the Twiggs County Board of Welfare has lost a faithful member in the passing of William Warren Johnston, who served continuously on the Board of welfare from his appointment in June ,1937 and as Chairman from June, 1938 until his death, June 18, 1951, and

Whereas, always present at every meeting except in case of illness, he was known to be loyal in his friendship, fair and just in his decisions, forthright in his thinking, sound and unbiased in his judgment. Honor and honesty, truthfulness and kindliness were manifested in his every act, and

Whereas, his love of people and his loyal service to his community were expressed in his early life as a teacher, later as a trustee of the school in his community, as a member of the Board of Education, the Board of Welfare, and as a steward and trustee of his beloved Beech Spring Methodist Church; and

Whereas, love of his family, his wife, his sons and daughters and their loved ones—was reflected in his daily life. His sincerity of purpose, his sense of right and justice and his fine Christian spirit served as a guide to others who sought a better way of life; therefore

Be it resolved that we, the members of the Twiggs County Board of Welfare and the staff of the Twiggs County Department of Public Welfare, express to his loved ones our heartfelt sympathy; and

Be it further resolved that a copy of these resolutions be presented to the family, a copy be sent to the local paper, and a copy become a part of our minutes.

Claud E. Mercer, Vice-Chairman
D. S. McGee
O. T. Chapman
Mrs. H. L. Chance
Mrs. Louise B. Hicks, Director
Mary Evelyn Wimberly, Stenographer
Approved July 25, 1951

Our mother who has been spared to us thus far was a wonderful companion to our father. So closely were their lives knitted that it is hard to think of one without the other. Until his death hers was a busy life, ministering to her large family, striving to "bring them up in the nurture and admonition of the Lord." The Church has indeed been her first love, her greatest cross now being that of insufficient strength to attend its services. She and our father celebrated their Golden Wedding at church services at Beech Spring November 2, 1941, Rev. J. Frederick Wilson honoring them with a special message. On that day a newspaper reporter who was present worte of her: "Mrs. Johnston wore a becoming fall dress with a corsage of yellow rose buds and tuberoses—not one of her daughters looked more 'chipper' nor moved about with more agility on this memorable occasion than did the bride of fifty years ago."

*Children of William Warren and Mary Lowe Johnston*

(1) Ruth Ethelyn, educated in Twiggs schools and Kaigler's Business College. Business woman for many years. Married John W. Burch of Odell, Illinois, who spent a greater part of life with Georgia Power Co. as Field Engineer; died at Gray, Georgia, August 17, 1955. Member of W. S. C. S., D. A. R., U. D. C. (No children). Two stepsons, Col. Charles H. Burch, Fort Huachuca, Arizona, Dr. John Ellis Burch, Joplin, Mo.

(2) Ruby Alleine, died in infancy.

(3) Cornelia Louise, educated in Twiggs schools, married John Thomas McCormick, Hawkinsville. (See sketch in Pulaski County History by Harris). Member of W. S. C. S., D. A. R., U. D. C., pianist and worker in Beech Spring Church for many years. (No children).

(4) Thomas Felix, educated in Twiggs and was attending Ga. Tech when he was victim of fatal accident August 23, 1921. Enlisted in Navy during World War I, was postal clerk at Camp Wheeler and later in Atlanta P. O. A young man of keen intellect and held promise for a bright future. Died in his twenty-third year.

(5) Francis Marion, received his education at Bullard School and Ga. Tech. Served with honor in World War I with Co. C, 151st Machine Gun Bat. (The famous Rainbow Division), the first to leave Camp Wheeler and commanded by Gen. John J. Pershing. Was gassed in Battle of Marne, injury from which he never recovered. Married Daisy Rees of Shellman, graduate of Bessie Tift College and a teacher for many years. In the employ of the government when death came at the age of 48. A Chesterfield in appearance and manner; his refreshing sense of humor and engaging personality drew for him numberless friends. (No children). Interred in Riverside Mausoleum, Macon.

(6) Mary Elizabeth, educated in schools of Twiggs, married George E. Ray, successful business man of Twiggs County, who died April 27, 1951. She continues the management of her husband's estate and is noted for her kindness and acts of benevolence.

(7) John Mims, educated in schools of Twiggs and Powder Springs A & M. Married Blanche Capps, of Macon. Her parents are Ethel Lamble, who was reared

in New York City, and William P. Capps. Connected for many years with Collins Bakeries in Montgomery and Macon. In 1951 he returned to Twiggs County, making his home on Cochran Short Route; he now operates Ray's Country Store.

(8) William Warren, Jr. received his education in Twiggs schools, Powder Springs and Augusta Business College; has held a responsible position in Atlanta P. O. for many years. Was with Seabees in Pacific Theatre of War for two and one half year during World War II. Married Linda Mangham of Columbus, graduate of LaGrange College and Peabody Library School; librarian of Federal Reserve Bank, Atlanta. In 1959 listed in Who's Who in American Business Women—(No children).

(9) Nellie Pauline, attended schools in Twiggs, Hawkinsville High, Young Harris College, Kaigler's Business College, Macon. First married to Edgar R. Zachary, Milledgeville, whose death occurred May 5, 1938. On October 20, 1944, she married George Welton Patterson, of Yakima, Washington, then athletic director at Cochran Field during World War II. They have since made their home in Walla Walla, Washington, where he is connected with Boys' High School of that city.

(10) Cicero Austin, attended school at Bullard High, Hawkinsville High, graduated from Young Harris College with honors. Married Helen Landers, of Hapeville, daughter of W. A. Landers, regional vice president of Coca Cola Co., and also graduate of Young Harris and University of Georgia. Both active in Chamblee Methodist Church. Own and operate Johnston's Home Furnishings, on Buford Highway, North Atlanta.

(11) Paul Eugene, educated at Bullard High and Young Harris College. Spent ten years in Baltimore and New York in food and restaurant business. Married first, Sybil Reynolds, Edgefield, S. C., second, Marguerite Hamil of Atlanta. Employed by City of Atlanta for many years, own and operates Johnston's Antiques, a business he started as a hobby, but has reached large proportions.

(12) Albert Sidney, educated Bullard High, Twiggs High, attended Law School, Macon, Printers' School, Nashville, Tennessee. During World War II was with the Navy, located at Jacksonville, Florida, later Fort Lauderdale. Here he was married to Mona Robinson, reared in Iowa, but at that time resident and busines woman of that city. It is here that they now own and operate a business. (No children).

(13) Mildred Alleine, graduated with honor from schools of Twiggs. Youngest entrant and graduate of Young Harris College, A. B. degree from LaGrange College, Library Science degree from Emory University. Librarian and high school teacher at Cochran High, Twiggs High and Bullard High. Married Rev. W. Robert Richerson, Crenshaw, Miss., graduate of Milsaps College and Candler School of Theology, Emory University; Chaplain in Army Air Corp during World War II, located in the Aleution Islands and Alaska, later in Marfa, Texas. Member of Mississippi Methodist Conference and has filled some of its best appointments. In his fourth year at Kosciusko First Methodist. He has recently won considerable recognition in the field of art, a hobby to which he is devoted. His paintings are being placed in some of the leading Art Exhibits over the South and are winning much favor from critics.

(14) Hilda Evangeline, graduated with honor from Bullard High, Young Harris College, and LaGrange College. Graduate work at Emory University and George Washington University. Taught at Tatum High, LaGrange, Lumpkin High, Gray High, and ten years at Lena Cox in Atlanta. Married Harry Augustus Mills, Cumberland, Maryland, Electronics Engineer, graduate of University of Maryland, attended St. John School, Johns Hopkins University—Episcopalian. He is the great-nephew of

Ralph Waldo Emerson, famous essayist and philosopher, and writes with much the same style—(Works are unpublished); holds important position with F. C. C. in Washington, where he and his family reside.

### Fifth Generation

*Children of John Mims and Blanche Capps Johnston*

(1) John Mims, Jr., attended public schools in Macon, Twiggs High, graduate of Jones County High School. Had college training at Middle Georgia, University of Georgia, and Mercer University. Spent three years in Eleventh Airborne Div. of U. S. Army. Married Marian Elizabeth Durden of Twiggs County, a graduate of Twiggs High, later studying voice; talented singer—reside in Macon, where both hold positions.

(2) Thomas Kenneth, educated a Jones County High (receiving many honors) and Twiggs High, where he graduated with distinction. Enlisted with the Eleventh Airborne Division Medical Corp, spending almost three years in Munich, Germany. Upon his return, married Jeannette Moore, Macon, where they reside and have positions. He will enter college this fall.

*Children of Nellie Johnston and Edgar R. Zachary*

(1) Zoe Johnston, educated at Gray High, Walla Walla High, and graduated from Washington State College, Pullman, Washington. Majored in dramatics. Married William A. Lloyd, also graduate Washington State and is connected with his father in the insurance business and wheat growing. Children: Steven Clark and Melissa Zoe.

(2) Ruth Gail, attended Gray Elementary, graduate of Walla Walla High, also studied at Washington State. Married Donald Tucker, also a graduate of Walla Walla High and Washington State College; associated with his father in extensive wheat growing business. Children: Kathleen and Zachary.

*Children of Nellie Johnston and George W. Patterson*

(1) Vicki Genelle, age 12

(2) Georgene (Dee Dee), age 11

*Child of Mary Johnston and George E. Ray*

Joseph Hamilton Ray, born September 10, 1933

*Children of Cicero A. and Helen Landers Johnston*

(1) Infant son (deceased)

(2) Joyce Edna, first honor graduate Chamblee High School, class of 1954. University of Georgia graduate; married Charles Melton Eberhart of Atlanta, Mercer University graduate. One child, Elaine. Reside in Savannah.

(3) Thomas Austin, Chamblee High student.

*Children of Paul E. and Sybil Reynolds Johnston*

(1) Paula Eugenia, student, University of Georgia

(2) Jeannene, student, Atlanta High School

*Children of Mildred Johnston and W. Robert Richerson*

(1) Mary Neal, born September 20, 1944

(2) William Robert, Jr. (Robin), born April 10, 1948

*Child of Hilda Johnston and Harry A. Mills*

Ralph Waldo Emerson, born February 21, 1955 and namesake of his famous great-great uncle.

Written by Cornelia Johnston McCormick, May, 1959
Route 1, Dry Branch, Ga.

## COWAN E. JONES

Cowan E. Jones was born in the home on the S.W. corner of Church and Main streets in Jeffersonville December 10, 1890; his parents were the late Dr. Thomas S. Jones and Georgia Burns Jones. At the age of less than a year his mother passed away and at about two and one-half years of age his father remarried to Grace Carroll Chapman, the mother of Nelly Day Chapman (Mrs. W. L. Thompson of Wrightsville). Out of this union he had three half-brothers, the late I. G. Jones, Thomas S. Jones, Jr., and Campbell Jones who died in infancy, and one half-sister, Mary Lillian Jones, who passed away at the age of two years. He was the grandson of Major Thomas S. Jones and Mary Cowan Jones, Joseph K. Burns and Fannie Everett Burns.

He attended public school in Jeffersonville, Rhodes Military Institute, Kinston, North Carolina, Dana's Preparatory School, Highland Falls, New York, and Georgia Tech. He was editor and publisher of the Twiggs County Citizen from January, 1912 to June, 1913, and in September of that year he entered the medical department of the U. S. Navy, first serving at the U. S. Naval Hospital at Newport, Rhode Island, followed by serving on board the U. S. S. Utah, U. S. S. Alabama, at the U. S. Naval Hospital, Charleston, South Carolina. At the beginning of World War I he was promoted to chief pharmacist's mate at that hospital and in that year (December 26, 1917) he was married to Isabella Thompson of Newport, Rhode Island, and on that day he was ordered to sea duty on board the U. S. Hospital Ship Mercy on which he served in American waters and overseas. After the close of the war he was ordered to return to duty at the U. S.Naval Hospital, Charleston, South Carolina.

In 1922 he was ordered to duty with the American Legation Guard, Managua, Nicaragua, later to the U. S. Navy Hospital Corps School, Norfolk, Virginia, as instructor; while on duty there his son, Cowan E. Jones, Jr., was born on December 31, 1924 in Newport, Rhode Island, two years later he was ordered to duty on board the U. S. S. Richmond (the original U. S. S. Richmond was a sailing sloop that served during the War Betwen the States), the U. S. S. Trenton, and later to duty at the Bureau of Medicine and Surgery, Navy Department, Washington, D. C. as editor of the Hospital Corps Quarterly, and assistant editor of the Hospital Corps Handbook, U. S. Navy, 1930.

His daughter, Georgia Elizabeth Jones, was born at Walter Reed Hospital, April 5, 1930, in Washington, D. C.

In 1930 he was ordered to duty with the Public Health Service in the Republic of Haiti, upon recommendation of the State Department, as Public Health Officer (An unusual distinction wherein he retained his identity and pay in the U. S. Navy and held a commission in the Haitian Government. Such distinction is not held by anyone in the United States at this time—1959), and later he was appointed as Member of the American Scientific Mission in that republic. After completion of that duty he was released from the Navy to U. S. Naval Fleet Reserve in 1934, after more than 20 years active service. Following that he served as editor and publisher of the *Barnesville News-Gazette* (1934-35); later he entered the real estate business in Clearwater, Florida, and remained there in that business until he was recalled to active duty in 1940. He served a short time at the U. S. Naval Hospital, Parris Island, South Carolina, after which he was ordered to the Bureau of Medicine and Surgery, Navy Department, Washington, D. C., and was commissioned and ordered to duty in connection with the professional division as administrative assistant in the preparation of courses for newly appointed medical and dental officers of the Navy, and as assistant in the revision of the Hospital Corps Handbook for the Hospital Corps, associate editor of the Hospital Corps Quarterly, assistant in the preparation of the Hospital Corps Drill Book, and assitant in the preparation of courses of instruction for the Hospital Corps of the Navy.

At the close of World War II, he was released to retirement as lieutenant after 33 years of combined service. He received five decorations for service during World War I, World War II, and peace time.

Cowan E. Jones, Jr. completed high school at McKinley Tech in Washington. He served in the Navy during World War II and attended Cornell University one semester, after which he was transferred to Rensselear Polytechnic Institute and completed the course in Naval Science and Tactics. He was commissioned Ensign in the Navy at the age of 20. He served on board the U. S. S. Philippine Sea (this vessel took Admiral Byrd to the South Polar area together with his supplies and equipment), the U. S. Wright, and served as executive officer of one of the Navy's PCS vessels. Following this duty, he was transferred to Massachusetts Institute of Technology for a postgraduate course. While attending MIT he was married on August 25, 1951, to Lois Wolf of Boston, and on July 28, 1952, their daughter, Nancy Dianne, was born. Following the three-year course at MIT, he was graduated as Naval Architect and Engineer. Following that, he was ordered to duty at the U. S. Navy Shipyard at Long Beach, California, and later to duty in connection with the construction of the atomic powered submarine, the U. S. S. Nautilus at Groton, Mass. Following this duty he resigned his commission to accept a position as hydrodynamics engineer with Convair, a division of General Dynamics Corporation, in San Diego, California.

Georgia Elizabeth Jones completed high school in Clearwater, Florida, attended Florida State University at Tallahassee, Maryland University, at College Park, and on December 22, 1951, she was married to Lieut. (jg) Moreland S. Knapp, U. S. N., at the chapel at Walter Reed Hospital, Washington, D. C. As mentioned before in this sketch, she was born at this hospital. Lieut. Knapp passed away on March 17, 1954, as result of an injury received in line of duty. In September of that year she entered Florida Southern College at Lakeland to complete her college training and in August, 1956 she was graduated there with B. S. degree. On the 25th of that month she was married to Lieut. James R. Bentley, USAF, of Bolivar, New York.

Submitted by: The C. E. Jones Family

## JOHN WALKER JONES

John Walker Jones was born January 23, 1866 in Twiggs County, Georgia; he died November 23, 1933 and is buried at the Jones- Denson Cemetery in Twiggs.

Walker was the youngest of eight children born to Mary Cowan and Major Thomas S. Jones of the Confederacy from Twiggs; grandson of Stephen Jones, and great-grandson of John Jones, veteran of the American Revolution. (See John Jones Ancestral Diagram).

On January 23, 1889 he was married to a cousin, Claude Leone Jones, and they had seven children, three of whom, John Walker, Jr., Mattie Clyde, and Laura Leone, died in infancy.

The four sons surviving are: William (Willie) Ernest, born November 10, 1889; Stephen Shedrick, May 31, 1893; John Levering, August 1, 1896; Henry Grady, July 28, 1898.

J. Walker Jones attended school at "old Lodge Academy" near Marion and Georgia Military College at Milledgeville. He worked and served as a farmer, merchant, community leader and steward in the Methodist Church. His farm comprised part of the old Jones plantation, he owned and operated a general store at Ripley and served also as postmaster. He was treasurer of Twiggs County from 1904 to 1912 and was a promoter in building the Rosebud Methodist Church at Fitzpatrick.

On April 30, 1900, Claude, the wife of Walker Jones, died. Later he married Bessie Fitzpatrick (1904) of Fitzpatrick, Georgia and she bore him four sons: Earl, Fitzpatrick, Julian and Roy.

William (Willie) Ernest Jones, born November 10, 1889, attended school at Fitzpatrick, old Auburn Institute and Brewton-Parker Institute at Mt. Vernon, Georgia. He is a veteran of World War I, having served in the Air Corps with the A. E. F. On August 9, 1922 he married Clifford Corinne Lunceford of Woodbury, Georgia, and they have three children: William Ernest, Jr., born March 20, 1924; he graduated from Twiggs High, attended North Georgia College, graduated from Middle Georgia College, and attended Mercer Law School. He served with the 101st Airborne Division during World War II, received the Purple Heart, four Battle Stars, Bronze Star and a citation from the Belgian Government. Milbrey Lunceford Jones, born November 22, 1929; graduated from Twiggs High School, West Georgia College and Georgia State College for Women. She also graduated from Emory University with a degree of Master Librarianship. Dorothy Corinne Jones, born Sept. 9, 1931, graduated from Twiggs High and Georgia State College for Women with a Bachelor of Science degree. She also attended West Georgia College, University of Georgia and the University of North Carolina. Dorothy married Luther Pierce Bridgeman, born June 3, 1924, of Griffin, Georgia, December 25, 1949. They have two children: Elizabeth Harden, born January 19, 1951, and Barbara Ann, born October 10, 1953.

Stephen S. (Jack) Jones, born May 31, 1893, received his public schooling at Fitzpatrick and Twiggs High School. He is a graduate of the Atlanta School of Pharmacy with a PhG diploma and Mercer University with a Pharmaceutical Chemist diploma. He worked as chemist in the Republic of Cuba; resident pharmacist at Bartow, Millen, Gray and Dry Branch, Georgia. He is a veteran of World War I. On October 14, 1923, he married Emma Opal Tharpe of Twiggs County and they have three sons: Billy Walker, Morris Jasper and Thomas Reid. Billy Walker, born November 3, 1925, graduated from Smith High School, Georgia Teachers College and the University of Georgia. He served in the Navy during World War II. On July 21, 1956 he married Bernice Jeannette Lindsey, born Sept. 26, 1929, and they have two daughters, Janet Elise, born November 30, 1957, and Elizabeth "Beth" Rachel, born December 9, 1959. Morris Jasper (Jackie), born September 12, 1927, graduated from Smith High School and attended several electronic schools. He married Betty Dorman August 31, 1947 and they have two children: Brenda Carol, born January 29, 1949, and Stephen Morris, born July 21, 1952. Thomas Reid, born January 20, 1931, graduated from Smith High School. He is a veteran of the Korean War. On July 2, 1955 he married Sybil Adel Worsham and they have one daughter, Kathryn Adel, born July 29, 1957.

John Levering Jones attended the Jeffersonville Public School and served in the Navy during World War I. He married Mary Cornelia Methvin June 10, 1920. To this union three sons were born: Willie Joseph, Claude and John Clifton. Willie Joseph (Joe) was born May 8, 1921. He graduated from Twiggs High and served in the Navy during World War II. He married Billie Faulk Harrell December 6, 1958. Claude was born September 29, 1924 and he attended Twiggs High School. He married Peggy Simmons September 29, 1948. They have two children: Elizabeth Ann, born June 30, 1951, and Mary Helen, born February 9, 1956. John Clifton was born January 4, 1931. He is a graduate of Twiggs High and Mercer University. He is a veteran of the Naval Air Corps. On May 4, 1959 he married Romona Tucker.

Henry Grady Jones attended Jeffersonville Public School and graduated from Poole's School of Morticians in Atlanta. Grady is a veteran of World War I, having served in the Navy. He married Birdie Kornegay of Tuscaloosa, Alabama May 11, 1923. Their children are Cordelia Elizabeth and Iris Leone. Elizabeth was born December 17, 1924. She is a graduate of Tuscaloosa Public Schools and the Grady Hospital School of Nursing in Atlanta. On December 1, 1947 she married Ernest Guy McKinley, and they have three children: Betty Kay, born November 11, 1948;

Henry Kenneth, born June 8, 1951, and Thomas Michel, born April 16, 1955. Iris Leone was born November 2, 1926. She is a graduate of Tuscaloosa Public Schools and business college. On March 22, 1947 she married Sam Alexander Mills of Bessemer, Alabama. They have two children: Sam Grady, born August 17, 1948 at Mobile, and Judity Ann, born June 2, 1950 at Selma, Alabama.

Prepared by: Mrs. W. E. Jones and B. W. Jones

Submitted by: W. E., S. S., J. L. and H. G. Jones

DIRECT ANCESTRAL LINE
JOHN JONES—SOLDIER OF THE AMERICAN REVOLUTION
By B. W. Jones—Twiggs County, Dry Branch, Georgia, January, 1955
Ref: Family Bibles and Cemetery Records
Submitted by the Family

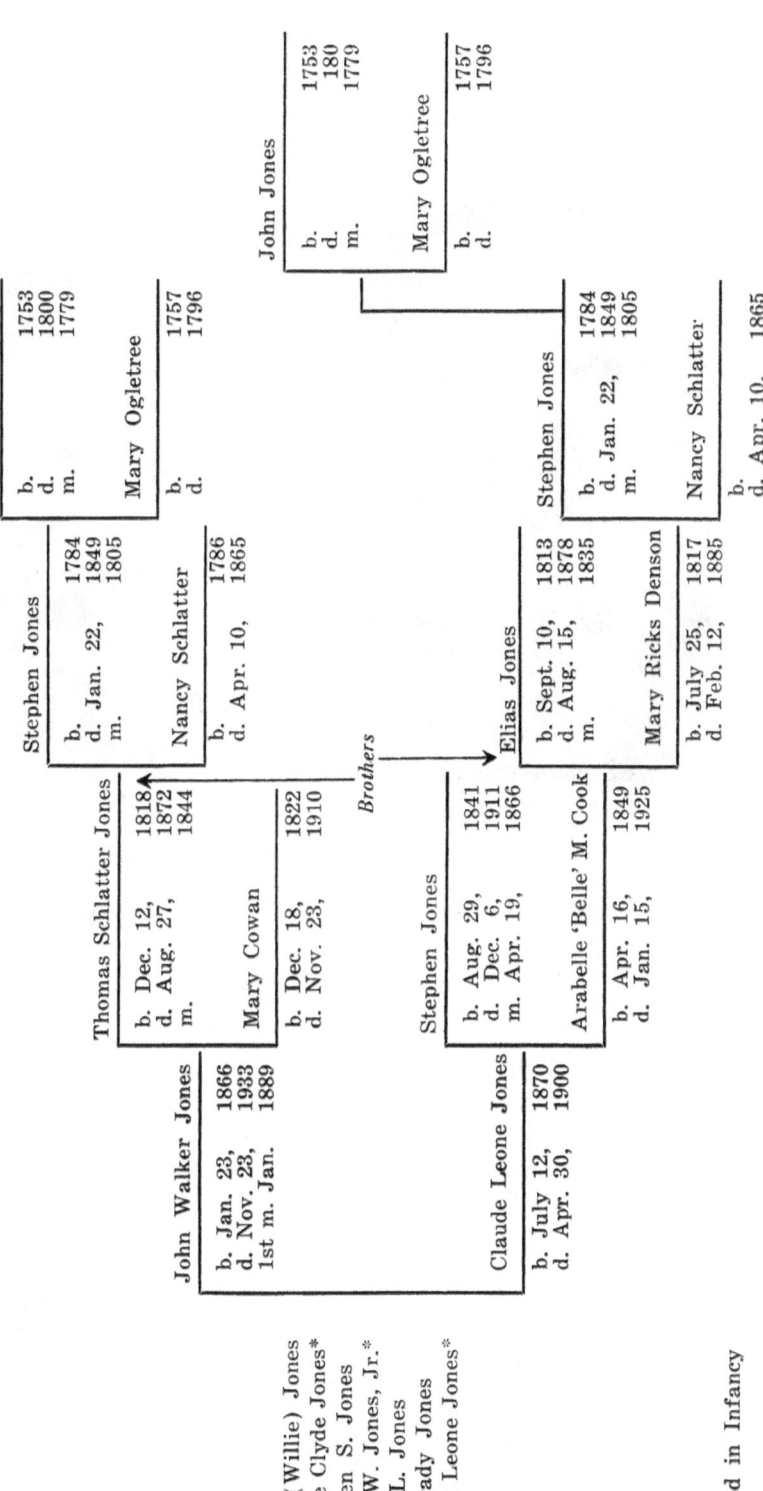

Wm. (Willie) Jones
Mattie Clyde Jones*
Stephen S. Jones
John W. Jones, Jr.*
John L. Jones
H. Grady Jones
Laura Leone Jones*

* Died in Infancy

## SHEDRICK ELIAS JONES
### February 7, 1857-July 27, 1930

Shedrick E. Jones

Mary E. Solomon, 1st wife

Shedrick E. Jones was the oldest son of Mary Cowan and Thomas Schlatter Jones, living in Twiggs County all of his life. He attended school in the "little log school house" near their home, about nine miles from Jeffersonville. Later he attended the University of Georgia, Athens, Georgia.

On January 15, 1885 he was married to Mary Elizabeth Solomon, daughter of Avarilla Fitzpatrick and William Lazurus Solomon. Mary graduated from Wesleyan Female College, Macon, in 1881 and all her life was a very active member of Richland Baptist Church. Their children are Kathleen and William Solomon. Mary died November 10, 1891. He married Anna "Mitt" Carswell on February 12, 1902. Their daughter is Dorothy Carswell.

At the age of 25 he was elected a member of the General Assembly of Georgia, serving in two sessions. Then in 1895 was made sheriff, serving two terms. Again he was elected as a county officer, 1905, as Tax Collector. In 1907 he started the several terms as Mayor of the City of Jeffersonville. About this time he was named as one of the Trustees of the newly created Twelfth District A. and M. School located at Cochran, Georgia.

He helped organize and was Vice President of the first Bank in Twiggs County. Then in 1913-14 served as State Senator. He was one of ten men that started the water works for the town, with the pumping of water beginning on September 16, 1910, from several springs; later aided in developing a system for the entire town by means of deep wells.

For many years he operated a General Merchandise store in Jeffersonville but farming was a lifetime business with him. He was one of those pioneering in the county in introducing registered cattle, Jerseys, and purebred hogs, Duroc-Jerseys; many of the firsts started on his farm—the planting of soy beans, velvet beans, as well as the use of the tractor for farming purposes.

As a tribute to his interest in young people a perpetual endowment was made to the Twiggs County Library by his son, Dr. William S. Jones, Menominee, Michigan.

### ANNA TALLULAH "Mitt" CARSWELL JONES
### July 30, 1873-August 22, 1944

Anna T. "Mitt" Carswell, 2nd wife
of Shedrick E. Jones

"Mitt" was born in Wilkinson County, daughter of Anna Tallulah Chapman and Captain William Edward Carswell, and moved to Twiggs County with her family at the age of three. She received her education at Auburn Institute, Jeffersonville, and Wesleyan Female College, Macon, graduating in the School of Fine Arts in 1895. She taught art in Dublin, Georgia for a short time, coming home to devote her time to homemaking. Her paintings preserve much of her efforts in growing beautiful flowers during this period. This hobby of growing things followed her all of her life using them to brighten her church, home, and for the enjoyment of the neighbors.

She married Shedrick Elias Jones February 12, 1902. To them was born a daughter, Dorothy Carswell. Her contributions toward the cultural and religious efforts in the community was expressed through her voice, time, other talents and money. She was a tireless worker in the Jeffersonville Methodist Church.

Her cheerful and sunny disposition endeared her to all and was affectionately known as "Miss Mitt".

Submitted by: Mrs. Kathleen Jones Carswell
Jeffersonville, Georgia

### THE NAME AND FAMILY OF LAMB

Thanks to the "Daughters" of dear old Twiggs, the County is putting its house in order, bringing to light precious things that have been tucked away in the recesses of many minds of Twiggs County citizens concerning their family trees and things of historic interest.

Mrs. Mary Shine Johnston Lamb

I am happy to present a sketch of the Lamb family whose name I bear, and wish that I could make mention of every member of this honorable household, for we are many in all its branches, but this would be a volume in itself, and as space is limited, I will confine my sketch more or less to the immediate stream of my family life with a glance backward from whence we came.

The name of Lamb is stated by some authorities to have been originally taken from the Celtic word Uan meaning Lamb, and they state, the family descended from one Arca-Dearg, who was the great grandfather of Uan, an Irish warrior of ancient times, most of whose descendants used the surname Lamb.

Families of this name were resident at early dates in the counties of England, in the city of London and in Scotland. These branches are believed to have been descended from the Irish parent stock.

These families were, for the most part, of the yeomanry and landed gentry of Great Britain, and were represented in the artistic, as well as in the civic and military life of England. Probably the most famous of the name in England was Charles Lamb, poet, critic, and essayist of London in the late 18th and early 19th centuries.

The earliest definite records of the name in England include those of William Lamb, Richard Lamb and Ingrida Lamb in 1273, and John Lamb in the latter 15th century, also Ann Lamb, who was buried in 1665.

Matthew Lamb, Esq. had two sons, Sir Matthew and Robert Lamb, of whom the first was created a Baronet by George the Second in 1755.

Sir Matthew served as a member of Parliament. He left a son, Sir Peniston, and a daughter, Charlotte.

Sir Peniston Lamb was created a Peer of Ireland by the title of Baron Kilmore in 1770. About this time John Lamb emigrated from Ireland to New Jersey. He married Patience Scull and they had nine children.

Probably the first of the name in New England was Thomas Lamb who came from London to Roxbury, Massachusetts about 1630. He had six children by his first wife and four by the last one. There were other emigrants also of this name and their children have scattered throughout the United States. They have been characterized, on the whole, by courage, wisdom, power of will, integrity, and, in many cases, the ability to lead others.

Among the Lambs who served in the war of the Revolution were Colonel Gideon Lamb and Lieutenant Abner Lamb of North Carolina, Colonel John Lamb of New York, Captain Richard Lamb of Pennsylvania, Lieutenant Thomas Lamb of Massachusetts, and Captain Nathan Lamb of Virginia.

More recent members of this family have distinguished themselves as Physicians, Artists, Professor, Lawyer and Author.

An ancient coat of arms of the Lamb family is described as follows:

*Arms*—"Sable, a fesse or, between three cinquefoils ermine, charged with a lion passant gules between two mullets of the field."

*Crest*—"A semi-lion rampant gules, collared or, holding in the dexter paw a mullet sable."

*Motto*—"Virtute et fide" meaning "By bravery and faith."

My grandfather Henry Lamb and his brother Reuben Lamb came from North Carolina and settled in south Twiggs County where they owned much land and many servants.

Henry married Allie Howell, daughter of Sanders Howell, and to them were born eight sons, seven of whom fought in the Civil War. Five were killed and only two returned home, my Father, the seventh son, and his brother Henry. Ira was too young to enter the army.

My Father at birth in 1846 was given the name of the family physician, Doctor Taylor, of Hawkinsville, and he was called "Doc" throughout his lifetime.

My Mother, born July 20, 1849, was Mary Shine Johnston, daughter of Felix Andrew Johnston and Elizabeth Jones of Dooly County. She was named for her aunt Mary Shine who was married to John Shine, an early prominent settler in Twiggs County. Mother's great-grandfather Thomas Johnston, our Revolutionary ancestor, came to Georgia from South Carolina and settled in Columbia County. His son Greene Berry Johnston moved to Twiggs County and married Sarah Vaughn. They had nine children, Felix Andrew being the oldest one.

Sarah's brother William Vaughn was father of Clayton and Jack.

Clayton married Mother's sister Sarah and her sister Susan became the second wife of Jack Vaughn.

Mother had two whole sisters, Sarah and Susan, three whole brothers, Cicero, Frank, and John, also two half-sisters, Mattie and Josie and three half-brothers, Will, George and Eugene. A family of dignity and honor. I remember as a child how I enjoyed the visits of Uncle Frank and Aunt Cordelia who lived in Jeffersonville. He was so sweet and genteel and she was so beautiful and gracious. She was Cordelia Hunter of Virginia and studied music at Boston Conservatory. Her art was an inspiration to me.

After Grandmother Elizabeth died, Grandfather Johnston moved his family from Marshallville to south Twiggs County about 1865 and Mother met my Father soon afterward while they were out horse back riding. They were married April 8, 1866. It was on this date in 1946, her 80th wedding anniversary, at 96 years of age, she quietly fell asleep to await the coming of her Lord Whom she loved.

My Father passed on in 1899. There were nine children to bless this union. Two died as infants. Fuller (1868-1925) married Hattie Petty. There were four children, Julius, Mabel, Kirkland and Ethyle.

Charles (1870-1951) married Carolyn Ward. To them were born four children, Byron, Doc, Maye and Charles. Eola (1872-1924) married Thomas Everett. They had five children, Estes, Taylor, Russell, Harry and Mary Frances. Donna (1875-1919) married William Everett, and there were three children, Gladys, William and Dorothy. Naomi (1880) married Thomas Momand. Claudia, a graduate of Wesleyan College, married Ross Childs, a member of the faculty, University of Georgia. Frank 1893-1945) married Lillian Smith and they had one child, Miriam.

Grandfather Lamb's brother, Reuben Lamb (1798-1852) married Elizabeth Rouse (1799-1846) about the year 1818. They had eleven children and I shall mention three of them. Andrew Jackson Lamb (1835-1898) Physician, who studied medicine at Belleview Hospital, New York City, and practiced his profession successfully in Cochran, Georgia. His sister Nancy married Daniel Johnston, Mother's uncle. James Madison Lamb (1819-1864) married in 1840 Asenath Hughes (1822-1844), a sister of Dan Hughes and aunt of Dudley M. Hughes.

Two of their children were James Madison Lamb II, who married Anna Perry in 1876 and their children were Hughes, Jack, Evelyn and Mary, the last one being Mrs. Hampton Rowland of Athens, Georgia.

Then the daughter of Madison and Asenath Lamb was Mary who married William Chapman and their children were William, James, Joe and Carrie Mae.

There are great and great, great grandchildren in our family, but I will leave the story for them to continue weaving the threads of this interesting coverage of the honorable family of Lamb.

Twiggs County is a dear bit of soil on which our loved ones lived and wrought and died in the Faith once delivered to the Saints.

Mother's picture, taken late in life, past eighty years, is enclosed with this sketch, and her favorite song was, "It is better farther on."

Our Heavenly Father said, "earth is my footstool, and I will make the place of my feet glorious," so, even though Twiggs County should experience some change in topography, it will share in God's plan for the restoration of Edenic beauty and glory to the earth.

To our Father and His Son Jesus our Savior and coming King, I dedicate this sketch with thanksgiving for life and all its attendant blessings.

Now unto Him who created all things for His pleasure and our good, I would say HOW GREAT THOU ART!

Written and submitted by: Claudia Lamb Childs
Holman Hotel, Athens, Georgia

## LATSON

In the late 1790's, Edward Latson and his brother Simon, interested in the cotton future of the South, left their home in New York, and settled in Twiggs County, Georgia. One brother made this cross country journey by ox cart. The other arrived at Savannah, Georgia by boat, later they met as pre-arranged in Twiggs County

They were prominently associated with the building of Stone Creek Baptist Church, constituted in 1809 before the city of Macon was incorporated and when Georgia itself was only 75 years old. It is the Mother of the first Baptist church of Macon.

Prior to 1850, Stone Creek Church, then only a small log building, was located near the creek from which it derived its name. Due to traveling problems the church was moved nearer the center of the community.

In 1850, Simon Latson was awarded the contract to build the white frame building which stood until 1953.

A Northerner by birth, Simon Latson, not believing in slavery, employed local slaves for construction of the church on land given by C. A. Thorpe and P. W. Edge.

On April 30, 1953, a tornado demolished the church. After this tragedy, its faithful members rebuilt historic Stone Creek Church. Today a modern brick structure stands on the same site as the former church.

Edward and Simon brought the first cook stove into Twiggs County. Curiosity brought people from all parts of the county to see this "wonder".

Simon moved to Texas to live. Edward remained in Twiggs County; dates of his birth, marriage and death are unknown.

Land, consisting of approximately 200 acres in Twiggs County, known today as the Latson estate, was equally divided between Edward's six children.

Edward Latson's 6 children were:

William, married Sallie Love. Estelle, married Solomon Wood. Adeline, married _____ Coleman. Ellen, born November 17, 1854, died April 27, 1929, married John Bowden. Leathea, married John Love.

Benjamin Madison Latson, born Twiggs County, April 18, 1849, died June 30, 1913, married Lucinda Annette DeFore, Oct. 18, 1874. She was born Feb. 20, 1854, died March 1, 1935. 7 children:

1. Adeline, born Aug. 24, 1876, died 1891.
2. Anne Elizabeth, born June, 1878, died_____.
3. Annette Gertrude Latson, born Twiggs County, March 1, 1880, died July 26, 1945, married Charles Bowden, Dec. 26, 1912. 2 children:

a. Eddie C. Bowden, born Dec. 21, 1913, married Nannie Mae Hattaway, Sept. 28, 1935. She was born May 17, 1913, died Sept. 23, 1957. 5 children:

(1) William Darrell, born Nov. 1, 1936, married Betty Jo Hinson, Aug. 18, 1957.
(2) Benjamin Milton, born March 24, 1938.
(3) Edward Carl, born Aug. 28, 1940.
(4) Jerry Lee, born Nov. 21, 1943.
(5) Wayne Allen, born Jan. 6, 1950.

b. James Benjamin Bowden, born Jan. 12, 1917, married Louise Tidwell, 1941, served as corporal in U. S. Army in the European Theater during World War II. 4 children:

(1) Benny C., born 1942.
(2) Evelyn L., born 1944.
(3) Jimmy F., born 1946.
(4) Jackie T., born 1947.

4. Carrie Latson, born Twiggs County, July 12, 1882, married Daniel Britt O'Neal, Jan. 16, 1901. He was born May 13, 1871. 3 children:

a. Maggie Lee O'Neal, born Jan. 29, 1902, married Corporal John Floyd Curry, Aug. 24, 1918. He served overseas in World War I. 2 children:

(1) Carl Daniel (Dink), born Oct. 31, 1920, married Dorothy Elizabeth McMullan, Nov. 23, 1941. He enlisted in U. S. Army, May 11, 1942; served as MM/2c in Asiatic-Pacific, Philippines and American Theaters until discharged Oct. 29, 1945. 3 children:

(a) Carl Donald, born July 8, 1942.
(b) Russell Clyde, born July 12, 1944.
(c) Anne Elizabeth, born March 4, 1950.

(2) Doris Evelyn, born March 30, 1924, married Leon Thomas Chester, Oct. 5, 1941. He was M/Sgt. in U. S. Army Medical Corps; served overseas in World War II in Hawaii and the Philippines. 2 children:

(a) Thomas Milton, born Aug. 23, 1942.
(b) Evelyn Theresa, born April 26, 1945.

b. Edward Daniel O'Neal, born Oct. 22, 1904; died Dec. 16, 1933.

c. Myrtle Virginia (Joe Brown), born July 24, 1905, married Harry G. Green, Sept. 9, 1922. He was born May 15, 1894; killed May 15, 1925 in line of duty as Deputy Sheriff of Bibb County. Myrtle later married Stephen Henry Simmons, Aug. 14, 1935. He was born May 11, 1894.

5. Bennie Latson, born Twiggs County, Jan. 9, 1884, died June 12, 1957, married James M. Rogers, Jan. 31, 1906. He died July 18, 1914.   7 children:

    a. Laval Rogers, born_____, died_____.

    b. Mary Evelyn Rogers, born Jan. 24, 1908, died Jan. 24, 1959, married John S. Cranford, Aug. 21, 1935.   6 children:

        (1) Jackie S., born June 18, 1936, married Edna Lyles, Sept. 13, 1958; served as GM/3c in U. S. Navy in Japan and China 1952-1956.

        (2) Marjorie Wynelle, born April 9, 1938.

        (3) James Heyward, born Feb. 9, 1941.

        (4) Joyce Marie, born Feb. 6, 1943.

        (5) Larry Osman, born March 30, 1944; died Sept. 4, 1944.

        (6) John Wayne, born July 25, 1945.

    c. James Madison Rogers, born Nov. 23, 1910, lost at sea in line of duty, Oct. 1943. Formerly a Petty Officer in U. S. Navy, he transferred to Merchant Marines in response to a request for volunteers from President Roosevelt.

    d. Mammie Belle Rogers, born June 23, 1912; died Aug. 5, 1945, married Hershel Mixon, July 29, 1933.   1 child:

        (1) Mary Carolyn, born June 18, 1934, married A/3c Robert F. Hardman, Dec. 25, 1957.   1 child:

        (a) Margaret Roberta, born March 1, 1959.

    e. Virginia Rose Rogers, born July 25, 1914, married George B. Nelson, Nov. 30, 1935.   2 children:

        (1) Bennie Lee, born Nov. 7, 1936, married S/Sgt. Travis C. West, June 17, 1956. 1 child:

        (a) Jimmy Lee, born Jan. 12, 1958.

        (2) George Sidney, born Aug. 19, 1938.

Virginia later married Floyd Green, Aug. 3, 1942. Aug. 3, 1942.

    f. William Lee Rogers, born June 24, 1934, married Christine Upshaw, June 17, 1955; served as Fireman in U. S. Naval Reserve 1952, remaining in In-Active Reserve.   2 children:

        (1) Cathy Darnell, born Feb. 11, 1956.

        (2) William Randolph, born Dec. 7, 1957.

    g. Robert Lee Rogers, born June 24, 1934, married Geraldine Adams, Jan. 28, 1957; served as Fireman in U. S. Navy 1952-1956.   1 child:

        (1) Teresa Darlene, born Nov. 11, 1958.

NOTE: William Lee and Robert Lee Rogers (twins) were adopted by Bennie Latson Rogers.

6. Edward B. Latson, born and died 1886.

7. Jennie Latson, born Twiggs County, Aug. 31, 1887, married Obie O'Neal, Jan. 31, 1906. He was born Aug. 10, 1887.   7 children:

    a. Mary Annette O'Neal, born April 26, 1909, married Thomas Harkness Edwards, April 16, 1933.   3 children:

        (1) Infant son, born and died Nov. 2, 1947.

        (2) Thomas O'Neal, born Nov. 4, 1949.

        (3) Benjamin Brown, born Dec. 14, 1950.

    b. Etta Pauline O'Neal, born Feb. 22, 1911, married N. Dixon, Aug. 13, 1927. 1 child:

(1) Etta Ann, born Sept. 12, 1928; served as a WAVE in U. S. Navy about 1949, married James D. Collins, 1953. Pauline later married Sgt. Hershel L. Taylor, Oct. 25, 1942. He selected the Army as a career after serving overseas in World War II.

c. Ola Mae O'Neal, born May 5, 1913, married Woodrow Wilson Davis, Jan. 16, 1956.   1 child:
(1) Wilse Russard, born May 17, 1957.

d. Benjamin Latson O'Neal, born April 8, 1915; died Sept. 21, 1957, married Marion Toney, June 15, 1937. He served in U. S. Navy as S/2c in World War II, 1944-1945.   4 children:
(1) Betty Ann, born Dec. 13, 1940, married Kenneth John MacKay, Aug. 2, 1958.
(2) Benjamin Latson, Jr., born Feb. 20, 1942.
(3) Margaret Elizabeth, born Jan. 11, 1947.
(4) Barbara Ann, born May 11, 1954.

e. Obie Wood O'Neal, born Nov. 21, 1917, married Dee Dee Hudson, June 1942. He served in U. S. Army as 1st Lt. in European Theater, World War II. He selected Army as career. Now M/Sgt. U. S. Air Force. Enlisted 1942, will retire 1962.   2 children:
(1) Obie Dee, born Aug. 23, 1943.
(2) Patricia Anne, born Sept. 21, 1944.

Obie Wood later married Lucie Charlotte Cagny, Jan. 29, 1948. 1 child: lotte Cagny, Jan. 29, 1948.   1 child:
(1) Charlton G. C., born June 28, 1958.

f. Lorie Kirby O'Neal, born Sept. 27, 1923, married Elizabeth Jessup, Aug. 8, 1942. He served in U. S. Navy as Moulder/3c, from Jan. 14, 1943-Dec. 18, 1945 during World War II in American, Asiatic-Pacific and European Theaters. Also, Philippine Liberation.   2 children:
(1) Adena Gail, born Sept. 23, 1946.
(2) Lorie Kirby, Jr., born March 18, 1948.

g. Willie Russell O'Neal, born Feb. 27, 1928, married Betty Jo Etheridge, March 19, 1950. He served in U. S. Navy as Storekeeper/3c from Feb. 15, 1947-Dec. 23, 1948 on the Aleutians.   3 children:
(1) Rebecca Anne, born Aug. 22, 1951.
(2) Sandra Janice, born April 30, 1956.
(3) Michael Russell, born Aug. 17, 1957.

Submitted by: Mrs. Myrtle O'Neal (S. H.) Simmons, Macon, Ga.

## LONG AND CROCKER FAMILIES

Among the early settlers of Twiggs County, Georgia were the Evans Long and William Crocker families. They came from Culpepper and Spotsylania Counties, Virginia.

Samuel Long, born in England, removed to Ireland and later to America, settling in Spotsylania County, Virginia, where he died Feb. 14, 1739. He and his wife Mary were the parents of Bromfield Long who died in 1778. Bromfield and his wife Sara were the parents of Reubin Long (1730-1792) who married Mary Harrison, daughter of John Harrison, Reubin and Mary being second cousins.

(Will of Bromfield Long recorded in Will Book B., page 263, and that of Reuben Long in Will Book D., page 52, Culpepper County.) Reuben Long served in a campaign against the French and Indians some time between 1753 and 1755. He was "a patriotic soldier and officer in our war of the Revolution as was also his father Col. Bromfield Long of St. Marks Parish, of Culpepper County, Va." (Green's Culpepper County, Va., Vol. 5, page 239.)

"Reuben Long entered the army as an Ensign in 1776 in the 11th. Virginia Regiment and marched from Virginia to join the army under Washington in York. He was commissioned a Lieutenant May 10, 1779, serving until the surrender of Cornwallis. He received a grant of 3,000 acres of land." (Heitman's Historical Register, Officers of The Continental Army; Virginia Court Records, Vol. I, page 20, Green's Culpepper County, Va. Reg. N.S. D.A.R. No. 154379, page 47.)

The children of Reuben Long and his wife Mary Harrison were:

1. Gabriel, R. S. (1751-1827)—(Reuben³ Bromfield² Samuel¹) married first Lucinda Slaughter and secondly Ann Slaughter, sisters.

2. Nimrod, R. S.—(Reuben³ Bromfield² Samuel¹) married Eleanor Eltinge Williams, daughter of John Williams III, and his wife Lucy Clayton. (See Williams family in "Some Prominent Virginia Families" by Louise Peoquet DuBellet)

3. Anderson, R. S., 1759-1840 (Reuben³ Bromfield² Samuel¹ married Mildred Ann Slaughter, whose mother was Sally Coleman Slaughter.

4. Fanny 1760-1796 (Reuben³ Bromfield² Samuel¹) married Daniel Richardson, R. S., born in England, came to America and settled in Culpepper County, Va., removed to South Carolina and then to Hancock County, Ga., where he and his wife died in 1796. He served as a Lieutenant in Capt. Levine's Co., 9th. Virginia Regiment.

5. Peggy—(Reuben³ Bromfield² Samuel¹) married Robert Kay. Issue: James

6. Evans 1765-1819 (Reuben³ Bromfield² Samuel¹) married Lucy Apperson, daughter of John Apperson (Epperson).

7. Polly Harrison—(Reuben³ Bromfield² Samuel¹) married John Nash. Two of the above sons of Reuben Long served as body guards to George Washington, one of whom Rev. Gabriel Long was a major in the Revolutionary Army. His brothers Anderson, Nimrod, and Evans, and his cousin Nicholas also served in the Revolution. In 1775 Gabriel served as a Captain, fighting at Hampton and Norfolk. Later he was commissioned a Major in Morgan's Rifle Regiment and was noted as one of the celebrated marksmen commanded by Morgan. (William and Mary Quarterly, second series Jan.-Oct. 1921).

Evans Long, the youngest son of Reuben, served in the Revolution under his brother Maj. Gabriel Long. In 1775 he was only thirteen years of age and attained the rank of sergeant. (John H. Gwalthmey's "Virginians In The Revolution", page 482 II C. L. and records of St. Marks Church, Culpepper County, Va.)

Following the close of the Revolutionary War, Evans Long married Lucy Apperson (Epperson) and they removed from Culpepper to Twiggs Co. Ga., where he died in 1819. A granite pillow marker inscribed "Evans Long, son of Reuben Long and Mary Harrison" is located in the Ezekiel Wimberly cemetery, two miles north from Jeffersonville on U. S. Highway 80.

Sara Simms Edge in "Joel Hurt and the Development of Atlanta" says "Three of the great-grandparents of Joel Hurt, maternal and paternal, the William Hurts, the Reuben Longs and the John Appersons were evidently closs friends and were all residents of Spotsylvania and Culpepper Counties, Virginia where their families had lived for generations and from where many of their children moved to settle as leading citizens of Georgia and later Alabama."

The children of Evans and Lucy Apperson Long were:

1. Mary Evans Long, born 4-25-1783 died 10-20-1872 (Evans⁴ Reuben³ Bromfield² Samuel¹) married (Major) William Crocker, born 9-1-1777 in Virginia and died 6-22-1835. Both are buried in the Crocker cemetery on their former plantation near the dead town of Marion, Ga. Their original home is owned and occupied by a descendant of Thomas Jones Faulk. Quoting from *"The Bench and Bar of Georgia"* Vol. I, pages 7 and 247-259, published in 1858 by Stephen F. Miller, "William Crocker had perfect title to sound judgment and unquestionable integrity. He was a teacher, studied law under Judge Early, was licensed to practice by Judge Carnes

in 1810, member of the bar from 1811 to 1825, served several terms in the Legislature and was appointed Judge-Advocate. He gradually obtained a good practice, much of it commercial paper, and in eight or ten years his march to prosperity was quite rapid. This period of fifteen years embraces the practice that was most profitable to Mr. Crocker. The largest number of suits he ever brought to one term was in the Spring of 1820, of Twiggs Superior Court. Of the five hundred placed on docket by all the members of the bar, two hundred were returned by Mr. Crocker and the dockets show that he was concerned in the defense of about two hundred more, making four hundred cases requiring his personal attention at the same term of court.

William Crocker Cemetery

In the future the title of Major will be applied, as he was known by that distinction when the author first became acquainted with Maj. Crocker in 1824. He had formerly belonged to the staff of Major-General Ezekiel Wimberly as Judge-Advocate with the privilege of wearing a rich uniform equal to that of his chief, except the two stars on the golden epaulettes of the latter. This office was next held by the eldest son of Major Crocker (Elijah Evans Crocker, Esq.) who removing out of the division, it was conferred upon the author by the same noble hearted patron. This privity of rank will excuse the introduction of matter here which is connected with the sword worn by the Judge Advocate (Major Crocker) and which sword was destined to figure in a scene fully as romantic, in a military point of view, as any that this poor world ever afforded."

Of this historic sword and LaFayette's triumphant tour through the Southern States, Louise Frederick Hays in her *History of Macon County (Ga.)* said: "When the Marquis de LaFayette came to visit America as the Nation's guest in 1825, he honored Georgia by visiting Milledgeville, the State Capitol, while the most colorful of Governors, George M. Troup, was in the executive office. All Georgia assembled to express their delight in her guest and every possible detail was arranged for his entertainment; a set of china was even made with a special design for the banquet.

There is a story full of human interest regarding a company called "The La

Fayette Volunteers"; John J. Slappey, Capt. Theophilus M. Chamberlin, Hamilton R. DuPree and Francis W. Johnson, Lieutenants; Stephen F. Miller, Orderly Sergeant.

This company was organized in Twiggs for the occasion, and after adopting cheap uniforms they secured a drum and fife. The ladies made them a beautiful handpainted white silk flag. They fitted up a carriage for the three living Revolutionary soldiers, Daniel Shine, William Duffel and Charles Raley. Thus equipped they started their march for Milledgeville. Enroute they halted at the home of Maj. William Crocker who was known to possess a beautiful sword and Stephen M. Miller, Orderly Sergeant, borrowed that sword. The company made a great hit at the celebration, where the Orderly Sergeant, Stephen Miller, paraded with the sword at the banquet and the ball, and came near having to use it in order to get Lieut. Chamberlin in the ball room with the flag. In his *Bench and Bar of Georgia* Miller gives a most interesting account of La Fayette's visit and of William Crocker's sword. A search was made for this historic sword and it was found in possesion of the great-great- grandson of William Crocker, Harmon Crocker, who lives in the Old Home of Dr. William N. L. Crocker, son of William Crocker. It is not surprising that the LaFayette Volunteers could parade with such flare with such a sword. The handle is hand-carved ivory and the blade is etched in gold, which even time and rust have not obliterated."

"Another unique antique was found at the Crocker home, a doll seventy-five years old. It had an old fashioned bisque head and a rag body with hand-made wooden hands and feet. Its clothes were made from homespun cloth, the embroidered ruffles done by hand. The doll belonged to Lou Crocker Walker, daughter of Evans Crocker.

Another story of this house is that Mary Crocker, daughter of Dr. W. N. L. Crocker, afterwards Mrs. W. Hamilton Felton, was born there the night the stars fell. This was on Nov. 13, 1833."

We now review LaFayette's visit to Culpepper County, Va., quoting from Green's notes on Culpepper County, Dr. Slaughter's St. Marks Parish, part II, page 157, "LaFayette made four separate visits to America; first in 1777, then 1780, after which he returned to bring money and men to aid the Colonists. His third visit was in 1825, when he accepted the invitation of Congress to become the guest of the Nation. It was during this latter visit that he was a guest of Culpepper. The town of Culpepper sent a committee composed of LaFayette's old comrades in arms, Gabriel Long and Capt. Philip Slaughter to convey to him their invitation, he being at the time at Monticello, the home of Jefferson, where he was meeting his old friends, Madison, Monroe, William Wirt and others. That evening LaFayette journeyed with Mr. Madison to Montpelier where the Culpepper committee found him and delivered their invitation."

Col. Gabriel Long who with Capt. Slaughter delivered Culpepper's invitation to Gen. LaFayette was the uncle of Mary Evans Long, who married Major William Crocker whose sword played a colorful part in LaFayette's visit to Twiggs County, Ga.

"The property of Major Crocker, says the historian Stephen Miller, had increased to a large estate, which enabled him to give liberally to his children as they settled in life. He was a prudent manager even to the most rigid economy, yet provided a good education for his sons and daughters, and whatever was necessary to support their positions in society. All of them formed advantageous matrimonial connections. One of his daughters, Lucy, married Samuel Williams, late of Stewart County; another, Mary, married Allen Belcher, M.D., after whose death she intermarried with Tomlinson Fort, late of Stewart; and the youngest, Frances, married James Solomon, and several years after his death she became the wife of Hugh L. Dennard of Houston County. The daughters are still living, all of whom have grandchildren. The sons of Major Crocker are Elijah Evans Crocker who resides near the old homestead, Dr. William N. L. Crocker of Macon County, formerly a senator in the Legislature and Peter Early Crocker yet of Twiggs County.

In person Major Crocker was of the ordinary size, well formed, had blue eyes, fresh complexion and a round, well developed forehead. He was very plain in his manners, which resembled those of a farmer, and was quite a favorite among the people, who honored him the more for his quiet, social deportment. He died at his residence near Marion, Twiggs County, June 22, 1835 at the age of fifty-eight years."

The children of Major Crocker and his wife, Mary Evans Long, were:

1. Col. Elijah Evans Crocker, born 3-20-1803, died 9-24-1867, married Betsey Bryan Wimberly, born 5-13-1810. Issue: Martha Howard (1833-1853), married S. S. Mellon; Sallie Jones (1835-1908), married John Rockwell of Stewart County, son of Stoddard Rockwell and his wife Clara McCarta of Putnam County. Their children were I. Stoddard (1858-1927); Henry (1864-1898); Fanny, born in 1867, married R. T. Humber of Stewart County and resides in Lumpkin; John (1869-1921).

2. Frances, who died in 1888, married James Solomon (1800-1842). Issue: James C. killed serving the Confederacy; Cinderalla, who married Paul Tarver; William L., born in 1834; Josephine, born 12-27-1837, died 2-23-1903, married Charles Reynolds Faulk of Twiggs County. Issue: Carey E. Faulk. Secondly Frances Crocker Solomon married H. L. Dennard of Twiggs. Issue: Mary who married Dudley Hughes of Twiggs. "Mrs. Dennard was a woman of shrewd business sense and by her energy and good judgement quite a competency was accumulated." (Memoirs of Georgia, Twiggs County sketch of Solomon.)

3. Dr. William N. L. Crocker. Hay's *History of Macon County, Georgia*, published in 1933, "Dr. Crocker was an outstanding physician of Twiggs Countty, later moving to Macon County, where he practiced his profession and served in the State Senate (1847). He married Louise Stapler, daughter of John Stapler, Macon County pioneer. Issue: Evans S. who married Ann Elizabeth Harmon and settled near old Lanier but a few years later bought the home of his father known as the old Crocker place built over 110 years ago, situated about eight miles north of Montezuma, Ga., on the Marshallville Road. Evans Crocker and his wife had two children: Lou Evans who married W. J. Walker of Marshallville; and Miles William who married Eula McKinney of Gatesville, Texas. Issue: Miles Harmon Crocker and Nancy Louise who with their children constitute the fourth and fifth generation of Crockers living in the Crocker home. The other children of Dr. Crocker and his wife were Lou, Victoria, and Mary. Lou married Charles A. Walker and had J. C. Walker; Gertrude who married Prof. T. E. Hollingsworth; Victoria who married Dr. J. D. Wade; Henry; Charlie and Eugenia. Victoria Crocker married _____ Tomlinson and Mary married W. Hamilton Felton."

(Today the Crocker home is 136 years old.)

4. Peter Early Crocker.

5. Lucy Avery Crocker, born 3-2-1808 in area now knowns as Twiggs County, died 11-20-1889 Montgomery County, Ala., married Samuel Williams (1793-1839). They were among the early settlers of Stewart County, Ga., where Samuel Williams was a large land and slave owner. He was appointed by the Governor to conduct the first census of Stewart County and represented that county in the Georgia House and Senate. Their children were:1. William Alexander Williams, M.D., born 1-30-1826, died 3-10-1857, married Mary Harwell and had Samuel Harwell who died in infancy; William (1856-1920) married Anna Carter (1859-1934) daughter of Dr. Jardine Carter; John Alexander (1852-1918) married in Texas, Mary Hammond in 1885. She died in 1915 and both are buried at Boswell, Oklahoma. Issue: a daughter born 1886, died in infancy; Mary Frances born 1887 now living in Paris, Texas; William Hammond born 1889; Leonora Eugenia born 1891; John Alexander born 1899, died 1929. After the death of Dr. William Alexander Williams his widow married James A. Fort. Issue: George and Tomlinson (Lynn). 2. John Samuel Williams born 11-29-1827,

died 1-20-1854 unmarried. 3. George McIntosh Williams born 1-27-1830, died 2-10-1900, was an attorney and Judge of the Inferior Court of Stewart County where he resided and later lived in Rome, Ga. At the outbreak of the War-Between-the-States he removed his family to Macon County, Ala., in order to leave them near his wife's father, Col. Benjamin F. Borom while he served in the Confederate Army. He married Margaret Elizabeth Borom born 8-16-1838, died 2-11-1911. 4. Evans Uriah Williams born 7-27-1832, died 3-16-1901, married first Jane Callen, daughter of Dr. William Callen of Florence, Ga. and secondly Cornelia Bethune of Alabama. 5. Mary Margaret Williams born 3-17-1835, died in 1875, married Judge James M. Clark of Americus, Ga. 6. Theophous Early Williams, died in infancy. 7. Frances Anderson Williams, born 11-6-1838 in Stewart County, died 4-1-1900 in Montgomery County, Ala., married Joseph Calloway of Wilkes County, Ga.

After the death of Samuel Williams his widow, Lucy Crocker Williams, married May 28, 1874 Col. Simon Holt and following his death she married Judge Loverd Bryan. (See Terrell- Dixon *History of Stewart County, Ga.*, Vol. I, pages 633-670.)

6. Mary Epperson Crocker born 8-13-1810, died 5-20-1899, married Dr. Allen Belcher of Twiggs. Issue: Mary Epperson born 12-30-1827, died 12-10-1857, married James Arthur Fort (1822-1898); Louisa Frances (1830-1832). Secondly Mary Epperson Crocker Belcher married 9-15-1831 Tomlinson Fort of Stewart County, Ga. (See Terrell-Dixon *History of Stewart County, Ga.*, Vol. I, page 469).

7. Martha Margaret Crocker born 2-6-1813 married George W. Kidd. Issue William James, Missouri and Cora.

8. David Evans Crocker born 3-9-1818, died 3-20-1862, married Frances Pace, daughter of Hardy and Frances Pace.

2. Margaret Long (Evans$^4$, Reuben$^3$, Bromfield$^2$, Samuel$^1$) married Elijah Clark, Jr., son of Gen. Elijah Clark. "Elijah Clark, Jr., graduated at Yale in 1801 and received the degree of Master of Arts in the first class to graduate at the University of Georgia. Like his father and his brother, Gov. Clark, he entered politics and served in the House of Representatives, the Senate and as solicitor general. He ran for Congress and was defeated, whereupon he decided to leave the State. Disposing of his enormous acreage, and accompanied by thirteen slaves, he moved his family to Louisiana where he became a Circuit Judge and died there. He is buried at Parish Church of Parish Points Coupee. His son, Alfred Clark, died at Yale while a student there in 1827." (Biography of Elijah Clark by Louise Frederick Hays). Another son married his first cousin, Lucy Motley Long.

3. Frances Long (Evans$^4$, Reuben$^3$, Bromfield$^2$, Samuel$^1$) born Oct. 19, 1789, died Oct. 5, 1853, married Aug. 28, 1806 William Hudson, born Jan. 12, 1786, died 1834, eldest son of Irby Hudson and his wife Phoebe Featherstone who died Dec. 16, 1820. The Hudson family came from Culpepper and Dinwiddie Counties, Va., to Hancock County, Ga., later settling in Putnam County. (Copied from the family Bible of William Hudson). Irby Hudson, father of William, served in the Revolution. He was in Capt. Robt. Bollings Company, Dinwiddie County, Va., marching with troops in actual service under Col. Parker of Gen. Muhlemburg's brigade and held position in Norfolk and Portsmouth. He served until after the surrender of Cornwallis. (Account of his troops service written by Capt. Bolling 1835. Reference Pages 129 and 130, Section 143, McAllister's *(Virginia Militia of the Revolutionary War)*.

The children of William Hudson and his wife Frances Long were: 1. Lucinda Hudson born 12-4-1807, married William G. Green 12-18-1823. 2. Sarah Hudson born 6-11-1809. 3. Irby Hudson born 3-1-1811, married Martha W. Walker 2-20-1840. 4. Jane Hudson born 6-19-1813, married Dr. Thomas G. Harwell 8-25-1829 and after his death she married Benjamin F. Borom. 5. William Hudson born 12-17-1815, married Martha W. Lawrence 1-4-1838. 6. Mary F. Hudson born 2-25-1818, married Francis F. Boykin 2-23-1837. 7. Julia A. Hudson born 7-27-1820, married_____Ross and removed to Alabama. 10. Charles A. Hudson born 9-17-1828, married Mary L. Ga. 9. Nimrod Long Hudson born 2-17-1825, married Annah A. Harris 4-3-1852 and removed to Alabama. 10. Charles A. Hudson born 9-17-1828, married Mary L. Brown 6-1-1850. 11. Anna Louise Hudson born 1-8-1831, married Rev. James R. Thomas, D.D. and removed to California. 12. Fannie Hudson married_____Banks.

4. Lunceford Long (Evans[4], Reuben[3], Bromfield[2], Samuel[1]) born Aug. 10-1792, died Feb. 24, 1864, married Sept. 17, 1813 Nancy Daniel Jackson (1797-1859). Both are buried in the family plot near Millbrook, Ala. He served in the War of 1812. Their children were 1. Temperence Apperson born Feb. 8, 1816, married May 17, 1836 Marcus Young. 2. Lucy Motley born April 18, 1818, died Aug. 13, 1841, married Edward Clark, her first cousin. No issue. 3. Evans Apperson born Nov. 23,1820, died Feb. 2, 1861, married Feb. 2, 1841 Mary Young of Tennessee. 4. James Oliver born Nov. 5, 1822, died June 6, 1870, married Sept. 14, 1848 Sarrah Ann Lewis. He served in the Mexican War. 5. Walter Clark born Jan. 5, 1826, died Mar. 17, 1842. 6. Nimrod Washington born July 8, 1831, married Sept. 6, 1859 Ila Bynum. He was a dentist and served in the Confederate Army from 1861 to 1865. 7. Lunceford Crawford born Sept. 30, 1836, died Jan. 1891, married May 6, 1858 Cenora Jackson. He served in the Confederate Army a short time but was dismissed due to deafness.

5. Lucinda Long (Evans[4], Reuben[3], Bromfield[2], Samuel[1]) married John Owens.

6. Sarah Ann Long (Evans[4], Reuben[3], Bromfield[2], Samuel[1]) born Sept. 25, 1797 in Wilkes County, Ga., died May 25, 1884, married Tuttle Moreland. She is buried in Hurtsboro, Ala.

7. Nimrod Washington Long (Evans[4], Reuben[3], Bromfield[2], Samuel[1]) born Feb. 17, 1800 in Georgia, later removed to Russell County, Ala., married March 22, 1821 Catherine Davis of Lenoir County, N. C. (Nov. 3, 1804-Aug. 20, 1840) daughter of Malachi Davis and his wife Mary Wooten. He lived in Twiggs and Upson Counties, Ga. until 1835 when he removed to Uchee, Russell County, Ala., where he died Dec. 22, 1874. His home at Uchee was burned during the Indian trouble in 1836. He fought against the Indians in Florida, served in the Alabama legislature in 1837 and again in 1845 and was a member of the Convention of 1831 from Twiggs County, Ga. Anne Kendrick Walker in *Russell County In Retrospect* devotes many pages to Nimrod Washington Long. She says in part, "Few men ever made any better preparation for housing a family and taking care of a plantation than Nimrod W. Long." In 1836 as we know, occurred the Indian Uprising. An account is preserved of the exodus of Russell County's pioneers into Georgia. She describes the flight in detail and says in part, "Nimrod Long was one of the most notable men in Russell County. He was one of the founders of the Uchee Baptist Church and represented the county in the State Legislature. He was married three times and the father of thirteen children.

Nimrod Washington Long at the close of the war had one thousand bales of cotton that were seized and confiscated by the Federal authorities. When the raiders came through they took all of the plantation mules and horses with the exception of one old blind mule. Nimrod Long was the owner of two hundred and fifty slaves which were signed into the Freedman's Bureau at Montgomery, Ala. He had already given to each child land and slaves to maintain it. His plantations were self sustaining. A man from Boston was employed as overseer."

The children of Nimrod Washington Long and Catherine Davis Long were: 1. Evans Davis, (April 8,1824-Sept. 16, 1851) married Elizabeth Nuckells (Nichols). Issue: Evans Davis, Jr., Thomas N., and Catherine Louisa who married Barton Burts and had Joseph D., George, Archibald, Anna, Reuben, Nimrod, Thomas, and Gatsy. 2. Lucy Apperson born May 11, 1822, married Joel Hurt. Issue: Nimrod N., Charles H., Emma, Henry, Sarah F., Fletcher E., Joel, Louise, Fanny, George, James W.

(See *Joel Hurt and the Development of Atlanta* by Sara Sims Edge).
3. George Washington born Sept. 25, 1825 Twiggs County, Ga., died June 18, 1880 Hurtsville, Ala., buried in Uchee cemetery. He married Margaret Johnson and had Catherine S. and Scott J. Catherine married Exto Tucker.
4. Mary Ann Sarah married Dr. Oliver B. Walton and removed to Florida. Issue: Nimrod Long, Byrde W., Catherine, Charlie, George, Frances, and Ernest.
5. Malica Lunsford born Dec. 13, 1827, died Oct. 21, 1910, married Julia Cobb and after her death married her cousin Sophia Dickinson (1832-1887). He was a physician and graduated from the "School of Medicine", New York City, about 1850. Later this college merged with Bellview. He served as a surgeon in the 15th. Ala. Reg. Confederate Army. Issue: Gertha married Rev. Charles K. Henderson; Edgar Thomas married Mary Rhodes and had Gertha who married Phelham McKlery Couric.
3. Tululah Catherine married Alex Stephens and had Thomas Lunsford.
4. Arminta born Jan. 20, 1866, married Thomas Moffett Flourney (1859-1913). Issue: Eugenia who married Preer Walton; Robert who married Elizabeth Molder and had Mary Josephine who married Major Stephen W. Mulkey; Mary who married Harbin P. Park; Rebecca who married Charles Dexter Jordon and had Charles D., Jr. and Thornton; Thomas Moffett who married Nell Kimbrough and had Rebecca, Thomas Moffett and Barbara.
6. Margaret Aisley born March 10, 1833, died June 3, 1928, married James Jackson. Issue: Catherine L., Emma B., Mary F., and James, Jr.
7. Nimrod William Ezekiel (1834-1923) married Martha J. Gamble. Buried in Hurtsboro, Ala. Issue: Jackson Edward, Jessie L., Nimrod W., Frances, Lunsford and Quenell.
8. Catherine Lucinda born Sept. 11, 1836, died Oct. 18, 1883, married Leonidas Sherrod Thompson (March 14, 1833-July 6, 1893). Issue: Henry Bradford born May 23, 1855, died Aug. 23, 1926, married Mary Alice Shoptaw; George Lancaster born May 16, 1857, died a bachelor; Catherine Long born March 16, 1859, died March 20, 1881, married Bunjan Davee; Leonidas Sherrod born July 23, 1863, died Feb. 24, 1928, married June 6, 1886 Caladonia Coleman (1863-1896) buried at Hatchechubbee, Ala.; Nimrod Washington Long born May 19, 1866, died Sept. 23, 1945, married June 20, 1894 Lula Slaton.
9. Frances Elizabeth born Dec. 31, 1838, died Sept. 7, 1889, married Edward N. Brown of Hurtsboro, Ala. Issue: Laura Nimphia married Charles M. Owens, died in 1892; Edward Norphlet, Jr., married Thacker Walker and removed to Mexico where he was President General of the Mexican National Railroad. Later he and his family resided in New York where he established connections with railroad systems in this country, had a seat on the New York Stock Exchange and was appointed by President Roosevelt to a responsible position in administrative affairs of the railroads during the depression; Gatra Nimrod Washington Long married Marian Johnson; Lucy married Dr. W. B. Hendricks; Frances Catherine married C. R. Reid; Margaret married in 1900 Dr. Walter B. Hendricks.

Nimrod Washington Long's first wife died in 1840 and he married secondly Sophia Thomas in 1841. Issue: Grigsby Thomas (1842-1898) who married Priscilla Bird; Dr. Frederick B. married Nellie Calhoun; Laura R. (1846-1885) married Dr. Simon A. Holt; and James W. married Josephine Walker.

Submitted by: Mrs. Maude Williams Brewer (Mrs. Willis), 1033 S. Hull St., Montgomery, Ala.

## LOWE - MIMS

The Lowes are of English, some of German, origin. Variants of the name are Loew, Loewe. all having the same meaning—one with lion-like characteristics, bold, dweller at the sign of the lion. Lowe Coat of Arms, Co., Worcester, Thomas Lowe, Esq. of Lowe was chief of his family temp. Queen Elizabeth. Motto: Spero Meliora (I hope for better things). Information found in *General Armory by Burke* in the Library of Congress and in *Armorial Families* by Fox-Davies.

Twiggs County Lowe ancestors coming to America from England first settled in Virginia in Colonial days. Historical records show that some migrated to the Carolinas and Georgia, settling in Hancock, Jones and Twiggs Counties. One of these was the father of Thomas Lowe of Twiggs, the subject of this sketch. Bible containing dates and names having been destroyed, I cannot go further back for definite data than Thomas Lowe, born Dec. 26, 1826, died Jan. 17, 1880 at his home at Bullard. I do have reason to believe that his father's name was Elick. His brothers were Reuben, John (Jack) Frank; his sister, Martha. (There may have been others). In 1851 he married Cornelia Ann Mims, born in Edgefield, S. C., July 26, 1829, daughter of Martin and Charlsie Ferguson Mims, and granddaughter of Drury Mims, Revolutionary soldier. The Mims family of Edgefield County, S. C. is one of its oldest and most prominent. Since 1835 they have edited the Edgefield *Advertiser*, oldest newspaper in South Carolina.

Children of Thomas and Cornelia Mims Lowe:

William T., born Oct. 2, 1853, died April 20, 1873; Julia Augusta (married William Andrews. Children: Amanda Cornelia and John Thomas, born May 2, 1855, died June 11, 1883; E. Martin, born Feb. 26, 1858, died Oct. 1, 1885; John, born Sept. 2, 1862, died Oct. 17, 1869; Thomas, born May 26, 1864, died June 18, 1950; Cornelia Elizabeth ("Mitt"), born Dec. 1, 1866, died July 26, 1882; John Mims, born Sept. 29, 1870, died July 10, 1955; Mary Jones (married William Warren Johnston), born Dec. 24, 1871.

Children of Thomas and Mattie Lord Lowe:

John Burke, Connie Lee (deceased), Wilma, (Mrs. Ira Stucky), Tom II, Thelma, (Mrs. Carl Thomas), Helen, (Mrs. Graves Williams), Harry, (deceased).

Ellen, (Mrs. Tom Odom) is the adopted daughter of John Mims and Hattie Beard Lowe.

Children of Mary Jones Lowe sketched in Johnston biography.

The Lowe plantation, located in the Bullard community and comprising lands joining the present home of the youngest child, Mrs. W. W. Johnston, was one of the most productive in the county. It had its private cotton gin and other facilities common to the home life of that day.

One of the old time family negroes who remembered Thomas Lowe told the writer, "Marse Tom growed the finest cotton and corn and the biggest hogs to be found anywhere." Their family orchard hung in fruit from early summer until late fall, for the enjoyment of the neighborhood.

In 1862, he left home and family as thousands did, to enlist in the Confederate Army, he being a private in Company I, Fifth Georgia Regiment. He was wounded in the Battle of Bentonville, N. C., remaining a cripple until his death. Broken in body but not in spirit, at the close of the War, he resumed his occupation, devoting his attention to his plantation. He built for his family a new home after his return from the War in a different location from the old which was "across the branch" from the present homestead. Beech Spring Academy stood nearby, and it was here that the Lowe children received their schooling. Later, in 1878 Beech Spring Methodist Church was founded and this family was among its charter members.

After the death of her husband, Cornelia Lowe was both mother and father to her family, carrying on the business with her sons. A woman of unusual ability and moral stamina, her neighbors, many of them, looked to her for council and advice. Her services were sought after and freely given. She lived to see her eleventh

Johnston grandchild born and they all adored her.

To their descendants, Thomas and Cornelia Mims Lowe left a rich legacy of lives well spent.

Written by a granddaughter, Mary Elizabeth Johnston Ray (Mrs. G. E.) Route 4, Macon, Ga.

## JAMES ARCHIBALD McCALLUM

According to Bain in the Clans and Tartans of Scotland the McCallum clan originated in Argyllshire, Scotland. We first hear of them in the early fifteenth century.

It was during the reign of King George III of England that Angus McCallum was given a grant of land in America and he was the father of Archibald McCallum, the grandfather of James Archibald.

Archibald McCallum owned many slaves and much land around McCallum's Pond, and lived in the two-story house on the hill above the pond. This house was destroyed by fire several years ago. A portion of land owned by him is now in possession of Arthur McCallum.

Archibald McCallum was married twice. First to Mary Ware whose children were Archibald, James Ware, Addie, and Mary. Second to Miss Emily Banner whose children were Henry, Hugh, and Kate.

James Ware McCallum was born August 15, 1841, died November 1, 1875. He married Miss Nannie Elizabeth Jackson of Wilkinson County. Their children were:
 1. James Archibald McCallum, born Nov. 28, 1871, died 1949.
 2. Carrie Louise McCallum, unmarried, died Aug., 1933.
 3. Addie Elize McCallum, who died at 12 years of age.
 4. Mary McBride McCallum, who died at 6 years of age.

James Archibald McCallum's mother bought a small farm for him when he was 17 years of age. By hard work, good planning, and thrift he added many acres to his original holdings.

It was when this third child was a baby that he opened a small country store near the same spot where his son Hugh now has his place of business.

James Archibald hauled his merchandise by two horse wagon from Macon until the MD & S R.R. was built. He would leave home long before day and return the next day.

He built his business on the principle that "Honesty is the Best Policy", "Let the Other Fellow Have a Share", and "Never Turn One Away Who is in Need".

He brought up his children in this store where they came in contact with all types of people which was an education in itself.

James McCallum believed that each child should have a task after school and required obedience. If they failed they were disciplined. His children rise up and call him blessed and realize that they shall not see his like again. He was witty, wise and wonderful.

He was affiliated with the same Baptist Church of which his grandfather was one of the seven charter members.

James Archibald McCallum married Kate Leila Storey on Jan. 1, 1894. Their children are:
 1. Nannie Elizabeth McCallum born Oct. 24, 1894. Graduated G. S. C. W., Milledgeville. Taught school 13 years in Twiggs County. Married James Howell Whitehurst, cashier of Farmers & Merchants Bank and of Bank of Gray, and Clerk of Superior Court of Twiggs County for 22 years. Their children are:

Katye Frances Whitehurst, born Nov. 8, 1920, attended Bessie Tift College and Wesleyan. Married W. M. Chamberlain of Knoxville, Tenn. Their children are:

Nannie Whitehurst Chamberlain, born Feb. 14, 1948.
Marsha Wyl Chamberlain, born Feb. 26, 1953.
James McCallum Whitehurst, born June 13, 1930, graduate of North Georgia College, employed in Personnel Department at Huber Corporation (Twiggs Co.). Married Elaine Wood, May 12, 1953. Their children are:
James Howell Whitehurst, born July 7, 1958.
2. James Ware McCallum, born Jan. 1, 1897. Living on farm near Ailey, Ga. Married Maurene Meadows. Their children are:
Betty McCallum, born June 16, 1936. Married Harold Allen Bivins, Jet Air Pilot. Has M.A. degree. Have two small daughters, Betty Anna and Catherine Maurine.
James Archibald McCallum, born Oct., 1940, a student at Brewton-Parker Institute.
Ware McCallum, born July, 1942, high school.
3. Arthur Storey McCallum, born Aug. 26, 1898. Physician, graduate of Emory University, Atlanta, and Jefferson Medical College of Philadelphia. Living Sanford, Fla. Married Josephine Graves of Rome, Ga. Their children are:
Margaret McCallum, married Dr. Wm. Anderson of Haddow Heights, N. J. Have three little girls, Leslie, Anne and Shelley.
Anne McCallum, married Dalton McCay, Druggist of Norfolk, Va. They have two little girls.
James Archibald McCallum, senior at Jefferson Medical College. Married Ardeth Manfork. Have two little girls, Christen and Karen, and one son, James Blair McCallum.
4. Hugh Archibald McCallum, born May 23, 1900. Married Mary Faulk, Danville, Ga., Oct. 19, 1932. Farmer and Merchant near Jeffersonville, Ga. Their children:
Mary Jane McCallum, born June 19, 1936, graduate Mercer University, teacher in Dekalb County school.
Frances McCallum, born May 9, 1940, student Mercer University.
Carrie McCallum, born Sept. 16, 1943, high school student.
Hugh Arthur McCallum, born July 15, 1950.
5. Linton Eliot McCallum, born Jan. 4, 1902. Works for *The Times*, Asheville, N. C. Has three sons, Dale, James Hiden and Ware McCallum.
6. Sarah Kathryn McCallum, born Aug. 31, 1910. Graduate Shorter College, Rome, Ga. Taught English in Richland, Ga. Married Brigham White of Dublin, Ga. Living in Hawkinsville, Ga. Their children are:
Beth White, born Aug. 25, 1937, a senior at Mercer University.
By: Nannie McCallum Whitehurst (Mrs. J. H.)

## McCREA - HENDRICKS

Among the early settlers of Twiggs County will be found the family of Gustavus McCrea. He moved into this new country while yet a frontier county and established his home along its southwestern boundary. Through his industry and thrift he accumulated substantial land holdings and built up a large commercial business. His home, which was located on a high bluff on the old Marion road, was the last residence east of the ferry. Here the stagecoaches often stopped as the drivers were welcome to tie their horses and the weary travelers could rest and secure food, water or sleep. It is told that on one occasion a merchant traveling west with a caravan containing two covered wagons of slaves tied his horses in the yard overnight; in the morning he began bargaining with the old gentleman who went into the house and brought out $40,000.00 in gold with which he bought the entire cargo of slaves. His grandchildren lived to tell stories of going back to the old homeplace and seeing the Indians come up to trade their wares of skins or pottery in exchange for merchandise in the commissary that had been shipped by boat up the Ocmulgee River from Savannah. The trading center which he established was continued by his son and an associate operating under the name of McCrea and Jarvis. Something of the size of this business can be seen from the pages of an old ledger which lists General Tarver as one of his customers buying shoes by the hundreds of pairs, pepper by the pounds, etc.

Gustavus McCrea was born Sept. 10, 1800 and married Wealthy Ward Jan. 15, 1823. She was the daughter of Elijah Ward who served as a private in Ballard's Company, North Carolina Troops during the Revolutionary War. He was born March 15, 1753 and died June 7, 1823. He was married on March 15, 1783 to Perubia Knight who was born June 4, 1768 and died Dec. 18, 1827. They are believed to have been buried in the family cemetery near West Lake, Ga. Gustavus McCrea died July 1, 1869. His wife, Wealthy Ward, who was born Nov. 21, 1800, died on Feb. 2, 1884.

The children of Wealthy Ward and Gustavus McCrea who lived to maturity were Pherubia Ann Caroline who married Virgil Perry; Phenelophie Elinder who married James H. Forehand; Cherry Elizabeth who married Wilson Hendricks; Martha Lassie who married Hixon Lee; Thomas E. McCrea who married Josephine A. Hughes; Catherine who married Thomas B. Pace; Mary Frances who married S. T. C. Murray; John A. McCrea who served as a lieutenant with Co. G, 48th Reg., Georgia Infantry, was wounded at Chancellorsville, Va. and surrendered at Appomatox, Va., April 9, 1865; Benjamin G. McCrea who served in the C.S.A. Army and was killed in the Second Battle of Manassus in Virginia; and Hilliard W. McCrea, the youngest.

Wilson Hendricks, the son of Tignall and Elizabeth Hendricks, was born in North Carolina April 18, 1811. Left an orphan he migrated as a young boy to the Richland section of Twiggs County with a group of early settlers to whom he was related by blood or marriage. He was married to Cherry Elizabeth McCrea on July 3, 1845 and established his home near what is now Cary in old Pulaski (now Bleckley) County. He was a large landowner, a prosperous farmer and a proponent of the live-at-home standard. He was a valued member of old Evergreen Church during its early history and served on the committee to plan for the erection of the beautiful building still used by its members. He reared his family on the plantation, a portion of which is still in the possession of lineal descendant. During the War-Between-the-State he served as 1st Lieut., Co. F, 7th Ga. Regiment with Gen. J. F. Redding. He enlisted May 4, 1864 and was discharged at Bentonville, N. C., April 9, 1865. He was known for his kindness and consideration of others as well as his proud and indomitable spirit. Beloved by the old family servants, many remained with him after being set free. After his death on Aug. 22, 1878 his widow moved to Cochran in order to educate her children. She died May 1, 1904.

The children of Cherry Elizabeth McCrea and Wilson Hendricks who lived to maturity were Gustavus Wilson, born Aug. 27, 1846 who served as a lieutenant with the C.S.A. during the entire war and married Nannie E. Wilkinson, April 30, 1872; Colliton L. born March 16, 1848, married Vick Clarke Oct. 20, 1876; George Franklin born, Jan. 8, 1850, married Emma Schilling May 7, 1884; Thomas Ruffin Daniel, born July 5, 1853, married Henderson Raiford and after her death married Lillie Farrar; Lucy McMitchell, born Jan. 25, 1857, married David T. Coley Jan. 11, 1874; Polly Martha, born March 11, 1858, married J. M. Snell Jan. 23, 1875; Benjamine L., born Oct. 9, 1866, married Zaidee Morris; Julia Belle, born Aug. 28, 1864, married Dr. P. L. Hudson May 16, 1881; Charity Lila McZelle, born Oct. 8, 1872, married Elijah Cook, Jr., Dec. 29, 1895.

George Franklin Hendricks, son of Wilson Hendricks, moved to Cochran where he reared his family. Although he did not pursue politics he was known to have had a fine legal mind and accumulated a good law library. He was civic minded and contributed his interest and influence to the development of Cochran and Bleckley County. For many years he was engaged in the mercantile business with farming interests. He died June 19, 1921. The six children of George and Emma Hendricks who grew to maturity were as follows:

Annie Lorena, who married D. Gorham Jackson and presently is living in Decatur, Ga. She has two daughters, Emerine, the wife of Stephen Freeman McMichael, whose children are Elizabeth, Emerine, Elaine and Stephen; the second daughter, Loraine, is the wife of Major James W. Allen, Jr., and the mother of two children, Jacqualine and Jimmie Allen.

Barney Wilson Hendricks married Margaret Celete Cook. He is a Methodist and for many years was secretary and treasurer of the Kiwanis Club. He served throughout the first World War as First Class Sergeant, Co. C, 106 Field Signal Battalion and was stationed in Northern France at the cessation of hostilities. He was organizing commander of Bleckley County Post 107, American Legion. Now retired, he was formerly a wholesale grocer and produce buyer in Cochran. Their only son, Barney Wilson Hendricks, Jr., serving with the Air Transport Command, was stationed in North Africa during WW II. He graduated from the Middle Georgia College, Cochran and is a past president of the alumnae association of that institution. He received his B.S. degree in business administration from the University of Georgia in 1949; he was elected to the Beta Gamma Sigma, honorary fraternity and Alpha Tau Omega, social fraternity. Presently, he is associated with The Lenkerd Company, wholesale dealers of heavy farm implements. He is Chairman of the Commission on Education, Cochran Methodist Church, Chairman Bleckley County Chapter, American Red Cross, past president of the Cochran Lions Club, member of the Cochran Housing Authorities, the American Legion, Jaycees and a former assistant scoutmaster. He married Dorothy Carolyn Hitchcock of Moultrie, Ga., and is the father of twin daughters, Montie Maure and Margaret Hardeman Hendricks.

Emmie Elizabeth married Thomas Howard Reeves and lives in Cochran.

Lillie Lila married Andrew Jackson Thompson and lives in Cochran. Her two sons are Andrew Franklin and Kindred Hendricks Thompson who married Mattie Nell Fair and has a son, Kenny.

Hennie May Hendricks is unmarried and lives in Cochran.

Frederick Sommers Hendricks is superintendent of the Cochran Water Department. He married Emmie Lee Witherington.

Lila McZelle, youngest daughter of Cherry Elizabeth McCrea and Wilson Hendricks, was born on the family plantation eight miles north of Cochran and moved to Cochran when quite young. She received her early education at the old Ebenezer College in Cochran. This institution began in January, 1887 and at the end of the first term she was one of the ten students who made the "Honor Roll." In September, 1894 she accepted the position as art teacher at the Freddie Shipp College in Cordele, Ga. and on Dec. 29, 1895 she was married to Elijah (better known as Lige) Cook, Jr., by Rev. P. A. Jessup of Cordele. She was a member of the Cochran Baptist Church and held many offices in its auxiliaries. In 1922 she compiled a History of the Cochran Baptist WMU. She entered on Roll No. 26, Cochran Chapter No. 764, United Daughters of the Confederacy June 9, 1909 and served as president of the Cochran Chapter in 1913 and later as treasurer. Her life of service to church, town and family brought her in touch with varied groups and organizations in which she was a leader and friend. Her passing on March 12, 1938 brought sadness to a host of friends as she was known and loved by many.

The children of Lila McZelle Hendricks and Elijah Cook, Jr., were Louise Madoline (deceased), infant son (deceased), Maree Cecil (deceased), and Madge Elizabeth.

Maree Cecil married J. P. Davis, Sr., of Chipley, Ga. Their children are J. P. Davis, Jr., Lila Claire Davis, Cecil Cook Davis, and Daphne Davis.

Madge Elizabeth married T. H. Kimbrough of Chipley, Ga., son of H. B. and Eva Mobley Kimbrough of Chipley, Ga. Most of their married life has been spent in Cochran, Ga., where he is a prominent business man and she a popular young matron active in the church, civic and social activities of the city. Their only daughter, Beth Kimbrough, married Donald E. Stewart of Columbus, Ga. Their children are William Haywood Stewart, Donna Elizabeth Stewart, La Wanna Stewart, and Rodney Duane Stewart.

Submitted by:<br>
Miss Hennie May Hendricks<br>
Madge Cook Kimbrough (Mrs. T. H.)<br>
Cochran, Georgia<br>
(Members of the Hawkinsville Chapter, D.A.R.)

## THE McNAIR FAMILY OF TWIGGS COUNTY

The McNair family of Twiggs County had its roots, as had many other Twiggs County families, in Wilkinson County. Early in the nineteenth century, William C. McNair settled there and married Sarah Chapman. There were eight children of this marriage, of whom the youngest was Ezekiel, born Aug. 14, 1849.

Ezekiel farmed his share of his father's plantation when he grew up, studied medicine for one year at the University of Virginia, and graduated from the Medical School of the University of Georgia. He married Miss Lucy Ann Josephine Pope of Jones County Feb. 1, 1871. Six children were born to them, only three of whom lived beyond babyhood. These were Idus Lafayette, born Jan. 26, 1874; Wiley Pope, born May 17, 1876; and Emily Lucy, born April 11, 1884.

This family became the "McNair family of Twiggs County" about 1876 when Dr. Ezekiel moved his family to Jeffersonville so that his children could attend school, there being none very near the Wilkinson County farm. In Jeffersonville, Ezekiel continued to serve as doctor, literally to the day of his death, and to serve Jeffersonville as a participator in civic affairs. For a number of years, he had a joint office in "Sandy Bottom" with Dr. B. S. Carswell. Later he built an office next to his home and continued his practice alone. And at his side always was "Miss Jo," kind, gentle and beloved. Ezekiel died Sept. 13, 1913; Josephine, Feb. 17, 1926.

The oldest son, Idus, went on to graduate from Emory College in 1893. He returned to Jeffersonville in 1894 to become for a short time the Principal of Auburn Institute. During that short time he, as Principal, and his father, as a member of the Board of Trustees, secured as music teacher for the Institute, Miss Julia B. Hilton of Yarmouth, Nova Scotia, graduate of the New England Conservatory of Music. Idus McNair and Julia Hilton were married April 5, 1895. After several years of teaching, Idus made Macon his home and started learning the cotton business. He went overseas with the Y.M.C.A. for one year in World War I. He died in Miami, Florida, Feb. 13, 1953; Juila in Miami, Jan. 4, 1956. Of this marriage, there is one daughter, Marjorie Harris, born May 10, 1896. She is now living in New York and is a Senior Employment Manager of the New York State Employment Service.

The second son, Wiley, attended Georgia-Alabama Business College in Macon and went immediately into the cotton business. He married Penelope (Nell) Boynton of Macon on Nov. 18, 1904. Eventually Idus and Wiley joined forces with their own firm, The Spinners Cotton Company, which they operated for a number of years. Wiley died July 22, 1934; Nell, Jan. 21, 1940. Of this marriage, there is one son, Sidney Boynton, born June 2, 1913. He married Katherine Alfriend of Macon Oct. 16, 1937. Sidney served overseas two and a half years in World War II, and is now a Colonel in the Air Force Reserve. There are two children, Katherine Alfriend, born Dec. 31, 1946, and Marjorie Boynton, born March 29, 1951. Sidney is now a CPA in Macon and is a partner in the firm Clifton and McNair.

The daughter Emily (Emie) graduated from Georgia Normal and Industrial College and taught school for several years. Following that she went to the Macon Hospital for training and graduated as a trained nurse, a profession she followed for a number of years in Macon. She returned to Jeffersonville to live and on Sept. 5, 1926 married George Washington Jackson, originally of Jones County. He was killed while on duty as deputy sheriff in Jeffersonville Jan. 5, 1934. Emie died July 5, 1952. There were no children.

Submitted by: Marjorie McNair, New York City, N. Y.

## JAMES THOMAS McCOY

J. T. McCoy

James Thomas McCoy was born Dec. 27, 1838 in Washington County, near Milledgeville. He served as a soldier in the Army of the Confederacy for the duration of the War-Between-the-States. Shortly after the war, he made his most fruitful decision. He chose Mary Ann Mercer for his life companion. Mary Ann was born near Jeffersonville, Oct. 13, 1850. Left motherless at the age of ten, she was raised by a devoted uncle, Jim Harrell, and his good wife, Mary. Their marriage was blessed by one son, Andrew, three daughters, Gertrude, Florence, Mabel, all attended Auburn Institute, where their mother was educated. James and Mary Ann were determined to rear a family of the highest type of citizenship. Their children have never forgotten their efforts.

Having received his apprenticeship as a wheelwright, Tom established his own business in Jeffersonville, a carriage, wagon, harness and blacksmith shop. His business prospered from the beginning, due to his ability and conscientious dealing with all mankind. He was honored by election to the Twiggs County Board of Education, serving over twenty years, part of the time as Chairman. In this service he was deeply interested in giving to all the children the very best educational advantages. From young manhood, he was a faithful Deacon in the Baptist Church. To know

Tom and Mary Ann was to revere them. He was called to receive his greatest reward March 24, 1912. A few months later, on Nov. 27, 1912, Mary Ann joined him in death.

Submitted by: L. L. Lowe

## ISAAC NEWTON MAXWELL

"Isaac Newton Maxwell, merchant and planter, Danville, Twiggs County, Georgia, is clearly entitled to representation in this volume. From poverty and obscurity as a young man he was destined to take a position both financially and socially among the best men of his county. His people were from the old tarheel state, where his father, Uriah, was born in 1806, the son of William Maxwell, he being of Irish-Swiss extraction. Uriah married Mary A. Walkins and moved to Twiggs County (near Dry Branch, Ga.) where a family of eight children were reared. A daughter and three sons died in youth, the latter during the War, either in battle bravely defending their Southland, or of disease contacted in the Service. The last surviving children were: Mrs. Lucinda Kennington, Charity, Susan and Isaac. The last named was born Sept. 22, 1847. The War found him still in his "teens" with a limited education, but loyal to his section, and anxious to do battle for an idea. He became a member of Captain B. D. Lusman's Company, which went out from Macon, and served faithfully to the end of the War. With naught but his two hands and a willing heart, in 1865, he began the new battle, this time with the world; soon he won the victory. As a tiller of the soil on rented land, then as overseer of the large plantation of D. M. Hughes, and subsequently as an owner himself, he continued to prosper, reared and educated an interesting family. He added merchandising to his farming interests in 1890, which venture met with success. He was in politics, a Democrat, and in faith, a Baptist. Isaac was a great reader of good literature and added to the limited education received in his youth. In 1865 Mr. Maxwell was joined in matrimony to Mary J. Champion, to whom was born the following children: Lula (Mrs. J. C. Johnston), Leona, John T., Harvey H., Oscar N. and Edgar D. Maxwell.

He was Chairman of the Board of Commissioners in 1902 when the present Courthouse in Jeffersonville was erected; served in the Georgia House of Representatives from Twiggs County in 1905 and 1906."
Reference: Prepared sketch by Dr. J. C. Solomon, 1936.

Submitted by: E. D. Maxwell

## ALEXANDER NELSON—PIONEER

Alexander Nelson lived in Twiggs County, Ga. from 1812 until the time he died.

He joined the Stone Creek Baptist Church near Dry Branch, Ga. in 1812, and applied for "letters of dismissal" for himself and wife Sarah, daughter of Joseph Collins (Rev. Sol.) in Oct., 1831. He was treasurer for many years, and served on committees to "cite the erring members" on numerous occasions. Alexander Nelson served as one of the spies employed by Major Patton, Jones Co., Fort Pickney—in the Fifth Regiment on the Frontiers of Jones Co. in pursuance of orders from Lt. Col. William Jones, Aug., 1813. Each man furnished his own horse, arms, and provision. (Reference: "Georgia Military Records 1779-1814" by Hays, Page 188).

Alexander Nelson owned many hundreds of acres of land in Twiggs, Jones & Baldwin counties where they converged. He was a taxpayer in Baldwin County in 1808.

The comodius 11-room Nelson home built before 1830, crowns the top of a high hill overlooking acres of pine forest, is one of the oldest houses in Twiggs County. Nearby is the walled Nelson Cemetery where Alexander and Sarah sleep under a native stone marker, surrounded by more than 40 of their descendants. The slaves were buried outside of the walled cemetery.

Lumber and farming interests occupied the Alexander Nelson family in early times—later Kaolin mines were developed on this property which is still owned by descendants of a son John Alexander Nelson, who served two terms in the State Legislature from Twiggs County.

The children of Alexander and Sarah (Collins) Nelson were:
Ruth, born 1802, married Thomas Simeon Chappel, both buried in Nelson Cemetery.
Betsy, married Archibald Spears (lost three sons in the War-Betwen-the-States"), both buried in Alvarado, Texas.
Sarah, married_____ Green and had, issue: Sally and a son.
John Alexander, born 1807, married (1st) Martha F. Eppes, (2nd) Mancy H. Smith, all buried in Nelson Cemetery.
William, born 1809, married (1st) Elizabeth Hoskins (the mother of all his children), (2nd) Cornelia C. DeLoach, William and Elizabeth H. Nelson are buried in Abberville, Lafayette County, Miss.
Mary Jane, married Dr. Rudolphas McEwin Williams (who died in the War-Between-the-States). Mary Jane is buried in Barnesville, Ga.
Jack, married and raised a large family in Meridian, Miss.
Research has been done by a descendant of William and Elizabeth (Hoskins) Nelson whose lineage is proven—namely—
William and Elizabeth (Hoskins) Nelson had issue:
Alexander, born March 12, 1834, Georgia—died unmarried Oct. 22, 1855, Choctaw County, Ala., buried in Christopher Chapel Cemetery.
Nancy, married John Goins
Sarah, married Tobe Beall
George Washington, born June 18, 1840, Georgia—married Laura Elizabeth Miller Dec. 14, 1865, Choctaw County, Ala.—died 1918, Caperville, Tenn.
Mary Lou, born Georgia, married John Roberts
William C., born Georgia, married Dora Walton
Alice, born Georgia, married (1st) Frank Cooper, (2nd) Ed. Hussey
John Albert, born Alabama, married Mary Houston
Felix, born Alabama, married Eunice Burt
George W. and Laura M. Nelson had Issue:
A.  William Miller, born Dec. 1, 1866, Choctaw County, Ala., married Nov. 22, 1893 (LaFayette County, Mississippi) Susan Elizabeth Ferrell, died March 30, 1935, Holly Springs, Miss.—had Issue:
Benjamin Ferrell, born Nov. 6, 1894 in Marshall County, Miss.—married Nov. 17, 1928, Elizabeth Bennett
Edward Dale, born Jan. 17, 1897 in Marshall County, Miss.—married Feb. 12, 1927, Mable McLendon
William Miller, Jr., born Aug. 18, 1899 in Marshall County, Miss.—married Jan. 16, 1924, Elma Louise Foster
Frank Wall, born May 22, 1902 in Marshall County, Miss.—married Jan. 19, 1924, Betty Freid
Ivy Mitchell, born Jan. 19, 1905 in Marshall County, Miss.
Lalla Elizabeth, born Feb. 4, 1910 in Marshall County, Miss.—married William Chester Briggs
George Azmond, born Dec. 6, 1912 in Marshall County, Miss.—married March 27, 1937, Elizabeth Whitson.
B.  Azmond A., died unmarried
C.  Walter A., died aged 5 years
D.  Carrie E., died aged 3 years

E. Minnie Gertrude, born Aug. 7, 1875, married Perino Colbert and had Issue. Miss Jessie Rice, a descendant of John Alex. Nelson, and Mrs. Eleanor Davis McSwain of Macon, Ga., assisted Mrs. William Miller Nelson in compiling the Alex. Nelson genealogy. References used were, Bible, tombstones, U. S. Census, Court Records, family knowledge, and "Stone Creek" Baptist Church minute book.

Research by: Mrs. William Miller Nelson, 212 Grand Ave., Yazoo City, Miss.

## WILLIAM O'DANIEL

William O'Daniel, M.D.

"Well-known to the medical profession of Georgia as a man and physician, for his good qualities and high mental attainments, is Dr. William O'Daniel, of Twiggs County. He was born May 2, 1839, in that county, and has always lived there, excepting four years' residence in Atlanta, when holding a public position. His grandfather was born in Ireland and settled in Georgia when Daniel O'Daniel, his father, was born. Daniel O'Daniel lived all his life in Twiggs County, dying there, aged sixty-five years. Dr. O'Daniel received his education in the "old field" schools of Twiggs County, and at Auburn Institute, taught by James E. Crosland, located near his home. He then taught several years in Marion Academy in Twiggs County.

In 1862 he laid down the ruler and the rod and enlisted in the Confederate service as a noncommissioned officer in the commissary department, in Col. D. G. Hughes' regiment. After the war he continued the study of medicine, which he had begun when officiating as an educational instructor, and in 1866 was graduated from the Atlanta Medical College. He returned to his old home in Twiggs County, where he has since practiced his profession. Dr. O'Daniel is a member of the State Medical Association, of which he is ex-president; a member of the American Medical Association, of the Tri-state (Georgia, Alabama and Tennessee) Medical Association, member of the National Association of Railway Surgeons, was a member of the Ninth International Medical Congress, and was a delegate from Georgia in 1893 to the Pan-American Medical Congress, which met in Washington, D. C. He has frequently been a delegate from Georgia to the meetings of the American Medical Association, and is a member of the Macon Medical Association.

Dr. O'Daniel has been a frequent contributor to medical journals, principally the *Atlanta Medical and Surgical Journal,* and has read many valuable papers before the State Medical Association. He received the honorary degree of A. M. some years ago from Emory College of Oxford, Ga., and the degree of M. D. from the medical department of the University of Georgia, located at Augusta, and the honorary degree of M. D. from the Kentucky School of Medicine in 1885.

Dr. O'Daniel for many years solicited by friends to permit his name to be used for public office, always declined, but finally gave in in 1875, when he was elected State Senator from the Twenty-first Senatorial District, serving during the sessions of 1875-76-77. He also served two years as Clerk of the Superior Court of Twiggs County. In April, 1891, Dr. O'Daniel was appointed by Gov. Northen principal physician to the state penitentiary, which position he held until the spring of 1895, when he resigned and returned to his farm. The compliment of his selection was of the dignity of an honor, as there were a number of candidates for the position. Dr. O'Daniel gave an excellent administration, his wide experience and professional skill, together with his kind nature, enabling him to effect several reforms which have long been commended by humanitarians and the national prison reform congress. He is a Knight Templar Mason and for many years was Worshipful Master of Twiggs Lodge No. 164, F.&A.M. He also belongs to Constantine Chapter No. 4, Royal Arch Masons, and St. Omar Commandery No. 2, Knight Templars. He is a steward of Beech Spring Methodist Church in Twiggs County.

Dr. O'Daniel was wedded Nov. 4, 1860, to Elizabeth M. Land, daughter of Henry Land, a leading farmer of Twiggs County, and to them were born two sons and two daughters, who now survive. His sons are Dr. Mark H. O'Daniel, of Macon, who was for eight years assistant physician in the insane asylum at Milledgeville, and Dr. William O'Daniel, who succeeded his brother to the place mentioned. His daughter is Miss Mollie L., who was graduated from the Wesleyan Female College at Macon. A fine country residence is the home of this eminent citizen and physician who, when desirous of freeing himself from the exactions of a public career, can find retirement by his fireside and the enjoyment of all the pleasures and contentment of a happy domestic life."

The above information was copied from *Memoirs of Georgia,* by Knight. evidently written during the lifetime of Dr. O'Daniel. Following is additional information submitted by the undersigned, who knew the family.—Mattie, also a daughter of Dr. William O'Daniel, was a graduate of Wesleyan College and was married to Judge C. C. Smith of Hawkinsville, Ga. Children born to this union: Clara Crisp, died young; C. C. "Cap". "Cap" was married to Evelyn Slocum of Sumter County, Ga. Issue: Sheffield.

    Submitted by: O. T. Chapman, Jeffersonville, Ga. and Cornelia Johnston McCormick, (Mrs. J. T.), Dry Branch, Ga.

## PAUL FAMILY

In the early 18th Century a family by name of Paul migrated from North Carolina and settled in Jones County, Ga., near what is now Wayside. Two of the brothers of this family, John W. Paul and Robert Paul, journeyed further south and settled in the Bluff District of Twiggs County. Robert Paul, his wife and the entire family have long since passed on and their bodies appropriately marked with gravestones—some still legible—lie in the cemetery at old Richland Church.

On Sherman's notorious march through Georgia, the Bob Paul home was directly in his path and the main house and barns sacked and burned, stock killed and everything laid waste. A small home was rebuilt and occupied until about the turn of the century when death took the last member of the family.

John W. Paul settled about two miles north of Robert and created quite a homestead for those early primitive days, maintaining a fine farm and wonderful orchard together with cattle and livestock. He married Sarah Lucretia Taukersley, a member of a well known and gentle family. To them were born several children: Alice, Sally, Julia, Hugh and John William Paul, Jr., all living to maturity, each one marrying and raising a family with the exception of Julia. She had no family.

John William Paul, Jr. was married in 1881 to Sally Lucretia Land and they settled in a beautiful oak grove only about a mile from the old Paul place. This family grew to be quite large with nine girls and boys reaching maturity. The home came to be known as "Fair Oaks" and was near Friendship Baptist Church. John Paul, Jr. and his wife, Sally, were known far and near for their neighborliness and hospitality. Mr. Paul always kept the finest of hunting dogs and was quite a hunter, providing much game for his table which was always set bountifully for anyone who cared to visit "Fair Oaks" and they were many. The farm surrounding the homesite was one of the finest in Twiggs County and abounded in the finest of fruits and vegetables at all seasons of the year. The sugar cane syrup made by Mr. Paul was a much sought after commodity, as were his hickory smoked hams.

The children of John and Sally Paul are as follows: James Land, buried in Jacksonville, Fla.; Lulye Maye; Wiley Price, buried in the cemetery at Friendship Church; Margaret; Oscar; Emma Land; Roy Adams; Evelyn Turpin; John William Paul, II.

The bodies of John W. Paul, Jr. and Sally lie in the cemetery at Friendship Baptist Church, he having passed on in 1927 and Sally being laid to rest beside him in 1958.

Submitted by: Oscar Paul, Macon, Ga.

## THE POPE FAMILY

Among the early settlers of Twiggs County, was Jesse Pope, born in Virginia Nov. 5, 1791, of English descent. His wife, Elizabeth Disharoon, was born in North Carolina Sept. 12, 1796. Her father was William Disharoon.

Jesse Pope was in the War of 1812. He volunteered at Snow Hill, Green County, N. C., July 15, 1813, and was honorably discharged at Fort Hampton, Cartwright County, N. C., January 15, 1814.

He married Elizabeth Nov. 28, 1814, and they moved to Twiggs County in the early part of 1816, bringing their first child and only daughter, Winifred, who was born in North Carolina. They joined Old Richland Baptist Church, by letter, the same year and, according to records, he later moved his letter to Bersheba Baptist Church, where he was appointed a Deacon. They had ten boys, two of whom died in infancy. All of their boys were born in Twiggs County. Seven of them became Confederate soldiers. Redman, Turner, and Reuben lost their lives in the service.

Their children were Winifred, John Miller, Redding and Redmond, the last named being twins, Turner, David Bynum, Reuben, and Benjamin Franklin. Jesse Pope was on the Twiggs County Tax Digest, 1818-1836. He moved with his family to Pulaski County in 1846.

The son, Redding Pope, was a Baptist minister of great spiritual power and convictions, and contributed much to the spiritual life of his community. Pope's church, of lower Pulaski County near Pineview, Ga., was named in his honor.

A great-grandson, James Pinckney Pope, was for two terms, mayor of Boise, Idaho, and was elected to the United States Senate from Idaho. After serving one term in the Senate, he was appointed by President Roosevelt a director of T.V.A., when he moved to Knoxville, Tenn. and served more than twelve years.

>Contributed by: Ex-Senator James Pinckney Pope (grandson of Reuben Pope), Knoxville, Tenn., and Mrs. Elizabeth Pope Causey (granddaughter of Redmond Pope), Duncan Ave., Macon, Ga.

## RUSSELL FLOYD READ

Russell Floyd Read

Russell Floyd Read was born at Read's Station, Twiggs County, Ga., Sept. 6, 1844, the son of Mary Bridges and William Humphrey Read. She was born in Wilkinson County, Ga., 1805, died 1851, buried in Old Ogletree Cemetery, Twiggs County. William Humphrey Read was born in North Carolina March 3, 1799, died Oct. 30, 1870, buried in Read Family Cemetery, Twiggs County. He was educated as a medical doctor but after several years of practice, became a cotton planter. As early as 1825, he operated a grist mill on Stone Creek. He had six sons in the Confederate Army, four of whom gave their lives.

One of his sons, Russell Floyd Read, joined Company G, 48th Regiment, Georgia Infantry, Wright's Brigade, Longstreet's Corp. At the Battle of Gettysburg, he lost his right arm and was taken prisoner. He was exchanged at City Point, Va. After his discharge, he attended Hodge's Institute at Hawkinsville. There he joined the Baptist Church and was baptized by Rev. George R. McCall.

On May 23, 1871, he married Mary Jane Phillips, who was born March 6, 1852, Twiggs County, died March 29, 1930, Macon, Ga., buried Read Cemetery. She was the daughter of Henry Haywood Phillips (Confederate soldier) and Martha Catherine Durden Phillips, both members of pioneer Twiggs County families. As a young man, Russell Floyd Read taught a private school. Although his principal interest was farming, he served as County Tax Receiver for several terms.

For many years he was a member of Stone Creek Church, however, when Friendship Church was formed, he joined as a charter member and served on the official board until his death June 3, 1904. He is buried in the Read Cemetery which is near the old Read homesite about one mile east of Read's Station and near the Cochran highway.

Children of Russell Floyd Read and his wife: Mary Wilkes, William Floyd, Martha Lorena, Bessie Julia, born May 23, 1884, Twiggs County, married Herschel Johnston Vaughn, John Gordon, and Russell Floyd.

Submitted by: Bessie J. Read Vaughn (Mrs. H. J.), 154 Oakridge Ave., Macon, Ga.

## READ GENEALOGY

(Read Cemetery, located near Read's Station, Twiggs County, Ga.)
Before William Humphrey Read started this cemetery, the family was interred at Ogletree Marsh.
William Humphrey Read 1799-1870
William Hamilton Read 1833-1864, son of William Humphrey, husband of Virginia
    Virginia A. Robutson
Julia Ann Read (two infants) 1834-1879, daughter of William Humphrey, wife of
    Tilmon S. Denson and John Phillips
Lucinda Rebecca Read (and infant) 1834-?, daughter of William Humphrey, wife
    of Wiley M. Pearce
William Joseph Colquitt Read 1871-1895, son of Benjamine Franklin Read and Anna
    Hinson
Four infants of Louisa Ellen Read and John Horne
Benjamine Franklin Read 1830-1893, son of William Humphrey, husband of Georgia
    Blow and Anna Hinson
George Munroe Read 1848-1888, son of William Humphrey, husband of Willis Jeffers
Russell Floyd Read 1844-1904, son of William Humphrey, husband of Mary Jane
    Phillips
Mary Jane Phillips 1851-1930, wife of Russell Floyd, daughter of Henry Heywood Phillips and Martha Katherine Durden
Alpheus LaFayette Read 1872-?, infant son of Russell Floyd Read
Katherine Belmont Read 1877-?, infant daughter of Russell Floyd Read
William Floyd Read 1879-1916, son of Russell Floyd Read
Mary Wilkes Read 1875-1926, daughter of Russell Floyd Read, wife of Lowry Rice; Lowry Rice died 1930, husband of Mary Wilkes Read.

*Sons of William Humphrey Read who served in the Civil Wars*
1. Alpheus LaFayete Read—killed, place of burial unknown. Melvina E. Solomon, wife.
2. John Forsyth Read—died, buried in Culpepper, Va., Nov. 9, 1861
3. Joseph Alexander Read—died, buried in Richmond, Va., Dec. 13, 1862
4. William Hamilton Read—died from wound while home on furlough, Sept. 28, 1864. Virginia A. Robutson, wife
5. Russell Floyd Read—lost right arm at Gettysburg
6. Benjamine Franklin Read—received head wound.

John Gordon Read (son of Russell Floyd) June 5, 1888-May 29, 1951. Married
    Lillie Bell Petty, May 29, 1913. Children:
        John Gordon, March 30, 1914-April 15, 1914
        Floyd Robbie, March 16, 1916
        Joan, December 14, 1923

Floyd married Elizabeth Graham Dec. 16, 1942. Daughter Currie born April 13, 1946. Second marriage, Mary Lou Shouper Dec., 1951. Daughter Lou born March 19, 1952.

Joan married James Robert Atwater April 24, 1941
    Daughter Gail Read born Feb. 16, 1942

Son James Robert born April 16, 1951.
Martha Lorena Read, daughter of Russell Floyd Read, married Charles Albert Harris, Sept. 29, 1901:
    William Floyd Harris, Nov. 3, 1902
    Charles Albert, Jr., March 27, 1911
    Kenneth Richard, Oct. 10, 1913
William Floyd Harris married Anna Johnson Owens of Tennessee
    William Floyd Harris, Jr.    1925-1925
    Anne Owens    1927-1928
    Betty Jean    1928
    Charles Richard    1933-1933
Charles Albert Harris, Jr., married Rita Frances Delaney of Massachusetts
    Ellen Lawton Harris
Kenneth Richard Harris married Ruth Roland Mahone of Macon
    Martha Ruth Harris
Betty Jean Harris, only daughter of William Floyd and Anna Johnson, married Joseph Patrick McGoldrick, Jr. Children:
    Joseph Patrick McGoldrick, III    1950
    Mary Eugenia    1951
    William Robert    1952
    Phillip Michael    1955
    Submitted by: Mrs. Martha Read Harris, 186 Parkwood, Macon, Ga.

## SAULS

Theophalaus Sauls, Sr. was married to a Miss Hart and they settled near the present location of Prospect Church. The land for a school house and Prospect Church was given by him. Their children were Cebron Sauls, Kinchen Sauls, Theophalaus, Jr., Anne, Penny, and Nettie. Theophalaus Sauls, Jr. married a second time; his wife's first name was Abbie; her surname is unknown to this writer. To this marriage was born one son, Martin Sauls.
    Cebron Sauls, wife unknown.
    Kinchen Sauls was married to a Miss Susan DeShazer, school teacher of this area.
    Theophalus Sauls, Jr., married Martha Jane Floyd.
    Anne Sauls, married William Pardon.
    Penny Sauls, married Henry Manning.
    Nettie Sauls, married Sam Berryhill.
    Martin Sauls, wife unknown; children were Milton, Henry, Warren.
                  By: John H. Holliday, Jeffersonville, Ga.

## DUDLEY HUGHES SHANNON

Dudley Hughes Shannon, the youngest child of Virginia Faulk Shannon and John Carey Shannon, was born in Jeffersonville, Ga., Sept. 23, 1894.
He attended school here, and later Gordon Military College at Barnesville. Following this, he entered banking business and was employed in this capacity when he enlisted for duty in World War I. He served approximately two years. He is a member of the Jeffersonville Baptist Church, a Mason and a Shriner.
On Jan. 15, 1920 he was married to Miss Annie Johnson Lanier of Bartow, Ga. They have one daughter, Leonora Shannon Hart (Mrs. Angus), and one granddaughter, Annie Shannon Hart.
June 1, 1933, "Dud" Shannon was appointed Deputy U. S. Marshal for the Middle District of Georgia. Later he served as U. S. Marshal.
During his term of office it was said of him that he never lost an opportunity

to help a man back to the right track.

After twenty-three years of faithful and efficient service he retired. His interest remains keen in any phase of progress and upbuilding, especially in this community.

Submitted by: Mrs. Laurie Shannon Boyd, Jeffersonville, Ga.

## JAMES DOUGLAS SHANNON

James D. Shannon was born in Twiggs County in the Old Marion Community, then the county seat, on June 24, 1888. He was the son of James Carey and Virginia Faulk Shannon. His mother died when he was a child, leaving him and several brothers and sisters. The family moved to Jeffersonville with the other early settlers of this community. Jeffersonville then became the county seat of Twiggs County.

Shannon attended Twiggs County public schools and later attended Mercer University in Macon, Ga., where he received his L.L.B. degree in 1910. He was admitted to the Bar in 1910 and became a practicing attorney.

He became active in politics when he finished college. He is a Democrat. He was first elected to the Georgia House of Representatives in 1915. In 1917 he fought for the Hughes Vocational Act. In 1937-38 he was Senator from the 21st District. During this time he served on 16 committees. He sponsored, fought for and aided in the passing of the Cancer Control Bill. He favored a bill to boost pay for school teachers. He was the author and composer of a bill permitting women to serve on juries and a bill permitting women to practice law. He was Chairman of the Georgia House Committee on Corporations, Chairman of Special Judiciary of the House, and Chairman of the General Judiciary of the Senate. He served four terms in the House of Representatives and two terms in the State Senate of Georgia.

Other positions he has held are: Chairman of the Board of Trustees of Twiggs High School for over twenty years, County Attorney, Clerk of County Commissioners, and County School Superintendent for seven years.

One of the latest achievements of James D. Shannon is that he was highly instrumental in getting the bridge across the Ocmulgee River between Twiggs and Houston Counties.

In June, 1920, James D. Shannon married Lily Eolyne Wall, daughter of Dr. Jasper MacArthur Wall and Tussie Bennett Wall. They have three children, all in life: James D., Jr., Mary Eolyne and Laurie Virginia Shannon.

James D. Shannon, Jr. served as a captain in the Eighth Air Force during World War II. He is now a captain with Eastern Air Lines. He was married to Frances Muse in August, 1947, and to this union was born four children: James Douglas, III, Nancy Eolyne, Frances Virginia, and Dudley Hughes, II.

Mary Eolyne was married to Thorborn Ross Tolleson, with the Tol. son Lumber and Supply Company in Perry, Ga., in October, 1948. To this union was born four children: Laurie Ann, Gorgelle McKibbon, Mary Shannon, and Thorborn Ross, Jr.

Laurie Virginia married Ferdinand Vogt Kay, to be a practicing medical physician in the forthcoming year, in June, 1952. To this union has been born one child, Lilly Shannon.

James D. Shannon is still an active lawyer. His college fraternity is A.T.O. He is a W. O. W. member of the Knights of Pythias, Mason and Alshiah Shriner.

He is a member of the First Baptist Church of Jeffersonville, where he is on the Board of Deacons and teacher of Men's Bible Class in Sunday School.

Submitted by: Mrs. Frances Shannon, 1214 Young Drive, College Park, Ga.

(J. D. Shannon deceased since sketch was submitted.)

## JOHN CAREY SHANNON

John Carey Shannon, one of the most prominent men of this section, was born in Columbia, Mo., July 22, 1853. He was the son of Frances Carey Moore of Athens, Ga., and James Shannon.

His father came to America in 1821, after he was graduated from the Royal Institute of Belfast to take charge of a school at Sunbury, Ga. During his career as an educator, he served as president of Richmond Academy at Augusta, State University of Louisiana, Bacon College at Harrodsburg, Ky., University of Mo., and Christian University, now known as Culver Stockton, and was Prof. of ancient languages at Franklin College which later became the University of Georgia.

After the death of his parents, Carey Shannon spent several years with relatives. Mr. and Mrs. Daniel Hughes in Twiggs County, he returned to Columbia to work in the office of his brother, Dr. Richard D. Shannon, who was State Supt. of Schools.

Coming back to Georgia he was married to Virginia Faulk, daughter of William and Virginia Solomon Faulk. Their home was Laurel Hill, at Marion. Eight children were born to this union: John Carey, Ethel Belmont, William Faulk, Virginia, James Douglas, Laurie, Mary Lou and Dudley Hughes.

About 1891 he built a home in Jeffersonville where he spent the remainder of his life. Losing his wife in March, 1896, he later married her sister, Miss Mary Lou Faulk, who survived him four years. The home is now occupied by his two daughters, Mrs. R. I. Butler (Ethel) and Mrs. J. M. Boyd (Laurie).

Mr. Shannon was a member of the Christian Church. A man whose life was filled with noble deeds prompted by a broad understanding and love of his fellowman. He was the first mayor of Jeffersonville, accepting no pay for his services. In the welfare of his town and county, and its advancement, he was actively interested.

He died December, 1929.

Submitted by: Mrs. Laurie Shannon Boyd, Jeffersonville, Ga.

## DR. JOHN G. SLAPPEY

Dr. John G. Slappey's life was spent in Twiggs County, Ga. He was a member of the Methodist Church, serving as a Steward, with tender faithfulness, he discharged every duty. With his medical skill he ministered to the sick and always carried in his heart and mind thoughts of the public good.

Dr. Slappey was born Feb. 26, 1853, died June 27, 1932. He was graduated from Atlanta Medical College in 1875. He was married to Annie Carter, Dec. 26, 1876. She died Nov. 23, 1892. Children: Mark Fred, born July 1, 1881, died Aug., 1950; Henry Carter, born Dec. 28, 1883, died 1898; John George, Jr., born Sept. 21, 1890.

John George Slappey, M.D., married March 15, 1893 Mary Coffee, born April 10, 1869, died July 11, 1951. Children: Mary Annie, born June 7, 1894; Rebecca Georgia, born Aug. 6, 1896; Robert Coffee, born Aug. 21, 1898; Joshua Wimberly, born Jan. 13, 1901; Nancy Exum, born March 3, 1905; Peter Harrison, born Dec. 12, 1907.

Submitted by: Rosa L. Faulk Slappey (Mrs. J. G.), Jeffersonville, Ga.

## BIOGRAPHIES OF DR. AND MRS. JAMES CARY SOLOMON

The history of any county is, by its very nature, wholly dependent upon the people who lived in it, their dreams and aspirations, their individual efforts in building a community in which to rear their familes, and their ability to organize and support one another in concerted action. Because this is especially true of

Twiggs County, which is limited by size, and which is predominantly rural in its population, the people of each generation who were outstanding leaders, really make its history.

The biographies of Dr. and Mrs. J. C. Solomon, who spent most of their lives in Twiggs County, are inescapably linked with every facet of the county's growth. Its political life, its agricultural and educational problems, its church and spiritual life—all were affected by the fine schoarship of Dr. Solomon, by his impassioned oratory, and by the subtle humor which were woven into the pattern of day by day living of the two parents of a fine family. As an author Dr. Solomon reached many, not only in Twiggs County, but also outside his home county; as an inspired preacher he had a direct grip upon the spiritual lives of thousands of people; but as a friend and neighbor he most gloriously lived his faith and convictions among the people whom he knew and loved best. He said in "A Love Letter to Twiggs County", published in the New Era in Jeffersonville, Ga., Jan. 10, 1941, "To The Dear People of Twiggs County:

The year 1940 was not all easy sailing. There were tough places in the channels—some snags and whirlpools and other obstacles. However, taking it all in all, it has been a good old year. We have had more smiles than tears, more hopes than fears, more laughter than scorn.—We have a good people, a good county, scores and hundreds of persons whose veins are full of the milk of human kindness, men and women who know how to forgive and forget, ladies and gentlemen of the sweetest spirit. So let us bear no malice in our hearts, nor cherish revenge against another, but with clean hands and pure hearts let us leave the old year and step into the new with gratitude to God, with kind words on our lips for the friendless, with love and sympathy for the sorrowing, and with prayers for the lost. Here's my hand and heart for you all, and for all whom you hold dear."

Dr. James Cary Solomon was born Jan. 28, 1861, in Twiggs County on the Solomon homestead near Old Marion, the former county seat, a place long noted for the warm southern hospitality that reigned in its cultured homes. He was the son of the late Hon. Wm. L. Solomon and Avarilla E. Fitzpatrick, representing two of the oldest and most prominent families in Georgia. His primary education was obtained principally in Marion Academy. His uncle, the Hon. B. S. Fitzpatrick, who for fifty years was school Superintendent of Twiggs County, was his instructor for a large part of his early school life. While quite young he was graduated from Mercer University, Macon, Ga., with an A.B. degree and later received both an A.M. and an honorary D.D. degree from this institution. After receiving his literary education at Mercer he studiesd at the Atlanta Medical College, where he was given his M.D. degree. He was graduated in medicine with honors and was valedictorian of his class. His father equipped an office for him on his plantation in Twiggs County, where he established his first medical practice, and where he travelled by horse and buggy over the entire county as a country doctor. Soon he extended his practice to Houston County, where his uncle, Mr. Erwin Dennard, and his grandmother, Mrs. Frances Dennard, and many other relatives lived. It was while he practiced medicine here that he met Miss Maggie Tharpe, whom he soon married. Like her husband she was reared on a lovely southern plantation. She was educated with her cousins by governesses. A log cabin school house was erected between the plantation of her father and that of her uncle, Mr. Wm. Tharpe, for the purpose of educating the children of their two families. Each governess lived six months in one house and six months in the other. Mrs. Solomon's education was finished at Houston Female College in Perry, Ga. After Dr. and Mrs. Solomon were married they came back to the home of Dr. Solomon's parents to live. It was here the two eldest daughters, Maggie and Janie, were born.

Dr. Solomon's interest in religion had been life-long. As a boy he gave his heart

James C. Solomon, M.D. & D.D.

Mrs. Maggie Tharpe (J. C.) Solomon

to God and united with the Stone Creek Baptist Church in Twiggs County under the pastorate of the Reverend P. W. Edge. Later, even while practicing medicine, he was ordained to the ministry in Old Richland Church near the plantation home of his parents, and it is interesting that he ended his active ministry as pastor of Stone Creek Church where he was baptized.

Following his ordination, he soon moved to Flovilla, Ga., where he continued with his practice of medicine, but filled pulpits in both Flovilla and Indian Springs. Here two other daughters, Esther and Mary, were born. The first bereavement of the family came with the death of little four month's old Mary. At about this time Dr. Solomon made his important decision to give up the practice of medicine and to devote his entire life to the ministry. His full time pastorate after this decision was in Macon, Ga. It was here that another daughter, Ruth, was born. After four happy, useful years in Macon, he accepted a call to the First Baptist Church in Dublin, Ga., where his youngest daughter, Jimmie, was born.

Dr. Solomon's call to an Atlanta pastorate led to his making Atlanta his residence for nearly twenty years. It was here that he became Superintendent of the Georgia Anti-Saloon League and that he did some of his most vigorous and far-reaching work, affecting all of Georgia and the nation. It was mainly due to his efforts that the victory was won toward making Georgia a dry state. Here he got to know the Georgia political leaders; and his pen was continually ready to champion the cause of prohibition and to oppose its repeal both locally and nationally. He was frequently invited to speak in other states when prohibition became a national political issue.

His interests were always many and varied. Dr. Solomon was for many years on the Board of Trustees of Mercer University and of Bessie Tift College; and for a year or more he served as Dean of Cox College in College Park, Ga. He continued to study through the years along denominational lines. He took several courses at Northfield, Mass., and spent one summer studying at the University of Chicago. Later he was elected, in 1936, as Vice-President of the Georgia Baptist Convention; and he was a speaker at a Baptist Convention in Havana, Cuba.

In May of 1917, Dr. and Mrs. Solomon lost their large, beautiful home during the great Atlanta conflagration, which destroyed 73 city blocks and 1,938 homes. The financial loss to the Solomon family was great. But was nothing to compare with the loss of precious keepsakes and possessions. Among the treasured possessions destroyed were the trousseaux of two of the daughters, Esther and Ruth. The spirit with which Dr. and Mrs. Solomon carried on in the face of such losses may be found in an article that he wrote on the "Inner Tragedies of the Great Atlanta Fire" for the Christian Index. It was after this great destructive fire that Dr. and Mrs. Solomon moved back to their beloved Twiggs County, where they spent their declining years.

The period of Dr. Solomon's greatest literary production was after his return to Twiggs County. Here he had published his book of poems, "Lights and Shadows", and some of his other books, "The Bugle's Blast", "St. Pierre's Reign of Fire", "Johannes, or the Other Boy Born in Bethlehem", all of which had religious bearing. The story, "The Deep South", which is a historical novel about Twiggs County, was never formally published, but has been typed and bound and is in the possession of the family.

From 1926—1936 Dr. Solomon served as moderator of the Ebenezer Association. He was a frequent contributor to the Christian Index and a voluminous writer to the Twiggs County paper and to the Macon Telegraph. He never failed to express himself during this era when national political policies became injurious to the local farmer, and he never failed to commend or to condemn political frieinds when he took issue with them on practical matters.

His friends gave him an eight weeks' trip to Europe because of his achievements in helping the state of Georgia to become dry. In this connection he was asked by the editor of the Twiggs County paper, "The New Era" to write for publication his travelog and experiences on his trip. These letters to his home paper were later published in booklet form at the request of Dr. Arch C. Cree, a prominent Baptist minister and conductor of the tour. Dr. Solomon's writing continued up to the time of his death; and as county historian, he was collecting material for the History of Twiggs County which he had hoped to see published.

As much as he loved his church, his county, his state, and his nation, it was primarily in his love for his friends and his family that his life really unfolded. The beautiful and inspirational ideals of Dr. and Mrs. Solomon have been carried out in the lives and work and achievements of their five daughters, their four grandchildren and their many great-grandchildren. The fine Christian spirit and the thirst for knowledge instilled in them in their Twiggs County home can never die. Truly the echoes from the lives of these consecrated parents will "roll from soul to soul, and grow forever and forever".

The two eldest daughters, Maggie and Janie, spent most of their lives as prominent educators in the Atlanta Public Schools. In addition to her work as teacher and as an elementary school principal, Maggie served as supervisor of the Atlanta Elementary Schools and as principal of Girls High School. She also taught for ten summers at the University of Georgia. For many years Janie was supervisor of Physical Education in the Atlanta Public Schools. After receiving their A.B. and their M.A. degrees Maggie and Janie did post graduate work at the University of Wisconsin, Columbia University and at Harvard University. Esther, after finishing her work at Girls High School in Atlanta, spent many years both at college and in art centers studying art. She and her husband, Mr. Samuel Emory Young, have in their home in Atlanta many of her beautiful pictures and much of her lovely hand painted china. Ruth received a diploma from the Atlanta Normal Training School and also a diploma in music. After one year's work as a beloved primary teacher in Atlanta she married General Letcher O. Grice. Jimmie, the youngest daughter, after being graduated at an Atlanta Business College and after attending the University of Utah, was for several years a most popular and successful secretary in the Atlanta Public Schools.

Dr. and Mrs. Solomon inspired their four grandchildren to be good students. Margaret Young was graduated at the University of Georgia and did post graduate work at Emory University. Sharpe Grice is a young Major who was graduated at West Point. Margaret Ruth Grice and James Grice both received their degrees at the University of Utah.

All of Dr. and Mrs. Solomon's children and grandchildren have shown much of the beautiful Christian spirit that had been instilled in them around the fireside in Twiggs County. Dr. and Mrs. Solomon celebrated their golden wedding anniversary in their country home surrounded by their family and by their devoted friends and relatives in "dear old Twiggs".

In a letter of birthday greeting written to Dr. Solomon on Feb. 3, 1944, Dr. Spright Dowell, President of Mercer University, said: . . . "What a joy it is to recite to you my personal admiration of the record of your long, fruitful, distinguished, and glorious life as a good minister of Jesus Christ! You have received your crown on this earth from scores of admiring friends and you are ready for the real experience of translation that awaits the just made perfect. . . . You have made an imperishable contribution to mankind and you will be greeted when you say good-bye here with the welcome from the Lord of Life, 'Well done, thou good and faithful servant, enter into the joy of Thy Lord' ".

Dr. Solomon died June 24, 1945, just about a year after receiving this letter from Dr. Dowell. Mrs. Solomon died in her daughter's home in Atlanta in Feb., 1950.

Submitted by: Miss Margaret Solomon, 1515 N. Highland Ave., N.E., Atlanta 6, Ga.

### BILLIE DUNN THARPE, SR.

B. D. Tharpe was born Sept. 25, 1879 in Twiggs County, Ga.; died June 24, 1946 at his ancestral home in Smith District of Twiggs; buried at Stone Creek Church Cemetery. Bill Dunn was the only child of Frances "Fannie" Margaret Hinson and Alexander C. Tharpe, both families being pioneer settlers of Twiggs. B. D.'s father, Alexander C. Tharp, was a soldier of the Confederacy from Twiggs; his grandfather, Jeremiah A. Tharp, was an outstanding citizen, community leader, and Deacon in Stone Creek Church; his great-grandfather, Rev. Vincent A. Tharp, was a veteran of the Revolutionary War and the pastor of Stone Creek Baptist Church from 1811 until his death in 1825.

Bill Dunn was active in church and community activities. He served as Treasurer (1919-1939) and Deacon in his beloved Stone Creek Baptist Church. He was for many years a member of the Smith School Board of Trustees and the Twiggs County Board of Education. His business interest included farming and mining. He owned and managed a kaolin mine and processing plant at Dry Branch, Ga. for many years—he later leased his kaolin interest to a larger mining concern. His hobbies were fishing and hunting.

On Feb. 12, 1903, Bill Dunn married Elizabeth "Bessie" Bond of Bibb County and to this union was born five children: Opal, Frances, Edna, Jere and B. D., Jr.

Opal Tharpe married Stephen Shedrick "Jack" Jones Oct. 14, 1923 and to this union three sons were born: Billy Walker, Morris Jasper and Thomas Reid. Billy married Bernice Jeanette Lindsey and they have two daughters, Janet Elise, born Nov. 30, 1957, and Elizabeth "Beth" Rachel, born Dec. 9, 1959. Morris "Jackie" married Betty Dorman and they have two children, Brenda Carol, born Jan. 29, 1949, and Stephen Morris, born July 21, 1952. Reid married Sybil Adel Worsham and they have one daughter, Kathryn Adel, born July 29, 1957.

Frances Tharpe married Vivian Elton Wood Feb. 12, 1937 and they have two daughters: Shirley Jean and Ann Tharpe. Shirley married Sept. 1, 1956 and has one son, Douglas Elton (Powell), born June 2, 1957.

Edna Tharpe married Robert L. Powell June 6, 1936 and they have one child, a son, Warren Thomas Powell, born Oct. 19, 1942. Warren married Sherry Floyd (1959) of Dudley; issue: a son, Jeffery Thomas, born Aug. 5, 1960.

Jere A. Tharpe married Mildred Barnwell Jan. 20, 1950 and they have two sons: Allen, born Nov. 8, 1953 and Billy, born Dec. 23, 1954.

B. D. Jr. married Jeanette Bailey of Macon Dec. 27, 1952 and they have two children: Linda Jeanette, born Dec. 5, 1953 and Bill Dunn, III, born March 22, 1959. They reside at Forsyth, Ga.

Submitted by: The children of B. D. Tharpe, Sr.

### HERSCHEL JOHNSON VAUGHN

Alexander Vaughn (1743-1797) and his wife, Jane (1745-1829) came to Warren County, Ga. from Virginia near the close of the Revolutionary War.

Their son, Daniel Vaughn (1780-1854), married Sara Staples (1782-1853), daughter of Stephen and Mary Starke Staples of Hanover County, Va. Stephen Staples, a Revolutionary soldier, settled in Wilkes County, Ga., during the Revolution. Daniel Vaughn, Lieutenant, War of 1812, moved from Columbia County, Ga. to

Twiggs County in 1832. He was a planter and a large landowner.

William Thomas Vaughn (1821-1901), son of Daniel and Sarah Staples Vaughn, born in Columbia County, Ga., married first, Sarah Sanders (1826-1863); second, Mrs. Elizabeth Sanders Herring (1814-1895). He was a successful planter and owned land in several Georgia counties. He was a devoted member of Richland Baptist Church and served as deacon for many years. Too old for military service, he furnished slaves to work on the Confederate fortifications at Savannah. Buried Vaughn Cemetery.

John Shine Vaughn (1851-1924), son of William Thomas and Sarah Sanders Vaughn, married March 20, 1875, Emma Jane Armstrong (1855-1889). She was the daughter of Isham Hand Armstrong (1830-1896), Confederate soldier, and Mary Jane Woodson Armstrong (1834-1894). Isham Hand Armstrong came to Georgia from North Carolina. Mary Jane Woodson Armstrong was the daughter of Jonathan and Margaret Barfield Woodson of Jones and Bibb Counties, Ga. John Shine Vaughn was a successful farmer, merchant, and postmaster of Twiggsville, Ga. Also, he represented Twiggs County in the State Legislature. Buried Jeffersonville Cemetery.

Herschel Johnson Vaughn, son of John Shine and Emma Armstrong Vaughn, born Dec. 16, 1880, received his education in the public schools and Emory College. After teaching school for two years, he entered the service of the Post Office Department at Macon in 1900 and retired Nov. 1, 1948. He married Bessie Julia Read of Twiggs County, Sept. 2, 1900. (See Read family). She was a charter member of the Twiggs County Chapter, United Daughters of the Confederacy. They are members of Vineville Baptist Church, Macon, Ga.

Their children:
1. Herschel Read Vaughn, born Nov. 16, 1901, Macon, Ga., married Selma Inez Pritchett Oct. 2, 1922, died July 3, 1937, Atlanta, Ga. Their children:
   a. Herschel Read Vaughn, born March 15, 1924, married Margaret Brown, June 10, 1942. Their children: Stephen Read, born April 9, 1943; Glenn Winston, born March 20, 1947.
   b. Jacquelin Vaughn, born Feb. 10, 1930, married Bradley Braley Feb. 12, 1949. Their child, Lynne, born March 23, 1950.
2. Emma May Vaughn, born April 26, 1904 in Macon, Ga., was married Dec. 15, 1922 in Macon, Ga., to Glenn Thomas Carthron, born Dec. 24, 1895 near Talbot, Tenn. Their children: Mae Vaughn Carthron, born Jan. 26, 1925, Macon, Ga.; Betty Read Carthron, born Oct. 29, 1928, Macon, Ga. Glenn Thomas Carthron, Jr., born Sept. 1, 1933, Macon, Ga.
   Mae Vaughn Carthron was married May 23, 1943 in Savannah, Ga., to Walter Cambridge Murray, born July 17, 1923, Savannah, Ga. Their children: Mae Jane Murray, born Oct. 29, 1944, Hobbs, New Mexico; Jennifer Vaughn Murray, born Nov. 15, 1945, Savannah, Ga.; Walter Cambridge Murray, Jr., born Nov. 6, 1946, Savannah, Ga.
   Glenn Thomas Carthron, Jr., was married Dec. 27, 1956 in Savannah, Ga., to Rebecca Iris Adams, born Feb. 18, 1937, Orangeburg, S. C. Their child: Julia Adams Carthron, born Nov. 29, 1957, Savannah, Ga.
3. Russell Felder Vaughn, died in infancy.
4. Bessie Neva Vaughn, born Macon, Ga., May 23, 1915, married Feb. 4, 1933 to Francis Goulding Clark. (See Clark history). Their child: Francis Goulding Clark, Jr., born July 8, 1940, Macon, Ga., now a student at Emory University.

Submitted by: Herschel J. Vaughn, 154 Oak Ridge Ave., Macon, Ga.

## WILLIAM V. WATSON

William Vance Watson was born Sept. 4, 1899 in Laurens County, Ga., and moved to Twiggs County in 1929. His first marriage was to Effie Pearl Wasden, and their children are William Fred, Robert Syntell, Vernon Ray and Holbert Vance. After her death he married Mrs. Kemper Manning Bozeman. They have one daughter, Myrtice Ann.

He is now serving as Chairman of Board of Commissioners of Twiggs County, is active in the Jeffersonville Baptist Church, in city and county civic affairs, and is a successful farmer and dairyman.

Submitted by: The Watson Family

## WILKINSON MABERRY WHITEHURST

W. M. Whitehurst

Wilkinson Maberry Whitehurst, Mayor of Jeffersonville from Sept., 1923 until death—almost 21 years. Born March 12, 1875, Whitehurst Homestead, Longstreet, Twiggs County. Died Jan. 19, 1944, at home. Buried Jeffersonville Cemetery.

Studied at private schools, Longstreet; Auburn Institute, Jeffersonville; and business college, Newnan, Ga. Merchant from Sept., 1896, until death. Served in Georgia State Senate 1931-'32.

First Twiggs Countian to own an automobile, called Autobuggy, in 1907. Soon traded for Reo, 4 cylinder, right-hand steering, chain drive, and side crank. Third car, a Buick was bought in August, 1910, see picture.

Married April 25, 1911, in Baptist Church, Tennille, Ga., Henri Louise Ivey (Aug. 14, 1888, Millen, Ga., graduated Tennille Institute, 1904, and Brenau College, A. B. degree, 1907), daughter of Henry Jones Ivey (Feb. 11, 1847, Warren County, Ga., April 3, 1917, Tennille, Ga.) and his second wife, Eliabeth Lucinda (Lingo) Ivey (July 11, 1860, Twiggs County, married Nov. 2, 1880 in Wilkinson County, died April 23, 1930, Tennille, Ga.); and granddaughter of Zaccheus Ivey and Eliza-

W. M. Whitehurst and Miss Louise Ivey of Sandersville, Ga., who later became his wife, seated in his new 1911 model Buick.

beth( Grenade) Ivey, and of William Slaughter Lingo and Gabriella Louisa (Nash) Lingo

Children: Frances Elizabeth (Jan. 27, 1912, graduated Bessie Tift College, 1933, died Aug. 20, 1943); Henry Ivey (Nov. 21, 1913, Oct. 8, 1915; and Mary Hart, Feb. 9, 1918, graduated University of Georgia, 1939).

His parents: Morgan LaFayette Whitehurst (June 18, 1825, Wilkinson County, died Aug. 7, 1893, Twiggs County) and his second wife, Mary Frances (Burke) Whitehurst (March 16, 1843, Wilkinson County, married Feb. 25, 1869, died June 26, 1886, Twiggs County). Grandparents: Josiah Whitehurst, Sr., and Thulia Ann (Wilkinson) Whitehurst, and Nimrod Burke and Elizabeth (Butler) Burke, all from Wilkinson County, Ga.

Submitted by: Mary Hart Whitehurst

## MAJOR GENERAL EZEKIEL WIMBERLY

Ezekiel Wimberly, an illustrious pioneer settler in Twiggs County, Ga., settled here about the time the county was created by an Act of the Georgia Legislature, Dec. 14, 1809. He moved to Twiggs from Washington County Ga., where he resigned as sheriff of that county on Oct. 15, 1809.

His home was built on the ridge which runs through the central portion of the county and divide the waters of the Oconee River and the Ocmulgee River. Along this ridge the Macon-Dublin-Savannah Railroad, which was constructed some years later, runs in front of this old home. In the county his children were born and reared. He is one of the few early settlers of the county who have progeny that have lived continuously in the county to the present day building their homes and rearing families with creditable records.

His paternal ancestor, John Wimberly, Gentleman, born in England, was a Commissioner for the County of Lincoln, England, by Charles II, King of England, in

1660 and 1666. He emigrated to America between 1670-1672 and on Dec. 16, 1673 obtained a land grant in Nansemond County, Va.

Ezekiel was the son and grandson of Revolutionary soldiers. His father's grave, John Wimberly, being marked with a Revolutionary marker by John Ball Chapter, Daughters of the American Revolution, can be found in the Wimberly Family Cemetery where repose the remains of Ezekiel, on his home plantation, on the east side of the railroad paralleling U. S. Highway No. 80, two miles north from Jeffersonville, along with the remains of other members of the "clan".

Ezekiel bore arms in the War of 1812, commanding the Twiggs Militia. His ready response as a defender of freedom's cause can be substantiated by his letter dated Marion, 27th July, 1836, to His Excellency, Governor Schely. . . . "feeling always willing to serve my country and more particularly in the field in its defense in time of danger, I avail myself of the earliest opportunity to make known to you my desire to enter into the military service . . ." Upon receiving orders from Brigadier General David Blackshear in 1813, he erected and garrisoned three forts along the Ocmulgee River as frontier protection to the inhabitants who were terrorized by threat of enemy invasion.

He served as a member of the House of Representatives 1811, 1812, 1813, as Senator from Twiggs for 14 years and twice as Presidential Elector. A Major of the 80th Battalion, Georgia Militia; Lieutenant Colonel of the Light Dragons, Twiggs County; Colonel of the First Militia Major General Adams Division of Georgia Militia; Colonel at Fort Hawkins and a Major General of the Sixth Division, Georgia Militia, the post from which he resigned Nov. 27, 1840.

As a tribute to his valor, the Major Phillip Cook Chapter, United States Daughters of 1812, sponsored the bill which was passed by the Georgia Legislature in 1956, naming the bridge which spans Savage Creek near where the creek flows into the Ocmulgee River on State Highway No. 96 GENERAL EZEKIEL WIMBERLY. He was one of the first white settlers in the county to cross the Ocmulgee River in the wilderness days, having an Indian as a guide. Knowledge no doubt which proved profitable during the War of 1812.

Ezekiel, son of John Wimberly and Penelope Perry, was born in Bertie County, N. C., Sept. 1, 1783, died Twiggs County, Ga., May 5, 1843. Married first to Sarah Mims of South Carolina, issue, daughter "Sally" born Jan. 22, 1806, married to John Jones, a banker of Macon. Second marriage to Mary "Polly" Bryan, daughter of Blake Bryan, a Revolutionary soldier, and Elizabeth Blackshear, on July 18, 1809, Washington County, Ga., by David Blackshear, Justice of the Peace, an uncle of "Polly." "Polly" was born Oct. 12, 1787, North Carolina, died Oct. 22, 1875, Twiggs County, Ga. Children born to this union: Betsey Bryan, May 13, 1810, married Elijah Evans Crocker; John James, Oct. 24, 1813, married Eleanor Watson; Martha, Nov. 23, 1815, married Augustus Howard; Joseph William, Jan. 29, 1822, married Amanda Brown; Robert Rutherford, Oct. 27, 1823, married first, Elizabeth Cullen, second Penelope Boynton, third, Zilla Peacock, fourth, Sarah Jessup; issue by last three wives: Henry Howard, July 31, 1826, married Betsey Walker; Ezekiel Abner, born April 7, 1820, died June 2, 1885, born and died in Twiggs County, Ga. Being cripple, he served the Home Guards during the War-Between-the-States.

Ezekiel Abner Wimberly married first, Ann E. Denson, daughter of Joel and Nancy Denson, on April 16, 1845. She was born April 3, 1825, died July 18, 1853. Children: Martha Howard married Willis Hearn; MeDora married \_\_\_\_\_ McGowen; Ann E. married Henry Jackson Pipkin; Nancy Joel died young.

Ezekiel Abner Wimberly married second on May 20, 1857, Louisa Almyra Horne, daughter of Turner Horne and Margaret Cross, born Feb. 1, 1836, Bertie County, N. C., died Oct. 13, 1900, Twiggs County, Ga. Children born in Twiggs County: Ezekiel Turner, married Virginia King; William Evans; George Henry married Beatrice Defore; Beniah Carswell, hereafter; Augustus Howard; John Joseph, married first Beatrice Harrison, moved to Selma, Ala., three daughters born to this union, Lucile, Tess, Mary John; second marriage to Mrs. Donnie Breckenridge Lanier, June 1, 1953; Margaret "Maggie" L., born Feb. 18, 1879. "Maggie" married on Feb. 12, 1903 to James Thomas O'Neal, by J. B. Andrews, Justice of the Peace, uncle of J. T., at Macon, Ga. James Thomas "Jim Tom" born June 8, 1881, Twiggs County, died July 30, 1945, Macon, Ga., son of Thomas O'Neal (O'Neill) and Sarah M. Andrews. Thomas O'Neal descends from the royal line of O'Neills of Ireland. He served in Company G, 48th Regiment, Georgia Infantry, Confederate States of America during War-Between-the States. Children of "Jim Tom" and "Maggie" born in Twiggs County:

I. J. Lanette, born May 23, 1905, married May 5, 1935, by Reverend S. B. Wingfield, at Macon, Ga., to Hugh Lawson Faulk, born Aug. 29, 1907, Twiggs Co., son of Henry G. Faulk and Laura T. Wimberly. Two sons were born to this union at the Macon Hospital, Macon, Ga.: 1. Hugh Lawson Faulk, II (Junior), Nov. 9, 1937, enlisted United States Army May 8, 1959, Serial Number RA 14698988, married to Doris June Barden July 26, 1959, at Chamblee Baptist Church, Chamblee, Ga.; 2. Thomas Henry Faulk, born Sept. 18, 1941, enlisted United States Navy, Nov. 20, 1958, Service Number 522-58-91.

II. Ruby and Jewel O'Neal (twins) born Oct. 15, 1908. Jewel died Dec. 17, 1908. Ruby married James Lamar Cullen of Dublin, Ga., June 3, 1934, by Reverend John Warren, Macon, Ga. Ruby is a graduate of the Macon Hospital School of Nursing.

Beniah Carswell" Dock" Wimberly, born Jan. 23, 1871, Twiggs County, Ga., moved to Dallas County, Ala., the latter part of 1896 or early 1897, letters from his mother date back to Feb. 1897, married Maud Williams of Summerfield, Ala., March 2, 1910. Later moved to Selma, Ala., and died there Dec. 20, 1948. Children: James T. and Ruth R., both live at Selma, Ala.

Lanette O'Neal Faulk, Ruby O'Neal Cullen, and Ruth R. Wimberly

## EZEKIEL JENKINS WIMBERLY

Ezekiel Jenkins Wimberly, the son of Ezekiel Turner and Jennie (King) Wimberly, was born at Vidalia, Ga., March 29, 1904. On Sept. 12, 1933, he married (Miss) Helen Domingos at Centenary Methodist Church, Macon, Ga. He died Dec. 11, 1951 in the full vigor of manhood and usefulness.

His span of life was short but he lived "in deeds not years." In the words of a prominent minister "It is not so much life's decoration as life's donation." Zeke's work is not measured by the span of his life but by the great amount he accomplished and the good he did. He had everything to live for, and for him to live was to serve. He contributed richly to his own church, the Jeffersonville Baptist and to the other churches in the community, to his county and to every worthy cause.

The Wimberly family is an old and honorable one, which through the years gave freely to the educational, social, financial, and Christian development of the United States and to the South in particular. None of his forebears were more honorable than the subject of this biography. The lineage of E. J. Wimberly is traced to William Wimberly who married Ann Harwarden, about 1500 and through their grandson, Sir Thomas Wimberly of Beechfield in Lincolnshire, England, who was knighted May 16, 1588, by Queen Elizabeth in the 30th year of her reign. Major General Ezekiel Wimberly, notable in the War of 1812 and one of the founders of Twiggs County was the great-grandfather of Ezekiel J. Wimberly.

Among his progenitors were such outstanding men as Needham and Blake Bryan,

E. J. Wimberly

James Blackshear, John and Ezekiel Wimberly, Sr. Through his mother's line John Ball, the Kings, Methvins, Glovers, and others of note both paternal and maternal.

(The early Wimberly records are recorded in the Doomsday Book and the Visitation Book of England).

His pastor, Rev. Nelms, said of him, "It goes to the head of most people who create an estate, but it went to Zeke's heart." That is the keynote of his character—doing good with what he had. As a young boy, he came to live in Twiggs County, where he received his education. Living among the trees he loved, his life's work shaped itself: that of forestry and conservation.

For three terms he served as a Twiggs County Commissioner, owned and successfully operated the Wimberly Lumber Company, a director and stockholder of the Four County Bank, Chairman of the Twiggs County Forestry Fire Commission, Treasurer of the Jeffersonville Baptist Church, an active member of the Men's Bible Class, and a Mason.

When the Calloway plan of farming was put into effect in Twiggs, he was one of five or six men who gave $1,000 each for the project. Mr. Cason Calloway, who originated the farming method, invited the donors, throughout the state, to take a trip, as his guests, to see his methods in operation. Places visited were the Experiment Station in Beltsville, Md., the Hershey Farms and plant at Harrisburg, Pa., notable farms in a radius of 30 miles from Columbus, Ohio, and last, the U. S. Steel mills at Pittsburgh. Later he attended a National Conservation Convention in Denver, Colo., where there, as elsewhere, he eagerly sought means of conserving our natural resources. He was a man of sound business judgement which he used for his church, his county, and his business.

As one who knew him well, I soon learned that he loved people, took a delight in having his friends, and loved ones, in his home. A man of great courage, both physical and moral, and at the same time full of humility. A man in whom there was no quip. He was a faithful husband, loving father and son, and a kind brother— a helpful friend to all. His faith grew stronger and brighter as the days passed by— ready at all times to proclaim his belief in the Gospel of Christ. His love of home, his devotion and companionship with his wife and children were outstanding marks of his character.

The year following his death, the Twiggs County Forestry Commission in co-operation with the Macon Chamber of Commerce and the Georgia Forestry Commission sponsored a demonstration in memory of E. J. (Zeke) Wimberly with a wood lot and fire control demonstration. This took place on Jeffery-McElrath forest lands where 150 people gathered. Hon. J. D. Shannon said of Zeke, "His time, his energy, and his talent went to the world of forestry. He planted the seed of good conservation with many of us Central Georgians and it is a seed that has grown and matured."

The living monuments of Ezekiel J. Wimberly are his two children: 1. Charlotte Wimberly, born 11-26-1935 at Macon, Ga., was married at Centenary Methodist Church in Macon, Ga., 6-7-1959 to Thomas Robert Smith of McRae, Ga. 2. Ezekiel Jenkins Wimberly, Jr., born 2-7-1943, Macon, Ga.

Patience is a virtue that one has often great occasion to use, and he who expects to get along comfortably through the world would do well to lay in an early stock. The most agreeable of all companions is a simple, frank man, without any high pretensions to any oppressive greatness; one who loves life and understands its uses; obliging alike at all hours, above all a golden temper, and steadfast as an anchor. For such a one, we gladly exchange the greatest genius, the most brilliant wit, the profoundist thinker. Zeke's life was made up of these traits.

Though this good man has gone from among us, the incense of his life and character remains with us who knew and loved him best.

Submitted by: Mrs. W. D. Domingos

## WIMBERLY

The history of the Wimberlys in America began with John, coming to the colonies from England. John Wimberly, gentleman of Pinchbeck and Beechfield, England, was granted four-hundred acres of land in Nansemond County, Va., in 1673, said land being due him for transporting eight persons into the colony.

The Wimberlys moved to North Carolina between 1700 and 1720, and descendants of John came to Georgia on the great wave of immigration from Virginia and North Carolina in 1800. The early records of the Wimberlys will be found in *Domesday Book* and also in *A Pedigree of the Family of Wimberly of Lincolnshire* copied from the Visitation Book of that County, in the Heralds College, London, and attested by Bevill Wimberly, Esq., in 1634.

The arms and crest were confirmed to Sir Thomas Wimberly of Beechfield, England, and Ascoughfee Hall, County Lincolnshire in the Thirtieth year of the reign of Queen Elizabeth on the 16th of May, 1588. The motto on the scroll reads above the large buckhead "BYDAND", (Remaining).

On the scroll beneath the shield are the words "NON OMNIS MORIAR," (We shall not wholly die.)

Sir Thomas was an ancestor of John.

The Twiggs County history of the Joshua Rhodes Wimberlys began with the pioneering of Joshua Rhodes Wimberly, M.D., to the County shortly after its creation. He was the son of Fred Davis Wimberly and Alice (Rhodes) Wimberly of North Carolina, and was married to Caroline Henrietta Starr on May 10, 1832, in Twiggs County at the residence of George W. Welch, Esq. Dr. Joshua Rhodes Wimberly was born in North Carolina in 1796 and died January 24, 1844, in Jeffersonville. Caroline was born in 1805 in Connecticut and died in Jeffersonvile after the 1870 census. Both are buried in the Wimberly cemetery, Jeffersonville. Their children were George, Frederick Ezekiel, John Lowry, Joshua Rhodes, and Henry T. George and Frederick Ezekiel were killed in the Civil War. George is buried in the Wimberly cemetery in Jeffersonville, and Frederick was killed at the Battle of Sharpsburg. His body was never recovered.

## THE FAMILY OF JOHN LOWRY WIMBERLY

John Lowry Wimberly, born Jan. 24, 1841; died Sept. 28, 1908; on Nov. 20, 1867 married Mary Jane Griffin, born May 31, 1849; died Dec. 16, 1909; daughter of Colonel Eli Short Griffin and Averilla Margaretta Nash. To this marriage 11 children were born, five of them lived to maturity. They were:

I. Henry Bunn Wimberly, LLB, b. March 7, 1870; d. July 28, 1930; married Bethenia Maury. Of this union there were three children: (1) Mathew Fontaine, (2) John Lowry and (3) Hariett Bunn. Bethenia Maury is the granddaughter of Mathew Fontaine Maury whose bust is in the Hall of Fame for charting the floor of the Atlantic Ocean.

II. George Welch Wimberly, M.D., b. Feb. 6, 1875; d. Oct. 26, 1929; married Erma Pearl Bez-de-check. Their children are: (1) William and (2) George.

III. Caroline Griffin Wimberly, b. Sept. 1, 1876; d. Dec. 26, 1940; married Daniel Shine Faulk. (See Faulk sketch within.)

IV. Averilla Margaretta Wimberly, b. July 20, 1887; d. April 7, 1959; married John Louis Schulz, living at Custer, Washington. Their children are: (1) John Wimberly, (2) George Louis and (3) James, who died May 2, 1958.

V. Alice Lowry Wimberly, b. Sept. 4, 1893.

## THE FAMILY OF DR. JOSHUA RHODES WIMBERLY

Joshua Rhodes Wimberly, M.D., b. Nov. 6, 1843; d. Jan. 10, 1904; married Adelaide America Steely, daughter of Rev. W. R. Steely and granddaughter of James Steely, a Revolutionary Patriot; b. Nov. 15, 1848; d. Oct. 6, 1890. Their marriage took place in 1866. Of this union five children survived:

I. Frederick Ezekiel, b. Nov. 25, 1868; d. Aug. 12, 1932; unmarried.

II. Lucy Graves Wimberly, b. Jan. 11, (Tuesday), 1870; d. April 13, 1934; married Jan. 20, 1890 to James Jackson Wall, b. Dec. 31, 1864; d. Jan. 22, 1923. There were three children born to them: (1) Adelaide Wimberly, b. Dec. 20, 1890; (2) Lilly Caroline, b. Sept. 7, 1892 and d. Feb. 8, 1896; (3) Jasper McArthur, b. Aug. 31, 1894.

III. Joshua Rhodes Wimberly, b. July 19, 1871; d. July 19, 1924; married Bessie Leonora Burke on Jan. 22, 1895; the daughter of John Franklin Burke and Leonora Carswell Burke of Wilkinson County, Ga. Bessie Leonora Burke was born Oct. 25, 1873 and died Aug. 28, 1910. She was a graduate of Wesleyan College, class of 1894. Their only child, Leonora Irene Wimberly, was born Nov. 21, 1895. On July 19, 1923 she married Charles Chevrier Gleeson at the Jeffersonville Baptist Church. The latter mentioned, Charles Gleeson, was born on Dec. 2, 1897 and was the son of Lydia Paul Eastlack and Charles Chevrier Gleeson, Sr., of Thorofare,

N. J. He was graduated from Temple University and a veteran of World War I. He died Aug. 27, 1950. Two daughters were born of this marriage: Elizabeth Pauline and Charlotte Irene. (Bessie) Elizabeth Pauline Gleeson was born on Oct. 12, 1925 and graduated from Pennsylvania State College with an A.B. degree. On Sept. 6, 1946 she married Ellis A. Hall, a graduate of the University of Cincinnati, B.S. degree, and the Cincinnati Conservatory of Music with a Master of Music degree. Ellis Hall was born Aug. 6, 1924 in Oil City, Pa. Their children and the dates of their birth are: Lawrence Ellis Hall, Sept. 6, 1952; Randall Gleeson Hall, July 28, 1954; George Charles Hall, July 8, 1957; and Laura Elizabeth Hall, March 7, 1959.

Charotte Irene Gleeson was born on June 22, 1929. Upon graduation from the University of Georgia with the degree of B.Sc. in Pharmacy, she first married Lamar James Jackson on Aug. 27, 1950. Lamar J. Jackson was born Dec. 14, 1928 and a graduate of University of Georgia with a B.Sc. degree in Pharmacy. He died May, 1952 while in the U. S. Army in Korea. A son, Charles Lamar was born of this marriage on Nov. 22, 1951. On Jan. 1, 1954, Charlotte Irene Gleeson Jackson married George Richardson Spears, a graduate of Alabama Polytechnic Institute with a B.Sc. degree. On Dec. 8, 1954, a son, George Richardson Spears, Jr., was born. A daughter, Judith Anne, was born Dec. 1, 1956.

Joshua Rhodes Wimberly, III, was married the second time to Winifred Locke of Jeffersonville on Dec. 21, 1911. To this union two children were born: Joshua Rhodes IV, and Mary Evelyn. Joshua Rhodes IV was born Nov. 29, 1912. His wife, Agnes Bragg of Hawkinsville, was born April 20, 1917. She and Joshua Rhodes IV were married Nov. 20, 1938. Their daughter, Harriet Evelyn, was born Nov. 26, 1944.

IV. Mary Adelaide Wimberly, twin sister of Caroline who died in infancy, was born on Sept. 7, 1874, died May 28, 1913; married in the First Baptist Church, Jeffersonville, Ga., Sept. 6, 1900 to Mathew James Carswell, son of Mathew James and Ellen Dupree Carswell. He was born Jan. 15, 1873 and died Aug. 18, 1929, a graduate of Mercer University Law School. Three children were born of this union: (1) Ellen Huff, born Feb. 12, 1906; died May 25, 1958. She was graduated from Eastman High School and attended both the University of Georgia and Georgia State College for Women; (2) Courtney Wimberly Carswell was born March 7, 1909 and is a graduate of Eastman High School and the Atlanta Law School; (3) George Henry Carswell, born Dec. 10, 1912, was graduated from Boys High, attended Tech, graduated Woodrow Wilson Law School of Atlanta. He married Julia Porter of Danville, Ga., daughter of Mary Eliza Taylor and William T. Porter. The marriage was solemnized in the Danville Baptist Church Oct. 6, 1937. Julia Porter was born on Oct. 10, 1913. Their two children are: Judy Ann Carswell, born Dec. 12, 1938 and George Henry Carswell, III, born Jan. 31, 1943. Judy Ann is presently a senior at the University of Georgia.

V. Major Albert Courtney Wimberly, born Oct. 2, 1879; died Feb. 14, 1953; a graduate of West Point U. S. Military Academy, class of 1904. He and his wife, Alta Midkiff Wimberly, are buried in Arlington National Cemetery.

Mrs. C. C. Gleeson
Jeffersonville, Georgia

## ISAAC WATERS WOOD

Isaac Waters Wood was born March 30, 1845; died March 9, 1925 at his ancestral home in Twiggs County; buried in Wood-Waters Cemetery near Fitzpatrick.

Isaac was a studious boy although being limited with books and teachers, he became a self-made, self-educated man. He was one of the best mathematicians of his day. An old arithmetic ledger in family records shows his first math teacher was John Vinson. It is recorded that while he was tilling the soil, he would stop his mule at the end of a row and sit beside his plow and work arithmetic problems. He was a prosperous farmer, school teacher and community leader and a life long member of his beloved Antioch Baptist Church, where he served as church clerk for many years. He, too, was instrumental in founding and building Oak Grove Community Sunday School House on the Kennington Place near Fitzpatrick. For many years this little house was filled to capacity every Sunday evening with children and parents from the surrounding neighborhood. Isaac was a veteran of the Civil War, serving in Company A, 5th Georgia Reserves, Confederate States of America Infantry.

Isaac Wood married Mary Sophia Wood Feb. 22, 1877. Mary Wood was born Oct. 15, 1854 and died Aug. 7, 1917. To this union were born eight children, however, only two lived to reach maturity. They are Dr. Arthur Eugene Wood, born Nov. 20, 1885 and Jennie Nora Wood, born March 12, 1890.

Dr. Arthur E. Wood

Dr. Arthur Eugene Wood received his education at the Fitzpatrick Public School of Twiggs County, Locust Grove Institute in Henry County, Mercer University, Vanderbilt and the University of Pittsburgh. For 39 years Dr. Wood has been head of the Chemistry Department at Mississippi College, Clinton, Miss. In addition to his college work, he was mayor of Clinton for 26 years. Dr. Wood has been the recipient of many honors and awards in his capacity as Science Professor at Mississippi College and as mayor of Clinton.

On Aug. 5, 1914, Dr. Wood married Anne Marie Powers of Florence, Ala. Anne Powers was born Aug. 6, 1889 and died Aug. 12, 1957. To this union were born Eleanor Hardaway Wood, Aug. 16, 1915; Louise Wood Jan. 16, 1918, died July 23, 1918; James Powers Wood Dec. 20, 1920 and Arthur Eugene Wood, Jr., Sept. 26, 1926.

Jennie Nora Wood received her education at Fitzpatrick Public School of Twiggs County and Bessie Tift College at Forsyth, Ga. She has always led a busy life—active in the affairs of her home community and County in addition to her home duties and responsibilities. Nora married Davis Sawyer McGee of Knoxville, Ga. (Crawford County) Aug. 10, 1913. They made their home in Twiggs County where Mr. McGee was one of the first County Agricultural Agents. Mr. D. S. McGee was an active leader in all school, church and civic affairs. He served as a member of the Twiggs County Board of County Commissioners, Welfare Board and the Board of Tax Assessors. He, too, served on the Twiggs County Local Selective Service Board throughout World War II. For 33 years he was a member of the Board of Trustees of his beloved Smith High School at Dry Branch, Ga., in which capacity he served as Secretary and Treasurer of the Board. Davis was born Sept. 16, 1885; died Nov. 8, 1957 and is buried in Crawford County.

Children of Davis and Nora McGee are Elnora, born June 12, 1914; Davis Sawyer, Jr., born Oct. 13, 1915; Eva Rosalyn, born Aug. 7, 1919 and died Oct. 10, 1921; Dent Waters, born July 28, 1922; and Patrick Lindy, born July 10, 1927.

Elnora McGee married James P. Beamer of Calhoun, Ga. To this union were born Dorothy Marie, July 24, 1938; James Philip, Jr., July 17, 1941; Anita Elnora, May 25, 1943.

Davis S. McGee, Jr., married Eula Wallace of New Jersey. To this union were born Mark Allen, June 9, 1948, and Philip Andrew, Feb. 2, 1953.

Dent Waters McGee married Virginia Morris of Marietta.

Patrick Lindy McGee married Betty Wells of Senatobia, Miss. To this union were born Linda Adrienne, Nov. 12, 1955, and Patrick Lindy McGee, Jr., 1959.

Isaac Waters Wood was the son of Green Berry Wood, Sr., who served the Confederate Government as guard at the Andersonville, Ga. prison. Isaac was also the grandson of Rev. David Wood, a pioneer settler of Twiggs County.

Green Berry Wood, Sr. married Margaret Waters in 1841. Children born to this union were Martha Elizabeth Wood Pickle and Isaac Waters Wood. After the death of his wife, Margaret, Green Berry, Sr. married Margaret's sister, Catherine Waters. To this union were born William Fitzpatrick Wood; Jennie Wood; Doctor Andrew J. Wood, a life long practicing country doctor of Twiggs County; John Thomas Wood; Mary Wood Mercer; Ella Wood Floyd; Green Berry Wood, Jr.

Rev. David Wood, grandfather of Isaac, married Elizabeth Towles. He was a Baptist minister and early settler of Twiggs, where he was instrumental in founding and building the once flourishing Wood's Meetinghouse near Ripley in Twiggs. This church became inactive just prior to the War-Between-the-States.

Respectfully submitted,
Mrs. D. S. McGee, Sr.

# INDEX

*Note about the indexing.* To have completely indexed each name which appeared within this book would have required more space than the limited budget would permit.

It will be noted that portions of the book are arranged in alphabetical order or in chronological order, therefore, the names found therein are not listed in the index. Such portions as the cemeteries, census, county officers, deed abstracts, letters testamentary, Lottery of 1805, representatives, senators, Roster of Soldiers of Wars and the tax digest are indexed by subject. The biographical sketches are arranged by family name. (Initials have been used for many given names.)

Abercrombie, J. S., 162, 169.
Academies, 115-116, 262, 265, 273, 275.
Adams, Abram, 32; A. S., 138; A. W. (Mrs.), 164, 168; D. C., 48, (Mrs.) 168; E. V. (Mrs.) 178; H. K. 125; Jewel B., 1; John Q., 269; Kathleen (Mrs.) 180; Obidah, 36; Pat, 182; Richard, 36; Roy C., 39.
Adams Park (Settlement), 39-40, 157.
Adkins, John, 32, 33.
Agriculturial Extension Service, 170-175.
Agriculturial Society, 183.
Ainsworth, J. T., 139; W. N., 139.
Aldredge, J. H. (Mrs.), 124.
Alexander, Samuel, 30, 275.
Allen, Andrew Y., 42; John F., 39; T. E., 123; Wm., 180.
Alley, J. M. (Mrs.), 176.
Allman, Jeremiah, 32.
Anderson, Andrew, 52; Belle B. (Mrs.), 39; Earl (Mrs.), 176; J. J., 36; J. T. B., 129; Thomas, 182; Thomas W., 116; Reuben, 32, 33; W. C., 36; Willis, 274, 275.
Andrews, 361; Abisha, 116, 134; I. G., 134; Joe A., 123; Robin, 88; W. H., 134.
Anglin, Nathan, 36; John, 277.
Antioch Baptist Church, 127-128, 26, 462.
Antioch Cemetery, 292-294.
Appendix, General, 187-358.
Ard, (Arde), A. W., 146, 180, 185.
Armstrong, Sarah, 141.
Arnold, J. D., 182; J. H., 122; J. J., 122.
Asa (Settlement), 40.
Asbell, 361; Clora (Mrs.), 131; C. O., 131; F. B., 53, 132, 361; Georgia, 131; Inez (Mrs. Lee), 131; I. G., 54; Jerry W., 182; John, 116; J. R., 53; L. Z., 131.
Asbury, Francis, 135.
Atkinson, Robert, 32, 34.
Atteway, Josiah, 35.
Attorneys (see Lawyers).
Auburn Institute, 117-119, 264.
Austin, Bessie F., 186; G. F., 137.

**B**

Bailey, Henry, 32; James, 32, 34; Mary W., 164; Stephen, 36.
Balcom (Balkcom), Estelle J., 164; Ichabod, 41, 104; J., 180; J. H., 152, 173; Jimmy, 166.

Balkcom Home, 156.
Baldwin, J. J., 129.
Ball, Wade H., 270.
Barbree, S., 134.
Barclay Home, 156.
Barclay, John A., 41, 117; Nancy E., 137.
Barker, William, 30, 32.
Barksdale, John, 129.
Barkwell, David, 39, 43.
Barnabee, B., 88.
Barnett, Lewis, 36.
Barnum, (Dr.), 186.
Barrentine, Agnes, 181; C. B., 122; James 182; W. B., 181.
Barrett, Eula, 122.
Barrs, Ray, 181.
Barton, Elizabeth, 263.
Bartree, Nell M., 43.
Bateman, Greenwood, 36; Green W., 265; Jesse, 265; John, 31; John E., 36; Simon, 31.
Bauxite, 96.
Bayne, Miller (Mrs.), 178.
Beach Springs Baptist Church, 136.
Beck, James, 166, 181; James E., 134; J. E., 129, 144, 169; Sara E., 48.
Beckam (Beckom), A. F., 136, 137, 185; E. G., 139; Ella J., 137; Wm. H., 112.
Beckham-Fort Cemetery, 296.
Beckom Home, 156.
Bedingfield (Beddingfield), Gideon, 363; Hardy, 32; Harmon, 36; Robert, 34.
Bedingham, Nedham, 32.
Beech Springs Academy, 137.
Beech Springs M. E. Church, 135-138, 407.
Beech Springs Cemetery, 295-296.
Bell (Beal, Beall), Bessie, 181; Harry, 181; Jane, 47, 137; Jane (Mrs.), 138; Joseph, 37; M. A., 186; Robert A., 50, 89; Wm., 180.
Belcher, Allen, 185.
Belk, S., 88.
Belton, Solomon (Capt.), 282.
Benjamin, G. F. (Mrs.), 177, 178; G. F., 265.
Bennett, Eula (Mrs.), 181; Mary (Mrs.), 175; Mary C. (Mrs.), 173, 177; W. R., 181.
Benson, Thomas W., 32.
Berry, Nathan, 55.
Bersheba Church, 141.

Bessina (Post Office), 54.
Betton, C. F. M., 89.
Bickley, C. T., 137.
Bichum, W. H., 52.
Big Sandy (Settlement), 40-41.
Billhimer, Delia R., 137.
Biographical Sketches, 360-463.
Bird, John G., 266; Thomas, 32, 33.
Birdsong, Betty S., 186; W. R. (Dr.), 185.
Bishop, I. L., 138.
Blacke, Alfred, 55.
Blackshear, D., 29; David, 26, 27, 28, 34; Ezekiel, 266; General, 30; Joseph, 116; Wm., 180.
Blackwell, John W., 267; John V., 267.
Blair, J. A., 158; (Mr.), 263.
Bloodworth, T. E., (Mrs.), 166.
Blount, James P., 36.
Bobbitt, James, 180.
Bollinger, R. H., 156; Ruby (Mrs.), 1.
Bond Cemetery, 294.
Bond Home, 156.
Bond, J. T., 54; S., 186.
Bonds Mill (Post Office), 54.
Bonner, John, 1; Lillian, 118.
Booth, R. M., 87, 137, 142; Louise F., 186.
Bostwick, Lawson, 182; Stephen, 32, 33.
Bowers, Charlotte (Mrs.), 180.
Bowman, A. G., 169; A. G. (Mrs.), 168; F. L., 36; Gladys, 181.
Bowles, H. R., 124.
Boy Scout Troops, 181-182.
Boyd, James, 186; J. M. (Dr.), 265.
Boynton, Sidney H., 47; S. H., 129.
Bozeman, C. H., 122; David, 31; D. H., 55.
Brack, G. M., 181; Mabel (Mrs.), 180.
Bradshaw, J. W., 162, 169.
Brady, L. E., 136, 138.
Branch, G. D., 173.
Brannen, Cora B. G., 186; E. E. (Mrs.), 178.
Branscomb, M. B., 125.
Brazeal, Mary (Mrs.), 129.
Bridger, G. B., 53.
Briggs, Hortense, 121.
Briley, Annie, 121.
Brown (Browne). Isaac, 32, 34; J. M., 149; Joseph E., 100; Jennye W. (Mrs.), 122, 123; J. W., 137; Kathleen, 173; Margaret (Mrs), 180; Robert F., 42; W. F. N., 180; W. O., 124; Wm. W.,17.
Brownlow, W. G. (Rev.), 278.
Brundage, A. J., 159; Helen, 121.
Brunsman, H. G., 188.
Bryan, Blake, 142; Councell S., 270; Elijah, 31; James, 267; James A., 269; James C., 267; James W., 269; Levi, 36; Mary G., 1; Matthew, 38; S., 141; Sidney, 36; Wm., 35.
Bryan Cemetery, 296.
Bryant, E. D., 141; Philip W. (Mrs.), 1, 25.
Bryson, C. E., 124.
Buchannon, J. E., 138.

Bull, 364; John H., 265; Jesse J., 265; Mary M., 265; Wm., 117.
Bullard, 363; Allen, 26; Cora, 137; D., 141; Daniel, 41; Dora, 137; Victoria, 137; Wiley, 363.
Bullard H. D. Club, 175-176.
Bullard School, 123-124.
Bullard (Settlement), 41.
Bullock, Jasper, 45; Jesse, 141.
Bugby, N., 88.
Bunn, Henry, 36, 53, 115, 267.
Burgess, J. B., 129.
Burke, Effie, 118; Ellington, 118; John, 32, 34; Kate, (Mrs.), 176; Ora Kate R., 174; William, 30, 34.
Burkett Cemetery, 294.
Burkett, Elizabeth S., 45; George W., 45, 134, 162; H. A., 134; Joe, 154; Joseph B., 45; J. U., 45, 180, 277; K. F., 180; Kate, 119; Lizzie, 119; Louise (Mrs.), 55; Nannie, 119; Nell, 181; S. T., 122, 162; Walter (Mrs.), 122; Washington J., 45.
Burns, H. B., 26; Henry B., 118; J., 185; J. E., 131; J. K., 54; Joseph, 38; Julia, 26; Mary, 118; Mercer, 131, 133; Willie J., 118; W. P., 170.
Burnham, Reba (Dr.), 91.
Burns (Post Office), 54.
Busby, Nimrod, 32, 33.
Bush, Abram, 31; Gidon, 32; Moses E., 31.
Butler, C., 36; Champion, 116; F. M., 121; R. I. (Dr.), 186, 262; Thomas J., 45.
Buzzard Roost (Settlement), 42-43.

C

Cadden, Virginia H., 164.
Cain, James, 32.
Caldwell, James, 31.
Califf, 365; E. F., 133; D. Y., 48, 129, 169, 182; J. P., 68, 129; W. H., 365.
Camp, R. E., 89.
Campbell, Archibald M., 263; J. H., 127, 129, 132.
Cannon, Beulah, 181; Frank, 130; G. F., 68; J. H., 134; O. C., 129; W., 134.
Cannon H. D. Club, 176.
Carden, B. F., 122; F. D. (Mrs.), 176; Olin (Mrs.), 178.
Carlisle, M., 34; Michael, 32.
Carr, Jos., 137; Wm., 88.
Carroll Home, 143.
Carroll, I., 127; Isaac, 143, 180; R. C., 53, 185; R. E., 131.
Carswell, 372; Beniah, 144, 185; B. S., 179; DeWit, 47; Ellen H., 132; Iverson, 118; Kathleen, 1, 175, 372; K. J. (Mrs.), 130, 164, 167, 168, 169, 172, 176; M. J., 22, 90, 118, 262; Mary L., 47; M. L. (Mrs.), 183; Nelson, 144; Rufus, 118; W. R., 163.
Carswell-Beck Home, 144.
Carter, Joel, 31; John F., 42.
Carver, Wm. B., 47.
Cash, John, 38.

Carson, Kenneth, 181.
Casten, Quincy, 182; Roy, 182.
Cauley, Wm., 16.
Cawthorn, Major, 28.
Celebrations: Centennial, 22; Fourth of July (1826), 267-271; LaFayette Volunteers, 282-284.
Cemeteries, 292-324.
Centennial, 22.
Census, 188-193.
Central of Ga. Railroad, 157, 51.
Chairmen, Commissioner Roads & Revenue, 68.
Champion-Epps Cemetery, 299.
Chamberlin, Theophilus M., 282.
Chance, 374; Burton (Mrs.), 177; George (Mrs.), 177; H. L., 176; H. L., (Mrs). 170; H. J., 43; Josh, 141; Sarah, 130; Silas (Mrs.), 177; Rufus (Mrs.), 177; Wm., 130; W. H., 374.
Channel, J. E., 138.
Chapel Hill (Post Office), 54.
Chapman, 365, 366, 367; C. T. (Mrs.), 178; Elizabeth G. C., 164; Geo. E. (Dr.), 185, 365; John, 139, 144, 366; Nell, 183; O. T., 170, 367; O. T. (Mrs.), 138, 183, 367; Ruth, 145, 164.
Chapman-Duggan Home, 144-145.
Chappell (Chappel), 376; J. J., 116; R. A., 89; Thomas, 54, 115; Thos. S., 116; T. S., 134.
Childers, 373.
Chiropractors, 186.
Christian, G. W., 136.
Christenbery, G. F. (Mrs.), 168.
Churches, 127-142.
Civil War, 19-20; 99-114, 43; "War Tax", 263.
Clance, H. L. (Mrs.), 170; Reuben, 127, 143.
Clark (Clarke), 371; Aaron, 37; Abi, 119; A. L., 123; A. J., 119; Council, 271; (Gen.), 283; James, 32; R. H., 89; S. H., 263; William, 270.
Claxton, J. L., 123, 124.
Clay (see minerals), 93.
Clay, George, 124; Miss, 121.
Clements, J. A., 53.
Clerks, County Commissioners, 68; Inferior Court, 62-63; Superior Court, 63-64.
Climate, 98.
Clopton, A. G., 89.
Cloud, Wm., 88.
Clubs, 164-184.
Coach, Wm., 31.
Coats (Coates) E., 129; Wm., 132.
Cobb, Joshua, 32.
Cochran, Frances, 124; J. M., 124.
Cole, C. B., 89.
Coley, Mary E. (Mrs.), 42.
Coleman, Isiah, 38.
Collins, 141, 368; Eli, 31; H. R., 160; I. F., 1; James, 32; J. D., 130; John, 38; Jonathan, 266; Joshua, 38; J. W., 116; Moses, 38; Nettie A., 137.

Colquitt, W. T., 89.
Colwell, Glenn, 181.
Comme . ., 38.
Combess, Lollis, 121.
Commissioners, Roads and Revenue, 68.
Communication, 157-163.
Communities, 39-57.
Compilers (Twiggs History), V, 381.
Compton, Erastus, 182; W. D., 125.
Concord Cemetery, 297; Church, 142.
Conrad, Henry, 32.
Cook (e), 369, 370; B., 123; Cornelius E., 137; Julian Porch, 371; J. R., 136, 137, 151, 369; J. R., (Mrs.), 175; Laura A., 137; Laura J., 137; Lula 137; Lulie, 137; Minnie N., 137; Nancy (Mrs.), 263; Phillip, 21; (Major), 263; T. J., 137.
Cook Home, 156.
Cool Spring Church, 141; Lodge, 179-180.
Coombs Cemetery, 297.
Coombs (Combs), Daniel, 36; J. R., 130, 179; Lucy, 122; W. F., 46.
Cooper, Bro., 129.
Coppage, Lewis, 32, 33.
Coroners, of County, 69-70.
Cornish, S. G., 125.
County Officers, 58-84.
Court House, 50, 85-87, 266.
Cowan, W. A., 116.
Coward, Henry, 33.
Cowart, J. E. (Mrs.), 183; Joe, 140.
Cox, J. V. (Dr.), 1; W. C., 125.
Craig, James L., 31.
Cranford, E. C., 180; Edward F., 40, 122; Elizabeth, 122; Henry J., 40; John, 180; J .M., 143; Lelia, 118; Lewis, 41; Mary, 148; Mary Poole (Mrs.), 122-123.
Cravey, H. O., 123.
Crawford, George W., 104; Grace T., 164; Joel, 89; Louis F., 41; Mary J., 41; William, 32, 33.
Crawley, C. E., 137.
Creeks (water course), 98.
Crocker Cemetery, 298, 425.
Crocker Home, 145.
Crocker, 423; E. E., 51, 157; Wm., 50, 88, 115, 145, 275; (Major), 282, 283; Wm. H., 47, 265, 277.
Crooms, C. C., 124.
Crosby, A. F., 122; Edward D., 36; John S., 41; John W., 122; Tullie G., 40.
Crosland Academy, 116, 43, 125.
Crosland, James E., 116; J. E., 265.
Cullen, Ruby O., 186.
Culpepper, Joseph, 31; Sampson, 31.
Cummins (Cummings), Robert, 88, 115, 185, 274; (Dr.), 275, 276.
Curru, Jno., 38.

**D**

Dallmus, E. G. (Mrs.), 122, 178.
Dame, Lou L. (Mrs.), 180.
Daniel, James, 31; Josiah, 35; Lewis, 31; Orman, 185; Orman (Mrs.), 168; Thomas, 115, 273.

Danville: Boy Scout Troop, 181-182; Chapter O. E. S., 180-181; PTA, 178; School, 116, 125; Settlement, 43, 116, 159; Telephone System, 162.
Daughters of American Revolution (Chapter), 164-167.
Davidson Academy, 116, 128.
Davidson (Davison), E. J., 162; Joseph, 116; William, 30, 37, 128; Victor, 23, 135.
Davis, A. S. (Mrs.), 175; Eleanor, 281; Elisha, 17, 115; Josiah, 32; J. T., 122; S., 141; Wm., 85, 115, 134, 272, 275, 277.
Day, J. T., 122; Lucile W., 164.
Dean, John, 31, 32, 34; Minton, 32, 34; W. A., 124.
Deed Records, 231-258.
Defore, H. F., 122; J. F., 122; M. T., 134.
Delacy, J. F., 86, 87.
Delk, S., 50.
Delphas (community), 54.
Delzel (Post Office), 54, 152.
Denean, J. H., 129.
Dennard, Hugh L. (Mrs.), 157; Isaac,
Dennard, Hugh L. D. (Mrs.), 157 Isaac, 29, 30, 32; John, 36; John D., 269; John F., 115; Marshall, 36; Thomas, 26.
Denson, A. M., 128; Elizabeth, 128; E. H., 185; E. J., 54, 136; Elias J., 128; Eliza J., 128; J., 132; John, 160; J. H., 116, 128, 136; John H., 116; Joel, 116; Mamie R., 46; Sarah, 132.
Denson-Jones Cemetery, 309-310.
Denson's Mill (Post Office), 54.
Dentist, 186.
Desazo, Richard, 35.
DeSoto, Hernando, 23.
DeSoto Trail, 23.
Diana (Post Office), 55.
Dick, Samuel, 15, 17, 115, 275.
Dickey, J. E., 21, 139; J. M., 139.
Dickens, J. C. (Mrs.), 178; Sallie (Mrs.), 180.
Dickson, Sampson, 32.
Dixon, R. M., 137; Sara R. (Mrs.), 1.
Doctors, 185-186.
Domingos, J. W., 137.
Dominy, Laura M., 43.
Dorman, C., 141.
Dotson, E. R. (Mrs.), 188.
Doughtrey, H., 123.
Dowsing, Wm., 24, 25.
Driscol, D. O., 138.
Dry Branch: Boy Scout Troop, 182; PTA, 178; School, 122-123; Settlement, 43-45, 159; Telephone System, 161-162.
Duckworth, Adnah, 171, 176.
Dudley, L. T., (Mrs.), 123.
Duffel, William, 282.
Duggan, C. A., 129, 145, 169, 185; C. A. (Mrs.), 168; L. Annette, 164.
Dunevant, Bertha, 171.
Dunlap, Mary (Mrs.), 123.

Dunn, Jeremiah, 32, 34; William, 32, 33, 275.
Dunwoody, James, 31.
Dupree, Benj., 115; D. H., 186; Edmund, 115; Frances (Mrs.), 129; Ira E., 53, 125, 129, 185, 267; (Dr.), 270, 271; Hamilton R., 282; James M., 22; Jeremiah, 275; Stuting, 269; Wm. H. (Rev.), 268.
Durden, Alice W. (Mrs.), 124; H., 128, 136; Henry, 112; M. C., 112; M. D., 128.
Durham's Bluff, 26; Home, 145; Post Office, 55.
Durham, Caroline, 147; Hardy, 36, 55, 116, 145, 147; Mary, 145; Samuel, 145; Thomas, 26.
Durham-Wimberly Cemetery, 297.
Dye Cemetery, 299.
Dye, J. M., 128; Mary, 128.
Dyess, Christopher, 37.
Dykes, J. I., 130.

E

Eady, John, 16.
Eanes, John, 55.
Early, Peter, 88; J. T., 169, 182; J. T. (Mrs.), 164, 179; Raynor, 166; Wilma A., 164.
Easom (Eason), Charles, 51; C. S., 138.
Edge, Peter W., 90; P. W., 129.
Edmonson, Bill, 138.
Edwards, Allen, 51; Andrew, 182; E. A., 125; Harry Stilwell, 85; Troy, 181, 265; Vernon, 138.
Ellis, P. W., 137.
Elmore, Frank (Mrs.), 179.
Emerson, Ruth, 122.
Epps-Champion Cemetery, 299.
Epps-Finney Home, 146.
Epps Home, 156.
Epps, Cliff, 128; Henrietta V., 45; Herbert, 128; Hubert, 128, 182; J. C., 116; Levenia B., 41; Travis, 127; Walter, 181, 182; Will, 146; Winfred, 128; W. V., 122.
Eppinger, John, 188.
Esley, Levi, 32.
Etheridge, A., 141.
Evans, E. J. (Mrs.), 53; George, 38; J. 141; James, 277; John, 88; John S., 53; J. T., 53; Lemuel, 32; Robert, 50; R. A., 89.
Everett, 378; J. E., 123; Robert A., 21; Taylor L., 378; W. E., 122.
Ezell, H. A., 134; L., 36; Mills, 32; Wm. H., 36.
Exam (Exum), Wm. H., 53, 270.
Extension Service, 170-175.

F

Fairchild, Loftin, 37.
Family (Biographies), 360-463.
Fannin, James W., 21.
Fargason, D. J., 169; D. J. (Mrs.), 168, 178; L. H., 124; Sallie J. (Mrs.), 168.

Faulk, 381, 387; Austelle S., 164; Carlton S., 182; Celina Hodges, 262; Charlie, 118; Cletia A., 164, 165; C. R., 112, 131, 132; Dorothy, 131; D. S., 129; G. W., 122, 131, 132, 152, 153, 182; Hallie W., 132, 153; Henry, 116, 262, 265, 278; H. G., 153; H. D. (Mrs.), 133; H. L. (Mrs.), 175; Hugh L., 1, 90; Jane, 147, 164; Joe (Mrs.), 131; John, 38; John C., 182; J. W., 131, 145; Lanette O., VI, 2, 124, 132,, 164, 381; Laura W., 132, 147, 164; Lucy W. (Mrs.), 174; Mark, 153, 381; Mark B. (Mrs.), 168; M. Jane, 164; (Mrs.), 24; Mary, 89, 118; M. G., 133; M. S., 68, 131; Sally V., 153; Sara, 132; Shine, 131; Shines (Mrs.), 168; Thomas H., 166; Tom, 118; T. J., 145; Wm., 107, 112, 113, 183, 266; W. C., 55, 129; William Charles (Judge), 387; Wm. T., 133.
Faulk Cemetery, 299-300; Home, 153; Post Office, 55.
Feagan, Aaron, 26.
Fenn, John, 31.
Fern, S. D., 141.
Finch Cemetery, 300.
Findlay, C. D., 54, 185.
Finney, Bessie, 146; Charles, 146; E. C., 265.
Fitch, Thomas, 89.
Fitzpatrick, 387; Avarilla, 264; B. S., 21, 22, 45, 87, 119, 140, 146, 170, 265; (Mrs.), 183; C. B., 39, 151; Duross, 133; Edwin H., 39; Fleta, 22, 45; Irwin, 39; I., 132; J. B., 146; Jane L., 133; John 104, 264; L. A. 132; Madge, 122; Mark W., 132; O. B. T., 151; Ora B., 138; O. B. (Mrs.), 175; Rose, 140; T. E. (Mrs.), 137; W. F., 137; Will, 182.
Fitzpatrick Cemetery, 300-301; Home, 146; Settlement, 45.
Flemming, Allen, 51; John, 274; Lucy, 124.
Floyd, Brady (Mrs.), 178; Hildon, 182; L. E., 140; Minnie (Mrs.), 176; R. F. (Rev.), 166.
Ford, Wm., 88.
Forest, 91.
Forsyth, John (Gov.), 276.
Fort, Arthur, 15, 18; (Jr.), 18, 88; Elizabeth, 18; Moses, 18, 50, 89, 115, 274, 275; Owen Charlton, 18; Sarah, 18; Tomlinson, 18; Zachariah, 18.
Forts, (Jackson, Telfair, Twiggs), 29, 30-34, 49.
Fortner, 32, 34.
Fountain, Bill, 182 Laverne, 186; Sybil, 186.
Fourth of July Celebration (1826), 267-271.
Fowler, Frank (Mrs.), 177; J. S. (Mrs.), 177; Mary (Mrs.), 176; Ruby (Mrs.), 177; T. E., 159.

Fox Hunters, 182-183.
Franklin, Bedney, 89; J. B., 159.
Frazer (Frasier), Daniel, 38; Patricia W., 164; Simeon, 36.
Frederick, John, 32, 34.
Frebrel, Abeom, 38.
Friendship Academy, 116; Baptist Church 128, 443.
Frierson, J. S., 89.
Fulbright, H. M., 124, 179; (Mrs.), 179.
Fulghum, M., 132, 141; Micajah, 127.
Fullers Earth, 96-97.
Fullerton, Robert J., 43.
Fullilove (Fullilore), C. L. (Mrs.), 121, 123.
Fullingame, Wm., 32, 33.
Fullwood, John, 32, 33.

G

Gaddis, M. R., 130.
Gainer, Samuel, 89.
Gainey, Amanda, 147; John, 180; Wm. A., 180; W. H., 147.
Gainey-Ard Home, 146.
Gallemore (Gallimore), 389; G. R., 119; J., 185; J. S., 54; S. M., 130, 142.
Gallemore's Mill, 389.
Galloway, Eleazar, 31.
Gammel, Thomas, 137; T. E., 137.
Garrard, John, 31.
Garden Clubs, 168.
Garrett, James, 31, 277.
Garrison, R. C., 159.
Gates, 391; Albert, 118; A. M., 129; A. M. (Mrs.), 168; Albert M., 21, 126; Paul, 186.
Gathright, Miles, 275.
Genealogical Appendix, 359-463.
General Appendix, 187-358.
Georgia Messenger (Letters), 56-57.
Gentry, Pleas, 137.
Gettys, William Bryson, 392.
Gibson Home (Dr.), 156.
Gibson, O. C., 185; Will, 185.
Gilbert, Thomas, 31.
Gilmer, George R. (Gov.), 277.
Gilstrap, Levin, 31.
"Gleesom Hall" (Dr. Wimberly Home), 147, 384.
Gleeson, Irene W., VI, 132, 164.
Glenn, David, 270; Robert 88, 115, 267, 269, 273; Sara, 132; William D., 270.
Glover Home, 148.
Glover, J. T., 112, 117; John, 263, 277; Thomas, 90, 116, 148.
Goodwin (Godwin), B. W., 130; J., 130; John S., 262.
Goff, John H., 24.
Golden, Wm., B., 109.
Golucke, J. W., 87.
Goss, C. C., 123, 182; S. E., 125.
Government, 87-90; (Leg. Acts), 272-279.
Grace, J. D., 122; (Mrs.), 178.
Gragg, Henry, 274.

Graham, Callie, 181 David, 270; E. D., 89; James, 31.
Granberry (Granbery), J. M., 55; S., 277.
Granberry (Post Office), 55.
Granny, M. M., 36.
Grantham, Benjamin, 31.
Gregory, J. C. (Mrs), 176.
Greene, A. H., 134; Donald, 182; J. F., 182; R. F., 182.
Griffin, 393; Addie W., 47; Bill, 135; B. S., 263; Carrie C., 186; David, 125; Eleanor, 184; E. S., 180; Ethelred, 35, 36; H. F., 47, 169; H. F. (Jr.), 22, 89, 262; H. P., 162; Johnny, 118; Larkin, 276; L. L., 21, 122; Luther Lawrence, 393; L. S., 55; Mary Y., 264; Short, 128; S. H., 122; William, 29, 30, 32, 33, 117, 138, 140, 180; Yancy, 41.
Grimes, Wm., 88.
Grimsley, C. G. (Mrs.), 176.
Griner, Samuel, 50.
Griswoldville, Battle of, 104.
Guerry Home, 156.
Guerry, James, 115, 263; James (Sr.), 276; T. L., 36.
Gulen, P. C., 263.
Gurly, Miss, 122.

## H

Haigler, Mabel, 121.
Haines, James G., 31.
Hair, John, 32, 34; Thomas, 32, 34.
Hall, J. J. D., 169; J. M., 129; Mary L., 119; O. D., 171; Sanders (Mrs.), 178; W. L., 159.
Ham (Hamm), A. U., 122; (Mr.), 127; Virginia (Mrs.), 180; W. C., 122.
Hammock, Anna, 132; E., 132; E. F., 122; J., 127, 128; James, 148-262.
Hammock Cemetery, 301; Home, 148-149.
Hammond, Abner, 116.
Hamrick, Howard P., 43; James, 179; Jimmy, 182; J. Y., 185; Roscoe, 182; W. E., 59.
Hancock, J. M., 138.
Hand, J. R., 116.
Hardeman, R. V., 262.
Hansell, A. H., 89.
Hardie, J. S., 122.
Hardin, (Harden), Betty, 174; John, 85, 88, 272, 273, 275; W. L., 159.
Hardy, Charles (Rev.), 263.
Hargrave, Lemuel, 274.
Hargrove, Martha, 130; Zachariah B., 50, 276; Z. B., 89.
Harly, Joseph, 37.
Harrell, Belle, 118; Bessie, 118; David, 28; Dewitt, 174; Eunice, 118, 183; Everett, 118; Frank, 42; James T., 41; John, 32; John L., 41, 129, 137; Mary L., 118; W. H., 41, 129, 139; W. H. (Mrs.), 183; W. W., 68.
Harris, Jesse, 32; John, 32 Stephen W., 88, 89; Thomas, 50; Thomas W., 88, 89, 274; Virginia S., 1, 23.

Harrison, Cornelia C., 186; H. F., 89; James, 35, 36; J. G., 137, 138, 140; Mary F., 132; R. A., 89, 90, 132; Richard A., 262; Wm. C., 35, 36; Zachariah, 40.
Harrison Cemetery, 301.
Hart, Angus (Jr.), 91; Edwin, 141; Angus (Mrs.), 178.
Hartford Road, 26.
Hartley, J. M., 185.
Haskins, E. A. (Mrs.), 124; Earl (Mrs.), 175.
Hatcher, Linton, 68, 129.
Hathern, Joshua, 34.
Hathhorn, M., 141.
Haughton, Amos, 31.
Hawkins, B. L., 131; C. C., 181; Dessie, 131; K. J., 89; Lavania, 17; Ruth (Mrs.), 180.
Hawthorn (e), John, 88; Joshua, 32;
Hayden, James, 269.
Haygood, Myrtle, 121.
Haynes, W. R., 159.
Hayes, J. E. (Mrs.), 37; John, 26.
Hearn, Laura R., 186; S. A., 137.
Heidleburge, Thos. C., 88.
Hembree, A. J. (Dr.), 262; J. A., 162, 185; M. D., 186.
Hemphill, William, 29, 30, 32.
Henderson, Lillian, 104.
Hendricks, 395; C. F., 132.
Henry, Patrick, 115.
Herring, Frederick G., 32, 34; John A., 45; J. R., 134.
Herring Cemetery, 301.
Herrington, C. D., 138.
Herrishall, Wm., 88.
Hicks, Harris, 32; Louise B. (Mrs.), 170.
Higgs, A., 55; Anna, 47; Anna H. (Mrs.), 149.
Higgs-Horne Home, 149.
Higgsville (Post Office), 55.
Hightower, Ephriam, 31.
Highways, 160-161.
Hill, Barnard, 89; Ben, 87; Estelle (Mrs.), 177, 180; E. L., 122, 180, 181; Francis, 182; H. H., 182; Lois, 180; Moses, 32, 34; T. G., 140; T. L., 159, 180; Roy, 181.
Hillman, David, 39.
Hines, David, 38; Wm. L., 159.
Hinson, Caleb, 33; Elam, 35; J. F., 265; Jas. F., 52; John, 32, 33; John E., 182; H. T., 182; Paul (Mrs.), 168.
Hinson Cemetery, 302.
Hodges, C., 35; C. L. (Mrs.), 179; H. C., 159; Jno. L., 36, 269; R. J., 35; Robert, 204.
Hogan (Hoegen), Anthony, 39; Inez, 186.
Hogins, Wm., 38.
Holder, J. W., 137; J. N., 160.
Holland, Carl, 186; Jethro, 32, 34.
Holliday, 397; Faye R. (Mrs.), 125; J. H., 140; J. H. (Mrs.), 179; J. T., 122; Roger (Mrs.), 178.

Hollingsworth, Cornelius, 116; Dixon, 230; J., 141; James, 32, 33, 34, 141; Jesse, 141; John, 32 33.
Holmes, A., 141; D., 141.
Holt, T. G., 50, 88, 89.
Holzandorf, Wm. H., 47.
Hooten, Henry, 127.
Horn (Horne), 397; Abishia, 36; I., 134; J. T., 129; Joseph, 149; W. D. (Rev.), 47, 127, 128, 129, 149, 397.
Horton, Milton, 182; T. K., 159.
"Hollywood" (Home), 144-145, 392.
Home Demonstration Ext. Service, 170-175, 372.
Homes (old), 143-156.
Hopewell Church, 141.
Hoss, Wm. A., 39.
Howard, David, 180; James, 32, 33; J. H., 89, 124.
Howe (Mrs.), B. F., 168.
Howell, Clarence, 43; Ethleen H., 164; M. A., 112; Wm., 141.
Hoyle, W. E., 48.
Huber, J. M., 46; Masonic Club, 181; Settlement, 45-46.
Hudson, Irby, 276.
Huff, W. G., 186.
Hughes, 399; Agnes G., 147, 157, 164; Agnes (Mrs.), 176; Dan, 116; Dennard, 158; D. G., 22, 43, 140, 155, 158; D. M., 87, 117, 130, 150, 157, 158; D. M. (Mrs.), 130; Dudley M., 21, 22, 43, 125, 159, 266, 399; G. B., 129, 130; H., 35, 152; H. L. D., 182, 404; H. L. D. (Mrs.), 178; Hayden, 35, 55; Haywood, 129; Hennielu, 158, 38; Lucy, 140; Mary Dennard, 399.
Hughes Home(s), 43, 150, 155, 266.
Hughlen, John, 31.
Hulm, J., 185.
Humphrey, Robert H. (Mrs.), 164.
Humphries, C. C., 265; Charlie C., 162; W. C., 40, 128.
Hunt, Thomas, 31.
Hutchins, J. S., 137.
Hutchinson, James, 275.
Hyser, J. F., 159.

I

Irma Post Office), 55.
Indians, 23-38; Bluff Trail, 24; Passports, 37-38; Seminole War, 35-36.
Ingraham (Ingreham), David, 267; Kate, 122, 123.
Iverson, Alfred, 89; Robert, 274.
Irwin, Jared, 272.

J

Jackson, Emmie M., 186; James, 162.
Jaillette, Peter F., 282.
James, Hattie, 119; J., 141.
Jamison (Jameson, Jemison), George, 31; Robert, 38; William, 28, 30.
Jefferson, Academy, 46, 115, 276; Inn, 156.

Jeffersonville: Baptist Church, 129-130, 384, 387; Boy Scout Troop, 54, 182; Cemetery, 302-309; Methodist Church, 138-139; Schools, 115-125, 178; Settlement, 46-48, 159-262; Telephone System, 162; Woman's Club, 167-168.
Jenkins, Lawrence, 36.
Jessup (Jessop), Isaac, 127; J., 180; J. E., 181; John H., 40; Mattie, 181; Roger (Mrs.), 178; S., 134.
Jobson, Francis, 267; Francis W., 282.
John Twiggs Chapter, D. A. R., 164-166.
Johnson, A., 137; Andrew, 112; Ann E., 137; Benjamin, 31; B. F., 137; Brady, 138, 169; Carrie D., 137; C. F., 122, 137; C. G., 180; Charlie, 135, 140; Corine, 181; Edward, 32; E. H. (Mrs.), 177; Evie, 137; F. J., 140; Jackson, 137; James 32; J. D., 137; J. H. (Mrs.), 183; Laura, 137; Lemon, 32; M., 137; Marie M. (Mrs.), 124; Martha F., 137; Mary M., 124; McCoy, 138; Nancy S., 137; Otelia, 137; Quinton, 181; R. E., 137; Reid, 182; Robert, 29, 30; R. L., 124; Stephen, 16; Wayne, 182; W. B., 122; William, 262; W. O., 124; W. O. (Mrs.), 183 Vernon H., 171.
Johnston, 405; James, 273, 274; J. M., 138; Lillian T., 166; Robert, 30; T. J. (Mrs.), 168; William, 32, 33; William W., 123, 137, 170, 405; W. W. (Mrs.), 138, 405.
Joiner (Jiner), B., 88, Billy, 182; J. B., 128, 181; Julia, 181; Lula, 118; Nathan, 38; R., 159; Tilman, 138.
Jones, 411, 412, 416; A. B., 128; Anna Tullalah Carswell, 417; Bennet, 128; Bernice L., 1; Boderick, 137, 185; 405.
B. W., V, 2, 100, 123, 134, 182; Cecil, 118, 128; Cowan E., 162, 169, 411; H. A., 122, 134; Iris, 118; James, 32, 34; John, 32, 33, 34; John L., 282; J. W., 52, 54, 122, 137, 140; James W., 55, 68; John Walker, 52, 412; Jonathan, 32; Kathleen, 118, 122, 183; M. J. (Mrs.), 178; Mackie L., 123; Nancy A., 137; Opal, 181; Opal Tharpe (Mrs. S. S.), 122, 164, 178; S. C., 68; S. E., 48, 55; Shedrick Elias, 416; S. E. (Mrs.), 183; Sara Hendry (Mrs. J. W.), 128; Seaborn, 89; Stephen, 54; Stephen C., 42; S. S., 170, 181, 182, 186, 265; Thomas, 182; Tom, 185; T. H., 180, 263; T. J., 91; T. S., 48, 138, 185, 264; Thomas S., 122; T. W., 125; W. E., 54, 118, 155; W. E. (Mrs.), 168, 414; Wm. S., 118; W. S., (Dr.), 167, 185.

Jones, John, Ancestral Chart, 415.
Jones-Denson Cemetery, 309-310.
Jones-Pearce Cemetery, 310.

Jordan, Abigail (Mrs.), 52; Daniel, 31; G. Walker (Mrs.), 42; J. R., 137; Warren, 277.
Joyner, Sallie, 130; T. J., 180; W. A., 68.
Justice, Isaac, 180.
Justices of Inferior Court, 59.
Justices of Peace, 71.

## K

Kanahest, Jacob, 31.
Kaolin, 93-96.
Keener, John, 32, 33.
Keith, John, 262.
Kellogg H. H., 124.
Kelley W. C., 162, 169, 184.
Kennedy, Roy (Mrs.), 168.
Kennington, J. N., 185
Kent, J. L., 89.
Ketchum, W. H., 138.
Keys, Henry C., 52.
Kibbee, C. C., 89.
Kieser, Keturah, 181.
Kemball, R. H., 119.
Kinchen, Uriah, 31.
King, Alex E., 54; Clayborn, 118; Elizabeth, 184; Gordon, 138; Ira (Mrs.), 168; John, 26; Lizzie, 119; Neva, 164; R. J., 182.
Kingsley, J., 32.
Kirkland, Moses, 32.
Kirksey, Isaac, 32.
Kitchens, Arthur, 182; B. G., 134; Dwight, 181; Grady, 122, 181; Harold 182; H. L., 128; H. M., 122; Jere, 182; Jewell, 181; Maude, 181; Julia P. (Mrs.), 132, 173, 177; M. C., 122; Mary L., 181; Reba, 181; R. B., 182; Sallie B., 26, 104; S. G., 59; W. C. 122; Virgil, 182.
Knight, Lucian L., 51, 280.
Kolb, Martin, 88, 274.

## L

LaFayette Gen., 152, 156, 282; Volunteers, 282-284, 425-426.
Laine (Lane), Marion, 124; W., 137; Walter M., 39; W. M., 46; W. M. (Mrs.), 175.
Lamar, H. G., 89; L. Q. C., 89.
Lamb, 417; C. E., 91; James, 182; John, 32, 33; Mary J., 141; Rella (Mrs.), 180; W. H., 170; W. R., 181.
Land, A. J., 54, 122, 134, 152; Arthur J., 134, 152; Arthur J. (Mrs.), 152; A. T., 169, 176; A. T. (Mrs.), 168; Edward, 31; Henry (Mrs.), 137; H. F., 137; John, 137; J. T., 53, 137; Lou, 52; Mourning L., 137; Nathan, 35; Susie, 137; Land-Robertson Home, 151-152.
Land Lottery, 325-358.
Langlois, H. P., 138.
Langston, W., 137.
Lanier, Lemuel, 31.
Lansdell, R. A., 129.

Larsen, M. V., 132; W. W., 89.
Lassiter, A., 32.
Latson, 420; B. M., 122.
Lawrence, Lila R., 137; Wm. R., 137.
Laws, Georgia, 272.
Lawson, Davenport, 145; Hugh, 267, 270; H., 271; John, 31, 88; Roger, 275; Sabrina, 145.
Lawton, Gen., 109.
Lawyers, 50, 88-90, 262, 266.
Lee, J. E., 125; Thomas, 182; W. W., 179.
LeGrand(e), Wm. Thomas, 37; Home, 156.
Legislative Acts, 272-279.
Lenton, Jos. L., 36.
Leonard, C., 32, 33; Thos. E., 137.
Leslie, B. A., 134; B. A. (Mrs.), 168, 179; George, 130.
Lester, Ivan, 178; Ivan (Mrs.), 178; M. A. (Mrs.), 123; William, 32.
Letters Testamentary, 259-261.
Lewis, Corrine, 122; Daniel, 31; D. F. (Mrs.), 168; J.. S,, 137; M., 31.
Liberty Hill: Cemetery, 310-311; Chapte,r, O. E. S., 181; Masonic Lodge, 180, 128; Methodist Church, 138.
Library, County, 167.
Limestone (natural resource), 97.
Lincoln, Abraham, 99.
Lindsey, D. Z., 159; J. F., 124; V. E., 173.
Lineberger, O. B., 162.
Lingo, Bill, 127; Mary E., 45.
Lipham, E., 132.
Little, J. F., 141; W. M. 122.
Livingston, Martin, 32; Pat (Mrs.), 168.
Llwellyn, T. C., 173.
Lochrane, O. A., 89.
Lofton, Elkanah, 16.
Long, 423; Ellis, 47; Mary E., 145; S. R., 129.
Lord, Wm., 132.
Lovell, Effie, 122.
Lovejoy, Imogene, 137.
Lowe, 430; Cornelia A., 137; Cornelia E., 137; E. M., 137; J. M., 137; Mary J., 137; Thos., 137.
Lowrie (Lowry), John R., 115, 276; Samuel, 87, 162, 169.
Lowther, Samuel, 89.
Loyless, Henry, 88; H. M., 112; Henry, 274.
Lucas, Arthur, 35; John, 122; Jonas, 36.
Luckett, Elanor (Mrs.), 180; H. F., 125.
Lucy Chapel Church, 140, 407.
Luke, Frances, 123.
Lunceford, H., 123.
Lundy, C. A., 182.
Lyles, James, 128, 182; J. G., 134; R. A., 52.
Lyons, S. C. (Mrs.), 168.

## M

McBryant, O. L., 159.
McCall (Bro.), 129; Geo. R., 127, 128, 132, 265.

McCallum, 432; Archibald, 129; A. S., 185; H. A., 90, 129.
McCann, Xillo Y., 39.
McClendon, Frank P., 42.
McConnell, F. C., 129.
McCormick, Cornelia J., 1, 151, 164; James 85, 115, 272, 273, 276; J. T., 138; J. T., (Mrs.), 100, 138.
McCoy, 437; Coot, 138; G. 123; I. A. L., 47; Mable, 118.
McCoy Home, 156.
McCrary, B., 26; H. G., 138; Lucy, 118; Walter (Mrs.), 183; W. H., 186.
McCrea, 433; T. E., 53.
McCrory, C. C., 162, 169; Lois W., 139, 169.
McCullers, James W., 32.
McDonald, C. J., 89; J. E., 55.
McDowell, Thomas, 38.
McEachin, J. C., 118, 264.
McGee, Dent, 182; D. S., 122, 170, 171; D. S. (Mrs.), 178, 463; Lindy, 182.
McGinity, Thomas, 26.
McIntyre (McIntier), Archibald, 88, 115, 273, 275, 276, 283; Judge A. T. (Sr.), 50.
McLain, A., 182; Howard, 180; Keith, 182; Yvonne, 181.
McKibben, Mary, 121.
McKinley (Post Office), 55.
McKinney, Caleb, 30, 32, 34; Robert W., 31.
McKinnon, Florrie H., 68.
McLendon, B., 31.
McMannus, Arcy, 38.
McMullars, H., 134.
McNair, Ezekiel, 436, 186.
McRee, J. E., 119.
McSwain, Eleanor D., 166, 315, 322, 440.
McWilliams, Emory, 182.
Mabry, Alfred, 43.
Macker, John O., 38; Sarah (Mrs.), 38.
Maclese, W. H., 39.
Macon and Brunswick Railroad, 157.
Macon-Dublin-Savannah Railroad, 157-160, 366, 389.
Maddox, Jas., 159; J. G., 90; Nathan, 31.
"Magnolia Plantation" (Hughes Home), 150, 266.
Mail Service, 39-57, 163.
Mallary (Mallory), C. D., 127, 129; E. Y. (Mrs.), 178; G. M. (Mrs.), 181; Georgia S. (Mrs.), 143.
Manning, Rube, 182.
Marcy, J. O., 45; T. S., 41; Wm. Z., 41.
Marion Academy, 115, 275; Cemetery, 311; Settlement, 48-52, 274.
Marion, Francis, 48.
Mars, Alexander, 32.
Martin, A. F., 47; Clyde, 130; Denson, 118; Gus, 118; John, 32; J. H., 89; Joseph, 36; P. W., 154, 162; W. H., 169.
Mary Chapel Church, 142.

Masonic Lodges, 179-180, 277.
Mathis, Levi, 127.
Matthews, Budcaid, 37; J., 32, 33; John, 88; Thomas, 31; Timothy, 204.
Maulden, J. D., 137.
Maxwell, 438; E. D., 170; E. D. (Mrs.), 147; Frankie, 182; Harvey H., 43; Hugh, 143; I., 127; I. N., 68, 87; Isaac N., 43; James, 143; John, 180; John (Mrs.), 178, 179; Lelia W., 43; W. F., 68.
Maxwell Home, 156.
May, Dread, 38; S. J., 158.
Mayfield, D. T., 159; R. E., 129.
Mayo, James, 31.
Melton, B. D., 68; B. H., 128; D. B., 128; Elisha, 112; G. M., 128.
Mercer, C. E., 170; Elizabeth, 186; Howard, 186; H.W., 265; J. P. 140; Jones, (Mrs.), 183; Pink, 138; W. G., 170; W. H. (Mrs.), 138, 179; Will (Mrs.), 175.
Mercer Cemetery, 311.
Methodism in Twiggs, 135.
Methvin, Anna B., 137; Bertha D., 167-168; F. C., 137; George W., 265; Lucille, 170; Mary L., 137;Robert, 118, 119; S., 277; S. A., (Mrs.), 137; Sara J., 137; Tom, 118; Will, 182; William, 36.
Miller, Clara C., 164; Cliff, 119; F., 123; Fidell, 119; J. C., 134; Jere C., 90; Samuel, 31 Stephen F., 21, 50, 281, 282; S. F. 89, 262, 267, 270.
Millirons A. Jane, 137; E., 136, 137; D. V., 137.
Millman, Nate, 181.
Mills, Herod, 32.
Milton, Clement, 32, 34.
Mims (Family), 430.
Mincy, R., 36.
Minerals (resources), 93.
Minshaw, R., 35.
Mitchell, David, 27, 85; D. B. (Gov.), 274; David B., 17, 28, 38, 263; Governor, 88, 272,275; Henry, 17.
Mobley, Benjamin, 31.
Mock, Horman, 31.
Moffett, Craven P., 38; Henry, 38.
Monk (Dr.), 140.
Moon, Clara C., 186; Jno. B., 36; J. P., 170.
Moore, Henrietta C., 155; Lewis, 32, 33; S. E., 160; S. M., 122.
Morgan, A. A., 89; Cecil, 162; George, 32; John, 31.
Morris, Geraldine E., 174.
Morse, H. S., 159.
Morton, Wm. M. (Dr.), 263.
Mosely, D. F., 173; Maude, 121; Robert (Mrs.), 177; Ruth, 181.
Moses, G. D., 137; J. E., 162, 169.
Mount Moriah Church, 141.
Mount Pleasant Church, 141.

Mount Zion: Cemetery, 312-314; Church, 24, 130, 374, 401.
Moye, Edwin, 32; Idelle K., 186; Roger (Mrs.), 178; Vivian J., 186.
Murphey, Jesse, 32; Josiah, 47.
Murray, T. E., 138.
Myrick, Henry, 182; J. W., 53; Richard, 35.
Myricks Mill, 40-41.

N

Nash, A. E., 117; E. A., 180; (Dr.), 127, 128; L. A., 180; R. A., 36, 116, 122, 186.
Natural Resources, 91-114.
Nease, C. L., 138.
Neel (Neal), John, 267; Wright, 52, 229, 277.
Neeland, David, 31.
Nelson, 438; A., 134; J. A., 116; John, 32; John H., 45; Wm., 36, 116.
Nelson: Cemetery, 314-315; Home, 156.
Newberry, Thomas, 32.
Newby, H. J., 53; J. I., 266; J. L., 182; H. S., 54; R. R., 54; W. J. (Mrs.), 53.
New Haven Baptist Church, 130; Cemetery, 315-317.
New Hope Church, 142.
New Richland: Baptist Church, 130-131; H. D. Club, 176-177.
Newspapers, 162, 169; "Pickin's from the Press", 262-271.
Newsom, Kreuches, 38.
Nipper, Abram, 32.
Nix, E., 132.
Nivens, E. N., 134.
Nobles, C. L. (Mrs.), 177; Hade (Mrs.), 179; J., 141; Jim, 141; R., 141.
Noles, John D., 41.
Norris, R. B., 159.
Notable Citizens, 21.
Nurses, 186.
Nutt, R. S., 186.
Nutting, Annie, 118.

O

Ocmulgee Academy, 53, 115.
O'Daniel, 440; Daniel, 150; Elizabeth L., 137; Marcy C., 137; Mark H., 262; M. H., 137, 186; M. H. (Mrs.), 183; W., 183; Wm., 111, 136, 151, 440; Wm. A., 137; (Dr.), 266; O'Daniel Cemetery, 317-318; Home, 150-151.
Odom, Archibald H., 31.
Officers (County), 58-84.
Oglethorpe, Gen. James Edward, 15.
Oil Drilling, 265.
Old Homes, 143-156; Oldest Home, 43, 154, 266.
"Old" Marion, 48-52, 274.
Old Marion Chapter, D.A.R., 167.
Oliver, James, 269; J. H., 129; Thaddeus, 21; Wiley, 142.

O'Neal, Benj. P., 39, 46; G. A., 134; Harriette, 181; John, 134; J. T., 134; J. T. (Mrs.), 156; Kirby, 182; Margaret W., 164.
Opry, George, 31; Hugh, 36.
Order Eastern Star Chapter, 180-181.
Ordinaries (County), 61-62.
Organizations, 164-168.
Outler, J. M., 137.
Oxford, W. D., 124.

P

Pace Cemetery, 318.
Pace's Station (Settlement), 39-40.
Page, W., 141.
Paramore, Wm. H., 31.
Parent-Teacher Associations, 178-179.
Parker, John, 154; Theophilus L., 270.
Parrott, Sally, 132.
Pascell, Myrtle L., 186.
Passports (Indian Country), 37-38.
Pate, A., 32, 33; A. C., 89.
Patillo, R. L., 186.
Patton, James, 30.
Paul, 441; Geo., 137; J. E., 137; J. W., 122, 137, 128; Laura T., 137; Mary S., 137; Oscar, 39; Robert, 100; Sallie L., 137; Sarah, 137.
Payne A., (Rev.), 278; Ernest, 182.
Peacock, J. A., 162, 169; Howard, 36.
Pearce, Addie R. (Mrs.), 128; Alex, 36; E., 36; Henry, 134; John M., 128; J. M., 128; Theo., 127, 134; Wiley M., 112; Theophilus, 265; Pearce Cemetery, 318; Pearce-Jones Cemetery, 310.
Pearson, James, 35, 116, 277; J., 134; T., 138.
Peck, Henry K., 52; Ira, 50, 52.
Pennington, Margaret C., 186.
Perry, Arthur C., 275; Cora S., 137; Cordelia, 137; D. M., 137; Ida B., 137; Ira E., 180; Thornton, 31.
Perryman, G. L., 123; Robert, 50; R. L., 89; Robert L., 263, 283; Thos. I., 35.
Pettis, E. F., 68; Hattie, 119; J. W., 182; Mark, 32, 33; Minnie, 119; Sallie D., 47; Wilson, 180; W. J., 122.
Pharmacist, 186.
Phillip: Cemetery, 318; Settlement, 45-46.
Phillips, Pearl, 124; W. R., 157.
Physicians, 185-186.
"Pickin's from the Press", 262-271.
Pierce, Bishop, 135; Elizabeth H., 164; E., 132; E. H. (Mrs.), 124; Ken, 132; Madge R., 164.
Pine Ridge (Post Office), 55.
Pioneers, 18-20.
Pitman, Philip, 16.
Plantation System, 19.
Planters Academy, 116.
Pleasant Grove Academy, 116.
Poe, Washington, 89.
Pleasant Mount Academy, 262.

Pope, 442; Brev't, 86; Clara W., 132; J., 141; Jesse, 442.
Population, 118-193.
Posey, Dennis, 32.
Post Masters, 39-57.
Post Offices, 39-57.
Porter, Clara B., 147, 164; Clara (Mrs.), 178.
Pouncey, S., 141; Sarah, 141.
Powell, Edna Tharpe, 45, 122, 164, 166; Diana Kearney, 21; Francis, 88; J. E., 129; L. C. (Mrs.), 183; L. R., 159; Kinney, 32; Nancy, 132; Quincy, 33; R. L., 134, 159.

R

Powers, A. P., 89.
Prewett, Prior, 32.
Price, Edmond, 38.
Prince, O. H., 89.
Prospect Church, 139, 397, 445.
Pruett, Lemuel, 31.
Pulsifer, Nathanel W., 39.
Rabun, I. C. C., 137 Wm., 275; William (Gov.), 276.
Radford, James, 36.
Railroads, (Central, M. D. S., Macon and Brunswick, Southern, Sparks), 41, 51, 157-160, 266, 400.
Raines, Robt. H., 36; R. H., 47.
Raines Store (Jeffersonville), 46, 115.
Rainey, Signal, 269.
Raley (Raly), Charles, 282; John 36.
Ramey, H. L. (Mrs.), 137; Reese, 41, 42, 128, 137; Sparks, H., 42.
Ramsey, W. S., 129.
Randall, James, 32, 34.
Rankin, Issie, 122.
Rawlins, Walter, 128.
Ray, F. J., 68; S. W., 186.
Read (Reed), 443; A. B., 185; Billy, 182; Joseph H., 109; M., 130; Russell F., 55, 443; Wm., 116.
Read: Cemetery, 319, 444; Post Office, 55.
Reddy, T. G., 159.
Reece (Reese), Daisy, 124; Grace (Mrs.), 181; Harold (Mrs.), 177; J. D., 138; J. H., 162, 169; J. W., 138.
Reeves, N. G., 159.
Renfroe, C., 134.
Representatives (County), 83-84.
Revolutionary War Record, 280-281.
Reynolds, Martha, A. E., 104; H., 180; Peyton, 51, 116, 151; Wilbur, 118.
Reynolds-Fitzpatrick Home, 151.
Rhodes, Wm., 141.
Rice, John, 122; U. A. (Mrs.), 47; T. M. C., 180, 186.
Richards, Elibazeth, 173.
Richardson, Amanda Beckom, 26; Bruce (Mrs.), 141, 168; B. K., 132; Stephen L., 104; S. L., 137, 186; Susan A., 137.

Richerson, Mildred J. (Mrs.), 124.
Richland: Academy, 116, 365; Baptist Church, 26, 131-132, 266, 361, 362, 381, 442, 450; Cemetery, 319-320; Restoration League 132-133.
Ricks, Jacob, 85, 131, 272, 273, 275; James, 115; Susannah, 132.
Riggins L., 127.
Ripley (Settlement), 52.
Roach, Allaway, 31.
Robbins, Isoline W., 132.
Roberts, D. M., 86, 87, 89; Georgia (Mrs.), 176; John, 37.
Robertson, J. T., 54, 151; T. J., 54, 151.
Robertson-Land Home, 151-152.
Robinson, Boling H., 35; J. C., 186.
Rockmore, J. G., 47, 48, 129.
Rockwell, Samuel, 89; Wm. S., 109.
Rockwelt, Wm. S., 179.
Rogers (Rodgers), G. F., 138, 170; G. F. (Mrs.), 168, 176; H. A., 186, James M., 45; Jim, 159; Josiah, 267; Ora Kate, 173; Richard S., 116.
Rolland, William, 39.
Rooks, C. T., 134.
Rosebud Methodist Church, 140, 412.
Ross, David, 36; F. G., 159.
Roughton, John, 38; Zacharias, 38.
Roundtree, Ruth, 159.
Rozier, David; E. E., 169; E. F. (Mrs.), 167; E. J., 179.
Pulk, Peter, 38; Samuel, 38.
Rural Development Program, 174-175.
Rush, John M., 43.
Rushing, Matthew, 37.
Rutherford, Robert, 89, 283.
Rutland, Spurgeon, 118.
Ryles, Dan, 138; D. J., 180.
Ryan, Capt., 157.

S

Sabine (Settlement), 52.
Safford, Adam G., 89.
Salter, Benjamin, 32; James, 38; Samuel, 38.
Sand (Natural Resource), 97.
Sanders (Saunders), Clara W. (Mrs.), 124; Claude (Mrs.), 168; D. S., 142; Frank (Mrs.), 178; Harold, 182; J., 127, 128; Johnnie (Mrs.), 68; J. G., 122; John W., 186; J. R., 122; R., 141; Rabun C., 125; Sue W. (Mrs.), 48.
Sanderson, G. K., 86.
Sanford, Britton, 32.
Sapp, M. P., 134.
Sappington, Florine, 124.
Sassnett, Helen, 137.
Sauls, 445; Theophalaus, 139.
Sawyer, Joseph, 36; William, 36.
Saxon, Joseph T., 35.
Scarborough, J. J., 89; Willie F., 182.
Schley, William, 36.
Schools, 115-126; 264, 265, 278, 279; Commissioners, 82.

Scoates, H. W., 138, (Rev.), 182.
Scott, Leonard, 37.
Senators (County), 82.
Settlements (County), 39-57.
Settlers (County), 18-20.
Sessions. Mr., 147.
Shackleford, Edmund, 43.
Shannon, 445, 446; 447; D. D. 267; Dudley H., 113, 129, 445; J. C., 22, 48, 55, 129, 264; J. C. (Mrs.), 183; James D., 21, 68, 89, 90, 129, 132, 152, 262, 446; John Carey, 447; L. D., 87; 90; W. F., 47, 183.
Shannon Home, 152.
Sharpe, J. E., 129.
Shawes, J., 134.
Shedd, Inez R., 164.
Shell, Mr. 140.
Sheehan, John C., 36.
Shepherd, Alexander, 32.
Sheriffs (County), 58-59.
Sherrod, Robert, 26.
Shine, D. W., 53, 152; John, 152, 268, 282; John F., 47; Mary A., 152 153.
Shine Home, 152.
Shire, Isiah, 132.
Shorter, Eli, 89.
Shurling, H. F., 174, 182.
Simmons, Alonzo, 122; James, 31; John F., 36.
Simpson, A. N., 138, A. N. (Mrs.), 138; Frank, 138; Frank (Mrs.), 179; Sergt., 30; Simon, 31; Solomon, 31; Uriah, 31.
Sims, Annie, 118; John, 31; Nancy S., 54; W. R., 182.
Singletery, Thomas N., 32.
Singleton, Austelle F., 164.
Sinquefield, Mattie, 118, Theo., 118.
Sistrunk, Mary H., 43.
Slappey, 447; Carter, 118; Dr., 160; Fred, 118; John G., 53, 135, 137, 186, 262, 271, 282; John G. (Dr.), 447; Marianna, 22; Mark F., 42; Mary Faulk, 135; R. R., 42; Robert R., 42, 43; R. R. (Mrs.), 183; Va., 186.
Slavery, 19-20, 99, 101-103, 267.
Sloan, Joshua, 32, 34.
Smith, Alexander, 38; A. K., 162, 169; Ben B., 35, 277; B. S., 124; B. T., 52; C. C., 89; Charles, 38; Charlotte W., 164; Clara T. (Mrs.), 177; David, 38; Doss, 141; D. S., 141, Earl, 169; F. M., 122; George Gilman, 19; James, 32, 33, 89; James M., 21; J. H., 141; John, 31, 168; John T., 47; J. W., 159; Lonnie, 182; Lonnie (Mrs.), 176; Lovett B., 30, 31, 85, 272; Lovey B., 275; Mack B., 45, 134; Polly (Mrs.), 176; Powell, 32, 33; Ralph, 47, 178; R. J., 150; Thomas, 31; T. P., 179; Wm., 32, 38.
Smith: P.T.A., 178; School, 122-123.
Scouts, 182.
Smith-Hughes Vocational Act, 402.

Snipes, Kate, 123.
Soldiers, (see Veterans), 30-34, 104-112, 280-281, 285-289, 290-291.
Soils, 92.
Solomon, 447; C. A., 47, 112; H., 127, 128; Hardy, 277; Henry, 46; H. F., 134; James C., (Dr.), 21, 22, 129, 137, 185, 447; L., 127, 141; Lewis, 112, 128, 262, 263, 264; Lucy 130; Marcus E., 47, 52, 129; Virginia, 137; William, 23, 24, 134; W. L., 112, 183; William L., 264.
Solomon-Faulk Cemetery, 320.
Solomon (Post Office), 55.
Somersall, Henry, 34.
Sonicera (Post Office), 55.
Southern Railroad, 157.
Spann, Francis, 49; James, 88, 274.
Sparks Railroad, 160, 400.
Spears, Eli, 179; W. G., 162.
Spence, Leon, 137; Sara M., 137; Wm. H., 137.
Spillers, Grady, 128.
Stanford, Samuel, 32, 34; William, 32, 33.
Starr, Caroline H., 155, 263.
Steeley, Adelaide, 90; William, 129; Wm. R., 130.
Stephens, A., 36; A. H., 87; Alexander H., 99; E. N., 122; Holman, 31; James, 31; Johnson, 16; Mr. 162; Richard, 270; R. I., 89; Samuel, 271; William, 271; Wm. J., 52.
Stevens, J. B., 36; M. H., 43, 130; M. H. (Mrs.), 176, 178; R. L., 130; R. L. (Mrs.), 176.
Stewart, Charles, 32; Josiah, 32.
Stiles, J. G., 143.
Stokes, Essie, 122; J. A., 55; John, 139; Mary A., 55; W. H., 138, 180.
Stone, Doyle, 182.
Stone Creek: Academy, 115, 134, 277; Baptist Church, 44, 115, 134-135; 166, 177, 266, 361, 398, 420, 438, 452; Cemetery, 320-322; Community H. D. Club, 177.
Straham, Mr., 38.
Street, Reecy, 36; Wm., 36.
Streetman, Samuel, 32, 33; William, 32, 33.
Strickland, C. B., 179.
Stocks, Thomas, 276, 277.
Strong, C. B., 89; C. B. (Mrs.), 115; Christopher B., 88; T. D., 137.
Strother, Holland, 125.
Stubbs, J. M., 158.
Students: Auburn Institute (1890), 119; Class of 1897, 118.
Studfield, William, 32.
Summerall, Henry, 32; William, 32, 33.
Summers, J. W., 179.
Sumner, F. C., 159.
"Sunnyside" (Mark Faulk Home), 153.
Superintendents of Education, 126.
Superior Court, 63, 88, 89.

Sutton, Charles, 31; W. A., 172.
Swearingen, James, 269; Thomas, 31.
Swearinger, H. C., 186.
Swinney, E. N., 130, 131; Myrtle J., 186.
Symonds, H. L., 134.

T

Talbot, Matthew, 274, 276.
Talley, J. N., 89.
Talmadge, Eugene, 90.
Tare, Elisha, 33.
Tarver, Benjamin M., 53; Elisha, 32; F. R., 53; Hartwell H., 42, 52, 53, 268, 277; William M., 53, William W., 270.
Tarversville (Settlement) 52-53.
Tate, Rowland, 31.
Tax Collector, 66-67.
Tax Digest (1818-1826-1853), 194-230.
Tax Receivers, 64-66.
Taylor, A. W. (Mrs.), 181; C. E., 180; Dan H., 186; George, 36; H. T., 182; J. J., 36.
Teal, Spencer, 125.
Telegraph Service, 162.
Telephone System, 161-162.
Television Station, 163.
Terrell, Henry M., 274; Thomas W., 115, 276.
Tharp (Tharpe, Thorp), 452; A. C., 154; Bessie, 181; B. C., 122, 134; B. D. (Sr.), 122, 134, 153, 162, 166, 182; Billie Dunn (Sr.) 452; C. A., 101, 116, 127; Charnick, 154; T., 129, G. W., 22, 45, 117, 129, 130, 162; J. A., 115, 134, 154; Jeremiah, 153, 277; Jere A., 166; John, 32 154; John A., 133; Joseph, 134; Simeon, 112; T. J., 47; T. S., 52, 68, 122, 134, 161, 162; Wm. A., 115, 277; V. A., 43, 127, 154.
Tharpe Cemetery (J. A.), 322.
Tharpe Home, J. A., 153-154; V. A. (Rev.), 43, 154.
Thigpen, Joshua, 269.
Thomas, Capt. Charles N., 91; John, 31.
Thomason, C. R. (Mrs.), 178; F. J., 134; F. J. (Mrs.), 177; J. E., 171.
Thompson, Alfred, 36; Dr., 186; Ellen (Mrs.), 177; Joseph D., 269; Mr. 162; Richard E., 40.
Tice, Georgia (Mrs.), 168.
Tison, Sterling, 269.
Todd, William, 32, 34.
Tomlin, Myrtle F., 186.
Tomlinson, Jared, 269; Susannah, 18.
Toney, G. M., 182.
Toole, Julian, 136; J., 137; R., 123; Ruth, 119.
Tooke, Colonel, 28, 29.
Toombs, Robert, 43, 155.
Tornabene, Charles, 123.
Torrence, W. H., 89.
Town and Country Garden Club, 168.

Towns, 39-57.
Townsend, J. E., 130, 131; William S., 53.
Tracy, E. T., 89.
Transportation, 157-161.
Treadwell, F. H., 45.
Treasurers (County), 67-68.
Trentman, Henry, 33.
Trimble, Dr., 186.
Troup, George M. (Gov.), 268, 269.
Troutman, Henry, 32.
Truluck, E., 132; John, 32.
Trunell, J. W., 42.
Turk, J. L., 171.
Tweedle, C. E., 169.
Twiggs, John, 17, 18; Judge, 87.
Twiggs and Branch Garden Club, 168.
Twiggs County: Academy, 115, 274, 275; Area, 91; Calvary, 35-36; Climate, 98; Created, 15-17; Defense Corps, 265; Development Corporation, 169; Doctors, 185; Flag, 284; Government, 85-90; High School, 124, 264; Lafayette Volunteers, 282-284; Natural Resources, 91-114; Notable Citizens, 21; Nurses, 186; Officers, 58-84; Origin of Name, 17-18; Pioneers, 18-21; Schools, 115-126; Settlements, 39-57.
Twiggs Elementary School P. T. A., 178-179.
Twiggsville Settlement, 53-54.
Twiggs-Wilkinson, P. T. A., 178; School, 125, 404.
Tyson, M., 141; S., 141.

U

Underwood, Robert, 31; Thomas, 31.
Union Hill Academy, 116.
United Daughters of the Confederacy, 183-184.
Upton, John, 31.

V

Vandergriff, R. W., 180.
Varner, Alexander, 31.
Vaughn, 452, C. E., 131; Dan (Mrs.), 131; Fannie, 122; Fannie M., 47; F. M., 133; Herschel Johnson, 452; Jack (Mrs.), 176; John (Mrs.), 183; J. H., 68, 119, 177; J. S., 53, 86; J. S. (Mrs.), 183; Norman (Mrs.), 176; W. E., 137.
Vaughn Cemetery, 322.
Vernado, Samuel, 38.
Veterans, Civil War, 104-112; Revolutionary War, 280-281; War of 1812, 30-34; War World I, 285-289; World War II, 290-291.
Vickars (Vickers), Ashley, 116; James, 31, Young, 31.
Vinson, J. N., 123.

W
Wade, Isaac, 31.
Wagner, Fred, 87.
Wall, E., 34; Ezekiel, 32; J. G., 116; James J., 162; Lizzie K., 164; Lillian W., 159; Lowe (Mrs.), 168; W. T., 135.
Walker, C. W., 124, R. A., 159; W. D., 130.
Walters, Coley, 131, Thelma, 181.
Walton, Ensign, 283.
War Between-The-States, 19-20, 43, 99-114; Tax, 263.
War of 1812, 26, 27-34, 49.
Ward, Ed., 122; James, 32; J. E., 122; H. C., 47; L. W., 36; P. H., 182; S. C. (Mrs.), 183; Seth, 32; Willis, 31.
Ward Home, 156.
Wardlaw, George W., 36.
Ware, B. S., 130; James, 275; Mary T., 130.
Warfield, S. D., 158.
Warner, Hiram, 89.
Warren, J. S., 129; Lott, 89; Sergeant, 100.
Wars: Seminole, 35-36; War of 1812, 27-34, 49, 456; War Between-The-States, 43, 99-114; Revolutionary, 280-281; World War I, 285-289; World War II, 290-291.
Washburn, A. C., 131; A. V., 131.
Water (Resource), 97-98.
Waterhouse, N., 132.
Watkins, Benjamin, 32; B. F., 186; Ben F. (Dr.), 264; C., 141; James M., 36.
Waters, Dr., 186; George W., 68; Georgia (Mrs.), 181; H. J. (Mrs.), 176.
Waters-Wood-Lanier Cemetery, 322-323.
Watts, Isaac, 17.
Watson, Frederick, 32, 34; Wade, 125; W. V., 169.
Webb, E., 31, Dawson, 31.
Welch, C. S., 134; George W., 36, 263, 269.
Welfare Department, 170.
Wells, Ottie W. (Mrs.), 122; Samuel, 31.
Wellman, Francis H., 38.
Welton, J. T., 180.
Wessinger, V. E., 124.
West, John, 37, 38; Johnathan, 32, 33; Nancy, 262.
West Lake (Settlement), 42-43, 157.
Wester, W. H. (Mrs.), 168, 179; Wm. H., 134.
Wheat, Moses, 276.
Wheeler, John (Jr.), 269; N., 141; Reuben, 32.
Whitaker, Benjamin, 17, 272, 275.
White, Alton, 131; Alton V., 43; A. V., 132, 182; A. V. (Mrs.), 132, 164, 168; Alton V. III, 166; Ira (Mrs.), 183, 184; Rosaline D., 164; R. E., 162, 169; W. F., 183; William, 32, 33.

Whitely, J. B., 181.
"White House" (Hughes Home), 43, 155.
Whitehurst, 454; Bessie, 186; J. H. (Mrs.), 167, 433; Joel (Mrs.), 152; L. I., 133; Mary Hart, 169, 179; R. S., 133; Rebecca S., 135; W. M., 48; W. M. (Mrs.), 179; Wilkinson Mayberry, 452.
Wild Life (Resource), 92-93.
Willey, G. E., 134.
Williams, 125; A. S., 186; Benjamin, 276; Clarissa, 152; Corene (Mrs.), 181; Crosby, 118; Drury, 28, 30; Evie, 181; H., 128; Hansel, 181; H. B., 180, 181 J. A., 31; J. C., 181; John, 31; J. W., 182; Mitt (Mrs.), 162; Myrtle (Mrs.), 181; Margie N., 159; R. A., 159; Roy, 181.
Williamson, Dr., 283; W. W., 115.
Willis, James, 115, 276; Mary W., 263.
Willis Settlement, 54.
Wills (Letters Testamentary), 259-261.
Wills, B., 159.
Wilkinson, 371; J., 88; Wm. G., 36.
Wilson, J. F., 138; John, 32, 33; John B., 37; Mary E. H., 164.
Wimberly, 455, 457, 459, 460, 461; A. C. (Lt.), 264; Avie, 118, 122; A. Courtney, 162; Alice L., 133; A. T., 129, 179; B. B., 152; Bob, 139; Captain Ezekiel, 270; Caroline (Mrs.), 129; Clara, 22; Charles M., 182; Col., 29; Doris, 181; E. A., 277; Ezekiel, 21, 27, 28, 30, 31, 33, 34, 47, 156, 182, 274, (Major General), 455; E. J., 132, 156; E. J. (Mrs.), 164, 168; Ezekiel Jenkins, 457; F. D., 117; F. D. (Mrs.), 100; Forest, 152; Fred, 90; Frederick D., 270; George W., 186; Dr. George W., 264; Hal B., 262; Henry (Dr.), 139; H. H. (Mrs.), 179; Henry S., 147, 186, 270; J., 129; Jennie, 47, 164; J. H., 129; John J., 36; J. L., 129; John Lowry, 460; J. R., 90, 129, 155, 186, 267; Joshua R., 47; Dr. Joshua R., 263, 271; Dr. Joshua Rhodes, 460; Lucy G. 130; Maggie, 118, 119; Mary, 90; M. Evelyn, 164, 170; Minter, 90, 158, 262; Robert, 152; Warren, 186; William, 36.
Wimberly-Durham Cemetery, 297.
Wimberly, Ezekiel: Cemetery, 323; Home, 156.
Wimberly-Jones Home, 155.
Wimberly, Dr. Joshua Rhodes, Cemetery, 323-324.
Wirth, F. P., 112.
Wolf, Charles, 31; John, 31.
Womack, W. A., 124.
Wood, 461; A., 88; Abraham, 37 ,115, 273; Ann, 166; A. J., 186; Ashlet, 88; B. J., 180; David, 127, 142; Elton, 181 Frances, 181; Frances L., 164; G. B., 134; Isaac Waters,

461; Jones, 134; Laura, 137; Martin, 38; Mathew, 37; M. W. (Mrs.), 137; Olline N., 45; R. N., 159; Thomas (Mrs.), 168; V. Elton, 134; Winnie, 186; William Thomas, 45; W. W., 170.
Wood's Meeting House, 142, 463.
Woodruff, Elias, 38; L. C., 151.
Woodson, Simon, 31.
Woodward, Aaron T., 43; Lamar, 124.
World War I, 285-289; II, 290-291.
Worsham, H. L., 122; Tom (Mrs.), 168.
Worthwhile H. D. Club, Danville, 177; Jeffersonville, 167.
Wright, B. W., 169; J. T., 158.

Y

Yarborough, James, 31.
Yaughn, James, 299; Leonard, 181; L. M. (Mrs.), 176, 179.
Young, David, 36; Edward B., 51; J., 141; John, 88.

Z

Zachery, Dr., 186.
Zellner, Elizabeth, 173.

HISTORY OF TWIGGS COUNTY

ERRATA

Page 35--For Desago, read Deshago

Page 59--For 1902, read <u>1929</u>-1941

Page 75--For Sept. 16, 1930, read Sept. 16, <u>1830</u>

Page 85--For page 80 (below picture), read p.<u>50</u>

Page 186--Omitted: (PHARMACISTS) "Patsy" Charlotte I. Gleeson Spears

Page 188--For 2nd Asbell, Elisha, read Asbell, John

Page 189--For Corsn, read Cowan, William A.

Page 194--For Beckman, read Beckham

Page 208--For Horne, Joan, read Horne, Joab

Page 233--For Payten, read Peyton Reynolds

Page 300--Omitted: Henry Glenn Faulk, Sr.
July 15, 1858-Oct. 29, 1947

Page 369--For Albert Goodwyne, read Albert Mitchell

Page 369--Omitted: after McGruder, read Irma Baynard married James Roland Goodwyne

Page 370--Omitted: after Ann, read Mary Elizabeth, after Ingram, read Debroah Jean

Page 385--For Aug. 14, 1935, read August 14, <u>1936</u>

Page 451--For Sharpe Grice, read Tharpe Grice

www.ingramcontent.com/pod-product-compliance
Lightning Source LLC
Chambersburg PA
CBHW020633300426
44112CB00007B/102